MW00809888

Ibn ʿArabi
in the Later Islamic Tradition

SUNY Series in Islam
Seyyed Hossein Nasr, Editor

Ibn ʿArabi in the Later Islamic Tradition

The Making of a Polemical Image in Medieval Islam

Alexander D. Knysh

State University of New York Press

Published by
State University of New York Press, Albany

Printed in the United States of America

For information, address State University of New York Press, State University Plaza, Albany, N.Y., 12246

Production by Diane Ganeles
Marketing by Nancy Farrell

Library of Congress Cataloging-in-Publication Data
Knysh, Alexander D.
Ibn ʿArabi in the later Islamic tradition : the making of a polemical image in medieval Islam / Alexander Knysh.
p. cm.—(SUNY series in Islam)
Includes bibliographical references (p.) and index.
ISBN 0-7914-3967-4.—ISBN 0-7914-3968-2 (pbk.)
1. Sufism—Controversial literature. 2. Ibn al-ʿArabī, 1165-1240.
I. Title. II. Series.
BP189.36.K58 1999
297.4′092—dc21 98-3407
CIP

10 9 8 7 6 5 4 3 2 1

To My Wife Anna

CONTENTS

TABLES

PREFACE

This book was written over a period of almost seven years, during which it benefited from the advice and financial help of many individuals and institutions. To all of them I owe an enormous debt of gratitude. Thanks are due, in the first place, to my colleagues in the Department (Sektor) of Near Eastern Studies, the Institute for Oriental Studies in St. Petersburg (former Leningrad), Russia, who witnessed the beginning of this project and whose warmth and friendship remained a major inspiration long after my departure to the United States. I am especially indebted to my supervisors, Prof. Anas Khalidov and Dr. Stanislav Prozorov, who introduced me, respectively, to Arabic and Islamic studies and who were the first readers and critics of my academic works. The early chapters of the book, however, were written at the Institute for Advanced Study in Princeton, which generously provided me with excellent research facilities, a stimulating intellectual environment, and an opportunity to focus single-mindedly on my research. It would be impossible to mention by name all of the wonderful colleagues I met there. However, I must acknowledge my deep indebtedness to Profs. Oleg Grabar, Gerhard Böwering, and Ulrich Haarmann, whose presence and advice did much to clarify my thinking and to broaden my knowledge. The last chapters of the project were completed thanks to a grant from the Rockefeller Foundation for the Humanities, which gave me a full year of support at the Center for the Study of Islamic Societies and Civilizations, Washington University, St. Louis, Missouri. At the Center I found many congenial and competent colleagues who contributed significantly to my project. In particular, I am grateful to Profes. Cornell Fleischer and Peter Heath, who placed their faith in my work when it was still a jumble of loosely strung and poorly digested facts and observations. As great a debt is owed to the other

Rockefeller fellow, Dr. Thomas Burman, as well as Dr. Garay Meniccuci, of Marshall University, WV, both of whom kindly read the manuscript over in draft and saved me from many stylistic errors and solecisms. The final version of this book was completed at the Department of Near Eastern Studies, the University of Michigan, whose faculty and staff were invariably supportive of my writing and research. Particular thanks are due to Prof. Brinkley Messick and my research assistant Margaret Sullivan, who spent a whole summer smoothing my style and making sense, together with my wife Anna, of the hundreds of disparate catalog cards and illegible scraps of paper, which I was stubbornly referring to as "my bibliography." Finally, I had the good fortune to meet and discuss my work with the foremost experts on Ibn ʿArabi, Profs. William Chittick, Michel Chodkiewicz, James W. Morris, and Michael Sells, whose suggestions and corrections have been invaluable. In most cases, I benefited from their advice and assistance through the good services of the Muhyiddin Ibn ʿArabi Society, which invited me to its annual conferences in Oxford and Berkeley. To all of the members of the society, and especially to Prof. Elton Hall, Chris Ryan, Martin Notcutt, Stephen Hirtenstein, and John Mercer, goes my deep appreciation. Last but not least, I would like to dedicate this book to my wife Anna—hardly an adequate compensation for her boundless patience and constant encouragement.

LIST OF ABBREVIATIONS

BSOAS	*Bulletin of the School of Oriental and African Studies,* The University of London.
EI	*The Encyclopedia of Islam,* 1st ed.: 4 vols., Leiden and Leipzig, E. J. Brill, 1913–1934.
EI[2]	*The Encyclopedia of Islam,* new edition: vols. 1–9, Leiden, E. J. Brill, 1954–.
IES	*Islam: Entsiklopedicheskii sovar'* (*Islam: An Encyclopedic Lexicon*): Ed. by S. M. Prozorov, Moscow, Nauka, 1991.
REMMM	*Revue du Monde Musulman et de la Méditerranée*: Éditions ÉDISUD, Aix-en-Provençe.
MRM	Ibn Taymiyya, *Majmūʿat al-rasāʾil wa ʾl-masāʾil:* 4 vols., ed. by Muḥammad Rashīd Riḍā, Cairo, Maṭbaʿat al-Manār, 1922–1930. Reprint: Cairo, Lajnat al-Turāth al-ʿArabī, 5 vols., 1976.
RWW	Al-Taftāzānī, *Risāla fī waḥdat al-wujūd.* In *Majmūʿat al-rasāʾil:* Istanbul, no publisher, 1294 A.H.

A NOTE ON TRANSLITERATION AND DATES

In this book I follow a simplified version of the transliteration of the *International Journal of Middle East Studies* (*IJMES*) for Arabic and Persian words. Although I retain the *ʿayns* (ʿ) and the *hamzas* (ʾ) in the main text, I omit dots under certain letters, which, in academic literature, represent velarized, or "emphatic," Arab consonants. Nor do I use macroned letters to convey long Arabic vowels. These omissions are made in order to facilitate the production of a lengthy text such as this one, and by no means reflect my negative attitude toward any transliteration system current in my field of specialization. A full transliteration of the Arabic and Persian names and titles is provided in the bibliography.

All dates are given according to the Muslim lunar calendar (*hijra*), which are followed by a backslash and the Common Era equivalent.

INTRODUCTION

Few personages of Islamic intellectual history enjoy the fame of Muhyi ʾl-din Muhammad Ibn ʿAli Ibn al-ʿArabi, or simply Ibn ʿArabi (560-638 A.H./1165-1240 C.E.), as he was known in the Muslim East. Fewer still are as controversial as this outstanding exponent of Islamic mysticism. Already in his lifetime and especially after his death, Ibn ʿArabi's mystical ideas became a stumbling block for Muslim scholars who have tried to find a key to the "Ibn ʿArabi enigma" ever since. In the process, they have often clashed over the meaning of Ibn ʿArabi's breathtaking insights into the mysteries of the cosmos, the Islamic Scripture, and religious faith. Today, as before, Ibn ʿArabi's legacy continues to bewilder his readers, both Muslims and non-Muslims alike. Although his vast work has been analyzed in dozens of academic monographs and in hundreds of articles, Ibn ʿArabi still poses a major intellectual challenge to his investigators. More significantly, an aura of mystery and controversy that has enveloped his name over the last seven centuries has attracted to him not only academics but also a broad nonspecialist audience in the Muslim countries and in the West.[1] In the Muslim world, Ibn ʿArabi's abiding importance is attested by a vast body of polemical literature around his name. It is not surprising: from the 7th A.H./13th C.E. centuries onward practically every Muslim thinker of note took it upon himself to define his position vis-à-vis the controversial Sufi master.

The present book, however, is not a study of Ibn ʿArabi per se. His doctrines have been analyzed in scores of scholarly dissertations, some of which will be surveyed further on.[2] It is not my intention to augment or to correct the conclusions reached by my predecessors, who have furnished an accurate, if not always impartial, summary of Ibn ʿArabi's ideas. My purpose here is to examine the perception of Ibn ʿArabi's personality and teaching by Muslim scholars throughout the four centuries following his death. This, therefore, is a study of image-making and polemics in premodern Islam. With this goal in mind I will inquire into the methods and motivations of Muslim scholars, since, as we shall see, Ibn ʿArabi's posthumous image was molded largely against the backdrop of the theological controversy over his intellectual legacy.

Another issue to be addressed in this work is the Islamic notion of "heresy" as opposed to "true belief." It will be treated in the context of the fierce intellectual confrontations between the upholders of communal, nomocentric Islam and those who espoused a more subjective, imaginative, and personal approach to the meaning and implications of Islamic faith. It is in this context that I will discuss the perennial conflict between the exoteric and esoteric interpretations of religion that we find in all monotheistic traditions.

In discussing the "orthodoxy" versus "heterodoxy" dichotomy in medieval Islam I will touch upon a number of related dichotomies: Sunni legalism versus Sufi vision, conformism and orthodoxy versus innovation and freethinking, communalism versus individualism, cold rationalism versus mystical raving, and so forth. I will also tackle such issues as the objectivity of the Muslim biographical literature, the role of anecdotes in prosopographical and theological texts, the literalization and fictionalization of polemical discourse, and the dynamic tension and dialogue between various interpretations of the Muslim dogma. In the end, more questions will be raised than answered. Nevertheless, my hope is to achieve the following objectives:

1. to highlight the principal stages of the scholarly debate over Ibn ʿArabi's legacy and the evolution of polemical arguments employed by the participants;
2. to describe the reasons for a striking, almost inconceivable, tenacity of his mystical teaching;
3. to unravel the motives of the parties to the controversy over Ibn ʿArabi and his ideas.

Finally, I would like to assess the impact of the Ibn ʿArabi issue on medieval Islamic thought and to try and understand how his life and ideas were used by various theological and political factions vying for ascendancy.

In the genre, the present book is yet another exercise in the noble science of "ulamalogy,"[3] being focused as it is primarily on the Muslim scholars, whose interests, it is to be recalled, are by no means identical with those of the other strata of the medieval Islamic society, namely the military, the merchants, the craftsmen, and the peasants. The focus on the *ʿulama*ʾ inevitably takes a toll on the other critical participants in "the venture of Islam" whose conspicuous absence from the pages of scholarly monographs has been justly bemoaned in recent Western scholarship.[4] Yet, in my mind, the sheer bulk and complexity of the *ʿulama*ʾ literary output and the important roles they played in medieval Muslim societies prevent us from proclaiming closed the study of their weltanschauung. Whereas their social status and reproduction, their relation to property, and their access to power have been treated in some detail by the Western scholars mentioned in note 3 of this section, their intellectual concerns, doctrinal disagreements and factional differences merit further examination. The need for such an examination is pointed out even by the critics of "ulamalogy," who acknowledged that here also much remains to be done.[5] And this is precisely my goal in the present book.

This study does not claim to be linguistically, chronologically, and geographically comprehensive. Despite its wide scope—from 7th/13th-centuries Ayyubid Egypt and Syria to their Mamluk successors in the 8th/14th–10th/16th centuries, from 8th/14th Timurid Central Asia to contemporary al-Andalus, North Africa, and Rasulid Yemen—it still fails to give full justice to the tumultuous and eventful history of Ibn ʿArabi's legacy. By all standards, the corpus of literature devoted to Ibn ʿArabi is enormous: it features dozens of book-length apologies and refutations, not to mention hundreds of biographical notes and passing references to his teachings in medieval Muslim literature. Many, if not most, of these writings are still in manuscript form or have appeared in obscure, often inaccurate, editions.[6] Finally, I limit my inquiry to Arabophone works, ignoring numberless pertinent treatises in Persian, Turkish, Urdu, Tatar, Uzbek, Malay, and in the other languages of Islam. However, one can argue that the Arabic material is generally representative of the view of Ibn ʿArabi found in non-Arabic literatures. First, most Arabic tracts in defense or refutation of the Greatest Master, as he was known among his admirers, were written by Persians, Hindus, and Anatolian and Central Asian Turks. Second, the seminal theological and polemical works on Ibn ʿArabi and his school were written in Arabic—the language par excellence of Islamic scholasticism.[7] This is not to say that there have been no important discussions of the Ibn ʿArabi issue in the other languages of Islam. Such discussions, however, are by and large commentaries on, or popularizations of, Ibn ʿArabi's writings rather than original contributions to the polemic. In any case, when non-Arab authors defended or refuted the teaching of the Greatest Master in their native tongues, they relied heavily on their Arabophone predecessors for arguments.

Originally, I intended to trace the history of the controversy over Ibn ʿArabi and his teaching from its inception up to the present day. However, halfway through the project, I realized that such a task cannot be accomplished in one book. With every new century the volume of literature on Ibn ʿArabi and his followers grew exponentially, making an exhaustive survey impossible. More importantly, much of the material from the later period remains unpublished and may take many more years to accumulate and classify. Therefore, instead of giving a sketchy account of the entire corpus of writings on Ibn ʿArabi over the last seven centuries, I decided to concentrate on those writers who shaped the polemic over the Ibn ʿArabi issue.

Although the present study covers the period between the 7th A.H./13th C.E. and the 10th A.H./16th C.E. centuries, one should not assume that subsequently the debates around Ibn ʿArabi suddenly subsided. On the contrary, with the rise of the Ottoman state, whose rulers came to view Ibn ʿArabi as a patron saint of their dynasty,[8] the controversy gained fresh momentum. As under the Mamluks, the leading scholars and government officials of the greatest Islamic empire continued to debate Ibn ʿArabi's "orthodoxy." An official ban on public defamation of Ibn ʿArabi throughout the Ottoman realm issued by the noted Ottoman scholar and statesman Kemal Pashazade (d. 940/1534) is just one example.[9] Likewise, Sultan Selim I commissioned the Meccan theologian Abu ʾl-Fath Muhammad Ibn Muzaffar, known as Shaykh Makki to compose an official apology for the Greatest Master.[10] Many Ottoman *ʿulamaʾ* followed suit, producing a substantial body of pro-Ibn ʿArabi literature.[11] Finally, perhaps the most influential apology for, and popularization of, Ibn ʿArabi's teaching was written by the great scholar and Sufi of Ottoman Egypt, ʿAbd al-Wahhab al-Shaʿrani (d. 973/1565).[12]

Ibn ʿArabi's legacy, which occupied scholars throughout the Ottoman age, made a remarkable comeback in the 14th/19th-20th centuries, when the problem of Ibn ʿArabi was once again propelled to the forefront by political and ideological developments.[13] The other areas of the Muslim world—the Maghrib, Iran, India, and, to a lesser extent, Central Asia—did not remain immune to the Ibn ʿArabi controversy. In India, for instance, debates over Ibn ʿArabi's legacy took on the form of a bitter antagonism between the followers of the doctrine of the unity of being (pro-Ibn ʿArabi) and those who supported the unity of witnessing (anti-Ibn ʿArabi), first formulated by ʿAla al-dawla Simnani (d. 736/1336) and later refined by the great Indo-Muslim reformer Ahmad Sirhindi (d. 1034/1624).[14]

Why was Ibn ʿArabi so important to the Muslims of such varied backgrounds in such diverse societies and historical epochs? This study will try to give an answer to this question.

The first two chapters of this book examine the beginnings of the anti-Ibn ʿArabi debate in the late 7th/13th–early 8th/14th centuries. This was a seminal period for Ibn ʿArabi's legacy—a time when his metaphysical, theological, and exegetical tenets were closely scrutinized and evaluated by the educated classes of the Muslim *umma.* In coming to grips with his open-ended, often contradictory statements, the scholars forged the first polemical arguments (both pro and contra), laying the groundwork for one of Islam's most enduring doctrinal controversies. Since then, these arguments, substantially augmented and refined, became the stock-in-trade of the later writers on this topic.

In reviewing the development of the argumentative strategies deployed by the polemicists I shall occasionally depart from a strict chronological order. Such departures are especially numerous in Chapter 2, where the discourse oscillates freely between the historical present and the historical future. This technique allows us to observe how the original narrative motifs were restated by later writers, highlighting the use of his statements and the facts of his biography for polemical purposes.

Throughout my study, I am trying to demonstrate that the scholarly discourse around Ibn ʿArabi's teaching hinged on a set of thematic axes that remained unchanged in different historical and theological contexts. In line with this approach, comparisons will be drawn between the first occurrence of a given motif or fact of Ibn ʿArabi's life and its subsequent "creative" evolvements, and occasionally outright abuses, by later disputants. This diachronic method is less prominent in the later chapters, where it is supplanted by a more consistently synchronic perspective. In each case, the shifts in chronological framework are dictated by the nature of material under discussion.

Ibn ʿArabi's Life and Work

Although this is not a study of Ibn ʿArabi himself, at least some general idea of his life and work is essential to make sense of the polemic over his legacy. Without this background knowledge, the argumentation adduced by both sides engaged in the disputation may be lost on the reader.

Muhammad b. ʿAli b. Muhammad Ibn al-ʿArabi, as he styled himself in his writings, or Muhyi al-din Ibn ʿArabi, as he was known among eastern Muslims, was born in 560/1165 in the Andalusi town of Murcia.[15] When he was still a child, the Almoravid kingdom that had ruled the Maghrib and al-Andalus for almost two centuries was overthrown by another Berber dynasty, the Almohads. At the time of this momentous transition from one dynastic rule to the other, Ibn ʿArabi's father, an Arab of noble pedigree, held an important office at the court of the sovereign of Murcia named Ibn Mardanish.[16] Following the death of this ruler, Ibn ʿArabi's father and his family moved to Seville where he was taken into government service by an Almohad ruler. Under the Almohads Seville experienced an unprecedented cultural florescence, replacing the old capital, Cordoba, as the main center of Muslim culture and learning in al-Andalus.[17] The young Ibn ʿArabi made good use of this cultural ambience. He studied the traditional Muslim sciences under the guidance of the best Andalusi *ʿulama'* of the epoch and soon excelled in all fields of intellectual endeavor, especially in the Arabic belles-lettres.

Little is known about that "profane" period of his life, which he later viewed as an insignificant prelude to his subsequent conversion to mysticism.[18] There are some indications that he was employed as a secretary to the governor of Seville, although the exact circumstances of his early career remain obscure. In Ibn ʿArabi's own words, at that time he led a life typical of a wealthy young man of noble Arab stock and vaguely alluded to the profligate carousels and merry pastimes in which he indulged together with his aristocratic boon companions.[19]

Then, unexpectedly, came a conversion to the Sufi path that was precipitated by an unearthly voice commanding Ibn ʿArabi to abandon his ungodly ways and to devote himself to what he was created for—the service of God.[20] Deeply shaken by this miraculous episode,

Ibn ʿArabi parted company with the people of his class, and started to attend the gatherings of ragtag ascetics whom the snobbish Muslim scholars and king's courtiers dismissed as illiterate bumpkins, tricksters, and worthless beggars.[21]

Unheedful of the repeated admonitions and even ridicule by his former friends and relatives, Ibn ʿArabi stubbornly refused to relinquish his new brethren in God. The sincerity and finality of his conversion is attested to by the rest of his life. Following the example of his Sufi friends, Ibn ʿArabi engaged in the ascetic exercises associated with the initial stages of the mystical path. We see him practicing the constant invocation of God, vigils, fasting, vows, retreat, and meditation. Parallel to the practical training, he vigorously pursued the study of the classics of Sufi literature under the renowned mystical masters of Seville. Judging by Ibn ʿArabi's own accounts (which, it should be noted, are often self-serving and chronologically inconsistent), he soon learned all he could from the Sufis of Seville and started to crisscross the Iberian Peninsula in search of a more advanced spiritual direction. His quest for mystical knowledge took him to the Maghrib, where he benefited from many outstanding representatives of Western Sufism, who pursued the mystical path established by the great North African saint Abu Madyan (d. 594/1197).[22] According to Ibn ʿArabi's own testimony, he soon outstripped his Maghribi teachers in the degree of spiritual attainment as well as in the mastery of the Sufi tradition. Still a young man, he reportedly achieved the status of an accomplished Sufi *shaykh* surrounded by a reverential retinue of disciples.[23]

At the age of thirty-five, Ibn ʿArabi left al-Andalus on a pilgrimage to Mecca never to return to his native land that was shrinking in the face of the Christian Reconquista. In the East, Ibn ʿArabi journeyed extensively and studied under the most prominent religious teachers of his time. He spent several years in the Hijaz, whereupon he visited Palestine, Syria, Iraq, and Anatolia. Wherever he wandered, he was accompanied by a small group of devoted disciples, some of whom became major exponents of his teachings.[24] In addition to studying *hadith*—a preoccupation he pursued until his last days—Ibn ʿArabi taught his own works to the Sufis of the Hijaz, Aleppo, Konya, Siwas, Baghdad, and Damascus. His expertise in esoteric and exoteric sciences won him many followers including a few Muslim sovereigns who lavishly supported him and his disciples. In Syria, Ibn ʿArabi enjoyed the patronage of the Ayyubid princes who granted him generous allowances in money and property. In Anatolia also, he made friends with the local Saljuq sultans and their courtiers, including the father of his foremost disciple, Sadr al-din al-Qunawi (d. 673/1274).[25] His decade-long sojourn in the Saljuqid kingdom left a deep imprint on the intellectual life of Muslim Anatolia (Rum), which became an important center of the transmission and dissemination of his mystical ideas. While there, he wrote many Sufi works and trained numerous disciples. Simultaneously he counseled the sultan of Rum on religious and political issues and composed for him a letter of practical advice.[26] Unlike many of his learned contemporaries who craved royal favors, Ibn ʿArabi seems to have firmly adhered to the Sufi principle of staying away from secular authorities. Although he did occasionally accept royal patronage, he neither amassed a fortune nor entered the official service of any ruler.

From 620/1226 until his death in 638/1240 Ibn ʿArabi lived in Damascus where he enjoyed the protection of the local Ayyubids. He made friends with some influential religious officials of Damascus, who proudly counted themselves among his disciples. Thanks to these connections Ibn ʿArabi was free to promulgate his esoteric teachings in spite of occasional protests of some concerned local *ʿulamaʾ* such as ʿIzz al-din Ibn ʿAbd al-Salam.[27] His teaching sessions, however, were confined to a narrow circle of close followers and admirers who alone were able to make sense out of his difficult discourses. Only after his death did his esoteric writings acquire a wider readership. Some conservative *ʿulamaʾ* were scandalized by his bold insights and hastened to condemn them as outright "heresy," setting in motion the torrid controversy that is the subject of this study.

In Damascus, Ibn ʿArabi wrote his controversial masterpiece titled "The Bezels of Wisdom" (*Fusus al-hikam*)—a brilliant, if extremely opaque essay on prophethood, mystical metaphysics, exegesis, and the nature of religious faith. In this comparatively short essay Ibn ʿArabi addressed many critical issues of Muslim theology and laid down his metaphysical views that evince strong monistic tendencies.[28] To make matters worse, he did this in a way that baffled and antagonized many of his traditionally minded readers, exposing him to harsh criticism.

Parallel to the *Fusus* Ibn ʿArabi completed a final recension of his magnum opus, the "Meccan Openings" or "Meccan Revelations" (*Al-Futuhat al-makkiyya*)—a multivolume project he started during his stay in Mecca and continued to revise until his last years. The end result was a colossal (no hyperbole in this case) book that combines the characteristics of a spiritual diary and an encyclopedia of the traditional Islamic sciences seen from an esoteric perspective. With the two major works of his life successfully accomplished Ibn ʿArabi passed away peacefully in 638/1240, surrounded by his disciples and relatives. Today, his domed shrine in one of the suburbs of Damascus attracts numerous admirers of his genius who come to visit him from far and wide.

Ibn ʿArabi is justly regarded as among the most prolific Muslim writers ever: his legacy consists of an estimated 300 to 400 works. Their length vary from slim two-page pamphlets to medium-size tracts to such monuments as his unfinished Qurʾanic commentary and the *Futuhat.* The subjects of Ibn ʿArabi's writings are extremely diverse.[29] Moreover, he approached the traditional Islamic subjects from a peculiar angle that was dictated by his deeply personal vision of God and of the world. To wit, he seems to have been interested not in the subject as such as in its relevance to a set of moral, theological, and cosmic insights that he wanted to illuminate. At the same time, neither in the *Fusus* nor in the *Futuhat,* nor in any other work, does he provide a succinct and unequivocal account of his teaching. On the contrary, his discourse is deliberately crafted so as to obfuscate its essence.

In line with this discursive strategy, Ibn ʿArabi couches his favorite motifs and ideas in the lexicon and imagery of traditional Muslim disciplines, especially *kalam* and *fiqh.* Additionally, he availed himself of the terminology and topoi of Arabic poetry, literary criticism, mythology, and occult sciences. In an effort to convey to the reader his elusive mystical insights and fleeting experiences, Ibn ʿArabi often resorted to "symbolic images that evoke emergent associations rather than fixed propositions."[30] Although he occasionally did use syllogistic reasoning, he considered it to be incapable of expressing the dizzying fluidity and dynamic that characterize his vision of reality. To compensate for the perceived inadequacy of syllogistic arguments Ibn ʿArabi deliberately loaded his discourses with shocking antinomies and involved allegories that defy any rational explanation. Little wonder that his works often strike his reader as a mishmash of themes and topoi operating on several parallel discursive levels ranging from poetry and mythology to jurisprudence and speculative theology. These are, in a nutshell, the major features of Ibn ʿArabi's narrative method that account for the difficulties one encounters in trying to elucidate or summarize his ideas.

Recent studies of his work have expressed doubt over the stereotyped view that portrays him as a thoroughgoing esotericist who was completely oblivious to the external aspects of Islamic religion.[31] Supporters of this approach argue that Western scholarship has been insensitive to the more exoteric aspects of Ibn ʿArabi's work, namely his unflagging preoccupation with the *hadith, fiqh,* and the minutia of the Muslim ritual. In rejecting this one-sided view of the Greatest Master, the revisionist scholars point out that the topics of many of Ibn ʿArabi's "esoteric" treatises are in fact quite traditional. Consequently, so the argument goes, the more conventional aspect of his legacy has been underestimated by both Ibn ʿArabi's followers and his antagonists who tended to focus on the more controversial aspects of his work.

A closer examination of Ibn ʿArabi's purportedly "exoteric" writings reveals that his treatment of such traditional issues as speculative theology and *fiqh* betrays the same underlying commitment to his favorite mystical ideas and esoteric topoi.[32] However, one cannot but agree with the revisionist scholars in that the exoteric or traditional facet of Ibn ʿArabi's legacy has not yet received the attention it deserves. For all intents and purposes, the stark reality is that students of the Greatest Master in the East and in the West continue to concentrate on the sensational esoteric ideas of the *Fusus* at the expense of the more conventional elements of his oeuvre.

Unsurprisingly, to the general Muslim and Western reader, Ibn ʿArabi remains first and foremost the author of the *Fusus al-hikam,* "The Bezels of Wisdom"—an abstruse and elliptic work that recapitulates the cardinal themes of Ibn ʿArabi's theosophical discourse. Although the much more detailed *Futuhat* is also viewed as a hallmark of Ibn ʿArabi's weltanschauung, it is too lengthy, technical, unstructured, and repetitious to attract anyone but the most devout investigator. Apart from these two writings, the Muslim reader is also likely to be aware of Ibn ʿArabi's poetry that purports (misleadingly) to represent the gist of his complex doctrine. Disparate poetic fragments from Ibn ʿArabi's *diwan* are often quoted by his antagonists as proof of his radical departure from the "true Islam."[33]

As regards Ibn ʿArabi's other writings, they are known only to a narrow circle of specialists.[34] Some of them are little more than essays and rough drafts that were later polished and incorporated into the monumental *Futuhat.* Ibn ʿArabi's minor tracts from the Andalusi period contain elaborately veiled predictions about the imminent advent of a divinely inspired messiah (*mahdi*) from the "house of the Prophet." They reflect a preoccupation with messianic eschatology that Ibn ʿArabi shared with the mystical masters of the Maghrib and al-Andalus whose ideas he developed in his later writings.[35]

In short, all of these writings, including the voluminous collection of Ibn ʿArabi's poetry, have been overshadowed by the controversial *Fusus.* No wonder that this work has elicited most of the polemical responses that are discussed in the chapters that follow. As we shall see, in the polemic over Ibn ʿArabi's legacy, his other writings were rarely, if ever invoked.

What is, then, the essence of his doctrine in the *Fusus?* The question is not as innocent as it might appear at first sight. The text of the *Fusus* stubbornly eludes any summarization through abstract terms to the extent that some scholars have doubted whether Ibn ʿArabi had any meaningful philosophical doctrine at all.[36] In the words of a Western investigator, Ibn ʿArabi "integrally combined the contrasting approaches of earlier Islamic intellectual traditions that had focused respectively on spiritual disciplines and contemplation, intellectual and scientific inquiry, and the elaboration of scriptural and prophetic teachings" in a way that "was never really repeated or adequately imitated by any subsequent Islamic author."[37] In the *Fusus,* Ibn ʿArabi's discourse is particularly (perhaps deliberately) arcane, presenting the reader with a tangle of disparate theological and metaphysical propositions cast in mythopoeic parables and recondite terminology.[38] Throughout the *Fusus,* Ibn ʿArabi couches his intensely personal experience of God and the universe in a variety of discursive garbs from scriptural exegesis to speculative theology to *fiqh* and romantic poetry. Paradoxically, these discursive show windows are not easily interchangeable: they color the very visions and experiences that Ibn ʿArabi endeavors to convey, making it difficult to neatly separate the content from the form. True, an experienced reader may identify a few recurring motifs that permeate Ibn ʿArabi's entire narrative. Yet, one can never be sure whether in reformulating these motifs their original meaning is preserved intact. On the contrary, it often seems that the new verbal shells transform the very meaning of these motifs. Nor can one be sure whether a given formulation is final or just another rephrasing of the same recurrent theme. The goal of this deliberately elusive discourse is to "carry the reader outside the work itself into the life and cosmos which it is attempting to interpret."[39] This effect is achieved through breaking the shackles of habitual human perception by a kaleidoscopic change of perspective—a method that a Western scholar aptly described as "mystical dialectic."[40]

Further adding to the specificity of the *Fusus* is the way in which its elliptic narrative compels the reader to engage in the constant process of decoding in order to unravel its underlying import. Faced with the absence of an unequivocal referential framework or a conventional syllogistic argumentation, the reader has to make use of his personal resources, such as educational background, world-outlook, and intuition. As Morris put it, Ibn ʿArabi's esoteric texts "are meant to function as a sort of spiritual mirror, reflecting and revealing the inner intentions, assumptions and predilections of each reader . . . with profound clarity."[41] It is, therefore, hardly surprising that each Islamic generation offered its own understanding of the *Fusus,* though, as we shall see, in the end several authoritative trends within the interpretive tradition triumphed over creativity. Given Ibn ʿArabi's discursive strategy, one can see why these numerous interpretations have failed to exhaust the potential of his polyvalent and multilayered text. A recent rediscovery of Ibn ʿArabi's "contribution to mankind" by some Western intellectuals is the best testimony to this remarkable feature of his oeuvre.[42]

In light of the foregoing, one can see why Ibn ʿArabi's narrative method continues to puzzle the students of his thought. This, however, is not to say that his principal ideas cannot be expressed in a language of abstract philosophical categories. Shorn of its deliberate obfuscation and confusing digressions, Ibn ʿArabi's discourse in the *Fusus* boils down to a limited number of cut-and-dried philosophical propositions that very often appear to be in conflict with the exoteric Muslim dogma. This impression is further enhanced by Ibn ʿArabi's exegetical paradoxes that he employed to awaken his readers to the hidden dimensions of the revealed texts. By actualizing the conceptual and spiritual potentialities of the Qurʾan and the Sunna, Ibn ʿArabi creates what amounts to a new, esoteric prophesy.[43]

Obviously, his daring interpretations of the Qurʾan and *hadith* did not go unheeded. Like his metaphysical and theological propositions they aroused the ire of exoterically minded scholars. As we shall see, his "allegorical" exegesis was continually denounced by his critics not only as farfetched and arbitrary but also as one that cast doubt on the finality of the revelation.

At the same time, it is obvious that Ibn ʿArabi's discursive methods and esoteric exegesis are uniquely well suited to his ultimate goal—to convey to the reader an intuitive perception of the intense polarity within the originally unique and indivisible Divine Absolute that unfolds its properties in an astounding multiplicity of the empirical universe. It is this spontaneous self-polarization within the unique Divine Godhead that Ibn ʿArabi found particularly fascinating. Anxious to express the evasive interplay of the primordial, immutable oneness, and the multiplicity and change inherent in its empirical manifestation, he experimented with nonconventional discursive methods. Since he applied his experimentation to the sacred texts of Islam, he inevitably laid himself open to accusations of heresy and unbelief. What we call "the problem of Ibn ʿArabi" can be explained, in part, by the fact that his theological opponents were neither willing nor able to accept his rules of the game. Briefly put, whereas Ibn ʿArabi's paradoxes and antinomianism were deliberately geared to disrupting the conventionalities of scholastic reasoning, his opponents continued to test his statements by the very conventions he sought to dispel. Hence, the inevitable collision of world-orienational philosophies in which the opponents were simply unable to see eye to eye.

Should we for a moment ignore the peculiarities of Ibn ʿArabi's discursive method and present his abstruse narratives in conventional terms we would wind up with an assortment of trite philosophical propositions that evince neo-Platonic inspiration. Like many religious thinkers before and after him, Ibn ʿArabi was captivated by the idea of the universe as a temporal and spatial unwinding of divine perfections that he equated with the manifestation of divine attributes or names. In his scheme, these attributes/names are primordial exemplars, the matrix upon which God shaped the empirical universe into being. This concept of creation is akin to the medieval Christian doctrines that also emphasized the exemplary structure of the universe. One immediately thinks, for example, of medieval Christian "realism" positing an intimate correspondence between the *modus intelligendi* and *modus essendi* as the key to understanding the world around us.[44] In a like vein, Ibn ʿArabi viewed his immutable entities (*aʿyan thabita*) as paradigmatic creative possibilities, which are eternally fixed in God's knowledge.[45]

According to Ibn ʿArabi, the unfolding of the divine perfections in space and time was occasioned by God's primeval desire to contemplate himself in the mirror of the cosmos—a notion that is intimately linked to the pervasive medieval analogy of the micro- and macrocosm. This analogy, in turn, evokes the *homo imago Dei* motif of ancient Greek philosophy.[46] Each divine attribute or perfection, in Ibn ʿArabi's view, is manifested in the universe in accord with each individual creature's primordial predisposition to receive it. This predisposition, or readiness, is itself predicated on the creature's primordial essence that is part of God's knowledge of himself and the world prior to creation. Hence, in line with the neo-Platonic doctrines, which were embraced by medieval European theologians as well as by their Muslim colleagues, the world can be seen as a theophany, or manifestation of God's potentialies and perfections.[47]

Ibn ʿArabi's metaphysics describes the world as a product of the divine self-reflection that prompts God to manifest himself in the things and phenomena of the empirical universe. This idea shocked his opponents who (mis)took it for a veiled acknowledgment of the substantial identity between God and the world that effectively disposed with divine transcendency and self-sufficiency. In such a theory, God was no longer the absolutely otherworldly and impregnable entity of mainstream Muslim theologians. He rather becomes part and parcel of, and immanent to, His creation. Hence, the widespread association of Ibn ʿArabi with the doctrine of the oneness of being (*wahdat al-wujud*) which is generally understood as an Islamic prototype of Spinozian pantheism.[48]

Likewise, Ibn ʿArabi's theory of the immutable entities (the primordial concepts of future creation that had eternally existed in the divine consciousness) was construed by many Muslim scholars as springing from the "heretical" doctrine that posited the eternity of the world (*al-dahriyya*).[49] By recognizing that God had created the cosmos in accordance with a preestablished pattern determined by these immutable entities (considered somehow independent from God), Ibn ʿArabi, in the opinion of his critics, effectively did away with divine omnipotence. The Sufi, however, never plainly stated this: rather we see that he constantly focuses on the ever-changing manifestations of the immutable entities without, however, specifying the nature of their relationship with the Godhead.

In addition to the critical concepts of existential oneness (*wahda*) and the immutable entities, the *Fusus* outlines a few other theological propositions that raised the hackles of his learned readers. Among such irritative propositions is Ibn ʿArabi's notion of two conflicting modes of divine volition: one pertaining to the creative command, the other—to the obligating command. The former stresses the role of God as the creator of the universe, while the latter is concerned primarily with the moral and normative imperatives of the divine dispensation.[50] From the perspective of the creative command, all human actions are a product of the Divine Will and, therefore, are equally "pleasing" to God. The obligating command, on the other hand, conditions human actions by declaring them either "good" or "evil." In other words, it urges humans to comply with legal rulings and moral precepts promulgated in the *shariʿa,* threatening punishment to those who disobey. Many theologians rejected this dichotomy of the Divine Will as a gateway to antinomianism and moral irresponsibility.[51] The other objectionable ideas in the *Fusus* are, for the most part, corollary of the seminal theological and metaphysical propositions that were just outlined.

Our description of Ibn ʿArabi's principal themes would be incomplete without referring to his famous concept of the perfect man (*in-*

san kamil) which is explicated in several chapters of the *Fusus*. In Ibn ʿArabi's view, the perfect human being forms the critical link between the two diametrically opposed aspects of the unique divine reality. Neither an animal nor an angel, man hovers between the world of corruption and the world of immutability by combining in himself the characteristics of both realms. By virtue of his intermediary position, man becomes a microcosmic reality in which God contemplates himself in the most adequate form. As Austin, put it: "the Perfect Man is that human individual who has perfectly realized the full spiritual potential of the human state, who has realized in himself and his experience the Oneness of Being that underlies all the apparent multiplicity of existence."[52] For Ibn ʿArabi, the perfect mystical man constitutes the very cause, and the ultimate goal of creation.

In Ibn ʿArabi's writings, the perfect man presents himself not only as a purely metaphysical abstraction, but also as a quite real supreme saint (*wali*), or the spiritual "pole" (*qutb*), of the epoch, who was entrusted by God with leading humanity to salvation. In some of Ibn ʿArabi's texts, this perfect individual is placed in the context of the historical experience of the Muslim community and identified with the awaited world-restorer, the eschatological *mahdi* who appears at the end of time to revivify religion and to prepare the ground for the final arrival of the Qurʾanic Jesus, the harbinger of the final hour.[53] In several poetic passages, Ibn ʿArabi identified himself with this supreme saint of the epoch, although it is not clear whether this was his genuine conviction or just a figure of speech. Nevertheless, the very fact that he toyed with this idea incensed the Muslim scholars who were anxious to protect the Muslim community from sedition by self-proclaimed saviors.

Whatever messianic pretensions he had, Ibn ʿArabi entertained them in private. At least, he never disclosed them publicly. His discretion helps explain why his espousal of such potentially disruptive ideas did not get him into trouble during his lifetime. Ibn ʿArabi's cautious religio-political stance and preoccupation with inner experiences and visions explains why, in an age that witnessed the formation of the major Sufi brotherhoods, he founded neither an organized *tariqa* nor a popular school of Sufism.[54]

Ibn ʿArabi's failure to attract a large popular following is due in part to the obscurity and elusiveness of his teaching. Unlike the founders of popular Sufi orders (e.g., ʿAbd al-Qadir al-Jili, al-Suhrawardi, Najm al-din Kubra, and al-Shadhili), the Greatest Master offered no clear-cut practical guidelines that could be readily translated into popular patterns of social behavior. Although he occasionally does give some practical recommendations for beginning

Sufis, Ibn ʿArabi's works were too recondite for the majority of his coreligionists and, therefore, remained confined to, and fully appreciated by, a relatively small intellectual elite. Paradoxically, the very difficulty of Ibn ʿArabi's teaching seems to have determined its extraordinary pervasiveness and tenacity, since it presented a continual problem for every new generation of Muslim scholars.

1

DEFINING THE APPROACH

Ibn ʿArabi has no reason to complain about biographers ignoring him in their works; this is not usually the case in Muslim prosopographical literature.[1] The accounts of his life and work by his younger contemporaries resurface in the subsequent centuries, "enriched" with details not found in the original sources. Such later elaborations indicate the abiding importance of Ibn ʿArabi for later generations of Muslim writers. As understandable as these elaborations are in view of the subsequent theological disputations surrounding Ibn ʿArabi's name, they considerably complicate the task of reconstructing an objective portrait of the Greatest Master.[2]

At the same time, for a researcher looking into the process of image-making in medieval Islamic society the numerous biographical notices on Ibn ʿArabi are a treasure chest of information that reveals the critical aspects of his personality and intellectual heritage as viewed by medieval observers. Following Chamberlain's incisive suggestion,[3] the impersonal and formulaic character of medieval biographies widely bemoaned by Western Islamicists is precisely the one that helps to get valuable insight into the self-image and intellectual universe of the *ʿulamaʾ*. Rather than ascertaining the accuracy of single anecdotes that constitute biographical entries, I shall try to bring out their uses in medieval biographies of the Greatest Master and their intended effect on the readers.

In Chapter 2, I shall review the testimonies of Ibn ʿArabi's biographers from the 6th/13th centuries onward with special reference to the anecdotal material contained therein. This review will help to determine how Ibn ʿArabi's personality was reimagined and reproduced in the collective memory of the Muslim community over time. This approach seeks to render justice to the concerns and order of priorities of the society of which Ibn ʿArabi was an outstanding, if somewhat atypical, representative. Before turning to these issues, it is necessary to situate this study within the vast corpus of academic literature on Ibn ʿArabi and on his work.

To a large extent, this study was motivated by the dramatic disparity in the way in which Ibn ʿArabi is portrayed by Western and Muslim scholars. Even a cursory glance at the studies of the Sufi master by such Western or Western-trained researchers as Nyberg, Asin Palacios, Nicholson, Afifi, Corbin, Burckhardt, Landau, Nasr, Izutsu, and more recently Austin, Chittick, Chodkiewicz, and Addas reveals that, despite the diversity of their personal backgrounds and methodologies, they tend to present Ibn ʿArabi as a great genius of Islamic mystical thought who stood head and shoulders above both his Muslim contemporaries and later his critics. In a similar way, these Western investigators see Ibn ʿArabi as a individual who was grossly misjudged by his narrow-minded coreligionists.

With this notion of Ibn ʿArabi as their starting point, the Western scholars mentioned above set about conveying to the uninitiated the unfathomable greatness and subtlety of Ibn ʿArabi's thought. In so doing, they diligently dissected Ibn ʿArabi's principal works with Western analytical tools, leaving out the native Muslim opinions of Ibn ʿArabi and his work that are scattered across innumerable biographies, theological treatises, and polemical tracts.

Western Islamicists' disregard for the Islamic material on the Greatest Master was dictated in part by their belief that Muslim views of his legacy are inherently biased, simplistic, and therefore irrelevant to the task of reconstructing his sophisticated doctrines. One result of this disregard was that the assessments of Ibn ʿArabi by Muslim authors were effectively banished from the pages of Western monographs, which relegated the authority to interpret Ibn ʿArabi to a handful of his Muslim followers who were handpicked by Western investigators. The testimonies and commentaries of Ibn ʿArabi's followers have since dominated Western discussions of Sufi philosophy, which rely on them for the elucidation of obscure passages and terminology found in Ibn ʿArabi's works. Consequently, the Western audience has been presented with a thoroughly sanitized (and generally sympathetic) portrait of the Sufi thinker and his teaching.

Naturally, Western exponents of Ibn ʿArabi have focused on the more sensational aspects of his thought. Such an approach has tended to reduce Ibn ʿArabi's complex legacy to a few "congenial" topics, which fascinated Western writers but which were not necessarily representative of how Ibn ʿArabi was assessed in his own environment. Through addressing such favored topics, several principal approaches to Ibn ʿArabi have crystallized in Western scholarship. Western humanist scholars with a solid background in the history of classical and European philosophy were attracted primarily to Ibn ʿArabi's metaphysical speculations and cosmology. Consequently, they usually occupied themselves with gauging the extent to which Ibn ʿArabi was influenced by neo-Platonic philosophy or its Christian interpreters.[4]

A different view of Ibn ʿArabi was taken by European clergymen who were concerned with detecting the underlying affinities between Christian and Islamic theology with a view to advancing an Islamo-Christian dialogue. Such Christian scholars treated Ibn ʿArabi, if not exactly as a crypto-Christian, then at least as a freethinker open to other religious confessions, especially Christianity.[5] However, a scrutiny of Ibn ʿArabi's attitude toward other confessions, reveals little direct indebtedness to, or sympathy for, Christian doctrines. As in the case of the philosophically oriented students of Ibn ʿArabi, the ideological agenda that motivated the Christian scholars rendered them oblivious to his assessment by his own community.

The pioneering studies of the Greatest Master by Corbin and Izutsu in the 1950s and 1960s provided a more objective glimpse into how Ibn ʿArabi was perceived by his fellow Muslims. Both scholars brought into sharp focus the heretofore neglected aspects of Ibn ʿArabi's thought, consciously abandoning the Eurocentric perspective that shaped the work of their predecessors. While Corbin justly questioned the long-established tradition of treating Ibn ʿArabi as a neo-Platonic thinker par excellence and underscored the Islamic origins of his doctrine, Izutsu carried out an excellent analysis of Ibn ʿArabi's philosophical views as interpreted by his Persian follower, al-Qashani. Chittick's illuminating analysis of the strengths and weakness of their methodological assumptions[6] absolves me from the need to detail them here. Suffice it to say that their views of Ibn ʿArabi were too personal, colored as they were by the scholars' spiritual and intellectual commitments, to serve as a foundation for a balanced academic examination of his weltanschauung.

More recently, new trends in the study of Islam's greatest mystical thinker have asserted themselves. They are determined by the realization that, while the recondite text of the *Fusus* has been studied backward and forward, the rest of Ibn ʿArabi's vast oeuvre has been overlooked by investigators. This realization caused some scholars to redirect their attention to his neglected writings, which, as they soon discovered, were much more lucid than the *Fusus* and, additionally, more in concert with mainstream Sunni theology. Blazing the path for future investigators, Yahia compiled a massive catalog of Ibn ʿArabi's works that has become an excellent introduction to the transmission and reception of Ibn ʿArabi's written legacy in the centuries following his death.[7] More importantly for our purpose, the Egyptian scholar was the first to draw the attention of the researchers to the polemical and interpretative literature around the *Fusus* and, to a lesser extent, the *Futuhat.* Finally, he furnished a helpful list of Ibn ʿArabi's advocates and critics.[8]

Yahia's next project—a critical edition of "The Meccan Revelations"[9]—invigorated academic interest in this unique monument of Sufi literature. Exploiting its riches Chodkiewicz provided a brilliant analysis of Ibn ʿArabi's theory of sainthood, which was based almost entirely on a close reading of his magnum opus.[10] Later, Chodkiewicz supervised an ambitious Franco-American project that led to an annotated translation of several chapters from the *Futuhat* by the leading Western experts on Ibn ʿArabi's thought.[11] In his latest book, *An Ocean Without Shore,* the French scholar continues to make extensive use of the *Futuhat* in an effort to prove that Ibn ʿArabi was a perfectly orthodox scholar, who was misinterpreted by his obscurantist critics.[12]

Efforts to shake off the deeply ingrained obsession with the *Fusus* and to work out an understanding of Ibn ʿArabi grounded on a broader textual basis culminated in Chittick's recent study of the *Futuhat.*[13] His "Sufi Path of Knowledge" introduces the Western audience to the original complexity of Ibn ʿArabi's thought, making no concessions to the expectations and tastes of the Western reader.[14] At the risk of snubbing the feelings of those who consider Ibn ʿArabi to be a bearer of some universal, supraconfessional spirituality Chittick boldly reclaims him for Islam. As with Chodkiewicz, he calls in doubt the view that Ibn ʿArabi was a thoroughgoing freethinker bent on undermining the foundations of Sunni Islam. Chittick's study depicts Ibn ʿArabi as a mainstream Sunni thinker of the highest integrity who was maligned by a few stick-in-the-mud Muslim divines led by Ibn Taymiyya.[15] For Chittick, Ibn ʿArabi's message was to impart to his coreligionists a new, deeper understanding of the Qurʾan and Sunna, without, however, departing from the letter of the Muslim revelation.[16]

Chittick emphasizes that Ibn ʿArabi's respect for the revealed Law, which is evident from the *Futuhat,* was his genuine concern, not just "a window dressing," as some Western writers suggested.[17] Supported by Chittick's brilliant translations and vast Islamological erudition, his vision of the Greatest Master seems very compelling indeed. Yet, like his predecessors, Chittick focuses almost exclusively on Ibn ʿArabi's self-image, making short shrift of how Ibn ʿArabi was judged by the majority of Muslim *ʿulamaʾ*. His attempt to cast Ibn ʿArabi as a mainstream thinker rests for the most part on the internal evidence thoroughly culled from the Shaykh's own works.[18] But then again one can hardly expect Ibn ʿArabi to present himself as someone other than a faithful adherent of the *sharīʿa*. As the fierce polemic around his name abundantly shows, Ibn ʿArabi's protestations of his orthodoxy failed to lull his learned critics into taking this self-portrait for granted. They judged him on the basis of his theological and metaphysical propositions and of their implications (perhaps unintended) for the Muslim community at large. It is here that the cleavage between Ibn ʿArabi's self-perception and his assessment by others is at its widest.

Who, then, was the "real" Ibn ʿArabi and what determines his continuing relevance for the Muslim community? The present study is an attempt to answer this question. Anticipating the discussion to follow, I would tentatively describe him as a gifted religious reformer—not unlike al-Ghazali—with a unique spiritual message to convey to his community. The essence of this message seems to have consisted in curing the Muslim community of the perceived spiritual malaise which, in Ibn ʿArabi's mind, afflicted it as a punishment for a barren, literal interpretation of the Islamic revelation by his coreligionists. In line with this grand scheme, Ibn ʿArabi offered the Islamic community an esoteric panacea, for the most part unsuccessfully.[19] This overriding reformist concern provides a helpful clue to Ibn ʿArabi's personality and thought.

In tracing the fate of his legacy through the centuries,[20] this study gives his opponents and skeptics an opportunity to plead their case. Until their voices have been heard, one can hardly give the "Ibn-ʿArabi problem" the justice it deserves.

Ibn ʿArabi in Recent Western Scholarship

One feature that contemporary Western Islamicists share with their 19th-century forbearers is a genuine admiration for the great intellectual and cultural achievements of Islamic civilization. From this perspective, the great complexity and sophistication of Ibn ʿArabi's teaching makes an especially rewarding subject of scholarly inquiry. Not surprisingly today, as before, Islamicists continue to focus on the works of the so-called Ibn ʿArabi school of thought whose major representatives have been discussed by Morris and Chittick.[21] To these U.S. scholars goes the credit of providing an illuminating account of the ideas, problematics, and terminology of Ibn ʿArabi's later commentators, many of whom were original and important thinkers in their own right. While Morris and Chittick concentrate primarily on the Muslim East, Chodkiewicz has given a useful overview of the "traces" of Ibn ʿArabi's ideas and terminology in the popular religious lore of the Maghrib and Africa, namely religious poetry, Sufi litanies, and *tariqa* manuals. Chodkievicz has shown that Ibn ʿArabi's influence—often indirect and anonymous—on many important Sufi leaders of the Muslim West was profound and often critical.[22]

Ibn ʿArabi's reception by later Muslim scholars was addressed by Addas who analyzed several accounts of Ibn ʿArabi's life and work in Muslim biographical dictionaries. Since Addas's goal was to reconstruct an "historical" portrait of the Greatest Master, she carefully cleansed it from the legendary and fictitious layers that had adhered to it over the centuries. In light of this objective, Addas gave preference to Ibn ʿArabi's autobiographical narratives over his image in later biographies, which she dismissed as biased and inaccurate.[23] Apart from Addas's work, the evidence from the later biographical and polemical literature is examined in Chodkiewicz's *Ocean Without Shore,* which evinces an obvious apologetic agenda in presenting Ibn ʿArabi as an orthodox Muslim.[24]

By contrast, the present study avoids any presuppositions regarding Ibn ʿArabi's "orthodoxy"/"heresy" and focuses on the polemical discourse generated by both his admirers and antagonists. Accordingly, it relegates to the background the Greatest Master's understanding of himself and brings out those elements of his work and personality that his Muslim critics found particularly disconcerting or puzzling. For this purpose, the deliberate polemical distortions and fanciful anecdotes that surround his name are particularly useful. The blatant prejudices and unbridled biases of the later sources reveal how stereotypes, images, and symbols were formed and sustained in the Muslim scholarly milieu and how they were integrated into the dialogues and theological debates within the Islamic intellectual tradition.

In a sense, the present work follows in the footsteps of Massignon's painstaking inquiry into the vicissitudes of the controversial legacy of al-Hallaj, the famous mystic of Baghdad executed in 309/922.[25] To anyone familiar with Massignon's magisterial study this parallel will soon become obvious. There are, however, substantial differences between my approach to Ibn ʿArabi and Massignon's treatment of "the first mystical martyr of Islam." Massignon took an intense personal interest in al-Hallaj, whom he considered to be a model Muslim mystic. His study, therefore, is overtly sympathetic with his protagonist and presents the latter's teaching and career as the culmination of Islam's spirituality.[26] In other words, Massignon took for granted the validity of al-Hallaj's understanding of Islam as well as the authenticity of his religious message to the community of Islam. As one Western scholar put it, Massignon's "goal was not to establish a chronology of al-Hallaj's actions, but somehow to penetrate the core of his spiritual personality, and to see it as a vital response to the totality of his milieu."[27] Faithful to this hermeneutical methodology, Massignon dismissed or chastised those Muslims who dared to question the authenticity of his hero's vocation as well as his compliance with the *shariʿa*. In contrast to Massignon, this book gives a careful consideration to the voices coming from both sides of the debate over Ibn ʿArabi's contribution to the Muslim tradition.

This nonaligned approach is likely to bar me from appreciating fully the psychological and experiential motives that determined the actions of the characters depicted in my study. Yet, in my estimation, this lack of "empathetic" understanding is more than compensated by the sympathetic portraits of Ibn ʿArabi created by Yahia, Addas, Chodkiewicz, Deladrière, and Gilis—portraits that often verge on partisanship. In consciously avoiding any ready-made suppositions regarding Ibn ʿArabi's teaching, I will try to look at him from different perspectives. As for the *sym-pathesis* and *compassion,* which were so vigorously promoted by Corbin as the surest way to better understand the Greatest Master,[28] they are not entirely absent from my study. However, I try to spread them more evenly among the parties to the debate.

Another feature of my approach to Ibn ʿArabi is determined by the nature of the sources at my disposal. Trite as this statement may sound, one need not be misled by the ostensibly "neutral" genres of historical, chronological, and biographical narratives that form the textual basis for this study. Very often it is impossible to distinguish between a purportedly "objective" historical and biographical document and a "subjective" polemical tract written by a Muslim scholar in defense or refutation of a theological cause.[29] This is not surprising, since both texts were often produced by the same people—that is, the professional *ʿulamaʾ* whose intellectual preferences and factional commitments left an imprint on all of their writings regardless of the genre. In other words, a work that we would normally class according to its outward features as either "history" or "biography" is often little more than a platform for making one's polemical point or for settling scores with one's learned rivals. Upon closer scrutiny, many of the historical and biographical works from the epoch under discussion turn out to be thinly camouflaged polemical treatises with clear-cut religio-political, and occasionally personal, agendas. Wittingly or not, their learned authors intruded their personal predilections quite bluntly and without much regard to impartiality. Another methodological problem arises from the thoroughly selective way in which medieval writers organized their prosopographical narratives. This process is often comparable to literary portraiture, so loaded it is with the author's personal biases and commitments. My study of numerous accounts of Ībn ʿArabi and his work has compelled me to believe that many of the sources in question should be treated as bona fide literary discourses.

2

THE BIOGRAPHICAL PRELUDE

Passionately you spoke of deaths,
as you registered them,
Until, one day, I saw your own name registered
among the dead.

An epitaph appended to the
autobiography of al-Fasi (d. 832/1459),
a great historian of Mecca.
Al-Fasi. *ʿIqd,* vol. 1, p. 363

Ibn ʿArabi's Biography: From Early Accounts to Later Interpretations

The portraits of the Greatest Master reconstructed by Corbin and, more recently, by Addas are largely based on autobiographical passages garnered from Ibn ʿArabi's *Futuhat.*[1] Another important source for Ibn ʿArabi's theological and spiritual background is his "Holy Spirit" (*Ruh al-quds*) and "The Glorious Pearl" (*al-Durra al-fakhira*),[2] which feature hagiographic sketches of his Sufi teachers in al-Andalus, the Maghrib, and the Middle East. Although revealing of Ibn ʿArabi's character and ambition, these narratives are often subjective and self-serving, insofar as they were dictated by Ibn ʿArabi's desire to impress Eastern mystics and to extol his Western masters.[3] All of these texts bear a remarkable testimony to Ibn ʿArabi's all-consuming preoccupation with spiritual and visionary experiences, meetings with departed saints and prophets, and similar miraculous events in his *mundus imaginalis.* Implicitly, these narratives present him as the foremost Sufi gnostic (*ʿarif*) of the age.

Regrettably, there is precious little evidence to allow us to have a more impartial view of Ibn ʿArabi. His companions fully shared his otherworldly orientation and never questioned the veracity of his statements, however extraordinary. Hardly anything can be learned from the short deferential remarks that punctuate the writings of his admiring companions: Badr al-din al-Habashi (d. 618/1221),[4] Ismaʿil Ibn Sawdakin (d. 646/1248),[5] and Sadr al-din al-Qunawi (d. 673/1274).[6] Additionally, some facts about Ibn ʿArabi's life and teaching methods are mentioned by al-Qunawi's direct disciple, Muʾayyad al-din al-Jandi (d. 690/1291).[7] It stands to reason that such testimonies are mostly epigonic and biased toward Ibn ʿArabi—the earliest hagiographical anecdotes that picture Ibn ʿArabi as a great miracle-worker and saint originated amid this circle of devout friends and disciples.[8] The paucity and tendentiousness of these accounts make especially important any evidence from contemporaries who were not part of his immediate milieu.

Unfortunately, such external testimonies are tantalizingly laconic. Surprisingly, Ibn ʿArabi, who spent more than two decades in Damascus and who paid only a few brief visits to Baghdad, is first mentioned in the annalistic writings that originated in Iraq. The renowned Hanbali *muhaddith* Ibn Nuqta (d. 629/1231)[9] must have been the first to include the following terse obituary of the Sufi master into his "Registry" (*Kitab al-taqyid*):

> He lived in Konya and Malatya for a while.[10] He composed [prose] writings and poetry, though I dislike his verses.

This brief notice has come down to us in the recension of al-Dhahabi, a bitter opponent of the Greatest Master, who obligingly explains the reason for Ibn Nuqta's dislike:

> It seems to me that he [Ibn Nuqta] referred to the unity [of God and man] (*ittihad*), the wine [themes], [Christian] churches, and [ancient] maxims which abound in [Ibn ʿArabi's] poetry.[11]

Some eighty years later, Ibn Hajar al-ʿAsqalani (d. 852/1449), another great *hadith* scholar critical of Ibn ʿArabi,[12] further specified al-Dhahabi's remark by quoting the very lines that allegedly irritated Ibn Nuqta. Curiously, they happen to be perhaps the most frequently cited verse from Ibn ʿArabi's "Interpreter of Desires" (*Tarjuman al-ashwaq*):[13]

> My heart has become capable of every form:
> It is a pasture for gazelles and a convent
> for Christian monks,

> A temple for idols and the pilgrim's
> Kaʿba and the tables of the Torah and the manuscripts
> of the Qurʾan. . . . [14]

Now it is impossible to determine what verse Ibn Nuqta actually had in mind. While a later biographer obligingly supplies an answer, its reliability raises serious doubts due to his opposition to Ibn ʿArabi's teaching. One therefore wonders whether Ibn Nuqta indeed was resentful of these lines, or else we are dealing with a deliberate polemical interpolation by Ibn ʿArabi's opponents.

The other Iraqi scholar to include Ibn ʿArabi in his biographical work was Ibn al-Dubaythi (d. 637/1239 or 639/1241),[15] who dedicated to Ibn ʿArabi a relatively detailed entry that is featured in his "continuation" (*dhayl*) of the history of Baghdad.[16] Ibn al-Dubaythi met Ibn ʿArabi during his brief visit to Baghdad. It was part of his method as a biographer to personally interview scholars whom he intended to mention in his annals,[17] which makes his account all the more valuable:

> Muhammad b. ʿAli b. Muhammad b. al-ʿArabi Abu ʿAbdallah[18] was born in the West. He visited Baghdad in 608. He had a unique mastery of [mystical] gnosis *(maʿrifa)*[19] and was dedicated fully to the path of the People of Truth,[20] ascetic discipline, spiritual exertion,[21] and [writing in] the language of the Sufis. I have seen many Sufis from Damascus, Syria, and the Hijaz who ascribed to him preeminence and a high rank among the people of the [Sufi] Path. He had many companions and followers. I have read some of his works that contained accounts of the dreams in which the Prophet appeared to the sleeper and spoke to him in his dream. [Ibn ʿArabi] related such dreams on the authority of those who had experienced them.[22] [When we met], he recorded a few such accounts from me, while I, in turn, took down from him *(ʿallaqtu ʿanhu)* a couple of them. In that year, Muhammad Ibn al-ʿArabi left Baghdad for Mecca on a pilgrimage. He then settled there, and I have not met him since.[23]

Characteristically, al-Dhahabi (d. 748/1348) later restates Ibn al-Dubaythi's account in an attempt to bring it in line with his strictly negative attitude toward the Greatest Master:

> [Ibn ʿArabi] was mentioned by Abu ʿAbdallah al-Dubaythi, who said:
>
> "He studied with many religious teachers of his [native] country. He was interested in [polite] literature (*adab*) and served as a

Table 1
Ibn ʿArabi's Early Biographers

Direct disciples	Neutral historians
Anatolia and Syria	Iraq/Baghdad
Ibn ʿArabi (d. 638/1240)	Ibn Nuqta (d. 629/1231), possibly the earliest mention of I.ʿA.
al-Habashi (d. 618/1221)	Ibn al-Dubaythi (d. 637/1239 or 639/1241), personal acquaintance; interview in Baghdad in 608
Ibn Sawdakin (d. 646/1248)	
al-Qunawi (d. 673/1274)	Ibn al-Najjar (d. 643/1245), personal meeting (?); quotes poetic lines recited to him by I.ʿA.
	Syria/Egypt
	Sibt Ibn al-Jawzi (d. 524/1256) mentions I.ʿA.'s esoteric propensities, details of the funeral, friendship with Ibn Zaki
al-Jandi (d. 690/1291)	Abu Shama (d. 665/1268) writes a lauditory notice; takes part in the funeral procession; condemns Ibn Zaki, but does not hold I.ʿA. responsible for his "transgressions"
	Ibn al-Musdi (d. 663/1265) praises I.ʿA.'s achievements, stresses his dual allegiance to Zahirism and to esoteric gnosis
Portrayed Ibn ʿArabi as a great saint and miracle-worker; major source of the hagiographic *topoi* that were later incorporated into, and amplified in, the Anatolian/Syrian folklore and apologetic literature.	al-Qazwini (d. 682/1283) depicts I.ʿA. as a great sage;
	Ibn Abi ʾl-Mansur (d. 862/1283), the first Sufi biographer
	al-Andalus
	Ibn al-Abbar (d. 258/1260) focuses on the Andalusi period of I.ʿA.'s life; shows no clear understanding of his subsequent importance.

NOTE: Except in Table 2, where they represent lines of transmission, vertical arrows stand for teacher-student relationships.

> secretary to one of the rulers of the Maghrib. He then left the Maghrib on the *hajj,* and never returned. He studied in this country too. He transmitted the works of al-Silafi[24] on a general authorization.[25] He excelled in the study of Sufism, and composed many books. A great number of scholars and Sufis met him and studied under his guidance."[26]

Another early author who included Ibn ʿArabi in his biographical dictionary is Ibn al-Dubaythi's disciple, Ibn al-Najjar (d. 643/1245). A renowned historian and *muhaddith* of the time, Ibn al-Najjar composed a sequel to his teacher's history entitled "A [Useful] Extract from the Continuation of the *Taʾrikh Baghdad*" *(al-Mustafad min Dhayl Taʾrikh Baghdad).* As his teacher before him, Ibn al-Najjar arranged to meet Ibn ʿArabi during the latter's brief stay in the ʿAbbasid capital: the famous Sufi *shaykh* was a likely candidate for his ongoing biographical work on the celebrities who visited Baghdad. When the two scholars met, Ibn al-Najjar conducted what appears to be a quite professional interview during which he obtained biographical data from the future subject of his book. In the aftermath of the interview, he wrote the following entry:

> "Muhammad b. ʿAli b. Muhammad b. al-ʿArabi,[27] Abu ʿAbdallah al-Taʾi came from al-Andalus. He was born and raised in Murcia, then travelled to the East and Syria (al-Sha'm). He also resided in Rum (Anatolia). He composed works on Sufi sciences and a number of biographies of [his] Sufi masters.[28] He was a righteous individual who renounced this world completely.
>
> [When we met,] Abu ʿAbdallah Muhammad b. al-ʿArabi recited to me a verse he had just composed:
> Oh you, who wavers bewilderingly between
> true knowledge and passion!
> These two opposites merge
> for him, who has attained
> the highest degree of realization.
> As for the one who has never smelled
> a whiff of the pleasant odor,
> He will never understand that mixed
> musk[29] is far superior to dung!'.
>
> He was born on the 27th *ramadan* 560, at Murcia, and died on Friday, the 22d of *rabiʿ al-awwal* 638, in Damascus. He was buried at Qasyun.[30]

Al-Maqqari (d. 1041/1632), the famous Maghribi biographer and litterateur who meticulously collected all accounts of Ibn ʿArabi he could get his hands on, provides a longer, possibly embellished, version of Ibn al-Najjar's text:[31]

> Ibn al-Najjar said: "He [Ibn ʿArabi] studied (*sahiba*) under Sufi masters and possessors of hearts.[32] He entered upon the path of poverty and wrote extensively on the science of the Sufis, including biographies of the Sufi masters of the Maghrib and of the Sufi ascetics. He also wrote elegant poetry and his speech was pleasant. I met him in Damascus on a visit to that city. I took down some of his verses. What a perfect *shaykh* he was! He told me that he had entered Baghdad in 601 and spent twelve days there. He had visited it again, in 608, while going on a *hajj* with a caravan [of pilgrims]. He recited to me his verses. . . . I asked him about his birth. He said: the night of 17th *ramadan*[33], in the year of 560, at Murcia, a city in al-Andalus.[34]

Among the Syrian historians who mention Ibn ʿArabi in their works is Sibt Ibn al-Jawzi (d. 654/1256), an acclaimed Damascene preacher who had personal knowledge of the Sufi master. Sibt Ibn al-Jawzi's famous annalistic history "Mirror of the Age" *(Mirʾat al-zaman)* features the following obituary of the Sufi master:[35]

> In that year [i.e., 638 A.H.] died Shaykh Ibn ʿArabi, who excelled in the science of mystical realities *(haqaʾiq)*[36] and composed a great number of famous works [on that subject]. Somebody told me that he used to say: "I know [God's] Greatest Name[37] and alchemy through [divine] revelation, not through [rote] learning!"
>
> He died in the house of *qadi* Muhyi al-din Ibn al-Zaki. His body was washed by al-Jamal b. ʿAbd al-Haqq and Muhyi al-din, while al-ʿImad b. al-Nahhas was pouring water. He was then taken to Qasyun, and buried in the family shine of *qadi* Muhyi al-din.[38]

This account may be the first to mention the *qadi* Muhyi al-din Ibn al-Zaki's friendship with, and patronage of, the Andalusi master. According to later biographers, Ibn al-Zaki granted him a lavish daily allowance of thirty *dirhams,* which Ibn ʿArabi used to give away to the poor.[39] Ibn al-Zaki[40] was a controversial figure who reportedly entertained pro-ʿAlid leanings and considered ʿAli to be superior to ʿUthman.[41] This fact was later exploited by the historian Ibn Kathir in order to forge a link between Ibn Zaki's pro-Shiʿi propensities and his association with the Greatest Master.[42]

The ties of friendship between the future *qadi* of Damascus and the Sufi master elicited a flurry of comments from the later historians and biographers who cited Ibn Zaki's Shiʿi leanings as the cause of his "treacherous" conduct during the Mongol invasion of Syria in 658/1260, which ruined his career after the Mamluk restoration.[43] The story has it that Ibn Zaki led a delegation of Damascene jurists to Hulagu, whose troops were camping outside the besieged city. During the negotiations, Hulagu took a fancy to Ibn Zaki, and following the city's surrender appointed him chief *qadi* of the conquered lands stretching from Qinnasrin to al-ʿArish.[44] Ibn al-Zaki reportedly seized this opportunity to stock the religious colleges (*madaris*) with his protégés and scholars from his (i.e., Shafiʿi) *madhhab*. Because prior to his taking the office teaching posts were distributed more evenly among the members of all four legal Sunni schools,[45] his policies caused an uproar among the members of the disadvantaged *madhhab*s.

Among his critics was the Maliki jurist Abu Shama (d. 665/1268), who inserted into Ibn Zaki's obituary a long list of the *madrasa* positions "usurped" by Ibn al-Zaki's relatives and cohorts.[46] Although resentful of Ibn al-Zaki's perceived "unscrupulousness," Abu Shama saw no connection between his "misdeeds" and his friendship with Ibn ʿArabi. On the contrary, in his "Biographies of the Men of the Sixth and the Seventh Centuries" *(Tarajim rijal al-qarnay al-sadis wa ʾl-sabiʿ)* he shows high regard for the Greatest Master:[47]

> On the 22d *rabiʿ al-akhar*[48] in Damascus [died] al-Muhyi Ibn al-ʿArabi. His [full] name was Muhammad b. ʿAli, . . . as I saw written in his own hand. He was buried in the shrine of the *qadi* Muhyi al-din [Ibn Zaki] near Mount Qasyun. I attended the funeral prayer which was recited over his body in the Great Mosque of Damascus on Friday, whereupon I accompanied his bier to the square at Suq al-Ghanam.
>
> That was a befitting procession. [Ibn ʿArabi] wrote many works, and composition was easy for him. He composed fine poetry and long works in prose on the path of the Sufis and on their sciences. He was a native of al-Andalus. He traveled widely both in the East and in the West. He stayed at Mecca for a while.[49]

As we have seen, Sibt Ibn al-Jawzi's obituary of the Greatest Master mentions *qadi* Ibn al-Zaki among the three individuals who performed the last rites over the body of the deceased—a fact that corroborates the intimate ties of friendship between the two men, cited by the sources.[50]

The protection extended to Ibn ʿArabi by Muhyi al-din Ibn al-Zaki and by other Syrian nobles, including a number of Ayyubid princes, accounts for the lack of his persecution at the hands of self-proclaimed defenders of the *shariʿa*. As we shall see, when the controversy over Ibn ʿArabi's teaching came to the fore and his critics started to scour histories for evidence of opposition to his teaching among his contemporaries, their efforts bore little fruit.[51] Such was their frustration that they came to hold Ibn ʿArabi's influential supporters responsible for deliberately encouraging what they saw as a heinous heresy. Not surprisingly, Ibn al-Zaki, whose "collaboration" with the Mongols made him a convenient target,[52] was singled out by the polemicists as the major culprit. It is against this background that we should consider al-Dhahabi's scathing remark that the *qadi*'s "admiration for Ibn al-ʿArabi defied any description." The same sentiment was expressed by al-Dhahabi's disciple Ibn Kathir, who unequivocally linked Ibn al-Zaki's perceived "transgressions" to his infatuation with Ibn ʿArabi:

> The Ibn Zaki family embraced him entirely: they thought of no one but him, and believed that everything he said was the truth.

Ibn Kathir's suggestion that Muhyi al-din Ibn al-Zaki embraced Shiʿism under the "pernicious" influence of his Sufi protégé may be seen as part of the strategy aimed at forging a causal connection between Ibn ʿArabi's "aberrant" teaching and Ibn al-Zaki's "betrayal" of Sunnism and Islam. In amplification of this idea, the widespread dissemination of Ibn ʿArabi's doctrine came to be viewed by his later detractors as a sign of the spiritual malaise that afflicted the Muslim community on the eve of the Mongol invasion. Hence, their tendency to present their struggle against Ibn ʿArabi's doctrine as a sort of *jihad* incumbent upon every Sunni scholar.[53]

Such a frankly hostile attitude toward Ibn ʿArabi was a relatively late development that came to the fore in the age of Ibn Taymiyya and his partisans in Syria and Egypt. Yet, already in the second half of the 7th/13th centuries one can discern the first stirrings of the future polemical storm. In response to the attempts of Ibn ʿArabi's critics to besmirch his image, his supporters mounted an apologetic campaign to cleanse him of accusations of heresy and unbelief.

Conflicting descriptions of Ibn ʿArabi's funeral by his advocates and critics permit an illuminating insight into the discursive strategies utilized by both sides. Before comparing the treatment of this motif by both sides of the Ibn ʿArabi dispute, let us return to the eyewitness accounts of this event. Abu Shama, a sympathetic observer, mentions the wake at the Great Mosque of Damascus and the subsequent funeral procession to Mount Qasyun that he joined out of respect for the deceased. Abu Shama, it is to be remembered, described the bier and the procession simply as "befitting," or "beautiful" (*janaza hasana*)—a rather standard phrase under the circumstances.

A similar account of the funeral that is devoid of any dramatic details and exaggerations is furnished by Sibt Ibn al-Jawzi (or perhaps by al-Yunini), who limits himself to mentioning the place and the names of the washers of Ibn ʿArabi's body. Later, when the controversy over Ibn ʿArabi was in full swing, al-Qari al-Baghdadi, the author of a hagiographic account of the Greatest Master's life, which will be discussed further on,[54] changes the funeral scene beyond recognition:

> When he died on the night of *rabiʿ al-akhar* the 22d in the year 638, his funeral became a memorable day, one that bore happy tidings. The ruler of Damascus himself escorted [Ibn ʿArabi] to his resting place on foot. With him [the ruler] were princes, viziers, *ʿulamaʾ*, and Sufis. There was not a single person in Damascus who did not come to accompany him to his resting place. To express their grief, the people of the bazaar shut down their stores for three days. He was laid to rest in the [family] shrine of Muhyi al-din Ibn al-Zaki in the Salihiyya [district] of Damascus, at the foot of Mount Qasyun. A large building was erected over his tomb, which became the object of pious visits. . . . [55]

The discrepancy between the three accounts of the same event—two by sympathetic eyewitnesses, the other by a later partisan of the Greatest Master—is not fortuitous. In al-Qari's version, the funeral is depicted as an event of tremendous consequence, one that shows beyond doubt the exalted, saintly status of the deceased. This effect is achieved by the inclusion into the picture of the highest religious and secular functionaries of Damascus: the ruler himself is described as a humble participant in Ibn ʿArabi's last rites—a detail that we do not find in the simple narratives provided by Abu Shama and Sibt Ibn al-Jawzi.

The symbolic potential of the funeral scene—the prelude to the imminent reckoning in which the real worth of the deceased comes to light—was not lost on Ibn ʿArabi's opponents. Little wonder that

Ibn Taymiyya (d. 726/1326), Ibn ʿArabi's celebrated nemesis,[56] made use of the funeral motif in his theological refutation of Ibn ʿArabi's philosophy:

> Shihab al-din Mizzi told me on the authority of Sharaf al-din b. Shaykh Najm al-din b. al-Hakim, who heard this from his father. He said: "My arrival in Damascus coincided with the death of Ibn ʿArabi. As I watched his bier, it seemed to me that it was all covered with ashes. Only later did I realize that it was not how the funeral processions of God's friends look like!"[57]

In stark contrast to al-Qari's report, which was designed to prove Ibn ʿArabi's high status in the Muslim community of Damascus, Ibn Taymiyya's narrative casts doubt on Shaykh's status as a saint, whom God protects from any error. Each narrative exhibits an underlying polemical agenda: whereas al-Qari seeks to portray Ibn ʿArabi as the great saint of the age, Ibn Taymiyya implicitly exposes him as an imposter. In both cases, the polemical uses of the funeral scene have little to do with the laconic accounts provided by eyewitnesses.

Ibn ʿArabi in the Biographical Works of Western Muslims

So far we have discussed the testimonies of the scholars from the central lands of Islam, more precisely, Baghdad and Damascus. Given Ibn ʿArabi's Andalusi background, it is instructive to examine how he was assessed by Western Muslims. Luckily, we do have a biographical sketch of the Master from the outstanding Andalusi historian, *muhaddith*, and poet Ibn al-Abbar (d. 658/1260):[58]

> Muhammad b. ʿAli . . . the Sufi. He was born in Murcia and resided in Seville. He was known as Ibn al-ʿArabi . . . and studied with the scholars of his country. He had a predisposition to literature and served as secretary to one of the rulers until he set off to the East on a *hajj*. After he had fulfilled his religious duty, he did not return to al-Andalus. He heard *hadith* from Abu ʾl-Qasim al-Harastani[59] and and studied the *Sahih* of Muslim[60] with our master Abu ʾl-Hasan b. Abi Nasr[61] in *shawwal* 606. He transmitted *hadith* on the authority of Abu Tahir al-Silafi. He excelled in Sufism, and composed many works on this subject. A great number of scholars and devout men sought his company. A teacher of ours gave us a general authorization which he [Ibn ʿArabi] had granted to anyone who wanted to transmit *hadith* reports on his authority. He died after 640.[62]

Ibn al-Abbar's account is typical of Ibn ʿArabi's image in the Muslim West. It shows that even a well-informed local biographer was unable to overcome the limitations imposed on him by the remote geographical position of al-Andalus. Although Ibn al-Abbar is well-informed about the Andalusi period of Ibn ʿArabi's life, he seems to be unaware of the latter's subsequent notoriety in the Muslim East. Hence the most controversial part of Ibn ʿArabi's career that was critical for the shaping of his posthumous image in the central lands of Islam and in the East receives here a surprisingly short shrift. Ibn al-Abbar's ignorance of Ibn ʿArabi's later life finds further proof in his failure to provide the exact date of his subject's death. For the *muhaddith* Ibn al-Abbar, Ibn ʿArabi's worth as a scholar is determined by his expertise in *hadith* studies that he acquired under his Andalusi teachers. The other aspects of his personality and career, no matter how controversial, lay outside Ibn al-Abbar's geographic and intellectual purview, and, as a consequence, remained unassessed. This is hardly surprising, for when Ibn ʿArabi was making his last preparations for a trip across the Gibraltar, his most controversial works—the *Fusus* and the *Futuhat*—were yet to be written. Although Ibn al-Abbar does mention Ibn ʿArabi's Sufi background, for him and his Western compatriots the Greatest Master's credentials as a *hadith* scholar definitely took precedence over his Sufi leanings.[63] Only much later, when Ibn ʿArabi's principal works made their way into the Maghrib and al-Andalus, did his countrymen become cognizant of the acute theological polemic they had stirred up in the East. Once the wave of the polemic had hit the coasts of the Maghrib and al-Andalus, local scholars had to decide where they stood vis-à-vis this prickly issue.[64]

It would be instructive to get a glimpse of the subsequent development of Ibn ʿArabi's image in the Muslim West. In the following excerpt Ibn ʿArabi's personality is evaluated by a famous Maghribi scholar Abu ʾl-ʿAbbas al-Ghubrini (executed in 704/1304), whose tragic death at the hands of a Hafsid ruler is an uncanny replica of Ibn al-Abbar's cruel execution. As chief *qadi* and chronicler of Bougie (Bijaya), al-Ghubrini took it upon himself to mention all the celebrities who had ever passed by his native town.[65] Since Ibn ʿArabi stopped in Bougie on several occasions on his way to Tunis and back and even studied with some local *ʿulama*ʾ, al-Ghubrini saw it fit to include him in the biographical dictionary titled "The Epitome of Knowledge":

> Among them [scholars] was the distinguished [Sufi] teacher and jurist, *hafiz*[66] and accomplished master (*muhaqqiq*)[67] Abu ʿAbdallah Muhammad . . . also known as Ibn Suraqa. His honorific title was

Muhyi al-din, but he was better known as Ibn al-ʿArabi. He was born in Murcia, but resided in Seville. He composed many writings on Sufism and was an eloquent and perceptive individual, who was strong in quoting; whenever [an argument] was required of him, he was always able to adduce [it] with facility. He crossed the sea and landed on the Maghribi coast, whereupon he visited Bijaya in the *ramadan* of 597. He met Abu ʿAbdallah al-ʿArabi[68] and many other notables. I was told that when he entered Bijaya on the above date [an event occurred] which he later described as follows:

On that night I dreamed as if I were married to all celestial bodies and that I consummated my marriage with them. Thereupon I married all letters [of the alphabet] and I consummated my marriage. On the next day, my story was mentioned to a local seer who specialized in interpreting dreams. I asked the man to whom I had disclosed my dream not to divulge my name [to the seer]. When the story was recounted to him [i.e., the seer], he was totally overwhelmed. He said: "This is a sea whose depth can never be measured! To the man who has seen this dream, God Most High will disclose such sublime sciences, such knowledge of mysteries and of the properties of the stars,[69] which no one in his epoch will ever attain!" He fell silent for a moment, then said: "If the man who had that dream is in town now, he cannot be anyone but that Andalusi youth who arrived the other day!"[70] He [Ibn ʿArabi] set off on a long journey to the East where he eventually settled and where his home could finally enjoy the quiet of his presence. He wrote scores of books and multiplied the number of his works unceasingly. "In them is what is in them."[71]

Should God guide someone who is forgiving, benevolent, and eager to search for a plausible excuse, he would have no trouble achieving the goal. This attitude is approved by the most distinguished and noble-minded of scholars. However, should he be one of those who judge from outward appearances and brook no forgiveness in their opinions, then the issue would become difficult for him and the attainment [of the truth] would be all but impossible. When the people of Egypt accused him [Ibn ʿArabi] of some [heretical] utterances they had heard from him and were about to shed his blood in an affair that resembled that of al-Hallaj and his likes,[72] he was saved from that predicament (*qadiya*) through the good services of Shaykh Abu ʾl-Hasan ʿAli b. Nasr Fath b. ʿAbdallah al-Bijaʾi,[73] who rescued him from an imminent ordeal (*mihna*). The Shaykh Abu ʾl-Hasan ʿAli . . . spared no effort to save him. He interpreted his words allegorically *(taʾwil),*[74] in order to minimize the gravity of his errors and to solicit indulgence for his slips of the tongue. When he

> came to visit Ibn ʿArabi following his release, the latter—may God have mercy on him!—said: "Is it possible to imprison someone in whose humanity (*nasut*) divinity (*lahut*) has taken residence"[75]? In reply [Abu ʾl-Hasan] said: "O my lord, these are but ecstatic utterances (*shatahat*),[76] which are articulated in the state of drunkenness, and one cannot blame the drunk!" He [Ibn ʿArabi] died around 640. He transmitted *hadith* from Abu Tahir al-Silafi on a general authorization as well as through individual scholars. He himself used to issue teaching licences to the people of his epoch who wished to transmit [al-Silafi's] *hadith* reports on his authority.[77]

Al-Ghubrini's notice is problematic on several accounts. In the first place, the biographer makes a blatant mistake by confounding Ibn ʿArabi with Ibn Suraqa (d. 663/1265), a well-known *faqih* and Sufi, who, like the Greatest Master, was born and educated in al-Andalus, but who later emigrated to the East.[78] Although Ibn ʿArabi, to my knowledge, did not mention Ibn Suraqa in his works, he may well have met his compatriot in either Aleppo or Damascus.[79] In any case, later narratives bring the two men together in a curious anecdote cited by al-Safadi on the authority of ʿIzz al-din Ibn ʿAbd al-Salam, whose ambivalent view of the Greatest Master is the subject of the next chapter:

> Once Ibn al-ʿArabi and Ibn Suraqa were walking through the Bab al-Faradis.[80] Ibn al-ʿArabi said: "After so many thousand years, another Ibn al-ʿArabi and another Ibn Suraqa will be walking through this same gate, and they will have the same appearance!"[81]

This anecdote was apparently meant to underscore Ibn ʿArabi's ability to foresee the future, which found its most spectacular expression in his purported prediction of the rise of the Ottoman Empire.[82] In any case, al-Ghubrini's identification of Ibn ʿArabi with Ibn Suraqa is a blatant error which, as Addas justly pointed out, casts doubt on the accuracy of his account of Ibn ʿArabi as a whole. Seen from this perspective, his mention of the alleged persecution of the Greatest Master at the hands of the narrow-minded Egyptians appears doubtful.[83]

Whether or not al-Ghubrini's story is his invention, it casts light on the image of the Sufi master in the century following his death. Clearly, al-Ghubrini's (rather awkward) attempt to exonerate Ibn ʿArabi from accusations of heresy came in response to the ongoing controversy over Ibn ʿArabi which, as we shall soon see, was especially acute in that age (the late 7th/13th-early 8th/14th centuries). In this controversy, al-Ghubrini sided squarely with Ibn ʿArabi's advocates, articulating what was to become a standard line of defense used by Ibn ʿArabi's advocates, namely, his words and writings should be not be treated at face value but explained allegorically; the accusations of incarnationalism leveled at him by his enemies spring from a misunderstanding of his real intentions; he was a great saint whom God endowed with clairvoyance and other miraculous faculties. Hence, in al-Ghubrini's mind, the Greatest Master should not be judged by the criteria applied to the Muslim man in the street.

The Account of Ibn [al]-Musdi

Among the earliest biographers of Ibn ʿArabi quoted extensively in later biographical dictionaries is the Andalusi scholar Muhammad b. Yusuf al-Gharnati, better known as Ibn Musdi. Like Ibn Suraqa and Ibn ʿArabi, he spent most of his life in the East and his work falls squarely into the Eastern biographical tradition. His "Biographical Dictionary of [*hadith*] Scholars" *(Muʿjam al-shuyukh)* contains a brief but perceptive evaluation of Ibn ʿArabi's personality. As many other reports about the Greatest Master, it has come down to us in a later recension by al-Dhahabi:[84]

> I found in Ibn al-Musdi's handwriting the following [note] on Ibn al-ʿArabi: "He plunged bravely into the sea of [esoteric] allusions (*isharat*).[85] He also excelled in the sciences, which use [conventional] expressions (*ʿibarat*), and aspired towards the lofty peaks [of knowledge] until he satisfied all his wishes and realized all his aspirations. Knowledge (*al-ʿilmiyya*) put up its tent over his head, and his fame spread throughout the world to its farthest reaches. He roamed its [the world's] vast expanses, meeting its inhabitants. He excelled in both abstract reasoning and minute exposition and mastered many different sciences in a sure, reliable manner. In literature, he reached the heights that are never attained by other climbers. He studied under Ibn al-Jadd,[86] Ibn Zarqun[87] and Najba b. Yahya."[88] He said that he had met ʿAbd al-Haqq at Bijaya,[89] though this seems doubtful, and he had a teaching license from al-Silafi, which, in my mind, was a general license. He also claimed to have heard [*hadith*] from Abu 'l-Khayr Ahmad b. Ismaʿil al-Talqani, while I [i.e., al-Dhahabi] hold this to be a plain lie, because they could not possibly have met each other![90] Ibn Musdi also said: "His writings testify to his imposing stature and his boldness. They show that he has achieved the uppermost degree [of knowledge], where

> the feet of other [scholars] slip. He acquired an extraordinary mastery of theological discourse (*kalam*), and let's hope that this was a correct discourse. Many wondrous things are being told about him. He belonged to the Zahiri school[91] in matters of ritual practice (*ʿibadat),* but he adhered to esoteric teachings as regards doctrinal beliefs *(iʿtiqadat).* This is why I have no misgivings about him. However, God knows better what his heart concealed![92]

This biographical entry epitomizes a balanced view of Ibn ʿArabi taken up by many of his later biographers.[93] As such, it merits a closer scrutiny. Clearly, Ibn [al-]Musdi, whose *Muʿjam* was composed some fifteen to twenty years after Ibn ʿArabi's death, is already aware of the controversy around his name. Ibn al-Musdi's response is a subtle one. Avoiding the sensitive issue of Ibn ʿArabi's orthodoxy, he begins with a standard eulogy that underscores Ibn ʿArabi's mastery of the technical terminology of Islamic theology and mysticism. His observation is quite pertinent: the complex technical terminology is indeed a salient feature of Ibn ʿArabi's work.[94] Ibn Musdi then drops several hints about the scholastic (rather than practical or experiential) nature of Ibn ʿArabi's Sufism. Significantly, he neglects to mention Ibn ʿArabi's asceticism, exemplary piety or feats of self-mortification—the stock-in-trade motifs of Sufi biographies. Ibn Musdi's reticence in this regard indicates that he did not view these characteristics as central to Ibn ʿArabi's Sufism. Instead, he focuses squarely on Ibn ʿArabi's contribution to mystical philosophy.[95]

Ibn Musdi is at pains to explain the contradictory opinions of Ibn ʿArabi's work that were circulating in the Muslim scholarly milieu already in his age. His solution to the Ibn ʿArabi puzzle is to describe the Sufi as one who combined two widely disparate religious attitudes, that is, literalism in matters of practice and ritual, on the one hand, and esotericism (*haqiqa*-mindedness)[96] in matters of theory on the other. It is this unusual amalgamation which, in Ibn Musdi's mind, makes Ibn ʿArabi's work so difficult and therefore susceptible to misunderstanding. Anticipating the arguments of Ibn ʿArabi's later advocates, Ibn Musdi suggests that, unlike most Muslim scholars who normally stick to one pole of the spectrum, Ibn ʿArabi hovered between both, thereby defying normal evaluative criteria. Consistent with this conclusion, Ibn Musdi presents Ibn ʿArabi primarily as a Sufi gnostic and makes light of his credentials as a *hadith* scholar, which, as we have seen, were crucial to his other biographers. No wonder that this approach provokes al-Dhahabi's sharp reprimand: a famed *hadith* transmitter, he considered expertise in *hadith* to be indispensable for establishing the worth of any Muslim scholar. For al-Dhahabi, any blemish on Ibn ʿArabi's reputation as a *muhaddith* added to his overall disrepute—an opinion al-Dhahabi shared with the majority of his colleagues.

It is therefore only natural that Ibn ʿArabi's *hadith* expertise was so vigorously defended by his advocates. Al-Maqqari, whose enthusiastic support for the Sufi master has already been mentioned, hastens to counter al-Dhahabi's comment:

> There is no doubt about that [i.e., about the possibility of Ibn ʿArabi's studying under ʿAbd al-Haqq al-Ishbili]. Our lord and master Muhyi al-din said the following in a copy of the transmission license which he presented to the al-Malik al-Muzaffar Ghazi b. al-Malik al-ʿAdil b. Ayyub:[97] "Among our Andalusi teachers was Abu Muhammad ʿAbd al-Haqq b. ʿAbd al-Rahman b. ʿAbdallah al-Ishbili—may God have mercy on him! He transmitted to me all of his writings on *hadith*...and gave me a license to transmit all the books by Imam Ibn Hazm . . . .

Thus, despite the insistence by Ibn ʿArabi's followers that he should not be measured by the yardstick of traditional scholarship they were nevertheless not prepared to cede the issue to his detractors without a fight.

The Anecdotal Evidence from al-Qazwini

Some vivid touches to the portrait of Ibn ʿArabi are added by the great Muslim geographer Zakariyya b. Muhammad al-Qazwini (d. 682/1283), who met Ibn ʿArabi in Damascus as a young man and who included his recollection of that memorable meeting in his celebrated geographical work "Monuments of the Countries and the History of [Their] Inhabitants" *(Athar al-bilad wa akhbar al-ʿubbad)*.[99] In his description of Seville, the city where Ibn ʿArabi spent his Andalusi years, al-Qazwini writes:

> One of its inhabitants was the distinguished Shaykh Muhammad b. al-ʿArabi, known as Muhyi al-din. I met him in Damascus in 630. He was a distinguished [Sufi] master, man of letters, sage, poet, gnostic and ascetic. I heard that he had composed a great many works that contain marvelous things. Thus I heard that he wrote a book about the calamities [described] in the Qurʾan.[100] Among the marvelous stories he tells therein, was one about a palm-tree that grew in the street of Seville. It so happened that the tree started to

> tilt until it obstructed the way of passers-by. So people began to consider cutting it down and finally agreed to do this on the next day. He [Ibn ʿArabi] said: "On that night, I saw in a dream the Messenger of God—may God bless and greet him!" He stood next to that tree and it complained to him, saying: "Oh Messenger of God, the people have decided to cut me down because I block their passage!" The Messenger of God touched the tree with his blessing hand, and, lo, it straightened up. As soon as I woke up on the next morning, I went to the palm-tree and found it to be upright. I told the people about what had happened to that tree. They were fascinated with it so that they made it the object of pious visits (*mazar*).[101]

In another passage, al-Qazwini quotes Ibn ʿArabi's curious explanation of why the ancient Egyptians were so preoccupied with building the pyramids:

> Muhammad Ibn al-ʿArabi, whose honorific title was Muhyi al-din said: "Those people [the ancient Egyptians] believed in the transmigration of souls. Therefore, they set the pyramids up as their signposts, in order to mark the age in which they departed from this world [from the one] in which they [expect to] return."[102]

Unlike Ibn Musdi, who depicted Ibn ʿArabi as a Sufi gnostic par excellence, al-Qazwini's sketches showed him to be a sage and a visionary—an image that dovetails neatly into the accounts of the Shaykh's personality that we observed in the works of Sibt b. al-Jawzi (or al-Yunini) and al-Ghubrini.

Predictably, Ibn ʿArabi's detractors were not as indulgent of his extravagant claims, which freely mingled dreams and visions with reality. As we shall see, Ibn ʿArabi's imagination more than once exposed him to harsh accusations and ridicule. One such dream led to Ibn ʿArabi's fateful clash with the prominent Damascene divine ʿIzz al-din Ibn ʿAbd al-Salam al-Sulami in an episode that proved to be particularly harmful to his posthumous reputation.[103]

A Sufi Perspective: Ibn Abi ʾl-Mansur

A sympathetic portrait of Ibn ʿArabi is found in what appears to be his earliest biography by a fellow Sufi, Safi al-din Ibn Abi ʾl-Mansur (d. 682/1283) of Egypt, who met the Greatest Master in Damascus:[104]

> While in Damascus I met the Shaykh, the *imam*, the gnostic Muhyi al-din Ibn ʿArabi, who was the great master of the Sufi path.

> He was graced with all the knowledge God has ever bestowed on His [elect] servants.[105] His fame was wide-ranging, and his writings numerous.[106] He had a complete understanding of God's oneness and was so completely consumed by it that it came to permeate his knowledge, character, and spiritual state. [As a result,] he grew totally oblivious of the world around him whether in propitious times or adversity. He had many partisans among the people of ecstatic raptures (*mawajid*)[107] as well as the authors of [mystical] works. He cultivated the company of our lord and master al-Harrar,[108] and they became intimate friends and companions.[109]

At first sight, Ibn Abi ʾl-Mansur's testimony adds little to what we already know from the other biographies of the Greatest Master. Despite his personal contact with Ibn ʿArabi, the Egyptian Sufi depicts him in a somewhat aloof and clichéd manner that tells us little about Ibn ʿArabi as an individual. Yet, Ibn Abi ʾl-Mansur's account does give some new details that are ignored by the other biographers of the Greatest Master we have consulted. As a practicing Sufi, Ibn Abi ʾl-Mansur lays special emphasis on Ibn ʿArabi's indifference to the external circumstances of his life—a feature essential to every accomplished mystic. Furthermore, unlike the non-Sufi biographers, who usually limited themselves to a general observation about Ibn ʿArabi's numerous disciples, Ibn Abi ʾl-Mansur described them specifically as individuals who combined mystical experience with an interest in mystical theory. This is indeed typical of many of Ibn ʿArabi's partisans, who took an intellectual approach to Sufism, for instance, al-Qunawi, Ibn Sawdakin, ʿAfif al-din al-Tilimsani (d. 690/1291),[110] Ibn Israʾil al-Hariri (d. 677/1278),[111] and Ismaʿil b. ʿAli b. Abi ʾl-Yaman (d. 689/1290),[112] all of whom were contemporaries of Ibn Abi ʾl-Mansur.

Curiously the other references to Ibn ʿArabi in Ibn Abi ʾl-Mansur's *Risala* contain some veiled, almost imperceptible reservations about his status as a Sufi shaykh. These reservations, however, are so thoroughly disguised that one can only speculate as to their provenance. One possible explanation lies in the ambivalent relations between Ibn ʿArabi and Ibn Abi ʾl-Mansur's Sufi teacher, Shaykh al-Harrar. Despite their long companionship that had started in al-Andalus, later on the two masters seem to have allowed rivalry to cloud their friendship. The older, less educated, and not-so-brilliant al-Harrar, whose life otherwise bore a close resemblance to that of his younger contemporary, seems to have grown envious of Ibn ʿArabi's fame and enormous literary output. In any event, he must have had doubts that this fame was well deserved. While teaching his students in Egypt, al-Harrar implicitly conveyed his misgivings to his audience, couching them in the form of anecdotes and parables. These narratives were diligently recorded by his respectful student, Ibn Abi ʾl-Mansur, who later included them in his *Risala*. Whether or not Ibn Abi ʾl-Mansur pursued a hidden agenda is impossible to ascertain. Whatever his intention, the anecdotes in question are crafted so as to enhance al-Harrar's lofty spiritual state by contrasting it with Ibn ʿArabi's "inflated" repute.[113]

The first story, which Ibn Abi ʾl-Mansur recounts on the authority of al-Harrar, is set in al-Andalus. It shows al-Harrar together with Ibn ʿArabi and a group of local Sufis worshiping God in a deserted area in the environs of Seville. As they engaged in a collective prayer they noticed al-Khidr, the immortal, prophetlike figure widely considered by the Muslim mystics to be their saintly patron.[114] Awestruck and demure, the men watched al-Khidr approach them "without touching the surface of land." When the saint greeted them, the Sufis were so intimidated that none was able to return his greeting, except al-Harrar, who quickly regained his composure and uttered some words of reply. Satisfied, al-Khidr departed. "All this," al-Harrar later explained to his students, "happened because those people [i.e., his companions] still had on them outward signs of vainglorious pretensions."[115] The moral of al-Harrar's story, although indirectly stated, is clear: as the most serene of his companions in thought and deed, he alone was ready for the portentous encounter. It is no accident that of the whole group of the anonymous mystics only Ibn ʿArabi was singled out by name. The story has a double subtext: on the one hand, it extols the spiritual maturity of Ibn Abi ʾl-Mansur, on the other, it belittles Ibn ʿArabi's, calling in doubt his sincerity.

In Ibn Abi ʾl-Mansur's second story, the message is more straightforward. It portrays Ibn ʿArabi—by that time a venerated Sufi elder residing in Damascus—as a humble supplicant who sought al-Harrar's help in interpreting a perplexing vision. After some vacillation, al-Harrar grudgingly conceded, casting his reply in an even more perplexing puzzle, which further confused the supplicant and caused him to ask for another explanation. Al-Harrar politely condescended, demonstrating beyond doubt his superiority over the Greatest Master. Upon hearing al-Harrar's reply, Ibn ʿArabi felt so embarrassed by his inability to grasp the matter at hand that he vowed never again to annoy al-Harrar with such petty requests.[116]

In both episodes, the Greatest Master's status is ambiguous, to say the least. Although in the biographical notice Ibn Abi ʾl-Mansur duly praised Ibn ʿArabi, the two anecdotes he recounted on his teacher's authority intimate that Ibn ʿArabi's spiritual state was not without a flaw and that there were other mystical masters in his age who were at least equal, if not superior, to him, yet too modest to seek cheep popular acclaim.

Al-Qastallani's Polemical Twist

The last biographical sketch of Ibn ʿArabi to be discussed in this chapter is extracted from a polemical treatise by the famous *faqih* and Sufi Qutb al-din al-Qastallani (d. 686/1287),[117] who set out to unmask the monistic tendencies within Sufism.[118] It, therefore, provides early evidence of the controversy around Ibn ʿArabi's legacy that started shortly after his death. Al-Qastallani's biography of the Greatest Master anticipates some features of the anti-Ibn ʿArabi discourse in the subsequent centuries by intruding a polemical agenda into an (ostensibly neutral) biographical entry.

The main target of al-Qastallani's work was not Ibn ʿArabi but Ibn Sabʿin, the renowned Andalusi thinker who spent his last years in Mecca. Ibn Sabʿin was more than al-Qastallani's theological opponent;[119] he was the latter's political rival for the influence on the Meccan governor. In any event, far from a stick-in-the-mud enemy of Sufism, al-Qastallani was himself a member of the Suhrawardiyya order and adhered to the so-called "moderate" trend within Islamic mysticism that was generally suspicious of the metaphysical speculation along the lines of Ibn ʿArabi and Ibn Sabʿin. It seems quite natural that al-Qastallani, who vied with Ibn Sabʿin for the leadership of the Meccan scholarly community as well as for influence on the governor, cast his opposition in a theological idiom aimed at undermining his rival's prestige as a Sunni scholar. His polemical strategy consisted in presenting Ibn Sabʿin as the foremost exponent of monistic philosophy after Ibn ʿArabi's death. Hence his attempts to demonstrate continuity between the doctrines of both mystical thinkers. In this polemical conceit, Ibn ʿArabi was forced to play the role of a founding father (along with a few others) of the monistic "heresy":

> Among those who lived in the time of Ibn al-Marʾa[120] was Abu ʿAbdallah Muhammad b. ʿAli b. Muhammad al-ʿArabi al-Taʾi al-Ishbili [*sic!*], who came to this country[121] in the late 570s,[122] and stayed in Mecca for a while. Here he studied *hadith* and wrote his *al-Futuhat al-makkiyya*. He was well versed in Sufism and had [extensive] knowledge of its sciences. However, he inflicted a great damage on it

> [Sufism] by embracing this teaching. He wrote many books in which he explained the essence of his beliefs. He took special interest in the method of this school, and himself composed a great number of works on this subject. He lived in Damascus for a while, then traveled to Rum, where he was well received [by the rulers] and given abundant wealth. Later he returned to Damascus, where he died. . . . [123]

This account leaves no doubt about al-Qastallani's hostility to the Greatest Master. Whereas the previous biographers invariably emphasized Ibn ʿArabi's prestige with temporal rulers as a sign of his acceptance by the contemporary religio-political environment,[124] al-Qastallani's assesses it in negative terms, implying that by receiving "abundant wealth" from the rulers the Sufi master violated the critical Sufi precept of staying clear of the corrupt secular authorities. This biographical entry clearly indicates that his real target was Ibn ʿArabi's doctrinal premises. In the subsequent passages he seeks to link Ibn ʿArabi to the strain of the monistic thought that originated in the Muslim West and that was brought to fruition in the work of Ibn Sabʿin.

Interestingly, the sincerity of al-Qastallani's condemnation of monistic Sufism was called into question by al-Safadi, who upon quoting samples from al-Qastallani's poetry, caustically pointed out its close affinity with the verses of Ibn al-Farid, al-Shushtari, and al-Tilimsani—the Sufi thinkers who had borne the brunt of al-Qastallani's antimonistic attack.[125] According to al-Safadi, "ʿAfif al-din al-Tilimsani in his poetry said precisely the same or very similar things and this is exactly the method of the Sufis which he [al-Qastallani] had so strongly condemned. Only God penetrates the secret thoughts of men and only He knows their secret intentions!"[126]

As we shall see, al-Qastallani's duplicity is far from unique: many of Ibn ʿArabi's critics accused him of the views that they themselves entertained in private.[127] In al-Qastallani's case, it remains unclear whether he condemned monistic philosophy out of concern for doctrinal purity or, more likely, in an effort to besmirch his rival, who was closely associated with the monistic school. On the surface, we are dealing with a purely theological controversy that may or may not conceal an underlying conflict of interest.

Conclusion

In reviewing Ibn ʿArabi's treatment in the early biographical literature, one can see that by and large it presents a fairly accurate, if extremely schematic portrait of the Sufi master. Biographical notices from Ibn ʿArabi's epoch uniformly stress his exalted rank as a scholar and as a mystic. Predictably, biographers place heavy emphasis on his credentials as a *hadith* expert—a fact that is usually neglected in Western studies of his life and work, which center on the more congenial (i.e., less Islam-specific) facets of his personality.[128] Later biographies of the Greatest Master present a more complex picture. One trait they have in common is their intense subjectivity that reflects the growing polarization among the *ʿulama*ʾ over the meaning of his legacy.

In spite of the rigid conventions imposed on writers by the biographical/prosopographical genre, the entries on Ibn ʿArabi in biographical annals display variations that allow us to see him from a variety of perspectives. In general, the early biographers appear to be nonpartisan and conscientious. They carefully shun sweeping condemnations in a conscious drive to remain neutral vis-à-vis the sensitive issue of Ibn ʿArabi's orthodoxy. Finally, many portraits of Ibn ʿArabi in the earliest layer of biographical literature are often based on the impressions gained through interviews or hearsay.

There is no evidence to suggest that the early biographers examined thus far were familiar with Ibn ʿArabi's two principal works, the *Fusus* and the *Futuhat,* which will become objects of heated debates several decades later. It seems likely that these controversial writings were still confined to the narrow circle of Ibn ʿArabi's closest disciples. At any rate, his works had not yet attracted a full-scale theological scrutiny that had such a drastic impact on his image in later biographical and polemical literature.

During Ibn ʿArabi's final stay in Damascus, his impeccable conduct marked by a meticulous piety and formidable scholarship gave his potential detractors little grounds for denunciation.[129] Since the full implications of his teachings were unknown to outsiders, they could not stir up trouble. By the same token, his close ties to the Damascene religious establishment, including the Ibn al-Zaki family and other high-ranking religious officials, as well as Ayyubid princes, effectively protected him from accusations or harassment.

Early sketches of Ibn ʿArabi's life describe his teachers and patrons, his literary and scholarly works, and his travels and disciples. They also give some glimpses of his personality by featuring some episodes from his life. Put together, such disparate shreds of information form a picture that is both incomplete and open to a variety of interpretations. Such scanty facts and motifs as found in these early biographies of Ibn ʿArabi were thoroughly collected by later authors, who started to rearrange and reinterpret them according to their positions in the Ibn ʿArabi dispute.

Already at the earliest stages of this dispute, the overall obscurity of Ibn ʿArabi's teaching caused some confusion among his biographers. In response, they tended to focus on what we, with the benefit of hindsight, might describe as the purely external and contingent aspects of his personality and work. This is understandable, since such material lay on the surface and was the least ambiguous. In a like vein, the biographical sketches that were just discussed consistently locate Ibn ʿArabi within the frame of reference current in the Islamic prosopographical tradition with its overriding concern for *hadith* reports and for the reliability of their transmitters.

In sum, in the prepolemical period, the discourse on Ibn ʿArabi still evinces little indication that within the matter of two decades his ideas will become both an object of heated theological debates and an epitome of monistic philosophy. A foretaste for this impending scholastic storm can, however, be gained from the later biographies of the Sufi master that we have used for comparison.

3

BETWEEN DAMASCUS AND CAIRO: THE AFFAIR OF IBN ʿABD AL-SALAM

The Historical Setting

By the mid-7th/13th centuries, the decline of the Baghdad Caliphate, compounded by the weakening of its Ayyubid protectors, made it an easy prey for the Mongol armies. The Mongol invasion of Iraq and Syria in 656-658/1258-1260 led to the shift of political power from a devastated Syria to Egypt, whose Mamluk rulers had successfully stemmed "the storm from the East." From that time on, the Ayyubid princes of Syria, who refused to accept Mongol sovereignty, looked to the newborn Mamluk state for support. In a crucial showdown at ʿAyn Jalut (658/1260), the well-trained and disciplined Mamluk army, using the same fighting techniques as their foes, routed the invincible Mongols and saved Egypt from imminent invasion. In the aftermath of that victory, which was perceived by many Muslims as Islam's triumph over a hostile pagan force, the Mamluks established themselves as "the uncontested hegemonic power in the Near East."[1]

Baybars al-Bundukdari (d. 676/1277), a ruthless and brilliant Mamluk commander who had distinguished himself in the battle of ʿAyn Jalut, eliminated his Mamluk rivals to become the leader of the new state. Not only did he succeed in beating off the occasional intrusions of the Crusaders into Muslim territories, but, in a series of masterful military campaigns, wiped out most of the Crusader strongholds in Syria.[2] Owing to Baybars's able generalship, the groundwork was laid for the ultimate expulsion of the last Crusaders from Syria, which was accomplished under the Sultan al-Ashraf Khalil (689/1290 to 693/1293).[3] Despite the Mamluks' successes, they failed to forestall repeated ravages of Syria by the still formidable Mongols. Sporadic Mongol incursions from Iran laid waste to many Syrian towns, resulting in the mass displacement and suffering of

Muslim urban populations, many of whom took refuge in Egypt, leaving behind their houses and possessions.[4] Under Baybars, the Egyptian capital became the seat of the revived Sunni Caliphate and Islam's metropolis.[5]

The havoc the Mongol armies wreaked on Syria created an atmosphere of profound despondency among local Muslims who viewed the Mongol invasion as divine punishment for their weak faith, indulgence in "strange beliefs," low morals, and neglect of the *shariʿa*.[6] Even though some Mongol leaders gradually embraced Islam,[7] their sincerity and orthodoxy remained suspect in the eyes of Syrian and Egyptian *ʿulamaʾ*. Mongol converts were commonly held accountable for the corruption of the true faith[8] and for the encouragement of reprehensible innovations, supposedly nonexistent prior to the Mongol conquest.[9]

The external dangers that beset the Muslim world in the second half of the 7th/13th century-early 8th/14th centuries[10] had a strong impact on the religious life and ideology of the Islamic community. In Syria in particular, it fostered a defensive spirit and conspiratorial outlook shared by many societies in crisis. More than ever, local *ʿulamaʾ* were keen to blame the political and social crisis on the spiritual and moral degradation and on the intrusion of "alien" elements that compromised the purity of primitive Islam. The external danger made some Muslim scholars particularly anxious to safeguard the "unadulterated" Islam of the pious ancestors *(al-salaf al-salih)* and to castigate the purported "deviations" it had suffered at the hand of heretical "innovators." This tendency partly explains the acuteness of scholarly debates around the notion of "authentic" Islam that grew particularly acute in that epoch.

The theological fray around what constitutes "true Islam" as opposed to "heresy" or "innovation" was further fueled by the propensity of the Mamluk rulers to adopt "vulgar beliefs and superstitions" and to cultivate charismatic figures of questionable repute—a trait they shared with their Mongol enemies.[11] Perhaps the most flagrant example of the Mamluks' attachment to charismatic religious leaders is the friendship between the pious sultan al-Zahir Baybars (r. 658/1260-676/1277)[12] and his extravagant spiritual director al-Shaykh al-Khadir b. Abu Bakr b. Musa, alias Khadir al-Mihrani.[13] So strong was the Shaykh's influence on the Mamluk sovereign that the latter visited him several times a week in search of advice and reassurance. On many occasions, al-Mihrani also served as the sultan's fortune-teller. In return for al-Mihrani's services, the sultan generously endowed Sufi lodges for his favorite disciples in Cairo, Damascus, Baʿalbakk, Hama, and Homs.[14]

Genuine Sufi masters also found generous patronage in the Mamluk court. Baybars was particularly fond of Ahmad al-Badawi (d. 675/1276), the future patron saint of Egypt.[15] It is possible that Baybars deliberately supported Sufis in order to offset the enormous influence of the established Shafiʿi scholars, though this is by no means certain.[16] A vivid example of the high status of the Sufi master under the Mamluks is Nasr al-Manbiji (d. 719/1319), whose overriding influence over the sultan Baybars II Jashnikir (r. 708/1309-709/1310) is often mentioned by the Muslim historians of the epoch.[17]

The Mamluks' tenacious fascination with all manner of charismatic individuals of Sufi inspiration is sometimes explained by "vestiges of the shamanistic tradition in which they had grown up as children before their arrival in Egypt," as well as by their "personal uprootedness in a remote and foreign country."[18] One should, however, keep in mind that in supporting Sufism and Sufis the new Egyptian rulers simply followed the precedents established by their Zengid and Ayyubid predecessors, who were anxious to enhance their status as Muslim rulers by extending generous patronage to Sufi brotherhoods and individual mystics, including such unconventional ones as Yahya al-Suhrawardi, al-Harrali, Ibn Hud, and, of course, Ibn ʿArabi.[19]

As in the Ayyubid epoch, in the Mamluk time also the rulers' predilection for various Sufi leaders became a matter of great concern for the high-ranking religious officials, who felt that freewheeling mystics with no formal education were ill-qualified to provide counsel to their royal patrons. Nevertheless, in the competition for the rulers' hearts Sufi masters often gained the upper hand.[20] The fashion set by the sultans was eagerly imitated by the lesser governors and emirs of the Mamluk state, many of whom generously supported the "poor" (*fuqara*ʾ), that is, the Sufis, and eagerly sought their advice.[21] A material embodiment of the growing Sufi prestige can be observed in the rapid proliferation of Sufi institutions—a process that had already begun under the Ayyubids. The number of humble Sufi lodges, hostels, and fully fledged monasteries erected under the Mamluks is staggering. The Egyptian authorities spent enormous sums on their construction and upkeep.[22]

The expansion of Sufism can be explained by the dissatisfaction of many Muslims with the institutionalized religion on the one hand

and the generous private and state donations allocated for Sufi institutions on the other. Many men and women became "full-time" mystics, who abandoned gainful employment in order to devote themselves completely to God. Their withdrawal from the world was usually accompanied by joining a Sufi brotherhood. In the Mamluk realm we find such brotherhoods as Shadhiliyya, Rifaʿiyya, Burhaniyya, and Qadiriyya, which became endemic and which witnessed an unprecedented florescence.[23]

The physical spread of Sufism was accompanied by its doctrinal transformation. Not surprisingly, Sufism's increasingly diverse audiences demanded a more elaborate theory than the stock-in-trade pieties attributed to the great ascetics and mystics of the first centuries of Islam. Responding to such varied needs, Sufism evolved into such a complex and heterogeneous system that in the 9/14th century Maghribi Sufi Muhammad Zarruq (846/1442-899/1493) was able to identify ten distinct strands within the contemporary Sufi movement. Each of these strands, according to Zarruq, had its distinctive spiritual discipline, textbooks, and authoritative exponents.[24]

Sufism and Sunni Islam: Concord or Expediency?

Already at the early stages of Sufism's history its adherents attempted to interpret mystical experience in philosophical and metaphysical terms. This effort was essential for situating it within a wider, existential context, thereby investing it with a cosmic meaning. Al-Ghazali's famous synthesis of Sufi ethics, theosophy, and metaphysics with mainstream Sunni piety marked a significant, if not entirely unprecedented step in that direction. Yet, it was his effort to reinvigorate Sunni Islam by infusing it with mystical elements that proved to be most successful with both the Sufis and the *ʿulamaʾ* alike.[25] Attempts to work out a comprehensive Sufi theology and world-outlook continued after Ghazali's death in 505/1111.[26] Of these, Ibn ʿArabi's teaching was just one, although extremely consequential example that shaped Sufism for centuries to come.

With the institutional and doctrinal expansion of Sufism in the Mamluk epoch, mystical theories came to enjoy a substantially wider currency than they had at the time of their inception. The diffusion of doctrinal Sufism now occurred not only through individual masters and their oral instructions, but increasingly through mystical literature as well. When Sufi theoretical works became available to learned outsiders, they were shocked by the daring insights they found there. What such external readers had only suspected was now explicitly confirmed by Sufi writers themselves. Even the most open-minded *ʿulamaʾ* grew increasingly concerned with the possible detrimental effect of Sufi doctrines on the faith of an unprepared audience. The wide dissemination of theoretical Sufism fueled the theological controversy around Ibn ʿArabi and his followers for many centuries.[27]

In defending their beliefs, mystical thinkers often availed themselves of the Qurʾan and the Sunna in order to prove Sufism's rootedness in the Islamic religion. Their exegetical methods however were repudiated by their opponents as "farfetched," "garbled," and dispensing with the literal meaning of the Scriptures in favor of its purported esoteric subtext. Equally alarming to the guardians of Islam's purity was the tendency of some Sufis to make use of the terminology of speculative theology (*kalam*) and Muslim philosophy (*falsafa*). Later Sufi doctrines indeed bear close resemblance to both *kalam* metaphysics and philosophical cosmology—a fact that worried the scholars ever distrustful of ideas that harked back to pre-Islamic intellectual traditions.

Outward pressures in the form of the Mongol and Christians invasions further stiffened the scholastic opposition to the non-Islamic (Greek) philosophical ideas represented by Ibn Sina and his followers. Even Ashʿari theologians, who are often viewed by Western Islamicists as paragons of Muslim orthodoxy,[28] were sometimes accused by conservative *ʿulamaʾ* of the excessive reliance on Hellenic methods of rational inquiry.[29] Particularly suspicious in the eyes of the guardians of Islam's purity was the Sufi notion of sainthood (*wilaya*), which, according to many Sufi theorists, renders the Sufi "friend of God" (*wali*) a natural heir to the Prophet, in as much as they have direct access to the source of divine revelation. This claim was vigorously rejected by those traditionalist *ʿulamaʾ* who considered themselves to be the only legitimate interpreters and custodians of the Prophet's authority. The articulation of the sainthood theory is associated with the Iranian gnostic al-Hakim al-Tirmidhi (d. ca. 298/910),[30] whose passionate advocacy of the Sufi gnostics (*ʿarifun)* ignited a fierce theological debate and, eventually, let to his expulsion from the city of Termez. Sufi pretensions to be God's elect servants possessed of revelatory knowledge set them at variance with those *ʿulamaʾ* who emphasized the equality of all of the members of the Muslim community and the absolute transcendence and inscrutability of the Godhead.[31] Such community-oriented *ʿulamaʾ*

never tied of warning against the dangerous implications of the *wilaya* theory, which they viewed as a handy excuse for political sedition. Their concern was often shared by secular rulers with their innate fear of popular movements under messianic slogans—a phenomenon quite common in medieval Islamdom.

Hence the rulers' ambiguity vis-à-vis Sufism: in taking under their wing its charismatic leaders, they kept in check its disruptive religio-political potential, persecuting those who dared to carry their speculation beyond the accepted limits. However, since Sufism had already established itself among other trends within the Islamic mainstream, such radical Sufis were usually persecuted as "philosophers," "atheists," "libertines," crypto-Shiʿi "extremists," and Ismaʿili "preachers."[32]

Religion and Politics in the Mamluk State

> The disposition of mankind, whether as rulers or as fellow citizens, to impose their own opinions and inclinations as a rule of conduct on others, is so energetically supported by some of the best and by some of the worst feelings incident to human nature, that it is hardly ever kept under restraint by anything but want of power.
> John Stuart Mill. *On Liberty,* London, 1913, p. 8

The Sufis rarely were the primary target of the antiheretic purges instigated by conservative *ʿulamaʾ* and *qadis* and carried out by secular authorities. On the contrary, protected by his respectable patched frock and by an aura of holiness, the Sufi was less likely to fall victim to the inquisitorial zeal of the *ʿulamaʾ* than other "heretics." As in Western Europe,[33] the 7th/13th and 8th/14th centuries were a time when religious trials were a common feature of the urban landscape: historical chronicles provide vivid descriptions of public trials that involved all manner of religiously suspect individuals. In the Mamluk realm, these trials were frequently conducted by the *shariʿa* courts of Cairo, Damascus, and of lesser cities. Accounts of the trials mention such offenses against religion as espousal of "subversive" religious beliefs, "atheism", libertine behavior, and the cursing of the Prophet and his companions. The latter accusation was normally brought up against imprudent Shiʿis and Christians.[34] The inquisitorial spirit of the epoch is graphically conveyed by Ibn Kathir, himself a passionate supporter of "the pure religion of the pious ancestors," who described several such trials in Cairo and Damascus.

Even within the so-called mainstream Islam, theological positions varied considerably, providing fertile soil for heated confrontations. Disputants strived to win rulers, princes, and state officials over to their side, in hopes of silencing their critics and forcing their views onto the community at large.

The institutions and religio-cultural patterns of the Ayyubid epoch persisted with great tenacity under the Mamluks. The Ayyubid models did more than just survive; they experienced a vigorous revival once Mamluk power stabilized. On the political and administrative level, the bureaucratic bodies and offices that existed under the Ayyubids, and, in many instances went back to the Saljuq and Fatimid epochs, were perpetuated by the new masters. This is not to say that there were no important changes to the earlier patterns. Thus, the hereditary principle of accession to power that the Ayyubids generally followed was abandoned under the Mamluks in favor of usurpation. Nevertheless, the new sovereigns held on to the regal titles of their predecessors, as well as their claims to be the patrons and protectors of the holy cities in the Hijaz. At the same time, their slave background created "the glaring deficit of . . . Islamic legitimization for government."[35] To make up for this disadvantage, the Mamluks forged close ties with the men of religion in hopes of securing the much-needed legitimacy. The *ʿulamaʾ* and literati, mostly Arabs in origin, usually served as civil administrators: in addition to fulfilling various bureaucratic and judicial functions, they controlled education and supervised the estates of orphans and the revenues generated by *waqf* properties.[36] Military posts, on the other hand, were as a rule held by the men of Turkic, Slavic, or Georgian background.[37] Most members of the learned elite started their careers at religious colleges (*madaris,* sing. *madrasa*),[38] that had come into being under the Seljuqs and that flourished throughout the Ayyubid and Mamluk period.[39] A wide network of *madrasa* institutions was in significant ways responsible for the smooth transition from the Ayyubid to the Mamluk epoch and for the subsequent reproduction of the earlier religio-cultural patterns throughout the Mamluk rule. In the absence of a stable political structure, the learned class "provided the low-level institutional continuity which gave cohesion to the society even in the face of political instability at its upper levels."[40]

In a recent study Chamberlain has shown that the *madrasa*s served more than just educational and ideological purposes. They had at least two other important functions: the protection of the learned elite's property through the *waqf* endowment, and the advancement and reproduction of the privileged status of the *ʿulamaʾ* and notables *(aʿyan)*.[41] In other words, the *madrasa*s and their graduates were crucial elements in the Islamic societies of the Middle East, which made these societies "Islamic."[42] Hence "the religious teachers, jurisconsults, Qurʾan readers, traditionalists, qadis, etc. . . . had gradually come to constitute the political core of the state."[43] Whether or not they indeed were *the* core,[44] their critical role in shaping the internal and, to a lesser extent external, politics of the Mamluk state is beyond doubt.

In light of recent research one can no longer treat the *madrasa* as an institution geared to producing aloof experts on Qurʾanic exegesis, *hadith* criticism, *fiqh* jurisprudence, and theological casuistry, although such scholars also existed. *Madrasa* graduates staffed various state departments (*diwans*); supervised *waqf* endowments and charity networks; counseled princes and tutored their sons, served as ambassadors, diplomats, and preachers at congregational mosques; and, of course, held teaching posts at large religious colleges and Sufi monasteries. Reports of appointments to high administrative offices in Cairo, Damascus, Aleppo, Homs, and other big cities throughout the Mamluk realm dominate late medieval chronicles. It is no wonder, for the authors of these chronicles were almost exclusively members of the learned class with a direct stake in such appointments.[45]

Last but not least, due to their proficiency in the Islamic law certain *ʿulamaʾ* were the only ones qualified to interpret and to apply the norms of the *shariʿa*.[46] From the humble rank of a district judge or even a notary one could rise to the highest judiciary post of the Mamluk state—that of chief *qadi (qadi al-qudat)* who was appointed by either the sultan himself or by his viceroys. Chief *qadi*s were in a position to provide a check on the otherwise unrestricted power of the sultan and his military commanders, although the extent and nature of their influence was largely determined by the personal qualities of individual holders of this office.[47] Although the judge could, on occasion, protect his constituency from excessive taxation and from other overbearing actions of the sultan and his military officers,[48] his autonomy was severely limited by his dependence on the ruler. On the other hand, many chief *qadi*s grew complacent and corrupt while in office and had to be replaced by the sultan to satisfy popular demand for equity.

Under these circumstances, it was the *ʿulamaʾ* of a relatively humble official standing, untarnished, as it were, by high-handed administrative dealings or by toadying to the secular ruler, who had the greatest moral authority among the townsfolk.[49] Preachers in the Friday mosques, *mufti*s, teachers of *hadith,* Qurʾan readers, and educated booksellers strived to dissociate themselves from the more unsavory aspects of political power[50] and therefore were favorably positioned to translate their ministry into a broad popular support and, on occasion, opposition to the oppressive government or its individual representatives.[51] The Mamluk sultans, as a rule, were able to placate, bribe, or intimidate such troublesome popular scholars; yet, in the case of the most recalcitrant ones, they had to resort to naked repression, including exile or incarceration.

The authority of the *ʿulamaʾ* class remained strong throughout Mamluk period, for, as mentioned, military rulers depended on the services of its members, from the chief *qadi* downward. Occasional quarrels notwithstanding, both elites were doomed to maintain a mutually beneficial symbiosis.[52] To be certain, the Mamluk sovereigns could and did manipulate the *ʿulamaʾ* when they felt their power was too great. Typical in this regard is Baybars al-Bunduqdari's attempt to curtail the paramount influence of Shafiʿi doctors of law on the affairs of the state by abolishing their monopoly on the administration of justice.[53]

It is scarcely surprising that scholars competed fiercely for the most lucrative positions (*mansab*s) in the religious and civil administration, which offered to their holders substantial material advantages and social prestige.[54] In this competition, the *ʿulamaʾ* often relied on the "old boy" network that they had developed in the course of their studies. At the early stages of their careers, they became part of one or the other faction rallied around an authoritative mentor with a distinct theological or legal teaching. The role of such a mentor in the career of an individual scholar is difficult to overestimate, since the latter's prestige was "the reflection of that of his masters, and the masters of his masters,"[55] all of whom formed a distinct scholarly tradition.

As the Islamic chronicles of the age finely show, the leader of a scholarly faction was often pitted against an equally influential opponent and, as a consequence, against the latter's following. In the factional conflicts that inevitably ensued, discrediting the teaching of one's opponent, as well as the religious authorities he relied on, meant more than just scoring a purely scholastic victory. With a bit of luck, a theological faction could win the ruler to their cause and thereby ensure the right to propagate their tenets freely and to occupy the most lucrative posts in the state hierarchy. Rulers, as we shall see, often deliberately supported a minority faction—a stratagem that allowed them to manipulate *ʿulamaʾ* more effectively by keeping them divided.[56] Therefore, while historians of the Ayyubid and Mamluk epochs tend to present numerous clashes between scholarly factions as academic debates over certain theological issues, more was at stake than simply doctrinal purity. The scholarly debates that punctuate medieval Muslim chronicles were often "merely ideological manifestations"[57] of more basic conflicts of interest. Among these underlying conflicts princely patronage and access to privileges and prestigious executive and teaching offices loom especially large.

With regard to the heated disputes around Ibn ʿArabi's doctrine, an awareness of these underlying agendas is thrown into high relief by the famous Egyptian scholar and Sufi ʿAbd al-Rahman al-Munawi (d. 1031/1621):[58]

> A group of scholars sought to refute him [Ibn ʿArabi] and his followers. [In doing so] they pursued their own selfish goals. A scholar [from such a group] would come to know that one of his rivals and contemporaries has a strong belief in him [Ibn ʿArabi] and supports [his views]. At this point the bigoted partisanship that has its origin in [pre-Islamic] ignorance (*al-jahiliyya*)[59] would cause this scholar to oppose [his rival] and feign an excessive dislike for Ibn ʿArabi, his followers and his devotees. In the end, however, these opponents [of Ibn ʿArabi] find themselves rejected and sink into oblivion. For, despite many sound ideas contained in their writings, and their profound knowledge, no one profit[s] from them [on account of their bigotry]."[60]

In what follows we shall test the accuracy of al-Munawi's observation by examining concrete polemical writings from his epoch. In the process, we shall try to unravel the underlying agendas that brought about and sustained the long theological debate around Ibn ʿArabi and shaped the polemical strategies employed by its participants.

Defending the Purity of Islam in the Mamluk State

The trial and execution of a heretic took place in Damascus in 741/1341. It was described by Ibn Kathir (d. 774/1373),[61] a leading historian and *muhaddith* of Mamluk Syria, whose monumental work, "The Beginning and the End" *(al-Bidaya wa ʾl-nihaya),* is a major source of miscellaneous information on that epoch:

> On Tuesday, the last day of *shawwal,* a council was convened in the Court of Justice at the Dar al-Saʿada.[62] I was in attendance on that day. As usual, the judges and men of distinction assembled there. On that day, there was brought to their presence ʿUthman al-Dakkaki—may God Most High maim him!—who was accused of such gross blasphemies as neither al-Hallaj, nor even Ibn Abi ʾl-Ghadafir al-Salqamani dared to utter.[63] A clear proof was furnished against him that he—may God damn him!—claimed divinity, disparaged the Prophet and consorted with the suspicious group of al-Bajariqiyya,[64] and their like—upon them be God's damnation! During the Council he misbehaved himself with the Hanbali *qadi,* who together with the Maliki accused him of unbelief. He, however, alleged that the witnesses were hostile and prejudiced towards him, and he was sent back to prison shackled, chained and disgraced. On that occasion, God granted him a respite through His power and support. On Tuesday, 13 *dhu ʾl-qaʿda,* the above mentioned ʿUthman al-Dakkaki was again brought to Dar al-Saʿada in the presence of the emirs and the *qadi*s who questioned him about the alleged prejudice of the witnesses. He failed [to substantiate] his claim, and produced nothing in his defense. The judges then began to deliberate on the verdict to be passed on him. They asked the opinion of the *qadi* of the Malikis. He praised God and extolled Him, blessed His Messenger, whereupon he demanded that his [al-Dakkaki's] blood be shed, even if he should repent. After that, the above mentioned person was taken to Suq al-Khayl in Damascus, where he was beheaded, as the town crier announced: "This is the recompense of those who profess the doctrine of incarnation!" This was a memorable day at Dar al-Saʿada that gathered many notables and learned men. Our master, the *hafiz* Jamal al-din al-Mizzi[65] was in attendance as well as our master, the *hafiz* Shams al-din al-Dhahabi.[66] Both of them looked into this case, actively instigated its consideration, and offered an ample proof of the heresy of the said individual. Another testimony was given by the Shaykh Zayn al-din, brother of the Shaykh Taqi al-din Ibn Taymiyya.[67] Finally, three judges, the Maliki, the Hanafi, and the Hanbali returned to the court-room and submitted their verdict to the Council demanding the execution of the above-mentioned individual. I saw this all with my own eyes from beginning to end![68]

Ibn Kathir's narrative is arrestingly revealing because it brings together the key members of the anti-Ibn ʿArabi faction who were largely responsible for his posthumous notoriety. The presence of Ibn Taymiyya, Ibn ʿArabi's most influential critic, is symbolic, since he is represented by his younger brother. Nevertheless, there is little doubt that Ibn Taymiyya's lifelong struggle against all manner of perceived "deviations" from the letter of the *shariʿa* contributed to the public atmosphere that made possible the execution on charges of doctrinal nonconformity.[69]

Ibn Taymiyya's major legacy to posterity was a tightly knit group of loyal followers, some of whom were to become the leading scholars of the age. They enthusiastically embraced his vision of the authentic Islam of the "pious forbearers" (*al-salaf al-salih*), and spent their lives trying to cleanse it from "heretical accretions."[70] Characteristically, al-Mizzi and al-Dhahabi—Ibn Taymiyya's closest associates[71]—are portrayed by their disciple Ibn Kathir not as simple onlookers, but as active participants in the trial. Ibn Kathir's own position on the issue is obvious from his schadenfreude that he does not care to conceal.

Ibn Kathir's narrative is relevant to our present purpose insofar as Ibn Taymiyya and his supporters routinely accused Ibn ʿArabi of propagating the doctrine of incarnation and unification—precisely the accusation that was cited in al-Dakkaki's trial.[72] As we can see, in some circumstances, the academic debate over Sufi teachings could have very serious implications for those involved.

Ibn ʿArabi's Opponents in Search of Precedents

Ibn ʿArabi's critics from Ibn Taymiyya on were anxious to discover signs of opposition to his doctrine among his contemporaries. To their great disappointment, such signs were scant. As we have seen, Ibn ʿArabi's early biographers avoided outright condemnations of the Greatest Master who was enjoying the patronage of kings, princes, and influential religious officials. Nor did his impeccable conduct throughout the last decades of his life give them much reason for personal attacks. Finally, as has been suggested, the silence of the sources may simply indicate that Ibn ʿArabi's contemporaries were ignorant of the essence of his teachings. In any case, such a reticence on the part of early writers was a matter of annoyance to Ibn ʿArabi's later critics. Ibn ʿArabi's supporters, on the other hand, were quick to point out that the theological writings from his epoch contained no straightforward condemnations of their hero. Building on the lack of overt criticism of Ibn ʿArabi by his contemporaries, they argued that his views were wholly acceptable to the scholars of his own epoch—a viewpoint that is articulated in the following statement by the great lexicographer al-Fayruzabadi:

> Ibn ʿArabi took up his residence in Syria, where he promulgated his knowledge without a single Syrian scholar [of that epoch] denouncing him for that.[73]

Al-Fayruzabadi's observation is echoed by another influential advocate of the Sufi master, Muhammad b. ʿAbdallah al-Makhzumi (d. 885/1480):[74]

> When the Shaykh Muhyi ʾl-din settled in Syria, all the Syrian *ʿulamaʾ* frequented him in his house, because they recognized his exalted rank and [the fact] that he was the preeminent master of those who attained the truth (*muhaqqiqun*). They never condemned him even though he lived in their midst for more than thirty years. [On the contrary] they copied the Shaykh's writings and passed them on among themselves.[75]

Enter Ibn ʿAbd al-Salam al-Sulami

In these circumstances, is was absolutely essential for Ibn ʿArabi's detractors[76] to present their opposition to his thought as the continuation of a long scholarly tradition that was in evidence already in his own time. With this goal in mind they sought to enlist his authoritative contemporaries to their cause. Eventually, they found such an early foe in ʿIzz al-din Ibn ʿAbd al-Salam al-Sulami (d. 660/1262), the flamboyant leader of Syrian Shafiʿis who went on record as a fearless critic of temporal rulers and "deviant" thinkers. Ibn ʿAbd al-Salam's vigorous protest against an Ayyubid prince's peace deal with the Crusaders led to his expulsion to Cairo in an event that uncannily foreshadows the Egyptian exile of Ibn Taymiyya.[77]

Ibn ʿAbd al-Salam's kinship with Ibn Taymiyya runs deeper than their shared exile experience suggests: his puritanical vision of Islam, coupled with a profound hostility to the teachings he viewed as heretical or un-Islamic, anticipates the rigorous religious program advanced by his Hanbali double. Yet, for all these similarities, the two men adhered to the radically opposed schools of theology. A bona fide Hanbali, Ibn Taymiyya harbored a profound distrust of the rationalist methods and allegorical exegesis of the later Ashʿari dogmatics.[78] Ibn ʿAbd al-Salam, on the other hand, is presented by the sources as a champion of Ashʿari speculative theology, whose convictions were to the fore in his defense of the conception of the created Qur'an[79] against some influential Hanbali doctors in the retinue of the Ayyubid sovereign of Damascus al-Malik al-Ashraf. Vexed by Ibn ʿAbd al-Salam's censure of his Hanbali favorites, al-Ashraf reportedly summoned the Shafiʿi theologian to his court in order to personally interrogate him regarding his beliefs. Unabashed, Ibn ʿAbd al-Salam held his own, and, moreover, took this opportunity to expose the Hanbali tenets as "anthropomorphism" (*tashbih*). In the end, so the story goes, Ibn ʿAbd al-Salam got the better of his rivals and won the ruler over to the Ashʿari cause.[80]

Theological differences notwithstanding, Ibn ʿAbd al-Salam's general religious attitude with its overriding emphasis on the community's unity and welfare anticipates that of Ibn Taymiyya and his followers. One vivid example is Ibn ʿAbd al-Salam's clash with the Andalusi theologian ʿAli al-Harrali (d. 638/1240) over the latter's allegorical interpretation of the Qurʿan.[81] Ibn ʿAbd al-Salam's aversion to mystical speculation is further attested by his eager participation, together with a group of like-minded scholars, in a public trial against the controversial Sufi Shaykh of Damascus ʿAli al-Hariri (d. 645/1247).[82] The self-imposed inquisitors charged him with unbelief and disregard for the *shariʿa*[83] whereupon they persuaded the Ayyubid prince al-Ashraf Musa to throw him in jail. Al-Hariri's imprisonment, however, did not last long. He was released on the orders of the new Ayyubid ruler al-Salih Ismaʿil, who soon ran afoul of Ibn ʿAbd al-Salam[84] over his "treacherous" peace deal with the Crusaders, and therefore hastened to annul all previous deeds associated with the refractory scholar. Ibn ʿAbd al-Salam himself landed in prison for a couple of months—enough time for the sultan to realize that no compromise with his critic was achievable and to expel him to Egypt.

In Egypt Ibn ʿAbd al-Salam was warmly welcomed by the rival Ayyubid sultan who nominated him to a number of prestigious religious offices. He retained these posts after the Mamluk coup d'état that put an end to Ayyubid rule. While in Egypt Ibn ʿAbd al-Salam displayed the same intransigence in matters of religious principle and defiant unwillingness to bend to the ruler's will. Over and over he found himself in trouble and on one occasion barely escaped with his life after refusing to grant the status of free Muslims to some senior Mamluk officers.[85] His calls for a *jihad* against the Franks and against the advancing Mongol armies prefigure the activism and militancy that were exhibited in similar circumstances by Ibn Taymiyya.[86]

Toward the end of his life, Ibn ʿAbd al-Salam's popularity had become such that the sight of his funeral procession that was surrounded by a great crowd of grieving townsfolk caused the all-powerful Baybars al-Bunduqdari to sign with relief: "My reign over this kingdom has finally become firmly established, for had this Shaykh ordered my subjects to rebel, he would have easily deprived me of my power."[87]

Ibn ʿAbd al-Salam and Sufism

Given ʿIzz al-din ʿAbd al-Salam's unswerving commitment to the well-being of the Sunni community, which accounts in part for his hostility toward Syrian mystics of monistic slant, it is highly probable that, at some point in his life, he may have clashed with Ibn ʿArabi, who resided in Damascus at that time. Even if he did not attack the controversial Sufi directly, Ibn ʿAbd al-Salam with his vigorous opposition to any deviation from the "true" Islam was too convenient a figure to be passed up by Ibn ʿArabi's later detractors.

However, I must stress that Ibn ʿAbd al-Salam's biographers do not describe him as an enemy of Sufism. Quite the contrary, they portray him as a moderate Sufi, who, during his stay in Baghdad, studied mystical manuals, such as al-Qushayri's "Epistle on Sufism" *(Al-Risala fi ʾl-tasawwuf)*, under no less a figure than ʿUmar al-Suhrawardi (d. 632/1234).[88] Under al-Suhrawardi's guidance Ibn ʿAbd al-Salam was initiated into the Sufi path and received a Sufi frock (*khirqa*) confirming his rank as an accomplished Sufi master. Ibn ʿAbd al-Salam's preoccupation with Sufi moral discipline, ascetic practices, and esoteric gnosis is lent further support by his own writings, some of which are abridgments of, and commentaries on, classical Sufi manuals.[89] In a similar vein, al-Dhahabi, who commended Ibn ʿAbd al-Salam's scholarship, mentioned—not without embarrassment—his strong penchant for Sufi musical sessions *(samaʿ)* as well as his approval of the ecstatic dances practiced by Damascene mystics,[90] which were routinely condemned by Sunni *fuqahaʾ* as flagrant violations of the *shariʿa*.[91] An apology for *samaʿ* can be found, for example, in his treatise, "The Unraveling of the Puzzles and [the Discovery of] the Keys to the [Hidden] Treasures" (*Hall al-rumuz wa mafatih al-kunuz*), in which he spelled out his attitude to Sufism. In this work, Ibn ʿAbd al-Salam presents himself as an ardent advocate

Table 2

Ibn ʿAbd al-Salam (d. 660/1262),
the earliest condemnation of I.ʿA.,
taken up by later polemicists;
his overall position vis-à-vis
Sufism ambiguous

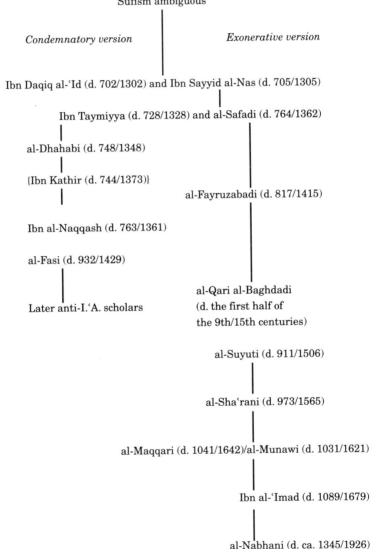

Condemnatory version | *Exonerative version*

Ibn Daqiq al-ʿId (d. 702/1302) and Ibn Sayyid al-Nas (d. 705/1305)

Ibn Taymiyya (d. 728/1328) and al-Safadi (d. 764/1362)

Condemnatory version:

al-Dhahabi (d. 748/1348)

{Ibn Kathir (d. 744/1373)}

Ibn al-Naqqash (d. 763/1361)

al-Fasi (d. 932/1429)

Later anti-I.ʿA. scholars

Exonerative version:

al-Fayruzabadi (d. 817/1415)

al-Qari al-Baghdadi
(d. the first half of
the 9th/15th centuries)

al-Suyuti (d. 911/1506)

al-Shaʿrani (d. 973/1565)

al-Maqqari (d. 1041/1642)/al-Munawi (d. 1031/1621)

Ibn al-ʿImad (d. 1089/1679)

al-Nabhani (d. ca. 1345/1926)

of the mystical gnosis. Taking up the line of thinking of al-Ghazali's *Ihya' 'ulum al-din,* Ibn 'Abd al-Salam not only depicted Sufism as a legitimate moral striving within Sunni Islam, but also as one that bestows on its adherents a higher knowledge that is unattainable through other religious disciplines. Furthermore, in tune with al-Ghazali's argument, Ibn 'Abd al-Salam praised Sufi friends of God *(awliya')* as carriers of this inspired knowledge.

In elaborating on this assumption, Ibn 'Abd al-Salam juxtaposed the adherents of the "external" religious law *(shari'a)* with those who aspire to its "inner" meaning (*haqiqa*). Ibn 'Abd al-Salam conceded that the behavior and statements of the latter group may sometimes contravene the external reading of the *shari'a*. However, in essence, this conflict is, in Ibn 'Abd al-Salam's view, illusionary, as illustrated by the famous encounter between the Qur'anic Moses (Musa), a typical bearer of the exoteric religious law, and al-Khidr, whom the Sufi tradition presented as an embodiment of the superior esoteric truth that eludes the rank and file.[92] The acts and sayings of the Sufi gnostic may indeed appear outrageous to an outsider. However, from the esoteric perspective, they are but expressions of a superior stage of awareness that can be obtained neither through inherited wisdom nor rational reasoning. To protect the tranquillity of those incapable of attaining it, its secrets are unveiled only to the elect Sufi gnostics, who should not divulge them to the commoners lest their belief in the finality of the *shari'a* be corrupted, resulting in antinomian excesses and disruption of the established social and moral order.

Neither in the *Hall* nor in any other work did Ibn 'Abd al-Salam level his criticism at Sufism as such—another feature he shares with his Hanbali counterpart, Ibn Taymiyya, who also attacked what he viewed as the recent heretical accretions to the "sound" Sufi tradition.[93] Although the Hanbali would have hardly agreed with Ibn 'Abd al-Salam's position on the *shari'a/haqiqa* relationship, on the miracles of the saints,[94] or on Sufi music and dancing, he would have approved of Ibn 'Abd al-Salam's persecution of al-Harrali and al-Hariri, who were closely associated with mystical speculations along the lines of Ibn 'Arabi and Ibn Sab'in.

It is true that Ibn 'Abd al-Salam's commitment to Sufism runs much deeper than that of Ibn Taymiyya. Yet, at heart, their general religious outlooks, as well as their biographies, are strikingly similar. In spite of their affiliation with the rival theological factions, both scholars share a common courage of convictions and vision of themselves as guardians of the pristine Islam bequeathed to them by the "pious ancestors." Hence their overarching solicitude for the letter of the *shariʿa* and their relentless drive to suppress the perceived blamable "innovations" in theory and practice.[95]

To sum up, what appears to be common premises and temperaments lead the two scholars to similar practical conclusions—ones that encouraged activism, religiously and politically. This common behavioral pattern marked by the lack of patience with theological opponents and intolerance of any deviation from the "orthodox" creed are behind their repeated campaigns against "alien" elements in Muslim theory and practice.[96] As we shall see, this perception of one's religious and social duty is endemic among most Muslim critics of Ibn ʿArabi, cutting across legal and theological allegiances. We find such community-minded activists among the Shafiʿis (Ibn ʿAbd al-Salam, Ahmad al-Wasiti, Ibn Kathir, and al-Mizzi); the Hanbalis (Ibn Taymiyya, Ibn Qayyim al-Jawziyya, and Ibn ʿAbd al-Wahhab); the Hanafis (ʿAlaʾ al-din al-Bukhari and al-Taftazani); as well as the Malikis (Ibn ʿArafa, Ibn Khaldun, and al-Fasi), all of whom ended up in the camp of Ibn ʿArabi's detractors.

Although both Ibn ʿAbd al-Salam and Ibn Taymiyya are united in their opposition to Ibn ʿArabi's abstruse esoteric teaching, their concrete responses to it are quite disparate, stemming as they were from different visions of Islam in general and Sufism in particular.

Ibn ʿAbd al-Salam's Denunciation of Ibn ʿArabi: An Essay on Contextualization

In his antimonistic treatises, Ibn Taymiyya portrayed Ibn ʿAbd al-Salam as the first critic of Ibn ʿArabi and his teaching. His objective was to use to the full the theme of Ibn ʿAbd al-Salam's purported denunciation of the Greatest Master.[97] His report was based on the authority of two reliable transmitters, Abu Bakr b. Salar[98] and Ibn Daqiq al-ʿId.[99] According to it, Ibn ʿAbd al-Salam declared Ibn ʿArabi "a master of evil" *(shaykh suʾ)*[100] and "a disgusting [man]" (*maqbuh*), who "professed the eternity of the world and did not proscribe fornication."[101]

This severe verdict, whose authenticity Ibn Taymiyya considered to be beyond doubt,[102] was pronounced by Ibn ʿAbd al-Salam upon his arrival in Egypt in 639/1241—that is, one year after the death of the Greatest Master. If authentic, this is probably the earliest reported instance of an unequivocal condemnation of Ibn ʿArabi by a contemporary, assuming that al-Ghubrini's testimony about his prosecution by unnamed Egyptian scholars is a polemical artifice or a legend.

Significantly, in Ibn Taymiyya's redaction, Ibn ʿAbd al-Salam's condemnation consists of two seemingly unrelated points: the first imputes to Ibn ʿArabi what may be described as moral laxity, whereas the second accuses him of adhering to a philosophical doctrine at variance with the creationist dogma espoused by the majority of Muslim theologians.[103] Strange as these charges may appear, they, in fact, constantly recur in the writings of Muslim heresiographers from ʿAbd al-Qahir al-Baghdadi and Ibn Hazm to al-Shahrastani and Ibn al-Jawzi, who often derive "erroneous" theological premises from the moral depravation (*ibahat al-maharim*) of their espousers.[104] Esoteric Sufi and Shiʿi groupings were especially liable to such dual accusations; their perceived moral crimes were often used as a pretext for their persecution by religious and temporal authorities.[105]

In this respect at least, Ibn ʿAbd al-Salam's denunciation of the Greatest Master is quite standard, although anyone familiar with Ibn ʿArabi's biography is likely to find it both unfounded and outright slanderous. More significantly, as it stands, the statement in question appears to have been taken out of a concrete historical and situational context. This context was indeed obligingly provided by later authors. Their elaborations cast new light on the matter, divesting Ibn ʿAbd al-Salam's remark of its unconditional bluntness. The versions of the story furnished by al-Safadi,[106] a cautious supporter of Ibn ʿArabi, and al-Dhahabi, his bitter critic, are especially helpful in placing Ibn ʿAbd al-Salam's censure into a meaningful historical framework.

Each of these writers traced his version of the story to Ibn ʿAbd al-Salam's most prominent disciple, Ibn Daqiq al-ʿId; the latter's credibility as a trustworthy *hadith* scholar (*thiqa*) was above suspicion in the Muslim intellectual milieu. Ibn Daqiq's words, in turn, were transmitted through his own disciple, the famous Egyptian theologian Ibn Sayyid al-Nas.[107] Both al-Safadi and al-Dhahabi insisted that they read the story recorded in Ibn Sayyid al-Nas's own hand. And yet, their versions vary.[108]

Both variants describe Ibn Daqiq al-ʿId's astonishment at his teacher's sharp critique of the acclaimed *wali,* which caused him to ask for proof of Ibn ʿArabi's lies. Ibn ʿAbd al-Salam obliged by the following reply (in al-Safadi's recension):[109]

> He used to deny [the possibility] of marriage between human beings and the *jinn,* since, according to him, the *jinn* are subtle spirits, whereas human beings are solid bodies, hence the two cannot unite. Later on, however, he claimed that he had married a woman from the jinnfolk, who stayed with him for a while, then hit him with a camel's bone and injured him. He used to show us the scar on his face which, by that time, had closed.

In al-Dhahabi's rendition, the story acquires a number of rather zesty details, which are missing (intentionally?) from al-Safadi's narrative:

> He [Ibn ʿArabi] said: "I married a she-jinni, and she blessed me with three children. Then it so happened that I made her angry and she hit me with a bone that caused this scar, whereupon she departed and I have never seen her again since."[110]

Al-Dhahabi's version reemerges in a censorious "biography" of Ibn ʿArabi by the famous Meccan historian Taqi al-din al-Fasi (d. 832/1429), who claims to have copied it from al-Safadi's work on the authority of the same scholars—Ibn Daqiq al-ʿId to Ibn Sayyid al-Nas, and so forth.[111] Al-Fasi's statement yields itself to two explanations. First, al-Fasi might have used a variant of al-Safadi's text that contained the missing zesty details. Alternatively, we have to assume that the text was edited in accordance with the polemical agenda. This suggestion is not improbable in view of the acuteness of the Ibn-ʿArabi controversy in the period under discussion.

The Ibn ʿAbd al-Salam story highlights the polemical strategies of the participants in the Ibn-ʿArabi polemic. One may hazard a guess that Ibn Taymiyya was aware of the whole version of the anecdote: having cited its abridged version, he went on to quote Ibn Daqiq al-ʿId's reference to Ibn ʿArabi's "loose imagination"—a perfectly logical response to the jinni-story from a sober and commonsensical individual.[112] If this reasoning is right, Ibn Taymiyya should have deliberately excised the jinni theme, retaining, however, the moral that Ibn ʿAbd al-Salam drew from it. In any event, the omitted narrative elements resurface tenaciously in most of the later recensions of the story unless they are derived directly from Ibn Taymiyya's edited text. For without the jinni topos, Ibn ʿAbd al-Salam's allegations ring hollow.

What, then, caused Ibn Taymiyya to edit Ibn ʿAbd al-Salam's condemnation? His interference might be attributed to the conventions of the genre of theological polemic, supposedly inimical to flamboyant stories such as this one. This suggestion, however, hardly stands up, for these same conventions did not prevent the Hanbali polemicist from availing himself of the anecdotal evidence detrimental to Ibn ʿArabi's reputation, including the funeral scene discussed in Chapter 2. A key to this puzzle may lie in Ibn Taymiyya's character, which Little attempted to deduce from the accounts of the scholar's personality by his contemporaries.[113] If Little's reconstruction is correct, one may assume that, Ibn Taymiyya's near obsessive fixation on his mission to purify Islam may have caused him to omit the trivia of the she-jinni story and to go straight to the heart of the matter. Or, perhaps, his grim determination and self-denying indifference to outside conditions,[114] made him immune to its obvious humorous overtones. Even if Ibn Taymiyya perceived them, he must have found them ill-suited for his serious discourse. As it stands, his redaction of the story retains only Ibn ʿAbd al-Salam's final verdict, discarding its dubious (or should we say, frolic) context as irrelevant to the all-important polemical goal.

Ibn Taymiyya's puristic attitude contrasts sharply with the lively interest in the jinni topos taken by other writers. The annalists al-Dhahabi and al-Safadi, and, later on, also Ibn Hajar and al-Fasi eagerly incorporate it into their otherwise dry and formulaic writings, adding to the corpus of similar titillating anecdotes, humorous sketches, and "insider" gossip that abound in the historical and prosopographical writings of the epoch.[115]

It is instructive to compare the conclusions that each of the three writers drew from Ibn ʿAbd al-Salam's story. Upon giving its truncated version, Ibn Taymiyya proceeded to pile up, in a malicious crescendo, disparaging opinions of the Sufi master culled from the works of his predecessors, citing, among others, Ibn Daqiq al-ʿId's derogatory remark about Ibn ʿArabi's "loose imagination" and mendacity—a remark that makes sense only when placed into the context of the jinni story expunged by Ibn Taymiyya.[116]

Whether or not aware of the context of the story, Ibn Taymiyya seems to have been much more concerned with Ibn ʿAbd al-Salam's assertion that Ibn ʿArabi professed the eternity of the world. Hence his corrective elaboration:

> [What Ibn ʿAbd al-Salam said] about him [Ibn ʿArabi] is true. This, however, is only one of the many heresies professed by Ibn ʿArabi. From [Ibn ʿAbd al-Salam's words] it is clear that he did not comprehend Ibn ʿArabi's real state. Nor did he grasp its real [implications]. Ibn ʿArabi did not argue that the Lord and the world are two

different entities, as did philosophizing theologians who taught that there are two things: the existence [of God], which is necessary-in-itself, and the world, which has no independent existence. On the contrary, he held that the existence of the world is identical with the existence of God. Thus, on this issue he concurred with the teaching of the materialists, who maintain that the world is eternal (*al-dahriyya al-tabaʾiʿiyya*). The materialists plainly deny that the Maker's existence is separate from that of the world. . . . In fact, Ibn ʿArabi's teaching is in agreement with the view of Pharaoh,[117] who, however, denied the existence of God altogether, while [Ibn ʿArabi] and [his] like confirmed it. At the same time, [Ibn ʿArabi] argued that God was nothing but existence—an idea upon which he is in agreement with Pharaoh. Hence they [Ibn ʿArabi and his followers] are more ignorant and more confused than Pharaoh who, however, surpasses them in unbelief due to his persistence and arrogance—something that is not characteristic of their unbelief.[118]

This passage shows Ibn Taymiyya's disagreement with Ibn ʿAbd al-Salam as to the nature of Ibn ʿArabi's heresy and questions the accuracy of Ibn ʿAbd al-Salam's opinion. Nonetheless, Ibn Taymiyya valued his authority too much to simply write him off—its inaccuracy notwithstanding Ibn Taymiyya consistently included Ibn ʿAbd al-Salam's censure of the Greatest Master into his antimonistic discourse as a much-needed authoritative precedent.

Al-Safadi takes a quite different position. Instead of seeking an explanation of Ibn ʿAbd al-Salam's story he recounts the already familiar anecdote about Ibn ʿArabi and Ibn Suraqa passing through the al-Faradis Gate.[119] By collating both stories, al-Safadi implicitly provided a concrete, if prosaic, reason for Ibn ʿAbd al-Salam's critique of Ibn ʿArabi's doctrinal beliefs. While the she-jinni story explains why Ibn ʿArabi was accused of mendacity and moral dissoluteness, the Bab al-Faradis narrative, in al-Safadi's mind, helps to account for his purported belief in the eternity of the world.[120] In juxtaposing both stories, al-Safadi subtly divests Ibn ʿAbd al-Salam's critique of its unconditioned character and commutes it into the casual response to a concrete, and comical, situation—a result that Ibn Taymiyya was so anxious to avoid.

Equally enlightening is an afterword to the jinni-story furnished by al-Dhahabi—the scholar whom Little describes as "objective rather than envious, fed up and frustrated rather than malicious."[121] These traits of his personality are indeed evident in the conciliatory conclusion he draws from Ibn ʿAbd al-Salam's censure of the Greatest Master:[122]

> I do not think that Muhyi al-din lied on purpose.[123] It is likely that all those spiritual retreats and fasting had a detrimental effect on him, inducing in him false dreams and even a sort of madness.[124]

The Ibn ʿAbd al-Salam motif receives a new twist in the work of the renowned Meccan historian al-Fasi. In his version of Ibn ʿArabi's biography written some fifty years after al-Dhahabi, al-Fasi provided a remarkably serious (and therefore naive) comment on the story, evincing the same insensitivity to its humorous subtext we have observed in Ibn Taymiyya:

> The blameworthy qualities which the *imam* Ibn ʿAbd al-Salam found in Ibn ʿArabi are inappropriate for the friends (*awliya*ʾ) of God Most High. The reason why he was accused of lying in the story we have just recounted is the following: It was not fitting for him to marry the she-jinni and not an ordinary woman, let alone be blessed with children by her afterwards.[125]

Obviously, the absence of the situational context in Ibn Taymiyya's version of the story confounded al-Fasi, causing him to muse over Ibn ʿArabi's philosophical position on the eternity of the world:

> As regards [Ibn ʿAbd al-Salam's] words about the "eternity of the world," one wonders whether that was indeed [Ibn ʿArabi's] real view, for the unbelief associated with it is well known. On these grounds alone the *faqih* Abu Muhammad [Ibn ʿAbd al-Salam] could have pronounced him an unbeliever. And this is in spite of the fact that at that time it was not yet obvious that, on top of it all, [Ibn ʿArabi] also taught that the world was identical with God in both image and essence. This, of course, is a much more serious delusion than one professed by the espousers of the eternity of the world who assert that there is an existence that is necessary-in-itself,[126] whereupon they proceed to assert that all possible existents [in the universe] have originated from this necessary existence.[127]

As with Ibn Taymiyya, al-Fasi felt that Ibn ʿAbd al-Salam's accusation had missed the target, since the profession of the world's eternity was routinely associated with the Muslim philosophers (*falasifa*), who, in turn, were assumed to have inherited it from ancient Greeks. In other words, by Ibn Taymiyya's time, let alone al-Fasi's, the nature of Ibn ʿArabi's teaching was too well known to credit him with the espousal of the eternity of the world as well. Therefore, for both Ibn Taymiyya and al-Fasi, Ibn ʿAbd al-Salam's criticism, although welcome as an authoritative precedent, rang hollow. While it kept resurfacing in the polemical writings of the anti-Ibn ʿArabi party, it definitely jarred the ear of the more discriminating scholars who attempted to bring it in line with the advanced state of the debate.

Ibn ʿAbd al-Salam on the Hierarchy of the Sufi Gnostics

The authenticity of Ibn ʿAbd al-Salam's disparagement of Ibn ʿArabi seems to find support in his "Epistle on the [Saintly] Substitutes and the [Supreme] Succor" *(Risala fi 'l-abdal wa 'l-ghawth)*.[128] This short polemical treatise targets the popular belief in the invisible hierarchy of the saints, through whom God sustains the world and protects it from destruction.[129] The "Epistle" did more than simply criticize the notion of "the men of the unseen," who constitute this imaginary hierarchy; it forthrightly disavowed the popular Sufi belief that each epoch has its own supreme saint, the spiritual "Pole" (or "Axis") of the epoch *(qutb al-zaman)*. According to the "Epistle," this erroneous belief led some Sufi theorists to posit the existence of "the seal of the saints"*(khatm al-awliya')*,[130] whose functions Ibn ʿAbd al-Salam found alarmingly similar to those of God's prophets and messengers:

> We have already laid bare the falsehood of the name "Succor" in general, including the one known as "Succor of the non-Arabs," who is said to reside at Mecca, or the [so-called] "Seventh Succor."[131] The same goes for the idea of the seal of the saints, which is equally false, for no proof can be adduced to support it. The first person to mention [it] was Muhammad b. ʿAli b. al-Hakim al-Tirmidhi,[132] who was followed by a group of scholars, each claiming to be the seal of the saints. Among them were Ibn Hamawayh,[133] Ibn ʿArabi and several misguided [Sufi] masters in Damascus. Each of them asserted that, in certain respects, he was superior to the Prophet. . . . All these claims sprang from the desire for the leadership (*riyasa*), which they thought belongs to the Seal of the Prophets. However, they made a grievous mistake, for the Seal of the Prophets is far superior to any of them, and there is ample evidence to prove this. . . . Anyone professing such a doctrine still remains a Muslim. However, such a person is an erring innovator (*mubtadiʿ dall*),[134] or a grave sinner. These individuals must be punished and restrained from indulging in such accursed beliefs, as it is usually done with regard to any other person who publicly professes a blamable innovation or [perpe-

> trates]dissoluteness. . . . The same punishment must be indiscriminately applied to everyone—the devout, the learned, the pious, the poor, the ascetic, the speculative theologian or the philosopher, as well as the kings, the ignorant, the scribes, the bookkeepers, the physicians, the clerks, and the commoners, because by supporting these views one inevitably strays from the straight path and abandons the true faith. . . . [135]

Ibn ʿAbd al-Salam's message is clear: he unequivocally rebuffed as fraudulent the claims to religious leadership and prophetic heritage made by some "misguided" Sufi leaders. Seen in a broader perspective, Ibn ʿAbd al-Salam's stance enshrined, in the context of Sunni Islam, "the traditional opposition of the powerful, formally educated religious officials (the *ʿulamaʾ*) and the more popular representatives of an authentic inner spirituality (the *ʿurafaʾ*), a tendency that was often somewhat antinomian and socially disruptive in its outward expression."[136]

On the face of it, the anti-Sufi tone of the "Epistle" fits in well with Ibn ʿAbd al-Salam's persistent defense of the prophetic mission of Muhammad, which he felt was endangered by the fraudulent claims of later impostors.[137] Similarly, it appears to be in tune with the author's censure of Ibn ʿArabi, whom he must have viewed as one such impostor irresponsibly propagating seditious doctrines. Ibn ʿAbd al-Salam's repeated reference to the absurdity of such unprovable beliefs as the hierarchy of the saints exhibits what may be described as a positivistic spirit *avant la lettre* with its ingrained suspicion of things mystical.[138]

Our previous conclusions are built upon the assumption that Ibn ʿAbd al-Salam was indeed the author of the "Epistle." His authorship, however, cannot be taken for granted, since the passage that was just quoted forms an integral part of Ibn Taymiyya's polemical treatise against the Sufi doctrine of the divine Pole and the invisible hierarchy of the Sufi saints.[139] It is, therefore, likely that the excerpt in question, which had circulated under separate cover, was, at some point, (mis)attributed to Ibn ʿAbd al-Salam.[140] If this is the case, the (mis)attribution is in itself revealing in bringing out the perceived affinity between the two eminent Sunni scholars in the minds of Muslim scholars, including the Syrian editor of the "Epistle."

The authorship of the "Epistle" notwithstanding, there is little reason to doubt the importance of Ibn ʿAbd al-Salam's acerbic testimony for Ibn Taymiyya's argument. Throughout his eventful life, the

Hanbali scholar posed as an uncompromising opponent of all manner of innovations in religious theory and practice. No wonder that he was always anxious to ground his views in the authoritative precedents of the pious forbears (*al-salaf al-salih*) or, at the very least, in the opinions of revered Sunni scholars. In the absence of such a supporting authority, his own onslaught against "innovations" might have been interpreted by his numerous opponents as unprecedented and arbitrary.[141]

In declaring war on Ibn ʿArabi and his monistic followers, Ibn Taymiyya was faced with the task of accounting for the lack of opposition to the Sufi among his contemporaries. Otherwise, Ibn Taymiyya's belated denunciations of his views could be (and, actually were) interpreted as an innovation.[142]

Sufi Responses to Ibn ʿAbd al-Salam's Censure

The importance of Ibn ʿAbd al-Salam's censure was not lost on Ibn ʿArabi's supporters. The popular Shafiʿi scholar was too weighty a figure to be ignored. To offset the detrimental effect of his derogatory remarks about their hero, Ibn ʿArabi's supporters circulated another story—ostensibly an amplification of the previous one, but, in fact, carrying a directly opposite message. The earliest version of this alternative story appears at the turn of the 7th and 8th centuries A.H., that is, roughly the time when the controversy over Ibn ʿArabi in Syria and Egypt had reached its peak. First invoked by the noted Egyptian Sufi ʿAbd al-Ghaffar al-Qusi (d. 708/1308,)[143] it resurfaces in the works of al-Fayruzabadi, al-Qari al-Baghdadi, al-Suyuti (d. 911/1505), al-Shaʿrani, al-Maqqari, Ibn al-ʿImad, and some other supporters of the Greatest Master. Despite minor variations in their accounts, all of them cite the same source: Ibn ʿAbd al-Salam's unnamed servant or student.[144] In al-Qusi's redaction, Ibn ʿAbd al-Salam and his servant were passing by Ibn ʿArabi, who instructed his disciples in the Great Umayyad Mosque of Damascus. Suddenly, the servant recalled that Ibn ʿAbd al-Salam had promised to reveal to him the identity of the supreme saint of the epoch, the "Pole of the Age" (*qutb al-zaman*). The question caught Ibn ʿAbd al-Salam off guard. He paused hesitantly for a moment, then pointed in the direction of Ibn ʿArabi, saying: "He is the Pole!" "And this in spite of what you have said against him?" asked the servant. Ibn ʿAbd al-Salam ignored this remark and simply repeated his reply.[145]

A hundred years later, the celebrated Muslim lexicographer al-Fayruzabadi (d. 817/1415),[146] cited a longer variant of the story in a *fatwa* written in Ibn ʿArabi's defense.[147] In his redaction, the story falls into two distinct episodes: in the first we witness Ibn ʿAbd al-Salam teaching jurisprudence *(fiqh)* to a gathering of learned men, apparently jurisconsults *(fuqahaʾ)*. When the issue of the origin and etymology of the word *zindiq*—"a Manichean," "a heretic"—was raised by the students, someone asked Ibn ʿAbd al-Salam for an example of a *zindiq* among his contemporaries.[148] Before he could open his mouth, a jurist next to him exclaimed: "Someone like Ibn al-ʿArabi in Damascus!" Ibn ʿAbd al-Salam did not protest and quickly changed the topic. The second episode is set Ibn ʿAbd al-Salam's house, with only himself and the servant present. As the two men were about to break their Ramadan fast, the servant asked him about the identity of the "Pole of the Age." After some hesitation, Ibn ʿAbd al-Salam named Ibn ʿArabi, prompting the perplexed servant to remind him of the way in which the Sufi master was treated in the recent teaching session. "Hold your tongue!" followed a brusque reply, "That was a jurists' assembly!"[149]

In al-Fayruzabadi's version of the story, Ibn ʿAbd al-Salam is presented as a secret admirer of the Greatest Master who was fully aware of the latter's exalted status in the Sufi hierarchy. However, as a public figure, Ibn ʿAbd al-Salam was careful to conceal his genuine opinion of the controversial Sufi in order to "preserve the outward aspect of the religious law" *(asun bi-zahir al-shariʿa)*. In so doing, he, according to al-Fayruzabadi, shrewdly avoided an inevitable confrontation with the "jurists," who viewed Ibn ʿArabi as a heretic.[150] The cautious position outlined by Ibn ʿAbd al-Salam is typical of many later Muslim writers who were sympathetic with Sufi wisdom, yet who were acutely cognizant of its potentially disruptive impact on an unprepared audience. In line with this position, they warned the uninitiated against jumping to hasty conclusions regarding the real meaning of Ibn ʿArabi's teachings.[151] Any other reaction, his supporters knew all too well, inevitably leads to fruitless debates, mutual accusations, personal confrontations, and, possibly, social unrest.

The apparent inconsistency of Ibn ʿAbd al-Salam's views concerning Ibn ʿArabi in the Sufi version of the story elicited a variety of explanations from the pro-Ibn ʿArabi faction. In accounting for the dubiousness of the issue, ʿAbd al-Ghaffar al-Qusi, the first transmitter of the story, remarks:[152]

> If he [Ibn ʿArabi] was the greatest among the saints, there is no contradiction in Shaykh ʿIzz al-din's opinion of him, because he [ʿIzz al-din] judged him according to his [Ibn ʿArabi's] outward actions and works, and in keeping with the *(shariʿa)* law. As for his innermost beliefs and intentions, they belong to the sphere of God's knowledge, so God will judge them as He wills. It is possible that Shaykh ʿIzz al-din was aware of Ibn ʿArabi's high spiritual rank, which no one could deny. However, whenever [Ibn ʿArabi] expressed an opinion contrary to the *shariʿa* law, ʿIzz al-din had no qualms about condemning him out of concern for the hearts of the weak and for the outward meaning of the *shariʿa*, which he wished to protect. Thus, he treated each individual situation accordingly.

In another elaboration, a sympathetic al-Qari al-Baghdadi willfully tailored the story to the *manaqib* genre, making it a pretext for praising Ibn ʿArabi's exceptional virtues:[153]

> To my mind, Shaykh ʿIzz al-din Ibn ʿAbd al-Salam sought to excuse the *fuqaha'*, who were swift to denounce that of which they had no inkling. At the same time, he intimated to his servant the [genuine] status of Shaykh Muhyi al-din [Ibn ʿArabi] by directing his [the servant's] attention to the loftiness of [Ibn ʿArabi's] rank and the greatness of his spiritual state.[154]

The importance of Ibn ʿAbd al-Salam's ambiguous evaluation of the Greatest Master for the subsequent polemic is further attested by the detailed treatment of this story in al-Fasi's massive biographical dictionary, "The Precious Necklace" *(al-ʿIqd al-thamin)*.[155] A bitter critic of Ibn ʿArabi's monistic views, al-Fasi rejected the Sufi version of the story as sheer fabrication. Yet, as a scrupulous *muhaddith,* he tried to justify his position through the methods current in *hadith* criticism:

> I have a strong suspicion that this story was invented by the extremist Sufis (*ghulat al-sufiyya*) who were infatuated with Ibn ʿArabi.[156] Thereupon the story gained wide diffusion until it reached some trustworthy people, who accepted it in good faith. . . . My suspicion regarding the authenticity of this story has grown stronger because of the unfounded supposition that Ibn ʿAbd al-Salam's praise of Ibn ʿArabi had occurred simultaneously with his censure of him. Ibn ʿAbd al-Salam's statement that he censured Ibn ʿArabi out of concern for the *shariʿ*a inescapably implies that Ibn ʿArabi enjoyed a high rank in the same moment as Ibn ʿAbd al-

> Salam was censuring him. Such a blunder could not have happened to any reliable religious scholar, let alone to someone as knowledgeable and righteous as Ibn ʿAbd al-Salam. Anyone who suspects him of this makes a mistake and commits a sin [by holding him responsible for] mutually contradictory statements. . . . One may try to explain Ibn ʿAbd al-Salam's praise of Ibn ʿArabi—if it indeed took place—by the fact that [Ibn ʿAbd al-Salam] was hesitating between praise and censure, because at the time he spoke Ibn ʿArabi's state had changed for the better.[157] If so, there is no contradiction in Ibn ʿAbd al-Salam's words. Were we to admit that the praise really occurred, it was nevertheless abrogated by Ibn Daqiq al-ʿId's report concerning Ibn ʿAbd al-Salam's [later] condemnation of Ibn ʿArabi. For Ibn Daqiq al-ʿId could only hear Ibn ʿAbd al-Salam in Egypt, that is, a few years after Ibn ʿArabi's death. This cannot be otherwise because he . . . was educated at Qus,[158] where he had studied the Maliki *madhhab,* until he mastered it completely. Only then he came to Cairo to study the Shafiʿi *madhhab* and other sciences under Ibn ʿAbd al-Salam's guidance. . . . His departure could only take place after 640, by which time Ibn ʿArabi had already been dead. . . . Now, Ibn ʿAbd al-Salam's praise, as the story itself testifies, occurred when Ibn ʿArabi was still alive. For did he not point to [Ibn ʿArabi], when that individual [the servant] asked him about the Pole or the [greatest] saint of the age?[159]

As convincing as al-Fasi's argument might appear, it failed to persuade Ibn ʿArabi's supporters, who were equally anxious to enlist Ibn ʿAbd al-Salam's authority to their cause. In any case, the motif keeps resurfacing with every new generation of Muslim scholars involved in the Ibn ʿArabi controversy, who debated its implications with equal vigor. Although not quite relevant to our present point, al-Fasi's comments reveal the techniques of *hadith* criticism with its focus on the identity and personal circumstances of transmitters as a means of verifying the accuracy of their reports.

Ibn ʿAbd al-Salam on the Relationship Between the *shariʿa* and the *haqiqa*

A key to Ibn ʿAbd al-Salam's puzzle is found in his own works, which are totally ignored by both parties to the debate. Nowhere is Ibn ʿAbd al-Salam's ambivalence toward speculative Sufism more evident than in his discussion of the relationship between the exoteric law *(shariʿa)* of the *ʿulama*ʾ and the esoteric perception of God and the world (*haqiqa*) of the Sufi sages *(hukama*ʾ*)*. This discussion clearly shows Ibn ʿAbd al-Salam's dubuous assessment of Ibn ʿArabi to be in line with his overall view of the tensions between higher mystical knowledge (*haqiqa*) and *shariʿa* Islam.

As many mystically minded Shafiʿi theologians before him, Ibn ʿAbd al-Salam considered the *shariʿa* and *haqiqa* to be complementary in assuring the proper functioning of the divine plan with regard to creation.[160] At the same time, he acknowledged the difference between their goals and orientations. While the former, in Ibn ʿAbd al-Salam's scheme, is concerned with the moral-ethical dimensions of faith and governs the day-to-day functioning of religious community, the latter is a more individualistic personal expression of one's religious sentiment, which is confined to the elect few. For Ibn ʿAbd al-Salam, the *shariʿa/haqiqa* dichotomy mirrors two different stages of the believers' spiritual attainment as well as two disparate visions of God and the world.

The mystical striver, who has reached an elevated degree of spiritual perfection, becomes witness to the higher truths of being that are concealed from the common herd of believers. Inescapably, he finds himself torn between two conflicting religious impulses: loyalty to the divine law and to mystical vision. When the latter gets the better of him, he may violate the *shariʿa* code and public propriety, thereby exposing himself to accusations of heresy or atheism. In elucidating the tension between the two levels of religious awareness, Ibn ʿAbd al-Salam wrote:

> When your feet are firmly established, your inmost self is consolidated, and your [ecstatic] intoxication diminishes, you say "He!" When, however, your ecstatic state prevails, and your intoxication takes you beyond the realm of constancy, you cry out "I!"[161] At the first stage, you are constant, at the second, you are transient. At this point, it becomes difficult for the human mind to solve the riddle implicit in the mystical utterances such as those just cited. One person may say [about you]: "He is a heretic (*zindiq*) who should be executed!" The other may object: "He is a trustworthy one who should be praised!" Still another will say: "He is overwhelmed [by a spiritual state] and should be left alone!" From the viewpoint of his spiritual state, he has indeed realized the supreme truth. At the same time, those who condemn him to death are justified, because the *shariʿa* has its limits, whose violators ought to be punished. . . . As for the *haqiqa*,

> the vision [associated with it] transcends the confines of this world. . . . And yet the *shari'a* and the *haqiqa* pursue the same goal, to wit, to be at God's service the way He wants you to serve Him. Hence, the *shari'a* is shallow without the *haqiqa,* and, likewise, the *haqiqa* is futile without the *shari'a*.[162]

In consideration of the foregoing, Ibn 'Abd al-Salam's ambiguous position vis-à-vis Ibn 'Arabi presents itself not only as logical but, in fact, as the only possible one.

Some Later Elaborations

As indicated, the figure of Ibn 'Abd al-Salam was claimed by each faction of the Ibn-'Arabi controversy due to his impeccable record as a staunch champion of the *shari'a*.[163] Some interesting reflections on his attitude toward the Greatest Master are featured in the work of Ibn 'Ata' Allah al-Iskandari (al-Sikandari), the renowned Maliki mystic and head of the popular Shadhili brotherhood. In the book, "The Delicacies of the Divine Favors" *(Lata'if al-minan),* the brotherhood's standard textbook, al-Iskandari depicted Ibn 'Abd al-Salam as a friend and great admirer of the founder of the Shadhiliyya, Abu 'l-Hasan al-Shadhili (d. 625/1258). According to al-Iskandari, while in Egypt, Ibn 'Abd al-Salam's attitude toward Sufism underwent a drastic transition from suspicion to wholehearted endorsement. This change, so the story goes, was precipitated by al-Shadhili's return from a pilgrimage, when he conveyed to Ibn 'Abd al-Salam personal greetings from the Prophet, who had visited the Sufi in his dream during his stay at the Meccan *haram*.[164] Interestingly, among those who witnessed Ibn 'Abd al-Salam's alleged conversion at the hands of al-Shadhili was a man, whom al-Iskandari described as a disciple of the Greatest Master *(ahadu ashab al-shaykh al-'arif Ibn 'Arabi).* Moreover, in al-Iskandari's narrative, this man is made to testify to the supernatural power of the Sufi shaykhs, especially of al-Shadhili, a testimony that is accompanied by a minor miracle to further persuade a skeptical Ibn 'Abd al-Salam of the veracity of Sufi claims.[165]

The theme of Ibn 'Abd al-Salam's "conversion" was later taken up by the great Egyptian polyhistor al-Suyuti, who took the side of Ibn 'Arabi's supporters in the debate over his teaching that was still very much alive in his epoch (the late 9th/15th centuries). As with Ibn 'Ata' Allah al-Iskandari, al-Suyuti made polemical use of Ibn 'Abd al-Salam's spectacular change of heart, ascribing it to the influence of al-Shadhili and to that of the latter's foremost disciple, Abu ʾl-ʿAbbas Ahmad al-Mursi (d. 686/1287).[166] In line with his position in the Ibn ʿArabi debate, al-Suyuti tried to prove that the exiled Damascene scholar eventually acknowledged the soundness of Sufi theory of sainthood and retracted his earlier denunciation of the Greatest Master.[167]

Regardless of whether Ibn ʿAbd al-Salam's conversion really took place, it is clear that the aim of both al-Iskandari and al-Suyuti was to exculpate such great Sufi saints *(awliyaʾ)* as Ibn al-Farid, Ibn ʿArabi, and al-Shadhili in the face of the repeated attacks on their teachings by Egyptian scholars. To this end, they brought into play Ibn ʿAbd al-Salam's impeccable credentials, in hopes of tilting the scale of scholarly opinion to Ibn ʿArabi's advantage. By focusing on Ibn ʿAbd al-Salam's supposed retraction, al-Iskandari and al-Suyuti sought to set an influential precedent for their learned contemporaries, inviting them to follow the example of Ibn ʿAbd al-Salam. Given the scholars' general inclination to follow authoritative precedents (*taqlid*), this polemical stratagem seems eminently reasonable.

Yet, al-Suyuti's ultimate goal did not necessarily correspond to that of the Shadhilis. While he consistently tried to forge a connection between Ibn ʿAbd al-Salam's alleged conversion to Sufism (which, as we know, had occurred long before his arrival in Egypt) and his condonation of Ibn ʿArabi, this did not seem to be high on al-Iskandari's agenda. In neither this passage from the *Lataʾif al-minan* nor elsewhere,[168] did al-Iskandari make a serious effort to exonerate Ibn ʿArabi personally from the accusations of heresy and unbelief. In fact, he had a quite different polemical ax to grind: to advance the cause of the Shadhili order and the saintly image of its founder. In keeping with this goal, his discursive strategy was geared to presenting al-Shadhili as the divine Pole and great miracle-worker of his epoch—a claim that was probably opposed by some Egyptian scholars who were not affiliated with the *tariqa.* It is in connection with al-Shadhili's purported "pole-hood" that al-Iskandari had recourse to the theme of Ibn ʿAbd al-Salam's retraction. In light of this goal, Ibn ʿArabi's appearance in the pages of the *Lataʾif* is a mere coincidence, a minor touch in a discursive scene designed for a quite different purpose.

Furthermore, there are indications that both al-Iskandari and his colleagues at the head of the Shadhili *tariqa* found Ibn ʿArabi's esoteric vision of Sufism uncongenial and outré.[169] Finally, Abu ʾl-ʿAbbas al-Mursi, al-Shadhili's first successor at the head of the brotherhood, is quoted by Ibn Taymiyya as referring to Ibn ʿArabi's adherents as "unbelievers who maintain that the created world is identical with the Creator."[170] This evidence suggests that while al-Suyuti, who wrote his polemical tract almost two centuries later and in a different religious and social climate, identified Ibn ʿArabi with Sufism as a whole, al-Iskandari and the Shadhili Sufis were careful to dissociate themselves from his metaphysical "excesses" and to emphasize their preoccupation with the issues of piety and moral living.[171]

If there is an affinity between Ibn ʿArabi and the Shadhiliyya, it is to be sought in their shared concept of sainthood. Both the *Futuhat* and the *Lataʾif* include very similar discussions of *wilaya,* the Sufi saints, and the mystical hierarchy[172]—precisely the notions that Ibn ʿAbd al-Salam attacked in the "Epistle." If he was indeed its author, then we are dealing with a very abrupt ideological volte-face, since, by acknowledging al-Shadhili's claim to pole-hood Ibn ʿAbd al-Salam should have completely forsaken the principal thesis of his treatise.

Where does all this leave us? On the one hand, we cannot rule out that Ibn ʿAbd al-Salam fell under the spell of al-Shadhili's charismatic personality to such an extent that he totally revoked his earlier condemnation of the Sufi hierarchy of saints. Alternatively, the "Epistle" was the work of Ibn Taymiyya, as we suspected. Yet, it is hard to imagine that his entire religious attitude was changed as a result of his meeting with al-Shadhili as the latter's disciples tried to make us believe. We have seen that he had been a moderate Sufi long before his expulsion to Egypt. Furthermore, his admiration for al-Shadhili did not necessarily imply his approval of Ibn ʿArabi (al-Suyuti's argument), since, by his time, the latter stood for a different strain of Sufism from that personified by the founder of the Shadhiliyya *tariqa.*

A polemical strategy reminiscent of al-Suyuti's is deployed by Ibn ʿArabi's later advocates, notably the famous Egyptian Sufi ʿAbd al-Wahhab al-Shaʿrani (d. 973/1565).[173] As with al-Suyuti, al-Shaʿrani sought to forge a logical link between Ibn ʿAbd al-Salam's "conversion" at the hands of al-Shadhili and his unconditional approval of Ibn ʿArabi and other *awliyaʾ*. To this end, he put in the mouth of Ibn ʿAbd al-Salam the following apology for the Greatest Master:

> Some of the [great] religious scholars condemn him [Ibn ʿArabi] in sympathy with the feeble-minded legists who are unable to appreciate fully the spiritual states experienced by the poor (*fuqaraʾ*).[174] They fear that [the masses] might find in the Shaykh's words something that contradicts the religious law (*sharʿ*), and thus be led

> astray. Had they cultivated the company of the *fuqara*ʾ, they would have learned their [Sufi] terminology and refrained [from charging Sufis] with violations of the *shariʿa*.[175]

The reader's first impulse is to dismiss this quotation as a flagrant apologetic fabrication—the impression reinforced by the absence of the usual chain of transmitters attached to it. Upon closer scrutiny, however, al-Shaʿrani's statement appears to be quite consistent with Ibn ʿAbd al-Salam's view of the inevitable tensions between the adherents of the *shariʿa* and the champions of the *haqiqa,* as well as with his insistence that the outward aspect of the *shariʿa* be protected at all cost.

Conclusion

To sum up our discussion of the polemical discourses generated by the Ibn ʿAbd al-Salam story, it is instructive to examine how the two great scholars interacted in real life in order to establish a benchmark against which all previous accounts can be understood. One thing is sure: they actually met each other. In one account, Ibn ʿAbd al-Salam borrowed from Ibn ʿArabi a copy of Ibn Hazm's (d. 456/1064) famous compendium of the Zahiri law, titled "The Adorned One" (*al-Muhalla*).[176] He is also said to have been witness to Ibn ʿArabi's supernatural perspicacity and ability to predict future events (*kashf*).[177] Finally, in Ibn ʿArabi's poetic *diwan,* we find a tantalizingly inconclusive account of a visionary meeting between Ibn ʿAbd al-Salam and the Greatest Master:

> In a dream I saw the Shafiʿi jurist ʿIzz al-din Ibn ʿAbd al-Salam, who was sitting on the stone bench—probably at a *madrasa*—and instructing people in [the teachings of] his school. When I sat down next to him, a person approached him with a question about the generosity of God Most High. He [Ibn ʿAbd al-Salam] recited to him a verse that said that divine Mercy embraces all His servants. I told him that I also know a verse pertaining to this subject which I had included in a poem of mine. However, no matter how hard I tried to recollect it, in that particular moment it eluded me. I said to him: "God Most High has just intimated to me something relevant to this matter and I would like to recite it!" He smiled and gave me permission to speak. And God Most High indeed inspired in me the following verses. . . . ʿIzz al-din kept smiling as I was reciting them. It

so happened that there was passing by us the *qadi* Shams al-din al-Shirazi, may God be pleased with him![178] When he noticed us, he dismounted from his mule and approached us. He sat next to al-ʿIzz Ibn ʿAbd al-Salam, then turned to me and said: "I wish you give me a kiss on the mouth!" He embraced me, and I kissed him on the lips. Al-ʿIzz Ibn ʿAbd al-Salam asked me about the meaning of this. I replied to him: "I am in a vision, and the kiss signifies the [final] approval that he seeks from me. He used to have a good opinion of me. Then it occurred to him that [some of] his goals eluded him, and he also became cognizant of [some of] his sins and of the approaching death hour." I then stood up and helped him [al-Shirazi] to mount his mule, whereupon he departed. Al-ʿIzz asked me by gesture and allusion, not in a usual manner,[179] about my wife's treatment of me. In reply, I recited two verses which were inspired in me in that same moment. . . . Here are these verses:

When my wife sees that my purse is lined

She smiles and approaches me coquettishly,

But when she sees it empty of *dirhams*

She loathes me and turns away with disdain![180]

As usual with Ibn ʿArabi's accounts of his visionary experiences, this one lends itself to many possible interpretations. Unfortunately, it gives little clue as to the exact nature of relations between the two men.

In sum, Ibn ʿAbd al-Salam's condemnation of Ibn ʿArabi as a professor of the doctrine of the eternity of the world reveals his ignorance of the Sufi master's real views. The anecdotal evidence that was just analyzed shows that his harsh censure of Ibn ʿArabi was, in all probability, provoked by a few fleeting encounters with the Sufi rather than a close study of the latter's works or, perhaps, by a couple of anecdotes that circulated among Damascene *ʿulama*ʾ. Hence the dramatic contrast between the harshness of his critique and his obvious lack of familiarity with Ibn ʿArabi's work.

It is unlikely that the relationship between the two men was particularly close or friendly. As religious teachers, they represented different types of authority, and, consequently, enjoyed disparate followings. The activist, inner-worldly attitude of Ibn ʿAbd al-Salam stands in sharp contrast to Ibn ʿArabi's contemplative, otherworldly stance. Conceivably, the latter's extravagant claims and visions may have been seen by the former as presumptuous, if not outright heretical. An heir to the long tradition of *shariʿa* Sufism personified by Shihab al-din al-Suhrawardi, Ibn ʿAbd al-Salam must have considered himself superior to the other mystical masters of the age, as evidenced by his Sufi works.

Clearly, Ibn ʿArabi's monistic propensities and interest in the more recondite aspects of the Sufi tradition did not resonate well with Ibn ʿAbd al-Salam's cautious, and relatively straightforward, *shariʿa / haqiqa* dichotomy. No wonder that Ibn ʿArabi's dream portrayed him as a "jurist" (*faqih*) par excellence, thereby implicitly denying him the status of an accomplished Sufi master. Ibn ʿAbd al-Salam had good reasons to dislike his overconfident contemporary or to treat him as a rival. This underlying conflict of ambitions and worldviews may well have sparked the altercation between the two leading scholars of the age that continues to puzzle Muslim writers.

Be this as it may, Ibn ʿAbd al-Salam's superficial judgment of the Greatest Master eventually became a problem for Ibn ʿArabi's later critics whose opposition to him sprang from a greater familiarity with his tenets.

The real meaning of Ibn ʿAbd al-Salam's invectives can be understood only in the context of the anecdotes about Ibn ʿArabi's marriage to the she-jinni and his enigmatic statement at the Bab al-Faradis. Barring this situational context, the truncated, out-of-context version of the story in Ibn Taymiyya's narrative is puzzling. In response, the *qutb* story was floated by the followers of Ibn ʿArabi, who were anxious to counter the harmful effect of Ibn ʿAbd al-Salam's sharp denunciations of the Greatest Master.

The matter may not be so simple, since Ibn ʿAbd al-Salam's duplicity of judgment tallies nicely with his ambivalent position vis-à-vis Sufi gnosis and experience, as laid out in his *Hall al-rumuz*. The story is further complicated by Ibn ʿAbd al-Salam's alleged change of opinion of the Greatest Master while in Egypt. Since this theme plays so neatly into the hands of Ibn ʿArabi's partisans, one is tempted to dismiss it as a fabrication. Yet, given Ibn ʿAbd al-Salam's ambiguous view of the *shariʿa/haqiqa* relationship one can never be sure. In the end, the narrative topoi discussed in this chapter are obscure enough to frustrate even the most dedicated inquirer. The same, unfortunately, goes for most other narrative clusters related to the Greatest Master that were subject to similar polemical distortions. In the end, one has to be content with an assortment of disjointed (and contradictory) legends, anecdotes, and "eyewitness" accounts, but with very little in the way of hard evidence from which to proceed. In these circumstances, to speak of an objective biography of the Andalusi Sufi is at best premature.

The Ibn ʿAbd al-Salam stories contributed to the atmosphere of ambivalence and conjecture that enveloped Ibn ʿArabi's image from the very start. The conflicting versions of the same story circulated by his friends and foes encouraged the ambiguity and caution that mark his treatment by later Muslim scholars. Whatever his genuine attitude to the Greatest Master, Ibn ʿAbd al-Salam became a personification of this painful duality.

A final remark concerns the polemical strategy utilized by the scholars whose works have been examined thus far. It is now clear that these scholars were interested less in Ibn ʿArabi's doctrines per se than in how Ibn ʿArabi was evaluated by earlier authorities, especially those who knew him personally. This preoccupation informs their tireless quest for opinions of the Greatest Master expressed by his contemporaries. For later writers, such opinions were absolutely indispensable in locating Ibn ʿArabi within the familiar frame of reference, namely, as a transmitter of received knowledge, a *faqih,* and a theologian. Judgments, statements, and intimations to this effect—either explicit or cast in the form of parables or anecdotes—came to constitute the database on which later scholars drew in constructing the image of the Greatest Master. The importance of these "firsthand" reports from authoritative scholars of his age is difficult to overestimate. It is over their meaning that the future generations of polemicists continually locked horns.

Ultimately, the "affair of Ibn ʿAbd al-Salam" sheds some light on the attempts of the Ibn ʿArabi party to exempt him and his fellow Sufi saints from the judgmental criteria applied to ordinary believers or exoteric *ʿulama*ʾ. A need for such an alternative yardstick was dictated by the apparent inadequacy of the traditional frame of reference, such as *hadith* criticism. In a sense, the controversy over Ibn ʿArabi, whose legacy could not be readily forced into the Procrustean bed of traditional scholarship, contributed to the emergence of an alternative set of evaluative criteria—one applied exclusively to "the friends of God."

4

IBN TAYMIYYA'S FORMIDABLE CHALLENGE

Despite the great importance of the Ibn ʿAbd al-Salam episode for the subsequent polemic over Ibn ʿArabi, it was put in the shade by the comprehensive critical attack on his legacy launched by Ahmad Ibn Taymiyya (d. 728/1328).[1] This celebrated Hanbali divine dealt monistic[2] Sufism a devastating blow, which made him undoubtedly the most implacable and consequential opponent of Ibn ʿArabi and his followers.[3] In his legal responsa (*fatawa;* sing. *fatwa*) and polemical treatises Ibn Taymiyya denounced the monistic trends within Sufism as a gross offense against the correct belief of the "pious ancestors" (*al-salaf al-salih*) and a dangerous innovation foreign to primeval Islam. Upon his death, his critiques of monistic philosophy became authoritative models for those who came in his wake.

Having carefully examined the foundations of the monistic metaphysics, Ibn Taymiyya struck at what he viewed as its weakest spots. His logical and straightforward approach[4] contrasts sharply with the deliberate ambiguities and understatements that characterize Ibn ʿArabi and his school. Yet outspoken as he was against certain practices and theories of the later Sufis, he should not be viewed as an enemy of Sufism understood as an ascetic practice and world-renouncing piety aimed at achieving moral self-perfection and the purification of the soul.[5] Nevertheless, while Ibn Taymiyya gave his seal of approval to the moral and ethical elements within mystical Islam, he still disagreed with most Sufi thinkers as to its ultimate objectives and the means to achieve them. For him, the goal of the Sufi path was not to gain the intimate knowledge of "God's essence (unknowable) but His command—in effect, the Shariʿah."[6] In keeping with this idea, Ibn Taymiyya energetically denied any possibility for human beings to penetrate God's unfathomable mystery, not to mention unite with it. For him, the goal of Sufism is to serve God more perfectly.[7]

On the practical level, Ibn Taymiyya took exception to what he viewed as Sufi "excesses" and "innovations," such as the worship of dead and living Sufi shaykhs, distinctive Sufi garments, affected ecstatic behavior, musical sessions, and miracle-working. For him, these were but idle diversions from the all-important salvational goals of communal Islam which, moreover, had no grounds in the Prophet's Sunna.[8]

In this chapter I will focus on Ibn Taymiyya's denunciation of philosophical mysticism (*tasawwuf al-falasifa*), with special reference to its metaphysical theories and exegesis. Since, in his epoch, they had become closely associated with Ibn ʿArabi, the latter bears the brunt of Ibn Taymiyya's attack. In his critique Ibn Taymiyya drew a careful distinction between the adherents of *shariʿa* Sufism and Ibn ʿArabi and his following. For him the latter are not Sufis but rather espousers of the doctrine that confuses God with his creatures (*ittihadiyya*). Conversely, he showed high regard for the *shariʿa* Sufis, whose striving to salvation through exemplary piety and mortification of the flesh he viewed as a legitimate "experiential . . . response to the message of the Qurʾan and the practice of Muhammad."[9]

In brief, Ibn Taymiyya's notion of "correct" Sufism was completely exclusive of metaphysics, which he considered a radical departure from the pious precepts of the "authentic" Sufis of the first Islamic centuries.

Structure, Method, and Contents of Ibn Taymiyya's Antimonistic Writings

Of all the attempts to come to grips with the complex phenomenon of Ibn ʿArabi, Ibn Taymiyya's was the most serious and consequential. Unlike Ibn ʿAbd al-Salam, Ibn Taymiyya displayed an intimate familiarity with Ibn ʿArabi's original texts, especially the *Fusus*. This is not to say that either hearsay or unverified accounts of Ibn ʿArabi's teachings were wholly absent from Ibn Taymiyya's works. They, however, on the whole, are auxiliary to his critical analysis of concrete theoretical propositions culled from Ibn ʿArabi's works.

Another source of Ibn Taymiyya's knowledge of the Greatest Master was his personal experience. He lived in an epoch that witnessed a rapid diffusion of Ibn ʿArabi's ideas among Muslim scholars of Anatolia, Persia, Syria, Egypt, and the Maghrib, with many of whom Ibn Taymiyya had direct contacts, and, occasionally, fierce disputes. The (mostly negative) impressions and conclusions that he drew from such encounters added personal overtones to his argumentation. In all, Ibn Taymiyya's discursive lucidity allied with his sharp mind and command of sources makes his critique of monistic philosophy a lively and engaging reading.

Ibn Taymiyya took issue with Sufi theory and practice in so many works that he simply could not avoid repetition. In what follows I attempt to bring unity to his disparate statements and to present his ideas in a more organized manner than they found in his original writings.

The doctrines of Ibn ʿArabi and members of his school are criticized in the following works by Ibn Taymiyya:

1. "The Exposition of the Falsity of the Unity of Being and the Refutation of Those Who Adhere to It."[10]
2. "The Denunciation of the Acts of Disobedience Through [the Doctrine] of Divine Predestination."[11]
3. "A Letter from the Shaykh al-Islam Ibn Taymiyya to the Divine Gnostic Shaykh Nasr al-Manbiji."[12]
4. "The True Reality of the Teaching of Unificationists, [also known as] the Unity of Being."[13]

In addition to these specialized refutations of monistic Sufism, Ibn Taymiyya condemned it in many of his legal responsa that took critical stock of the Sufi tradition as a whole.

Using his notion of "correct Sufism" as his measuring stick, Ibn Taymiyya singled out what he viewed as Ibn ʿArabi's tendency to obfuscate the critical God-man demarcation as his main target and as the starting point of his antimonistic critique.[14] In his view, this tendency put the Greatest Master amid the cohort of "heretics" and "grave sinners," responsible for such "vices" as the excessive influence on the Muslim state of its Christian and Jewish subjects, suggestive female dress, popular superstitions, the game of backgammon, the spread of Mongol customs among the Mamluks, the miracle-working of the dervishes, minor pilgrimages to saints' shrines, Shiʿi heresies, the exotic garments of wandering Sufis, hashish-smoking, the chivalric cult of *futuwwa,* state control of food prices, rationalist philosophy, and *kalam.*[15]

Among these varied transgressions, the excesses of latter-day Sufism took the pride of place: the space that Ibn Taymiyya accorded to them is roughly commensurate with the critique of Sufism in Ibn al-Jawzi's comprehensive treatise on various deviations from the *shariʿa,* titled *Talbis Iblis.*[16] Yet, in contrast to his predecessor, who focused on Sufi innovations in practical matters and life-style, Ibn Taymiyya's primary focus was on the Sufi metaphysics. This shift of priorities indicates that, in Ibn Taymiyya's time, doctrinal Sufism was perceived to be more dangerous to the community's welfare than the "innovations" in Sufi practice that preoccupied the Hanbali Ibn al-Jawzi one century earlier.

Before turning to Ibn Taymiyya's polemical strategy, it would be helpful to provide a brief outline of the structure and contents of his anti-Sufi treatises. Here they are discussed in the order in which they appear in Ibn Taymiyya's selected works edited by Rashid Rida (d. 1346/1935),[17] the famous Egyptian ideologue of the Salafiyya movement.[18] Interestingly, Rida's position vis-à-vis Sufism evinces the same hostility to monistic speculation that we observe in his Hanbali predecessor.[19]

The first treatise, "The Refutation of the Unity of Being, etc.," opens with an inventory of the controversial sayings in poetry and prose imputed to "extremist" Sufis (*ghulat*), such as al-Hallaj, Ibn al-Farid, Ibn ʿArabi, Awhad al-din al-Kirmani,[20] Ibn Sabʿin,[21] ʿAli al-Hariri, ʿAfif al-din al-Tilimsani, and Ibn Israʾil. According to Ibn Taymiyya, these and some other mystical thinkers, especially al-Niffari,[22] al-Busiri,[23] Saʿd al-din al-Farghani,[24] al-Shushtari,[25] al-Balabani,[26] and Ibn Abi ʾl-Mansur,[27] were the leading proponents of the doctrine of unification (*ittihad*) and absolute unity (*wahda multaqa*). Ibn Taymiyya holds them responsible for a panoply of abominable heresies, some of which, in his judgment, are greater than those of the Jews and Christians. In several polemical passages, Ibn Taymiyya directly equates *wahdat al-wujud* with the Christian theory of incarnation (*hulul*) and union (*ittihad*) between man and the divine, which Islamic theology holds to be sheer unbelief (*ilhad, taʿtil).*[28] This said, Ibn Taymiyya proceeds to demolish the metaphysical premises upon which these mystical thinkers rested their "heretical" tenets. In the process, he completely forgets about the controversial sayings and poetic lines he cited earlier in his treatise—at least, they play no role in his subsequent discussion. Instead, Ibn Taymiyya brings out the differences in the Sufi thinkers' views of the relationship between God and the world, arguing that their positions vary only in the degree of unbelief. These petty differences notwithstanding, their monistic and unificationist doctrines stem from the common confusion of the cosmos with its Creator. At the end of the treatise, Ibn Taymiyya tries to trace the origins of such doctrines back to the teachings of some Muʿtazila, who held that things that exist in our knowledge, should be treated as a special category of things, not as pure nonentities.[29]

In the introductory part of the second treatise, "The Denunciation of the Acts of Disobedience," Ibn Taymiyya addresses the perennial dilemma of divine omnipotence and predestination versus man's freedom of action and responsibility for his deeds. This notorious theological conundrum, which is closely linked to the thorny problem of the origin of evil in this world, was hotly debated in Islamic theology since its inception.[30] Ibn Taymiyya, too, regards it as central to the sound moral stance and spares no effort to defend it from the encroachments of the "fatalists" who relegated all initiative (as well as responsibility) to God. Simultaneously, he rebuffed the Muslim thinkers who considered human actions to be products of man's arbitrary and independent volition, especially of the Muʿtazila and the Ashʿariyya.[31]

Upon examining the solutions to this problem offered by the Ashʿari theologians, Ibn Taymiyya suddenly turns to the controversial utterances mentioned in the previous treatise. An explanation of this structural oddity may lie in the fact that disparate fragments of Ibn Taymiyya's original text were randomly assembled together by the editor, Rashid Rida, who apparently failed to respect its original structure.[32]

Be this as it may, this section of the treatise is entirely unrelated to Ibn Taymiyya's earlier discourse. In discussing the heretical statements by the monistic Sufis Ibn Taymiyya demonstrates their incompatibility with both common logic and the *shariʿa*. Simultaneously, he reinstates the transcendency of the Divine Godhead which, in his view, was compromised by the immanentist propensities (*tashbih*) of later Sufis. Ibn Taymiyya derives their immanentist concept of Deity from the incoherent utterances of early ecstatics, especially al-Bistami and al-Hallaj, who intimated the possibility for a perfected mystic to become one with God. Their personal experience of the divine presence was later taken to the metaphysical level by Ibn ʿArabi and his disciples and, in recent times, aggravated beyond remedy by those who pushed Ibn ʿArabi's assumptions to the extreme. In Ibn Taymiyya's interpretation, the Sufi utterances reflect the confusion and inconsistency of the monistic outlook. He therefore attempts to lay bare its genuine essence, which, he argues, is thoroughly masked by the ambiguous Sufi terminology, allegorical exegesis, meaningless paradoxes, and extensive use of symbols.[33] When purified of their verbal husks, the Sufi sayings prove to be at variance with Ibn Taymiyya's understanding of the central point of the Islamic revelation—the denial of God's likeness to, or affinity with, his creatures.

Turning again to the complex relationship between man's freedom and responsibility for his actions and God's axiomatic omnipotence, Ibn Taymiyya zeroes in on the doctrine of the two modes of Divine Will, which, in his opinion, Ibn ʿArabi shares with the Ashʿari theologians. This doctrine, argues Ibn Taymiyya, exaggerates the role of the creative divine Decree (*qadar*) to the detriment the moral Command and Prohibition (*amr wa nahy*) imposed by God on humanity, giving some "extreme" Sufis the pretext to indulge in licentiousness and socially irresponsible behavior.

Ibn Taymiyya's next argument is aimed at the perceived manipulation of the Qurʾanic text by monistic Sufis. In order to substantiate their fraudulent claims and to exempt themselves from the injunctions of *shariʿa* law, some Sufi theorists, so the argument goes, resorted to a farfetched allegorical exegesis that makes mockery of the Scripture's literal meaning, opening the door for its misuse by all manner of impostors.

In summary, Ibn Taymiyya bemoans the spread of the doctrine of oneness/monism (*wahda*) and unificationism (*ittihad*) among his contemporaries, many of whom, in his view, are deluded by the smoothly speaking Sufi elders who claim to have received their knowledge directly from God.

Ibn Taymiyya's third anti-Sufi work is a 704/1304 epistle to the influential Egyptian Sufi al-Manbiji, which became a reason for Ibn Taymiyya's expulsion to Cairo by the Mamluk authorities in 705/1305, as a punishment for propagating "extreme" religious views and popular disquiet.

The letter's addressee, Shaykh Nasr al-Manbiji (d. 719/1319), was head of a popular Sufi lodge in a suburb of Cairo who early in his life took to reading Ibn ʿArabi's works and became his ardent admirer. Al-Manbiji's political influence reached its peak under emir Baybars al-Jashnikir, master of the royal household (*ustadar*), who employed him as his confidant and spiritual adviser.[34] His closeness to Baybars al-Jashnikir gave al-Manbiji considerable political weight in addition to his powerful spiritual authority among the Cairene populace. According to the Mamluk historian Ibn al-Dawadari (d. after 732/1331-1332),[35] al-Manbiji was incensed by Ibn

Taymiyya's polite but presumptuous letter that contained harsh criticisms of the Greatest Master.[36] His anger was deftly exploited by Ibn Taymiyya's old antagonist, the leader of the Egyptian Malikis Zayn al-din Ibn Makhluf (d. 718/1318),[37] who persuaded the influential Sufi to have Baybars al-Jashnikir bring the belligerent Hanbali to trial. Ibn Taymiyya sent a similar letter to another influential scholar, Karim al-din al-Amuli (d. 710/1310-1311), director of the *Dar sa'id al-su'ada'*—the principal Sufi lodge in Cairo.[38] Both al-Manbiji and al-Amuli were disgusted by the contents and patronizing tone of the epistle.[39] Thus, although the followers of Ibn 'Arabi were only part of a broad scholarly opposition to Ibn Taymiyya's "extremism," it was they who took the lead in his persecution. That the Sufis indeed spearheaded the campaign to silence Ibn Taymiyya during the Cairene trial is attested by the frequent and exasperated references to the "Ibn 'Arabi faction" in Ibn Kathir's chronicle that carefully documents Ibn Taymiyya's tribulations (*mihan*) in Syria and Egypt.[40]

What exactly was the cause of al-Manbiji's indignation? Ibn Taymiyya's letter opens with an analysis of the Sufi notion of love of God (*mahabba*) which he views as the foundation of man's obedience to, and worship of, the Divine.[41] For Ibn Taymiyya, the love for God should not be allowed to become a convenient excuse for the antinomian tendencies and ecstatic behavior displayed by many later Sufis, especially the followers of Ibn 'Arabi. Nor should it lead to a meek acquiescence to the preordained course of events, since the Divine Decree does not absolve humans from carrying out God's commands and obeying his prohibitions. It is against this background that Ibn Taymiyya discusses the Sufi concept of "passing away from one's self" (*fana'*), which he, in contrast to those Sufis who described it as the mystic's ultimate self-annihilation in the Godhead, defines as "active obedience to God's will as manifest in the Qur'an and the Sunna of Muhammad."[42]

Having laid down his idea of "authentic" Sufism, Ibn Taymiyya contrasts it with monistic philosophy, or "unificationism" (*ittihad*). In examining the roots of monistic theories, Ibn Taymiyya traces them back to Ibn 'Arabi's *Fusus al-hikam*—a work in which the doctrine of unification and incarnation, which was only incipient in the ecstatic ravings of al-Hallaj and al-Bistami,[43] is brought to fruition.[44] Therefore, the *Fusus* constitutes the butt of Ibn Taymiyya's criticism, although he admits that the interpretation of Ibn 'Arabi's teaching by his later followers was even more perfidious than the original, for they supplanted Ibn 'Arabi's confused and disjointed ideas by outright heresy. This process was started by his direct disciple, Sadr al-din al-Qunawi and reached its apogee in the work of the "shameless" (*fajir*) al-Tilimsani, whose perfidy, in Ibn Taymiyya's opinion, is matched only by the abominations of Ibn Sabʿin and al-Balabani. Ibn Taymiyya's comparison between the *ittihadiyya* and those whom he considers "authentic" Sufis leads him to conclude that with al-Tilimsani and Ibn Sabʿin mystical speculation became the direct opposite of everything the authentic Sufism of old stood for.

Ibn Taymiyya's fourth treatise, "The [True] Reality of the Teaching of Those Who Espouse the Doctrine of Incarnation," is the longest of his antimonistic works discussed thus far. It is also more detailed and technical and contains long quotations from the writings of his Sufi opponents, especially the *Fusus*. The mere size of the work—a hundred pages in small print—indicates that it was designed as a comprehensive critique of monistic tenets. Its abrupt ending suggests that its final section was lost—an impression confirmed by the editor's perplexed remark: "this is the last part of this 'Epistle' which I have been able to find."[45]

In the preamble, Ibn Taymiyya sets out to unravel the epistemological foundations of the doctrine of unification, which, in his opinion, rests upon misinterpreted Qurʾanic verses, fabricated *hadith* reports, a faulty logic, and unsustainable metaphysical propositions. Yet Ibn Taymiyya concedes that although all unificationists proceed from a common starting point, their positions on concrete issues may vary. In ranking the monistic thinkers according to the extent of their departure from the correct Islam of the "pious ancestors," Ibn Taymiyya places Ibn ʿArabi among the less deluded due to the "many sound statements" found in his works. However, on balance, he classifies Ibn ʿArabi's overall vision of the God-world relation as downright unbelief. Ibn ʿArabi's delusion is to the fore in his concept of the immutable models of empirical things (*aʿyan thabita*), which the Sufi treated as full-fledged existents. Equally heretical, in Ibn Taymiyya's mind, is Ibn ʿArabi's assertion that God and the world share in the same existence.

Despite these obvious "delusions," Ibn Taymiyya places Ibn ʿArabi's followers much higher on the scale of "heresy and atheism." In particular, al-Qunawi's "outrageous" idea that God's absolute existence descends in stages into the empirical world where it becomes united with existential potentialities provokes Ibn Taymiyya's sharp rebuttal. For him, this idea reduces God to a generic and abstract notion with no independent empirical, or "external" (*khariji*), status. By consenting to al-Qunawi's vision of existence, says Ibn Taymiyya, one effectively throws out the Qur'anic notion of God as the absolutely transcendent being possessed of clearly defined attributes and characteristics.

Allied with al-Qunawi's erroneous conception of existence is what Ibn Taymiyya considers the unsustainable doctrine that presents absolute divine existence as inherent in all empirical things. For Ibn Taymiyya, this constitutes an outright denial of God's self-sufficiency and independence vis-à-vis the universe and, as a consequence, a divesture of God of any existence other than that *in concreto.* Logically, this view leads to yet another absurdity by implying that the absolute existence of God has no concrete locus or entity. In other words, the God of al-Qunawi's philosophy is a sheer mental construct with no independent ontological or epistemological status.

A further step toward negating God's role as the Creator and Sustainer of the universe was made by al-Tilimsani, whom Ibn Taymiyya accuses of failing to differentiate between the essence and existence of a thing—a proposition that leads to the confusion between absolute and concrete existence. To al-Tilimsani, says Ibn Taymiyya, everything is one, both essentially and existentially. Ibn Taymiyya denounces this doctrine as a wanton heresy, which was abhorred even by the "pagan" philosophers of ancient Greece. While Ibn ʿArabi's teaching, in Ibn Taymiyya's opinion, resembles the doctrine of mainstream Christian theology, especially the Melkites, who hold that divine and human natures form one substance with two different hypostases (*uqnuman*), he likens al-Tilimsani to the Jacobites (Monophysites), who posit that divine nature assumes human characteristics (*yatadarraʿ*) in the person of Christ. On the whole, both the Christian theologians and the supporters of unificationism share one thing in common: their argumentation throws them into the state of permanent perplexity and confusion (*hayra*), which Ibn ʿArabi indeed continually invoked in his writings.

This perplexity, in Ibn Taymiyya's mind, accounts for the logical absurdities of monistic thinking, which describes God as a self-sustaining and necessary entity, on the one hand, and one that needs His creatures in order to contemplate His perfections in them, on the other. In this confused epistemological and ontological perspective, the Divine Law and social order based on it are relativized, leading the monists to discard any difference between belief and unbelief, divine and human, truth and falsehood, licit and illicit.[46]

Next, Ibn Taymiyya sets out to refute the concrete metaphysical and theological propositions of the *Fusus,* which, in his words, were deliberately hidden behind the layer of technical terminology, allegorical exegesis, and obscure symbols. Here, Ibn Taymiyya takes special pains to rebuff Ibn ʿArabi's doctrine of sainthood and his claims to be the supreme saint of the Muhammadan community. In this connection, he resorts to the argument ad hominem outlined in Chapter 2, in which, it will be recalled, Ibn ʿAbd al-Salam's disparaging treatment of the Greatest Master played the pivotal role.

At the close of this long treatise, Ibn Taymiyya discusses Ibn ʿArabi's assertion that Pharaoh died a believer.[47] As we shall see, this view will become an object of the heated debates at the later stages of the polemic.

Ibn Taymiyya's Personal View of the Greatest Master

It is instructive to look at the concrete reasons for Ibn Taymiyya's polemical attack on the Greatest Master. Fortunately, Ibn Taymiyya makes them explicit in the works that were just summarized. The hints he drops here and there suggest that his favorable attitude toward Ibn ʿArabi underwent a dramatic change after his acquaintance with the *Fusus.* In accounting for this change of heart, Ibn Taymiyya writes:

> At first I was among those who held a good opinion of Ibn ʿArabi and praised him highly for the useful advice he provides in his books. This useful advice is found in the pages of the "Revelations,"[48] the "Essence,"[49] the "Tightly Knit and Tied,"[50] the "Precious Pearl,"[51] the "Positions of the Stars,"[52] and similar writings. At that time, we were unaware of his real goal, because we had not yet studied the *Fusus* and suchlike books.[53]

An independent testimony by Ibn al-Dawadari corroborates the critical role of the *Fusus* in Ibn Taymiyya's revision of his early opinion of the Greatest Master:

> The cause of the aforementioned troubles[54] is that one of the friends of Shaykh Taqi al-din Ibn al-Taymiyya [*sic!*] once presented him with a book by Shaykh Muhyi al-din Ibn al-ʿArabi titled *Fusus al-hikam.* This happened in the year 703 [1303]. Upon studying the book, Shaykh Taqi al-din discovered that it contained many

> statements that contravened his own views, whereupon, he began to condemn Ibn al-ʿArabi and revile those who believed in what he taught. In that year, during the month of Ramadan, Taqi al-din began to assiduously study [the *Fusus*] and eventually produced a refutation [of it].[55]

Having realized the "perversity" of the *Fusus,* Ibn Taymiyya was surprised to find out that similar beliefs were rife among his contemporaries. Some of these, according to Ibn Taymiyya, embraced these heretical beliefs in good faith, since they were unable to perceive their genuine implications. Others, however, were well aware of their heretical character and yet continued to promulgate them among the unwary and weak-minded. To Ibn Taymiyya, the danger of Ibn ʿArabi's tenets lay in the fact that they were diffused in the guise of Sufism, moreover, as the culmination of the mystical knowledge pertaining to the Sufi Path. Blind to the real implications of Ibn ʿArabi's speculations, many gullible Muslims mistook them for an expression of the "genuine" Sufi tradition. In an effort to dispel this confusion, Ibn Taymiyya sets about to demonstrate that Ibn ʿArabi's teaching has nothing to do with the "correct" Sufism of old.

Curiously, in several instances the Hanbali scholar portrays his struggle against the *ittihadiyya* as part of the Muslim holy war against the pagan Mongol (*tatar*) beliefs.[56] This parallel is not as far-fetched as it might seem at first sight, for Ibn Taymiyya saw a clear connection between the spread of Ibn ʿArabi's doctrines and the advent of the Mongol hordes, who, as pagans, ascribed divinity to such entities as idols, human beings, animals, and stars.[57]

As noted, Ibn Taymiyya's attitude toward Ibn ʿArabi is not devoid of ambiguity. Although he holds the Sufi master responsible for the heretical concept of an all-encompassing unity that blurs the crucial distinction between man and deity, he still did not consider Ibn ʿArabi to be outside the pale of Islam. Even though Ibn ʿArabi's monistic speculations were marked by incoherence and confusion, his intimate knowledge of the Qurʾan and Sunna prevented him from plunging headlong into infidelity. Rather, Ibn ʿArabi, in Ibn Taymiyya's view, constantly oscillates between truth and falsehood. In the final account, however, his errors outweigh his merits, especially in the *Fusus al-hikam,* which bristles with absurdities and fraudulent claims. Ibn Taymiyya's scruples vis-à-vis the Sufi master are further attested by his letter to Shaykh al-Manbiji:

> One of the two fundamental principles of his teaching laid down in the *Fusus* is that the existence of contingent and created entities is identical with the existence of their Creator. In other words, the former is neither different from God, nor is something other than He. He [Ibn ʿArabi] was the first to put forward this idea, in which he had precursors neither among Sufi shaykhs nor Muslim scholars. This teaching is currently shared by all espousers of [the doctrine of] unification. However, Ibn ʿArabi is the closest to Islam among them, and his teaching is, in many respects, better than theirs. He, at least, distinguished between the manifest One[58] and the concrete forms of His manifestation. Moreover, he affirmed the validity of the Divine Command and Prohibition and the Divine Laws as they stand.[59] He also instructed the travellers on the [mystical] path how to acquire high morals and the acts of devotion, as is common with other Sufis and their disciples. Therefore, many pious worshippers (*ʿubbad*) have learned [the rules of] their path through his instructions and thus have greatly benefited from him, even though they sometimes failed to understand his [mystical] subtleties.[60]

Similar statements can be found in Ibn Taymiyya's other antimonistic treatises, for example, in "The [True] Reality of the Teaching of the Unificationists," which opens with the following telling disclaimer:

> Despite the fact that [Ibn ʿArabi's first metaphysical principle] is sheer unbelief, he still remains the closest to Islam from among them all, because of the many sound things he says in his works. He was not as irreversibly grounded in the doctrine of unification as most of them. On the contrary, he showed much hesitancy in it. He was a captive of his loose imagination. In one moment, he imagined in it a right thing, in the other, a wrong one. Only God knows what state he died in.[61]

Such criticisms are quite moderate compared, for example, with the harsh condemnations Ibn Taymiyya hurls at the "impious and godless Ibn Sabʿin," whom he describes, in one instance, as "the greatest exponent of heresy, polytheism, sorcery, and unificationism." Ibn ʿArabi's case, in the eyes of Ibn Taymiyya, was a more complicated one, primarily due to the elusiveness of his theological positions, which makes it extremely hard for the critic to nail them down. While Ibn Sabʿin was outspoken in advocating the heretical doctrine of absolute oneness (*wahda mutlaqa*) and pushing it to its logical limits,[62] Ibn ʿArabi tends to blend various strands of Sufi speculation. In the same breath, he presents himself as an incarnationalist and a monist to the point that it is almost impossible to associate him with any of these heretical teachings.[63]

Yet, in the final account, Ibn Taymiyya finds Ibn ʿArabi's inconsistency irritating and misleading as to his genuine intentions. Hence his final conclusion that Ibn ʿArabi's entire argument rests on deceptive tactics of bringing together two contradictory statements and joining opposites. These tactics render his teachings totally indefensible from the standpoint of either syllogistic reasoning or the authoritative tradition of the pious ancestors.[64]

Although Ibn Taymiyya undoubtedly had some misgivings as to Ibn ʿArabi's exact position vis-à-vis Sunni orthodoxy, he did not allow them to cloud his final judgment of the Andalusi master. For Ibn Taymiyya, Ibn ʿArabi is a shameful heretic whose teachings led astray a great many Muslims. To illustrate his point, Ibn Taymiyya cites stories and learned opinions detrimental to the reputation of his Sufi opponent. Some of them are pertinent to our examination of Ibn ʿArabi's image in the eyes of posterity and, therefore, merit closer scrutiny.

Argumentum ad hominem

Most of the disparaging judgments of Ibn ʿArabi's personality figure in Ibn Taymiyya's fourth treatise, "The Reality of the Teaching of the Espousers of the Doctrine of Incarnation." They are concerned not only with Ibn ʿArabi but with the other controversial Sufi thinkers as well. As our discussion of the Ibn ʿAbd al-Salam affair has shown, Ibn Taymiyya spared no efforts to find authoritative critics of Ibn ʿArabi among the latter's contemporaries. That their negative opinions of the Sufi master were important to him is evident from the fact that he dedicates to them an entire chapter of his polemical work.

Following are a few typical anti-Ibn ʿArabi anecdotes cited by Ibn Taymiyya:

> I was told about Jamal al-din Ibn Wasil[65] and Shams al-din al-Isfahani[66] that they used to disapprove, denounce, and refute Ibn ʿArabi's teachings. Once al-Isfahani saw Ibn Wasil holding his [Ibn ʿArabi's] book in his hand. He said: "If I ever see you buy another book by him, don't even dare to show up in my house again!" . . . When Ibn Wasil recounted to [al-Isfahani] Ibn ʿArabi's story about

> the apple which turned around, as a scholar sat next to it,[67] he exclaimed: "By God, except Whom there is no god, he [Ibn ʿArabi] is a liar!" He [Ibn Wasil] was absolutely right![68]

Several other stories smearing Ibn ʿArabi's personal reputation or belittling his credibility as a scholar are recorded by Ibn Taymiyya on the authority of the famous Sufi master and popular preacher Ibrahim b. Miʿdad al-Jaʿbari (d. 687/1288).[69] Al-Jaʿbari who died in his eighties, had met Ibn ʿArabi on a visit to Damascus. His impression of that meeting is presented by Ibn Taymiyya as bluntly antipathetic:

> Ibn ʿArabi was an old man with a dyed beard. He was an impure teacher (*shaykh najis*) who denied every book that God had revealed and every prophet whom God had sent![70]

Furthermore, in a dream al-Jaʿbari claimed to have seen "Ibn ʿArabi and Ibn al-Farid, both blind old men, stumbling around and crying out: 'Where is the way? Where is the way?'"[71] In much the same fashion, other anecdotes quoted by Ibn Taymiyya describe Ibn ʿArabi as "Shaytan" and "*zindiq,*" whose works are to be abhorred by every pious Muslim, or better still, destroyed altogether. By sullying Ibn ʿArabi's integrity as a Muslim, such stories indirectly impugn the credibility of his doctrines.

An Argument from Metaphysics

On the metaphysical plane, the *Fusus al-hikam* forms the main target of Ibn Taymiyya's antimonistic critique, which turns on several basic assumptions repeated throughout Ibn Taymiyya's polemical discourse. In examining Ibn ʿArabi's metaphysics, Ibn Taymiyya describes it as one that consistently identifies God's existence with that of his creatures. According to the Hanbali scholar, Ibn ʿArabi makes no distinction between the existence of God and that of the "jinn, devils, unbelievers, sinners, dogs, swine." Hence, in his doctrine, God "assumes the attributes pertaining to deficiency and imperfection," which are shared by all the creatures no matter how lowly or despised.[72]

This general assumption, continues Ibn Taymiyya, effectively strips God of His attributes of Lordship that are ascribed to him by the Islamic Scriptures. It therefore reduces him to a pure existence devoid of any positive substance. Hence, argues Ibn Taymiyya, in Ibn ʿArabi's teaching God is both the lover and the beloved, the benefactor and the one enjoying beneficence, the provider and the one who is provided, the eater and the one who is eaten;[73] He prostrates himself, obeys, venerates, fasts, feels hungry and sick, sleeps, makes love, sins, rejoices, and so forth.[74] In a word, the crux of Ibn ʿArabi's teaching, as seen by Ibn Taymiyya, lies in its failure to distinguish between the Creator and his creature.[75]

According to Ibn Taymiyya, Ibn ʿArabi's second mistake is his attempt to blur the all-important difference between empirical existence (*wujud*) and what may be termed *noetic,* or *mental existence* (*thubut*).[76] In this scheme, noetic existence is identical with God's preeternal knowledge (or idea) of the empirical world prior to its actual creation. Basing himself on the concept of *thubut,* which had a long history in Islamic theology,[77] Ibn ʿArabi postulated that the "immutable entities," *(aʿyan thabita)* form a matrix after which God fashions the world into being. For Ibn ʿArabi, argues Ibn Taymiyya, these entities are as real as their empirical counterparts. It is here that the author of the *Fusus,* in Ibn Taymiyya's view, joins hands with those Muʿtazili thinkers who treated objects of God's knowledge *(maʿlumat)* as full-fledged realities, or simply as "things."[78]

In the light of this theory Ibn Taymiyya explains Ibn ʿArabi's proposition that God (*al-haqq*) "nourishes Himself on His creatures (*al-khalq*)," that is to say, actualizes the existential possibilities inherent in his Essence by manifesting himself in empirical things and phenomena. Since this actualization occurs in keeping with a preexistent noetic matrix, the differences among individual empirical things are predetermined by their immutable essences, *aʿyan thabita*. The only common characteristic they all share is existence—the absolute, all-encompassing reality of which they all necessarily partake. Hence, from the viewpoint of existence, all created things are identical. They, however, vary from one another in their particular properties encoded in their *aʿyan thabita*. In this scheme, God is in need of the immutable entities in order to manifest his perfections and qualities in the material Universe, whereas the immutable entities are in need of him for their concrete existence.[79]

Now, according to Ibn Taymiyya, Ibn ʿArabi's focus on the *aʿyan thabita* leads him to disregard the concrete names with which God described himself and which, consequently, are essential for understanding his revealed word.[80] In the *Fusus,* argues Ibn Taymiyya, the names are relegated to a secondary status—that of "relationships" (*nisab*) and "attributions" (*idafat*) which are mechanically inserted between God and the immutable entities. Outside this context, the Qur'anic names of God have no intrinsic value whatsoever: in contrast to the *aʿyan thabita* that actually exist, Ibn ʿArabi presents the divine names as pure nonentities.[81] This line of thinking, in Ibn Taymiyya's mind, robs God of his attributes, except one—existence, which, incidentally, is not ascribed to God by the Qur'an but arbitrarily imputed to him by Sufi philosophers in disregard for the Revelation.[82]

Ibn ʿArabi's "discovery" of the central role of existence instilled in him the false belief that he arrived at the mystery of divine predestination (*qadar*). In his mind, because the concrete existence of empirical things is determined by their preeternal noetic realities, "it was the essences that did good and evil, praised and blamed, while God conferred upon them only what they had already possessed in their state of non-existence."[83]

> Consider these words, exclaims Ibn Taymiyya, and [you will see] how he [Ibn ʿArabi] brought together two [heretical] theories, namely the negation of God's existence on the one hand, and the negation of His [status as the] originator of the creaturely world on the other. Thereby he denies that the Lord is the maker [of the world] and affirms that there is neither the existence of God, nor the act of creation. In so doing, he invalidated [the Qur'anic notion of] "the Lord of the worlds."[84] [For him,] there exists neither the Lord, nor the worlds over which He holds sway. In other words, there is nothing but the immutable entities and the existence that sustains them.[85]

This, argues Ibn Taymiyya, amounts to a denial of God's omnipotence, by presenting the divine acts as predetermined by the properties inherent in the *aʿyan thabita*, which shape God's knowledge of his creation. Such a theory renders God impotent of changing the course of events that is predicated by the properties encoded in the immutable entities. Thus, Ibn ʿArabi, in Ibn Taymiyya's interpretation, effectively limits God's role to the transferral of the immutable entities from the level of relative nonexistence to that of existence *in concreto*.[86]

This view, argues Ibn Taymiyya, entails a host of practical conclusions that are bound to "ruin the three pillars of faith, . . . that is, the belief in God, His messengers, and the Last Day." First, to claim that God's existence is identical with the existence of the world, necessarily implies that the world has no maker other than itself.

Second, in affirming that he receives his knowledge directly from God Ibn ʿArabi effectively dispenses with the divine messengers, including Muhammad, who received his revelation via an angel and therefore is, in the opinion of the Sufi philosophers, inferior to them. Third, according to the *Fusus,* God's threats to sinners and unbelievers are but empty allegories that eventually bode eternal bliss and happiness for all in a metaphoric and harmless hell. This thesis, as Ibn Taymiyya wryly observes, disrupts the divinely established order that rests on the human fear of punishment in the Hereafter.[87]

As Ibn Taymiyya repeatedly claims, the many flaws in Ibn ʿArabi's metaphysical reasoning stem from his misunderstanding of the relations between a mental construct (*ʿaqli)* and its concrete empirical manifestation (*khariji*). The fact that we have an idea (or a concept) of a thing, argues Ibn Taymiyya, does not necessarily imply its existence as an empirical entity. And yet this is exactly what some Muʿtazili theoreticians, such as Abu ʿUthman al-Shahham,[88] tried to prove.[89]

The concept of noetic existence first introduced by some Muʿtazili thinkers and later taken up by Ibn ʿArabi in his *Fusus* elicits Ibn Taymiyya's stern rebuke. He concedes that the mental image of a thing may indeed exist in one's knowledge. Yet he flatly denies that this mental image should be absolutely identical with its empirical, concrete manifestation, for imagining a man does not necessarily presuppose his existence as a concrete reality, possessed of the same properties as his noetic image. It is absurd, continues Ibn Taymiyya, to insist that mental realities are exact analogs of their concrete, empirical doubles. Rather, it is the faculty of abstraction that allows the mind to construct general notions (universals) which, however, never exist *in concreto.*[90] In support of his critique, Ibn Taymiyya argues that, in the surrounding world, one cannot observe an abstract (universal) man, animal, or tree. And yet there is no denying that such generic notions do exist in the human mind. The same goes for the concept of existence, which is abstracted from disparate individual existences of concrete things and phenomena by means of a complicated mental procedure. In real life, however, the thing's existence is identical with, and inseparable from, its essence or quiddity (*mahiyya*). Hence, we must not treat existence as something superimposed or grafted onto the thing's quiddity, since "in the outer world, a thing is a thing, for it constitutes its own entity, essence, and quiddity."[91]

In defending the sacred *creatio ex nihilo* principle of Islamic theology, which he felt was endangered by Ibn ʿArabi's doctrine of *aʿyan thabita*, Ibn Taymiyya adopts a radical nominalist stand. His polemical strategy consists in implementing the reductio ad absurdum method, known among Muslim theologians as "coercion" (*ilzam*).[92] Let us imagine, says Ibn Taymiyya, that the immutable entities are nonexistent in themselves, yet known to God in his foreknowledge, which is identical to his unique and indivisible essence. The question then arises whether God created them at the same moment when he bestowed existence upon them, or that they had languished in the state of nonexistence from eternity, whereupon they came into existence as concrete things. The latter supposition is absurd, because it contradicts the human senses, reason, and the Scripture that states that the world was created out of nothingness. For if things are originated in time, this means that their nature cannot be identical with the eternal and uncreated divine essence of God, attested by common logic and the Scriptures.[93]

Another point of Ibn ʿArabi's metaphysical discourse that Ibn Taymiyya undertakes to disprove is the nature of God's manifestation in the cosmos. Were we to admit, argues Ibn Taymiyya, that God's essence (*ʿayn dhatih*) is manifest *in* the material loci of manifestation (*mazahir wa majali*), we would have to acknowledge that God is identical with all of his creatures, including the most untoward ones. In Ibn Taymiyya's opinion, this notion inevitably places its espouser among the heretics and unbelievers. If, however, we admit that God manifests himself *to* the loci of manifestation in their state of nonexistence, one runs into yet another absurdity, because divine knowledge, power, and action cannot be applied to a nonexistent thing.[94]

To resolve this theological conundrum we should assume that God knows (and creates) the immutable entities as signs (*ayat*) pointing to Him. Ibn Taymiyya rejects this solution as being at odds with the purport of his imaginary opponent, who posits that the *aʿyan thabita* had been God's signs *before* he created them—that is, in their state of relative nonexistence—and that God appeared to them in preeternity. If the terms *manifestation* and *appearance* are to be understood in the strictly cognitive sense, as God's "perception" and "knowledge" of the immutable entities, such a usage, in Ibn Taymiyya's opinion, is logically unsustainable and, moreover, has no ground in the Qurʿan or in the Tradition.

Ibn Taymiyya's refutation of the monistic doctrine of divine manifestation is more than an exercise in scholastic hairsplitting. He clearly attempts to preclude the serious epistemological and practical implications of Ibn ʿArabi's metaphysics, which are brought into sharp focus in his attack on Ibn ʿArabi's idea that God manifests himself to every viewer in accordance with his primordial predisposition, or preparedness *(istiʿdad)*.[95] In keeping with this idea, the monistic viewer sees nothing but his own reflection in the mirror of Absolute (*al-haqq*), since each viewer's reception of divine manifestation is conditioned by the properties of his primordial self. As with the ordinary mirror, this self-vision prevents the human viewer from seeing the substance of the mirror—that is, God. However, Ibn ʿArabi's doctrine considers these properties to be identical with the divine names and attributes and, in the final account, with the Godhead. Ergo, argues Ibn Taymiyya, the viewer cannot see anyone else but God, whom Ibn ʿArabi thus holds to be identical with his creatures.

Ibn Taymiyya on the Doctrine of Sainthood

Summarizing Ibn ʿArabi's monistic speculations, Ibn Taymiyya insists that they led the Sufi to believe that he had attained the ultimate truth about God and the universe and thereby acquired a special status among humanity. It is from this perspective that Ibn Taymiyya sets out to discredit his claims to be "the seal of Muhammadan sainthood," from whose "niche" (*mishkat*)[96] the saints and, before them, God's messengers and prophets drew their knowledge of the divine mysteries. Ibn Taymiyya addresses a host of other claims made by Ibn ʿArabi, for instance, that sainthood, in contrast to prophecy, has no end and that it is a characteristic shared by both man and God[97], while the Qur'an attributes prophethood exclusively to man.[98]

Ibn Taymiyya points out that Ibn ʿArabi supports these audacious claims by misinterpreting the famous Muslim tradition that portrays the Prophet of Islam as the last missing brick in the wall of universal prophethood.[99] According to Ibn ʿArabi, the prophetic "brick" alone does not complete the wall—there still remains in it another recess that is to be filled with the seal of sainthood—that is, Ibn ʿArabi himself.[100] This interpretation of the brick motif provokes Ibn Taymiyya's bitter rebuttal in which he points to the source of this heretical doctrine—al-Tirmidhi al-Hakim, the first Muslim mystic to have given sainthood priority over prophethood.[101] This erroneous assumption, according to Ibn Taymiyya, was readily appropriated by many irresponsible and ignorant Sufi leaders who arrogantly placed themselves on an equal footing with the prophets.[102]

In general, much of Ibn Taymiyya's critique of the *Fusus* is devoted to exposing Ibn ʿArabi's methods of esoteric exegesis, which the Hanbali views as a deliberate strategy aimed at shoring up the questionable metaphysical assumptions and sainthood theory. For Ibn Taymiyya, the danger of allegorical exegesis lies in the relativization of the Islamic revelation, which is accompanied by an implicit denial of its finality. As a particularly egregious example, Ibn Taymiyya cites Ibn Arabi's interpretation of the *surat Nuh* (71)[103], which depicted the Qurʾanic polytheists (*mushrikun*) as the "true gnostics" (*ʿarifun*), who went beyond the "one-sided" transcendent vision of God propagated by the prophet Noah.[104]

According to Ibn Taymiyya, by deliberately ignoring the explicit meaning of the Qurʾan, Ibn ʿArabi, in tune with his metaphysical doctrine, contrived to erase the all-important line between the polytheists and the faithful, the righteous and the sinners. As with his metaphysics, his exegesis, in Ibn Taymiyya's phrase, makes a mockery of the religious obligations and norms that lie at the heart of the Muslim communal life. On these grounds, he holds Ibn ʿArabi responsible for a decline of morals in contemporary Islamic society.[105]

Thus, Ibn ʿArabi's equation of the existence of the world with that of its maker was seen by Ibn Taymiyya as fraught with polytheism and immorality, since it suggests that God can be adored in every existent thing, including idols, human beings, or even one's own passions (*ahwaʾ*). The monistic outlook effectively exempts polytheists, idolaters, and fornicators from the punishment they are liable to, according to the Qurʾan and Sunna. It is against this background that Ibn Taymiyya invites his reader to see Ibn ʿArabi's attempt to proclaim the Qurʾanic Pharaoh, the very embodiment of a wicked and arrogant tyrant, to be a true believer. For Pharaoh's outrageous claim to lordship,[106] is in full accord with Ibn ʿArabi's monistic vision of existence that posits the essential and existential unity of God and his creatures.[107] As with Ibn ʿArabi's interpretation of the Nuh story, here again Ibn ʿArabi's faulty metaphysics goes hand in hand with his garbled exegesis.

Ibn Taymiyya's Antimonistic Critique sub specie aeternitatis

Having examined Ibn ʿArabi's legacy, Ibn Taymiyya finds Ibn ʿArabi guilty of all charges brought against him by the earlier *ʿulamaʾ*. First, his concept of *aʿyan thabita* effectively divests God of his role as the Creator and Sustainer of the universe. Second, in treating every empirical thing as a manifestation or reflection of the eternal divine essence, Ibn ʿArabi slides into the doctrine of unification and incarnation—an abominable heresy in the eyes of Islamic theology. Third, his contention that the world was built after a preestablished model that God slavishly followed in his creation calls into doubt God's omnipotence. Fourth, Ibn ʿArabi's monistic metaphysics dispenses with the moral dimension of the Islamic revelation and throws the door open to immorality, fraudulent pretensions to religious leadership, and insidious polytheism. Fifth, Ibn ʿArabi's insistence on being the seal of the saints demeans God's messengers and prophets; additionally, it humiliates God's genuine saints—the world-renouncing ascetics of old. Finally, his claim to absolute sainthood is fraught with political sedition and popular unrest, because it encourages messianic movements and the proliferation of religious impostors. Last but not least, Ibn ʿArabi's exegesis is a blatant falsification of the literal meaning of the Scripture aimed at proving his heretical presumptions.

Ibn Taymiyya's criticisms of the Greatest Master are in perfect agreement with his overall conception of religion, the world, and the human condition.[108] On almost every point, his view is the direct opposite of that of his Sufi opponent—a fact that accounts for the harshness of Ibn Taymiyya's attacks on Ibn ʿArabi's monistic theorizing and its practical implications for the community of Islam. Standing in sharp contrast are not only the religious and intellectual orientations of the two thinkers (e.g., nominalism vs. realism, transcendency vs. immanence, nomos vs. eros, activism vs. quietism, literalism vs. an allegorical vision of the world, extroversion vs. self-centeredness, common sense vs. visionary experience), but their discursive methods as well. The deliberate obfuscation, fluidity, and open-endedness of Ibn ʿArabi's discourse contrasts starkly with Ibn Taymiyya's discursive lucidity and unswerving adherence to the point at hand.

Any unbiased observer has to acknowledge that Ibn Taymiyya's criticisms often strike at the pivotal points of Ibn ʿArabi's mystical weltanschauung. In a sense, his analysis of Ibn ʿArabi's metaphysical tenets has rendered a service to students of the Greatest Master in persuasively demonstrating the latter's indebtedness to Muʿtazili thought[109] with its emphasis on the reality of noetic images. Even more importantly, Ibn Taymiyya is astute enough to pinpoint the important differences among various strands within monistic Sufism which, until today, are often lumped together by less discriminating critics. In his taxonomy of monistic heresies, Ibn ʿArabi falls into the category of the less heterodox (though admittedly more confused) mystical thinkers, whose commitment to absolute unity does not prevent them from seeing a critical difference between God and his creatures. Ibn ʿArabi's constant vacillation between monism and theism, in Ibn Taymiyya's view, sets him apart from his ungodly followers, notably from al-Qunawi, Ibn Sabʿin, and al-Tilimsani, whose denial of God's transcendence bears the brunt of Ibn Taymiyya's antimonistic onslaught.[110]

A final judgment on the validity of Ibn Taymiyya's antimonistic discourse is in the eye of the beholder. One might agree with those Muslim and Western scholars who have insisted that Ibn ʿArabi's world-outlook is much more than a mere summa of abstract theological propositions to be dissected and systematized by rationalist tools.[111] In Ibn ʿArabi's work we are dealing with what Toynbee called "the Truth of the Subconscious Psyche" expressing itself in the language of "Poetry and Prophesy," rather than with "the Truth of the Intellect" whose natural medium, at least in the medieval period, is "Metaphysics."[112] In judging the former by the criteria of the latter, Ibn Taymiyya definitely confounds the two distinct modes of comprehension. From this perspective, Ibn Taymiyya's critique indeed seems to be shallow, reductionist, and one that thrives on an unwarranted simplification of the originally rich and complex insights. After all, Ibn ʿArabi's tortuous discursive strategy, frequent poetic asides, and deliberate ambiguity always allows one to argue that the Sufi did not actually mean what he said or that it was not his final articulation of the issue at hand.[113]

In support of this position one may cite Ibn Taymiyya's treatment of the *aʿyan thabita:* he first confuses them with universals, then proceeds to accuse Ibn ʿArabi of the failure to distinguish between the genera and the species, mental abstracts and concrete things, the universal and the particular.[114] While Ibn Taymiyya viewed Ibn ʿArabi's *aʿyan thabita* as some sort of archetypes, that is, as ideal models for many individual beings on the lines of the Platonic normative "ideas," a closer reading of the *Fusus* and the *Futuhat* reveals that this interpretation finds no support in the original texts. Rather, as Chittick has finely shown, "what corresponds to the Platonic ideas in Ibn ʿArabi's teachings is the divine names,"[115] and not the *aʿyan thabita* which, in Ibn ʿArabi's schema, are the immutable images of individual beings. In other words, in Ibn ʿArabi's teaching, the *aʿyan thabita* are "the things themselves 'before' they are given existence in the world;"[116] God has known them eternally;

he transfers them from the noetic plane to that of empirical existence. This transferral however does not affect their noetic status (*thubut*), which can be described as a relative nonexistence. Hence, in Ibn ʿArabi's interpretation, the *aʿyan thabita* are as particular and individual as their manifested counterparts. The difference between the two is the difference in ontological status, not in essence.[117] To view the *aʿyan thabita* as Platonic ideas, let alone as universal models for an infinite variety of individual things, is to seriously misrepresent Ibn ʿArabi's complex ontological argument.[118]

In a similar vein, Ibn ʿArabi offered a much more subtle explanation of the precedence of the *aʿyan thabita* vis-à-vis their empirical doubles than Ibn Taymiyya is ready to discuss.[119] More seriously, as noted, Ibn Taymiyya totally ignores the elaborate classification of the types of existent and nonexistent things that is laid out in Ibn ʿArabi's earlier writings. Such ignorance is all the more conspicuous, because it is precisely Ibn ʿArabi's theory of existent entities that Ibn Taymiyya singles out as the chief target of his criticism. In view of the foregoing, those champions of Ibn ʿArabi who have dismissed Ibn Taymiyya's critique as superficial and ill-informed appear to have had a strong case.

Yet Ibn Taymiyya's insensitivity to subtleties does not necessarily imply his failure to grasp the cardinal implications of Ibn ʿArabi's doctrine for the Muslim community. From the point of view of the unswerving loyalty to the community's welfare professed by the Hanbali leaders since Ibn Hanbal,[120] Ibn Taymiyya's position is an eminently logical one in its consistent effort to protect the homogeneity of the Sunni community against the disruptive individualistic and antinomian tendencies he perceived in the teachings of monistic Sufis. On the theoretical level, Ibn ʿArabi's bold forays into the realm of metaphysics and extensive use of its terminology made his status vis-à-vis the Poetical-Prophetic and the Metaphysical-Intellectual modes of apprehension extremely dubious, exposing him to the criticism of such metaphysically minded scholars as Ibn Taymiyya and al-Taftazani.

Thus, sub specie aeternitatis, any shortcomings of Ibn Taymiyya's antimonistic critique appear to be secondary to its main thrust. For there is little doubt that he did succeed in alerting his audience to the dangerous societal implications of monistic thought—admittedly at the expense of certain doctrinal nuances. For who would deny that Ibn ʿArabi indeed treated the cosmos not as created from absolute nothingness, but rather as an empirical realization of the preexistent mental images that are immutably fixed in God's foreknowledge? This metaphysical proposition is starkly at odds with the *creatio ex nihilo* axiom of the theological mainstream in all monotheistic traditions.[121]

Nor can one deny that Ibn ʿArabi's theory of sainthood and the hierarchy of holy men ruling the universe was rightly perceived by the Hanbali scholar as fraught with dangerous political and social implications. With the benefit of hindsight we can see that it was indeed widely used by various Islamic political and religious figures to substantiate and further their claims to political leadership and messianic guidance. Indirectly, therefore, Ibn ʿArabi may be said to have provided ideological underpinnings for a series of quasi-messianic, reformist, and schismatic movements in Islam including the Ahmadiyya-Idrisiyya and the other African *turuq* associated with Ahmad Ibn Idris (e.g., the Sanusiyya of Cyrenaica[122] and the Mahdiyya of Sudan),[123] the Tijaniyya of Algeria,[124] and, finally, the Indian Ahmadiyya.[125] Leaders of these and other movements availed themselves of Ibn ʿArabi's doctrine of the perfect man and supreme sainthood, which they viewed as a pretext for bringing Islam's message in line with changing times. By using Ibn ʿArabi's terminology, such religious leaders presented themselves to their following as infallible guides and seals of saints entrusted with the mission to reform or even supersede Islam.

All this said, one should point out that Ibn Taymiyya's own, purportedly "positive" and "orthodox" teaching has also proved to be potentially destructive, when appropriated and manipulated by religio-political leaders of the radical slant. Thus, his summary rejection of all "deviating" interpretations of the Islamic dogma provided an ideological foundation for a violent and devastating revolution launched by the Wahhabis of Central Arabia in the second half of the 18th century. These "Mongols of the Arabian Peninsula," as they were dubbed by their frightened Arabian neighbors, ushered in a reinterpretation of Islam along more radical lines, which was partially inspired by Ibn Taymiyya's exclusivist vision of Islamic "orthodoxy."[126]

More recently, Ibn Taymiyya's polemical writings were used as textbooks by the radical Islamic groups in Egypt directly implicated in the assassination of President Sadat.[127] One may, of course, argue that the Wahhabi "puritans" of the Najd or the radical religious reformers of Egypt were Islam's saviors, who strove to restore it to its pristine purity. This argument, however, would be a statement of one's personal vision of the "authentic" Islam, rather than an objective and balanced assessment of the movements in question.[128]

In the end, we have to content ourselves with a trite observation that, for their correligionists as well as for outsiders, the two thinkers represent two diametrically opposed views of the Islamic religion. Hence, any attempt to judge their respective faithfulness to the letter and spirit of the Muslim revelation inevitably compels us to fall back on our personal religio-political convictions, forsaking the ever elusive objective of impartiality.

5

IBN ʿARABI IN THE BIOGRAPHICAL LITERATURE FROM THE 8th/14th-9th/15th CENTURIES

Shaping an Ambiguous Image: al-Dhahabi

Although Ibn Taymiyya's critique of the Greatest Master had several antecedents in the works of Muhammad b. ʿUmar al-Kamili, al-Qastallani, and Ahmad al-Wasiti, in retrospect, it is obvious that their influence on the subsequent polemic was far less profound. Ibn Taymiyya's imposing stature as a champion of the *shariʿa* assured the broad acceptance of his polemical arguments by later generations of Muslim scholars. Due to their numerous elaborations on Ibn Taymiyya's critique, Ibn ʿArabi's teaching became "a burning intellectual problem of the time,"[1] which most writers felt obligated to address at least in passing. In positioning themselves vis-à-vis this scholastic debate, they willy-nilly aligned with either Ibn ʿArabi's partisans or opponents. For, in the aftermath of Ibn Taymiyya's harsh criticism of the Greatest Master, a mere mention of the latter's name came to demand of the writer a degree of involvement that he often found burdensome. To such neutral writers and biographers, the safest solution was to hide behind the thick fence of the opinions provided by one or another respectable scholar. As a result, the history of the Ibn ʿArabi polemic is one of the accumulation and rehearsal of a limited number of authoritative assertions or denials of his orthodoxy that were intermingled with anecdotes along the lines of the Ibn ʿAbd al-Salam story.

The continued centrality of the Ibn ʿArabi issue for later Muslim intellectuals is evidenced by the dramatic increase in the length of the biographical entries devoted to him by later authors. While the 7th/13th century biographers of the Sufi master were able to compress his life and work into half a dozen lines, it took up to a dozen pages to do the same job in the next century.[2] Authoritative statements about Ibn ʿArabi garnered from his earlier obituaries became the main building blocks for these lengthier biographical accounts of the Greatest Master.

As mentioned, Ibn Taymiyya's charismatic personality and his concerted effort to purify Islam of heretical ideas and practices, won him a large following among *ʿulamaʾ* as well as among the common folk. Even more importantly, he managed to assemble around himself a cohort of competent and influential scholars,[3] whose high standing in the Mamluk administration and in the world of Islamic learning made them critical players in the antimonistic controversy following his death in 728/1328. Standing out among them is al-Dhahabi, the celebrated historian, jurist, and biographer of the age, whose monumental works were the real treasure trove of information for those who came after him.[4]

Like many of his contemporaries, al-Dhahabi supported Ibn Taymiyya's struggle against all manner of deviations from the "pristine" Islam of the pious ancestors. This is not to say that in his writings he uncritically rehashed the opinions of the Hanbali doctor. An outstanding scholar in his own right, al-Dhahabi struggled throughout his career to forge independent theological positions on the pressing issues of Muslim scholarship. Since Ibn ʿArabi's controversial legacy loomed large among such issues, al-Dhahabi developed a distinct opinion of his personality and work. Characteristically, his assessment of the Greatest Master differs from that formulated by Ibn Taymiyya, mirroring al-Dhahabi's general disagreement with the latter's haughty intolerance of the other's opinions.[5] Al-Dhahabi's self-restraint finds a graphic expression in his handling of the Ibn ʿArabi issue, which elaborately mingles sharp condemnations with conciliatory declaimers that seem to be typical of his theological stance as a whole. Therefore, al-Dhahabi's writings present us with a much more nuanced portrait of the Greatest Master than the largely black-and-white one painted by his Hanbali predecessor. It seems probable that it was al-Dhahabi's balance of judgment that made him so popular with later writers on the Ibn ʿArabi issue, who, as we shall see, tended to avoid extremes.[6]

Al-Dhahabi's moderation notwithstanding, Ibn ʿArabi figured high on his list of those thinkers whose doctrines he considered to be at odds with Islam's fundamentals.[7] His negative attitude toward the Greatest Master is hardly surprising, since by al-Dhahabi's time Ibn ʿArabi had already become an emblem for the monistic tendencies in Islam.[8]

The accounts of Ibn ʿArabi's life and work in al-Dhahabi's monumental "History of Islam" (*Taʾrikh al-islam*) and in lesser biographical works reveal his intention to consider the controversial Sufi master from a variety of angles. To demonstrate his objectivity, al-Dhahabi thoroughly collected all the opinions of Ibn ʿArabi he could find in earlier biographical dictionaries, whereupon he reproduced them chronologically, thoroughly avoiding any critical comments. His only contribution to the polemic was his analysis of selected samples from Ibn ʿArabi's poetry and prose, which he carefully offset with the authoritative opinions from earlier scholars. The result of his examination of Ibn ʿArabi's poetic excerpts (mostly from the latter's *Diwan*) and theological statements (mostly from the *Fusus*) was thoroughly negative—he declared them irremediably heretical due to their assertion of the existential unity of God and the world.[9]

The reason for al-Dhahabi's negative assessment of the Greatest Master should be sought in his lifelong advocacy of the community-oriented, fideistic theology that was shared by most of Ibn Taymiyya's disciples. His understanding of the correct belief, which was firmly grounded in the thoroughly exoteric, pragmatic perspective,[10] inevitably clashed with Ibn ʿArabi's esoteric, individualistic outlook, which al-Dhahabi described as "the Sufism of the adherents of unity/oneness" (*tasawwuf ahl al-wahda*). In line with the strictly fideistic religious attitude enshrined in the "without asking how" principle (*bi-la kayf*), al-Dhahabi took exception to the elitist vision of Islam, which he identified with the Greatest Master:

> By God, for the Muslim who lives in ignorance, tending his cattle, who knows nothing of religious science but a few *suras* from the Qurʾan that he recites in his prayers, and who believes in God and the Last Day—his knowledge is much more beneficial than the obscure gnosis and all the subtle truths [one acquires] after reading a hundred books and staying a hundred days in retreat.[11]

In this remarkably terse statement, al-Dhahabi juxtaposed Ibn ʿArabi's arcane gnosticism with the serene, unquestioning faith of the ordinary believer, making clear his preference to the latter as more conducive to salvation and felicity. Much like Ibn Taymiyya, al-Dhahabi was particularly resentful of the antinomian tendencies he perceived in the *Fusus*—a book he once described as "the worst of all his [Ibn ʿArabi's] writings." While Ibn ʿArabi's other works yield themselves to an allegorical interpretation, the *Fusus* is too thoroughly heretical to merit such an excuse: if the teaching explicated there is not *kufr*, "then," exclaimed al-Dhahabi, "there is no *kufr* under the sun."[12]

Yet, unlike Ibn Taymiyya who took little interest in Ibn ʿArabi's personality, al-Dhahabi offered a psychological explanation of Ibn ʿArabi's "delusions," portraying him as a victim of excessive asceticism and self-mortification:

> I do not believe that his [Ibn ʿArabi's] lie was intentional.[13] It was the long retreats and constant fasting that had a harmful effect on him, leading to mental derangement, false imagination, and a madness of sorts (*tarf al-junun*).[14]

Elsewhere he elaborated on this theme in the following manner:

> This man converted to Sufism [early in his life]; he retreated [from the world], fasted, and practiced long vigils, until certain things were unveiled to him, which, however, became mixed with [his] loose imagination, with [his] fleeting states of mind, and with [his own] ideas. He was so obsessed by all this that, through his powerful imagination, he started to dream up things which he thought existed in the outside world [while, in reality, they were not there].[15]

Among the "things" that Ibn ʿArabi "dreamed up" according to al-Dhahabi was his "heretical" claim to be the "Seal of sainthood" and his assertion that he was able to "contemplate the Deity month after month until the end of time."[16] In al-Dhahabi's view, such irresponsible claims along with similar absurdities found in the *Fusus* fall under the heading of *kufr*. Yet, in contrast to his Hanbali colleague, al-Dhahabi was disinclined to declare Ibn ʿArabi a *kafir*. His qualms arose from his lack of certainty as to Ibn ʿArabi's state of mind at the end of his life—that is, whether or not he repented of his "sins" on his deathbed. Whatever his previous blasphemies, said al-Dhahabi, there was still a possibility that he recanted his heretical views and embraced the correct doctrine of the Sunni community (*ahl al-sunna wa ʾl-jamaʿa*).[17] Hence, in keeping with the ancient Muslim doctrine of respite or postponement (*irjaʾ*),[18] al-Dhahabi suggested that a final judgment regarding Ibn ʿArabi's faith or unbelief as well as his destiny in the afterlife be suspended. For, in al-Dhahabi's phrase, God is the only judge of the secrets hidden in his servants' hearts.[19]

Although, for al-Dhahabi, Ibn ʿArabi was a deluded individual afflicted with a severe mental illness, he by no means condoned the latter's monistic tendencies due to their potential harm to the Muslim community at large. Once Ibn ʿArabi's ideas had gained a foothold among *ʿulamaʾ*, wrote al-Dhahabi, they caused serious discord amid them. This discord was further aggravated by the tortuous nature of Ibn ʿArabi's writings, which easily lent itself to many conflicting interpretations. In summarizing the three major attitudes to the Sufi master that crystallized in the course of the debate over his legacy, al-Dhahabi wrote:

> He composed [many] works on the Sufism of the philosophers and adherents of oneness, which abound in erroneous statements. One group [of scholars] regarded these statements as sheer apostasy and heresy, while others considered them to be the allegoric allusions of the [Sufi] gnostics and the symbolic expressions current among the wayfarers on the mystical Path. Still another group believed that the problem lay in his ambiguous method of expression; its literal meaning appears to be unbelief and delusion, while its inner meaning is, in fact, nothing but truth and higher gnosis. . . . Most of the scholars, however, have agreed that his teaching is nothing but falsehood and delusion. And yet they have argued that it is impossible to prove beyond doubt that at the time of his death he was still clinging to his [heresies]. They went on to argue that his [pious] external state and conduct indicate that he should have turned to God in repentance. For was he not a great expert on the traditions and transmitted reports, who also had mastered many other religious sciences? Now, my position on this issue is as follows: it is quite possible that he was one of God's friends, who, on his deathbed, attained intimacy with the Divine and was thus assured a favorable outcome [on the Day of Judgment]. As regards Ibn ʿArabi's teachings, anyone who takes the trouble to look into them, bearing in mind the fundamental principles of the espousers of unificationism and the terminology of the Sufis, will discover—after he has put together the loose ends of the phrases—that the opinion of [Ibn ʿArabi's advocates] is contrary to the truth.[20]

Despite this rather straightforward rebuttal al-Dhahabi nevertheless strikes a reconciliatory note in his monumental "History of Islam." Written toward the end of his life, this entry may reflect al-Dhahabi's deep-rooted fear of being held responsible for slandering a friend of God on the Day of Reckoning:

> Ibn al-ʿArabi was characterized by such qualities as eloquence, acumen, good memory, mastery of Sufism, and proficiency in esoteric knowledge (*ʿirfan*). If it had not been for ecstatic utterances in his speech, he would certainly have been [approved] by scholarly consensus. His slips of the tongue may have occurred in a state of ecstatic intoxication and mystical rapture. Therefore, we wish him a favorable [outcome in the Hereafter].[21]

Apologetic Uses of al-Dhahabi's Ambivalence: al-Safadi and al-Yafiʿi

Al-Dhahabi's ambivalent treatment of the Greatest Master added further to the atmosphere of ambiguity that had surrounded his image from the very start. Writing shortly after al-Dhahabi, al-Safadi availed himself of this ambiguity to justify restraint in assessing Ibn ʿArabi's status vis-à-vis the *shariʿa*. Interestingly, al-Safadi's apologetic strategy consisted in presenting the Sufi as a faithful follower of al-Ashʿari,[22] while conceding that some statements from the *Fusus* indeed contained "reprehensible things, whose external meaning is at odds with the divine Law." Yet al-Safadi vindicated its author by making use of al-Dhahabi's discourse:

> He [Ibn ʿArabi] and his like are often susceptible to [mystical] states as a result of the privation caused by engaging in spiritual exercises during their retreats [from the world]. When they enter into such states, the Sufis are anxious to convey their experiences to others. However, often the meaning that they try to convey is too sublime and eludes [conventional] words.[23]

Another contemporary scholar to make use of al-Dhahabi's ambivalent assessment of Ibn ʿArabi was the famous Shafiʿi doctor and Sufi hagiographer ʿAbdallah al-Yafiʿi (d. 768/1367).[24] He described Ibn ʿArabi as a controversial scholar whose work formed a stumbling block for many *ʿulama*ʾ of the Islamic community. As a result, they accused him of a "grave sin" (*al-amr al-ʿazim*) or even *kufr.* In al-Yafiʿi's view, this condemnation was ill-founded and therefore rejected by Ibn ʿArabi's followers, who praised him to the heavens (*fakhkhamah tafkhiman ʿaziman*) and who ascribed to him many spectacular miracles. Following al-Dhahabi, who—it is to be recalled—relied on Ibn Taymiyya's antimonistic argument, al-Yafiʿi also viewed the *Fusus* as the principal reason for the *ʿulama*ʾ's suspicions about the faith of its author. Yet, unlike al-Dhahabi, al-Yafiʿi insisted that even this work could be brought in line with the *shariʿa* through an allegorical interpretation. As an example, al-Yafiʿi cited a commentary on the *Fusus* by the leader of Syrian Shafiʿis, Kamal al-din al-Zamlakani (d. 727/1327),[25] who, in al-Yafiʿi's judgment, had successfully dispelled the difficulties of the *Fusus,* thereby making it acceptable to any impartial reader.[26]

That being said, al-Yafiʿi suggested that, in the absence of conclusive proof of either Ibn ʿArabi's belief or unbelief, one should suspend (*tawaqquf*) any judgment on his status. Thus, although ostensibly reiterating the cautious position toward Ibn ʿArabi sketched out by al-Dhahabi, al-Yafiʿi was much more forward than the latter in defending the Greatest Master. Furthermore, al-Yafiʿi's pro-Ibn ʿArabi position is evidenced, for example, by his disregard for the vociferous condemnations of the Sufi's teaching by Ibn Taymiyya and his followers. Instead, he relied on the contemporary Shafiʿi scholar Ibn al-Zamlakani, thereby demonstrating both his loyalty to the Shafiʿi *madhhab* and dislike for the "extremism" of the Hanbali doctor.[27]

Apart from the standard Sufi version of Ibn ʿAbd al-Salam's censure of Ibn ʿArabi, al-Yafiʿi availed himself use of a number of similar "face-saving" narratives, such as the account of Ibn ʿArabi's alleged meeting with the great *shariʿa*-minded mystic ʿUmar al-Suhrawardi (d. 632/1235), who is made to testify to Ibn ʿArabi's lofty status among the Sufi saints.[28] Al-Yafiʿi's use of this anecdote did not go unnoticed by Ibn ʿArabi's critics, who challenged its veracity. One such skeptic angrily remarked that "the al-Suhrawardi story was transmitted from one anonymous [narrator] to another" and that al-Yafiʿi mentioned it because, as an advocate of Sufis, he was keen on "finding excuses for them no matter how far-fetched they may be."[29]

Al-Yafiʿi's defense of the Greatest Master is in full harmony with his lifelong effort to vindicate Sufism as a legitimate trend within Islam. In his numerous hagiographies, which celebrate the model piety and spectacular miracles of the Sufi saints,[30] al-Yafiʿi consistently set them apart from the shapeless mass of ordinary believers. For him, God's elect servants, should be exempt from the judgmental criteria that are commonly applied to the other members of the Muslim community. In al-Yafiʿi's apologetic discourse, every act or word of a saint carries a hidden meaning that can only be understood by one of their own—those who have had similar spiritual experiences.

The ambiguous attitude toward Ibn ʿArabi, delineated by al-Dhahabi (anti-Ibn ʿArabi) and refined by al-Safadi and al-Yafiʿi (pro-Ibn ʿArabi), struck a sympathetic cord with many moderate *ʿulamaʾ* who considered Ibn ʿArabi's teaching to be too subtle and vague to be properly understood by the uninitiated. Following in the footsteps of al-Yafiʿi, such scholars recommended that their fellow Muslims withhold judgment as to his status vis-à-vis the *shariʿa*.[31] This agnostic stance found an influential spokesman in the noted Egyptian polymath Jalal al-din al-Suyuti (d. 911/1505).[32] Responding to the condemnatory campaign against Ibn ʿArabi launched by Burhan al-din al-Biqaʿi (d. 875/1470),[33] al-Suyuti provides the following justification for this position:

1. The fact that Ibn ʿArabi really made the heretical statements for which he was condemned as an unbeliever can never be proven beyond doubt; there always remains a possibility that they were imputed to him by his detractors.
2. These statements may have been articulated in a state of ecstatic intoxication, whereas a drunk is not culpable of his words and deeds.
3. If one is unable to find a plausible explanation for such statements though a standard interpretation, he should turn to the people of esoteric knowledge (*ahl al-ʿilm al-batin*) who alone can explicate their meaning.
4. Finally, there is no way of knowing that the speaker really meant unbelief: his genuine intentions is a mystery that is known to no one but God.[34]

Al-Fasi: Between Biography and Polemic

A biography of the Greatest Master by the acclaimed Meccan historian and *faqih* al-Fasi (d. 832/1429) signals a significant development in the polemic over his legacy.[35] Unlike al-Safadi and al-Yafiʿi, al-Fasi was quite outspoken in his opposition to Ibn ʿArabi and monistic Sufism as a whole. His anti-Ibn ʿArabi stance is firmly grounded in the substantial body of negative opinions of Ibn ʿArabi accumulated by the Muslim prosopographical tradition over almost two centuries. The fact that al-Fasi quoted the opinions not available to al-Dhahabi indicates that in his time the controversy over Ibn ʿArabi still raged on unrelenting. Furthermore, it appears to have taken a new twist: whereas al-Dhahabi had largely drawn on the relatively neutral earlier biographies of the Greatest Master, al-Fasi's major source was the legal opinions (*fatawi,* sing. *fatwa*) on Ibn ʿArabi issued by the respected *ʿulama*ʾ of the age. The sheer volume of such *fatwa*s bears an eloquent testimony to the continuing acuteness of the Ibn-ʿArabi issue at the turn of the 9th/15th centuries.

By including the *fatawi* into his biographical narrative, al-Fasi, overstepped the boundaries of the prosopographical genre to plunge headlong into the realm of the unbridled partisanship that characterizes the Muslim polemical literature. Consequently, his treatment of Ibn ʿArabi does away with even the semblance of objectivity that one expects of biography writing. As a result, what al-Fasi describes—rather misleadingly—as a *tarjama* ("biography," or "obituary") of the Greatest Master is, in fact, polemic pure and simple.

Significantly, al-Fasi himself was aware of the fact that his piece hardly qualified as a conventional biographical entry:

> In this *tarjama* of Ibn ʿArabi we have mentioned things that have never been brought together in any other writing. One of our contemporaries, whom we find wanting in both intelligence and learning, has written a *tarjama* of Ibn ʿArabi. What he mentioned there is both doubtful and worthless.[36] We have already explained its falsity, upon the request of one of our companions, in another *tarjama* of Ibn ʿArabi. An abridged version of that longer *tarjama* is included in the present volume. . . . [37]

The briefest of looks at al-Fasi's narrative shows that it constantly blends biography with theological polemic, bringing to fruition the polemical strain that we already observed in most of the earlier accounts of Ibn ʿArabi's life.

Al-Fasi's extensive use of the *fatwa*s on the Ibn ʿArabi problem suggests that by the 8th/14th centuries the powerful mechanism of scholarly consensus (*ijmaʿ*) was set in motion to resolve it. In his "biography" of the Greatest Master, al-Fasi defined three major attempts to achieve a comprehensive and binding consensus (*ijmaʿ*) on the issue. The first occurred in 719/1319 or in 721/1321,[38] a period that was marked by the activities of Ibn Taymiyya and his direct associates. These scholars were the first to orchestrate the medieval Islamic version of a selective opinion poll. The biased character of the questionnaire that was sent to the leading *ʿulamaʾ* of the age indicates that it originated in the camp of Ibn ʿArabi's opponents. The addressees were asked to evaluate the following claims made by the Sufi master:

> —that the Prophet revealed to him the text of the book [*Fusus*] in a dream and ordered him to spread it among Muslims—a claim that is especially egregious because the content of this book effectively nullifies the teachings of the prophets as laid down in the Muslim Scripture;[39]
>
> —that Adam is called "man" (*insan*) because he is to God what the pupil is to man's eye;[40]
>
> —that the transcendent Divine Absolute is identical with, and immanent to, the creatury world (*al-haqq al-munazzah huwa ʾl-khalq al-mushabbah*);[41]

—that by abandoning their idols the tribe of Nuh (Noah)[42] became ignorant of God to the extent that they deserted them;[43]

—that God is present in each and every object of worship; therefore he is recognized and worshiped by the true gnostic in each and every form, whereas most people remain ignorant of his multiple manifestations;[44]

—that the multiplicity and differentiation observed in the cosmos stand in the same relationship to God as man's limbs and faculties to his essence;[45]

—that the tribe of Nuh (Noah) will eventually be spared the hellfire; like their counterparts in paradise, they will be brought into God's presence where they will enjoy the eternal bliss, since in their idols they worshiped no one but God, and therefore remained on "the straight path";[46]

—that the Qurʾanic threat of a painful punishment that awaits the sinners[47] should be interpreted allegorically as a promise of "pleasure"[48]—an interpretation implying that the transgressors of the divine law will not suffer in hell.

Based on the above propositions, the *mufti*s were invited to answer the following questions:

1. Whether anyone who believes in, and endorses, such claims should himself be treated as a *kafir.*
2. Whether anyone in his right mind who refuses to condemn such propositions by the word of mouth or in his heart remains a believing Muslim or becomes a grave sinner.

Plainly, the way in which this questionnaire was framed left potential respondents little room to maneuver.[49] Even those sympathetic to Ibn ʿArabi had no choice but to pass a condemnatory verdict or to stand accused for failing to denounce a blatant heresy.[50] Obviously, the questionnaire distorts Ibn ʿArabi's ideas by taking them out of their context. This selective procedure alone flies in the face of his open-ended discursive strategy, which turns on a constant perspective shift, intended to shock the reader into grasping the underlying esoteric truths.[51] Furthermore, the fact that the bulk of the statements are mechanically extracted from a particularly obscure chapter of the *Fusus,* which deals with Nuh's (Noah's) unsuccessful attempts to force a rigid notion of divine transcendence unto the immanence-minded idol worshipers, suggests a deliberately trivial reading, blind to the complexity of Ibn ʿArabi's thought.

It does not take a lot of imagination to see that the Nuh story, reduced, as it were, to the bare bones by the compilers of the questionnaire, came as a shock to the Muslim scholars with no prior exposure to Ibn ʿArabi's texts. This, it seems, was precisely the reason why the Nuh chapter was chosen by the authors of the questionnaire, for it is here that Ibn ʿArabi's allegorical exegesis clashes with the traditional interpretation of the Qurʾanic verses in question.[52]

Faced with the choice of condemning Ibn ʿArabi as an unbeliever or putting their reputations on the line by defending a flagrant heresy, the respondents nevertheless came up with a surprisingly wide variety of responses from unconditional condemnations to muted (and often pro forma) censures to tacit approvals. This gamut of opinions is all the more surprising since al-Fasi's open hostility to Ibn ʿArabi caused him to select for his polemical *tarjama* only the harshest criticisms of the Greatest Master.

Predictably, al-Fasi's list of rulings on Ibn ʿArabi opens with a terse *fatwa* by Ibn Taymiyya that summarizes his arguments against Ibn ʿArabi discussed in the previous chapter. In keeping with the requirements of the *fatwa* genre, which usually included a practical recommendation on the given issue, Ibn Taymiyya called upon all Muslims to fight the partisans of *wahdat al-wujud,* because "they poison the minds and faith of many believers, including Sufi masters, *ʿulamaʾ*, kings, and princes." For Ibn Taymiyya, their presence in the midst of the Muslim community is more harmful to the Muslims than the depredations of highway robbers, for while the latter simply steal Muslims' material possessions, leaving intact their faith, the *wujudiyya* rob them of something immeasurably more precious—their faith and hope for salvation.[53]

Ibn Taymiyya's *fatwa* is followed by that of the Shafiʿi jurist Badr al-din Ibn Jamaʿa (d. 733/1333), an influential scholar who occupied a number of important posts in the Mamluk administration.[54] A high-ranking government official, Ibn Jamaʿa simply could not condone the doctrinal "abominations" ascribed to Ibn ʿArabi by the questionnaire.[55] His response, therefore, is quite predictable:

> The aforementioned passages as well as those resembling them are nothing but a blamable innovation, delusion, abomination, and folly to which no believer must ever give ear or heed.[56]

In elaborating his harsh verdict, Ibn Jamaʿa brusquely dismissed Ibn ʿArabi's claims that the *Fusus* was communicated to him by the Prophet, stressing the detrimental effect of the book on Muslim faith. The real source of the *Fusus,* in Ibn Jamaʿa's view, is Iblis, whose goal is to confuse Muslims into embracing the blasphemous ideas set out in this heretical opus. Equally untenable from the standpoint of the Qurʾan and the Sunna was, in Ibn al-Jamaʿa's mind, Ibn ʿArabi's comparison of Adam with the pupil in God's eye—an image that Ibn Jamaʿa condemns as sheer anthropomorphism. Similarly, Ibn ʿArabi's identification of God with his creatures belies divine transcendence, which forms the foundation of *tawhid.* At the close of his *fatwa,* Ibn Jamaʿa takes exception to Ibn ʿArabi's attempts to exonerate the Qurʾanic idolaters by portraying Noah, a prophet of God, as a hopeless ignoramus who failed pitifully to comprehend the real purport of the divine injunction to worship God in every form. Upon reviewing the other propositions from the *Fusus* listed in the questionnaire, Ibn Jamaʿa found them equally heretical and inconsistent with the Sunni dogma, whereupon he proceeded to advise the ruler that all copies of the *Fusus* and other writings containing similar statements be destroyed in order to protect the community from a great temptation.

A similar view of Ibn ʿArabi was expressed by a scholar whose affiliation with the Hanbali school should have made him a natural theological opponent to the Shafiʿi *mutakallim* Ibn Jamaʿa. The individual in question, Masʿud b. Ahmad al-Harithi (d. 711/1311), whom the chronicles of the period describe as a renowned *muhaddith* and leader of the Cairene Hanbalis,[57] described the *Fusus* as a "great harm" (*darar ʿazim*) to the Sunni community, which is especially detrimental to Muslims with little knowledge of religion or of infirm faith. According to al-Harithi, the ignorant populace are especially prone to fall for the "ornate phrases" and "obscure allusions" of the *Fusus,* since their attractive attire disguises their underlying heresy. However, shorn of their verbal husks, Ibn ʿArabi's statements leave no doubt as to their real purpose. The practical conclusion al-Harithi drew from his examination of the questionnaire dovetails neatly into the fideist and literalist attitude of the Hanbali school: to hold fast onto the letter of the Qurʾan and the Sunna and to eschew any rationalist inquiry that might lead to doubt or apostasy.[58]

The next *fatwa* quoted in al-Fasi's *tarjama* was written by the renowned Shafiʿi jurist and polymath Muhammad b. Yusuf al-Jazari (d. 711/1311),[59] whose analysis of Ibn ʿArabi's claims in the questionnaire, brings him to the following conclusions that resonate finely with the previous responsa:

> —if someone, who is fully aware of Ibn ʿArabi's true purpose, still continues to defend him, he himself becomes a heretic;
>
> —if, however, someone embraces Ibn ʿArabi's views without understanding their true implications, he should be alerted to their perversity and discouraged from studying them.[60]

The next *fatwa* cited by al-Fasi belongs to the chief *qadi* of the Egyptian Shafiʿis ʿUmar al-Kattan (d. 738/1338).[61] Unlike the other *muftis*, who limited themselves to the trite observation that Ibn ʿArabi's propositions contradict the canonical interpretations of the Muslim Scriptures, al-Kattan emphasized that they are equally in conflict with the self-evident, innate knowledge (*ʿilm daruri*) shared by all humans regardless of their intellectual status. In his view, they are illogical and absurd and moreover akin to the incoherent ravings of a madman, who is totally oblivious to the information delivered to him by his senses and rational faculties. For no one in his right mind identifies the Maker with his creatures, or denies the multiplicity of the empirical world, as Ibn ʿArabi does in his *Fusus*. In al-Kattan's view, such groundless and preposterous propositions constitute a grave danger to Islam and should be condemned as blatant heresy. Anyone who approves of them, even tacitly, must himself be treated as a *kafir*.[62]

An extremely harsh view of Ibn ʿArabi was taken by the Shafiʿi jurist ʿAli al-Bakri (d. 724/1324), whose courageous criticism of the Mamluk policy nearly cost him his tongue (or, according to another story, his hand).[63] In dealing with the issues enumerated in the questionnaire, al-Bakri focuses on the delicate problem of meeting the Prophet in a dream, which Ibn ʿArabi claimed to have experienced prior to composing the *Fusus*. According to the Muslim scholarly consensus, seeing the Prophet in a dream is not only legitimate but also veridical, for neither Satan nor any other evil spirit could possibly impersonate him. Hence, any messages the Prophet communicates in such instances are to be taken as true guidance.[64] Now Ibn ʿArabi's assertion regarding the prophetic origin of the *Fusus* posed a serious problem to his opponents, since by contesting his theological views they indirectly questioned the soundness of this widespread belief and the authenticity of the *hadith* quoted in its support.[65] To overcome this predicament, al-Bakri suggested that

Ibn ʿArabi had distorted the genuine meaning of the message entrusted to him by the Prophet, which in its present shape is nothing but "an error and mischief."

On the issue of Ibn ʿArabi's status, al-Bakri was forthright: if the author of the *Fusus* really believed in what he wrote there, his *kufr* is proven beyond doubt. Even if his unbelief is unintentional—being, for example, a product of ignorance or imbecility—he still cannot be acquitted, since anyone who takes it upon himself to write about God's messengers must first consult the *ʿulamaʾ*. At the close of the *fatwa,* al-Bakri proclaimed that Ibn ʿArabi's blasphemies can never be reconciled with the explicit meaning of the *shariʿa*, because he "is too accursed (*alʿan*) and perverted" to deserve any such excuse.[66]

The last *fatwa* mentioned by al-Fasi as part of the first anti-Ibn ʿArabi campaign was issued by the famous Maliki judge ʿIsa al-Zawawi (d. 743/1342),[67] a scholar who unconditionally denounced the scandalous views imputed to the Greatest Master by the authors of the questionnaire. On the practical plane, al-Zawawi deemed it necessary to distinguish between two principal categories of Muslims who embrace the heresies laid down in the *Fusus.* To the first belong those who embrace them wittingly and intentionally. These, in al-Zawawi's classification, are manifest unbelievers (*kuffar*) who should be hunted down, put on trial and forced to recant their errors. More dangerous, however, are the covert professors of unificationism who pose as good Muslims, while secretly reveling in the monistic heresy. Al-Zawawi described them as "heretics" (*zanadiqa*) and called upon the rulers to exterminate them even though they should repent, for their sincerity cannot be trusted due to their previous concealment. In al-Zawawi's classification, the latter fall under the heading of "esotericists" (*batiniyya*), the category that also included the Ismaʿilis, whom most scholars viewed as the archenemies of the Sunni community. To stamp out the monistic heresy al-Zawawi demanded that the ruler order a search for copies of the *Fusus* and similar writings, whereupon they should be burned and their owners punished.[68]

Al-Zawawi's legal opinion ends the first round of the anti-Ibn ʿArabi campaign, as presented in al-Fasi's *tarjama.*[69] Its net result, according to al-Fasi, was the unanimous condemnation of the *Fusus* by the leading scholars of the age and their consensus that possessors of its copies be persecuted by the civil and religious authorities.

A second round of the anti-Ibn ʿArabi campaign took place less than two decades later—clear evidence that, despite al-Fasi's assertions to the contrary, the earlier efforts to stop the circulation of his ideas in Egypt and Syria proved to be unsuccessful. A interesting summary of the second campaign is given in the work of the Yemeni scholar Ibn al-Ahdal (d. 855/1451) who cites al-Dhahabi as his authority:[70]

> As for their writings,[71] they are worse than any unbelief. That's why the just rulers and those who guide on the straight way[72] prevent people from studying them and advise their destruction. They also prohibit people from selling or buying such writings. In the year 738 [i.e., 1337] the learned men of Egypt reached a consensus, according to which, these [writings] must be banned and their study be prohibited. The *qadi* Badr al-din al-Maliki[73] says that nowadays Ibn ʿArabi's books are not available in either Cairo or Alexandria, and no one dares to produce them in public places. If they are discovered [in somebody's house] they are confiscated and burned. As for the owner, he is tortured, and if proven to be an adherent [of Ibn ʿArabi], executed. Once, a copy of the *Fusus* was found in a book market. It was immediately confiscated, tied up with rope, then dragged along the street to the chief *qadi,* where it was burned for the common good.[74]

Similar episodes are attested for a later period, reflecting the same tensions and controversies around Ibn ʿArabi's legacy that we observed from the very start. If Ibn al-Ahdal's evidence is accurate, religious authorities did occasionally resort to violence to preclude the spread of monistic ideas. However, the limited success of such drastic measures is evident from the persistence of the Ibn ʿArabi polemic throughout the subsequent centuries. Moreover, as we shall see, when the partisans of Ibn ʿArabi succeeded in enlisting the support of the rulers, the antimonistic party occasionally found itself among the persecuted.

On a different issue, the foregoing discussion lends further support to our conclusion regarding Ibn Taymiyya's pivotal role in the antimonistic discourse of the 8th/14th-9th/15th centuries. Indeed, the first round of *fatwa* seeking, as described by al-Fasi, came on the heels of his sharp denunciation of Ibn ʿArabi and of other monistic thinkers.[75] It was Ibn Taymiyya, who narrowed the polemic to several theological and metaphysical propositions found in the *Fusus* and who formulated the theoretical objections to them in his antimonistic treatises.

The controversy over Ibn ʿArabi and his school raged unabated throughout the 8th/14th centuries. For the most part, it remained within the academic confines, although sometimes it did spill over into public life and politics, and with a vengeance. Much to the annoyance of Ibn ʿArabi's detractors, the campaign to discredit his ideas initiated by Ibn Taymiyya and taken up by his followers did not yield the desired result. On the contrary, the *Fusus,* and, to a lesser extent, Ibn ʿArabi's other works continued to be copied and read throughout the Mamluk lands as well as in Anatolia, Iran, Central Asia, and India, where Ibn ʿArabi's following was particularly well-entrenched. Helpless in the face of the remarkable resilience of his "heretical" doctrine, his antagonists tried to enlist the support of the secular authorities in hopes of intimidating potential and actual espousers of the philosophy of oneness.

The picture would be incomplete without referring to a third attempt to obtain a scholarly consensus on Ibn ʿArabi's unbelief that took place in 8th/14th-century Egypt[76] under al-Zahir Barquq (r. 784/1382-801/1399)—the first of the Circassian dynasty of Mamluk sultans.[77] There are indications that several scholars in al-Zahir's entourage were secret admirers of Ibn ʿArabi and were prepared to use their political clout to put a stop to the vilification of the Greatest Master by their colleagues.[78] As a result, the anti-Ibn ʿArabi faction found itself in the unfamiliar role of the defendant. According to al-Fasi, the movement to discredit Ibn ʿArabi's teaching was spearheaded by the renowned Shafiʿi scholar ʿUmar al-Bulqini (d. 805/1403),[79] who was seconded by his younger colleague Ibn Hajar al-ʿAsqalani (d. 852/1449).[80] Contrary to al-Fasi's opinion—later reiterated by al-Sakhawi—neither of these scholars seems to have written fully fledged refutations or issued *fatwa*s against the Greatest Master. In fact, sources describe al-Bulqini's alleged condemnation of Ibn ʿArabi as a rather casual response to a question posed by Ibn Hajar. At any rate, this was hardly a formal, binding *fatwa:* in answer to an oral query, al-Bulqini offhandedly described Ibn ʿArabi as a *kafir.* When pressed for details, he categorically refused to elaborate, citing the confusion over the issue generated by the decades of fruitless theological polemic.[81]

Thus, although al-Fasi in his *tarjama* took pains to depict both al-Bulqini and Ibn Hajar as implacable enemies of the Greatest Master,[82] their genuine positions vis-à-vis Ibn ʿArabi seem elusive. This is especially true of Ibn Hajar, whose sketches of Ibn ʿArabi's biography evince very little in the way of overt criticism.[83] Generally, Ibn Hajar adhered to the cautious and inconclusive position adumbrated by al-Dhahabi, whose impartiality and balance of judgment he valued.[84] As with al-Dhahabi, he attempted to present the widest possible spectrum of opinions on the Greatest Master, avoiding a clear-cut judgment of heresy or unbelief.[85] Ibn Hajar's study of the earliest biographical dictionaries persuaded him that their authors were, for the most part, well-disposed toward the Greatest Master. Musing over this strange phenomenon, Ibn Hajar observed that in Ibn ʿArabi's lifetime the *Fusus* had not yet gained wide currency, precluding his contemporaries from looking into the controversial aspects of his work.[86] As with the other critics of philosophical Sufism, Ibn Hajar was much more mistrustful of Ibn ʿArabi's followers, who, in his words

> Had a great, nay excessive belief in him and overstepped all limits [in his regard]. They, for example, held that he had achieved the rank of the prophets. Whenever someone became his disciple, he inevitably went to extremes in venerating him [Ibn ʿArabi] and never left him from that moment on. Nor would he ever prefer him [Ibn ʿArabi] to anyone else or recognize someone as equal to him. . . . [87]

Ibn Hajar's own assessment of Ibn ʿArabi's work is deliberately indecisive, betraying the typical bewilderment of an exoteric scholar who is confronted with the Sufi's legacy:

> Very little can be understood from them [Ibn ʿArabi's books]. However, the things one is able to comprehend are generally good and well-put. At the same time, his books abound in statements that are repugnant to the ear. His followers assumed that they [the statements] had a hidden meaning that was not readily evident from their outward wording. In sum, he had a great standing among the noblest of the Sufi teachers and possessed a complete knowledge of the divine names and of [the occult properties of] letters.[88] On all these [issues] he composed many unusual books and made many strange statements.[89]

In Ibn Hajar we find another example of the middle-of-the-road scholar who was hesitant to either condemn or absolve Ibn ʿArabi decisively, puzzled as he was over the seemingly incompatible facets of the Shaykh's personality—a literalist and an esotericist, a diligent *muhaddith* and an allegorical exegete, a talented litterateur, and a raving visionary.[90]

Among the many negative opinions of the Greatest Master in al-Fasi's *tarjama,* one by the influential Shafiʿi theologian Taqi ʾl-din al-Subki (d. 756/1355) merits special scrutiny.[91] An ardent adherent of Ashʿari *kalam,* al-Subki ran afoul of the sworn enemy of rationalist theology, Ibn Taymiyya.[92] Yet, on the issue of Ibn ʿArabi's "heterodoxy," al-Subki was, for once, in complete agreement with his lifelong theological opponent. His position is evident from his discussion of the two classes of the *mutakallimun* and the corresponding categories among the Sufi gnostics. For al-Subki, the majority of the *mutakallimun* and the Sufis are engaged in a legitimate quest for the knowledge of God's will, names, attributes, and commands in hopes of achieving a pure life and moral perfection. This conclusion, however, does not include the second class of theologians whom al-Subki placed in the same category with the "impious" Sufi thinkers led by Ibn ʿArabi. In al-Subki's mind, both the *mutakallimun* and the Sufis in this category were guilty of incorporating into their theoretical discussions the theological issues that cannot be resolved through rational speculation and, therefore, should be left untouched or taken on trust. Their preoccupation with things metaphysical, which they were ill-equipped to resolve, was viewed by al-Subki as having an adverse effect on their faith and loyalty to the community. On these grounds, he demanded that such *mutakallimun* and Sufis be excluded from the ranks of the Muslim scholars and treated as apostates.[93]

In addition to al-Subki, al-Fasi quoted a host of other critics of Ibn ʿArabi, who denounced him officially or in private. Their condemnations, however, add little to the standard *fatwa*s that have been already discussed. In a refreshing departure from the usual pattern, the famous Hanbali scholar Shams al-din Ibn al-Muhibb composed the following poetic lines that figure at the close of his ruling:[94]

> In a book of his, the little Ibn al-ʿArabi
>
> (Ibn al-ʿUraybi) invited people to take
>
> The crooked way of the one-eyed Antichrist
>
> (*al-dajjal*),
>
> And to follow the path of Pharaoh, whom
>
> he extolled as the master of those who have
>
> attained the truth (*muhaqqiqun*):
>
> May evil befall him and his clique![95]

Standing out among the critics of Ibn ʿArabi enumerated in al-Fasi's *tarjama* is the Sufi philosopher and proponent of "absolute oneness" Ibn Sabʿin, who, if al-Fasi's evidence is to be trusted, disdainfully dismissed Ibn ʿArabi's doctrine as "whimsical philosophy" (*falsafa jamiha*). Without delving into the complex issue of the relationship between the two pillars of monistic thought, it seems likely that Ibn Sabʿin referred to Ibn ʿArabi's undisciplined and tortuous narrative method, which obscured his real position on the issue of divine transcendence/immanence. If authentic, this is, to my knowledge, the only instance when Ibn ʿArabi is criticized by a more radical monist than himself.

A dissonant note in the otherwise harmonious chorus of accusations, assembled by al-Fasi, was sounded by the eminent Shafiʿi *faqih* and Ashʿari theologian ʿAlaʾ al-din al-Qunawi (d. 727/1327).[96] Contrary to the other *mufti*s cited in the *tarjama,* al-Qunawi admitted that the controversial statements of Sufi masters, such as ones quoted in the questionnaire, should be interpreted allegorically (*taʾwil*), in order to be reconciled with the literal meaning of the *shariʿa*. He, however, made an important reservation, arguing that *taʾwil* applies exclusively to the work of those individuals whose infallibility (*ʿisma*) is attested beyond doubt.[97] Yet, al-Qunawi was deliberately unclear as to whether Ibn ʿArabi fell into the category of those entitled to such a reconciliatory interpretation—a position that allowed him to avoid showing his true colors in the Ibn-ʿArabi debate. According to al-Qunawi, one cannot condemn Ibn ʿArabi on the strength of the heretical statements cited in the questionnaire, since there is a chance that they were imputed to him by his enemies. Echoing al-Dhahabi's scruples, al-Qunawi stressed that, even if the attribution is true, one can never be certain of Ibn ʿArabi's continuing adherence to his heretical views up to the moment of his death. In line with this position, al-Qunawi admitted that Ibn ʿArabi's statements, as presented in the questionnaire, fall under the heading of unbelief, yet refused to proclaim him an unbeliever.[98]

Al-Qunawi's qualms made al-Fasi extremely uncomfortable, because they undermined the very foundations of his polemical argument. Therefore, at the close of his *tarjama,* al-Fasi took special pains to refute them, arguing that the blasphemies imputed to Ibn ʿArabi were attested by his own writings. In a similar vein, with Ibn ʿArabi's heresies confirmed by a scholarly *ijmaʿ*, he can no longer be regarded as an infallible individual whose work is liable to an allegorical interpretation. Al-Fasi, therefore, calls on his colleagues to judge him as a common Muslim, in which case he cannot be anyone but a *kafir.* On top of this al-Fasi found no reliable evidence of Ibn ʿArabi's repentance at the end of his life. His own works, on the other hand, amply prove his delusion. Although al-Fasi did concede Ibn ʿArabi's exemplary life-style at the end of his life, he treated it as a deceptive strategy aimed at concealing his heresy. Blinded by Ibn ʿArabi's piety and acts of devotion, his contemporaries ignored the dangerous content of his works. Because of their ignorance of the real essence of his teaching, their statements do not carry much demonstrative weight.[99] Likewise the attempts of Ibn ʿArabi's supporters to interpret his work allegorically should be discarded as prejudiced.[100]

Like his predecessors, al-Fasi seasoned his monotonous list of derogatory opinions of the Greatest Master with anecdotes designed to corroborate his thesis. One of them features Ibn Hajar al-ʿAsqalani as the protagonist. Embroiled in a hot dispute with a loyal partisan of Ibn ʿArabi, Ibn Hajar, so goes the story, got the better of the rival due to his exceptional eloquence and versatility. Enraged by this humiliating defeat, Ibn ʿArabi's supporter threatened to lodge a complaint with the sultan regarding a matter potentially embarrassing to Ibn Hajar. As Ibn Hajar was reluctant to see the temporary ruler involved in a scholarly debate, he suggested that the contenders curse one another so that the erring party be afflicted with a divine punishment.[101] The two men having agreed on this solution, Ibn Hajar solemnly proclaimed that he be damned if Ibn ʿArabi is on the right path. His opponent, on the other hand, called damnation upon himself, should Ibn ʿArabi be an unbeliever. The next day, according to al-Fasi, the contestants meet at a Cairene park after the nightfall. At that very moment, Ibn Hajar's opponent felt "something soft" touch his ankle. In an instant, he lost his eyesight, and remained blind until his death, thereby "proving" Ibn ʿArabi's unbelief beyond doubt.[102]

In a macabre quirk of fate, al-Fasi himself became blind four years before his death,[103] although his blindness probably had nothing to do with the "mutual curse." After all that has been said about his hostility to the Greatest Master, one is surprised to learn that al-Fasi's position on the issue of his orthodoxy/heresy was not free from expediency. His lengthy autobiography clearly shows that al-Fasi maintained close contact with many famous scholars of Rasulid Yemen, some of whom were his *hadith* teachers.[104] As elsewhere, the *ʿulamaʾ* of Yemen were sharply divided over Ibn ʿArabi's legacy.[105] On his frequent visits to Yemen, al-Fasi met both pro- and anti-Ibn ʿArabi scholars and, according to the South Arabian historian Abu (Ba) Makhrama (d. 947/1540),[106] even attempted to mediate between them. Pressed to define his own position, al-Fasi proved surprisingly flexible. While dealing with the leaders of the anti-Ibn ʿArabi faction in Yemen, he showed his eager support for their cause and even presented them with a copy of his condemnatory "biography" (*tarjama*) of the Greatest Master.[107] Yet, on his visit to Zabid, which in that epoch was dominated by a powerful pro-Ibn ʿArabi faction, al-Fasi saw it fit to conceal his antimonistic position and even posed as Ibn ʿArabi's secret admirer. Moreover, if Ba Makhrama is to be trusted, in an attempt to curry favor with the wealthy and influential leader of the Sufi party, al-Mizjaji (d. 829/1425), al-Fasi volunteered to compose a laudatory biography of the Greatest Master, which he later presented to the pro-Ibn ʿArabi scholars. When Ibn al-Muqri (d. 837/1444), then the leader of the anti-Ibn ʿArabi faction in Yemen, asked al-Fasi for the earlier, critical biography, he declined, "out of concern for the Sufis [of Zabid]." However, deep at heart al-Fasi remained hostile to Ibn ʿArabi and his followers.[108] As we shall see, similar opportunistic behavior was demonstrated by many later participants in the polemic.

Ibn ʿArabi Through the Eyes of an Admirer: al-Qari al-Baghdadi's "Al-Durr al-thamin"

As previously stated, al-Fasi's polemical "biography" of the Greatest Master most likely came in response to the apologetic work by the latter's obscure partisan, named ʿAli b. Ibrahim al-Qari al-Baghdadi.[109] Another possible object of al-Fasi's retort may have been an apologetic *fatwa*-cum-biography of the Greatest Master that was composed by the celebrated Arab lexicographer Majd al-din al-Fayruzabadi (d. 817/1415) on the orders of the Rasulid sultan al-Nasir (d. 827/1423).[110] In this case, however, it is hard to explain al-Fasi's contemptuous reference to its author as "one of our contemporaries lacking in intelligence and learning," since al-Fayruzabadi's standing as a foremost philologist and scholar of the age was recognized even by his theological opponents, such as Ibn Hajar al-ʿAsqalani and al-Sakhawi.[111] Hence, it seems more probable that al-Fasi referred to the work of al-Qari al-Baghdadi, whose accomplishments in the field of Islamic sciences were indeed rather modest.[112]

Al-Qari's *Al-Durr al-thamin fi manaqib al-shaykh Muhyi al-din* is a typical example of the *manaqib* literature. It falls into two parts. In the first, the author outlines Ibn ʿArabi's vita (*ahwaluhu*) per se, presenting a highly idealized (and apparently fictitious) physical portrait of the Greatest Master.[113] This is followed by a sketch of his evolution from a godless, profligate youth to an accomplished gnostic whose exalted status was recognized by the greatest Sufi teachers throughout the Maghrib and al-Andalus.[114] Having described Ibn ʿArabi's travels across the Muslim East and the major events of his life,[115] al-Qari furnishes the improbable account of his fabulous funeral that we discussed earlier,[116] stressing the fact that Ibn ʿArabi's tomb became the object of pious visits by his admirers.[117]

The biographical—or, rather, hagiographic—part of al-Qari's work is followed by a summary of the polemic around Ibn ʿArabi with special reference to the three major approaches to his legacy adopted by Muslim scholars. Al-Qari attributes the first approach to Ibn ʿArabi's contemporaries who, as a rule, viewed him in positive light, for example, Fakhr al-din al-Razi, Ibn ʿAbd al-Salam (*sic!*), Shihab al-din ʿUmar al-Suhrawardi, Saʿd al-din Ibn Hamawayh, and Kamal al-din Ibn al-Zamlakani. To these renowned scholars al-Qari adds the biographers of the age who provided complimentary accounts of Ibn ʿArabi's life and work, namely, Ibn ʿAsakir,[118] Ibn al-Najjar, Ibn al-Dubaythi, and al-Qazwini.[119]

In an effort to exonerate Ibn ʿArabi from accusations of heresy, al-Qari spins a polemical discourse whose bias is particularly conspicuous in its fantastic account of the relationship between Ibn ʿArabi and the great Muslim theologian and exegete Fakhr al-din al-Razi (d. 609/1209-1210). Although the two scholars did correspond with each other,[120] there is absolutely no evidence to support al-Qari's claim that Ibn ʿArabi succeeded in converting al-Razi to his mystical weltanschauung.[121]

Al-Qari's selective use of the facts of Ibn ʿArabi's life is particularly conspicuous in his choice of anecdotes for the *Manaqib.* The briefest of looks at al-Qari's discursive strategy reveals his systematic deployment of carefully selected hagiographic topoi aimed at advancing his apologetic thesis. Simultaneously, we find al-Qari making light of, or downright suppressing, the narratives which, in his opinion, might weaken the thrust of his polemic argument. This strategy results in a highly idealized, if not outright fanciful portrait of the Greatest Master that was to have a lasting impact on the subsequent polemical literature.

Typical of al-Qari's attempts to rehabilitate Ibn ʿArabi's reputation is his systematic incorporation of anecdotal evidence from the Sufi's epoch, which finds no independent corroboration in contemporary sources. One example is the story of the unnamed ruler of Seville who set aside an enormous sum of money for the Meccan sanctuary on the condition that it be supervised and distributed by the most illustrious Muslim scholar of the age. In that year, as never

Table 3
Fatwa-deliverers (*muftis*)

Adversaries	Neutral	Advocates
ROUND 1		
Ibn Taymiyya, Hanbali;		[Ibn] al-Zamlakani (d. 727/1327), Shafiʿi;
al-Dhababi, Shafiʿi;		al-Safadi (d. 764/1362), Shafiʿi;
Masʿud al-Harithi (d. 711/1311), Hanbali;		al-Yafiʿi (d. 768/1367), Shafiʿi;
al-Jazari (d. 711/1311), Shafiʿi;		al-Hindi (d. 773/1372), Hanafi;
ʿAli al-Bakri (724/1324), Shafiʿi;		
Ibn Jamaʿa (d. 733/1333), Shafiʿi;		
al-Kattan (d. 738/1338), Shafiʿi;		
al-Zawawi (d. 743/1342), Maliki;		
al-Subki (d. 756/1355), Shafiʿi;		
Ibn al-Naqqash (d. 763/1361), Shafiʿi;		
Ibn al-Muhibb (d. 789/1387), Hanbali;		
	ʿAlaʾ al-din al-Qunawi (727/1327), Shafiʿi;	
ROUND 2		
Ibn al-Khayyat (d. 811/1408), Shafiʿi;		al-Fayruzabadi (d. 817/1415), Shafiʿi;
al-Bulqini (d. 805/1403), Shafiʿi;		
Zayn al-din al-ʿIraqi (d. 806/1403), Shafiʿi;		
	al-Bisati (d. 842/1438), Maliki;	
	al-Bukhari (d. 841/1437), Hanafi; studied with al-Tafatazani;	
		al-Qari al-Baghdadi (d. the 1st half of the 9th/15th centuries), Shafiʿi;
Abu Zurʿa (d. 826/1423), Shafiʿi;		
Ibn Hajar (d. 852/1449), Shafiʿi;		
al-Sakhawi (d. 902/1497), Shafiʿi;		Zakariya al-Ansari (d. 925/1519), Shafiʿi;
al-Biqaʿi (d. 885/1480), Shafiʿi.		Shaʿrani (d. 973/1565), Shafiʿi/Maliki.

before, Mecca attracted a particularly brilliant cohort of *ʿulamaʾ*, who arrived there on the *hajj*. However, when it came to choosing the greatest among them, all unanimously pointed to Ibn ʿArabi, who thus found himself in charge of the donation. Ibn ʿArabi reluctantly granted the wish of his peers, but made it clear that this charity was not for God, but rather for the sake of one's inflated ego. When pressed for an explanation, Ibn ʿArabi replied that he had unraveled the Seville ruler's hidden scheme—to show the Muslims that both the money and its distributer came from his kingdom. Not for a single moment had the king doubted that Ibn ʿArabi would be unanimously selected as the dispenser of his pious donation.[122]

A similar story is adduced by al-Qari to demonstrate Ibn ʿArabi's high status with the leading Damascene scholars of his age. Typically, he overstates Ibn ʿArabi's close ties with the Shafiʿi *qadi* of Damascus, Shams al-din al-Khuwayy (d. 637/1239), who is said to have paid the Greatest Master a weekly stipend of thirty *dirhams*[123] and placed himself completely at the Shaykh's service.[124] It should be pointed out that, while Ibn ʿArabi did indeed make friends with the *qadi,*[125] this could not have possibly been the case with the leader of the Damascene Malikis ʿAbd al-Salam al-Zawawi (d. 681/1282), whom al-Qari also describes as Ibn ʿArabi's "humble servant" and, eventually, father-in-law.[126] In the first place, al-Zawawi assumed the supreme *qadi*ship of the Maliki *madhhab* in 664/1266 (twenty-six solar years after Ibn ʿArabi's death), when it was created for the first time on the orders of Sultan Baybars.[127] Secondly, al-Qari's dating of Ibn ʿArabi's marriage to the *qadi*'s daughter is chronologically tenuous, because al-Zawawi would have to have lived for forty-two more years after the death of his son-in-law.[128]

This and many similar inconsistencies make us question the accuracy of the other "facts" mentioned in al-Qari's apologetic biography of the Greatest Master. It seems logical to suppose that his zealous desire to illustrate Ibn ʿArabi's high repute among the contemporary Syrian scholars made him unscrupulous in his choice of the argumentative means to support his thesis.

This, however, is not to say that al-Qari was wrong on all accounts. As was argued in Chapter 2, evidence from Ibn ʿArabi's epoch does indicate that he faced no organized opposition to his teaching in his lifetime, Ibn ʿAbd al-Salam's inconclusive criticism being something of an exception. The opposition emerged only later, when Ibn ʿArabi's works became accessible to a wider circle of readers many of whom were irritated by the possible implications of his daring insights. In his concerted effort to justify Ibn ʿArabi in the eyes of the Muslims, al-Qari consistently subjected the texts at his disposal to an apologetic censorship. So blatant was his tampering with the earlier assessments of Ibn ʿArabi's life and work that the frustrated editor of al-Qari's text, Salah al-din al-Munajjid, was compelled to provide in the footnotes the original texts of Ibn ʿArabi's biographies that were consistently misquoted in the *Manaqib*. Their cursory comparison reveals an extraordinary amount of subtle and not-so-subtle editing on the part of the apologist motivated by a clear polemical agenda.

Even the doctored evaluations of Ibn ʿArabi, which al-Qari puts in the mouth of authoritative scholars and historians, were not enough to satisfy this champion of the Greatest Master. On more than one occasion he reprimands his predecessors for being unduly restrained or ambiguous in asserting Ibn ʿArabi's orthodoxy:

> Whence then is this restraint after the recognition? Whence is this disavowal after the affirmation?[129]

Predictably, al-Qari comes down hard on Ibn ʿArabi's opponents, although his response to their critique is largely rhetorical—he all but ignores the concrete doctrinal objections to the views of the Greatest Master raised by the antimonistic *ʿulamaʾ*. Consequently, his spirited invectives against Ibn ʿArabi's critics carry little demonstrative weight—a weakness that haunts his entire apologia.

One merit of al-Qari's *Manaqib* is that it has preserved for us the famous *fatwa* in defense of Ibn ʿArabi issued by al-Fayruzabadi. The *fatwa* was requested from the great lexicographer by his patron, the Rasulid Sultan al-Nasir (d. 827/1424), amid a keen controversy over Ibn ʿArabi's legacy that split the scholarly community of 9th/15th-century Yemen into two warring factions. While the events of this controversy are detailed in Chapter 9 of this study, here it suffices to say that the sultan's attachment to Ibn ʿArabi and his Yemeni followers aroused the ire of many local *fuqahaʾ*, who took great pains to dissuade the ruler from supporting the Sufi "heresy." As with their colleagues in Egypt and Syria, the antimonistic party of Yemen resorted to the practice of *fatwa* deliverance (*istiftaʾ*) in hopes of mustering an unequivocal scholarly condemnation of Ibn ʿArabi and his followers. In an effort to counter the campaign against the monistic teaching spearheaded by the influential jurist Abu Bakr Ibn al-Khayyat (d. 811/1408),[130] al-Nasir commissioned al-Fayruzabadi, then the chief *qadi* of Rasulid Yemen, to write an apologetic *fatwa*. As one may expect, al-Qari is in full agreement with al-Fayruzabadi who condemned and ridiculed Ibn al-Khayyat's ban on the study and dissemination of Ibn ʿArabi's writings. For al-Qari, Ibn al-Khayyat's ruling is an "abominable act perpetrated by an unjust person, who did not know what he was talking about." Even though Ibn al-Khayyat opposed some of Ibn ʿArabi's statements, according to al-Qari, he had no right to prohibit others from studying his works on *fiqh, hadith,* Qurʾanic exegesis, and pious sermons, which were fully consistent with the Divine Law. Consequently, al-Qari calls upon his readers to ignore Ibn al-Khayyat's indiscriminate condemnation of Ibn ʿArabi's writings as totally illegitimate and ill-founded. In discouraging the study of the works dealing with the Qurʾan and the *shariʿa* law, Ibn al-Khayyat himself perpetrated a gross injustice to the Islamic religion that made him liable to the accusation of *kufr.*[131]

As a reason for the misgivings about Ibn ʿArabi's orthodoxy expressed by some scholars, al-Qari cites the obscurity of his texts, which elude a ready understanding either through the authoritative tradition (*sunna*) or speculative reasoning (*kalam*). This obscurity, in al-Qari's mind, gave rise to the controversy over Ibn ʿArabi's legacy between the advocates of inspired gnosis and those who relied on either of the two aforementioned sources. In responding to this dilemma, every intelligent person should grant the existence of the subtle mystrical mysteries and absolve the Sufi masters of the accusations of heresy hurled at them by the ignorant scholars who are prone to disparage anything that goes beyond their level of comprehension.[132]

Conclusion

The spread of Ibn ʿArabi's writings in the decades following his death exposed his ideas to a close scrutiny that it had avoided in his lifetime. Many readers learned about Ibn ʿArabi's teaching through the *Fusus al-hikam*—a difficult work characterized by a "great concentration of expression on the one hand, and extremes of exegesis on the other."[133] In this book more than anywhere else Ibn ʿArabi expressed himself in ways that were simply destined to confuse and scandalize the religious establishment. In provoking the heated debates over its meaning, this book soon became an embodiment of monistic thought against which its antagonists tended to direct their invectives, all but ignoring Ibn ʿArabi's other works.

Starting with Ibn Taymiyya, the *Fusus* came to be perceived by many *ʿulamaʾ* as a direct challenge to the conventions of the Islamic faith—a doctrinal time bomb that was bound to rip through the tissue of Muslim communal life. It is therefore only natural that theological propositions culled from the *Fusus* became the principal targets of several anti-Ibn ʿArabi campaigns throughout the 8th/14th-9th/15th centuries. In a drive to make their condemnation of the Greatest Master official and binding, his opponents strived to assemble the greatest possible number of negative judgments of Ibn ʿArabi from the leading scholars of the Muslim community. As we have seen, the tendentious procedures by which the propositions were selected for the questionnaire made his indictment a foregone conclusion. Yet, the validity of the *ijmaʿ* reached in the course of these campaigns was continually challenged by Ibn ʿArabi's partisans, fueling further controversy and advancing discursive elaboration.

In the polemical biographies of the Greatest Master by al-Fasi and al-Qari we find a singular hybridization of the biographical and polemical genres that became a hallmark of the Ibn ʿArabi debate in the subsequent centuries. The absence of opposition to Ibn ʿArabi in his lifetime was readily exploited by his supporters, who interpreted it as recognition of his orthodoxy by his learned contemporaries. This theme surfaces in most apologies for the Greatest Master written in that epoch, including al-Qari's *Manaqib.* Like its counterpart by al-Fasi, al-Qari's "biography" of Ibn ʿArabi displays all the typical characteristics of a polemical treatise. Both works intricately combine elements of the biographical genre with underlying polemical concerns.[134]

While it is true that the majority of Ibn ʿArabi's denouncers came from the circle of *ʿulama*ʾ associated with Ibn Taymiyya, hostility to the Sufi master transcended juridical *madhhabs* or theological affiliations: Ibn ʿArabi's monistic views were condemned equally by Muslim scholars who belonged to different and, sometimes, rival factions. Thus we see Ibn ʿArabi condemned by eminent Hanbalis as well as by their perennial opponents, the Ashʿari theologians of the Shafiʿi *madhhab.* The same goes for his defenders, who also formed a potpourri of legal schools and doctrinal allegiances.

The condemnation of Ibn ʿArabi in several *fatwa* campaigns failed to preclude Muslim intellectuals from studying and disseminating his works. In fact, these campaigns had the opposite effect: they placed Ibn ʿArabi in the scholarly spotlight, generating a host of complicated theological and ethical problems for his denouncers. Starting with al-Dhahabi's inconclusive assessment of Ibn ʿArabi's status vis-à-vis the *shariʿa*, the atmosphere of indecisiveness came to pervade the theological and biographical literature devoted to his legacy. Between the two opposing attitudes to the Greatest Master there gradually emerged an intermediary position that called for suspension of judgment (*tawaqquf*) and prudent abstention from either summary condemnation or blind support of his views. As with al-Hallaj, this position became the refuge of the neutral scholars who were anxious to stay away from the fray.

6

THE METAPHYSICAL ARGUMENT REVISITED: AL-TAFTAZANI

Historical and Intellectual Background

> When my thought dives into the
> sea of reasoning, then emerges with
> the pearl of a clue to a difficult puzzle,
> I look down upon kings, who
> about their rich booty brag,
> For [unlike them] I have obtained my fortune
> by books, not by battalions.
>
> Al-Taftazani. *Sharh al-maqasid,* vol. 1, p. 146

The stage for the next episode in the Ibn ʿArabi debate is set on the eastern fringe of Islamdom. It is here, in Khorasan and Khorezm, which in the second half of the 8th/14th centuries were overrun by the Turkic warlord Timur (d. 807/1405), that we find another influential critic of the Greatest Master, al-Taftazani. Before discussing his attack on Ibn ʿArabi's legacy, a word should be said about the times in which he lived and his background.

Timur's rise to power and ensuing conquest are generally seen by Western investigators as a revival, at a new historical stage, of the pagan Mongol tradition, albeit one diluted with the values of a settled Islamic civilization.[1] Timur's allegiance to Islam seems to have been profound and sincere. Yet, as with other ambitious rulers, it often was subordinate to his overriding political goal that was inspired in him by the idea of universal nomadic domination.[2] Emblematic of Timur's divided loyalties was his dual claim to Chingizid connection on the one hand and ʿAlid descent on the other.[3]

Apart from the military successes achieved at a horrendous cost,[4] Timur was famous for his singular interest in such diverse branches of knowledge as theology, medicine, geography, astronomy, and occultism. Timur's favorite subject, however, was history—a science that he viewed as essential to any successful ruler.[5] The noted Arab man of letters Ahmad b. ʿArabshah (d. 854/1450), an observer generally hostile to Timur, gives the following description of his preoccupation with historical science:[6]

> Whether travelling or at rest, he was assiduous in listening to the reading of chronicles, the stories of prophets—prayers and peace on them—the deeds of kings, and the accounts of men of the past, all in Persian. All these readings were repeated to him and their measures resounded in his ears. He so grasped and retained their substance that if a reader stumbled he would correct him—even a jackass learns from repetition!

In his religious attitude, Timur blended strict Sunnism with a pro-ʿAlid sentiment, which was not unusual for the eastern Muslims of that epoch.[7] He was also influenced by the shamanistic and animistic beliefs current in the nomadic milieu from which he rose to prominence.[8] Like many Mongol rulers before him, Timur, who was "much more familiar with the sword than with the pen,"[9] had high regard for men of religion, both *ʿulamaʾ* and Sufi dervishes. From his military expeditions he often brought renowned scholars and litterateurs back to Samarqand[10] to add to the splendor of his royal court.[11] Toward the end of his career, Timur counted among his retinue the leading Muslim scholars of the age, whom he consulted on various legal and religious issues.

Timur had a special liking for theological debates, in which he used to take an active part, arguing, in Ibn Khaldun's phrase, about what he knew and also about what he did not know.[12] The ruler's acute interest in such theological debates caused him to attract to his residence in Samarqand the most outstanding scholars and polemicists of the epoch.[13] Among them was Saʿd al-din al-Taftazani (d. 792/1390 or 791/1389).

Al-Taftazani was born in 722/1322 at Taftazan, a village located in the proximity of Nasa, a midsize town in Khorasan.[14] He left Taftazan at a very early age in search of knowledgeable instructors and traveled as far northeast as the Golden Horde. Among al-Taftazani's numerous teachers, of special importance was ʿAdud al-din al-Iji (d. 756/1355)—undoubtedly the greatest speculative theologian (*mutakallim*) of the epoch. It was primarily through him that al-Taftazani absorbed the long tradition of learning in Iranian Islam that combined Muʿtazili and Ashaʿri *kalam* with peripatetic logic and philosophy.[15]

Although, one anecdote portrays al-Taftazani as the most slow-witted of al-Iji's students, who was able to improve his academic performance only after a miraculous intervention of the Prophet,[16] this is probably but a legend designed to underscore his achievements later on. Actually, al-Taftazani wrote his first study of Arabic grammar—which received high acclaim from established scholars—when he was just sixteen years of age.[17]

To satisfy his craving for knowledge, al-Taftazani had to rely on the support of royal patrons, first at the Chagatayid courts of Central Asia, then among the Timurid warlords of Iran and Transoxania. His constant quest for wealthy patrons explains in part his long and presumably dangerous journeys across Iran and Central Asia. The geography of these journeys is reflected in the colophons of al-Taftazani's writings on grammar, rhetoric, logic, metaphysics, principles of jurisprudence, exegesis, and philology.[18] We find him in Samarqand, Damascus, Gurganj, Herat, Ghujuwan, and, finally, in Kalistan—an obscure town in Turkestan. In Khorezm, the major center of Islamic learning in Central Asia, al-Taftazani enjoyed the patronage of the ruling Chingizid family. To one of its princes, Mahmud Jani Beg of the Golden Horde, he dedicated his celebrated compendium on rhetoric, *Mukhtasar al-maʿani.*[19] During his stay in Fars, a prosperous province in south west Iran, in 779/1377-1378, al-Taftazani, by then an acclaimed scholar, is said to have commended his young colleague and future rival, al-Sayyid al-Sharif al-Jurjani (d. 816/1413), to the ruler of Shiraz Shah Shujaʿ.[20]

When Timur conquered Khorezm (780-781/1379), al-Taftazani was brought to his attention as an outstanding scholar, whereupon the ruler assigned him to a prestigious religious post in Sarakhs. Soon afterward, al-Taftazani was invited to Timur's court in Samarqand. As al-Taftazani was enjoying the amenities of Timur's capital, the latter's army invaded Fars and seized Shiraz. Among the human booty taken there was al-Taftazani's protégé, al-Jurjani, who was also shipped to Samarqand by the prestige-seeking ruler and joined his suite.

The two scholars, so goes the story, soon became embroiled in a protracted debate, in the course of which they furiously attacked each other's theological positions. Timur encouraged their constant rivalry, until he finally ordered them to settle the score in a public dispute.[21] As arbitrator he appointed the Muʿtazili scholar Nuʿman al-din al-Khwarizmi, who after long hesitation gave preference to the scholastic position advocated by al-Jurjani. Legend has it that on the strength of the arbitrator's judgment Timur proclaimed al-Jurjani the victor. He, however, qualified his decision by adding that even though both scholars were almost equal in terms of their knowledge of Islamic theology, al-Jurjani still had an edge over his rival as a descendant of the Prophet's family. According to the same legend, al-Taftazani was so humiliated by Timur's decision that he returned to Sarakhs and soon died of chagrin.[22] The bitter theological controversy started by the two scholars, was continued after their demise by their partisans, who came to be known as the Taftazanis and the Jurjanis.[23]

In the history of Islamic theology, al-Taftazani stands out as a man of broad intellectual interests who mastered a wide variety of scholarly subjects. His approach to the Islamic tradition was, in the words of a modern Muslim researcher, "marked with open-mindedness which seems to be rooted in his intellectual integrity."[24] Both Muslim and Western investigators have viewed al-Taftazani as a typical representative of the later Islamic fusion of the scriptural sciences, theological speculation, *falsafa,* metaphysics, and logic.[25] Due to the multiplicity of his intellectual interests, al-Taftazani is sometimes described as a philosopher-theologian type of Muslim thinker, "whose work was as much Falsafa as Kalam."[26] Nevertheless, until now al-Taftazani's rich intellectual legacy has been treated by the students of his thought as thoroughly epigonic, devoid of creative spirit, and one that contained "hardly anything original."[27] His was "an age [when intellectuals] wrote commentaries on earlier works,"[28] and al-Taftazani does not seem to have deviated from this general tendency that some European Islamicists tend to dismiss as a dispirited "recycling" of earlier ideas and theologemes. Seen from this standpoint, al-Taftazani's writings, though undoubtedly more succinct and lucid than the works of his contemporaries, indeed appear thoroughly traditional, demonstrating his tenacious commitment to the theological tradition exemplified by such seminal figures as Abu Hanifa, al-Ashʿari, al-Maturidi, al-Juwayni, al-Ghazali, al-Shahrastani, al-Razi, Nasir al-din al-Tusi, and al-Iji.[29]

Al-Taftazani's proclivity for orderly logical thinking helped him to clearly formulate even the most abstruse ideas of his predecessors. His lucidity made him popular with diverse audiences from beginners to experienced masters, many of whom used his works as textbooks and manuals. They were copied and circulated widely throughout the world of Islam, not just in its eastern part, where he left many direct disciples and followers.[30] An authoritative testimony to his widespread acceptance is borne by the following passage from Ibn Khaldun's "Prolegomenon" (*al-Muqaddima*):

> I found in Egypt numerous works on the rational sciences composed by the well-known scholar Saʿd al-din al-Taftazani, a native of Harat—a village [*sic*] in Khurasan. Some of them are on the *kalam* and the foundations of *fiqh* and rhetoric. They show that he had a profound knowledge of these sciences. Their contents demonstrate that he was well versed in the philosophical sciences and far advanced in the rest of the sciences which deal with Reason.[31]

In a similar vein, a contemporary Western scholar observes that already "by the time of his [al-Taftazani's] death or very shortly afterwards he was being studied and appreciated as a scholar in Cairo, which was in those days some months distant from the regions of Khorezm and Samarqand, where he taught and wrote."[32] With time, al-Taftazani's prestige not only did not diminish but grew rapidly: he came to be seen as a grand master of *kalam,* jurisprudence, rhetoric, and logic, and as "a potent (and controversial) inspirer of the philosophers who followed him."[33]

Those Islamicists who have described al-Taftazani as "in no sense an original writer,"[34] overlook at least one innovative aspect of his work. It lies not so much in the subjects he studied as in his overall theological position, which vacillated subtly between Ashʿari *kalam* and the Hanafi school of theology, which as we now know, was quite distinct from the strict Ashʿarism of the central lands of Islam.[35] Thus al-Taftazani contributed in significant ways to a final articulation of the principal tenets of Hanafi scholasticism named after al-Maturidi—a relatively obscure contemporary of al-Ashʿari (d. 324/935), who had been largely neglected by *ʿulamaʾ* prior to al-Taftazani. In bringing al-Maturidi out of obscurity as a cofounder (together with al-Ashʿari) of Sunni *kalam,* al-Taftazani placed Hanafi theology on an equal footing with the Shafiʿi-based Ashʿarism of Iraq and Syria.[36]

Although originally a bona fide Ashʿari scholar, al-Taftazani spent most of his life in the Hanafi intellectual environment which, as mentioned, was anxious to assert its distinct identity by advancing the Maturidian version of *kalam.* Consequently, he adopted a few distinctly non-Ashʿari views, especially those relating to the *qadar* versus *jabr* issue,[37] which have been a hallmark of the Maturidi theology ever since. Al-Taftazani's loyalty to the eastern school of speculative theology is epitomized in his commentary on the popular Hanafi creed by Najm al-din Abu Hafs al-Nasafi (d. 537/1142), *Sharh al-ʿaqaʾid al-nasafiyya*, which was to become one of the "chief textbooks of theology" in Islamic religious colleges of Central Asia and Iran.[38]

In the *Sharh,* al-Taftazani's divided loyalties are to the fore in his efforts to mitigate the differences between the Ashʿaris and the Maturidis, "sometimes taking one side and again the other."[39] His syncretic approach to Islamic theology is mirrored in his refusal to commit himself wholly to any particular school of Islamic law[40]—a feature that he, incidentally, shared with the Greatest Master. Given al-Taftazani's inclusive and broad-minded approach to religious issues, it is particularly interesting to examine the reasons for his implacable hostility to the monistic Sufism of the Ibn ʿArabi school, which, as we have seen, was influenced by Ashʿari and Muʿtazili ideas.[41]

Despite his vast expertise in various sciences, al-Taftazani placed *kalam* above them all. For him, *kalam* was the most noble pursuit and the ultimate goal of one's intellectual progress.[42] He sees the critical advantage of *kalam* over other disciplines in its subject matter—the general notions and concepts that make possible man's understanding of God and the universe. The task of *kalam,* according to al-Taftazani, is

> To examine the states[43] of the Maker, such as His eternity, oneness, power, will, and so forth. [It also studies] the states of body and its accidents, such as origination in time, the need [for a substantiator], the composite nature, the acceptance of corruption and the like—that is, the notions which form the Muslim doctrine or are implicitly alluded to in it.[44]

Kalam, in al-Taftazani's judgment, is

> beneficial for this world insofar as it regulates the life [of humans] by preserving justice and proper conduct, both of which are essential for the survival of this species[45] in ways that do not result in corruption. Equally [it is beneficial for] the hereafter in that it helps assure salvation from the painful punishment stemming from unbelief and delusion.[46]

Al-Taftazani's Refutation of Ibn ʿArabi

From the passages that were just quoted, al-Taftazani emerges as an outspoken champion of rationalist theology. His attitude toward Sufism is more difficult to assess, because, to my knowledge, he did not discuss it specifically in any of his major works. This is not to imply that he was unaware of, or indifferent to, Sufism's fundamental tenets. In contrast to al-Nasafi, who, like many Hanafi *ʿulamaʾ*, hued closely to the Muʿtazili *kalam*[47] and therefore denied the Sufi claims to inspired knowledge (*ilham*), al-Taftazani agreed with al-Ghazali and Ashʿaris that "in the way of the mystic there is perfection of belief and absolute knowledge."[48]

Al-Taftazani's sympathy for Sufism had its limits, however. He, for instance, flatly denied what he considered to be its "extreme" manifestations, especially the claims by some Sufis to have attained the knowledge of the unseen (*ghayb*), which the Ashʿaris regarded as God's exclusive prerogative. He, however, did not write off their accounts of their experiences as mere fantasy and delusion. What he did argue was that such subjective experiences could not serve as sound theological premises. In other words, mystical experience, as seen by al-Taftazani, has no epistemological or argumentative value at all. On the contrary, accounts of mystical insights by individual mystics often contradict the truths obtained through rational thinking or empirical observation.[49]

Al-Taftazani's overall attitude toward Islamic mysticism was nuanced. Like Ibn Taymiyya before him, al-Taftazani was careful to separate what he considered "sound" elements of Sufi theory and practice from what, in his mind, were "pernicious" elements resulting from inadequate reasoning or perception. Simultaneously, he put his stamp of approval to Sufi moral discipline with its emphasis on spiritual and bodily purification. In view of his strong opposition to the Sufi metaphysics, which he considered to be irreconcilable with the Ashʿari doctrine, al-Taftazani criticized Ibn ʿArabi primarily as an erring philosopher, who was deluded by his undisciplined imagination into adopting his personal insights as the foundation of a cosmological teaching.

On this and other points, al-Taftazani's criticism of Ibn ʿArabi's theory displays many parallels with the antimonistic discourse first articulated by Ibn Taymiyya. As his Hanbali predecessor, he also limited his criticism to the *Fusus,* paying little heed to the rest of Ibn ʿArabi's rich legacy.

Al-Taftazani's polemical agenda is conveniently captured in a poetic epigraph to his "Epistle on the Unity of Being":[50]

> The book called *Fusus* leads astray all men
>
> It is the rust upon the hearts[51] and the
>
> direct opposite of wisdom.

Once you start to blame it
The sea itself will rush to your help, flowing
and spilling over.
The plants of the earth that were dying of thirst
Will all drink abundantly as soon as you take the pen
in your hand.
[In return for your effort] you will be granted the
longest life ever lived by those before and
after.
Were you to lay on it only a tithe of the blame it
deserves,
Nay, a tithe of the tithe, there still would be
no blame on you![52]

In explaining the reasons for his condemnation of Ibn ʿArabi, al-Taftazani presented himself as a spokesman on behalf of the leading scholars of the Muslim community, especially his master, ʿAdud al-din al-Iji, who had advised his students not to learn about Mecca from the book[53] of "that Maghribi of the dry temperament" (*yabis al-mizaj*), who "apart from being an infidel was also a hashish-eater."[54] That al-Taftazani's description of his master's position was accurate is evident from the fact that elsewhere al-Iji indeed spoke of three types of "unificationism" and "incarnationism" professed respectively by the Christians, the Nusayris,[55] and the "extremist" Sufis, whom he described as "fumbling" (*mukhtabit*) between the former two. Within the latter type, al-Iji singled out "the Sufi monists," who, in an attempt to overcome all duplicity, deny that there was anything in existence save God alone. Al-Iji's negative view of monistic Sufis is further supported by his other disciple, al-Jurjani, whose fateful rivalry with al-Taftazani was just described. Despite their enmity to one another, both scholars seem to have concurred with their teacher in opposing the *wujudi* Sufis (*al-sufiyya al-wujudiyya*).[56] In short, al-Taftazani was just one of many critics of the Greatest Master and his followers in eastern Iran and Transoxania.

By way of ad hominem criticism, al-Taftazani made capital out of the theme of Ibn ʿArabi's drug addiction, suggested to him by al-Iji. In elaborating on al-Iji's allegation, he cited the introduction to the *Fusus* in which, as we remember, Ibn ʿArabi claimed to have written this controversial book on the Prophet's orders.[57] For al-Taftazani, this story was a typical product of Ibn ʿArabi's drug addiction and concomitant inability to separate fantasy from reality. Further pondering on this passage, al-Taftazani wondered whether, six hundred years after the Prophet's death, he could possibly have ordered Ibn ʿArabi "to promulgate that which was bound to ruin his [Prophet's] community for the sake of which he had struggled for twenty three years? . . ."[58]

Al-Taftazani imputed to Ibn ʿArabi and his partisans, whom he described as " the philosophizing unbelievers and heretics [adhering to] the unity of being" (*al-kafara al-zanadiqa al-wujudiyya al-mutafalsifa*), the following erroneous propositions:

—holding that everything in this world, including the most contemptible substances and creatures, is God;

—maintaining that God has no existence *in concreto,* which is the same as denying God as such;

—identifying divine existence with that of his creatures, and postulating, contrary to reason and sensory perceptions, that the world of multiplicity is but a figment of the imagination;

—assuming that the subjective experience of all-encompassing unity claimed by some Sufi visionaries is a mirror reflection of the actual state of affairs in the empirical universe;

—claiming for themselves a rank equal or higher to that of the prophets, which amounts to nullifying the mission of the Prophet of Islam;[59]

—practicing an allegorical interpretation of the Qurʾanic text in order to disguise or legitimize heretical beliefs.[60]

As we can see, most of the items on this list resonate with those brought up by Ibn ʿArabi's earlier critics starting with Ibn Taymiyya. To avoid repetition, I will focus on those points that were peculiar to al-Taftazani's polemical discourse. Of these, his insistence that mystical experience does not correspond to the way things are "in their essences" (*fi aʿyan*) merits special scrutiny.

As with most speculative theologians of an Ashʿari slant, al-Taftazani recognized the legitimacy of the inner quest for truth pursued by mystics (*ahl al-maʿrifa*).[61] The latter, according to al-Taftazani, may occasionally reach a state of mystical ecstasy in which they lose sight of everything save God. While in this state, they totally shut out the multiplicity of the empirical world and contemplate nothing but God's unfathomable Oneness. Such a unitive vision tends to completely absorb and overwhelm the mystic, a sensation that al-Taftazani likened to the experience of those who watch the light of the rising sun obscure the moon and the stars. Mystics call this visionary experience "absolute unity" (*al-wahda al-mutlaqa*), or "passing away from the self in [the contemplation of] divine unity" (*fanaʾ fi ʾl-tawhid*), in which the mystical witness is totally detached from anything other than the Deity. The unitive vision, in al-Taftazani's view, induces a state of mystical intoxication that renders its possessor oblivious to the surrounding world that he begins to treat as sheer illusion. Al-Taftazani conceded that mystical knowledge, attained via an irresistible emotional "attraction" to the Divine (*jadhba ilahiyya*), may indeed elude rational comprehension. Moreover, since this attraction is granted by God to the elect few, it can neither contradict nor invalidate the Qurʾanic dispensation. Nor can its possessors be absolved from the entailments of the divine law and religious obligations.

This said, al-Taftazani strongly protested that mystical intoxication, divine attraction, or unitive vision should mean that the cosmos is indeed identical with God. One proof of this is the obvious fact that, though the rising sun may overshadow the stars, they continue to exist as an objective reality. Put differently, the sun is not the single existent body in the empirical cosmos.[62]

Unitive visions and ecstatic experiences, which al-Taftazani dubbed the "*tawhid* of the gnostics," are, in his view, bestowed upon those Sufis who have attained the highest degree of self-perfection and have become God's intimate friends. Al-Taftazani, however, warned that their privileged position vis-à-vis God does not exempt them from the religious obligations incumbent upon every Muslim.[63]

According to al-Taftazani, "the Sufi espousers of the unity of being" (*al-wujudiyya al-mutasawwifa*), unlike their orthodox predecessors who never ventured into metaphysical speculations, insist that their subjective experiences mirror the real state of affairs in the universe. Hence their assertion that "the existence of originated things is identical with that of God Most High" and that "all [things] are nothing but God and there is neither a prophet or a messenger: neither the sender, nor one who was sent."[64] Based on this flawed metaphysical assumption, the *wujudiyya* make light of the prophetic mission of Muhammad and consider the *shariʿa* to be a transient dispensation that is to be superseded by universal sainthood. Moreover, according to al-Taftazani, some of the *wujudiyya* go so far as to proclaim themselves walking-talking manifestations of God, thereby withdrawing themselves from religious ordinances or social norms.

Turning to the principal objective of his critique—the monistic metaphysics of the Greatest Master, al-Taftazani declared the latter to be a deluded mystic, whose disorderly visions and ravings, were instilled in him by his addiction to hashish. Basing himself on his unruly imagination, Ibn ʿArabi developed a preposterous metaphysical doctrine that presents God and His creatures as two interdependent faces of a single reality. Another one of Ibn ʿArabi's "delusions" pointed out by al-Taftazani is his claim to have discovered the key to the inward meaning of the Qurʾanic revelation. By making this claim, Ibn ʿArabi, in al-Taftazani's view, placed himself above the Prophet, effectively reducing the latter to a mere exponent of its "outward" dimension, which is confined to the ignorant populace.

According to al-Taftazani, the principal danger of the *wujudiyya* for the community of Islam lies in their tendency to disguise themselves as Sufis and to couch their tenets in the terminology borrowed from the "authentic" Sufi tradition. Yet, their usage of the traditional Sufi terms is a far cry from that current among the "true" Sufis. As an example, al-Taftazani cited such terms as "absolute oneness" (*wahda mutlaqa*) and "passing away from one's self" (*fanaʾ*), which the *wujudiyya* apply to the objective reality around them rather than to their subjective visionary experiences. The same is true of such Sufi terms as "bringing together" (*jamʿ*) and "discrimination" (*tafriqa*), which, in al-Taftazani's view, have nothing to do with the state of affairs in the universe as a whole.[65] In summarizing his position on the *wujudiyya,* al-Taftazani wrote:

> You know well that all this is but heresy, atheism, and forsaking the Islamic religion. This is certainly not what the [true] Sufis meant by these and similar terms. We are dealing here with a teaching based on the law of expediency (*qanun al-sadad*), according to which, as you might have heard, there are no such things as heresy, nihilism, incarnation, and unification. This law makes [divine existence] identical with the existence of His contingent creatures, no matter how impure, and proclaims the existence of individual contingent things to be a pure illusion. Such propositions make a

> laughingstock of the *shariʿa*, for they disregard the explicit meaning of the true religious creed and proclaim the essences of all existent things to be non-existent. Moreover, they contradict the self-evident truths obtained through common reasoning. . . . What the [real] Sufi gnostics have in mind is that anything that is at odds with the *shariʿa* is but heresy, and that the secrets of mystical knowledge contain nothing that contravenes the external meaning of the Divine Law (*sharʿ*).[66]

In elaborating on the theme of the *wujudi* abuse of the conventional Sufi concepts, al-Taftazani turned to the notion of divine effusion, or emanation (*fayd; ifada*), in Ibn ʿArabi's metaphysics.[67] On the face of it, suggested al-Taftazani, this concept fits in well with al-Ghazali's theory that describes the process of creation as a "spilling over" of necessary existence from the source of divine munificence (*jud*) onto all receptive quiddities (*mahiyyat qabila*). However, unlike al-Ghazali who considered emanation to be a result of God's arbitrary will, Ibn ʿArabi described it as an obligation incumbent upon God, which allows him to manifest himself in concrete empirical essences. Al-Ghazali likens *fayd* to the fall of the sunrays (i.e., existence) upon the surface of the earth, which neither diminishes the body (*jarm*) of the Sun nor adds anything to the earth's surface. Furthermore, in al-Ghazali's theory, the relation between the beginning and the outcome of this process is that of causality (*sababiyya*) and not that of instrumentality, for the latter would inevitably compromise the notion of divine transcendence.

Although Ibn ʿArabi and the *wujudiyya* also use the concept of *fayd* they liken it to the spilling of water from a vessel upon somebody's hands. This image, according to al-Taftazani, unequivocally implies a separation of the substance of the effusion (=water) from its source and its subsequent contact with material receptacles (=hands). In this scheme, Absolute Existence is seen as multiplying itself according to the number of receptacles—a far cry from al-Ghazali's insistence that the multiplicity of causal relationships between the necessary Being and the individual empirical beings should not be taken to mean a union of essence.[68]

In al-Taftazani's view, the outward similarity between the al-Ghazalian metaphysics and that of the *wujudiyya* conceals the true implications of their teaching from their fellow Muslims, who are prone to mistake *wahdat al-wujud* for an unalloyed expression of primeval Sufism. Had they contemplated the matter more thoroughly, argued al-Taftazani, they would have discovered that al-Ghazali describes the divine effusion as a *bestowal* of existence on material receptacles, in contrast to the *wujudiyya* who claim that divine existence actually *pervades* the things and phenomena of the cosmos. In other words, the *wujudiyya* see Absolute Existence as identical with the transcendent divine essence on the one hand and with the existence of concrete creatury things on the other. Admitting this entails the following logical absurdities, which, in al-Taftazani's view, abound in Ibn ʿArabi's *Fusus:*

—the Qurʾanic idolaters worship no one but God;

—anyone claiming lordship is justified in his claim;

—the multiplicity of empirical things does not mean the multiplicity of their individual existences, but rather the plurality of relations and entifications (*taʿayyunat*) within the unique existence of God;[69]

—there is nothing in the empirical world except Absolute Existence and all individual empirical entities are but an illusion;

—in this life and in the Hereafter there will be neither a punishment for the sinners nor a reward for the righteous; all that exists is good and nothing is evil, hence there is neither a hell, nor a Judgment Day.[70]

According to al-Taftazani, as thoroughgoing heretics, the *wujudiyya* are unlikely to accept any argument based on the Scriptures, on transmitted texts, or on established religious authorities. Therefore, he reduced references to these sources to a bare minimum, relying instead on "rational demonstration and irrefutable logical proofs," in the way one would debate the Christians or Jews.[71] In practice, however, al-Taftazani did not always stick to his stated principle. When he felt his arsenal of syllogistic arguments was exhausted, he eagerly availed himself of the authority of the Qurʾan and the Sunna.[72] This may be interpreted as a sign of his inability to remain within the confines of a purely rational discourse, or, alternatively, his approach signals an attempt to maintain a precarious balance between faith and reason.

The Metaphysical Argument

Al-Taftazani's attack on the *wujudi* metaphysics opens with a discussion of the immutable essences (*aʿyan thabita*), which, as mentioned in Chapter 3, are the primordial images of empirical things eternally fixed in the divine knowledge. Al-Taftazani took exception to the *wujudi* treatment of both the *aʿyan thabita* and their empirical counterparts as "an illusion, a mirage that has no reality whatsoever" (*la haqiqa laha*).[73] He dismissed this idea as "a manifest sophism that is in conflict with both the senses and elementary rational reasoning."[74] The actual existence of the empirical things, in his opinion, is proven beyond doubt by empirical observation. As for the *aʿyan thabita,* if one agrees with the *wujudiyya* that they are "fixed" in the knowledge of God and that "His knowledge serves as a repository (*zarf*) for the noetic existence of the essences destined to become concrete things," one ends with a logical contradiction. For, argued al-Taftazani, "knowledge, being itself an [abstract] attribute, cannot serve as a repository for a mental construct."

Were the *wujudiyya* to restate their position to mean that divine knowledge attaches itself exclusively to the noetic entities, while having no relationship to their subsequent existence *in concreto,* it would necessarily follow that God's primordial knowledge of a thing is different from the thing's actual status in the empirical world—a proposition that al-Taftazani dismissed as absurd on logical grounds alone.

In approaching the *wujudi* ontology from a different angle, al-Taftazani focused on the concept of "entification," or "particularization" (*taʿayyun*) which was widely used by monistic thinkers.[75] In his view, entification can happen only to existent things in their actual, or empirical, state (*mawjudat kharijiyya*). Hence, entification itself is the concrete attribute of an empirical thing, although it may also exist as a mental abstract. Ergo, the *wujudiyya* implicitly admit that objects of divine knowledge *can,* under certain circumstances, exist in the empirical world *in concreto.* But here they run into an obvious absurdity, for they have just acknowledged that divine ideas can never acquire the status of "external" entities.[76]

Objectively speaking, al-Taftazani's criticism is leveled not so much at Ibn ʿArabi, who, characteristically, had never developed a clearly defined philosophical concept of *aʿyan thabita,* but rather at his later rationalist interpreters who gave it its final shape.[77] This al-Taftazani implicitly admitted, by quoting an interpretation of the first Qurʾanic *sura* by Sadr al-din al-Qunawi, rather than a passage from Ibn ʿArabi's own works.[78] To demonstrate that al-Taftazani's critical arrows are directed at Ibn ʿArabi as much as at his followers, it is necessary to recapitulate the major metaphysical issues addressed in his critique of the *wujudiyya.*

First, al-Taftazani denounced the *wujudi* thinkers for holding that Absolute Existence is a unique individual entity (*wahid shakhsi*) which can, therefore, assume existence *in concreto.* He found this idea preposterous, because it posits existence to be "an intelligible abstract of the second degree"—that is, one generated by the human mind through the process of abstraction (*taʿaqqul*). Consequently, like the other *intelligibilia,*[79] existence cannot take place outside the human mind—a proposition that compels the *wujudiyya* to admit that existence can only be abstracted by the intelligence from a totality of individual existents in the phenomenal world. Hence, in and of itself existence is not independent but contingent.

Second, al-Taftazani considered the *wujudiyya* to be guilty of positing that Absolute Existence—which they have already wrongly described as a concrete individual entity—is present in all of the empirical loci in which it occurs (*takarrar*) or manifests itself. And yet, in the same breath, they deny that Absolute Existence can either intermingle with or inhere in these loci. The result is the impossible situation in which Absolute Existence, in al-Taftazani's phrase, "multiplies in the eyes of observers, whilst remaining one and undivided in and of itself."[80]

This assumption, argued al-Taftazani, simply cannot be true: if one thing permeates (or occurs in) the other, the former inevitably breaks up into a multiplicity of individual entities. And yet, regardless of whether the *wujudiyya* envision Absolute Existence as a unique individual entity or as a necessary existent, they are adamant in denying that it is subject to either division or particularization, since this assumption would inevitably divest Absolute Existence of its absolute and necessary status by reducing it to a sum of concrete empirical entities. However, in accordance with the laws of logic, as al-Taftazani saw them, an individual entity can never appear, occur, or inhere in other things without intermingling with them. Nor can it multiply without simultaneously being split into a plurality of individual entities. Hence, the essence of Absolute and Necessary Existence can never identify with the individual concrete things it generates through emanation.

Third, by maintaining that the relationship of Absolute Existence to its concrete empirical manifestations does not involve its partition but rather its "attribution" (*idafa*) to them, the *wujudiyya* are still unable to save the day. For, in al-Taftazani's judgment, attributing one thing to the other, even when grammatically possible,[81] does not automatically mean that the things in question are bound by causality. Thus, in language, attributing a horse or money to Zayd does not imply that Zayd is derived from the horse or money and vice versa. If so, the *wujudi* insistence that the relationship between

Absolute Existence and individual existent things is attributive in nature inevitably nullifies their thesis that all individual things take their origin in Absolute Existence.[82]

Fourth, the *wujudi* concept that the word "existence" is a sign (*ʿalam*) pointing to the essence of the Necessary Existent Being, in the same way as the divine epithet "majesty" (*jalala*) points to the divine essence, is untenable either. Since "majesty," according to al-Taftazani, can have only one referent—the Divine Godhead, it disallows any duplicity or plurality, while "existence," on the contrary, is shared by an infinite multiplicity of empirical referents in the created world. Ergo, "existence,"—unlike "majesty," which presupposes uniqueness both linguistically and theologically (*lughatan wa sharʿan*)—designates an attribute *pertaining to* the essence, but not the essence itself. For this reason, existence per se cannot be conceived as being identical with the unique and undivided divine essence, because this would imply the plurality of the latter. In sum, concluded al-Taftazani, existence is nothing but a general idea (*maʿna kulli*) which pertains to a multitude of concrete existent things and multiplies in keeping with the number of the entities it describes. Thereby, in al-Taftazani's view, the metaphysical assumptions of the *wujudiyya* are proven false.[83]

Fifth, even if we grant together with the *wujudiyya* that Absolute Existence is identical with the existence of all originated individual beings, we shall arrive at yet another absurdity. For this would logically mean that Absolute Existence cannot influence empirical things, since a thing cannot exert influence on itself. Hence we admit that God, as Absolute Existence, has no commanding influence over the quiddities (*mahiyyat*) of originated things. This conclusion, according to al-Taftazani, is what Muslim philosophers and philosophizing Sufis mean when they maintain that the quiddities of things are not "made" (*majʿula*) the way they are by a maker (*jaʿil*) but "are what they are in themselves." In al-Taftazani's mind, this assumption effectively reduces the role of God in the universe "to merely bringing them into existence,"[84] and, consequently divesting him of his function as the omnipotent Creator. In illustration of this point, al-Taftazani put forward what he considered to be a self-evident proposition—namely, that the attribute of an essence necessarily derives from an inner property inherent in that essence, not from the essence as such. Now, if we grant that God's existence is identical with his essence and thus cannot be something that subsists through something else (e.g., through an attribute inherent in its essence), then we must rule out the possibility of its multiplication and particularization in concrete empirical existents. But this, argued al-Taftazani, is exactly what the *wujudiyya* try to prove.[85]

Sixth, existence, according to the *wujudiyya,* is united with, and inheres in, the totality of concrete empirical things. Hence the essences and attributes of these things allow no "empirical multiplicity" (*taʿaddud hissi*). This conclusion logically stems from the belief that Absolute Existence is an individual entity (*wahid shakhsi*) which al-Taftazani consistently imputed to his opponents. If so, then Absolute Existence can be united with only one entity at a time, but never with a multitude. This assumption, according to al-Taftazani, results in yet another absurdity, since our reasoning and sensory perception clearly show the multiplicity and variety of individual existent things. In sum, concluded al-Taftazani, one cannot imagine that such a subjective and derivative mental construct as existence—a hollow abstract with no reality outside our minds—is identical with either the Absolute Necessary Being of the *falasifa* or "the Lord of the Worlds" of the *ʿulamaʾ*.[86]

In defending their monistic vision of the universe, the *wujudiyya,* according to al-Taftazani, rejected the notion of Absolute Existence as a sum total of individual existents. They attributed the multiplicity of the empirical world to the inadequacy of the observer's perception that distorts the picture by presenting the unique Absolute Existence as multiple and variegated. In denying the accuracy of sensory perception, the *wujudiyya,* in al-Taftazani's judgment, join hands with the ancient sophists who doubted that the empirical world has any positive existence and treated it as a chimera devoid of a positive substance. Al-Taftazani condemned this view as being at odds with both the religion and the moral and social order it supports: "since all is God, all is good and all is permitted."[87]

A corollary of the *wujudi* denial of a positive religious and moral order is their assertion that humans are incapable of achieving a sure knowledge of God and the world. In line with their unitive vision of the world, the *wujudiyya* treat all empirical things as an undifferentiated mass in which "earth is identical with heaven, heaven is identical with water, water is identical with fire, fire is identical with air, air is identical with a human being, a human being is identical with a tree, a tree is identical with a donkey, a donkey is identical with man."[88] In this scheme of things, God assumes the same functions that the Divine Revelation ascribes to his creatures.[89]

In countering the antinomian implications of this theory, al-Taftazani formulated a positive credo that rested firmly on the Ashʿari dogmas:

—God does have positive existence and is the first cause and sustainer of all possible things;

—he directly interferes in, and has full control over, their concrete empirical existence;

—since the doctrine of *tawhid* declares God to be one in his essence, it permits no multiplicity or particularization within it;

—although Absolute Existence has a degree of reality, as any mental abstract in our minds, this does not presuppose its independent empirical status; nor can it be conceived as inherent in individual empirical things outside of our imagination.

The Problem of "Pharaoh's Faith"

While the first part of al-Taftazani's treatise deals primarily with the ontological implications of the monistic teaching, in the second[90] he turned to the already familiar problem of "Pharaoh's faith." This problem, only briefly mentioned by Ibn Taymiyya, became the linchpin of al-Taftazani's critique of how Ibn ʿArabi interpreted the Islamic tradition. He began by locating Ibn ʿArabi within the taxonomy of "heretics and unbelievers" developed in the Muslim heresiographical literature.[91] As his starting point he adopted the notion of *kafir*—a generic term that Muslim heresiographers apply to any unbeliever. More specific is the Qurʾanic word "hypocrite" (*munafiq*),[92] which describes anyone who denied or doubted the prophetic mission of Muhammad during his lifetime. For his epoch, al-Taftazani identified the latter with the Syrian Druse, who outwardly feign the acceptance of Muslim faith while secretly rejecting the finality of Muhammad's prophesy.[93]

Al-Taftazani then proceeded to discern some other types of miscreants, such as the "apostates" (*murtaddun*) who renege their religion, the "polytheists," and "the people of the Book."[94] He also mentioned the "materialists" who either deny the existence of the Creator or attribute his functions to time, or aeon (*dahr*), which they conceive as having neither a beginning nor an end.[95]

By far the worst type of unbelief is, in al-Taftazani's mind, one entertained in secret by those individuals who show outward compliance with the letter of the *shariʿa*. These disguised heretics, whom al-Taftazani described as *zanadiqa* (sing. *zindiq*),[96] pose a grave threat to the Muslim community, because they are intent on undermining it from within. They, therefore, merit capital punishment, and their repentance, unlike that of the apostates, should not be accepted. It is in this category that al-Taftazani placed the author of the *Fusus* and his followers.

Al-Taftazani saw the most glaring example of Ibn ʿArabi's heresy (*zandaqa*) in his portrayal of the Qurʾanic Pharaoh, this "archetype of unbelieving, arrogant, unjust, and self-deifying man,"[97] as a true believer, "who found consolation in the faith with which God endowed him when he was . . . drowned," and whom God "took to Himself spotless, pure and untainted by any taint."[98] In a long, repetitious discourse, al-Taftazani set about to rebuff this "hideous" theological misconception by using "the twenty four chapters of the Qurʾan in which Pharaoh is mentioned as well as the consensus of the leading scholars of the [Muslim] Community."[99]

Al-Taftazani presents Ibn ʿArabi's "advocacy" of Pharaoh as hinging on the analogy between him and the ungodly people of Nineveh in *sura* 10 of the Qurʾan. The Ninevehans, so goes the story, first rejected the admonitions of the prophet Yunus (Jonah), then changed their mind and recognized Yunus' prophethood at the sight of the "painful chastisement" about to befall them.[100] Basing himself on the story of the repentant Ninevehans, Ibn ʿArabi argued that Pharaoh, like them, was converted to the true faith, when he saw signs of his impending doom (i.e., his imminent drowning in the sea). In a sense, Ibn ʿArabi's argument was not as farfetched as it may appear at first sight: it takes its origin in the Shafiʿi view that the faith one embraces in peril (*hal al-yaʾs*) should be considered valid. Cognizant of the Shafiʿi position, al-Taftazani opted for a more stringent view of the matter taken by Hanafi scholars, who deny the validity of involuntary conversion. Due to the conflicting interpretations of the issue by the different schools of law, legal niceties form the centerpiece of al-Taftazani's criticism of the concept of Pharaoh's faith.[101]

Before discussing how al-Taftazani interpreted Ibn ʿArabi's view of the matter, a word should be said about the Greatest Master's original position. On the metaphysical level, he considered Pharaoh's conversion to be a symbol of God's all-encompassing mercy, which comes as a natural result of the Sufi belief in the underlying ontological unity of the universe. On the level of mystical gnosis, however, he took a more radical interpretation in presenting Pharaoh's swift change of heart as a result of not so much his fear of imminent destruction as of his recognition of the veracity of Musa's mission, which he, as a perfected gnostic, took pains to conceal in keeping with the divine scenario that always requires duality.

On the exegetical level, the peculiarity of Ibn ʿArabi's interpretation of the passage in question lies in his denial that Pharaoh was certain of his imminent death, since, according to the Greatest Master, he had just seen the Children of Israel crossing the sea by its bed. On this view, Pharaoh was not the irredeemable unbeliever forced into Islam under duress: his conversion was a voluntarily act which, in Ibn ʿArabi's phrase, "saved him both outwardly and inwardly."[102] As with the other exegetical paradoxes of the *Fusus,* this interpretation makes sense only when considered against the background of Ibn ʿArabi's worldview as a whole. In the case at hand, the key lies in the way in which Ibn ʿArabi understood the complex (and contradictory) interplay of God's creative will and his normative wish, which the dramatic encounter between Pharaoh and Musa was designed to illustrate.[103]

Due to al-Taftazani's ignorance of the underlying motives of Pharaoh's behavior that Ibn ʿArabi had in mind, his critical thrusts miss the mark. As with Ibn Taymiyya, al-Taftazani was not prepared to deal with the subtlety of the Pharaoh theme as presented in the *Fusus.* His critique, therefore, skims the surface of Ibn ʿArabi's pregnant discourse, giving us a glimpse into the wide disparity of perspectives that separates the Greatest Master from his detractor.

Characteristically, al-Taftazani began his critique by flatly dismissing any resemblance between the "people of Yunus" and Pharaoh, which, as mentioned, was at the heart of Ibn ʿArabi's argument. For him, there was no doubt that Pharaoh embraced Islam only when faced with an unavoidable death. His Ninevehan counterparts, on the other hand, recanted their unbelief several days in advance of the severe chastisement prophesied to them by Yunus. Hence, in contrast to their conversion, which the Qurʾan specifically describes as an exception to the rule, that of Pharaoh could not have been authentic, since it was simultaneous with his death. Furthermore, the Qurʾan explicitly says that the Ninevehans' punishment was deferred, which does not necessarily guarantee them salvation in the Hereafter. If anything, the relevant Qurʾanic verses suggest that the Ninevehans were simply granted a respite in this life, while their status in the Hereafter was still unknown. The fact that they professed faith by their tongues to divert the chastisement does not necessarily mean that their belief was sincere. Moreover the inefficacy of a belated or halfhearted repentance is abundantly demonstrated in the Qur'an. With regard to Pharaoh, al-Taftazani argued that the mere wording of his hasty proclamation of faith[104] is indicative of his insincerity. Ignorant of Musa's God, Pharaoh simply imitated the established custom (*taqlid*), whereas, for most Qur'anic commentators, such a perfunctory conversion will be of no value on the Day of Judgment. In addition, al-Taftazani pointed out that Pharaoh never affirmed the prophetic mission of Musa, which constitutes the conditio sine qua non of any monotheistic creed. Hence, his conversion was not only a sham but also incomplete.[105]

Finally, for al-Taftazani, Pharaoh, whose arbitrary arrogance and injustice violated all legal and moral norms, was a far greater sinner than the Ninevehans or, for that matter, than any other infidel mentioned in the Qur'an. Therefore, in al-Taftazani's opinion, God simply could not have seized Pharaoh's soul, as Ibn ʿArabi put it, "spotless and pure of any sin."[106] In conclusion, al-Taftazani provided the following summary of the Pharaoh issue:

> It is clear to the greatest scholars of Islam, as well as to the experts on the Sacred Law and legal issues that whoever states that the accursed Pharaoh died a believer thereby contradicts the Qur'an and gainsays the words of the Supreme Ruler and the Greatest Judge. He [who concurs with Ibn ʿArabi] thus negates the fundamentals of Islam as set down in the Sunna of the Prophet. Like Pharaoh and his godless people, [such a person] is an infidel and will be counted among those who lied and strayed from the right path.[107]

Conclusion

Al-Taftazani's critique of the *Fusus* demonstrates a rather selective and narrow response to the conceptual richness of the *Fusus* that is, in many ways, similar to Ibn Taymiyya's antimonistic attack. Of the many challenges posed by the book, al-Taftazani focused on two widely disparate issues: Ibn ʿArabi's metaphysics and Pharaoh's faith. This choice may have been dictated by his desire to defeat Ibn ʿArabi in two different fields of scholarly inquiry. Whatever his motive, these issues seem to have been rather arbitrarily pulled out of the overall context of Ibn ʿArabi's discourse—a factor that has rendered al-Taftazani's critique inconclusive, to say the least.

A major flaw in al-Taftazani's argumentation is his failure to discriminate between Ibn ʿArabi and his philosophically minded commentators, who are lumped together under the heading of *wujudiyya.* This is all the stranger if we recall a more sensitive approach to the subject taken by Ibn Taymiyya, who was continually at pains to separate the "confused" Ibn ʿArabi from his more "impious" followers. In the case of al-Taftazani, the situation is reversed: the blame is almost entirely on the founder, while his later interpreters receive only a fleeting condemnation.

Paradoxically, although al-Taftazani's stated goal is to refute the *Fusus,* a close textual analysis of this work shows that textual evidence plays a relatively minor role in his polemic. There are, for example, surprisingly few word-for-word quotations from the work that purports to be the main target of al-Taftazani's critique. Nor is his critique based on a careful examination of Ibn ʿArabi's mystical doctrine. Instead, the polemical discourse centers on several ready-made preconceptions regarding Ibn ʿArabi's thought which, moreover, are too broadly formulated to render justice to the complexity of the latter's *Gedankenwelt.*

In a casual remark, al-Taftazani revealed what appears to have been a major source of his knowledge of his opponent's views. Characteristically, this is the work of Sadr al-din al-Qunawi,[108] who, as mentioned, took a strictly rationalist approach to his master's legacy, treating it from the perspective of Avicennan philosophy with its persistent ontological bent.[109] As a result, the gravity of al-Taftazani's accusations stands in sharp contrast to his rather superficial acquaintance with the Sufi's original work. For this reason, his critical attack on the *Fusus,* in my view, falls short of its goal: one expects a deeper assessment of this difficult book from a scholar of al-Taftazani's caliber.

Al-Taftazani's superficiality is evident in the fact that, less than a century after Ibn ʿArabi's death, he directed his attack not against the Sufi master as such, but against the latter's polemical image, which had been molded by several generations of Muslim controversialists. In other words, al-Taftazani uncritically accepts the issues framed for him by his predecessors, dispensing with an independent examination of the work at issue. This is not to say that al-Taftazani was totally ignorant of the *Fusus,* since he occasionally quoted short passages and phrases from Ibn ʿArabi's masterpiece, especially in his discussion of Pharaoh's faith.[110] Amazingly, these appear to be the only direct quotations from a work that was supposed to be the sole target of al-Taftazani's critical attack on Ibn ʿArabi's doctrine.[111] Other references are so vague that one cannot readily locate them within the text of the *Fusus;* more often they are little more than facile paraphrases of the original concepts and themes.[112] Even direct quotations, which, as mentioned, are mainly related to the issue of Pharaoh's faith, can hardly serve as evidence of al-Taftazani's close reading of the *Fusus,* since they could have been borrowed from one of the numerous later refutations of the Greatest Master, most probably Ibn Taymiyya's. In sum, to anyone conversant with the world of ideas peculiar to the *Fusus,* al-Taftazani's treatment of this complex work appears narrow, dogmatic, and superficial.

In a colophon attached to the "Epistle," al-Taftazani indicated that it was composed in Damascus—a city that was home to both Ibn ʿArabi's bitter opponents and ardent supporters, who were locked in a fierce intellectual battle over his legacy. By al-Taftazani's time, their debates had generated a substantial body of scholarly literature that supplied him with a handy array of polemical arguments. Simultaneously, there had crystallized a pool of the controversial issues over which the disputants were crossing their polemical swords. It is from this pool that al-Taftazani crafted his antimonistic argument. This approach may have saved him the trouble of undertaking a thorough study of Ibn ʿArabi's thought. However, it undoubtedly took a heavy toll on his discourse by rendering it secondary, out-of-context, and oblivious to Ibn ʿArabi's original concerns.

This approach mirrors the selective, dogmatizing reception of Ibn ʿArabi's ideas that was characteristic of many Muslim theologians. Unable or unwilling to enter the highly complex thought-world of Islam's greatest mystic, they contented themselves with skimming the surface of his work, while neglecting its more recondite sides. By the same token, al-Taftazani's treatment of Ibn ʿArabi is typical of the general body of anti-Ibn ʿArabi literature in its singular focus on the text of the *Fusus* and concomitant disregard for the rest of his vast corpus. But even this relatively short work was then mercilessly reduced by Ibn ʿArabi's detractors to a handful of abstract metaphysical and theological prepositions that are hardly representative of his intellectual stance and method as a whole.

Due to al-Taftazani's lasting influence upon subsequent generations of Muslim theologians, his "Epistle" became a model for those who came in his wake. The next generation of critics will consistently target their criticisms at Ibn ʿArabi's monistic ontology or at the Pharaoh issue, or both. A fine illustration of the tenacity of the polemical pattern established by al-Taftazani is the work of his direct disciple, Muhammad b. Muhammad b. Muhammad al-Bukhari (d. 841/1437).[113] Yet, being al-Taftazani's disciple did not necessarily involve opposition to Ibn ʿArabi's thought. A significant treatise in defense of Ibn ʿArabi and his concept of Pharaoh's faith was written by Jalal al-din al-Dawani (d. 907/1501-1502)—a later exponent of al-Taftazani's work,[114] who sided squarely with the Greatest Master.[115]

In the first half of the 10th/16th centuries an influential Hanafi scholar, Burhan al-din al-Halabi (d. 956/1549), achieved notoriety as an implacable critic of the Greatest Master whose refutation of his doctrines exhibits a heavy indebtedness to al-Taftazani's *Risala*.[116] Later still, the pugnacious Hanafi polemicist Mulla ʿAli al-Qari (d. 1014/1606), who was famous for his intolerance toward any Sunni school of law other than his own,[117] refined al-Taftazani's critique of the Greatest Master, by adding his own arguments. Although undoubtedly inspired by al-Taftazani, his critique emanated from a much deeper understanding of the *Fusus* than its prototype. Nonetheless, Mulla ʿAli al-Qari's approach to Ibn ʿArabi's masterpiece is informed by the same polemical concerns: Ibn ʿArabi's ontology and the problem of Pharaoh's faith.[118]

Yahia names a few other Hanafi scholars from the 10th/16th centuries who went on record as bitter opponents of Ibn ʿArabi and his following—a fact that makes one suspect the Hanafi school of being particularly biased against the Greatest Master. Significantly, all of these antimonistic scholars drew freely from al-Taftazani's work.[119] The polemic grew especially sharp in the 12th/17th centuries, when Ibrahim b. Hasan al-Kurani (d. 1101/1690), a renowned Meccan theologian and *muhaddith* of Kurdish background, composed a series of metaphysical tracts aimed at reconciling the ontological teachings of Ibn ʿArabi and al-Qunawi and rebutting their detractors. In contrast to al-Taftazani, who disregarded the substantial differences between these two mystical thinkers, al-Kurani demonstrated that each of them adhered to a specific vision of monistic ontology. Yet, in an effort to disarm their critics, al-Kurani, himself an Avicennan thinker, glossed over their differences, arguing that both the teacher and his disciple shared a common notion of God and of the world.[120]

Al-Kurani's apology for the monistic philosophy provoked a massive stream of rejoinders that further fueled the already heated debates around Ibn ʿArabi and his school.[121] The scholastic controversy ignited by Ibn Taymiyya and al-Taftazani continued uninterrupted throughout the 12th/18th centuries, which witnessed the growing acceptance of Ibn ʿArabi that was, in great part, facilitated by the work of such brilliant pro-Ibn ʿArabi scholars as al-Nabulusi (d. 1143/1731) and Ismaʿil Gelenbewi (d. 1205/1791). Nevertheless, the polemic raged on throughout the 19th century,[122] when several rejoinders to al-Taftazani's critique were written by an influential Damascene scholar ʿUmar al-ʿAttar (d. 1308/1890).[123]

In sum, there is no reason to doubt that al-Taftazani generally supported Sufism as an ascetic and moral discipline and as a way to self-perfection. In many instances we find him praising its classic and contemporary representatives including such controversial ones as Abu Yazid al-Bistami.[124] At the same time, his notion of "authentic" Sufism was rigidly defined: it certainly did not include the mystical philosophy of Ibn ʿArabi and his followers. A thoroughgoing rationalist, al-Taftazani balked at the idea that the "oceanic" experiences of Sufi visionaries mirror the real ontological situation of the universe. It is this assumption that he regarded as the principal flaw in Ibn ʿArabi's ontology. For al-Taftazani, it enshrined a misguided epistemological procedure that confused personal experience—a legitimate perception of *tawhid* by certain elect gnostics (*ʿarifun*)—with objective ontology which, in his view, can be adequately comprehended only through a sound syllogistic reasoning and through a proper interpretation of the Islamic tradition. It was this confusion of experience and cosmology, and not Sufi gnosis per se, which al-Taftazani was so anxious to disprove.

Like Ibn Taymiyya, al-Taftazani was intensely aware of the dangerous social and moral ramifications of Ibn ʿArabi's ontological theory. This awareness caused him to try and salvage Islamic mysticism from the "corruptive" influence of monistic theories. His attack on the notion of Pharaoh's faith, on the other hand, was dictated by his opposition to the perceived tendency, on the part of Ibn ʿArabi and his followers, to relativize, through a "garbled" exegesis, the all-important borderline between faith and unbelief.

7

IBN ʿARABI IN THE MUSLIM WEST: A PROPHET IN HIS OWN LAND?

Ibn ʿArabi in Western Islamic Heresiography

Having discussed the reception of Ibn ʿArabi's legacy in the Muslim East, we must now turn to the Western lands of Islam, where his controversial teaching originated. His prominence in the local religious literature[1] bears the best testimony to the profound impact of his ideas on the intellectual life of Western Muslims. As in the East, Ibn ʿArabi's exponents in the Maghrib and al-Andalus often showed a rather superficial understanding of his teaching, which they further adapted to the understanding of the general reader. Typical of the popular literature that developed around Ibn ʿArabi's name are the "streamlined" paraphrases of the *Futuhat* by the celebrated Egyptian Sufi ʿAbd al-Wahhab al-Shaʿrani, who consistently glossed over its sticky points.[2] Ibn ʿArabi's original writings were confined to the few sophisticated Sufi leaders, who were careful not to advertise their interest in monistic philosophy.[3] The conservative Maliki jurists, who set the tone in the religious life of al-Andalus and the Maghrib,[4] were generally suspicious of Ibn ʿArabi's metaphysical and theosophical tenets. As a result, his ideas often circulated anonymously, in the form of disparate poetic lines and unattributed quotations that fill popular Sufi manuals and collections of litanies. The readership of this popular mystical literature consisted mainly of the rank-and-file members of the local Sufi orders, which gained great prominence in the Maghrib from the 7th/14th centuries on. Unable to appreciate the niceties of Ibn ʿArabi's work, ordinary Sufis and associated members of Sufi institutions usually contented themselves with its simplified renditions such as those of al-Shaʿrani's. Maghribi *shaykhs* never tired of warning their disciples against perusing Ibn ʿArabi's own writings for fear of confusing beginners on the Sufi path by the Shaykh's bold metaphysical ideas and exegetical paradoxes.[5]

In this respect at least, Ibn ʿArabi fared no better among Western *ʿulamaʾ* than he did among their Eastern colleagues.[6]

Yet, in contrast to the East, Ibn ʿArabi's mystical ideas were not viewed as something exceptional or unprecedented in the West. Many Maghribi and Andalusi heresiographers, whom Massignon somewhat ungenerously dubbed "witch-hunters" (*chasseurs de sorcières*),[7] tended to view Ibn ʿArabi as part of a sinister plot against Islam masterminded by a group of heterodox mystics. In any case, the writers of Maghrbi or Andalusi background rarely treated him as *the* founder and foremost representative of the monistic school in Islamic mysticism, as was often the case in the Muslim East.

In general, evidence is sparse about how exactly Ibn ʿArabi was viewed by his countrymen.[8] One thing is clear: like their Eastern colleagues, many Western *ʿulamaʾ* considered him to be a dangerous freethinker and heretic. Among the first to blacklist him, was the renowned Andalusi traditionalist and master of Qurʾanic recitation Ibn al-Zubayr (d. 708/1308)[9] who included Ibn ʿArabi in the polemical treatise "Safeguarding the Unaware from Going Astray in the Desert without Landmarks" (*Radʿ al-jahil ʿan iʿtisaf al-majahil*).[10] This work is an example of the scholarly opposition to the mystical and theological movement called al-Shudhiyya,[11] with which Ibn ʿArabi came to be firmly bound in the Western Islamic heresiography.[12] Ibn al-Zubayr had firsthand knowledge of the tenets of the Shudhiyya: he taught Arabic grammar to the children of Ibn Ahla (d. 645/1247)—the political and spiritual leader of this school in that age.[13] Ibn al-Zubayr's antimonistic convictions had at least one practical consequence: he took an active part in the public trial of a popular ecstatic al-Saffar, a suspected follower of the Shudhiyya, who barely escaped execution on charges of heresy.[14]

Ibn al-Zubayr's hostility toward monistic Sufism was shared by his noted disciple Abu Hayyan al-Gharnati (d. 745/1344),[15] who left al-Andalus for an illustrious career in Egypt, where he made a name for himself as the foremost Arab grammarian of the epoch.[16] Abu Hayyan's negative attitude toward monistic mysticism is evident from his Qurʾanic commentaries. Characteristically, many of the Sufi "monists" he mentions there are natives of al-Andalus, including Ibn ʿArabi who is cited alongside al-Hallaj, al-Shudhi, Ibn Ahla,[17] and Ibn al-Farid as the leaders of "the first generation of the impious Sufis." According to Abu Hayyan, the first Sufi "monists" were followed by radical adherents of "absolute oneness," such as Ibn Sabʿin and his closest followers, ʿAfif al-Tilimsani and al-Shushtari.[18] Abu Hayyan explained his negative view of these monistic philosophers by his "compassion for the feebleminded Muslims, so as to warn them against those [Sufis] . . . who reject God and His messenger, teach the eternity of the world, and deny the possibility of Resurrection."[19] This statement conveniently captures the position of the later Andalusi and Maghribi *ʿulamaʾ* who compiled similar lists of heretical Sufis. Curiously, in the Muslim West, such blacklisting became a trademark of the local heresiographical tradition. Similar rosters of heterodox mystics were drawn up by Ibn al-Khatib and Ibn Khaldun, who, though more sensitive to various shades within speculative Sufism, followed the same pattern.[20]

Interestingly, in the East, the tendency to blacklist "monistic" Sufis can be traced back to the famous Maliki-cum-Shafiʿi scholar Qutb al-din (Ibn) al-Qastallani (d. 686/1287).[21] He went on record as an uncompromising critic of al-Hallaj, Ibn al-Farid, Ibn ʿArabi, al-Shushtari, al-Tilimsani, and Ibn Sabʿin, whom he disparagingly dubbed the "adherents of nothingness" (*laysiyya*).[22] It should be stressed that al-Qastallani was a member of a noted Sufi family with strong Maghribi ties.[23] Is is from them that he inherited the Western Islamic notion of the "monistic conspiracy," which was allegedly introduced by al-Shudhi and refined by his direct followers. Furthermore it seems likely that al-Qastallani's critical account of the Shudhiyya inspired Ibn Taymiyya's momentous attack on monistic Sufism.[24] Thus, al-Qastallani's critique of the *laysiyya* forms a vital link between the Western and Eastern heresiographical traditions, whose representatives were equally anxious to stem the spread of monistic ideas.

Ibn ʿArabi Through the Eyes of Ibn al-Khatima

Ibn ʿArabi's impact on popular Sufi literature in the Muslim West has been surveyed by Chodkiewicz.[25] I, therefore, will limit myself to the more sophisticated reception of his legacy, as exemplified by three outstanding representatives of Western Islamic thought: the Andalusi litterateur and grammarian Ibn Khatima (d. 770/1369), the Granadine vizier Lisan al-din Ibn al-Khatib (d. 776/1375), and the Maghribi statesman and historian Ibn Khaldun (d. 808/1406). The former two were close friends who contributed in significant ways to the last efflorescence of Arab-Islamic culture in al-Andalus on the eve of the Muslim withdrawal.[26] Ibn Khaldun, whose family left Seville for Tunis shortly before his birth, can also be regarded as an heir to the Andalusi tradition.[27] His contribution, however, was

Table 4

Qutb al-din al-Qastallani (d. 686/1287), the first to "blacklist" I.ʿA. alongside the *Shudhiyya* Sufis; Ibn Sabʿin, his personal rival, the principal target of attack.

His critique of the monistic school *Shudhiyya* was taken up and developed by Ibn Taymiyya and Ibn al-Zubayr (d. 708/1308)

Abu Hayyan al-Gharnati (d. 745/1344) lists I.ʿA. among the leaders of "the first generation of the impious Sufis," i.e., al-Hallaj, al-Shudhi, Ibn Ahla, and Ibn al-Farid; distinguishes them from the *laysiyya*—the proponents of absolute oneness (al-Tilimsani, al-Shushtari, and Ibn Sabʿin).

Ibn Hisham (d. 761/1360) condemns I.ʿA.'s *Fusus* (see the epigraph to Chapter 8 of this study); includes him in a roster of "heretical" Sufis.

Ibn Khatima (d. 770/1369) suspects I.ʿA. of an unspecified "heresy"; stresses his penchant for allegorical style and obscurity, but does not associate him with the "monistic conspiracy"; ignorant of I.ʿA.'s career and importance following his departure to the East.

Ibn al-Khatib (d. 776/1375) provides a competent and imaginative account of Sufism's history; treats I.ʿA. among the "people of *tajalli*"; emphasizes and denounces their political activism, as exemplified by Ibn Qasi; dissociates them from the professors of "absolute oneness" led by Ibn Sabʿin; his empathy for monistic philosophy becomes a pretext for his execution.

Ibn Khaldun (d. 808/1406) draws a sharp line between the "authentic" early Sufis and his philosophically minded contemporaries; his account of I.ʿA.'s ideas is on many points inaccurate and based on secondhand renditions; emphasizes the underlying affinity between I.ʿA.'s *mahdi* theory and "extreme" Shiʿism; condemns both unequivocally in his Egyptian *fatwa*.

primarily to the social and political history of the Maghrib, which was his home for the first fifty years of his life. It should be noted that Ibn Khaldun cultivated the friendship of Lisan al-din Ibn al-Khatib, whom he met in Fez and Granada.[28] Given the similar intellectual and religious backgrounds shared by the three scholars,[29] it is instructive to examine their respective responses to the Ibn ʿArabi problem. They were, as we shall soon see, quite dissimilar, informed as they were by diverse intellectual concerns and personal preferences.

Ahmad b. ʿAli Ibn Khatima does not seem to have held any important public office in the Nasrid kingdom, although he did serve in the governor's chancery of Almeria.[30] His claim to fame was primarily as a refined poet and litterateur, who wrote a history of his native town which, unfortunately, has not come down to us.[31] Since Ibn ʿArabi paid a brief visit to Almeria in 595/1199,[32] Ibn Khatima felt obligated to include him in the list of the renowned visitors to that city. His short biographical notice was preserved for us by al-Maqqari, who was meticulous in collecting any data on the Greatest Master.[33] After a rather standard enumeration of Ibn ʿArabi's teachers and writings[34] Ibn Khatima gives the following evaluation of his work:

> We do not approve [of] some of his teachings and writings. Although he had the ability to express himself clearly, he [preferred] to speak from behind the veil, fortifying himself [by the use of] symbols[35] in an impenetrable mountain citadel and taking refuge in allusions of dubious import, rather than talking in a straightforward and accessible manner. A reliable companion of ours told us, citing a certain expert on the religious sciences whom he had met, that he harshly criticized [Ibn ʿArabi] and accused him of weak faith. Moreover, that scholar actually said that Ibn ʿArabi was weak all around. God knows better about the veracity of this opinion, for any speech that uses metaphors and figurative expressions without paired subjects,[36] is susceptible to many conflicting explanations. In short, he [Ibn ʿArabi] exposed himself to blame because he used vague [phrases] that elude easy comprehension and obstruct the path of those aspiring [to grasp their meaning].[37]

This assessment of Ibn ʿArabi's legacy leans heavily on the philological side—something one expects from a connoisseur of the Arabic belles-lettres such as Ibn Khatima. Although his own excessively florid literary style, amply documented by Ibn al-Khatib and al-Maqqari, was far from lucid and overloaded with labored metaphors and precious similes,[38] Ibn Khatima has no qualms about reproaching Ibn ʿArabi for his overindulgence in symbols and allegories. Furthermore, he cites the deliberate obscurity of Ibn ʿArabi's style as a principal reason for his condemnation by religious scholars. At the same time, Ibn Khatima obviously has no direct knowledge of what Ibn ʿArabi actually taught and wrote and, therefore, relies heavily on the opinion of an unnamed scholar. Elusive and ambivalent, Ibn Khatima's evaluation boils down to the trite (and already familiar) proposition that Ibn ʿArabi was a "difficult" writer, whose work was ambiguous to say the least.

Ibn al-Khatib The Vizier

The great Andalusi polymath and statesman Muhammad b. ʿAbdallah al-Salamani, better known as Lisan al-Din Ibn al-Khatib,[39] was born in 713/1313 of a family of Arab notables, whose members had traditionally been employed in the religious and civil service of Andalusi rulers. Ibn al-Khatib's father occupied a high office at the court of the emir Ismaʿil I (r. 713/1314-725/1325) of Granada (Gharnata)—the city where the young Ibn al-Khatib received an excellent education under the guidance of the best scholars of the epoch.[40] He studied a broad variety of subjects: the Arabic language and grammar, *fiqh* and exegesis, *adab* and poetry, medicine and *falsafa,* history and Sufism. Ibn al-Khatib's broad background is mirrored in a dazzling multiplicity of the topics he treated in his writings. His vast knowledge, noble pedigree, and the high post of his father, combined with his unique literary talent and extraordinary memory, destined him for a splendid career in the Granadine court. In 741/1340, Ibn al-Khatib was appointed personal secretary to Ibn al-Jayyab, vizier of the emir Yusuf I (r. 733/1333-755/1354) and, upon Ibn al-Jayyab's untimely death of a plague in 749/1349, took his office at the head of the royal chancery with the title of vizier. He was put in charge of the emir's diplomatic correspondence and was occasionally sent as Granada's envoy to the rulers in al-Andalus and the Maghrib. To all of these functions he later added those of master of royal household, which in his own words, gave him full authority over the financial, military, administrative, and political affairs of the Granadine court and state as a whole.[41] Ibn al-Khatib retained these posts and titles under the new emir Muhammad V al-Ghani bi-ʾllah (r. 755/1354-760/1359), who had been his disciple and confidant. In the service of the young sultan Ibn al-Khatib distinguished himself by successfully accomplishing an important diplomatic mission to the Marinid sultan Abu ʿInan. Impressed by Ibn al-Khatib's spirited panegyric, the powerful Marinid pledged to support the young Granadine emir in his bitter struggle with the *Reconquista.*[42] From then on, Ibn al-Khatib invariably steered Granada's foreign policy toward a closer cooperation and, eventually, political union with the powerful Marinid state.[43]

When in 760/1359 Muhammad V was deposed by his half brother Ismaʿil and by a group of disloyal courtiers and narrowly escaped with his life, Ibn al-Khatib, as doyen of the deposed regime, landed in prison with his property confiscated by the new ruler. However, he was soon released thanks to the interference of the Marinid sultan Abu Salim and joined his fugitive sovereign in his Maghribi exile. In Fez, they were welcomed by Abu Salim and his retinue that featured such great luminaries of Western Islamdom as Ibn Marzuq and ʿAbd al-Rahman Ibn Khaldun.[44] After a brief stay in Fez and a tour of the Marinid realm, Ibn al-Khatib finally settled in a quiet town of Salé, to which he had taken fancy on his earlier diplomatic trip to Morocco. He spent almost two years there, immersed in writing and pious meditation, yet not neglectful of his mundane interests. His residence in Salé gave him a rare occasion to nurture his predilection for Sufi spirituality. For once, he allowed his mystical propensities to outweigh his usual preoccupation with his political career and court intrigue—a preoccupation that cost him so dearly in the future.

Ibn al-Khatib's seclusion ended in 763/1362, when Muhammad V regained his throne with the help of the Marinid sultan. Summoned by the sovereign, Ibn al-Khatib returned to Granada to assume his former post at the head of the civil and military authority (*dhu ʾl-wizaratayn*) of the Granadine kingdom. Soon afterward, he ran afoul of several Maghribi politicians and generals residing in Granada, whom he viewed as his political rivals. In an effort to maintain full control over state politics and the military, Ibn al-Khatib launched a series of intrigues, including fabricated letters, aimed at besmirching the reputation of his Maghribi rivals in the eyes of the ruler. The intrigue bore fruit, and the rivals were expelled from the Granadine court.[45]

Ibn al-Khatib's triumphs, however, were not without cost, for his intense scheming aroused the hatred of the emir's courtiers sympathetic with the banished Maghribi émigrés and, moreover, alienated his former friends and disciples. In a drive to secure his undivided influence upon the emir, Ibn al-Khatib did not hesitate to trample upon even his most loyal friends. When Muhammad V showed favor to the Maghribi visitor ʿAbd al-Rahman Ibn Khaldun, who had successfully accomplished a delicate diplomatic mission to the court of Pedro the Cruel of Seville, Ibn al-Khatib's envy sent his old friend packing to the Maghrib in 766/1365.[46]

In the meantime, his position at the Granadine court began to erode due to the intrigues and hostile rumors instigated by his disciples and aides Ibn Zamrak and Ibn Farkun who joined hands with his powerful enemy, the grand *qadi* of Granada, ʿAli al-Nubahi.[47] Ibn Zamrak and Ibn Farkun craved their teacher's position, while ʿAli al-Nubahi was offended by Ibn al-Khatib's mystical ideas expounded in the *Rawdat al-taʿrif* as well as by his leniency toward those whom the *qadi* had declared "downright heretics."[48] More importantly, the emir, already in his forties, began to resent the vizier's overbearing control over the affairs of state as well as his single-minded loyalty to the Marininds, which, in the emir's mind, had come into conflict with Granada's own interests.[49]

Apprehensive of the emir's growing displeasure, Ibn al-Khatib entered into secret negotiations with the Marinid sultan ʿAbd al-ʿAziz. Having secured the sultan's support, in 773/1371 Ibn al-Khatib left the capital with his youngest son ʿAli on the pretext of inspecting fortresses in the western part of the Granadine kingdom. Instead, he headed for Jabal Tariq (Gibraltar), from where he set sail for the Maghribi coast. Thanks to ʿAbd al-ʿAziz's intervention, the family soon reunited with the fugitive vizier in Tlemsen.[50]

Ibn al-Khatib's sudden departure infuriated his enemies, especially Ibn Zamrak and al-Nubahi who hastened to accuse him of treason. The latter also declared him a heretic, who had belittled the reputation of the Prophet, espoused the "atheistic" teachings of the *falasifa,* and propagated the incarnationist doctrine (*hulul*) of the Sufi "heretics." Shortly after Ibn al-Khatib's escape to the Maghrib, al-Nubahi issued a *fatwa* calling for the destruction of the vizier's works and the confiscation of his property. The books were put to torch in Granada's market square in the presence of many eminent scholars, who had tacitly approved al-Nubahi's verdict. The latter then sent Ibn al-Khatib a letter exposing the vizier's alleged "abominations" and excommunicating him from the community of the faithful. The ad hominem nature of this letter, which apart from heresy and desertion accused Ibn al-Khatib of venality, unscrupulousness, and slander suggests that al-Nubahi had a personal grudge against the disgraced vizier. This impression is corroborated by his reference to the instances of Ibn al-Khatib's unsolicited interference with, or disregard for, legal rulings and criminal verdicts meted out by al-Nubahi.

Stung by these accusations, Ibn al-Khatib wrote a refutation of his detractor titled *Khalʿ al-rasan fi ʾl-taʿrif bi-ahwal Abi ʾl-Hasan* that ridiculed al-Nubahi by portraying him as an impish, apelike dwarf (*al-jaʿsus*), grossly ignorant of *fiqh* and of the Islamic tradition.[51] On al-Nubahi's instigation, Muhammad V demanded that the sultan ʿAbd al-ʿAziz either extradite or execute his heretical protégé. Unconvinced by al-Nubahi's accusations, the Marinid sultan declined the request as motivated by personal hatred. Although the Marinid died soon afterward, Ibn al-Khatib continued to enjoy the patronage of the vizier Abu Bakr Ibn Ghazi, who became regent on behalf of the minor son of ʿAbd al-ʿAziz. Ibn Ghazi's blunt refusal to extradite the fugitive vizier insulted Muhammad V and may have contributed to his decision to support the opponents of Ibn Ghazi and of his royal ward. With his military and political support the rebels soon gained the upper hand in the dynastic struggle that ensued and proclaimed Abu ʾl-ʿAbbas Ahmad al-Marini the new sultan.

With Ibn Ghazi no longer by his side, Ibn al-Khatib was left at the mercy of the victors who owed their triumph to the Granadine emir and were eager to repay their debt. They threw the disgraced vizier into prison until the arrival of a delegation from Granada headed by Ibn al-Khatib's disciple-turned-enemy Ibn Zamrak, who was appointed vizier following the former's escape to the Maghrib. Upon the delegation's arrival in Fez, the new sultan ordered a public hearing of Ibn al-Khatib's case, which was conducted by a council of scholars loyal to him. The members of the Granadine delegation took an active part in the trial. Undaunted by the cruel intimidation and torture, Ibn al-Khatib courageously protested his innocence and flatly denied the accusations of heresy and unbelief leveled at him by Ibn Zamrak.[52]

Although some ʿ*ulama*ʾ had found Ibn al-Khatib guilty of monistic heresy, the final vote was far from unanimous and no conclusive decision was reached by the council. Ibn al-Khatib was sent back to prison, where he was strangled at night by the thugs sent to him by his old enemy, the vizier Sulayman Ibn Dawud, who acted in collusion with Ibn Zamrak's Andalusi delegation. On the next morning (the end of 776/May-June 1375), his body was buried at Bab al-Mahruq in Fez. Unsatisfied, his vengeful enemies exhumed his corpse and threw it onto the bonfire, whereupon his charred remains were finally laid to rest on the same spot.

A detailed account of Ibn al-Khatib's ordeal was left to us by ʿAbd al-Rahman Ibn Khaldun, who remained his loyal friend and admirer despite the brief alienation that had occurred between them at Granada. At the close of his narrative, Ibn al-Khaldun quotes the poignant verses that the imprisoned vizier reportedly composed on the eve of his assassination:

> We travel far away, albeit the dwellings
>
> are near
>
> Although we have a message to deliver, we
>
> remain speechless

Our breath suddenly stops
As if a loud prayer was followed by
a silent recitation
Of noble ancestry we were, but, alas, we have
turned into a stack of dry bones[53]
We used to feed others, but lo, now we
ourselves are food [for worms]
We were like shining suns that travel high
in the sky above,
But, lo, the suns have set and
been lamented by the [orphaned] stars
Many a warrior armed with the sword was felled
by a rain of sharp-pointed arrows
Many a lucky one was suddenly failed by
his good fortune
Many a young nobleman, who used to don the
royal mantle, was put in the grave wrapped in
rags
So, tell the enemies: "Yes, Ibn al-Khatib is gone,
but is there anyone who will not be gone
one day?"
And tell those of you who rejoice at this
news: "Only he who thinks he will never die
can rejoice on a day like this!"[54]

Ibn al-Khatib on Love Mysticism

In his "Garden of Instruction in Noble Love" (*Rawdat al-taʿrif bi ʾl-hubb al-sharif*) Ibn al-Khatib demonstrates a much deeper understanding of Ibn ʿArabi's doctrine than we saw in Ibn al-Khatima's terse obituary notice of the Greatest Master.[55] This lengthy work was designed as a refutation of the "Anthology of Tender Loving" (*Diwan al-sababa*)[56] by Ibn Abi Hajala (d. 776/1375)—"a Sufi of sorts who does not seem to have adhered rigidly to any particular way of thinking."[57] The "Anthology," which, in Ibn al-Khatib's phrase, included numerous "descriptions of the frustration of lovers . . . in both poetry and prose," offended the sensitivities of his royal patron, Muhammad al-Ghani bi-ʾllah, who asked his vizier to refute it in a special dissertation.[58] Apart from his lack of affiliation with any school of law,[59] one personal feature known of Ibn Abi Hajala was his hostility to the *ittihadiyya* Sufis and especially to Ibn al-Farid.[60] Early in his career, he attempted to "imitate" (*ʿarada*) Ibn al-Farid's poems by using the same rhymes and meters but purging them of "all questionable content." The result was a rather forced and insipid replica of Ibn al-Farid's ingenious original, titled *Gayth al-ʿarid*, which earned its author "the scorn and ridicule of the powerful chief judge, Siraj al-din al-Hindi (714-773/1314-1372)," a great admirer of the poet and his *al-Taʾiyya al-kubra*.[61] Owing to Siraj al-din and to other influential supporters of Ibn al-Farid in Egypt, Ibn Abi Hajala suffered much harassment and was even put on trial on charges of slandering God's saints. As a result of this episode Ibn Abi Hajala developed such a deep repugnance toward Ibn al-Farid and other monistic Sufis that, on one account, on his deathbed he requested that he be buried with a copy of the *Ghayth* and his antimonistic manifesto in his hand.[62]

Little wonder that in repudiating Ibn Abi Hajala's love treatise, Ibn al-Khatib adopts a contrary view of monistic Sufism.[63] Moreover, he deliberately makes mystical experience the crux of his *Rawdat al-taʿrif*, which, in his own words, dealt with "a nobler subject, namely love of God that leads to the summit of happiness . . . and proximity to Him."[64] His approach is thus intentionally at odds with Ibn Abi Hajala's preoccupation with the profane love and anguish of earthly lovers.

In exploring the vast theme of divine love, Ibn al-Khatib uses an elaborate imagery in which the predominant role is alloted to the symbol of the tree.[65] In this conceit, love (*mahabba*) is likened to a luxuriant tree whose roots are deeply grounded in the earth—a metaphor for the human soul. Ibn al-Khatib discerns several types of love, which he compares with the tree's twigs. Love stories, in Ibn al-Khatib's metaphor, symbolize the leaves, love poetry stands for blossoms, and the lover's union with his divine beloved is the tree's sweet fruits. The growth and efflorescence of the tree, according to Ibn al-Khatib, are determined by the characteristics of the earth—that is, by the nature of the individual human soul. Parallel to the composition of the earth, the inherent qualities of the soul determine its fertility or barrenness. Elaborating on this metaphor, Ibn al-Khatib proceeds to discuss the optimal mixture of temperaments, dispositions, and faculties of the human body that makes possible the burgeoning of the tree of love.

In Ibn al-Khatib's conceit, knowledge of the soil and of other factors that favorably influence the tree's growth lies at the heart of the art of "gardening." Once you have discovered in your soul the seed of divine love, you should begin to cultivate it carefully. You must start out by watering it with the traditional Islamic and rational sciences, which help to cleanse the ground around the tree of soul of weeds and parasites. In a similar vein, Ibn al-Khatib demonstrates the necessity for the loving "gardener" to continually practice acts of devotion and to strictly observe the precepts of the *shariʿa*—measures that help to straighten up the tree/soul.

The author then proceeds to alert his reader to the dangerous philosophical and religious speculations which, in his opinion, may distract the lover from striving after his goal. Among the especially grave theoretical delusions Ibn al-Khatib points out the doctrine of the eternity of the world; of God's knowledge of universals;[66] and of the belief that God may dwell in, or unite with, his creatures. To avoid these pernicious views and to secure the growth of the sprout of love, one should, according to Ibn al-Khatib, practice the constant invocation of the divine name (*dhikr*) and concentrate singlemindedly on the contemplation of divine beauty.

Much of Ibn al-Khatib's work deals with the various definitions of love in the Arabic language and literature and with enumerating its multiple uses in poetry, prose, and rational sciences, all of which, in his view, testify to love's centrality to human life. But love, for Ibn al-Khatib, is more than this: the entire cosmos revolves around *mahabba,* since everything, in his words, issues from, and returns to, love. From this perspective, man's love of God constitutes just one manifestation of the all-encompassing phenomenon of cosmic love, albeit by far the most sublime one.

Although love naturally grows out of an ardent and unquenchable longing for the Deity, it requires of the lover constant self-exertion and self-sacrifice. For Ibn al-Khatib, moral uprightness is the indispensable condition of true love—one that is constantly reinvigorated by the beatific vision of the divine in the lover's soul. Ascetic practices are seen by Ibn al-Khatib as necessary stations on the path to intimacy (or friendship) with God (*wilaya*), which Ibn al-Khatib described as the ultimate fruit of divine love.[67]

In Ibn al-Khatib's metaphor, knowledge is presented as the second most important branch of the tree of love. He views all lovers of God as seekers of truth, who strive to make sense of their passion and to relate it to the surrounding world. Therefore, Ibn al-Khatib organizes such seekers-cum-lovers into six categories: (1) the ancient (Greek) philosophers; (2) the "Illuminati" (*al-ishraqiyyun*); (3) the Muslim *falasifa;* (4) the "accomplished [mystics], who consider themselves to be perfect" (*min al-mutammimin bi-zaʿmihim al-mukammalin*);[68] (5) the partisans of "absolute unity" (*al-wahda al-mutlaqa*); and (6) the genuine Sufis of old. Each group, in Ibn al-Khatib's scheme, vigorously upholds its own vision of love and of the Divine Beloved.

Like Ibn Abi Hajala, Ibn al-Khatib uses the form of a poetic anthology to illustrate the all-important role of divine love in human life. However, in contrast to his opponent, who is concerned with narratives depicting various mundane manifestations of human passion, the author of *Rawdat al-taʿrif* draws on Muslim philosophical and theological writings, Sufi textbooks, and collections of mystical poetry. Ibn al-Khatib makes especially heavy use of the contemporary mystical tradition[69]—a fact that accounts for the predominance of Sufi sources in his narrative.[70] Especially prominent among them are Ibn ʿArabi's *Fusus, Futuhat, Diwan,* and several shorter treatises from the Andalusi period.[71]

Despite his fascination with things mystical, Ibn al-Khatib never pretends to be a practicing Sufi himself.[72] Nor does he ever draw on his personal mystical insights and experiences, relying instead on the secondhand testimonies from the rich mystical literature of the epoch. In general his sources are a mixed bag that contains the daring paradoxes of the "drunken" Sufis alongside the humdrum ethical precepts of the moralizing early ascetics. As mentioned, Ibn al-Khatib saw his task in explaining how love of God was experienced and described by individuals of vastly different spiritual and intellectual backgrounds.[73] To this end, Ibn ʿArabi's work with its developed concept of divine love, proved to be especially helpful.[74]

Ibn ʿArabi in *Rawdat al-taʿrif*

Before moving onto Ibn al-Khatib's treatment of the Greatest Master, it should be remembered that *Rawdat al-taʿrif* became the cause (or, more exactly, the pretext) of the vizier's brutal execution by his political rivals that we described earlier on. The kangaroo court staged by his political rivals and personal foes accused Ibn al-Khatib of espousing the "doctrine of the people of unity" (*ahl al-wahda*) and "incarnation" (*madhhab al-hulul*)[75]—charges that are remarkably similar to ones routinely brought against Ibn ʿArabi and his followers. Although courtly intrigues and struggle for power at the Granadine court were the real reasons for Ibn al-Khatib's execution, his *Rawdat al-taʿrif*, provided his enemies with a convenient excuse for the permanent removal of the powerful vizier from the political scene. In any event, accusations of "monistic heresy" figured prominently in the death warrant that was announced in the marketplaces of Granada and Fez in the aftermath of his assassination.[76] One may say that Ibn al-Khatib fell victim to his imprudent use of controversial Sufi sources, most notably the writings of Ibn ʿArabi and other mystical thinkers of dubious credentials. This is especially ironic since in *Rawdat al-taʿrif* Ibn al-Khatib did his utmost to distance himself from their bold statements and ecstatic utterances.

Ibn al-Khatib's attitude to Ibn ʿArabi varies depending on the context in which he cites the latter's ideas. For instance, he makes extensive use of Ibn ʿArabi's opinions on such important issues of Sufi practice and theory as *dhikr, kashf,* and *mushahadat al-haqq.*[77] Though sometimes such quotations are unacknowledged,[78] the entire text of *Rawdat al-taʿrif* is virtually permeated by Ibn ʿArabi's terminology—a fact that need not surprise us in view of their wide spread currency among later Muslim thinkers, not limited to Ibn ʿArabi's adherents.[79] Ibn al-Khatib's use of monistic motifs did not escape the attention of his enemies, who hastened to portray him as a bona fide supporter of the monistic "heresy." What they overlooked, perhaps intentionally, is that in his classification of the types of "lovers" the devout early Sufis, not the *wujudi* mystics of Ibn ʿArabi's inspiration, are placed under the honorable heading of "truth realizers" (*mutahaqqiqun*). The *wujudi* mystics, on the other hand, fall under a deliberately dubious heading that may indicate an implicit censure as well as a veiled praise.

Ibn al-Khatib's treatment of various trends within mystical Islam leaves no doubt as to whom he considers to be the *muhaqqiqun.* They are explicitly identified as the representatives of the so-called "Sharʿi Sufism":[80] al-Ghazali (d. 505/1111), Ahmad al-Rifaʿi (d. 570/1175),[81] ʿAbd al-Qadir al-Jilani (d. 561/1166),[82] and Abu Madyan (d. 594/1198).[83] Of the Sufis of the Muslim West, Ibn al-Khatib pays special tribute to the founders and members of the Shadhili brotherhood, which by his time dominated Sufism on both sides of the

Straits of Gibraltar.[84] In this, he was in agreement with the majority of the *ʿulamaʾ*, who considered a strict observance of the *shariʿa* and avoidance of metaphysical speculation to be trademarks of the "authentic" Sufi. Plainly, on the latter point at least, Ibn ʿArabi and his followers hardly fitted the bill.

Ibn al-Khatib is quite forthright in declaring that only practicing Sufis, that is, those who maintain high moral standards and stringent spiritual discipline, deserve to be called the "best of the Muslims" (*sadat al-muslimin*). Their major achievement, in Ibn al-Khatib's view, is striking a delicate balance between the outward and the inward aspects of the *shariʿa*.[85] Their moderation sets them apart from speculative Sufis—primarily Ibn ʿArabi and his cohorts, who are ambiguously described as "accomplished [mystics] who consider themselves perfect." Besides Ibn ʿArabi, this category includes such controversial Sufis as Ibn al-Farid, Saʿid (Saʿd) al-din al-Farghani (d. 700/1300-1301),[86] Ibn Sawdakin (d. 646/1248),[87] Abu Bakr Ibn al-ʿArif (d. 536/1141),[88] Ibn Barrajan,[89] Ibn Qasi (d. 546/1151),[90] and al-Buni (d. 662/1225).[91]

Searching for one feature that all these mystics shared in common, Ibn al-Khatib singles out what he declares to be the pivot of their cosmology—the *hadith* of the "Hidden Treasure,"[92] which, in their interpretation, posits the primordial essence of God prior to creation as a pure and undifferentiated oneness. At some point in time, so the interpretation goes, this unique essence grew desirous of contemplating its infinite properties and perfection in an external object, causing God to differentiate and particularize his primordial oneness in a series of self-manifestations that Sufi theorists presented as God's gradual descent from the state of absolute transcendence and unity to the level of empirical multiplicity and relativity.[93]

For Ibn al-Khatib, the philosophical premises of the proponents of absolute oneness bear an unmistakable resemblance to the emanative metaphysics (*fayd*) of the ancient philosophers and their Muslim followers.[94] Yet, unlike the *falasifa,* who use rational abstractions, the adherents of unity couch their ideas and experiences in the terminology of the Muslim revelation. Thus, in Sufi speculation, the divine attributes of the *falasifa* (*sifat*) are replaced by "God's most beautiful names," which the Sufis treat as the vital link between the two opposite poles of the essentially unique Divine Absolute, that is, transcendency and immanence, incomparability and similarity, oneness and plurality. Explaining the nature of this polarity, in Ibn al-Khatib's opinion, constitutes the chief concern of the "accomplished mystics," who thereby endeavor to resolve the perennial problem of the duality of God and the world. Their solution is simple. They declare the duality of God and cosmos to be a matter of perspective: from the standpoint of its origination from a unique and undifferentiated Absolute the world is one, while as the empirical manifestation of the divine properties and names it is multiple and variegated.

Such are, in Ibn al-Khatib's view, the cardinal principles of the monistic cosmology as understood by Ibn ʿArabi and his monistic soulmates. His discussion of their metaphysical concepts exhibits a sure command of the terminology current in the Ibn ʿArabi school.[95] At times, his elucidations are directly inspired by either Ibn ʿArabi's original works or those of his followers.[96]

In a particularly bold passage, Ibn al-Khatib applies the dialectics of oneness/manyness to the prophethood/sainthood theory of the "accomplished mystics." In his explanation, the archetypal cosmic function of the saint or prophet is intimately linked to the self-revelatory aspect of the otherwise inscrutable Divine Absolute.[97] After the empirical universe was brought into being, this function has been manifesting itself in the chain of concrete historical prophets and saints, each entrusted with guiding a particular religious community through a specific revealed law. These historical prophets and saints epitomize one or another aspect of the primordial Muhammadan Reality (*al-haqiqa al-muhammadiyya*)[98] which determines the specific natures of their missions. In the end, however, the individual historical manifestations of the Absolute Divine Reality are reintegrated into the original unity in the personality of the Seal of Universal Sainthood.[99]

In summarizing his discussion of monistic theories, Ibn al-Khatib provides the following assessment of Ibn ʿArabi and his followers: whereas, on the practical level, they adhere to the same laudable tradition as the genuine Sufis of old (*sufiyya*), their metaphysics and soteriology are at variance with the *shariʿa* and exhibit non-Islamic influences. In his analysis of the theoretical foundations of the "accomplished mystics" Ibn al-Khatib describes them as a peculiar mixture of "Aristotelian"[100] (read "neo-Platonic") ontology with such traditional scriptural notions as "divine names," "presences," "pen," "guarded tablet," "throne," and "footstool." The end result of this admixture is, in Ibn al-Khatib's view, dubious, if not outright heterodox.

In addition to this syncretic ontology, the "accomplished mystics" occasionally put forth a distinct conception of prophethood that does not correspond to the mainstream Sunni creed. Ibn al-Khatib strongly warns the mystics against taking this fatal step, because, even though on certain points the metaphysical and soteriological tenets of the "accomplished mystics" agree with the Islamic tradition and syllogistic reasoning, their overall validity remains suspect.

In anticipating the inevitable opposition to their doctrine on the part of mainstream Sunni *ʿulamaʾ*, the "accomplished mystics" declared it to be the product of intuitive "unveiling" (*kashf*), which is inaccessible to outsiders. Since a literal reading of the Qurʾan cannot testify to the soundness of their experiences, they have to rely heavily on allegorical interpretation, which, in Ibn al-Khatib's view, is blatantly neglectful of the traditional exegetical methods; it, therefore, carries no argumentative weight.[101]

Nevertheless, the doctrine of Ibn ʿArabi and his followers is, in Ibn al-Khatib's view, closer to Islam than that of absolute unity, espoused by al-Shudhi,[102] Ibn Dahhaq (d. 611/1214),[103] Ibn Sabʿin (d. 669/1270),[104] al-Shushtari (d. 668/1269),[105] Ibn Mutarraf al-Judhami al-Aʿma (d. 663/1264),[106] Ibn Ahla (d. 645/1247),[107] al-Hajj al-Maghribi (d. 688/1289),[108] and the anonymous "people of wadi Riqut."[109] Despite Massignon's assertions to the contrary,[110] Ibn al-Khatib treats these mystics with great caution and consistently offsets the opinions of their admirers with those of their detractors. On one occasion, he even condemns them in no uncertain terms as "extremists" (*al-mutawaghghalun*), who "committed a grave error by advancing the [doctrine of] absolute oneness, by letting themselves be enraptured with it, by camouflaging and disguising it with symbols, and by haughtily scorning others on account of it."[111]

More importantly, Ibn al-Khatib draws a sharp distinction between the espousers of absolute oneness proper and the less consistent monists of the Ibn ʿArabi circle. In his view, although the mystics in the Ibn ʿArabi group adhered to a form of unitive metaphysics, they nevertheless strived to maintain a clear distinction between God and the world. Ibn Sabʿin and his followers, on the other hand, boldly carried the unitive implications to their logical conclusion—the idea that God is the only true reality, all the rest being but a figment of the imagination (*wahm*) and fanciful workings of the human mind. It is the imperfect imaginative and rational faculties of humans that break up and particularize the unique and indivisible reality of the Divine Absolute. In the absence of the subjective human observer, the cosmos regains its primordial oneness that is identical with the divine Godhead. In Ibn al-Khatib's interpretation, this concept effectively invalidates all of the previous prophetic laws, freeing its espousers from any moral or religious restraints. To the accomplished monist, the revealed laws are meaningless and therefore can be safely ignored.

Thus, in Ibn al-Khatib's scheme, although the "accomplished mystics" and the adherents of absolute oneness proceed from kindred metaphysical premises, their conclusions are disparate. He likens the latter to the ancient Sophists, citing Zeno of Elea, as a typical example. As for Ibn ʿArabi and the "accomplished mystics," Ibn al-Khatib views them as the Muslim successors to the neo-Platonic doctrine of divine emanation.[112] Doctrinally, the "accomplished mystics" are, in Ibn al-Khatib's judgment, less at variance with the *shariʿa* than the espousers of absolute oneness. Yet, the practical conclusions that the "accomplished mystics" draw from their teachings can be dangerous due to their proclivity to seek political leadership alongside religious authority. In pursuing this goal, several "accomplished mystics" instigated and led popular uprisings in hopes of wresting power from the "impious" temporal rulers. As a highly placed government official, Ibn al-Khatib condemns such claims in view of the grave political disturbances they might produce—a fact that explains his devastating critique of Ibn Qasi and of other politically active Sufis.

In the end, however, Ibn al-Khatib assumes an irenic position, admitting that all seekers of God mentioned in his work are pursuing the same goal—the True Reality, or God (*al-haqq*). Their difference, in his mind, lies in their distinct conceptions of this Reality. Thus, the philosopher sees God as an abstract First Cause, whose workings he endeavors to understand; for the "illuminated" mystic (*ishraqi*) God is a pure light amid the gloom of material nonbeing. As for the wise man (*hakim*),[113] he first approaches God through his intellect, but then turns to his intuitive insight as more conducive to eternal bliss. The jurist, on the other hand, aspires after the gardens of paradise and hopes that his legal expertise and scholarly "exertion" (*ijtihad*) will assure him a place close to God. Finally, the monistic Sufi sees God as an undifferentiated oneness, with which he strives to identify himself through an ecstatic vision. For Ibn al-Khatib, all these seekers are equally "lovers," although each of them loves God in his own way.[114]

Ibn Khaldun and Islamic Mysticism

Of the Muslim thinkers discussed here, Ibn Khaldun is perhaps the one least in need of introduction.[115] In his "Prolegomenon" (*al-Muqaddima*), he set out to explain the historical evolution of medieval Islamic societies on the basis of his study of North African history. This ambitious project alone assured him a unique place in Islamic intellectual history and made him a favorite object of European academic research. The vast volume of literature on Ibn Khaldun and his thought dispenses me from repeating the conclusions reached by my predecessors. Yet a brief survey of Ibn Khaldun's life and work is necessary in order to put his position vis-à-vis Islamic mysticism in general and Ibn ʿArabi in particular into a broader social and historical context.[116]

Born and educated in Ifriqiyya (Tunis), Ibn Khaldun first embarked on the dual career of courtier and politician. His experience as a high-ranking statesman provided him with firsthand insight into the functioning of the state government and into the factors that contributed to the success and decline of the North African dynasties. However, Ibn Khaldun's own political ambitions were repeatedly frustrated by the intrinsic instability of Maghribi political life that was rife with intrigue, treachery, and jockeying for power. A percipient observer, Ibn Khaldun eventually realized the great dangers involved in pursuing a political career in such a precarious environment. His worst fears came true when his brother Yahya, a brilliant scholar and courtier, fell victim to political intrigues and was brutally assassinated. The tragic fate of his old friend and rival Ibn al-Khatib further confirmed his disenchantment with Maghribi politics. At the height of his political career, Ibn Khaldun wisely withdrew from the courtly intrigue into a less spectacular scholarly profession. In retrospect, it is clear that this timely decision brought him far greater fame than any governmental post.

The Orientalist scholarship of the first half of our century routinely portrayed Ibn Khaldun as "the father of sociology," or, at least, as an historian with a pronounced "sociological" turn of mind.[117] Regardless of the labels, his writings reveal him to be a deeply disillusioned and pragmatic observer who took a remarkably poignant view of the political, social, and intellectual endeavors of his fellow human beings—a feature he shares with his contemporary, Ibn al-Khatib.[118] Little wonder that Western historians have repeatedly portrayed Ibn Khaldun as a thoroughgoing pessimist with a worldview that was both "dark and gloomy."[119]

With regard to Muslim theology, the great Arab historian had little patience for the hairsplitting bickering of both Muslim *falasifa* and rationalist *ʿulamaʾ* to the extent that he sometimes neglected the substantial differences between their intellectual positions. Nor was he particularly interested in their muddled discourses: each time he tried to reproduce them, he "got hopelessly entangled, and invariably failed."[120] This may be an overstatement, yet one can hardly deny that Ibn Khaldun treated the convoluted paths and technicalities of theological speculation as irrelevant to man's happiness in this world and in the Hereafter.[121]

In short, Ibn Khaldun's scholarly method is characterized by empiricism and pragmatism of a rather detached nature.[122] This is not to say that he was a simple collector and classifier of facts. On the contrary, Ibn Khaldun's entire work shows his sincere dedication to bringing out the universal laws and recurrent patterns of human behavior that determine the progress or decline of human societies. Once these laws and patterns have been identified, Ibn Khaldun seeks, at least in the *al-Muqaddima,* to test them against concrete historical phenomena and human collectivities. It is precisely due to his conscious and consistent application of this method that many modern Islamicists have praised Ibn Khaldun as "an astonishingly clear thinker"—an accolade he incidentally shares with Ibn Taymiyya. His methodology, however, is not without shortcomings, since he frequently achieves clarity through oversimplification.[123]

Ibn Khaldun's sympathetic treatment of Sufism contrasts sharply with his obvious dislike for speculative disciplines. Although there is no direct evidence that he himself was an active Sufi, he certainly was conversant with, and interested in, Sufism's history, theory, and practice. In any event, his proficiency in Islamic mysticism was sufficient to qualify him for a highly coveted position at the head of the Baybarsiyya *khanaqa*—the famous Sufi monastery in Egypt.[124] Additionally, Ibn Khaldun's familiarity with the Sufi tradition is attested by his own writings. Apart from a long chapter on Sufism in the *Muqaddima,*[125] Ibn Khaldun dealt with it in a special treatise, "The Cure of the Questioner Through the Clarification of the Problems" (*Shifaʾ al-saʾil li-tahdhib al-masaʾil*).[126] Written between 774-776/1372-1374, that is, shortly before the *Muqaddima,*[127] the *Shifaʾ* was a response to a query from the famous jurist of Granada Abu Ishaq al-Shatibi (d. 790/1388), as to whether or not a Sufi novice can dispense with a spiritual guide, relying entirely on Sufi books and manuals for his training.[128]

In broad outlines, Ibn Khaldun's view of Sufism and its development from a simple practical piety to a sophisticated worldview bears a strong similarity to that of Ibn al-Khatib. Moreover, the two scholars may have acquired their expertise in Sufism under the guidance of the same Sufi master—"the gnostic and chief saint in Spain," Abu Mahdi ʿIsa Ibn al-Zayyat.[129] On more than one occasion Ibn

Khaldun acknowledged his indebtedness to both Ibn al-Zayyat and *Rawdat al-taʿrif* for the sayings of early Sufi masters, especially, ʿAbdallah al-Ansari al-Harawi.[130] The case for Ibn Khaldun's dependence on *Rawdat al-taʿrif* is lent further support by his account of various trends within Sufism, which closely follows that of his Andalusi friend and colleague.[131]

Ibn Khaldun's vision of Sufism's history hinges on the notion of a constant interaction and conflict between two principal tendencies. The first fosters ascetic exercises, spiritual discipline, rigorous self-exertion, moral living, inner serenity, and meticulous observance of the *shariʿa*. This active tendency, which Ibn Khaldun dubbed the Sufism of "good works" (*ʿilm al-muʿamala*), enables the Sufi novice to "purify his heart from wickedness and turbidity by means of abstention from the carnal appetites."[132] It suppresses the "natural bodily instincts" and cleanses the heart from the rust of "hypocrisy" and "worldliness," as a result of which it becomes a polished mirror that reflects the sublime attributes and proprieties of the perfect Deity.[133] When fully realized, this exemplary godliness assures the mystical wayfarer happiness in this world and salvation in the next.

Although this Sufism, which was practiced by Islam's early "ascetics," "worshipers," and "world-renouncers," is in and of itself sufficient for salvation, most later Sufis went beyond it in an attempt to attain proximity with God that would open their souls to the outpourings of their divine beloved. This sincere and disinterested striving after "the greatest bliss" (*al-saʿada al-kubra*), constitutes, in Ibn Khaldun's phrase, the "inner *fiqh*" (*fiqh al-batin*)—a moral and spiritual code of behavior, which was first articulated by the Sufi and theologian al-Harith al-Muhasibi (d. 243/857).[134] With al-Muhasibi's successors, the "inner *fiqh*" grew into a fully fledged science of the "states" and "stations" of the mystical path as well as the means to achieve them. Originally a moral code and pure intuitive experience, Sufism became a complex theory with a set of standard rules, practices, and principles, as well as with its own technical terminology.[135] Since this later Sufism placed much value upon the direct vision of things experienced by some accomplished mystics, Ibn Khaldun termed it the Sufism of "intuitive unveiling" (*ʿilm al-mukashafa*). It found its principal exponent in the famous Sufi and theologian Abu ʾl-Qasim al-Qushayri (d. 475/1072).[136]

The two trends in Sufism—the path of piety (*tariqat al-waraʿ*), based on a strict observance of the *shariʿa* injunctions, and the path of supersensory unveiling (*kashf*), which privileged intuitive experience over the "externals" of the revealed law—were, according to Ibn

Khaldun, blended in al-Ghazali's monumental "Revivification of Religious Sciences" (*Ihyaʾ ʿulum al-din*).[137] In Ibn Khaldun's system, both paths are viewed as valid, though he acknowledged that advocates of the literal interpretation of the *shariʿa* are occasionally insulted by the statements and behavior of individual mystics. Furthermore, for Ibn Khaldun, following both paths simultaneously assured wayfarers "the very essence of happiness"[138] which one cannot attain through philosophical and theological reasoning.[139]

At the same time, Ibn Khaldun pointed out the negative consequences of the emergence of the two distinct trends within the originally homogenous Sufi movement, especially as they started to diverge from each other as time went on. Eventually, Sufism became the opposite of what it originally was: instead of helping Muslims to achieve a moral and pious life, it turned onto itself and became an arcane intellectual trend with a distinct metaphysical doctrine and vision of salvation. This new Sufism, in Ibn Khaldun's argument, was increasingly irrelevant to the immediate spiritual needs of the Muslims, which was especially deplorable because, in his words, "full salvation requires the performance of all demands of the divine law, externally and internally, with the additional provision that the internal states of the heart remain constant, without interruption or slackening."[140] When measured against this ideal, the evolution of latter-day Sufism was seen by Ibn Khaldun as "a change that went against the very character and intention of the original religion."[141] With time, the "science of unveiling" was appropriated by a narrow circle of select visionaries, who thoroughly concealed it from unprepared audiences behind an obscure and misleading terminology.

On the issue of the necessity of the spiritual guide, Ibn Khaldun asserted that his guidance is essential to every seeker in order to avoid the dangers and delusions that await Sufi novices.[142] As a vivid example of such delusions, Ibn Khaldun cited the blasphemous utterances attributed to some ecstatic Sufis. These "words of dubious import," as Ibn Khaldun called them, occur when Sufis endeavor to convey their ineffable mystical experiences to the uninitiated. Since the meaning of these utterances is often at odds with the externals of the *shariʿa*, the *ʿulamaʾ* hold their authors responsible for blasphemy and unbelief. Ibn Khaldun, however, exonerated the earlier Sufis from such accusations, arguing that Sufi experiences are often totally ineffable and should not be measured by ordinary theological yardsticks.[143] Ibn Khaldun, however, decidedly refused to absolve al-Hallaj—a Sufi who, in his view, deliberately divulged "the [ineffable] divine mystery" (*sirr Allah*) that should be confined to the initiated only. Since al-Hallaj's blasphemy was intentional, his excommunication and subsequent execution were well deserved.[144]

Ibn Khaldun on Monistic Philosophy

It is against this general background that one should examine Ibn Khaldun's attitude toward monistic philosophy. A pragmatic thinker who was acutely apprehensive of the ethical and social role of religion, he did not care for the convoluted metaphysics of the later monistic Sufis. In making *kashf* an end in itself, they have contaminated the primeval spirituality of classical Sufism with the rationalist speculations of *kalam* and *falsafa,* which were unknown to the authentic Sufis of old. These later Sufis put forward "a fully fledged theosophical cosmology of the emanationist type," mixing it with the subtle experiences of their pious predecessors:[145]

> A number of recent Sufis, who consider intuitive perceptions to be scientific and logical, hold that the Creator is one with His creatures in His essence, His existence, and His attributes. They recognize that this is basically the opinion of the [Greek] philosophers before Aristotle, especially Plato and Socrates.[146]

Whenever these mystics try to articulate their experiences discursively, they only "add obscurity to obscurity," which result in voluminous works whose subject, in Ibn Khaldun's parlance, straddles the "vague terrain" between rational philosophy and mystical vision. Despite their obscurity, these works find an eager audience among the people prone to sluggishness and inactivity. Such idle individuals "believe that the bliss lies in the knowledge of the mysteries pertaining to the Divine Realm (*malakut*),[147] which they can discover on the pages of those books. How wrong they are!"[148] In sum, according to Ibn Khaldun, one cannot attain the mystical goal through Sufi books alone. Under no condition can the mystical wayfarer be excused from the rigorous spiritual discipline and self-exertion that lie at the heart of the Sufi path.

In examining mystical metaphysics, Ibn Khaldun discerned two concepts of oneness upheld by Sufi philosophers. He likened the first to the Christian doctrine of incarnation and its Shiʿi analog, both of which hold that God can become incarnate in certain privileged individuals. A much more radical notion of oneness is upheld by those who consider this concept to be inconsistent with divine oneness: since incarnation presupposes two different entities, it inevitably implies duality and otherness (*ghayriyya*). To avoid this, some radical Sufis, whom Ibn Khaldun called "monists" (*ittihadiyya*) *stricto sensu,* posit the absolute oneness that excludes even the faintest notion of multiplicity and differentiation.[149] According to them, plurality pertains solely to human perception, while in reality the empirical world is a mere fantasy (*awham*). Ibn Khaldun dismissed this doctrine as contrary to sense-perceptions, Revelation, and rational argument.[150] In his words, "the monistic point of view cannot be adopted as a sound creed . . . similar to the other tenets of Islam, . . ." because it rests entirely on the subjective statements of "those who claim to have actually experienced this absolute oneness of all."[151]

Ibn Khaldun and the People of *tajalli*

One original feature of Ibn Khaldun's treatment of the Sufi metaphysics, which has no parallel in *Rawdat al-taʿrif*, is his emphasis on the notion of divine self-manifestation (*tajalli*),[152] which he sees as crucial for Ibn ʿArabi's version of speculative Sufism. Although the term *tajalli* is ubiquitous in Ibn ʿArabi's original writings, the author of the *Muqaddima* relied on its elaboration by al-Farghani, the author of a famous mystical commentary on Ibn al-Farid's *al-Taʾiyya al-kubra*.[153] Al-Farghani, however, was not Ibn ʿArabi's disciple. Rather, he belonged to the circle of Sadr al-din al-Qunawi, who, as I have repeatedly emphasized, interpreted Ibn ʿArabi's legacy within the framework of Avicennan ontology. Thus, in line with al-Qunawi's cosmology, al-Farghani also viewed the cosmos as an orderly unfolding of the divine essence in a series of self-manifestations (*tajalliyat*) from the highest level (or "presence") of the Universal Intellect (or "the Pen"), through the level of the Universal Soul or the "Nebulous Presence" (*ʿamaʾ*), down to the earthly sphere.[154]

Mindful of the preponderance of divine manifestation in al-Farghani's metaphysics, Ibn Khaldun consistently cited him among "the people of *tajalli*,"[155] along with Ibn al-Farid, Ibn Barrajan, Ibn Qasi, al-Buni, al-Hatimi (i.e., Ibn ʿArabi), and Ibn Sawdakin. All of these thinkers, in Ibn Khaldun's view, agreed that, in the final analysis, the divine essence accepts no description except that of oneness/unity (*al-wahda*). At the same time, they viewed this primeval oneness as impregnated with two opposite impulses, that of plurality and immanence, and that of singularity and transcendency. It is the former that causes the unique Absolute Existence to unfold into the empirical multiplicity of the material world. The latter, on the contrary, remains thoroughly occult and interior, concerned as it is with reestablishing the original oneness of the Divine Absolute. Ibn Khaldun interpreted the theory of two impulses as an attempt on the part of the exponents of [divine self-] manifestation to account for the transcendence/immanence dynamics that posed a perennial logical and philosophical problem.

Ibn Khaldun's account of the monistic theory followed, in general outlines, the relevant passages of Ibn al-Khatib's *Rawdat al-taʿrif*. The fact that Ibn al-Khatib's work was considerably more detailed, indicates that the Granadine vizier had a better command of the subject at hand. This impression is further reinforced by the fact that, unlike Ibn al-Khatib, Ibn Khaldun did not concern himself with the subtleties of a teaching which, in his opinion, found no support in either empirical observation or demonstrative argument. Like any pragmatist, he found the impossibility of testing these Sufi theories with positive criteria irksome. His annoyance finds an expression in his assessment of the *tajalli* school. Like the author of *Rawdat al-taʿrif*, he denounced their tendency to couch their teaching in the vocabulary of the Muslim tradition and/or speculative theology, which, in his view, further obfuscated the already difficult matter. Although Ibn Khaldun occasionally conceded that the unitive metaphysics may have some reality behind it, he still believed that it was much safer to treat it as a deviation from the orthodox dogma.[156]

A harsher assessment of the *ashab al-tajalli* is featured in Ibn Khaldun's later *fatwa*, which has come down to us via the critical "biography" of the Greatest Master by al-Fasi. Unlike the *Shifaʾ* and the *Muqaddima*, which were written in the Maghrib, the *fatwa* almost certainly dates back to his Egyptian years,[157] when he occupied the highest rank in the religious hierarchy of the Mamluk state. It seems reasonable to suggest that as the leader of the Egyptian *ʿulamaʾ* Ibn Khaldun could ill afford to simply reiterate his ambiguous early assessment of speculative Sufism. In any event, the tone of his Egyptian *fatwa* fits in neatly with similar antimonistic condemnations that originated in Ibn Taymiyya's circle:

> Among those Sufis (*mutasawwifa*)[158] were Ibn ʿArabi, Ibn Sabʿin, Ibn Barrajan, and those who followed in their steps and embraced their creed. They composed many works which they circulated among themselves. These works reek of downright unbelief and reprehensible innovation. [Any attempt to] explain their underlying

> meaning allegorically produces results that are as far-fetched as they are abhorrent. This makes the inquirer wonder whether these people can at all be treated as members of this [Muslim] community and counted among [the followers of] the *shariʿa*. . . . Now, as regards the books which contain these erroneous beliefs and are passed around by people, for example, the "Bezels" and the "Revelations" of Ibn ʿArabi, "The Removal of the Sandals" of Ibn Qasi, "The Eye of Certainty,"[159] and many poetic lines by Ibn al-Farid and al-ʿAfif al-Tilimsani, as well as Ibn al-Farghani's commentary on the "Taʾiyya" of Ibn al-Farid. The judgement with respect to these and similar books is as follows: when found, they must be destroyed by fire or washed off by water, until the traces of writing disappear completely. Such an action is beneficial to the religion [of Islam] because it leads to the eradication of erroneous beliefs.[160]

Another point Ibn Khaldun addressed in his Egyptian *fatwa* concerns the inquiry into the mysteries of the unseen, which he imputed to the later Sufis. For him, the knowledge of the unseen constitutes the prerogative of the prophets and messengers that should not be infringed by ordinary humans. What the faithful should know has already been delivered to them by the legislating prophets: any attempt to unravel the divine mystery may upset God's plan with regard to this world and shatter the faith of the inquirer. Echoing al-Dhahabi's statement quoted earlier on, Ibn Khaldun argued that the recondite ontological theories of the philosophizing mystics have no direct bearing on the faithful's ability to fulfill his essential religious obligations and to achieve salvation.[161] His call for the destruction of the objectionable works at the close of the Egyptian *fatwa* indicates the stiffening, for one reason or another, of his originally ambiguous position on the issue.

As mentioned, in his description of the doctrine of the "professors of absolute oneness" (*ashab al-wahda*) Ibn Khaldun followed closely the classification of Sufi groups already outlined by Ibn al-Khatib.[162] Yet, whereas Ibn al-Khatib was genuinely concerned with the doctrinal differences between the two schools of speculative Sufism, Ibn Khaldun gave them short shrift, focusing instead on the detrimental social and political implications of the monistic teachings—a concern for which doctrinal minutia were of little moment. In examining these implications he found what he considered to be an underlying affinity between Sufi *wilaya* and the Shiʿi doctrine of the infallible *imam*.[163] To prove this affinity, Ibn Khaldun turned to the early stage of Sufism's history, when the Sufi movement was, in his view, first exposed to the influence of the Shiʿi conception of the imamate. This influence, he argued, was already apparent in the excessive veneration of ʿAli by the early Muslim mystics who routinely traced their spiritual genealogy back to the Fourth Caliph and to the Prophet, bypassing the first three caliphs. This Shiʿi tendency grew especially strong in the teachings of the later Sufis that Ibn Khaldun described as "virtually saturated with Shiʿah theories."[164] The later Sufis did more than simply venerate ʿAli and his descendants; they shared the militant messianic teachings of the "extreme" wing of the Shiʿi movement—the Ismaʿilis. The only difference between the two was that in Sufism, the Fatimi messiah (*mahdi*) of the Ismaʿilis was identified as the supreme Sufi gnostic, the "pole" or "axis" (*al-qutb*) of the age. Barring this difference, in both Sufism and Ismaʿilism the *mahdi* plays essentially the same function, to wit, to instruct his followers in the hidden meaning of the *shariʿa* and to guide them to salvation.[165]

This said, Ibn Khaldun portrayed Ibn ʿArabi, Ibn Qasi, and Ibn Sabʿin as the foremost exponents, within Sufism, of the Shiʿi/Ismaʿili doctrine of the *mahdi,* detecting the Shiʿi influence in the Sufi doctrine of the invisible hierarchy of holy men whom these writers presented as the individual manifestations of the eternal Muhammadan Reality (*al-haqiqa al-muhammadiyya*).[166] In examining Ibn ʿArabi's ideas of prophesy and sainthood, Ibn Khaldun stressed two major theories espoused by the Greatest Master. The first, set out in "The Fabulous Gryphon on the Seal of the Saints and the Sun [Rising From] the West" (*ʿAnqaʾ mughrib fi khatm al-awliyaʾ wa shams al-Maghrib*),[167] posited that sainthood, like prophethood, has its seal (*khatm*)—the supreme Sufi saint of all time. Furthermore, in the *ʿAnqaʾ*, according to Ibn Khaldun, the seal of sainthood symbolizes the continuation of the prophetic mission on a new historical stage—when the message brought by the Seal of the Prophets (i.e., Muhammad) has been obscured and corrupted by mundane concerns.

In the *Muqaddima,* this theory is consistently put into the mouth of one Ibn Abi Watil, whom Ibn Khaldun described as an important follower of the Greatest Master.[168] In Ibn Abi Watil's interpretation, prophesy is inevitably followed by a Sufi-based deputyship (*khilafa*), or sainthood, which, in turn, is superseded by a temporal reign (*mulk*), based on raw force and coercion. As the *mulk* gradually degenerates into dire tyranny, materialism, corruption, and worldliness, God sends the seal of the saints to restore the world to its original moral and social harmony. The seal's pious reign, which Ibn Abi Watil called "sainthood" (*wilaya*), is however, short-lived, for it is soon supplanted by deputyship, which, in turn, is followed by the oppressive secular rule. At the end of time, the Antichrist (*al-dajl*) will appear to immortalize the tyranny and oppression associated with the godless *mulk.* He will be opposed by the ultimate *mahdi,* ʿIsa b. Maryam, who will destroy him in a final eschatological fight before the Day of Judgment.[169]

Although Ibn Khaldun's exposition of the tripartite prophesy/sainthood/*mulk* scheme is based on Ibn Abi Watil's work, he consistently claimed to have derived it from the *ʿAnqaʾ mughrib.* This confusion is to the fore in Ibn Khaldun's discussion of the theme of the bricks in the wall of prophethood, which we have cited in the previous chapters. According to Ibn Khaldun's interpretation, the Seal of the Prophets (= Muhammad) is identical with the golden brick,[170] whereas the seal of the saints is symbolized by the silver one. The disparity in the value of gold and silver, so goes the argument, indicates the comparative importance of their missions. For Ibn Khaldun, this image asserts the primacy of the prophet over the saint.

Ibn Khaldun's paraphrase, however, is at odds with the meaning of the brick motif in Ibn ʿArabi's original text. Although the *ʿAnqaʾ mughrib,* which Ibn Khaldun cited as his primary source, does contain cryptic predictions of the rise of the seal of the saints, it is conspicuously silent about the bricks' theme.[171] It is, to be remembered, featured in the *Fusus,* which Ibn Khaldun did not mention among his sources.[172] One may therefore venture the guess that Ibn Khaldun's real source was Ibn Abi Watil, who mentioned the topos in question in his commentary on the *Khalʿ al-naʿlayn.* In any event, in the *Fusus,* the brick image has a different meaning from that put into it by Ibn Khaldun. By all standards, Ibn ʿArabi's own interpretation of the brick image is both bolder and subtler: he saw the bricks as symbols of the two complementary aspects of the prophetic mission. On this view, sainthood is eternally relevant and thus takes precedence over legislative prophesy, which is confined to a specific time and space.[173]

Contrary to Ibn Khaldun's understanding of the brick motif, it is the legislative function of prophethood that Ibn ʿArabi likens to the silver brick, since the golden one, for him, is the symbol of sainthood.[174] Now it seems that Ibn Khaldun intentionally opted for a less shocking interpretation of the brick motif which, on balance, is quite in line with the mainstream Sunni dogma. Alternatively, Ibn Khaldun may have misunderstood its meaning, since, as mentioned, he learned about it through Ibn Abi Watil's commentary on "The Removal of the Sandals"—his major (and possibly only) source on the teaching of the Greatest Master. The latter seems even more likely, since the author of the *Muqaddima* unequivocally described Ibn Abi

Watil as a typical member of Ibn ʿArabi's school.[175] Another reason to suspect Ibn Khaldun's familiarity with Ibn ʿArabi's original works is the geomantic drawings and occult calculations that he attributed to Ibn ʿArabi, but that are different from those in the original text of the *ʿAnqa*ʾ.[176]

Thus, by all intents and purposes, Ibn Khaldun seems to have had, to put it mildly, only a secondhand knowledge of Ibn ʿArabi's original work. His ignorance, however, did not prevent him from attacking the Greatest Master's perceived "heresies," especially his belief in the early advent of the eschatological world restorer of Fatimi extraction. By the same token, in Ibn Khaldun's discussion of later Sufism, Ibn ʿArabi is consistently paired with the celebrated Maghribi astrologer, Ahmad al-Buni (d. 622/1225), whose grand eschatological predictions were condemned by many concerned Muslim theologians.[177] Whether or not this pairing is justified, it certainly reflected the popular perception of Ibn ʿArabi as an occultist and thaumaturge that was discussed in Chapter 2 of this study. In elucidating the principles of onomatomancy, the author of the *Muqaddima* relied almost exclusively on the writings of al-Buni, ignoring the wealth of material on this topic found in the *Futuhat*.[178] In general, his knowledge of Ibn ʿArabi's divinatory techniques is secondary and imprecise, derived, in all likelihood, from Ibn Abi Watil's commentary on the *Khalʿ al-naʿlayn*.[179]

Plainly, sociopolitical rather than theological considerations motivated Ibn Khaldun's severe criticism of the messianic theories imputed to Ibn ʿArabi and to other monistic Sufis.[180] These considerations determined his negative attitude toward Ibn ʿArabi, whose works, as we have shown, he knew largely from hearsay. Ibn Khaldun's misgivings should be seen against the background of the turbulent Maghribi history that was punctuated by popular uprisings led by self-appointed *mahdi*s who supported their claims through magic, thaumaturgy, and occult prognostication.[181] Outside this religio-political context, Ibn Khaldun's criticism is muted. Occasionally, he even seems to have been genuinely fascinated by the divination techniques, which he discussed in great detail in a special chapter of the *Muqaddima*.[182]

To sum up, Ibn Khaldun's position vis-à-vis Sufism was nuanced. He gave his stamp of approval to Sufi morals and spiritual self-discipline, which, in his view, were conducive to a greater personal awareness of God's oneness, and, eventually, to a blissful contemplation of God in the afterlife. He also set much value upon such mystical experiences as the direct vision of God (*mushahada*) and intuitive unveiling (*kashf*). Like many Ashʿari theologians sympathetic to Sufism, he asserted the reality of the saintly miracles.[183] At the same time, taking his lead from Ibn al-Khatib, he envisioned Sufism's history as the process of an inexorable decline from the originally laudable and sound principles that was occasioned by the infusion of alien metaphysical, rationalist, and esoteric elements. In the course of its evolution, Sufism became a religious doctrine complete with its own vision of *tawhid,* cosmology, eschatology, prophethood, divine names, and attributes. As a result, Sufism, in Ibn Khaldun's opinion, lost its *sharʿi* identity and strayed from the right path into downright heresy.

It is against this background that one should assess Ibn Khaldun's treatment of the Greatest Master that seems to have undergone significant changes over the years. His relatively tolerant and ambiguous view of Ibn ʿArabi, which we find in the *Muqaddima,* gave way to an energetic and unequivocal rebuttal in his Egyptian *fatwa,* written at the end of his life. One can only speculate on whether this change of heart reflected Ibn Khaldun's genuine convictions or was dictated by the exigencies of his post at the top of the Egyptian religious hierarchy.

Ibn Khaldun's early Sufi training and intellectual curiosity made him susceptible to the powerful attraction exercised by monistic Sufism.[184] Yet, as a top-ranking courtier and religious official, Ibn Khaldun was ever apprehensive of those aspects of Sufi speculation that might result in social and political unrest. This apprehension explains his decisive repudiation of the monistic metaphysics, sainthood theory, occult sciences, and divination techniques as incompatible with the intentions and goals of genuine Sufism and of the Muslim community.[185] In light of this overriding concern, doctrinal differences between the *ashab al-tajalli* and the *ashab al-wahda al-mutlaqa* were seen by Ibn Khaldun as being of minor significance. As with his theory of historical evolution, he focused on general, "objective" tendencies making short shrift of the multitude of concrete detail.

Similar to the other critics of Islamic mysticism, Ibn Khaldun used the classical Sufism of the 3d/9th-4th/10th centuries as a yardstick against which he measured later Sufi teachings. These he found wanting and strongly decried Sufism's devolution from the golden age of an untainted mystical experience and faithfulness to the *shariʿa* to the artificiality and outright heterodoxy that he observed among contemporary Sufis. Little wonder that they bear the brunt of his critique in the Egyptian *fatwa* and, to a lesser extent, in the *Shifa*ʾ and the *Muqaddima.*

Paradoxically, however, Ibn Khaldun was ill-equipped to evaluate their work—his knowledge of their theories was based, in part, on the oral lectures of his Sufi teacher, Ibn al-Zayyat, and, in part, on Ibn al-Khatib's *Rawdat al-taʿrif*. The only original Sufi texts he quoted in the *Muqaddima* are al-Farghani's commentary on Ibn al-Farid's "Great *Taʾiyya*" and a commentary on Ibn Qasi's *Khalʿ al-naʿlayn* by the obscure disciple of Ibn Sabʿin. Although he did cite Ibn ʿArabi's *ʿAnqaʾ mughrib,* he seems to have known it in a flawed and facile rendition that failed to do justice to the complexity of Ibn ʿArabi's original ideas.

Conclusion

The opinions of Ibn ʿArabi presented in this chapter indicate that in the Muslim West his legacy was not considered unique or exceptional. Neither Ibn al-Zubayr nor Abu Hayyan, not to mention Ibn Khatima, seem to have been aware of the great impression his teaching made in the Muslim East. Since Ibn ʿArabi left no significant following in either al-Andalus or North Africa, he was viewed by many of his countrymen as part of a larger group of heretical mystic philosophers, whose ideas were consistently exposed and condemned by local *ʿulamaʾ*. This vision of Ibn ʿArabi is in marked contrast with the way in which he was assessed by the Eastern *ʿulamaʾ* who treated him as the foremost exponent, if not the founder, of monistic philosophy.

This disparity of visions finds a vivid expression in the assessment of the Greatest Master by the Almerian litterateur Ibn Khatima, who demonstrates a lack of firsthand acquaintance with his work. At the same time, Ibn Khatima's focus on Ibn ʿArabi's use of symbols suggests not only a professional interest, but also an acquaintance with the Sufi's works from the Andalusi period, possibly the *ʿAnqaʾ mughrib* and "The Book of Ascension" (*Kitab al-israʾ*),[186] which are quite consistent with his comments on the allegorical, recondite style employed by the Greatest Master.

Of the three Western Islamic authors discussed in the second part of this chapter, Ibn al-Khatib shows the greatest familiarity with monistic Sufism in general and with Ibn ʿArabi's teachings in particular. Yet, even Ibn al-Khatib does not treat the Greatest Master as *the* founder of the unitive metaphysics, which, in his mind, constitute the hallmark of "the accomplished mystics." On the contrary,

Ibn al-Khatib's discourse leaves no doubt that the views that the Eastern *ʿulamaʾ* consistently ascribed to Ibn ʿArabi, were, in the Muslim West, associated with a larger group of Andalusi thinkers, the "al-Shudhiyya."

This is even more remarkable since Ibn al-Khatib invariably presents another Andalusi Sufi master, Ibn Sabʿin, as the leader of the adherents of absolute oneness, whom he calls "Sabiʿiniyya." It appears that, for Ibn al-Khatib, Ibn Sabʿin was a much more consequential figure for Western Islamic mysticism than the Greatest Master. Ibn al-Khatib's reticence toward Ibn ʿArabi may, however, indicate his conviction that the latter simply continued the old mystical tradition of Ibn al-ʿArif, Ibn Barrajan, and Ibn Qasi, while Ibn Sabʿin was the creator of an original philosophical system.[187] This of course was not the way Ibn ʿArabi was received in the Muslim East, where he was seen as the founder of *wahdat al-wujud.* Interestingly, this term was apparently unknown to the Western authors we have discussed. At least none of them, to my knowledge, applied it to Ibn ʿArabi's legacy,[188] although they did use the terms that we never meet in Eastern heresiographical works, most notably *ashab al-tajalli* and *al-mutammamun bi-zaʿmihim al-mukammalun*. A similar view of Ibn ʿArabi is taken by Ibn Khaldun in his *Muqaddima,* which also neglects to single out Ibn ʿArabi as either the founder of the monistic philosophy or the promulgator par excellence of the controversial seal-of-the-saints doctrine. On the latter issue Ibn al-Khatib and Ibn Khaldun also exhibit a remarkable unanimity: highly positioned courtiers and statesmen, they rejected it as a potential banner and ideology for violent messianic uprisings.

Both Ibn al-Khatib and Ibn Khaldun hold a similar idealized view of the beginnings of the ascetic and mystical movement in Islam. For them, early Sufism is synonymous with the unswerving loyalty to the *shariʿa* that was free from any political or intellectual ambitions. Conversely, they see Sufism's later evolution as an unmitigated corruption of the original values and standards. This assumption, of course, is in no way unique to these authors and constitutes the fulcrum of most of the accounts of Sufism's history by its advocates and adversaries alike.

In the idealized picture of early Sufism painted by Ibn al-Khatib and Ibn Khaldun, there is no room for an independent metaphysical theory. Likewise, they take exception to a specifically Sufi eschatology and prophetology. The picture of Sufism they assemble rests on the assumption that the genuine Sufis should never venture beyond the mainstream Sunni creed. In this vision of Sufi history, the early mystics are nostalgically portrayed as the exemplary believers who successfully maintained the balance between the inner and outer dimensions of Islamic revelation. On the other hand, Ibn ʿArabi and other philosophizing later mystics, with their complex metaphysics and ontology and their recondite occultism, are presented as dangerous innovators who have adulterated the pristine purity of early Sufism.

No matter how strongly Ibn al-Khatib and Ibn Khaldun oppose the later Sufi teachings, they implicitly acknowledge that no mystical quest is possible within the dual straightjacket of rationalist speculation and blind traditionalism, both of which are essentially alien to the mystical weltanschauung. Their ambivalent attitude toward theoretical mysticism is evident from the detailed discussions of the Sufi metaphysics and prophetology in both *Rawdat al-taʿrif* and the *Muqaddima*.

Ibn al-Khatib's remarkably competent and, for the most part, unbiased account of later Sufi doctrines furnished his enemies with a pretext to accuse him of monistic heresy. Ibn Khaldun, possibly mindful of his friend's tragic end, was more outspoken (if also less profound) in exposing the perceived "errors" and "excesses" of monistic Sufism. Nevertheless, the discussion of Ibn ʿArabi and his followers in the *Muqaddima* is ambiguous enough to make some modern scholars suspect Ibn Khaldun of being partial to the monistic thought.[189]

8

EGYPT: THE POLEMIC CONTINUES

> This is the book whose
> delusions
> Have led astray both the fathers and
> their sons
> Begone thee who thinkest
> otherwise, for thou surely
> art an unbeliever!

An inscription on the cover of
a copy of *Fusus al-hikam* by
Jamal al-din Ibn Hisham
(d. 761/1360)[1]

The 9th/15th centuries witnessed a dramatic escalation of the debate around Ibn ʿArabi's theology. The polemical "biographies" of the Greatest Master by al-Qari al-Baghdadi and al-Fasi are just two examples of the vast body of literature generated by the controversy, in which anti-Ibn ʿArabi works outnumbered those written in his defense. Whereas in the 7/13th and 8/14th centuries we find around ten full-scale refutations of the Greatest Master by six different authors,[2] the 9th/15th centuries alone produced at least nineteen works of this kind.[3] In addition, we find numberless legal *responsa* condemning Ibn ʿArabi and his followers.[4]

In quantity, if not in quality the Ibn ʿArabi faction lags far behind: throughout the 8th/14th-9th/15th centuries his partisans produced some eight to ten apologies, plus ten exonerating *fatwa*s.[5] A comparison of each side's literary output accurately reflects the balance of power between the parties to the debate. In what follows we shall discuss a few clashes between them that took place in the scholarly community of Mamluk Cairo.

Ibn ʿArabi in Mamluk Cairo

The theological confrontation over Ibn ʿArabi's legacy set off tremendous waves throughout the Muslim community, sweeping into its current the growing number of *ʿulama*ʾ. Although many of them had little personal stake in this moot issue, they tended to align with either his advocates or detrators. Not infrequently their ignorance of the complexity of the problem made such outsiders more intolerant and outspoken than the more sophisticated polemicists. A typical example is the Turkoman official Taghri Birmish b. Yusuf (d. 823/1420). Well-connected to the Circassian ruling elite, this self-proclaimed enforcer of orthodoxy spearheaded several popular campaigns against suspected deviators from the correct faith of "the pious forefathers" in Cairo and later on in the holy cities of Arabia. The historians al-Maqrizi and al-Sakhawi, who adhered to the opposite factions of the Ibn-ʿArabi debate, condescendingly portray Taghri Birmish as an energetic but superficial Hanafi scholar whose native density prevented him from learning anything but the basics of religious knowledge. As a result, he abandoned the scholarly career for government service, which did little to cool his inquisitorial zeal. During his study in Cairo Taghri Birmish learned about the Ibn ʿArabi polemic, which his teachers often mentioned in their lectures. Before long, he made the cause of the anti-Ibn ʿArabi faction his own and publicly denounced the latter's teaching as a gross insult to the "pure and simple" dogma of primeval Islam.

According to al-Sakhawi, after he was appointed to an office in the military administration of the Mamluk capital, Taghri Birmish called upon his religious teachers to support his vigilante campaign against Ibn ʿArabi by issuing condemnatory *fatwa*s. In his self-righteous zeal he demanded that all of Ibn ʿArabi's works be declared illegal and destroyed on the spot. Although himself no friend of Ibn ʿArabi, the great Egyptian historian al-Sakhawi[6] nevertheless speaks of Taghri Birmish's witch-hunting with a detached, even snobbish disapproval:[7]

> He constantly attacked Ibn ʿArabi and other Sufi philosophers like him, and went to such extremes as to burn whatever [Ibn ʿArabi's] books he could lay his hands on. Once he attached a copy of the *Fusus* to the tail of a dog. This made him very popular with the townsfolk, whereas his opponents strongly disapproved his actions. He did not, however, care for their opinion, though he himself was uneducated in the religious sciences.[8]

Al-Maqrizi, an Egyptian scholar empathetic with Sufism and the Greatest Master, adds that Taghri Birmish's hatred for Ibn ʿArabi became an obsession that he scathingly attributes to Taghri Birmish's native stupidity. Due to his denseness, says al-Maqrizi, he was unable to make sense of Ibn ʿArabi's works, relying blindly on the opinions of his teachers.[9] Ironically, both al-Maqrizi (pro-Ibn ʿArabi) and al-Sakhawi (anti-Ibn ʿArabi) equally disapprove of Taghri Birmish's involvement in the matter, which, in their view, was beyond his comprehension. For them, the uncouth Turkoman administrator was an unwelcome intruder who was throwing around his political weight to suppress a teaching of which he had no inkling.

In any event, in 9th/15th-century Egypt, autos-da-fé of Ibn ʿArabi's works similar to the one just described were nothing out of the ordinary.[10] Widely discussed among the conservative Egyptian *ʿulama*ʾ was the question of how one should dispose of the copies of the *Fusus* seized by the authorities. Some suggested that one cannot put to the torch books, no matter how heretical, if they contain Qurʾanic quotations. To avoid burning the word of God, some scholars demanded that the text of the *Fusus* be washed off, whereupon the blank pages be thrown into the fire.[11]

As the Taghri Birmish episode finely shows, some radical opponents of the Greatest Master occasionally had recourse to nonconventional methods of "humiliating" the *Fusus* and its author. At the same time, extreme solutions were not always appreciated by Ibn ʿArabi's learned advocates and adversaries alike, as is evident from the following story that took place in Egypt in 888/1483:

> In that year [888] Shams al-din al-Hulaybi[12] was taking inventory of the belongings of [the deceased] Yahya Ibn Hijji.[13] Among his [Yahya's] books he noticed the *Fusus* by Ibn ʿArabi. "This book," he said, "must be burnt, because Ibn ʿArabi was an unbeliever, who was worse than the Jews, the Christians and the idol worshippers!" One of his companions told: "How can you [order to] burn the text of the *Fusus* that contains verses (*ayat*) from God's speech?!" "So be it!" replied [al-Hulaybi]. His statement became public, and he himself was charged with unbelief. He hastened to throw himself [at the feet] of Ibn Muzhir the Chancellor,[14] who took al-Hulaybi's side [against his accusers]. Nevertheless, [al-Hulaybi] was strongly reprimanded and divested of his turban.[15] [In the end], however, he was pronounced a [believing] Muslim and his life was spared. As a result of all this, his fortunes changed for the worse. The poet Abu ʾl-Naja al-Qumani[16] ridiculed him in [the following poem]:

Oh Hulaybi! You were seated with a slap
on the back of your head
When you, unbeliever, arrogantly
demanded that the *Fusus* be burned
You have made a narrow escape
By producing two witnesses [who testified
to your innocence]![17]

This story[18] contravenes the statements of al-Sakhawi and of other critics of Ibn ʿArabi, who argued that his books and teachings were completely banished from Egypt in the second half of the 9th/15th centuries.[19] In fact, on several instances al-Sakhawi himself admitted that, despite the persecutions, Ibn ʿArabi's ideas continued to enjoy wide popularity among the Egyptian scholars of the age. As an example he mentioned one ʿAbd al-Wahhab b. al-Taj, who spread Ibn ʿArabi's teaching "in the learned gatherings and marketplaces" of Cairo. At the same time, most of the pro-Ibn ʿArabi scholars preferred to study his works (mainly the *Fusus*) in the privacy of their homes, although their friends and colleagues were usually well aware of their secret passion.[20] Such scholars seem to have always had a small but eager following, which helps to explain how Ibn ʿArabi's ideas survived in the overwhelmingly hostile environment described by al-Sakhawi and by other authors.

On the other hand, compared with the wide popularity that Ibn ʿArabi enjoyed in Anatolia and India, where his works were openly studied in the mosques,[21] Egyptian society was certainly far less tolerant of his ideas.[22] One is tempted to attribute this phenomenon to the conservative mentality of the Egyptian *ʿulamaʾ*, especially since Ibn ʿArabi's admirers were especially numerous among foreign scholars residing in Egypt.[23] Plausible as this explanation may appear, it is not without a flaw, since some of Ibn ʿArabi's most outspoken critics in Egypt were also outsiders. Outstanding among them were ʿAlaʾ al-din al-Bukhari and Burhan al-din al-Biqaʿi.

Al-Bukhari versus al-Bisati: A public dispute over Ibn ʿArabi's unbelief

ʿAlaʾ al-din Muhammad b. Muhammad al-Bukhari[24] was born and educated in Bukhara,[25] where he studied under Saʿd al-din al-

Taftazani. It was from him that al-Bukhari inherited a profound dislike for monistic philosophy, which he saw as synonymous with Ibn ʿArabi and his followers. Al-Bukhari traveled widely in Iran and Central Asia searching for competent religious instructors. From an early age he excelled in traditional and rational sciences such as the Qurʾan, *hadith,* rhetoric, logic, poetry, and dialectics. He also studied classical Sufi manuals and was seen by many as an accomplished Sufi master. A well-rounded individual with broad intellectual horizons, al-Bukhari for some time resided in India, where his preaching and lectures earned him great popularity among Indian Muslims. Having favorably impressed a local ruler, al-Bukhari was invited to serve as his personal religious tutor and advisor. However, a man of principle, he soon fell out with his Indian patron and left the Subcontinent for Mecca, where he lived for several years until the Mamluk sultan Bars Bay (r. 825/1422-841/1438) invited him to the Egyptian capital. Soon after his arrival, he was embroiled in a vociferous public dispute over Ibn ʿArabi's orthodoxy, in the course of which he clashed with the influential Maliki *qadi* of Egypt, Muhammad al-Bisati (d. 842/1438), who advised caution in this matter. Following a public altercation with his opponent, an angry al-Bukhari took ostentatious leave of Cairo to the great chagrin of his Egyptian partisans.

In Syria, where he settled after his departure, al-Bukhari kept thinking about his "humiliation" at the hands of al-Bisati and composed a lengthy refutation of Ibn ʿArabi and his school, titled "The Dishonoring of the Infidels and the Counselling of the Champions of God's Unity" (*Fadihat al-mulhidin wa nasihat al-muwahhidin*).[26] Simultaneously, he got himself involved in another fierce controversy. Ironically, this time his target was Ibn ʿArabi's archenemy, Ibn Taymiyya, whom al-Bukhari accused of certain juridical "innovations." Al-Bukhari's critique caused a great uproar in Syria that was home to many influential followers of the Hanbali scholar. Unmindful of the wide opposition to his critique among his Syrian colleagues, al-Bukhari boldly demanded that Ibn Taymiyya be divested of his honorific title of *shaykh al-Islam,* proclaiming everyone who refused to do so an unbeliever. His condemnation of Ibn Taymiyya drew severe criticism and eventually a book-size refutation by the Shafiʿi scholar Ibn Nasir al-din al-Dimashqi (d. 838/1434)[27] who sent his opus to Egyptian scholars for approval. As one might expect, upon receipt of this work, Muhammad al-Bisati seized the opportunity to denounce his former prosecutor as an ignoramus and troublemaker.

Al-Bukhari's acrimonious polemic with the Syrian supporters of Ibn Taymiyya did not cause him to forget about his hostility to the

Greatest Master, whom he continued to accuse of heresy and juridical incompetence. In the end, he gained notoriety as a vociferous critic of both Muslim thinkers who, as we have seen, exemplified diametrically opposed religious outlooks. The irony of this situation was not lost on some Muslim authors, who, not without malice, quoted al-Bukhari's statement that "Ibn Taymiyya is a *kafir,* and Ibn ʿArabi is [also] a *kafir!*"[28] Toward the end of his life, al-Bukhari is said to have been afflicted by an evil female spirit that haunted him under different guises. To repel her, this champion of orthodoxy was reduced to such unorthodox healing techniques as magic formulas, exorcism, and even outright sorcery. His reliance on these cures drew the malicious sneers of his opponents, who, depending on their theological position, attributed his affliction to his vilification of either Ibn Taymiyya or the Greatest Master. Eventually he was cured of his illness by a popular Egyptian saint Ibrahim al-Itkawi (d. 834/1430).[29]

Although I have not consulted the manuscript of al-Bukhari's refutation of the Greatest Master, some idea of this work can be obtained from its detailed paraphrase by another opponent of Ibn ʿArabi.[30] The briefest of looks at this treatise evinces al-Bukhari's heavy dependence on the "Epistle" of al-Taftazani, which he often quoted verbatim. Like its prototype, it deals mostly with Ibn ʿArabi's metaphysics. The similarity between al-Bukhari and al-Taftazani is to the fore in their treatment of the Sufi concepts of *fana*ʾ and *baqa*ʾ, which they understood as purely psychological phenomena with no underlying ontological reality behind it. As his predecessor, al-Bukhari argued that the original meaning of these Sufi terms was distorted by the monistic thinkers.[31] As with al-Taftazani, al-Bukhari did not doubt the reality of mystical experience. What he vigorously denied was that it provided an accurate insight into the structure of the universe, which, in his view, can be understood only through a proper application of theological reasoning.

In spite of his Hanafi background and lifelong opposition to Ibn Taymiyya, al-Bukhari evinced the same puristic view of the Muslim dogma that we observed in the work of his Hanbali antagonist and his followers. Another trait he shared with Ibn Taymiyya was his manifest lack of forbearance toward religious opinions other than his own. His intellectual kinship with Ibn Taymiyya is also obvious in his obstinate refusal to bow to, or accept the patronage of, the secular authorities. Al-Bukhari's strained relationships with the temporal rulers of the age, whom he repeatedly accused of condoning "un-Islamic" customs, illegal taxes, and unseemly pastimes call to mind similar remonstrations that punctuated Ibn Taymiyya's career.[32] The same holds for al-Bukhari's bitter struggle against popular beliefs and customs that he viewed as contrary to the *shariʿa*.[33]

Al-Bukhari's blunt rejection of "deviant" doctrines found a dramatic expression in his violent confrontation with al-Bisati over the issue of Ibn ʿArabi's "unbelief." Of direct relevance to our topic, this episode merits closer examination. Luckily, al-Sakhawi, who took personal interest in documenting the Ibn ʿArabi debate, left a detailed account of the encounter between al-Bukhari and al-Bisati at a scholarly gathering in Cairo in 831/1428:

> It so happened that Ibn ʿArabi was mentioned during that assembly, whilst [al-Bukhari] was one of those who had strongly denounced him and his followers, proclaimed them unbelievers and prohibited the study of their books. [When he heard Ibn ʿArabi's name,] he demanded that his condemnatory position [vis-à-vis Ibn ʿArabi] be made public (*ibraz*). Most of those present agreed with it except for al-Bisati. [Later on] people would say that he simply wanted to show him [al-Bukhari] his strength in conducting scholarly debate and disputation.[34] Al-Bisati admitted that [many] people disapproved of the external meaning of [Ibn ʿArabi's] words. However, he added, were one to interpret the meaning of his statements allegorically, one would find that there was nothing in [Ibn ʿArabi's] words that calls for blame. The scholars who were present began to debate this [subject]. Our Shaykh[35] told me: "I was more inclined to take the position of ʿAla' [al-din al-Bukhari], though I was of the opinion that we should not hasten to proclaim someone an unbeliever exclusively on the strength of the words of unbelief attributed to him." Here is a summary of their positions. Al-ʿAla' [al-Bukhari] demanded that all who professed [the doctrine of] absolute oneness be condemned unconditionally. To this the Maliki[36] replied: "You do not understand [the doctrine of] absolute oneness!" When al-Bukhari heard this [reply], he flew into a rage and cried at the top of his lungs: "You are dismissed [from judgeship], even though the sultan has not yet dismissed you [formally]!" By saying this [al-Bukhari] implied that his [al-Bisati's] position has rendered him an unbeliever. It is said that al-Bukhari told him plainly: "You are an unbeliever, for everyone who adheres to [the doctrine of] absolute oneness, which is the most heinous kind of unbelief, is beyond pardon!" Having said this, he kept shouting: "By God, if the sultan does not dismiss him [al-Bisati] from the office of the judge, I will leave Egypt immediately!" Thereupon al-Bisati was advised to take leave of the gathering in order to to preclude further scandal.[37]

On the next day the case was taken to the Mamluk sultan Bars-Bay, who was presented with the difficult dilemma of choosing sides in a theological problem of which he had no idea. The sultan, however, shrewdly deferred the matter to the council of the chief judges of Cairo[38] chaired by the chief *qadi*[39] of the Shafiʿis, Ibn Hajar al-ʿAsqalani. The latter opened deliberations by asking al-Bisati to explain his position. Satisfied with his answer, Ibn Hajar pronounced the Maliki scholar not guilty of holding Ibn ʿArabi's teaching (*maqalat Ibn ʿArabi*), especially since al-Bisati volunteered to denounce the Shaykh and his followers as unbelievers.[40] According to Ibn Hajar's ruling, al-Bisati's explanation was enough to disprove the accusation of unbelief hurled at him by al-Bukhari on the spur of the moment—a decision that the sultan was happy to endorse. However, when informed of the council's ruling, al-Bukhari left Cairo in disgust in 831/1427 never to return.

As for al-Bisati, his repentance seems to have been quite sincere. In the numerous works he wrote in the aftermath of that memorable episode, he invariably placed Ibn ʿArabi alongside the "heretical" *falasifa* who hid "their venomous delusions under the guise of Sufi piety and asceticism." As if to expiate his guilt, al-Bisati denied that allegorical interpretations of Sufi statements may bring them in compliance with the *shariʿa* and debunked Ibn ʿArabi's doctrine of the seal of the saints.[41] Moreover, numerous passages from al-Bisati's theological writings quoted by al-Biqaʿi suggest that the Maliki doctor was also critical of Ibn al-Farid, whom he suspected of adhering to the doctrine of incarnation and declared an infidel in his polemical commentary on the *al-Taʾiyya al-kubra*.[42] Yet, al-Bisati's genuine attitude toward Ibn ʿArabi and other controversial mystics remains unclear, especially since the antimonistic harangues are attributed to him exclusively by Ibn ʿArabi's opponents, who were anxious to prove that his momentous quarrel with al-Bukhari was caused exclusively by his desire to display his argumentative skills. In spite of al-Biqaʿi who vigorously denied that al-Bisati ever authored a sympathetic study of the *al-Taʾiyya,*[43] he almost surely did so. One, therefore, cannot help wondering whether his condemnation of Ibn al-Farid and Ibn ʿArabi later in life was but a smoke screen intended to throw his accusers off the trail. Following the fateful encounter with al-Bukhari that nearly ruined his career,[44] al-Bisati had little option but to toe the orthodox line.

As with the other public disputes over Ibn ʿArabi's orthodoxy, the clash between al-Bisati and al-Biqaʿi clearly shows that when confronted with this divisive issue both religious officials and temporal rulers tended to avoid extremes. In the case just described, neither Ibn Hajar, the chief religious authority, nor the Mamluk sultan supported the radical, and potentially disruptive, solution pressed by the irate al-Bukhari. As custodians of law and order, both the sultan and his chief justice strove to put a lid on the simmering public scandal to prevent it from spilling over into the streets. Several decades later, faced with a similar cause célèbre the majority of Egyptian *ʿulamaʾ* again opted for a peaceful resolution. This time, however, the theological controversy around monistic Sufism was aggravated by shifting political alignments and social tensions that rendered it particularly acute.

Al-Biqaʿi's "Destruction" of Monistic Philosophy

The controversy of 874/1469-875/1470 was provoked by a vigorous attack on monistic Sufism by Burhan al-din Ibrahim b. ʿUmar al-Biqaʿi (d. 885/1480)[45]—a scholar whose accounts of the al-Bisati-al-Bukhari affair were quoted in the previous section. Like al-Bukhari, al-Biqaʿi was an outsider, who hailed from the village Khirbat Rawha in the Biqaʿa valley between Homs and Damascus. According to al-Biqaʿi's own account, he barely escaped death at the hands of the members of a rival clan who raided his village at night, killing most of his male relatives. Fleeing the bloody vendetta that ensued, al-Biqaʿi settled in Damascus, where he studied with many renowned *ʿulamaʾ* of his time, including Ibn al-Jazari (d. 834/1430), the anti-Ibn ʿArabi scholar, whose role in the Ibn ʿArabi polemic will be discussed further on. Following his departure from Syria, al-Biqaʿi journeyed throughout the Middle East, until he finally settled in Cairo, where he became a student of Ibn Hajar, who "greatly praised him and . . . worked for his advancement," thereby sparking the envy of his other disciple, al-Sakhawi.[46] Upon the completion of his studies, al-Biqaʿi occupied a number of important teaching posts at Cairene mosques and religious colleges. His vibrant and occasionally acrimonious character, combined with his exaggerated sense of self-importance, soon irritated his peers, including such respected figures of the Cairene religious establishment as al-Suyuti and al-Sakhawi. Embittered by al-Biqaʿi's disregard for their opinions and reputations and possibly envious of his high status in the eyes of the great Ibn Hajar, al-Sakhawi later wrote an extremely hostile obituary of al-Biqaʿi which, in the words of one Western scholar, "amounts to a slander."[47]

Al-Biqaʿi's career in Egypt was marked by his relentless opposition to "the philosophy of the unity of being" and its founder.

However, it was Ibn al-Farid rather than Ibn ʿArabi who became the immediate reason for al-Biqaʿi's critical campaign against the monistic tendencies in Sufism.[48] According to al-Sakhawi, himself a bitter critic of the Greatest Master, in his animosity to monistic Sufism al-Biqaʿi went to extraordinary lengths, accusing even the respectable al-Ghazali of harboring monistic leanings.[49] This accusation proved to be especially detrimental to al-Biqaʿi's reputation that had already suffered due to his haughty disregard for his peers. If we trust al-Sakhawi,[50] there was hardly a man of religion in Egypt who escaped al-Biqaʿi's reprimands, which stemmed from his unshakable belief in his superiority as a scholar and writer. This attitude again conjures up the lack of patience with his colleagues that we observed in Ibn Taymiyya, who, incidently, himself fell victim to al-Biqaʿi's "spite" (*bughd*).[51]

For all of al-Biqaʿi's "extremism," real or alleged, it cannot be denied that his legacy bears witness to a rare talent and versatility. He distinguished himself as a perfect stylist[52] and expert on a wide variety of religious sciences as well as history and biography—a fact that even his detractors had to acknowledge. Al-Biqaʿi's varied talents apparently instilled in him an inordinate pride, setting him on a collision course with contemporary *ʿulama*ʾ, whom he tended to treat as his intellectual inferiors. Many episodes from al-Biqaʿi's eventful life demonstrate that, much like Ibn Taymiyya, he "did not have self-restraint and discretion enough to act in his own best interest, without constantly creating a public uproar."[53] Eventually, al-Biqaʿi alienated both his teachers and peers, who were no longer willing to tolerate his haughtiness and lack of indulgence to their slips of the tongue and pen. Faced with a broad scholarly opposition, he had to leave Egypt for Syria, retracing al-Bukhari's route a decade earlier. He passed his last years in Damascus, where, according to al-Sakhawi, he continued to intrigue intensely against local scholars.

Al-Sakhawi's ungenerous account of al-Biqaʿi's career portrays him as a troublemaker and as a man of no principles who thrived on dogmatic divergences, unscrupulously using them to further his selfish ends. His opportunism, according to al-Sakhawi, reached its peak when he persuaded a group of influential Egyptian scholars, including the chief Hanafi judge Ibn Shihna (d. 890/1485), his son ʿAbd al-Barr (d. 921/1515), the chief Hanbali judge ʿIzz al-din al-Kinani (d. 876/1471), and the renowned Shafiʿi jurist Ibn Imam al-Kamiliyya (d. 874/1469),[54] to publicly condemn the monistic views of Ibn al-Farid. By stirring up and prolonging this campaign, al-Biqaʿi was anxious to advertise his orthodoxy and erudition in hopes of "gain[ing] personal notoriety and advancement."[55] Posing as an uncompromising critic of the controversial Sufi poet, al-Biqaʿi, in al-Sakhawi's words, also hoped to undermine the credibility of his learned rivals. To achieve his goals, al-Biqaʿi reportedly was not too squeamish to ally himself with former adversaries. Yet, his efforts came to naught, when he failed to persuade his allies to form a united front against the Sufi "heresy"—a failure that al-Sakhawi attributes to his unscrupulous self-advancement and desire for leadership.[56]

We find yet another parallel between Ibn Taymiyya and al-Biqaʿi in the fact that the latter's expulsion (in this case from Cairo) was caused by his "extreme" stance on the Ibn al-Farid/Ibn ʿArabi issue, which, as we remember, had led to the indictment and exile of the Hanbali doctor. There are, however, differences as well: whereas Ibn Taymiyya's antimonistic drive was directed against Ibn ʿArabi, al-Tilimsani, and Ibn Sabʿin par excellence, al-Biqaʿi's primary target was Ibn al-Farid. This made al-Biqaʿi's task especially difficult: although many *ʿulama*ʾ had some misgivings about the poet and his work, his great poetic talent and reputation for holiness among the Egyptian lower classes as well as members of the ruling elite[57] made it extremely difficult to obtain a scholarly consensus on his supposed heresy. Several exceptions notwithstanding, the Egyptian biographers of the age routinely portrayed Ibn al-Farid as an exemplary saint, or, at least, as "God's fool," who was only loosely associated with the "unificationist" doctrine. Moreover, Egyptian *ʿulama*ʾ tended to view his religiously suspect statements as a result of his mystical intoxication and/or poetic inspiration, not as an intentional espousal of the objectionable monistic doctrine.

Given Ibn al-Farid's prominence in the world of Egyptian religiosity,[58] it is not improbable that his condemnation by a Syrian scholar was perceived by many Egyptians as an attack on their "national" saint,[59] especially since al-Biqaʿi's campaign was joined by other scholars of Syrian extraction—Muhibb al-din Muhammad Ibn al-Shihna and his son ʿAbd al-Barr.[60] Whatever their motives, their condemnatory campaign ran into stiff opposition. Enraged, al-Biqaʿi publicly demanded that both Ibn ʿArabi and Ibn al-Farid be "excommunicated," proclaimed infidels, and their works be destroyed. His demands, which were supported by Ibn Shihna, al-Kinani, Ibn Imam al-Kamiliyya, and the popular Sufi al-Matbuli, were seen by many scholars as being a bit outré. More importantly, it irritated the influential Mamluk officer Barquq (d. 877/1472), overseer of the pious endowments attached to Ibn al-Farid's shrine and a personal friend of the sultan Qa'it Bay. The scholars associated with Barquq, the sultan's court, and Ibn al-Farid's shrine, launched a counter-attack, accusing al-Biqaʿi and his supporters of unwarranted extremism and denigration of God's saints. As usual, they argued that the heresy of the great Sufi masters cannot be proven beyond doubt, which makes such an extraordinarily measure as *takfir* entirely unjustified.[61]

Following the familiar pattern, al-Biqaʿi attempted to muster a scholarly consensus confirming Ibn al-Farid's unbelief. To this end, he composed several lengthy polemical tracts aimed primarily at Ibn al-Farid, but criticizing other monistic thinkers as well. One of these tracts, titled "The Awakening of the Unaware to Ibn ʿArabi's Unbelief" (*Tanbih al-ghabi ila takfir Ibn ʿArabi*), was dedicated solely to the Greatest Master, whose teaching al-Biqaʿi depicted as being similar to Ibn al-Farid's poetic ravings. In the other work, "Warning the Servants of God Against Those Who Stubbornly Espouse the Innovation of Unificationism" (*Tahdhir al-ʿibad min ahl al-ʿinad bi-bidʿat al-ittihad*), al-Biqaʿi focused on Ibn al-Farid, although Ibn ʿArabi's "fallacies" were also addressed.[62]

Al-Biqaʿi's critical campaign galvanized Egyptian intellectual life and caused many secret admirers of Ibn ʿArabi and of Ibn al-Farid to openly side with the pro-Sufi faction.[63] This, incidently, was a safe (and reasonable) thing to do in view of the support extended to the Ibn al-Farid party by some top-ranking Mamluk courtiers and officials. The controversy swept through the entire Cairene society, as the advocates of the accused Sufi masters began to circulate verses in their defense among the populace.[64] The historian Ibn Iyas, whose sympathies were squarely with the Ibn ʿArabi/Ibn al-Farid party, cites a few lines from one such poem composed by the Hanbali poet Ahmad al-Mansuri (d. 887/1482) which were recited in the streets of Cairo:

> Verily, al-Biqaʿi is accountable for his words
>
> Do not think him to be in the right, for his heart
>
> will be tormented [in the Hereafter]![65]

To put an end to the agitation caused by the controversy, the sultan requested the expert opinion of the revered Sufi and Shafiʿi jurist Zakariya al-Ansari (d. 925 or 926/1519), who ruled that Ibn al-Farid's poetry, if interpreted properly, evinces no affiliation whatsoever with the heretical doctrines of unificationism and incarnationalism, and therefore should be pronounced orthodox.[66]

As the war of words over Ibn al-Farid and Ibn ʿArabi escalated, leading Cairene *ʿulamaʾ* grew increasingly wary of the potential implications of al-Biqaʿi's antimonistic crusade for the Egyptian community at large. In an attempt to defuse the tension, the noted Arab polymath al-Suyuti, who had a personal stake in Ibn al-Farid's shrine,[67] composed two forceful rejoinders to al-Biqaʿi's *Tanbih al-ghabi* in which he outlined what he declared to be the only proper approach to the issue. While in his *Qamʿ al-muʿarid* he defended primarily Ibn al-Farid, his second treatise is devoted exclusively to the Greatest Master. Although pro-Ibn ʿArabi and pro-saint in tone, this latter work was no doubt designed to achieve a reconciliation between the warring parties and put the matter to rest. Subtly, al-Suyuti advanced an irenic thesis that should be adopted by all the sensible *ʿulamaʾ* involved in the controversy: to withhold judgment regarding Ibn ʿArabi's "orthodoxy," and to discourage lay readers from looking into his works. The latter recommendation, in al-Suyuti's view, stems from the obscurity of Ibn ʿArabi's style, which is accessible only to those elect few who have themselves experienced the same spiritual states as the author. Therefore, al-Suyuti described Ibn ʿArabi's works as potentially confusing to outsiders who may misinterpret their meaning and thereby plunge into *kufr*.[68]

In hindsight, it is clear that al-Suyuti's irenic argument fell on deaf ears. According to al-Biqaʿi, Ibn ʿArabi's unbelief was obvious to anyone taking the trouble to read his works. Yet, he was perfectly aware that his blanket condemnations of the Greatest Master would not dissuade his supporters. Therefore, to prove his point al-Biqaʿi marshaled the methods employed by earlier Muslim heresiographers. His strategy was to provide several definitions of unbelief (*kufr*) and of the unbeliever (*kafir*), whereupon he endeavored to demonstrate that Ibn ʿArabi's statements unequivocally incriminate him as an infidel. Like other critics of Ibn ʿArabi, al-Biqaʿi relied exclusively on the *Fusus* as a source of his polemical ammunition—a fact duly reflected in the original title of his treatise.[69]

In seeking to determine the type of *kufr* peculiar to Ibn ʿArabi,[70] al-Biqaʿi ran into a serious impediment in the form of the complex nature of Ibn ʿArabi's supposed delusions. After long deliberations, he was finally able to situate the Sufi master in the shadowy area between the "extremist Sufis" (*ghulat al-sufiyya*), the philosophers, and the Ismaʿili "esotericists" (*al-batiniyya*).[71] In al-Biqaʿi's view, in comparison to all these heresies Ibn ʿArabi's were, by far the gravest. He accused Ibn ʿArabi of holding the following heretical tenets:

—The Creator is identical with his creatures.

—God's essence permeates the created world and there is no difference between them.

—All people are on the straight path and none of them will ever go astray.

—Pharaoh died as a believer.

—God is present in every object of worship, including idols and stones.

—There are no unbelievers who deserve to be punished in the afterlife, therefore, in the end, all mankind will enter into God's all-encompassing mercy.

—Since there are neither wrongdoers nor sinners, the afterlife will be an abode of everlasting delight, therefore God's "threat and promise," which constitute the kernel of the *shariʿa*, are but empty metaphors.

—Adam was created in God's own image.

—God needs his creatures to the same extent to which they need him.

—Noah (Nuh) deceived his people when he called them to worship the incomparable (transcendent) aspect of God, thereby ignoring the aspect of similarity (or immanence) which Ibn ʿArabi considered to be equally valid and important.

—God can take on the form of a human being.

—God is the governing spirit of the world and the world is a great man.

—Woman is part of man and his longing for her symbolizes God's longing for the universe as an estranged part of his self.

—Man can contemplate God most perfectly in woman.

—The text of the *Fusus* was written by its author at the Prophet's command.

Most of these charges, are not new to the anti-Ibn ʿArabi discourse. What sets al-Biqaʿi apart from his predecessors is that he, unlike, for example, Ibn Taymiyya, does not provide a comprehensive critique of Ibn ʿArabi's "misconceptions." Rather his criticisms are scattered throughout the lengthy text of his treatise and have to be gleaned from a disorderly jumble of long-winded quotations from, and comments on, Ibn ʿArabi's *Fusus.*[72] Logically, one would expect the author to analyze Ibn ʿArabi's statements in the second part of the work. This, however, does not happen. Instead, al-Biqaʿi simply cites the critical opinions of Ibn ʿArab extracted from the earlier polemical writings on the subject, interspersing them with anecdotes and vitriolic invectives against the Greatest Master.

Although Ibn ʿArabi occupies an important place in al-Biqaʿi's polemical discourse, he is never the only target. Since it was Ibn al-Farid's poetry that started the Egyptian debate, al-Biqaʿi continually pairs him with the Greatest Master in order to bring out what he describes as the undeniable affinity between the two. Al-Biqaʿi's main point is to convince his reader that, from the viewpoint of orthodoxy, the poet fared no better than the Sufi philosopher. As a result, his critical discourse constantly oscillates between the *Fusus* and the *Taʾiyya*—Ibn al-Farid's controversial poem celebrating the ecstatic mystical union between the human lover and his Divine Beloved.[73] The comparison between these works can therefore be seen as the foundation of al-Biqaʿi's discursive strategy in the *Tanbih.*[74] In al-Biqaʿi's view, Ibn al-Farid's poetry exhibits his debt to the monistic doctrines of Ibn ʿArabi—a fact that explains why the *Taʾiyya* became the object of numerous commentaries by the latter's followers, such as Saʿid al-din al-Farghani.[75] In a sense, al-Biqaʿi's remark was well taken, since, like Ibn ʿArabi, Ibn al-Farid was often portrayed by his later interpreters as a mystical philosopher par excellence.[76]

With the history of the Ibn ʿArabi controversy spanning almost two centuries, al-Biqaʿi easily anticipated the arguments of his future opponents. He took special care to forestall the argument from allegorical interpretation that indeed looms large in al-Suyuti's refutation of the *Tanbih.* Admitting that some of Ibn ʿArabi's "heretical" statements yield to an allegorical explanation would indeed threaten al-Biqaʿi's entire case. It is no wonder that he vigorously denied that one can find an allegorical explanation (*taʾwil*) for the texts whose meaning is blatantly at variance with the letter and spirit of the Islamic revelation. Al-Biqaʿi brings his point home by citing the anti-Ibn ʿArabi *fatwa*s from al-Fasi's polemical "biography" of the Greatest Master. However, his principal authority on the *taʾwil* issue was Abu Zurʿa al-ʿIraqi (d. 826/1423), the author of a widely circulated *fatwa* against Ibn ʿArabi and his school,[77] which denied that even the most sophisticated interpretation can bring the *Fusus* and the *Futuhat* in line with the literal meaning of the *shariʿa*.[78]

It is worthy to note that earlier on Abu Zurʿa's father, the prominent *hadith* scholar Zayn al-din al-ʿIraqi (d. 806/1403),[79] had gone on record as a bitter critic of Ibn ʿArabi's teaching. His *fatwa,* which is also cited in the *Tanbih,* merits special scrutiny since it brings out those exegetical passages from the *Fusus* that his critics found especially offensive. In the passage in question Ibn ʿArabi scolds Musa for his unjust treatment of his brother Harun (Aaron). According to the corresponding Qurʾanic verse, the Musa's ire was provoked by Aaron's permission for the children of Israel to indulge in the worship of the golden calf, while he was communicating with God.[80] In Ibn ʿArabi's exegesis, however, it was Moses, not Aaron, who was at fault, since he neglected the fact that God manifests himself in every possible form and image, including the golden calf. As a prophet of God, argued Ibn ʿArabi, Musa should have known better. Unfortunately, in a rush to punish his people, Musa did not take the time to look into the tablets that God had revealed to him shortly before the incident. Had he done that, so goes Ibn ʿArabi's exegesis, he would have discovered no reason for condemning either his people or his brother. Moreover, Ibn ʿArabi held Musa's wrath to be misplaced on yet another account—the Qur'an, in his view, explicitly states that Aaron *did* try to prevent his people from worshiping the calf, albeit unsuccessfully.[81]

Unsurprisingly, Ibn ʿArabi's interpretation of this Qurʾanic passage provokes Zayn al-din's energetic rebuttal, which al-Biqaʿi meticulously reproduces in his *Tanbih:*

> These words are a clear testimony to the author's unbelief for several reasons. First, he portrayed Musa as condoning the worship of the calf by his people. Second, he interpreted the divine words "thy God has decreed that thou shalt not serve any but Him"[82] as meaning that "He [pre]ordained that one *cannot* worship anything but Him alone."[83] To wit, the worshiper of an idol worships no one but God. Third, [Ibn ʿArabi proclaimed] that Musa reproached his brother Harun for opposing that occurrence.[84] This is a plain slander of Musa and a distortion of what God said about Musa's anger at His servants. Fourth, [Ibn ʿArabi held] that the [true] knower sees God in everything, nay sees Him to be the essence of everything. Therefore, he made the calf identical with the God worshiped [by his servants]. Anyone who hears all this cannot but resent this insolent statement, which can never be made by anyone in whose heart there is a single grain of faith.[85]

Upon reviewing Ibn ʿArabi's exegetical methods, Zayn al-din comes to the conclusion that Ibn ʿArabi was much more than a deluded man; he was a full-blown polytheist, whose "heresy surpasses that of the Jews and the Christians." In a sense, argues Zayn al-din, the latter are much closer to the correct faith than was Ibn ʿArabi, for they at least venerated God in the form of one of his most deserving human servants, whereas Ibn ʿArabi's logic led him to admit that God was identical with any object of the empirical world. In support of his conclusion Zayn al-din cites an anecdote that describes his friend's encounter with Ibn ʿArabi's follower in Alexandria. As the two men were debating Ibn ʿArabi's assertion that God is identical with everything:

> A donkey passed by them. [Zayn al-din's friend said]: "What about this donkey?" "Yes, and this donkey too!" exclaimed the other. At that moment, the donkey began to drop dung from his rear part. "What about this dung?" asked [Zayn al-din's friend]. "Of course, this dung too [is God]!" answered the man.[86]

Zayn al-din's *fatwa* offers a revealing insight into the polemical stratagems employed by Ibn ʿArabi's detractors. The discourse that opens with a theological critique of Ibn ʿArabi's exegetical methods, eventually turns into a burlesque that encapsulates, derisively, the essence of Ibn ʿArabi's weltanschauung, as seen by his opponents. The same combination of "serious" theological criticism with lampoon and caricature prevails in the antimonistic treatises from Ibn Taymiyya on. The provenance of anecdotes such as the one recounted by Zayn al-din is hard to establish. Whatever their origin, they clearly serve the same purpose—to expose the antinomian, disruptive implications of Ibn ʿArabi's monistic ideas. While Ibn ʿArabi himself was, in all likelihood, innocent of such flagrant statements, there is no denying that his teaching could, on occasion, yield itself to scandalous interpretations. It is, therefore, only natural that some of his imprudent adherents did occasionally indulge in this kind of intellectual brinkmanship in an effort to shock their literal-minded opponents out of their conventionality. In doing so, they came dangerously close to the delicate borderline that separates a communal-based positive religion from an uncontrollable and individualistic outbursts of the lovelorn ecstatics.[87]

The rashness of some later adherents of the Greatest Master and their lack of patience with exoterically minded scholars contributed in significant ways to the radicalization of the debate over his teaching. It was with the "donkey anecdote" in mind that Ibn ʿArabi's critics accused him of challenging the positive faith of the majority of Muslims and the social order it supported. Conversely, his champions had to continually downplay the possible antrinomisan interpretations of his teaching. This discursive tug-of-war, dictated by the diametrically opposed polemical perpectives, still remains at the heart of the Ibn ʿArabi controversy.[88]

In scrutinizing the arguments and examples from Zayn al-din's *fatwa,* which were diligently preserved by al-Biqaʿi, one cannot escape the impression that they have their origin in Ibn Taymiyya's antimonistic discourse. To this, both Zayn al-din and al-Biqaʿi have precious little to add aside from lengthier citations from the *Fusus* and a greater number of anti-Ibn ʿArabi opinions that had been expressed since Ibn Taymiyya's death. In their essence, their polemical strategies are closely modeled on those of the Hanbali scholar, reminding us once again of the latter's seminal role in the antimonistic debate.

Apart from Ibn Taymiyya's works, al-Biqaʿi makes extensive use of the other polemical writings discussed earlier in this study, including al-Qastallani, Ahmad al-Wasiti, al-Dhahabi, al-Taftazani, al-Fasi, Ibn al-Khatib, Ibn Khaldun, and ʿAlaʾ al-din al-Bukhari. Also quoted is the refutation of Ibn ʿArabi by the prominent Yemeni theologian al-Husayn Ibn al-Ahdal (d. 855/1451), whose contribution to the Ibn-ʿArabi controversy will be discussed in Chapter 9 of this study.[89] One of al-Biqaʿi's sources, however, deserves special mention, because it presents Ibn ʿArabi in a somewhat unusual light. It belongs to the ingenious *faqih* and Qurʾan commentator Ibn al-Naqqash (d. 763/1361),[90] a writer who anticipates Ibn Khaldun in linking Ibn ʿArabi to the tradition of occultism and fortunetelling, associated with al-Buni.[91] According to Ibn al-Naqqash, many Sufis and *ʿulamaʾ* were so fascinated by al-Buni's occult speculations that they themselves became students of the hidden properties of the letters of the Arabic alphabet and of the art of divination. In the course of their studies they came to realize that the Scriptures likewise conceal hidden predictions and allusions that may be elucidated through a special interpretative technique. The preoccupation with occultism eventually became a trademark of later Sufi thinkers in a development which, according to Ibn al-Naqqash, changed the entire physiognomy of Islamic mysticism by rendering it highly arcane and incomprehensible. In the last section of the *fatwa* he provides the following summary of contemporary Sufi thought:

> They [Sufis] gradually arrived at the oneness of being, which is the teaching (*madhhab*) propagated by such infidels as Ibn ʿArabi, Ibn Sabʿin, and Ibn al-Farid, who identified God's existence with that of His creatures. These individuals were not satisfied with proclaiming God to be one with the empirical world, because [the notion of] union [between them] would pre-suppose two interacting sides, while, in their opinion, existence is one, brooking no multiplicity whatsoever. They did not distinguish between something that was one [with something else] in essence and something that was one with other similar things due to its being part of the same species (*bi-'l-nawʿ*). They also claimed that all existent things of necessity partake in the notion of existence. However, [we know that] the existence of one particular thing is quite distinct from the existence of the other. What is shared by all things is the universal idea (*kulli*) which has absolute, unrestricted existence only in the human mind but never as a concrete reality. . . . According to the [adherents of the unity of being], those who strictly observe the *shariʿa* occupy the lowest rank. . . . These people [i.e., the adherents of the oneness of being] are given to imagination and fantasy, which they praise highly. This is especially true of Ibn ʿArabi,[92] who described the realm of imagination as the "land of the truth" (*ard al-haqiqa*).[93] Because of their [emphasis on] imagination they often speak of the coincidence of the opposites,[94] which is something only a misguided imagination can produce. Some Muslim scholars, such as the Shaykh ʿIzz al-din Ibn ʿAbd al-Salam, Ibn al-Hajib,[95] and others, who examined the status of these [people] and came to the conclusion that the jinn and lesser devils must have appeared to them, and they put down in writing what those creatures related to them in their visions. They also [spoke of] the lights which they contemplate [in their dreams] and took such [visions] for miracles that [God] grants to His saints, while these were in fact devilish temptations and not divine [graces]. . . . The real essence of their teaching is as follows: this world is the only thing in existence. But this is nothing but the teaching of Pharaoh. They, however, differed from him in that they held this world to be identical with God. . . . One can find all this in the teachings of Ibn ʿArabi and his ilk.[96]

Ibn al-Naqqash's *fatwa* shows a firsthand familiarity with the work of the Greatest Master, which one rarely finds in polemical accounts of his teaching. This alone sets Ibn al-Naqqash apart from the majority of the writers we have discussed. Perceptively, he puts his finger on imagination as the key to Ibn ʿArabi's epistemology—a fact that was largely ignored by his medieval critics. His mention of the phrase "the land of the truth," which does not occur in the *Fusus,* indicates that he may have had some familiarity with the *Futuhat.* Yet,

Ibn al-Naqqash's remarks are far too cursory to do justice to the complexity of Ibn ʿArabi's teaching. Thus he summarily lumps Ibn ʿArabi together with the exponents of absolute unity, whose doctrines, it will be recalled, were treated by al-Qastallani and Ibn Taymiyya as a distinct trend within the monistic school. In conclusion, Ibn al-Naqqash compares "the unificationist sect" with the Ismaʿilis and the Druse, emphasizing the grave danger to the Sunni community posed by the views of "these schismatics."

In failing to grasp the significance of, and to follow-up on, Ibn al-Naqqash's perceptive observations al-Biqaʿi misses a unique opportunity to deepen his thoroughly traditional criticism of the Greatest Master and thus to make a fresh contribution to the polemic. Consequently, Ibn al-Naqqash remains just another name in the long list of writers whose anti-Ibn ʿArabi *fatwa*s parade through the pages of the *Tanbih*.

At the close of his treatise, al-Biqaʿi calls for an unconditional condemnation of Ibn ʿArabi and his following. He debunks various intermediate solutions suggested by the learned advocates of Sufi *awliya*ʾ as a dangerous concession to the unenlightened opinion of the credulous masses, who consider the friends of God to be divinely protected from all sin. Al-Biqaʿi counts himself among the few conscientious scholars who have the courage to expose the destructive impact of monistic speculations on the Islamic community. In al-Biqaʿi's metaphor, such conscientious scholars are likened to the professional doctors who administer to their patients a bitter medicine. As is in real life, most patients prefer to be treated by ignorant and irresponsible quacks who give them poison in the guise of a panacea. Ibn ʿArabi's monistic potion, argues al-Biqaʿi, has far more severe consequences than the worthless amulets and ointments prescribed by the quacks. While the latter's patients put at risk their health, money or, in the worst case, their worldly lives, those "poisoned" by Ibn ʿArabi's doctrines forgo salvation in the Hereafter and proceed directly to hell.

As for Ibn ʿArabi's defenders, al-Biqaʿi sees them either as his devoted partisans or as people ignorant of his true views. Hence al-Bigaʿi's energetic repudiation of neutral positions vis-à-vis the Ibn ʿArabi issue:

> One must not say: "I abstain [from judgement]," or "I keep silent." Nor should one say: "I neither affirm [Ibn ʿArabi's heresy], nor deny [it]." Such [a position] itself implies unbelief since the unbeliever is he who denies what is generally accepted as the [correct] belief.

> Therefore, whosoever doubts that [Ibn ʿArabi's teaching] is unbelief, has himself become an unbeliever. This is why Ibn al-Muqri[97] said in his "Commentary on the *Rawda*"[98] that anyone who has any doubts regarding [the unbelief of] the Jews, the Christians, and the school (*ta'ifa*) of Ibn ʿArabi, is himself an unbeliever.[99]

As with most of Ibn ʿArabi's opponents, neither al-Biqaʿi nor his allies in the Ibn al-Farid/Ibn ʿArabi controversy opposed Sufism as such. On the contrary, some of them were themselves full-time Sufi masters,[100] who showed high regard for the Sufis of the classical epoch as well as for their later followers, such as al-Suhrawardi. In concert with Ibn al-Khatib and Ibn Khaldun, al-Biqaʿi adopted the same simplistic scheme of Sufism's development from the pristine, unquestioning faith of the early ascetics to the recondite metaphysics of Ibn ʿArabi, which, in their view, was ruinous to the religion of the pious ancestors.[101] To ward off the monistic threat, al-Biqaʿi advances Ibn Taymiyya's familiar thesis that "the pursuit of ecstatic experience must under no circumstances be allowed to interfere with the observance of the many obligations imposed by divine law."[102] In all, al-Biqaʿi's arguments are not new. Though the parallels he drew between Ibn ʿArabi and Ibn al-Farid can be treated as a novelty of sorts, his discourse generally replicates the polemical techniques and themes worked out by previous generations of anti-Ibn ʿArabi writers, especially Ibn Taymiyya and his followers.

At the end of his second treatise, al-Biqaʿi makes an attempt to strike out on his own by presenting the problem of Ibn ʿArabi in the form of a dialogue between a follower and an antagonist of the Greatest Master, which I would like to reproduce here. How can one, indignantly asks Ibn ʿArabi's follower, tarnish the reputation of the Sufi masters who have been recognized as great saints for the last two centuries? If they were heretics, how could they get away with their grave delusions in their lifetime? In reply, the opponent explains the lack of prosecution of Ibn al-Farid and Ibn ʿArab by their contemporaries by the fact that the latter were duped by the Sufis' outward piety and, therefore, failed to grasp the insidious implications of their teachings. The same lack of unanimity and resolve, argues the antagonist, is evident in the trial of al-Hallaj, which failed to establish an authoritative precedent for dealing with heretical Sufis. Thenceforth, they have been able to escape execution by exploiting the lack of unanimity among the scholars to their advantage. It is, in the antagonist's opinion, allegorical interpretation (*ta'wil*) that more than once allowed the Sufi heretics to escape the capital punishment they fully deserved. Thanks to *ta'wil* Sufi philosophers could always count on the support of gullible *ʿulamaʾ* who are easily misled by their elegant speeches and pious comportment. These are, in al-Biqaʿi's view, the reasons why heterodox Sufi doctrines, such as those of Ibn al-Farid and Ibn ʿArabi, have survived the two centuries of heated debates.[103]

Conclusion

The anti-Ibn ʿArabi campaigns of the 8th/14th centuries started by Ibn Taymiyya and perpetuated by his followers failed to eradicate Ibn ʿArabi's influence in Egypt and Syria. In any case, his works, especially the *Fusus,* continued to be copied and circulated in large numbers in the Mamluk lands and beyond. Moreover, judging by the numerous polemical treatises in defense or refutation of Ibn ʿArabi written throughout the 9th/15th centuries, interest in his legacy not only did not subside but actually increased. Ibn ʿArabi's continual renown was a thorn in the side of the *ʿulamaʾ* and statesmen who feared that his ideas might be exploited by political adventurers and persons with antinomian proclivities. In responding to their attacks, Ibn ʿArabi's advocates availed themselves of the notions of sainthood and allegorical exegesis to promote the image of Ibn ʿArabi as a Sufi gnostic and visionary who stood outside, if not above, the *sharʿi* norms applied to the ordinary believers. The confrontation between the two parties had far-ranging repercussions in the society at large and often took in its train lay outsiders.

Full-scale polemical refutations of Ibn ʿArabi's teachings were produced, for the most part, by the radical and activist *ʿulamaʾ*, rather than by those who can be described as mainstream. Their authors drew inspiration from different sources. While al-Bukhari adopted the argumentation from the metaphysics and ontology that was employed by *kalam* theologians (notably, al-Iji and al-Taftazani), al-Biqaʿi organized his discourse on al-Fasi's *responsa* model. In the final analysis, both approaches hark back to Ibn Taymiyya's seminal works, which continued to shape the antimonistic discourse throughout the 9th/15th centuries. Ibn Taymiyya's dominant influence is somewhat surprising, since both al-Bukhari and al-Biqaʿi were fierce theological opponents of the Hanbali scholar. This, however, does no not seem to have had any bearing on their position vis-à-vis the Ibn ʿArabi problem.

The unfavorable opinions of Ibn ʿArabi expressed by al-Bukhari and al-Biqaʿi provoked a stream of polemical responses that were written chiefly by the ʿ*ulama*ʾ of moderate views, not necessarily Ibn ʿArabi's admirers. Their stance is best represented by al-Suyuti, who advanced what may be described as an agnostic approach to the issue of Ibn ʿArabi's belief/unbelief, which rested on the notion of the infallibility of the Sufi saints. As most pro-Ibn ʿArabi scholars before him, he insisted that Ibn ʿArabi's statements can be brought into agreement with the *shariʿa* through a proper allegorical interpretation. At the same time, he called upon responsible scholars to limit the circulation of Ibn ʿArabi's works among the uninitiated in order to forestall further debates about his orthodoxy.

9

IBN ʿARABI IN YEMEN

YEMENI SOCIETY IN THE LATER MIDDLE PERIOD

The previous chapters have given us some feeling for the astounding pervasiveness and persistence of Ibn ʿArabi's legacy across time and space. Scarcely a part of the medieval Muslim world remained immune to the influence of his ideas and terminology. Ibn ʿArabi's works were widely copied and diligently studied by Muslims of remarkably diverse educational backgrounds and intellectual propensities from al-Andalus to Central Asia. Almost without fail his ideas met with stiff opposition orchestrated by certain factions within the *ʿulamaʾ* class. Since Ibn ʿArabi's advocates were themselves scholars of no mean standing, the two parties inevitably found themselves embroiled in the controversy over Ibn ʿArabi's status vis-à-vis the *shariʿa*. Woven into a tangled web of personal ambitions, court intrigues, and party factionalism, Ibn ʿArabi's persona came to serve as an important ideological symbol, a common frame of reference for various scholarly factions engaged in the incessant struggle for political influence, administrative and teaching sinecures, and control over pious endowments.

These general observations, as we shall see, are fully pertinent to the story of the acceptance and dissemination of Ibn ʿArabi's teaching in Yemen—a country whose religious history and culture in the Middle Ages received relatively scarce attention in Western scholarship. Due to its isolation from the traditional Muslim metropolises and centers of learning, the Yemeni society has often been viewed by Western investigators as a static backwater of Islamic civilization, which slavishly imitated the more sophisticated culture and institutions of central Islamdom. In this chapter I will test the validity of this stereotype, bearing in mind that a comprehensive history of Islam in medieval Yemen and South Arabia is still to be written.

We have a fairly comprehensive picture of the history of the Zaydi community of Yemen and, to a lesser extent, of that of the Yemeni

Table 5
Debates over Ibn ʿArabi's legacy in Rasulid Yemen.

Stage 1 (The second half of the 7th/13th centuries).

The Yemeni Sufis Ibn Jamil, Ibn ʿAlwan, al-Yahyawi, and, possibly al-Muqaddasi and Ibn Naba, introduce I.ʿA.'s ideas into the intellectual life of late Ayyubid-early Rasulid Yemen.

Stage 2 (The late 8th/14th-early 9th/15th centuries).

Al-Jabarti (d. 806/1403), a charismatic Sufi leader, and his disciple al-Jili energetically disseminate I.ʿA.'s works in Zabid, making them the pivot of Sufi education.

The renowned Yemeni scholar Ibn al-Khayyat (d. 811/1408) engages the grand *qadi* al-Fayruzabadi (d. 817/1415) in a theological debate over I.ʿA.'s orthodoxy, which is followed by an exchange of *fatwa*s and personal acrimony. The sultan sides with the I.ʿA. party.

Following al-Fayruzabadi's death, Ibn al-Raddad, the new grand *qadi,* gives his Sufi followers a free hand in spreading I.ʿA.'s teachings. The opposition to his policy, instigated by several distinguished Yemeni scholars, is brutally suppressed.

Stage 3 (The first half of the 9th/15th centuries).

Upon Ibn al-Raddad's death (821/1418), the opposition to the I.ʿA. party is led by the famous poet and scholar Ibn al-Muqri (d. 837/1444), who eventually succeeds in putting on trial the last exponent of I.ʿA.'s teaching in Yemen, al-Kirmani (d. 841/1437). Despite a temporary setback following the transition of power to al-Kirmani's royal supporter, Ibn al-Muqri's party is successful in eradicating the "monistic heresy."

Ismaʿilis.[1] The study of these communities has often been motivated by Western scholars' interest in the "deviant" Islamic doctrines—a hobbyhorse of European Islamology since its inception. This obsessive preoccupation with "deviancy" has led them to neglect the "platitudes" of mainstream Sunnism that was professed by the majority of medieval Yemenis.[2] As a result, we have a somewhat one-sided view of Yemeni religious history, in which Zaydism has consistently received the lion's share of academic attention. Such a view, however, obscures the historical fact that Zaydi political domination was a relatively late phenomenon. Moreover, it was never complete: for several centuries Yemen and South Arabia were ruled by the powerful

Sunni dynasties that energetically promoted Sunni learning in hopes of countering the influence of the Zaydi and Ismaʿili communities. In the late 7th/13th-8th/14th centuries the powerful Rasulid dynasty effectively reduced their Zaydi rivals to a handful of strongholds in the mountainous region of Saʿda, which had little bearing on the political life of the rest of Yemen.[3] The same policy of containment and suppression was implemented by the Rasulids with regard to the once formidable Ismaʿili community, which was swept aside in 569/1173 by the Ayyubid invasion of Yemen and never regained its former influence. The Rasulid sultans delivered the Ismaʿili community a coup de grace in the early 9th/15th centuries, by drastically reducing its authority over its traditional tribal allies.[4]

Once the obstinate notion of medieval Yemen as a predominantly Zaydi-Ismaʿili preserve is laid to rest, a comprehensive study of Yemeni Sunnism becomes a necessity. Unfortunately, our knowledge of its history is scant indeed. Here are the few facts that are known. From the 7th/13th centuries on, the majority of Yemeni Muslims, especially those in the areas south of Sanaʿaʾ and as far east as Hadramawt and Mahra, adhered to one or the other Sunni schools of law.[5] The Sunni state of the Rasulids was pitted against the "moderate" Shiʿi state of the Zaydis in Saʿda as well as the "extreme" Shiʿism of the few surviving Ismaʿili communities in the Haraz mountains west of Sanaʿaʾ. The Rasulids also fought against Ibadi Kharijism, whose adherents, based in Oman, occasionally attempted to spread their cause to Mahra and Hadramawt at the point of the sword.[6]

For centuries the Sunni *ʿulamaʾ* of Yemen vigorously pursued the study of religious sciences, producing a vast body of scholarly literature, much of which still remains in manuscript form. The importance of this literature is readily attested by its popularity in the core lands of Islam.[7] In their prodigious efforts to propagate religious learning and to advance the cause of Sunni Islam, Yemeni scholars were supported by local rulers of Sunni allegiance. The largesse of the Ayyubid and Rasulid rulers as well as their officials accounts for the rapid growth of religious colleges in the territories under their sway.[8] Alongside the mosques, the colleges became centers of a bustling intellectual activity and advanced religious studies.[9] Sunni scholars in major urban centers of Yemen and South Arabia such as Taʿizz, Zabid, Janad, Ibb, Aden, al-Shihr, and Tarim (Hadramawt) found themselves in an especially advantageous position. They were wooed and lavishly rewarded by prestige-seeking Rasulid princes and military commanders. With their needs provided for by governmental allowances and private donations, the scholars dedicated themselves fully to religious instruction and writing. To broaden their intellectual horizons, many Yemeni and South Arabian *ʿulamaʾ* traveled to Mecca and Medina, where they benefited from the learned visitors to the holy cities. From their journeys to the Hijaz the Yemeni divines brought camel-loads of books and new intellectual fads. For their part, Yemeni and South Arabian *ʿulamaʾ* contributed in significant ways to the intellectual life of the holy cities, where they spent lengthy periods and frequently filled important religious offices.

Sufism in Medieval Yemen

Parallel to the entrenchment of Sunnism in Lower Yemen in the aftermath of the Ayyubid conquest, the country witnessed a rapid spread of Sufism and its institutions, which theretofore had been relatively unimportant. As elsewhere, Sufism found an enthusiastic following in the Yemeni masses, who were attracted to its charismatic, miracle-working leaders. The popularity of Sufism was astutely exploited by the Ayyubids, who cultivated Sufi shaykhs and showered them with gifts and charitable donations.[10]

Unlike Muslim mystics in the central lands of Islam, their Yemeni colleagues did not organize themselves into large brotherhoods with centralized leadership and numerous regional branches. Rather, they tended to form small Sufi communities that resided in lodges under the auspices of revered masters. Such communities were often situated in the countryside, where Sufis could practice their rites unmolested. Medieval Yemeni writers mention numerous rural Sufi lodges (*arbita,* sing. *ribat*) scattered throughout the Tihama and the Southern Highlands.[11] Many Yemeni Sufis enjoyed the reputation of miracle-workers and rainmakers, which created great demand for their services both in the countryside as well as in the towns. Some Sufi shaykhs used their spiritual authority (*jah*) to mediate frequent conflicts between rulers and tribes and to protect the peasants from the exactions of both.[12] Sufis in big cities pursued a more sophisticated form of mysticism that not infrequently was tinged with the monistic ideas of Ibn ʿArabi and Ibn Sabʿin.[13] As in the other geographical areas we have discussed, mystical speculation of this kind was opposed by many *ʿulamaʾ*, who viewed it as a potential source of heresy and sedition as well as idleness and lax morals.

Not all Yemeni scholars shared this harsh view of theoretical Sufism. Some saw in it a welcome spiritual and emotional alternative to the dry scholasticism and orthopraxy of institutionalized religion and were ready to put their careers on the line defending it against its critics. As in the case with the Ibn al-Farid/Ibn ʿArabi controversy in Egypt, we are dealing here with the tensions within the Yemeni scholarly community and not with a conflict between the "orthodox" *fuqahaʾ* and the "heterodox" Sufis, as suggested by some investigators.[14]

Given the importance of Sufism for Yemeni Islam, it is amazing how little we know about its rise and development.[15] In what follows I will try to sketch out some episodes of its history with special reference to the struggle between Ibn ʿArabi's advocates and detractors in the 7th/13-9/15th centuries. My discussion, however, is entirely subordinate to the main task of this study and does not purport to substitute for a much-needed history of Yemeni Sufism, which is still to be written.

The Rasulid Kingdom

Geographically and chronologically, my discussion centers on Lower Yemen and the Tihama under the Rasulid dynasty (632/1235-858/1454). The Rasulids were the lieutenants of the Ayyubid sultans of Egypt and Syria, who proclaimed themselves independent of their masters and carved out a kingdom for themselves in Lower Yemen with centers in Taʿizz and Zabid, the cities located southwest of the present capital, Sanaʿaʾ. The latter was situated close to the Zaydi-controlled region of Saʿda and frequently changed hands in a constant tug-of-war between the Rasulids and the Zaydi *imam*s, supported by the warlike mountainous tribes.

Unlike the Zaydi *imam*s, who had been incorporated into the tribal society of Yemen since the 3d/10th centuries, the Rasulids were newcomers.[16] Although they later crafted a noble Arabian pedigree stretching back to the famed Ghassanids of northern Arabia, the Rasulids were, in all probability, professional soldiers of Kurdish or Turkoman background in the service of the Ayyubid princes of Yemen.[17] Having successfully unified the country and having established an efficient administration based on the Syrian and Egyptian models, the Ayyubids paved the way for their successors, who were astute enough to preserve and build on this solid foundation.[18]

The founder of the Rasulid kingdom, Nur al-din ʿUmar Ibn Rasul, was appointed as deputy to the last Ayyubid ruler of Yemen, al-Malik al-Masʿud, who left for Mecca in 626/1228 never to return. In anticipation of another Ayyubid sovereign, Nur al-din had successfully squashed a popular rebellion in the Tihama and beat off a Zaydi offensive in the north. The new Ayyubid sovereign, however, did not show up, since the Egyptian rulers, beset by domestic and external problems, were no longer interested in a remote and troublesome Yemen. Nur al-din ʿUmar seized this opportunity to throw off allegiance to his Ayyubid sovereigns and to proclaim himself independent of Cairo. To legitimize his new status, in 632/1234, he obtained an investiture from the caliph in Baghdad. His reign came to an abrupt and violent end when he was ambushed and assassinated by his relative who conspired to wrest power from him. ʿUmar's son, Yusuf, defeated the faction led by his father's assassins and outgeneraled other rivals in the struggle for power.[19] He then assumed the royal title al-Muzaffar and established himself as the undisputed ruler of the lands stretching from Mecca to Hadramawt—no small feat in such a fractious and forbidding country as Yemen.[20]

Under Yusuf's long rule (r. 648/1249-694/1295) Yemen witnessed an unprecedented political and social stability which led to the consolidation of the new state and its economy.[21] Under his immediate successors, the Rasulid state achieved its apogee, profiting greatly by the Red Sea transit trade via Aden and al-Ghulayfiqa, a port located near the city of Zabid. The rapid growth of the trade was facilitated by the sensible fiscal policy pursued by the early Rasulids. The economy also boomed due to the ambitious agricultural development programs instituted by the sultans, who promoted the massive cultivation of palms by the black slaves from Ethiopia. The prosperous economy allowed the Rasulids to buy the loyalty of the militant tribal confederations and the services of the mercenaries, who were essential for the preservation of order in their feud-ridden and volatile domain. For some time, the Rasulid kingdom became the major Arabian power, which competed even with the still powerful Mamluk state.

The Rasulid sultans could not count on the unruly and unreliable mountaineer tribesmen, relying instead on the more stable and law-abiding populations of the coastal Tihama and the Southern Plains, where their royal residences, Taʿizz and Zabid, were located. The Rasulid army was recruited from Abyssinian slaves and Turkoman mercenaries, who were not involved in local tribal alliances and rivalries. Even at the peak of their power, the Rasulids had to cope with the political problems faced by the other medieval Muslim states of the epoch: the fratricidal wars of succession, the anarchy of the tribal factions opposed to any centralized control, and the violence of their Turkoman praetorians. In addition, they were locked in a war of attrition with their principal political and religious antagonists, the Zaydi *imams,* who were almost impregnable in the mountains of Saʿda. In the zenith of their power the Rasulids successfully dealt with all of these challenges. However, the tribal anarchy and the depredations of the unpaid mercenaries, combined with a severe financial crisis that had started under the sultan al-Nasir Ahmad, brought about the collapse of the central government and, eventually, the dissolution of Rasulid power in 858/1454.[22] It was succeeded by the Tahirids, erstwhile governors of Aden, whose rule, in turn, was ended by the victorious Ottomans, who occupied Yemen in 933/1526.

The Rasulids and Islamic Learning

As mentioned, many Rasulid sultans were generous supporters of Islamic culture, education, and religious institutions, whose rule witnessed the emergence of a constellation of first-rank scholars who wrote on "numerous disciplines, ranging from history and biography to genealogy and agriculture, from medicine to farriery and equine affairs."[23] In subsidizing diverse intellectual and cultural activities, the Rasulids followed in the footsteps of their former masters, the Ayyubids of Egypt who had cultivated friendship with the learned elite as well as with charismatic Sufi leaders.[24] Although they tended to maintain a balance between the rival scholarly factions in their domain, some Rasulids occasionally became captives of their personal predilections and took one side against the other. Unlike the Mamluks, who, for the most part, shunned scholarship, leaving hair-splitting theological disputes to the *ʿulamaʾ*, the Rasulids hewed closer to the Ayyubid ideal of a versatile and cultured ruler.[25] Able statesmen and prolific writers on a wide variety of subjects, they took an active part in the scholarly life of their kingdom.[26]

The Rasulid sovereigns also distinguished themselves as builders of *madrasas*, mosques, and libraries who made Zabid and Taʿizz major international centers of Islamic learning. Their splendid palaces and elegant winter residences housed rich collections of Arabic manuscripts, both local and imported.[27] Men of learning and poets were held in great esteem at the Rasulid court and received lavish rewards for their theology and poetry. Some literati undertook arduous journeys from distant Muslim lands in search of the opportunities for advancement offered by the enlightened Rasulid rulers. Among such distinguished visitors we find the renowned *faqih* Muhammad Ibn Abi Bakr al-Farisi (d. 675/1276),[28] the great Egyptian biographer and *muhaddith* Ibn Hajar al-ʿAsqalani,[29] the celebrated lexicographer Majd al-din al-Fayruzabadi (d. 815/1415),[30] the acclaimed Meccan biographer and historian al-Fasi,[31] the master of Qurʾan recitation and *muhaddith* Muhammad Ibn al-Jazari (d. 833/1429),[32] and the great Muslim traveler Ibn Battuta (d. 779/1377), who left a spirited description of the splendor and wealth he observed on his visit to the Rasulid capitals.[33]

Of special interest for the present study is ʿAbd al-Karim al-Jili (d. 832/1428), "undoubtedly the most original thinker and the most remarkable and independent mystical writer . . . in the 'school' of Ibn ʿArabi,"[34] who spent the last decades of his life in Yemen under the patronage of the Rasulid sultans and their officials.[35] Despite the vigorous protests of some local *fuqahaʾ* opposed to speculative Sufism, al-Jili was given a free hand in promulgating his teachings among Yemeni Muslims.[36] Likewise, the local Sufis, Abu ʾl-Ghayth Ibn Jamil, Ahmad Ibn ʿAlwan, al-Jabarti, and Ibn al-Raddad were treated with great respect by different Rasulid sultans.[37]

Historical sources indicate that the Rasulid sultans were well versed in Sufi literature and actively encouraged its study. It is, therefore, not surprising that sooner or later they came under the influence of the Sufi masters of monistic leanings who found the cosmopolitan environment of Rasulid Yemen quite congenial to their intellectual dispositions. Sources also show that the sultans, their courtiers, and many members of the royal household assiduously collected mystical writings and generously recompensed their authors.[38] One result of their bibliophilic zeal is that today Yemen boasts several splendid collections of Ibn ʿArabi's manuscripts that still await their researcher.[39]

Some Rasulid sultans were more than simply collectors; they became diligent students of Sufi philosophy. Monarchs, it will be recalled, are often trendsetters in matters of taste and intellectual fashions. Unsurprisingly, the rulers' interest in speculative Sufism was eagerly imitated by the officials and religious functionaries of their state. Scholars and literati of a relatively inconspicuous standing also took to reading mystical works. Sources tell us that Ibn ʿArabi's *Fusus* and *Futuhat* were high on their reading list.[40] This is not to say that Ibn ʿArabi's writings were the staple read of the

Yemeni Muslims. Far from it. Even at the peak of Ibn ʿArabi's influence on Yemeni Islam (the late 8th/14th-early 9th/15th centuries), they were still confined to a narrow, albeit influential, circle of *ʿulama*ʾ, who could make sense of their recondite content and technical jargon. For the man in the street, as for most Muslims today, Ibn ʿArabi remained an enigma of dubious import, which was hotly debated by the highbrows. The great significance that Yemeni historiography ascribed to the Ibn ʿArabi polemic reflected the concerns of its learned makers rather than those of the rank-and-file believers.

This is not to say that the ascendancy of Sufism in Rasulid Yemen had no impact on popular religiosity. Sufi musical sessions (*dhikr, sama*ʿ) both in cities and in remote Sufi lodges drew crowds of enthusiastic onlookers.[41] They usually began in the mosques after the sunset and continued well into midnight, occasionally spilling into the streets in the form of festive processions. On religious holidays a throng of up to seven hundred Sufis marched through the streets of Zabid, piercing the night with loud mystical hymns, Qurʾan recitations, and drumbeats.[42] No wonder that Sufi activities drew the criticism of some conservative *ʿulama*ʾ who viewed them both as a frivolous pastime and as a serious infringement on the *shariʿa* prohibition of music and dancing. Scores of vehement confrontations between the Sufis and their opponents over the legitimacy of the loud *dhikr* are documented in contemporary Yemeni chronicles and religious poetry.[43]

One feature relevant to our present discussion is that the Sufi leaders who encouraged, and actively participated in, mystical concerts presented themselves as followers of Ibn ʿArabi, whose mystical poetry was often chanted during the *dhikr* sessions alongside that of Ibn al-Farid, al-Tilimsani, and Ibn al-Raddad.[44] For the advocates of religious sobriety, these sessions became emblematic of the "corruptive" influence of Ibn ʿArabi's teaching on the Muslim faith and mores—an accusation that hardly stands up if one considers his critique of *sama*ʿ sessions as a sign of immaturity.[45]

The ascendancy of Sufi teachings and practices in the Yemeni cities triggered several anti-Sufi campaigns that were instigated by the influential jurists (*fuqaha*ʾ) and preachers (*khutaba*ʾ) who presented themselves as defenders of Islam's "purity" against Sufi "innovations." As in the theological confrontations discussed earlier on, the Yemeni polemicists were not always driven by a disinterested concern for the correctness of the faith. Many of them had more mundane axes to grind, especially after they had realized that the sultan's support of the Sufi faction effectively barred those not affiliated with it from royal favors and high administrative posts. Again, as in the preceding chapters, the Yemeni debates over Sufism's orthodoxy present a familiar admixture of self-righteousness and a pragmatic prosecution of one's interests.

Whatever its causes, the struggle between the opponents and advocates of Sufi practice and speculation had a lasting impact on the intellectual and religious life of the Rasulid Yemen. The conflict grew especially intense following the wide dissemination of Ibn ʿArabi's tenets among the Yemeni intellectual elite and the support extended to their proponents by some Rasulid dynasts. The controversy over Ibn ʿArabi subsided after the fall of the ruling house, although its reverberations are still palpable in Yemen and South Arabia today.[46]

Ibn al-Ahdal on the Rise of Monistic Sufism in Yemen

To date, only a meager part of the vast literature on Islam in medieval Yemen is available to interested scholars. We are therefore lucky to have at our disposal a detailed account of the Ibn ʿArabi polemic in Rasulid Yemen by the noted historian and jurisconsult al-Husayn Ibn al-Ahdal (d. 855/1481).[47] A vociferous critic of Ibn ʿArabi and his followers, Ibn al-Ahdal left behind a vivid, if biased description of the reception of monistic thought by Yemeni scholars and rulers in the 8/14th and 9/15th centuries.

Al-Husayn Ibn ʿAbd al-Rahman Ibn al-Ahdal was born into a famous family of Yemeni *sayyid*s.[48] He studied Shafiʿi *fiqh* and *hadith* under the best scholars of his time, such as al-Fasi, Ibn al-Jazari, and al-Nashiri (d. 815/1412).[49] Apart from the traditional Muslim disciplines, Ashʿari *kalam,* and annalistic history, Ibn al-Ahdal also studied the Sufi tradition.[50] Ironically, among his first *shaykh*s was Ahmad Ibn al-Raddad, the foremost exponent of Ibn ʿArabi's teaching in Yemen, whom Ibn al-Ahdal later targeted in his polemical writings.[51] In any event, Ibn al-Ahdal was proficient in Sufi theory and practice: as is often the case with Ibn ʿArabi's detractors, he was not opposed to Sufism per se but to its supposed corruption by later mystical thinkers.[52]

Ibn al-Ahdal's scholarly career is closely associated with Abyat Husayn, a suburb of Zabid, where he was born and from where left for Mecca and the Hijaz in search of renowned teachers. From his long travels he returned as an accomplished jurisconsult and Ashʿari theologian, and spent the rest of his life in his native town. His expertise in *fiqh* and *kalam* earned him the position of the chief religious expert (*mufti*) of Abyat Husayn, whose authority was acknowledged by Sunni scholars throughout Yemen. A foremost religious authority of the age, Ibn al-Ahdal was often consulted on theological matters of broad public concern by the religious authorities of Taʿizz and Zabid. When the Ibn ʿArabi controversy broke out and his opponents rushed to obtain a scholarly *ijmaʿ* condemning his mystical teaching, Ibn al-Ahdal issued a detailed *fatwa,* in which he accused the Greatest Master of "heresy and unbelief." Later, he expanded the *fatwa* into a lengthy refutation of Ibn ʿArabi's doctrine that will be the focus of our discussion in this chapter. His anti-Ibn ʿArabi position is also evident in his major historical work *Tuhfat al-zaman fi taʾrikh al-Yaman* ("The Wonder of the Age in the History of Yemen") which contains numerous references to the struggle between Ibn ʿArabi's admirers and detractors in the late 8th/14th-early 9th/15th centuries.[53]

Firmly rooted in the tradition of anti-Sufi criticism dating back to Ibn Taymiyya and to his followers, Ibn al-Ahdal's polemical treatise surpasses most of the earlier writings of this genre in profundity and comprehensiveness. A self-conscious historiographer,[54] Ibn al-Ahdal provided not only a theological critique of Ibn ʿArabi's views, but also an accurate chronological account of how they were received at the various levels of medieval Yemeni society. To supplement Ibn al-Ahdal's valuable, if choppy observations, I will make use of medieval Yemeni chronicles and biographical dictionaries of local Sufis and *ʿulamaʾ*. The anti-Sufi bias of some of them and the pro-Sufi tendency of the others render them unreliable and require from the researcher a considerable amount of immunity from the blatant distortions they often exhibit. Yet, the bits and pieces of data found in these sources permit a more or less accurate reconstruction of the major stages of the Ibn ʿArabi polemic in medieval Yemen.

Ibn al-Ahdal's account of the diffusion of Ibn ʿArabi's teaching in Yemen forms part of his larger theological book "The Removal of the Cover from the Truths of the Profession of God's Uniqueness" (*Kashf al-ghitaʾ ʿan haqaʾiq al-tawhid*).[55] The book opens with a typical Ashʿari *ʿaqida* (profession of faith), whereupon Ibn al-Ahdal discusses various "deviant" Muslim sects which, in his view, are bound for perdition. Although Ibn ʿArabi is occasionally mentioned in the first two chapters as an example of a deluded "heretic," it is only in the third chapter of the *Kashf* that Ibn al-Ahdal provides a full scale critique of the Greatest Master. This critique is based entirely on the

Fusus. As noted, theologically Ibn al-Ahdal was heart and soul a champion of the Ashʿari dogma who consistently used it as a yardstick in gauging the degree of perversity of those whom he viewed as "deviators" from "the path of the pious ancestors." Ibn al-Ahdal's religious allegiance is quite typical of the Yemeni scholars of his epoch. In the earlier centuries, however, Ashʿarism was viewed with great suspicion by local *ʿulama*ʾ and had to hold fort against its numerous antagonists, mainly the Hanbalis.[56]

Ibn al-Ahdal doctrinal preferences are evident from his choice of sources among which we find the works of such staunchly Sunni scholars as al-Ashʿari, al-Ghazali, *qadi* ʿIyad, Ibn al-Jawzi (d. 599/1201), Fakhr al-din al-Razi, Ibn ʿAbd al-Salam, al-Nawawi, and al-Subki. Although Ibn ʿArabi absorbs the lion's share of the author's criticism, Ibn al-Ahdal also disposes of the other Sufi "heretics," especially al-Hallaj, Ibn al-Farid, and al-Tilimsani. Yet, as Ibn al-Ahdal was never tired of repeating, among these Sufi "heretics," Ibn ʿArabi was by far the most dangerous. In addition to the *Kashf* and the *Tuhfat al-zaman,* Ibn al-Ahdal attacks Ibn ʿArabi's teaching in several other treatises, one of which appears to be an abridgment of the chapter on Ibn ʿArabi from the *Kashf,* but may also be yet another version of his earlier antimonistic *fatwa.*[57]

Ibn al-Ahdal places the appearance of Ibn ʿArabi's works in Yemen around the middle of the 7/13th centuries—that is, shortly after the author's death. According to Ibn al-Ahdal, their diffusion was somehow or other associated with the semilegendary Sufi teacher and saint (*wali*) Abu ʾl-Ghayth Ibn Jamil (d. 651/1253),[58] whom the popular Yemeni lore credits with spectacular ascetic feats and saintly miracles. Why Ibn al-Ahdal considers him to be a follower of Ibn ʿArabi is not quite clear, although he vaguely alludes to Ibn Jamil's ecstatic utterances, describing his union with God (*shatahat*).[59] On the whole, however, Ibn al-Ahdal's view of the great Yemeni saint is ambiguous. Like most of his contemporaries, he shows a deep respect for Ibn Jamil, by calling him the mystical pole of the epoch (*qutb al-zaman*) and the greatest saint of his generation (*sayyid al-awliya*ʾ *al-muhaqqiqin*). Yet, as a theologian and heresiographer, he takes exception to Ibn Jamil's perceived "antinomian" statements and behavior, which he likens to the "blasphemous ravings" of al-Hallaj and Ibn al-Farid.[60] Ibn al-Ahdal may have been right. However, the samples of Ibn Jamil's *shatahat* cited by medieval Yemeni writers are entirely trivial, patterned as they are on the paradoxes ascribed to some inspired Sufi masters of old.[61] In any case, they evince no unmistakable correspondence with the sophisticated metaphysics, terminology, and esoteric exegesis that are the trademark of Ibn ʿArabi's school. Nonetheless, Ibn al-Ahdal is convinced that

> [Ibn Jamil's] sayings are reminiscent of those of Ibn ʿArabi and his followers in that they also deal with the union [of God with his creatures], the refusal to acknowledge that humans are responsible for their acts of disobedience, obedience and submission, the denial of the act of creation and of the Muslim religion, and [as a consequence] the denial that unbelief [really] exists.[62]

Whether or not Ibn Jamil was indeed guilty of monistic proclivities, Ibn al-Ahdal goes to extraordinary lengths to exonerate him from the *shatahat* under the pretext that they were foisted upon him by a later admirer of Ibn ʿArabi, Ibn al-Raddad. For Ibn al-Ahdal, this was but Ibn al-Raddad's stratagem[63] aimed at proving the continuity between the teachings of both Sufi masters in order to legitimize Ibn ʿArabi's teaching among Yemeni scholars. Ibn al-Ahdal's goal is to show the opposite. In his view, the affinity between the two shaykhs was deliberately concocted by his Sufi opponents.[64] What he does not deny is that Ibn Jamil was responsible for the introduction into Yemen of the Sufi *samaʿ*[65]—a practice which, in a curious quirk of fate, was to become emblematic of the Ibn ʿArabi party under the leadership of the flamboyant Shaykh Ismaʿil al-Jabarti.

Another important representative of Yemeni Sufism whose name is often mentioned in connection with Ibn ʿArabi's teachings is Ahmad Ibn ʿAlwan (d. 665/1266)—a revered Sufi of the Rifaʿiyya brotherhood that had established a firm foothold in Yemen around the late 6th/12th centuries.[66] Unlike the illiterate Abu 'l-Ghayth Ibn Jamil, Ibn ʿAlwan was born of a family of noted scholars[67] to become a leading Yemeni writer of his time. His biographers emphasize his proficiency in mystical literature, *adab,* grammar, rhetoric, and *fiqh* as well as his enthusiasm for theosophical discourses and esoteric exegesis.[68] His eloquent sermons drew big crowds, winning him the nickname "[Ibn] al-Jawzi of Yemen."[69]

Ibn ʿAlwan left behind a considerable body of writings, some of which are reported to have been composed in "strange languages" (*lughat ghariba*),[70] incomprehensible to his Yemeni disciples. According to his biographers, he learned them through his visionary interviews with the spirits of the foreign saints who visited him in his retreat. Ibn ʿAlwan's indebtedness to Ibn ʿArabi still remains tenuous, if not implausible.[71] In his *al-Tawhid al-aʿzam,* Ibn ʿAlwan presents himself as a thoroughly traditional Sufi moralizer, instructing Sufi novices in the basics of the mystical Path. There is, however, no denying that some of his more daring mystical paradoxes quoted by al-Sharji[72] are redolent of the ecstatic outbursts of al-Bistami and al-Hallaj—a fact that did not escape the attention of Massignon who included the Yemeni Sufi in his list of al-Hallaj's sympathizers.[73] Massignon had a strong case. A fragment of Ibn ʿAlwan's poem that he cited in his study of al-Hallaj reveals the Yemeni's debt to the Hallajian tradition of mythopoetic mysticism. On the other hand, the same fragment clearly shows that the celebrated Yemeni saint was no stranger to the speculative and metaphysical tendencies within Sufism personified by Ibn ʿArabi and his followers.

Whether or not Ibn Jamil and Ibn ʿAlwan actually experienced Ibn ʿArabi's influence (chronologically, at least, this seems feasible), it is certain that the religious climate of Yemen under the late Ayyubids and early Rasulids was propitious for the implantation of monistic speculation. When, in the late 7th/13th centuries, Ibn ʿArabi's exponents, who came from the holy cities of Arabia, began to propagate his ideas in Yemen, they found a surprisingly receptive and enthusiastic audience among both local Sufis and mystically minded *ʿulamaʾ*. Another reason for the rapid dissemination of Sufi ideas in Yemeni society lay in the policy of the Ayyubids, who consistently encouraged the Sufi movement and its leaders in an effort to securer a broader popular basis for their power. The Rasulids, it will be recalled, were faithful imitators of the Ayyubid sultans who copied their policies including the cultivation of popular Sufi leaders. At times, they tolerated even the most unconventional aspects of the Sufi outlook that many conservative *ʿulamaʾ* found irksome, if not downright heretical.[74]

If Ibn al-Ahdal's narrative is accurate, the first active proponent of Ibn ʿArabi's teaching in Yemen was ʿUmar b. ʿAbd al-Rahman b. Hasan al-Qudsi (or al-Muqaddasi) (d. 688/1289), a native of Jerusalem,[75] who studied under the renowned Rifaʿi Shaykh Najm al-din al-Akhdar.[76] Whereas the Sufi biographer al-Sharji portrays al-Qudsi as al-Akhdar's emissary to Yemen with the mission of propagating the Rifaʿi teaching,[77] for Ibn al-Ahdal, he was first and foremost a proponent of monistic ideas.[78] Upon arrival in Yemen, al-Qudsi (al-Muqaddasi) and his Yemeni companion and friend, Muhammad b. Salim Ibn al-Naba,[79] received flattering honors from the Rasulid prince al-Ashraf ʿUmar (d. 696/1297), who later became the ruler of Yemen after his pious father al-Muzaffar Yusuf

(d. 694/1295) voluntarily gave up the Rasulid throne.[80] While still heir apparent, al-Ashraf appointed al-Qudsi to the post of the professor (*mudarris*) of speculative theology (*kalam*) at the prestigious religious college Umm al-Sultan in Taʿizz. Al-Qudsi was assisted by Ibn al-Naba, who remained his closest companion until his death. Although Ibn al-Ahdal is anxious to depict both scholars as espousers of Ibn ʿArabi's ideas, it is evidently their teaching of (Muʿtazili?) theology that caused their conflict with the conservative *ʿulamaʾ* of Taʿizz. It seems, however, more likely that the local scholars were resentful of the generous royal patronage accorded to the newcomers. Whether al-Qudsi and Ibn al-Naba also propagated Sufi philosophy, as Ibn al-Ahdal tries to convince us, is unclear.

Events took a sharp turn when one Ahmad Ibn al-Safi (d. 707/1307),[81] who had attended Ibn al-Naba's lectures on the Qurʾan, lodged a complaint with the city's chief religious authority (*raʾs al-muftin*), Abu Bakr Ibn Adam,[82] accusing the lecturer of denying the uncreatedness of the Qurʾan (a typical Muʿtazili thesis) as well as of other unspecified "heresies" (*zandaqa*).[83] Ibn Adam and the *fuqahaʾ* of Zabid and Taʿizz, many of whom were offended by the swift rise of al-Qudsi and Ibn al-Naba, seized this opportunity to do away with the "upstarts" and concocted a plan to assassinate them during the congregational prayer at the Friday mosque. The two scholars, however, got wind of the plot, and asked the prince al-Ashraf for protection. The latter immediately instructed the governor of Taʿizz to provide them with an armed guard. When the sultan al-Muzaffar was informed about the plot, he sent the conspirators an angry and humiliating reprimand in which he exposed their bigotry and narrow-mindedness and threatened them with severe punishment unless they desist. The sultan's letter, which was then publicly announced in the Friday mosques of Yemen, achieved its expected effect: the frightened *fuqahaʾ* left their enemies alone.[84]

Upon al-Qudsi's death, Ibn al-Naba succeeded him at the head of the Umm al-Sultan college where he continued to teach the doctrines that had nearly cost him his life. His finest hour came with the accession of his patron and friend Prince al-Ashraf to the Rasulid throne in 694/1294.[85] According to Ibn al-Ahdal, toward the end of his life Ibn al-Naba allegedly recanted his doctrinal "delusions," though his repentance, cast in the form of a laudatory treatise on the ways of the "pious ancestors," was not accepted by his former enemies who remained doubtful of his sincerity.[86]

It should be stressed that neither al-Janadi (d. 732/1331) nor al-Khazraji (d. 812/1409)—Ibn al-Ahdal's principal sources, linked al-Qudsi (al-Muqaddasi) and Ibn Naba to monistic Sufism. For these historians, they were but exponents of a suspect theological teaching, apparently, of Muʿtazili inspiration. In other words, we have no clear evidence to support al-Qudsi and Ibn Naba's affiliation with Ibn ʿArabi and his school of thought, especially since their works have not survived. The fact that Ibn al-Ahdal mentions them in connection with the Ibn ʿArabi controversy may spring from his tendency to see continuity and interdependence between various forms of "heresy"—an idea that runs like a red thread across the entire narrative texture of his *Kashf.*

The first Yemeni scholar whose link with Ibn ʿArabi is beyond doubt is Abu ʾl-ʿAtiq Abu Bakr Ibn al-Hazzaz al-Yahyawi (d. 709/1309).[87] Unlike Ibn Jamil and Ibn ʿAlwan, who adhered to the ecstatic and mythopoetic mysticism of al-Bistami and al-Hallaj, this well-traveled Yemeni scholar took intense interest in Ibn ʿArabi's metaphysics.[88] During his long sojourn in Mecca and Medina he studied with some local followers of the Greatest Master and copied or purchased many of his works.[89] He then brought them to Yemen, where he lent them to those interested.[90] As with al-Qudsi and Ibn Naba, Abu ʾl-ʿAtiq enjoyed royal patronage and was on friendly terms with the sultan al-Muʾayyad Dawud, whose relatively long and stable reign lasted from 696/1297 to 721/1322.[91] Al-Muʾayyad's total reliance on Abu ʾl-ʿAtiq's judgment[92] in matters of religion and domestic politics did not sit lightly with many *fuqahaʾ*, who envied him for his influence on the ruler. In an attempt to discredit Abu ʾl-ʿAtiq, these scholars repeatedly charged him with "heresy" and "sorcery" (*sihr*) which, they claimed, he performed by manipulating the magic properties of the divine names and alchemy (*kimiya*).[93] Given Ibn ʿArabi's proficiency in occultism and numerology, such accusations do not seem entirely groundless.[94] Although Yemeni historians credited Abu ʾl-ʿAtiq with a number of Sufi treatises and mystical poetry, none of these has survived.

From the patchy and tendentious evidence furnished by Ibn al-Ahdal, Abu ʾl-ʿAtiq al-Yahyawi emerges as an independent scholar of high integrity, who used his influence with the Rasulid sultan to carry out a series of important reforms aimed at strengthening state control over charitable funds and endowments.[95] Curiously, al-Janadi ignored al-Yahyawi's monistic propensities, praising instead the strict measures he implemented against the breachings of the religious law in the Rasulid capital such as the drinking of wine, gambling, and other forbidden pastimes.[96] On the other hand, Ibn al-Ahdal, whose judgment of Abu ʾl-ʿAtiq was clouded by the latter's partiality to Ibn ʿArabi's teaching, takes a much harsher view of the scholar to the extent that he calls in doubt the sincerity of his intentions. To the author of the *Kashf,* al-Yahyawi's pious reforms were a smoke screen by which he intended to hide his indulgence in "heresies" and vainglorious pretensions (*al-raghba fi ʾl-dunya*), since, in Ibn al-Ahdal's opinion, a desire to curry favor with the rulers (*al-taqarrub ila ʾl-dawla*) was a trait he shared with the other members of the Ibn ʿArabi party.[97] By worming their way into the rulers' confidence, says Ibn al-Ahdal, Ibn ʿArabi's followers secured the license to propagate their "perverted" beliefs.

Impartial Yemeni historians, on the other hand, portray Abu ʾl-ʿAtiq al-Yahyawi as a tranquil person who shunned open confrontations with his learned detractors and stoically endured their repeated attacks on his theological views. This may have been a sign of his weakness in the face of the broad opposition to monistic speculation among the leading Yemeni divines. Although Abu ʾl-ʿAtiq al-Yahyawi remained faithful to his persuasions against all odds, he did not seem to be able to disseminate them among his contemporaries. Even if he had disciples, they failed to form a distinct school of thought after his death. Commenting on this situation, one of the Yemeni critics of Ibn ʿArabi, Ahmad b. Abu Bakr al-Nashiri (d. 815/1412), triumphantly observed that Abu ʾl-ʿAtiq al-Yahyawi was so important to the Sufi cause that "with his demise, Ibn ʿArabi's teaching here [in Yemen] came to an end."[98] In a similar vein, Ibn al-Ahdal asserts that Ibn ʿArabi's books disappeared from Yemen after Abu ʾl-ʿAtiq al-Yahyawi's departure. They were, however, to reemerge, and with a vengeance, a few decades later in the city of Zabid.[99]

Al-Jabarti and the Sufi Community of Zabid

In the last quarter of the 8th/14th centuries Zabid became an important center of Sufi activity. The number of local Sufi communities grew during the reign of al-Ashraf Ismaʿil (778/1376-803/1400), who outstripped his predecessors in his lavish patronage of Sufism. The weight of royal authority gradually tilted the balance of power in favor of the Sufi party, reducing its opponents to the unfamiliar role of the underdog. The triumph Yemeni Sufism was in large part due to the astute leadership of the charismatic Shaykh Ismaʿil al-Jabarti (d. 806/1403).[100] A popular spiritual tutor, whose lectures on Sufism drew large crowds, al-Jabarti was also the Sultan's closest friend and advisor.[101] Biographers concur that the

Sultan put his trust in al-Jabarti after the latter had predicted that the siege of Zabid by the powerful Zaydi Imam Salah al-din Muhammad Ibn al-Mahdi (r. 773/1371-793/1390) would end in failure, saving the beleaguered sultan from the inevitable disaster.[102] Following the Imam's "miraculous" withdrawal from the city walls, al-Jabarti was elevated to the status of the Sultan's personal confidant. Commenting on al-Jabarti's enormous popularity among the inhabitants of Zabid, al-Sakhawi contemptuously described him as an opportunistic ignoramus.[103] Whenever somebody turned to him for a cure or intercession, said al-Sakhawi, al-Jabarti would invariably recommend him the only panacea he knew—to recite the *Yasin* chapter of the Qur'an.[104] A similar ungenerous opinion of al-Jabarti was held by the great Yemeni scholar al-Shawkani (d. 1250/1832),[105] who described al-Jabarti's house as a refuge for the pious man as well as for the rogue.[106]

These ungenerous comments notwithstanding, there is no doubt that al-Jabarti was endowed with a strong charismatic personality that made him popular with both the ruler and the masses. The aura of sainthood, which surrounded al-Jabarti already at the early stages of his career, later helped him to hold his own against the fierce resistance of some *fuqahaʾ* who were envious of his wide popularity. Unabashed by their opposition, al-Jabarti succeeded in making his Sufi beliefs a legitimate and respected option for every believer in the Rasulid realm. His tireless efforts to promote the ideals of mystical Islam led to the rise of a Sufi school that derived its identity from an enthusiastic allegiance to the teaching of Ibn ʿArabi and to his later interpreters.[107]

Due to al-Jabarti's efforts, colorful Sufi festivities and *samaʿ* sessions became a common occurrence in Zabid and in its environs.[108] On the doctrinal plane, his admiration for Ibn ʿArabi was such that he reportedly made the study of the *Fusus* mandatory to his numerous disciples and demanded that they always carry at least one copy of this book and be able to produce it upon request. Should a disciple fail to obey, al-Jabarti, in the words of his biographers, would "reprimand him" (*yantaqid minhu*) and "turn his back on him" (*lam yaltafit ilayhi*).[109]

Alongside conventional Sufi manuals, such as al-Qushayri's *Risala* or al-Suhrawardi's *ʿAwarif al-maʿarif*, the *Fusus* and *Futuhat* as well as their commentaries became a standard read for al-Jabarti's *murid*s. Consequently, both books were copied and sold in large quantities, and, at al-Jabarti's instance, regularly recited at Sufi gatherings.[110] His "infatuation" with Ibn ʿArabi's mystical ideas aroused the ire of the more conservative Yemeni jurists that is graphically conveyed by Ibn al-Ahdal:

> Due to Ibn ʿArabi's books and the excessive belief in him the city of Zabid in Yemen has become an arena for severe trouble and temptation at the hands of the ignorant Sufis. They all are followers of Shaykh Ismaʿil al-Jabarti and Shaykh Ahmad Ibn al-Raddad, who place much faith in Ibn ʿArabi, praise him highly and study whatever of his books they can obtain. They also collect commentaries on the *Fusus* written by ʿAbd al-Razzaq al-Qashani,[111] Dawud al-Qaysari,[112] al-Muʾayyad al-Jandi and other such books of theirs.[113] They nurture strange, unheard of, beliefs that explicitly state that they have achieved union with God (*ittihad*). It is said that once a group of these Sufis got together for a drinking party. While they were passing around a goblet of wine, one of them called upon [his neighbor] in the following manner: "By my greatness, if you give me this glass [of wine], I will surely send you to my creatures [as a Messenger]!"[114] Here is another example. One of those Sufis used to call his friend "Your Greatness."[115] And when one of them cursed the other, they reproached him, saying: "[How dare you] to curse God?!" On yet another occasion, one of them said: "This wall is God!" Finally, some of those Sufis used to fornicate with the wife of their companion, telling her: "We are all one man on account of oneness!"[116]

Its outspoken anti-Sufi bias notwithstanding, one should not hasten to dismiss this testimony en bloc as malicious slander. There is no doubt that an adequate understanding of Ibn ʿArabi's ideas presupposes a great deal of spiritual and intellectual maturity and self-discipline on the part of their prospective recipients—a fact that was fully realized by those advocates of the Greatest Master, who insisted that the contents of his books should not be divulged to each and everyone. Since, in Yemen, Sufism was a relatively recent implantation that lacked intellectual sophistication, it is not surprising that some local adherents of Ibn ʿArabi could indeed have interpreted his ideas in antinomian terms. It is, therefore, not inconceivable that a fervid (if shallow) adoption of Ibn ʿArabi's daring insights by his Yemeni partisans might indeed have resulted in the excesses and immoral conduct that gave rise to grotesque anecdotes such as those I have just reproduced.[117] Whether Ibn ʿArabi can be held responsible for these scandalous episodes or if they were invented by Ibn al-Ahdal is a totally different matter.

Ibn al-Ahdal's angry diatribe renders us a valuable service by enumerating the Sufi works that were read by the mystics of Zabid.

The three authors mentioned in the passage are prominent representatives of the rationalist interpretation of Ibn ʿArabi's legacy that became closely entwined with the Islamicized neo-Platonic philosophy of Avicenna. Such rationalizing commentaries became the main vehicle through which Ibn ʿArabi's ideas were disseminated throughout the Muslim scholarly milieu.[118] In this regard at least, the Yemeni disciples of the Greatest Master followed in the steps of their counterparts in Egypt, Anatolia, Iran, and India, where the same commentaries laid the groundwork for the rise of the philosophy, known as *wahdat al-wujud*.[119]

It appears that his intimate knowledge of Ibn ʿArabi's teaching made al-Jabarti cognizant of the dangers attendant upon its uncritical and superficial acceptance by the uninitiated. He is said to have repeatedly emphasized to his disciples that the breathtaking mysteries of the great Sufi gnostics may prove to be detrimental to the weaker souls and to those lacking background in the traditional Islamic knowledge.[120] Such warnings, however, fell on deaf ears, for some of his followers continued to indulge in "strange beliefs" that exhibit a rather bizarre mixture of the Sufi doctrine of the Perfect Man, incarnationalism, and the messianic tenets of the "extreme" Shiʿa. In an uncanny quirk of fate, the Sufi leader of Zabid himself became the object of these "heretical" beliefs. With great disgust Ibn al-Ahdal reports that many of al-Jabarti's followers considered him to be a personification of the divine attributes; the most fervent of them went as far as to proclaim him God incarnate.[121] Claims to lordship were reportedly also entertained by some lesser figures in al-Jabarti's inner circle such as one Shaykh Mahmud of Persia (*min al-ʿajam*), who, when asked to introduce himself, replied that the name of the attribute was "Mahmud," while the name of the essence was "God."[122]

Ibn al-Ahdal claims that al-Jabarti and Ibn al-Raddad, al-Jabarti's successor at the head of Sufi movement in Zabid, did nothing to discourage such exorbitant attitudes among their overzealous followers. On the contrary, both shaykhs implicitly condoned what Ibn al-Ahdal describes as "blasphemous gibberish" by publicly musing over the issue of whether the Sufi saint can identify himself with the attributes of the Divine Essence or just with the those pertaining to the Divine Actions.[123] If Ibn al-Ahdal's testimony is to be trusted, al-Jabarti should have belonged to the so-called extremist trend within Sufism (*ghulat al-tasawwuf*) which was represented by al-Bistami, al-Hallaj, al-Kharaqani, Abu Saʿid Mayhani, and some later Sufi masters. While most Sufi shaykhs admitted that the perfect mystic may assume properties of the divine actions (*sifat al-afʿal*), they denied that he could become one with God's transcendent essence. The fact that al-Jabarti did not rule out this possibility, which is confirmed by no less an authority than Ibn al-Raddad and al-Jili,[124] put him in the company of the "extremist" mystics who claimed to have achieved an essential union with God.[125] Ibn al-Ahdal argues that al-Jabarti borrowed this scandalous idea from Ibn ʿArabi's works, which, as we know, allowed a great variety of interpretations. In the absence of al-Jabarti's own statements to this effect, Ibn al-Ahdal's accusation cannot be ascertained.

If Ibn al-Ahdal's account of al-Jabarti's views is accurate, it seems feasible that the leader of Yemeni Sufis adhered to the aspect of Ibn ʿArabi's teaching that underscored divine immanence, and, as a consequence, was given to the shocking mode of expression this often entailed. By giving preference to immanence over transcendence al-Jabarti upset the delicate balance between these two aspects of divine existence, which Ibn ʿArabi was so keen to preserve.[126] In view of al-Jabarti's importance for the shaping of Yemeni Sufism, his "immanentist" interpretation of Ibn ʿArabi's legacy had far-reaching implications. In disseminating the immanentist thesis among Yemeni Sufis he encouraged, perhaps unwittingly, the excesses described in Ibn al-Ahdal's account.

In discussing al-Jabarti's "delusions," Ibn al-Ahdal never raises the obvious question of whether Ibn ʿArabi was properly understood by his Yemeni partisans. On the contrary, he seeks to excuse al-Jabarti by laying the entire blame at Ibn ʿArabi's door. Ibn al-Ahdal's choice of culprit may have been determined by al-Jabarti's posthumous popularity that was still much alive, when the *Kashf* was being written.[127] Mindful of this popular reverence for the deceased shaykh, Ibn al-Ahdal excuses him on the grounds of his lack of a sound theological training that allegedly prevented him from grasping the "heretical" essence of Ibn ʿArabi's doctrine.[128] Rather than a conscious follower of the Greatest Master, al-Jabarti, in Ibn al-Ahdal's account, was a gullible victim of Ibn ʿArabi's disguised heresy. In blindly trusting Ibn ʿArabi's self-description as an infallible friend of God, al-Jabarti, according to Ibn al-Ahdal, swallowed an attractively packaged poison.[129] Hence the following verdict:

> How abhorrent is the Sufi who is ignorant of the principles of the divine law to the extent that he cannot discern things permitted [by the law] from those prohibited [by it]. And yet his ignorance does not prevent him from discussing the attributes of the Divine

> Essence and the properties of Divine Unity. It should, however, be made abundantly clear with regard to the divine attributes and names and with regard to what one can and cannot say about Him, that one should always turn to the authority of the scholars who study the fundamentals of religion. For they are the only ones who combine the knowledge of the divine law with rational examination, as did, for example, Abu ʾl-Hasan al-Ashʿari and his followers.[130]

Contrary to what one would expect from his inimical treatment of Ibn ʿArabi's followers, the author of the *Kashf* concludes his evaluation of al-Jabarti and Ibn al-Raddad on a reconciliatory note:

> One is well advised not to consult them [i.e., al-Jabarti and Ibn al-Raddad] on matters of the divine law. . . . True, they may well have been great Sufi masters who were admired [by their disciples]. Yet they never studied the sciences pertaining to the divine law or the fundamentals of religion. On the contrary, they were preoccupied with the Sufi concerts, the study of [mystical] works and the collection of teaching licenses. . . . We thus believe that these two masters were the saints [whose deeds were] beneficial to Islam and to those Muslims who profited from their knowledge. We, however, wish that they had repented from the delusion they were in.[131]

Al-Jabarti's Associates: Ibn al-Raddad and al-Jili

I will now turn to the other members of the Ibn ʿArabi faction, who made possible the unprecedented efflorescence of speculative Sufism under the Rasulids. I have already mentioned the name of Ahmad [Ibn] al-Raddad, the scholar-turned-Sufi who succeeded al-Jabarti at the head of the Sufi community of Zabid. In what follows I shall take a closer look at this remarkable individual.

Born of a noble Meccan family[132] in 745/1346 or 748/1348, Ibn al-Raddad received the best education available in his age.[133] His noble origin, connections in the higher circles, and solid education destined him for a brilliant career at court or in the state administration. This, however, was not to be. Around 767/1365 Ibn al-Raddad made his first trip to Yemen. On a visit to Zabid, he made the acquaintance of al-Jabarti and his Sufi followers. Deeply impressed by the charismatic master, he abandoned his mundane career for mysticism. On al-Jabarti's advice he cut off ties with his influential friends at Mecca and embarked on the path of humility and pious meditation. Initially Ibn al-Raddad subjected himself to austere ascetic exercises aimed at humbling his ego. When this aim was successfully achieved, he turned to the study of "philosophical Sufism" (*tasawwuf al-falasifa*) under the guidance of al-Jabarti. He made such rapid progress that al-Jabarti soon put the still young Ibn al-Raddad in charge of his *murids*. Soon afterward, in recognition of Ibn al-Raddad's outstanding achievements, al-Jabarti invested him with a Sufi frock of the Qadiriyya brotherhood and declared him his successor.[134] From then on, the master and the disciple were inseparable. Ibn al-Raddad's conversion to mysticism was profound and final. His new vocation distracted him completely from his own family to the extent that al-Jabarti had to interfere in order to provide for the starving wife and children of the new *murid.*

Ibn al-Raddad's teaching method is remarkable in its focus on a diligent study of Ibn ʿArabi's works. Because of this, both Ibn Hajar and al-Sakhawi lashed out at him as

> An extoller of this blamable innovation,[135] of which he had direct experience, of which real implications he was fully aware, and on account of which he attacked [those who opposed it], favoring only those who agreed with it. Whenever he learned that someone had purchased a copy of the *Fusus,* he would encourage him and hold him in high regard.[136]

Owing to al-Jabarti's influence at court, Ibn al-Raddad was introduced to the sultan al-Ashraf Ismaʿil (d. 803/1401), who made him a close companion (*nadim*).[137] Although frequently invited to the ruler's wild carouses, Ibn al-Raddad, as al-Sakhawi grudgingly conceded, neither drank wine nor engaged in any other canonically forbidden pastime.[138] While at court, Ibn al-Raddad was befriended by al-Fayruzabadi, the grand *qadi* of Yemen, who commended his talents to the sultan, indicating that he would like to see Ibn al-Raddad as his successor.[139]

Unlike al-Jabarti, whose chief contribution to Yemeni Sufism was his numerous disciples, Ibn al-Raddad was a prolific writer on a variety of subjects, especially those related to the Sufi Path. In his treatises, he promoted Ibn ʿArabi's ideas and encouraged both advanced Sufis and novices to look into the mysteries of *Fusus* and *Futuhat.* In a book on the practice of wearing and passing on the Sufi robe (*khirqa*), he energetically rebuffed the condemnations of licentiousness brought against his fellow mystics by some scholars of Zabid.[140] Apart from rather pedestrian didactic verses directed at Sufi novices,[141] Ibn al-Raddad's legacy contains elegant mystical poetry describing the mystical lover's unrequited longing for God.[142] This part of Ibn al-Raddad's literary work elicited the following disparaging comment from Ibn Hajar:

> He wrote much poetry and prose in which he propagated this manifest delusion[143] until he completely corrupted the faith of the inhabitants of Zabid, except those whom God protected. His poetry and prose bleat with unification [with God]. [Sufi] reciters learnt his poems by heart and sang them at Sufi festivals in hopes of achieving through them proximity with God.[144]

In the Sufi community of Zabid, Ibn al-Raddad's authority was complete and uncontested.[145] Following the transition of power to al-Nasir Ahmad (d. 827/1424), Ibn al-Raddad successfully reasserted his influence upon the new ruler, whom he gave his daughter in marriage. On al-Fayruzabadi's advice, the sultan eventually appointed the leader of Zabidi Sufis to the supreme judgeship of Rasulid Yemen.[146] This appointment evidently caused a great uproar among Yemeni *ʿulama*ʾ, most of whom supported the candidacy of the non-Sufi scholars al-Nashiri and Ibn al-Muqri (d. 837/1444). At any rate, most *ʿulama*ʾ strongly resented such a flamboyant figure as Ibn al-Raddad, whom they treated as an incompetent upstart. The sultan, however, had his way. In response, the disgruntled *ʿulama*ʾ started a campaign to discredit the new grand *qadi* and to persuade the ruler to reconsider the appointment. Their intrigues focused on Ibn al-Raddad's widely known predilection for Ibn ʿArabi's teaching, which they hastened to present as a grievous heresy. However, the scholars miscalculated. Unlike the dovish Abu ʾl-ʿAtiq al-Yahyawi, who humbly tolerated the critical attacks on himself and on the Greatest Master, Ibn al-Raddad, once in office, turned the tide, visiting severe reprisals upon his learned antagonists. These events will be discussed a little further on.

Alongside Ibn al-Raddad and al-Jabarti, we find ʿAbd al-Karim al-Jili (d. 832/1428), the noted Sufi theorist whose fame rests on his refinement of Ibn ʿArabi's concept of the Perfect Man as well as his widely read commentary on the first chapter of *al-Futuhat al-makkiyya*.[147] The life and career of this Sufi master, who arrived in Yemen from India, is all but ignored by Yemeni chronicles.[148] Therefore, any information on al-Jili's activities in Yemen is of great importance. Luckily, in his account of al-Jabarti's companions, Ibn al-Ahdal provides a cursory glimpse of al-Jili's character and theological beliefs, as seen by his detractors. It shows that al-Jili blended in smoothly with the landscape of Yemeni Sufism:

> Among those doomed to be lost in this sea more than anyone else is ʿAbd al-Karim al-Jili, the Persian. A reliable and honest scholar told me about him that he had accompanied him [i.e., al-Jili] in one of his travels, during which he heard him praising profusely Ibn ʿArabi's books and teachings. This person [i.e., the informant] also heard him overtly ascribing lordship (*rububiyya*) to every human being, bird, or tree which he happened to see on his way.[149]

In another passage Ibn al-Ahdal mentions his personal meeting with al-Jili during the latter's visit to Abyat Husayn, where Ibn al-Ahdal was chief *mufti.* At that time, he was as yet unaware of al-Jili's affiliation with the Ibn ʿArabi school and therefore did not engage the Persian Sufi in a theological dispute. This may mean that al-Jili kept secret his monistic views. Al-Jili's own remarks, on the other hand, indicate that he made friends with all of the major figures in the al-Jabarti circle: al-Jabarti, Muhammad al-Mukdish, Ibn al-Raddad, and al-Mizjaji, and took an active part in their Sufi sessions. Yet, his exact role in the local Sufi community and in the Ibn ʿArabi debate remains obscure. What we do know is that he was constantly on the move and did not settle for a long period in any one place. It is however clear that his main residence was in Zabid, from where he made trips to Sanaʿa', Mecca, and even as far as Cairo.[150] Al-Jili's death at Abyat Husayn in 826/1421 or 832/1428, coincided with the decline of the Sufi community in Zabid that was caused in part by the activities of the famous Yemeni scholar and poet Ibn al-Muqri. Al-Jili was buried in the shrine of the local holy man named Ibrahim al-Jabali (or al-Bijli?),[151] whose descendants hosted him during his frequent visits to Abyat Husayn.[152]

Further details about al-Jili's activities in Yemen can be found in his own writings. Apart from the mystical metaphysics and sainthood theory, which constituted the crux of his mystical doctrine, al-Jili occasionally addressed the issues of the practical training of Sufi novices. As with other Sufi thinkers, he was not just a theorist, but also a practicing Sufi *murshid* with an entourage of devoted followers, whose needs he addressed in his mystical works. Thus, in the introduction to his "Book of the Forty Degrees," al-Jili advised his disciples to seek mystical wisdom in the writings of the great Sufi saints rather than to try to achieve it through the mortification of the flesh, seclusion from the world, and pious meditation.[153] In support of this method al-Jili quoted a dialogue between al-Jabarti and one of his disciples in Zabid. According to al-Jili, al-Jabarti recommended that the disciple should start his education by perusing Ibn ʿArabi's works, which he described as the surest path to mystical knowledge. When the perplexed disciple replied that he would rather wait until God disclosed to him these mysteries through a mystical unveiling, al-Jabarti's objected by saying, "what you search for is exactly what the Shaykh [i.e., Ibn ʿArabi] tells you in his books."[154]

This story gives valuable insight into the teaching methods employed by the Sufi masters of al-Jabarti's school. Their insistence on the study of Ibn ʿArabi's writings is revealing insofar as it reflects the latter's role as the source of identity for the local Sufi community. Elsewhere, al-Jili asserted that Ibn ʿArabi's ideas can save the novice the difficulty of classifying and formulating the elusive mystical experiences and symbolic visions he encounters on the Sufi Path. On this view, the *Fusus* and *Futuhat* are handy shortcuts for the beginner, because they give him a greater conceptual clarity, and, as a consequence, a more advanced degree of spiritual and intellectual maturity. To illustrate this point, al-Jili cited the example of the Sufi poet Abu Bakr Muhammad al-Hakkak (who died in the last decade of the 8th/14th centuries).[155] As a young man al-Hakkak took to reading Ibn ʿArabi's books and in several days attained the degree of perfection that one acquires after decades of ascetic practices and self-exertion. With the help of Ibn ʿArabi's books, the young Sufi soon outstripped established Sufi masters, who relied exclusively on their subjective experience, while ignoring mystical writings. Al-Jili's narrative is especially revealing, since Yemeni biographers consider al-Hakkak to be al-Jabarti's first instructor in Sufism—it was from him that the future leader of the Yemeni Sufis received his first Sufi robe as well as permission to guide *murid*s (*tahkim*).[156] It must be emphasized that al-Hakkak belonged to the Qadiriyya brotherhood, an affiliation he shared with both al-Jabarti and al-Jili.[157] One may, therefore, argue that the Yemeni Qadiriyya, and to some extent the Rifaʿiyya (which was the Sufi affiliation of Abu ʾl-ʿAtiq al-Yahyawi), was especially active in the preservation and diffusion of Ibn ʿArabi's ideas in Yemen.[158]

In his treatise on the Sufi Perfect Man,[159] al-Jili made further references to his Yemeni experiences. One of them evinces deeper reasons for his veneration of al-Jabarti than a simple commitment of the *murid* to his spiritual master. In discussing the central topic of his work, the manifestation of the essence of Muhammad in the personality of the Perfect Man of the age, al-Jili wrote:

> [The] Universal Man is the pole around which revolve the spheres of existence, from the first to the last. . . . He, however, puts on different dresses . . . and is named according to this or that garb of the time. It is thus that I encountered him in the form of my master Sharaf al-din Ismaʿil al-Jabarti. At that time I did not know that he actually was [a manifestation of] the Prophet [Muhammad],[160] and I thought him to be my master. This was one of the many [revelatory] visions in which I witnessed him in this capacity during my stay in Zabid in 796 (i.e., 1393).[161]

Elsewhere, al-Jili praised al-Jabarti as "the universal master" (*ustadh al-dunya*), "the perfect [saintly] axis" (*al-qutb al-kamil*), "the locus of this world on which God's gaze is ever fixed" (*mahall nazar Allah ila hadha ʾl-ʿalam*), and "the precious elixir" (*al-kibrit al-ahmar*).[162]In a similar vein, he dedicated to his revered master a number of laudatory poems that present al-Jabarti as "the possessor of the perfect essence and attributes."[163] Such an extravagant praise is all the more surprising given al-Jili's view of himself as the greatest Sufi gnostic and perfect man of the age as well as his haughtily refusing to acknowledge the tutelage of any living Sufi master.[164] His adoration for al-Jabarti is not unique to Sufi history. It immediately conjures up the intimate relationships between Rumi and Shams-i Tabriz or between al-Shadhili and Ibn Mashish.[165]

Excerpts from al-Jili's treatise, such as the one that was just quoted, demonstrate the lack of a clear-cut boundary between abstract metaphysical speculation and personal mystical experience, which, incidentally, characterizes Ibn ʿArabi's entire worldview.[166] In this respect at least, al-Jili seems to have been the Greatest Master's faithful follower: he too drew no sharp line between the Perfect Man, as an abstract manifestation of the universal *al-haqiqa al-muhammadiyya*, and its quite concrete embodiment in the personality of his Yemeni master. This lends support to Ibn al-Ahdal's claim[167] that al-Jili's near-worship of al-Jabarti was shared by the latter's enthusiastic adherents.[168] Not surprisingly, many Yemeni scholars were scandalized by such a gross violation of the notion of divine transcendence, which they classified as plain incarnationalism (*hulul*). Since al-Jili was one of the most well-educated mystical thinkers of his age, one cannot even fathom what exuberant forms the veneration of al-Jabarti should have assumed among his less sophisticated followers. After al-Jabarti's death, al-Jili made his master's claims his own, although we have no evidence that he achieved a comparable prominence among the Yemeni Sufis. These claims, as al-Jili's writings finely show, naturally flow from his metaphysical speculations about the all-important role in the universe of the Sufi Perfect Man.[169]

Emboldened by the sultan's support, the Sufis of Zabid began to openly defy their detractors among the *fuqahaʾ*, who continually attacked the noisy Sufi gatherings in the mosques that were accompanied with much drumbeat, singing, and dancing. Ecstatic behavior was not uncommon among the participants. One Sufi, Shaykh ʿUmar al-Musinn, was so excited during such a gathering that he hurled himself from the high roof, but miraculously survived the fall, which was immediately ascribed to the salutary effects of the *samaʿ*. In another episode, he reportedly tore out the eye of the singer but, upon recovering from trance, managed to put it back in its socket.[170] Finally, several people in the audience are said to have given up the ghost as a result of the emotional shock they suffered during the Sufi sessions presided over by al-Jabarti.[171]

Such scandalous goings-on in the city mosques alarmed many *ʿulamaʾ*, who felt that they were losing ground to al-Jabarti's followers. Yet with the sultan's sympathy squarely on the latter's side, the *ʿulamaʾ* had to toe a fine line. The growing prestige and power of al-Jabarti found a graphic illustration in the story of Shaykh Salih al-Misri.[172] When he publicly condemned al-Jabarti's mystical teachings and condonation of the ecstatic behavior in the city mosques, the Sufi complained to the sultan, who ordered al-Misri to be arrested, flagellated, and forcibly put on a ship bound for India.[173] As a result of this incident al-Jabarti detractors were cowed into silence.[174]

Scholarly Disputes over Ibn ʿArabi: The *fuqahaʾ* versus the *sufiyya*?

In his account of the dissemination of Ibn Arabi's teaching in Yemen Ibn al-Ahdal identifies several foci of the debate. One of them involved the two leading figures of the Yemeni religious establishment—Majd al-din al-Fayruzabadi (d. 817/1415) and Abu Bakr b. Muhammad Ibn al-Khayyat (d. 811/1408). As mentioned, al-Fayruzabadi arrived in Yemen at the invitation of the sultan al-Ashraf Ismaʿil, who appointed him chief *qadi* of the Rasulid kingdom.[175] His opponent, Ibn al-Khayyat, was the principal expert in Yemen on the Muslim tradition and jurisprudence, whose lectures in the colleges of Taʿizz attracted crowds of students from all over Arabia.[176]

A long and acrimonious quarrel between the two eminent scholars was sparked by al-Fayruzabadi's commentary on the classical collection of Islamic traditions by al-Bukhari. To please the sultan and his Sufi favorites, al-Fayruzabadi laced his work with quotations from the *Futuhat,* provoking Ibn al-Khayyat's severe criticism. Supported by a number of Yemeni scholars, Ibn al-Khayyat accused al-Fayruzabadi of holding a heretical teaching, which, in his words, had been repeatedly condemned by the scholarly consensus. Ibn al-Khayyat's supporters asked the sultan to arbitrate between the two men, apparently in hopes of casting doubt on the validity of al-Fayruzabadi's judgment and, possibly, in an attempt to dislodge him from his post. In the *fatwa,* which Ibn al-Khayyat issued in the aftermath of this episode,[177] he called upon the sultan to ban the study, purchase, and copying of Ibn ʿArabi's books. Furthermore, at the close of his ruling, he bluntly proclaimed Ibn ʿArabi an infidel whose heretical tenets placed him outside the Islamic fold. The text of Ibn al-Khayyat's *fatwa* has not come down to us.[178] Judging by its paraphrase in al-Fayruzabadi's rejoinder, it faithfully reproduced the antimonistic arguments we discussed in Chapters 5 and 8. Al-Fayruzabadi's response was framed as an eloquent apologia for the Greatest Master, which proclaimed him "the leader of those who have realized the ultimate truth" (*imam al-tahqiq haqiqatan*), whose works are "overflowing seas whose pearls are so numerous that one is unable to tell where they begin and where they end."[179] Al-Fayruzabadi concluded his *fatwa* with a verse that was to became the motto of the admirers of the Greatest Master:

> So, why should I be afraid to make plain
> what I firmly believe in:
> (And let the fool interpret this straightforward answer
> as an offence, if he so wishes)
> By God, by God, by God the Greatest and the One,
> Who made him [i.e., Ibn ʿArabi] His evidence and proof.
> What I have said is only [a grain] of his many virtues;
> I have added nothing, unless I have made them less
> perfect than they really are.[180]

In explaining Ibn al-Khayyat's hatred of Ibn ʿArabi, al-Fayruzabadi attributed it to his ignorance, bigotry, and prejudice. Al-Fayruzabadi's critique got personal, when he described Ibn ʿArabi's detractors as too stupid to be able to grasp the subtle meaning behind his allegorical expressions and sophisticated technical terminology.

The publication of both *fatwa*s provoked further mutual recriminations. Whereas Ibn al-Khayyat suggested that al-Fayruzabadi's defense of Ibn ʿArabi was dictated by his unscrupulous desire to curry favor with the sultan[181] rather than concern for the community's well-being, al-Fayruzabadi portrayed his opponent as a double-talking rabble-rouser seeking self-advancement. He also added that by smearing the reputation of such a great saint as Ibn ʿArabi, Ibn al-Khayyat[182] become guilty of slander—a sin punishable in the Hereafter. Mystical experience and gnosis, so goes al-Fayruzabadi's argument, have always been present in the Muslim community, though he advised discretion in discussing them in front of an unprepared audience. On the question of the legitimacy of Ibn ʿArabi's works, he ruled that they should be available to all interested in perusing them.

Al-Fayruzabadi's quarrel with Ibn al-Khayyat was as much about the Greatest Master as it was about personal rivalry. There are some indications that al-Fayruzabadi was indeed anxious to curry favor with the sultan, whose Sufi sympathies we knew well. Moreover, as Ibn al-Khayyat repeatedly pointed out in his rejoinder, al-Fayruzabadi acted, at least at the early stages of the controversy, on the sultan's direct orders.[183] Later on, when his competence as an interpreter of the *shariʿa* was openly called into doubt by Ibn al-Khayyat, al-Fayruzabadi had no option but to hold his own. This explanation of al-Fayruzabadi's motives is lent further support by Ibn Hajar al-ʿAsqalani, who met the great lexicographer on a visit to Zabid in 800/1397.[184] While there, Ibn Hajar was informed about the encounter between the two divines,[185] which he summarized in the following way:

> I do not suspect him [al-Fayruzabadi] to be a faithful espouser of the aforementioned teaching [i.e., that of Ibn ʿArabi]. [I however admit] that he was very fond of passing for someone he was not (*mudarat*). Besides, he himself demonstrated to me his repugnance and deep aversion toward the teaching in question.[186]

Whatever their motives, the conflict between al-Fayruzabadi and Ibn al-Khayyat had far-reaching repercussions for the subsequent intellectual history of Yemen, anticipating a series of scholarly feuds that grew particularly fervent under the sultans al-Ashraf Ismaʿil and al-Nasir Ahmad.

Among Yemeni scholars who sided with Ibn al-Khayyat in his campaign to stamp out the "Sufi indecencies" was the famous scholar and *mufti* Ahmad b. Abu Bakr al-Nashiri (d. 815/1412),[187] whose vast expertise in Islamic law earned him several high posts in al-Ashraf's administration. After he was promoted to the post of the chief *qadi* of Zabid, al-Nashiri ordered a crackdown on all manner of violations against of the *shariʿa*. As a result, he clashed with the sultan's retainers (*ghulman*) who retaliated by initiating a series of court intrigues that led to his dismissal. Despite the temporary reversal of fortunes, al-Nashiri continued to teach at the prestigious colleges of Zabid and was later reappointed to his former office by al-Nasir Ahmad.

In the debate over Ibn ʿArabi's legacy al-Nashiri threw his lot with the opponents of the Greatest Master, alienating the influential Sufis in the Rasulid administration, including the powerful al-Fayruzabadi. Following in the steps of his teacher Ibn al-Khayyat, al-Nashiri composed a polemical treatise aimed at exposing "the perfidy of Ibn ʿArabi's teaching" (*fasad ʿaqidat Ibn ʿArabi*).[188] Upon examining the testimonies of Ibn ʿArabi's critics, al-Nashiri declared Ibn ʿArabi and his followers "infidels" (*kuffar*) and "apostates" (*murtaddun*) who have fallen away from the Muslim community and therefore can no longer marry Muslim women.[189]

Al-Nashiri's vehement attacks on the reputation of the Greatest Master send the Sufis of Zabid running to the sultan, who prohibited the *faqih* from engaging in public denunciations of his Sufi opponents. As for al-Fayruzabadi, he was so embittered by al-Nashiri's tract that after al-Nashiri's death his son saw it fit to destroy the controversial work in order to placate his father's powerful foe.[190] Nevertheless, al-Nashiri's antimonistic legacy survived beyond his death: a popular teacher, he left many disciples, including some twenty first-rank scholars[191] who inherited his enmity toward the Greatest Master. At least three of them became Ibn ʿArabi's vociferous critics when the next generation of Yemeni *ʿulamaʾ* came of age.

With the departure of the old actors, new characters appeared on the Yemeni scene. Among them was Muhammad b. ʿAli al-Khatib (d. 825/1421), a native of the town of Mawzaʿ, where he held the post of preacher at the town's Friday mosque.[192] A disciple of al-Nashiri, he was already prejudiced against monistic Sufism in general and Ibn ʿArabi's teachings in particular. His prejudice turned into an active resistance when he learned that Ibn al-Raddad, who had recently been appointed the grand *qadi* of Yemen, put his stamp of approval on the dissemination and study of Ibn ʿArabi's work in all areas under his jurisdiction. Appalled by the prospect of the unrestricted diffusion of Ibn ʿArabi's "heresy," al-Khatib warned his parishioners against it from the pulpit of his mosque in Mawzaʿ. His public condemnation of the Greatest Master did not go unnoticed. He was summoned to Zabid, where the irate Ibn al-Raddad had him reiterate his statements before an audience that included the leading members of the Ibn ʿArabi faction. It seems that Ibn al-Raddad grossly underestimated al-Khatib's oratory and discursive skills: in the public dispute (*munazara*) with the leader of the Sufi party al-Khatib scored what some anti-Ibn ʿArabi authors described as a decisive victory, provoking the intense hatred of his powerful rival. On the latter's orders al-Khatib was thrown into prison, from which he was rescued by his friend, the emir Muhammad Ibn Ziyad, and hastily withdrew to his home town.[193] There, beyond the reach of his enemies, he composed a polemical tract, "The Removal of Injustice from this [Muslim] Community" (*Kashf al-zulma ʿan hadhihi ʾl-umma*),[194] which Ibn al-Ahdal describes as a detailed refutation of the *Fusus*.[195]

Ibn al-Raddad's appointment to the post of grand *qadi* of Yemen became a tangible sign of the ascendancy of the Sufi party. The legitimization of Ibn ʿArabi's teachings by the new grand *qadi,* came as a shock to the followers of Ibn al-Khayyat and al-Nashiri. Disoriented by the demise of their teachers, the anti-Ibn ʿArabi party were desperately looking for a leader. They found him in Ismaʿil b. Abu Bakr al-Muqri (or Ibn al-Muqri), a famous polymath who went down in Yemeni history primarily as the greatest poet of the Rasulid epoch.[196] Ibn al-Muqri's variegated talents quickly won him the favor of the sultan and his courtiers who accorded the poet respectful treatment and a lavish pension. These favors, however, did not satisfy Ibn al-Muqri's ambitions: he set his mind on succeeding al-Fayruzabadi at the head of the Yemeni religious hierarchy. In an attempt to persuade the sultan of his superior polemical and poetical skills, Ibn al-Muqri engaged the elderly scholar in a dispute, which led to a keen rivalry between the two men accompanied by acrimonious jabs in prose and poetry. Unimpressed by Ibn al-Muqri's intrigues against his grand *qadi,* the sultan allowed al-Fayruzabadi to execute his duties until his death.[197]

In the course of his altercation with al-Fayruzabadi, Ibn al-Muqri developed an aversion to Ibn ʿArabi, whom his elderly opponent had so vigorously defended against Ibn al-Khayyat and other critics. Following al-Fayruzabadi's death, Ibn al-Muqri was anticipating the imminent promotion to the post vacated by his rival. So strong was Ibn al-Muqri's desire to become supreme *qadi* that he declined a lucrative invitation by the sultan to lead a diplomatic mission to Mamluk Egypt. Then, out of the blue, came the news of Ibn al-Raddad's appointment to the coveted post. Deeply offended by al-Nasir's choice, Ibn al-Muqri spearheaded a campaign to discredit and eventually dislodge the new grand *qadi*. Since Ibn al-Raddad was an avowed partisan of the Greatest Master, Ibn al-Muqri had no option but to cast his frustration in the form of anti-Ibn ʿArabi diatribes. He started out by criticizing Sufi practices, especially the *samaʿ*, which he classified as the worst kind of *bidʿa*. Given Ibn al-Raddad's enthusiasm for the *samaʿ*, Ibn al-Muqri hoped to undermine his reputation as the leader of the scholarly community of Yemen. In addition, by initiating this polemical campaign Ibn al-Muqri wanted to make the sultan aware of the broad opposition to his new grand *qadi* among the *ʿulamaʾ*. This goal required stronger measures than a usual theological hairsplitting—a fact that accounts for the radical stance Ibn al-Muqri assumed on the issue of Ibn ʿArabi's orthodoxy. Not only did he demand that Ibn ʿArabi himself be declared an unbeliever, but he also wanted the same ruling to be applied to anyone who refused to testify to Ibn ʿArabi's unbelief.[198]

Thanks to Ibn al-Muqri's leadership, eloquence, and poetic talent he secured the success of his anti-Sufi campaign among both scholars and ordinary Muslims. For the laymen, Ibn al-Muqri's ranting had a special attraction due to his ability to present the nebulous theological argument in tangible and accessible images. Nor was his critique entirely groundless: he put his finger on the pretenses to the knowledge of divine mysteries that were entertained by many of Ibn ʿArabi's followers. Likewise, he masterfully exposed the greed and worldliness of some Sufi leaders, their faked ecstatic behavior, and ignorance of the Islamic tradition. Here is an example of a satire aimed at one Ibn Harun, a noted member of the Sufi faction:

> The news about Ibn Harun's deeds in his mosque is
> sad indeed.
> It fills with tears the eyes of every weeper:
> The daily bread of the learned men in his hand has
> become
> A snare for anyone who, by chance, comes near him.
> Those of them who joined their idle
> pastimes,[199] were given a lavish treat, whereas

those who piously abstained, were left starving!

Many a wearer of the turban[200]

Had to agree with him concerning the *Fusus* and its

teaching in hopes of getting a little food that they

imagined they would find there.

Alas, they have found nothing but fatigue.[201]

Although in exposing Ibn ʿArabi's "fallacies" his previous critics had occasionally availed themselves of a verse or two, with Ibn al-Muqri poetry became the principal vehicle of the debate.[202] Al-Fasi, Ibn al-Ahdal, and the later Yemeni scholar al-Maqbali were quick to notice the efficacy of Ibn al-Muqri's polemical poetry, which they quoted profusely in their polemic against Ibn ʿArabi's teachings.

Even a cursory glance at Ibn al-Muqri's verses reveals his unique mastery of mockery and the grotesque, which, to reiterate, proved to be especially effective with those readers and listeners who had never looked into the *Fusus* or the *Futuhat,* but who were aware of the fierce controversy around Ibn ʿArabi's legacy. Brimming with wit and humor, Ibn al-Muqri's poignant satires were not meant to unravel the complexities of Ibn ʿArabi's doctrine. Nor was his choice of arguments especially original—most of them are already familiar to us from the works of Ibn ʿArabi's earlier critics. Rather his contribution to the polemic consists in presenting these tried arguments in a striking and memorable way, making them the table talk of the Yemeni households as well as of scholarly assemblies.

Paraphrasing poetry is a notoriously inadequate way to convey its meaning. I can therefore do no better than to quote a few excerpts from Ibn al-Muqri's anti-Sufi satires:[203]

A gruesome calamity has afflicted the Muslims:

It makes even the gravest sin look like a minor

slip.

It hides in the books—may God declare

war on their author!—by which entire cities

are led astray.

There the little Ibn ʿArabi speaks of God with

astounding insolence and extreme audacity,

Claiming that the Lord and His servant are one,
and that the Master and His slave are entirely
identical with one another![204]
He thus denies [the necessity of] religious
obligations (*taklif*), because man, in his
view, is both God and servant, and this,
of course, is the denial of a deranged man.[205]
In the blaze of the argument, he denounces everyone
who does not consider the creatures to be one with
their Maker both in form and essence.
God, he says, dwells in every form;
When He manifests Himself to a specific locus,
it becomes [the site of] a divine manifestation.
He also denies that God is independent of
man and that men are in need of Him—a clear
defiance of the Divine Law.
He makes a mockery of the negation and the affirmation
[in the phrase] "there is no diety but God,"[206]
to the great delight of every sinner.[207]
If you look carefully, he claims, the one who is denied
is the same as the one whose existence is asserted!
He thus has corrupted the meaning of the phrase by
which people submit to God, nay, he nullified
it completely, replacing clear proofs with
an abominable confusion. . . .
He then proclaims that divine punishment is nothing
but sweetness,[208] and that in the Hellfire our Lord bestows delight
on every evildoer.
Creatures, he says, cannot disobey God—hence
there is no need for either pardoner or forgiver.

God's Will, in his eyes, is in complete accord
with His [creative] Command, hence in existence there
can be no unbeliever, since everyone obeys
the [divine] orders.
In other words, our divine Protector is pleased
with everyone, and everyone will, in the end, enjoy
felicity [in the Hereafter], for he [Ibn ʿArabi] asserts
that the sinner will suffer no harm.
All unbelievers, he says, will not die until
they have become believers, except those who have suffered an
unexpected death which overtook them unawares.[209]
This is why Pharaoh was not the only one honored with
faith in the moment of his death, nay this is true of
every unbeliever!
So, my friend, declare him a liar, and you will
be among the cream of the faithful, if, however, you
think him to be in the right, then you yourself are a
wretched unbeliever![210]

In the remainder of this long poem Ibn al-Muqri proceeded to portray the disappointment and anguish awaiting those who have heedlessly embraced Ibn ʿArabi's heretical tenets. His unwary supporters, said the poet, will soon discover that the torments of Hell are as real as they are described in the Qurʾan and that humans are indeed divided into the felicitous and the wretched, the latter doomed to suffer a painful punishment in hell. This discovery, concludes Ibn al-Muqri, will be all the more exasperating since, as perpetrators of an abominable heresy, the followers of Ibn ʿArabi will surely be among the damned.

As with Ibn Taymiyya, in his early career Ibn al-Muqri, according to Ibn al-Ahdal, felt indifferent to either Ibn ʿArabi or monistic theosophy as a whole. His complacency, however, changed to an active resentment with the demise of al-Nashiri, when he became aware of the heretical tenets propagated by the monistic party. Upon a thorough consideration, he found the *Fusus* and the *Futuhat* to be meaningless and heretical[211]—a change of heart that is too closely patterned on that experienced by Ibn Taymiyya to be given much credit. It seems more likely that Ibn al-Muqri simply did not have any option but to attack Ibn ʿArabi, whose name was attached to the banner of his rivals, al-Fayruzabadi and Ibn al-Raddad. In exposing Ibn ʿArabi's "heresy," Ibn al-Muqri hoped to achieve a theological victory over al-Jabarti's party, by then at the peak of its influence.[212]

In fulfillment of his plan, Ibn al-Muqri set out to bring together the opponents of the monistic "heresy" by instituting an *istifta*ʾ. As with the Egyptian scholars discussed in Chapter 5, he made a synopsis of Ibn ʿArabi's statements in the *Fusus* and *Futuhat,* which he sent to the major religious authorities of Rasulid Yemen, asking them to determine Ibn ʿArabi's status vis-à-vis the *shariʿa*. Predictably, in the course of the *istifta*ʾ the scholars, who had been handpicked by Ibn al-Muqri, issued condemnatory rulings that denounced Ibn ʿArabi as an unbeliever and demanded that his works be destroyed.[213] Ibn al-Muqri's scathing satires combined with the publication of these legal opinions incited the population of Zabid and other Yemeni towns against the monistic party, laying the groundwork for mass riots. When he was informed about the anti-Sufi campaign, Ibn al-Raddad vigorously complained to al-Nasir and asked his permission to punish the agitators. With the sultan's consent granted, Ibn al-Raddad unleashed the sultan's soldiery against the leaders of the anti-Ibn ʿArabi party. Some were intimidated and forced into silence; others hurried to recant their condemnation of the mystical teachings; still others chose to flee from Zabid, leaving behind their possessions, which were immediately confiscated by the authorities.[214] However, with Ibn al-Raddad's death in 821/1417-18, his punitive campaign came to an abrupt end. Had it not been for his death, remarks Ibn al-Ahdal, the sanctions against Ibn ʿArabi's critics would have been carried out on a larger scale and with much more disastrous results.[215]

Bemoaning the suffering of his supporters, Ibn al-Muqri wrote:

> Oh, Lord, Your immaculate Law has fallen
>
> Into a trap from which it contemplates its utter plight
>
> No truth is left on the face of the earth,
>
> Except the words of al-Hallaj, Ibn al-
>
> Tilimsani,[216] and [Ibn] al-ʿArabi. . . . [217]

Ibn al-Raddad's successor at the head of the Sufi party was Shaykh Muhammad b. Muhammad al-Mizjaji (d. 829/1425), a wealthy nobleman who owned many palm groves and estates in Zabid and its environs.[218] Al-Mizjaji studied Islamic sciences under al-Fayruzabadi, who introduced him to Sufi literature. His principal Sufi tutor was al-Jabarti, whom al-Mizjaji greatly admired and lavishly supported. He also made friends with Ibn al-Raddad: the two men made several arduous journeys on foot to the holy cities carrying with them only a bare minimum of water and provisions. Despite his attachment to the ragged world-renouncers, al-Mizjaji was a very rich man, who spent his fortune freely on his fellow mystics in Zabid. Under the influence of al-Jabarti and Ibn al-Raddad he took to reading books on mystical philosophy and actively disseminated Ibn ʿArabi's works by retaining several skilled scribes who diligently copied the *Fusus* and the *Futuhat.* He also maintained a large library at his private mosque, which was open to everyone. Its shelves were abundantly stacked with books on speculative Sufism. That the owner of the library was himself well versed in Islamic mysticism is evident from his apology for Sufi theory and practice titled "Guiding the Wayfarer to the Most Sublime Path" (*Hidayat al-salik ila asna ʾl-masalik*)—a major source for the history of Yemeni Sufism under the Rasulids.[219]

Despite his leadership of the Sufi party, al-Mizjaji remained on friendly terms with Ibn al-Muqri. Later on, when Ibn al-Raddad became the great *qadi* and the Ibn ʿArabi controversy reached its peak, al-Mizjaji and Ibn al-Muqri found themselves on different sides of the barricade. Even that did not completely dissolve their friendship. In poetic epistles that they exchanged about that time they remind one another of the "good old days," when the scholarly fray had not yet stood between them.[220] Although al-Mizjaji felt uneasy about his friend's hostility to Ibn ʿArabi, he definitely lacked Ibn al-Raddad's resolve. A close friend of, and advisor to, three Rasulid sultans—al-Ashraf, al-Nasir and al-Zahir Yahya (r. 831/1428-842/1438)[221]—al-Mizjaji was reluctant to use his political and financial clout to silence the critics of the Sufi party.[222] Al-Mizjaji's restraint was duly appreciated by his opponents. His biographers, many of whom belonged to the anti-Ibn ʿArabi faction, deliberately minimized his monistic leanings, praising instead his charitable acts, such as the building of mosques and the assignment of charitable funds to religious colleges.

To meet Ibn al-Muqri's poetic challenge, the Sufi side needed an equally talented spokesman. They found him in Yahya Ibn Rawbak (d. 835/1431), a noted poet and litterateur, whose eloquent panegyrics of the sultan al-Nasir had secured him royal protection and a sinecure in the Rasulid administration.[223] In throwing his lot with the Ibn ʿArabi party Ibn Rawbak must have been motivated by his resentment of Ibn al-Muqri, his principal rival for the sultan's affections,[224] although one cannot rule out that he was genuinely sympathetic with the Sufi cause. In his acrimonious rejoinders to Ibn al-Muqri's attacks he ridiculed the bigotry and intolerance of the stick-in-the-mud legists and extolled the virtues of al-Jabarti and his followers.[225] A contemporary observer aptly described the conflict between the poets as "a raging war that was waged not by the thrusts and strikes [of weapons] but by the tongues."[226] Ibn al-Muqri accepted Ibn Rawbak's challenge and repaid him in kind, prolonging the poetic duel.[227]

Ibn al-Muqri versus al-Kirmani: Final Episodes of the Long Struggle

Although the precise chronology is far from certain, the debate between the two poets must have occurred around the time when Ibn al-Muqri was trying to eliminate the last eminent Sufi thinker of the Rasulid Yemen, Ahmad [Ibn] al-Kirmani the Persian (d. 845/1441). Al-Kirmani's biography prior to his arrival in Zabid is obscure. His name suggests that he hailed from Kirman in Persia, where he must have acquired proficiency in the mystical philosophy of a monistic bent. Ibn Rawbak, who wrote a poem in his defense, vaguely referred to his long peregrinations across the Muslim lands prior to his settling in Yemen.[228] In Zabid, al-Kirmani was warmly received by the Sufis of the al-Jabarti circle. He, however, did not have personal knowledge of the venerable Sufi master, whom he missed by a decade or so. Al-Kirmani's familiarity with the mystical teachings of Ibn ʿArabi and of his Persian commentators soon attracted the attention of al-Jabarti's successors, Ibn al-Raddad and al-Mizjaji, who took him under their wing. In this respect at least, al-Kirmani's experience in Yemen was similar to that of al-Jili, another Persian exponent of monistic doctrines. If Ibn al-Ahdal's dating of al-Jili's death is correct,[229] it is conceivable that the two Persian exponents of the Greatest Master should have met.

As with the other leading Sufis in the Ibn ʿArabi faction, al-Kirmani was introduced to the sultan al-Nasir, whose sympathy for mysticism seems to have increased over the years.[230] Yet, unlike the dovish al-Mizjaji, al-Kirmani had no scruples using his influence with the aging sultan when he felt that the position of his fellow Sufis was threatened. In the middle of the vocal anti-Sufi campaign orchestrated by Ibn al-Muqri, al-Kirmani asked al-Nasir to interfere, pointing to the possibility of a popular revolt against his rule. The sultan responded vigorously, ordering his mercenaries to raid the houses of al-Kirmani's detractors, including Ibn al-Muqri's own residence.[231] A number of Ibn al-Muqri's disciples were arrested, although the scholar himself managed to slip out of Zabid and take refuge in Bayt al-Faqih, a sacred village under the protection of the Banu ʿUjayl, a famous Yemeni clan of holy men.[232] Ibn al-Muqri's exile lasted less than one year, whereupon the sultan invited him back to Zabid and generously compensated him for the tribulations he had suffered.[233] Ibn al-Ahdal explains al-Nasir's decision to make peace with Ibn al-Muqri by the rumors that the scholar might enter the service of the Zaydi *imam* of Saʿda, the principal political rival to the Rasulids. Given Ibn al-Muqri's wide popularity, his siding with the Zaydi leader would have been extremely damaging to the Rasulid state, which was already going through a severe political crisis. To forestall this dangerous alliance the sultan swallowed his pride and disregarded the demands of his Sufi protégées to punish the recalcitrant scholar.

The persecution of Ibn al-Muqri and his followers marked the last stage of the Sufi ascendancy in the Rasulid kingdom. In the economic and political turmoil that followed al-Nasir's death in 827/1424 the Sufi party rapidly began to lose ground. At the instigation of Ibn al-Muqri—now the undisputed leader of the scholarly establishment—the new sultan al-Mansur ʿAbdallah (r. 827/1424-830/1427), whose sovereignty over Yemen was continually jeopardized by rebellious Rasulid princes and tribal leaders, abandoned the pro-Sufi policy of his predecessors. Seeking the support of the majority of the *ʿulamaʾ* class, he ordered a crackdown on the Sufi party. Backed by the leading *mufti*s of Zabid and Taʿizz, Ibn al-Muqri urged the sultan to issue a degree banning the study of Ibn ʿArabi's works. Simultaneously, Ibn al-Muqri publicly accused al-Kirmani of professing a heinous heresy. In an uncanny reversal, al-Kirmani's house was sacked by the sultan's men, his disciples arrested, and his possessions sequestered. Disgraced and vilified, al-Kirmani barely escaped summary execution. Ironically, he took refuge at Bayt al-Faqih, where he came under the protection of the same holy clan that had sheltered his persecutor a few months earlier.[234]

Al-Kirmani, it seems, did not have patience enough to wait for the storm to blow over, and set his mind on returning to Taʿizz. This was an ill-judged move, for after the death of al-Mizjaji (829/1425) the Sufi party had lost its influence at court and was left face-to-face with its longtime enemies, who unleashed against them the populace and the state retainers. On hearing about al-Kirmani's return, Ibn al-Muqri hastened to arrange for another learned consensus that declared al-Kirmani not only a "heretic" (*zindiq*) but also an apostate (*murtadd*)—a charge which, according to the *shariʿa*, called for the total disfranchisement and execution of the culprit. Ibn al-Muqri's condemnation of al-Kirmani and of Ibn ʿArabi's teaching was supported by a condemnatory *fatwa* issued by the teacher of al-Biqaʿi, Muhammad Ibn al-Jazari (d. 834/1430), who was visiting Yemen at the sultan's invitation.[235] Similar rulings were delivered by many local scholars including Ibn al-Ahdal, who later used his *fatwa* as the blueprint for a detailed refutation of Ibn ʿArabi and his school.[236]

When these accusatory rulings were presented to the sultan al-Mansur, he ordered al-Kirmani to be arrested and put on trial. During interrogations conducted by his adversaries, al-Kirmani was forced to "repent" and to "return to the true faith," whereupon he was dismissed on the condition that he should neither study nor teach Ibn ʿArabi's books. Such leniency may be explained by the timely intersession of Ibn Rawbak, whose spirited apology for al-Kirmani dissuaded the sultan from executing the Sufi leader. The text of his "repentance" was announced in the mosques of three Yemeni towns, Zabid, Mahjam, and Taʿizz. In Zabid, the preacher of the city's Friday mosque publicly demanded the excommunication of all of Ibn ʿArabi's followers and the immediate destruction of their books.[237] Preachers of the minor mosques followed suit. When the trial was over, al-Kirmani was forced to leave Yemen for Mecca. Those of his adherents who stayed on kept a low profile.

Unhappy with the sultan's decision to spare al-Kirmani's life, Ibn al-Muqri vented his anger in the following verses:

> Had you cut off his [al-Kirmani's] head
> the other day, God's religion would have
> been delivered from at least one minor ailment.
> No sacrifice in the eyes of God is more preferable
> than spilling the blood of al-Kirmani
> It is an insult to God that he walked away
> safe and sound on his own feet
> For was not he the one who blasphemed?!

By God, oh, the best of kings, that was
a grave mistake, but it will no doubt be redressed
With the sword, after the men of learning
have concluded that the likes of him must
not be spared![238]

As this and other verses clearly testify,[239] scholarly consensus or not, the ruler remained the final judge of how a controversial religious issue was to be resolved: it was to him that both parties vigorously appealed throughout the trial.

In the meantime, the Rasulid kingdom was inexorably approaching its final eclipse. The protracted struggle among pretenders to the Rasulid throne led to a political and economic collapse that the new monarchs were unable to remedy. Deprived of revenues from the sea trade and agriculture, they could no longer pay their mercenaries, who started to recompense themselves by pillaging the settled populations of the Tihama. The tribesmen too were making up for the termination of the state allowances by robbing the defenseless peasants. Both the mercenaries and the tribes became involved in the power struggle by supporting different claimants to the Rasulid throne, who were reduced to helpless puppets.

In 830/1427, during the interregnum following the death of al-Mansur, al-Kirmani returned from his Meccan exile. Once in Zabid, he proclaimed his previous repentance null and void, and, according to Ibn al-Muqri, returned to his old ways. Nothing is known about his activities at that time except that he was successful in winning the young sultan al-Ashraf Ismaʿil (r. 830/1427-831/1428) over to his cause and was given a free hand in spreading the his teachings.[240] In an attempt to avenge himself for the humiliation he had suffered at the hands of Ibn al-Muqri, al-Kirmani derided his antagonist in a long poem. Ibn al-Muqri answered with an epistle exposing al-Kirmani's "double-faced" demeanor and censured him for taking advantage of the inexperienced ruler. Ibn al-Muqri also circulated several poetic epistles among the *ʿulama*ʾ and officials of Zabid warning them not to be "beguiled" by al-Kirmani's doctrine.[241] These letters indicate that al-Kirmani and his followers still had many supporters in high places, especially among Rasulid princes, military commanders, and some religious administrators.

Al-Ashraf's reign was short-lived. A few months after his ascension to the Rasulid throne he was imprisoned by a group of rebellious mercenaries who were frustrated by his inability to pay their salaries.[242] The new sultan, Yahya, who assumed the regnal title al-Zahir, banished al-Kirmani from Zabid either due to the latter's close affiliation with the deposed al-Ashraf, or, perhaps, in order to put an end to the continuing quarrels among the scholars. Once again, al-Kirmani and his fifty disciples had to seek refuge in the sacred village of the Banu ʿUjayl family. In a drive to deliver the Sufi movement a fatal blow, Ibn al-Muqri continued to agitate for the trial and execution of his Sufi opponent.[243] In the meantime, al-Kirmani attempted to regain his former influence by taking part in the intrigues within the ruling dynasty. He put his hopes on al-Zahir's brother, Prince al-ʿAbbas—one of several claimants to the Rasulid throne. When the plot to depose al-Zahir failed, al-Kirmani barely escaped the sultan's reprisal and had to flee to the distant region of Jazan, where he died in 841/1437.

Al-Kirmani's flight and subsequent death marks the final eclipse of the Ibn ʿArabi party in Yemen. However, Ibn al-Muqri's efforts notwithstanding, neither he nor his followers were able to banish the monistic "heresy" completely from the intellectual life of Yemeni Muslims. Some Yemeni scholars continued to adhere to it. Among them was ʿAli b. Muhammad Qahr, or Ibn Qahr (d.845/1441), an acclaimed scholar and *faqih* who held the office of the *qadi* of Zabid after Ibn al-Muqri's death.[244] Ibn Qahr was a close friend, or perhaps a disciple, of al-Kirmani and wrote a commentary on the latter's work.[245] The fact that al-Zahir held Ibn Qahr in high regard and lavishly paid him for his services may indicate that the ruler's enmity toward al-Kirmani sprang from the latter's role in the political intrigues rather than from doctrinal considerations. Ibn Qahr appears to have been the last important follower of Ibn ʿArabi in Yemen, since Ibn al-Ahdal, who died in 855/1451, invariably speaks of the monistic party in the past tense. Nor does he mention any Sufi school either in Zabid or in other Yemeni cities in that age. It must not be thought, however, that with the fall of the Rasulids Sufism in Yemen sank into total oblivion. In 868/1463, during the reign of the Tahirids, the noted Sufi preacher Ibrahim b. Ahmad al-ʿAsqalani appeared in Zabid and in Taʿizz; his lectures on mysticism and the miracles of the saints drew enthusiastic crowds. To forestall the resurgence of the pro-Sufi sentiment among the masses, the concerned *ʿulamaʾ* of Taʿizz hastened to put a stop to al-ʿAsqalani's public preaching and eventually had him banished from the Tahirid kingdom.[246]

Conclusion

When Ibn al-Ahdal was writing his account of the struggle surrounding Ibn ʿArabi's legacy in Rasulid Yemen, his goal was to prevent a revival of the monistic "heresy." Analyzing the reasons for the temporary triumph of the Ibn ʿArabi party, he pointed his accusing finger at both al-Ashraf and al-Nasir, whom he held responsible for the cultivation of such "outright heretics" as Ibn al-Raddad, al-Jili, and al-Kirmani. In extending his protection to these and other Sufi philosophers, so ran Ibn al-Ahdal's argument, al-Nasir in particular forfeited his royal obligation to uphold the *shariʿa* and thus became liable to deposition. In a manner typical of many Muslim polemicists, Ibn al-Ahdal, however, stops short of proclaiming al-Nasir an unbeliever. Rather he berated the sultan's policies obliquely, by portraying him as an imperfect Muslim. Ibn al-Ahdal deployed this strategy in both the *Kashf* and in several historical chronicles that depicted al-Nasir as an irresponsible drunkard and debauchee who could not care less for the community's welfare. Ibn al-Ahdal's bias against al-Nasir was noticed by a later historian of Yemen, Ibn al-Daybaʿ (d. 944/1537), who dismissed his charges as unfair and dictated by tendentiousness and bigotry.[247]

The historical evidence related to the conflict between the Ibn ʿArabi party and their opponents in Yemen is too fragmentary and partial to permit any definitive conclusions. About the only statement that one can make with certainty is that royal patronage played a critical role in the brief but vigorous efflorescence of Ibn ʿArabi's teaching under the Rasulids. At the zenith of Rasulid power the thriving and cosmopolitan populations of Zabid and other urban centers were tolerant of various manifestations of Sufism including those that drew the censure of some conservative scholars.[248] In promoting the exponents of Ibn ʿArabi's doctrines to the positions of authority, the rulers stepped on the toes of many members of the Yemeni religious hierarchy. The rulers' patronage of the Sufi party, which carried Ibn ʿArabi's name on its banner, was motivated in part by the personal interest they took in his doctrines. At the same time, there is no denying that the Rasulid sovereigns derived tangible political advantages from supporting one scholarly faction against the other—a strategy that kept their potential learned critics divided. As mediators in the conflict between the pro-and anti-Ibn ʿArabi parties, the sultans were favorably positioned to manipulate outspoken *ʿulamaʾ*, such as Ibn al-Khayyat and al-Nashiri, and to divert them from criticizing their politics and, possibly, from stirring up popular unrest.

The scholarly opposition to the monistic teachings of Ibn ʿArabi and his followers in Yemen was strong and, at times, ferocious. The wide circulation of Ibn ʿArabi's works among Yemeni intellectuals was already perceived as a shocking affront by many exoterically minded local *ʿulamaʾ*. The fact that the Yemeni mystics not only taught such works to their disciples but recommended them to the general reader was seen by such scholars as an act of unprecedented audacity. By shrewdly winning the cultured sultans over to their side, the Sufi party led by al-Jabarti and Ibn al-Raddad not only survived the campaign of verbal and physical harassment instituted by their numerous adversaries but was able to turn the tables against them under al-Ashraf and al-Nasir.

The decline and eventual fall of the Rasulid kingdom did not automatically entail the demise of the Ibn ʿArabi school in Yemen. However, with the withdrawal of royal patronage it was reduced to a narrow circle of the initiated. At the same time, as evidence from Yemeni and South Arabian libraries abundantly shows,[249] the interest in Ibn ʿArabi's legacy among Yemeni and South Arabian scholars has persisted throughout the following centuries and up to this day. Unfortunately, in the absence of accounts such as one provided by Ibn al-Ahdal, it is impossible to determine whether or not there was another resurgence of Ibn ʿArabi's doctrine in Yemen after the Rasulids had vacated the historical scene.[250]

GENERAL CONCLUSION

> Among the [Muslim] thinkers bewilderment (*hayra*) is much greater than among those of the other religious communities. When a [Muslim] thinker gets tired of thinking, he stops where fatigue has overcome him. Some of them have stopped at the stripping of God of His attributes (*al-taʿtil*), others have stopped at the secondary causes,[1] still others have stopped at similarity (*al-tashbih*).[2] A group [of thinkers] has stopped at bewilderment, and said: "We do not know!" Yet another group has hit upon one aspect of truth, then stopped in exhaustion. So, each man has stopped at the point where fatigue has overcome him, whereupon he turns to his mundane needs in order to have a rest and satisfy his natural desires. Having rested from his fatigue, he returns to the point which he has reached in his consideration and proceeds from there to wherever his thought takes him until he either gets tired again or dies. . . .
>
> Ibn ʿArabi. "ʿUqlat al-mustawfiz,"
> in Nyberg. *Kleinere Schriften,* p. 90[3]

The atmosphere of bewilderment, ambiguity, and confusion has surrounded Ibn ʿArabi's legacy since Muslim scholars started to grapple with it. Their predicament can be viewed through a complex series of lenses. I am inclined to see it primarily as a manifestation of the uneasy coexistence and potential conflict between the communal-legalistic and gnostic-individualistic interpretations of faith, or, in other words, between nomocentric theology and contemplative mysticism.[4] This major divide has engendered a host of related oppositions, of which the validity of mystical experience vis-à-vis the "objective" world, as postulated in the Scriptures, sense-perception, and/or syllogistic reasoning, takes pride of place. It is over this issue that the participants in the Ibn ʿArabi debate have clashed throughout the centuries following his death. Although even the most bitter opponents of the Greatest Master did not doubt the existence of mystical experience, they did disagree with his supporters over its role in, and practical implications for, a society based on the revealed law. What the anti-Ibn ʿArabi scholars opposed most was his unitive metaphysics that he posited as the culmination of *tawhid* but that they viewed as a grave threat to the community's faith and way of life. Apprehensive of the dangerous social consequences of monistic theory, Ibn ʿArabi's critics strove either to delimit it to the realm of personal experience or to subordinate it completely to the mainstream Sunni dogma, primarily Ashʿarism. Their opponents, on the contrary, considered mystical experience to be integral, if not superior, to the exoteric dogma.

Closely allied with the issue of the religious and social role of mystical experience is the notion of sainthood which, as we have seen, was widely used by Ibn ʿArabi's defenders to assure him a privileged status within the Muslim community, exempting him from the regular evaluative criteria. The response of Ibn ʿArabi's antagonists was not to reject the authenticity of sainthood, which by that time had been taken for granted by most Sunni *ʿulama*ʾ, but to expose Ibn ʿArabi as a false saint and heretical philosopher who used sainthood as a cloak.

On the metaphysical level, the crux of the disagreement between the pro- and anti-Ibn ʿArabi *ʿulama*ʾ lies in their distinct visions of God's transcendence/immanence vis-à-vis the created world and, as a consequence, of the possibility of achieving direct contact with the Divinity in the postprophetic epoch. In laying emphasis on divine immanence and accessibility, Ibn ʿArabi and his followers created a gnostic school of thought complete with its own cosmology, exegetical techniques, terminology, symbolism, epistemology, and belief in salvation by esoteric knowledge. For reasons I have tried to make clear, this school's vision of Islam was condemned as heretical by many, although by no means all, Sunni scholars across the medieval Muslim world.

The irresistible tendency of modern Western and Muslim investigators to dichotomize phenomena at hand has led to the description of the Ibn ʿArabi controversy in terms of the static bipolar oppositions between *nomos* and eros,[5] "ecstasy" and "control,"[6] "orthodoxy" and 'heresy,"[7] "esotericism" and "exotericism,"[8] "conformism" and "freethinking."[9] While these dichotomies do highlight some important facets of the Ibn ʿArabi problem, they tend to understate the painful ambiguity and ambivalence that pervade the works of medieval Muslim writers who tried to resolve it. The task of Ibn ʿArabi's critics was complicated by the general vagueness of the notion of sainthood that was widely used by its advocates to justify phenomena and statements which, under normal conditions, would have been condemned as outrageous and unthinkable.[10]

On the personal level, the critics of Ibn ʿArabi were hampered by the fear of the price to pay on Judgment Day for having summarily condemned a fellow Muslim as a *kafir.* These two factors, to my mind, help to explain why, in dealing with the issue of Ibn ʿArabi's "unbelief" many, if not most, *ʿulamaʾ* found themselves astride the fence, avoiding both unequivocal endorsement and outright condemnation. In so doing, they left the door open for retractions, which are richly documented not only for neutral scholars but for Ibn ʿArabi's bitter enemies as well.[11] This ambivalence is still quite common among Muslim academics who often follow in the footsteps of Ibn ʿAbd al-Salam by publicly condemning the Greatest Master, while showing respect for him in private.[12]

Despite this ambiguity and vacillation, prodigious efforts were exerted by the leading Muslim scholars of the 7th/13th-9th/16th centuries to protect the faith of the Sunni community from what they viewed as the subversive influence of Ibn ʿArabi, Ibn al-Farid, Ibn Sabʿin, and their commentators. The sheer volume of polemical literature produced by the participants in the Ibn ʿArabi debate belies the widespread concept of Islam as an "orthoprax" religion par excellence—one which, in contrast to Christianity, pays little heed to doctrinal questions as long as the ritual decorum is observed by adherents of different dogmatic persuasions.[13] The evidence presented so far indicates exactly the opposite: Ibn ʿArabi's numerous critics consistently ignored his impeccable personal piety and meticulous observance of the Islamic rites, focusing instead on his theories.

In medieval Islamic societies, Ibn ʿArabi's mystical weltanschauung was not always pitted against the positive, community-oriented Islam of the Sunni *ʿulamaʾ*: the relations between the two have ranged from complementary and even harmonious to outright antagonistic and were determined by the complex interplay of social, political, and cultural factors as well as by scholars' personal backgrounds, temperaments, and intellectual preferences. As we have seen, in most cases it was the support of the temporal ruler rather than the scholarly consensus that determined the acceptance or rejection of Ibn ʿArabi's legacy in a given state. It is also clear that, with a few significant exceptions, both the scholars and the rulers sought to avoid pitched confrontations in dealing with this divisive and potentially disruptive issue. Like other contested theological issues, Ibn ʿArabi's legacy served as a convenient rallying point for various religio-political factions vying for power and supremacy. While no universal *ijmaʿ* has ever been reached on the problem of Ibn ʿArabi's belief/unbelief,[14] local campaigns to either vindicate or condemn him show that a relatively effective machinery was created by the *ʿulamaʾ* for defining and formulating an authoritative position on a given doctrinal issue.

Over the centuries the problem of Ibn ʿArabi attracted Muslims from all walks of life: *fuqahaʾ* and charismatic Sufis, historians and biographers, litterateurs and princes, men of the bazaar and courtiers. In explaining its continual relevance Chittick, the leading Western expert on his thought, suggested that Islam be viewed as consisting of three basic dimensions: works, faith, and perfection. To each of them, in Chittick's interpretation, corresponds a group of religious specialists responsible for its proper functioning—works are the preserve of the jurists; faith is the domain of the rationalist theologians, philosophers, and some philosophically minded Sufis; while perfection is maintained by the active Sufis, who concern themselves with the spiritual well-being of humanity in an effort to attain the loftiest degree of awareness.[15]

While this tripartite schema indeed highlights important aspects of the Ibn ʿArabi controversy, as any intellectual construct, it detracts from the complex personal identity of the real participants in the debate. Ibn ʿArabi's adversaries were neither the dry-as-dust jurists nor the narrow-minded scholastics: most of them, as we have seen, were themselves Sufis of various stripes. At any rate, with a few insignificant exceptions, they were not opposed to Sufism as such, but to the way in which it was interpreted by Ibn ʿArabi, whom they, incidentally, denied the status of the authentic Sufi. We are faced here with the uneasy task of separating "true Sufism" from "false Sufism," or "authentic Sufism" from "deviated Sufism"—a task which, as Chittick himself has acknowledged, is probably insurmountable. The history of the Ibn ʿArabi controversy shows that the "pure jurists," the "pure theologians," and the "pure Sufis" are just abstractions in our minds, since most of the historical figures we have discussed were all three in one. If we agree with Chittick in that Ibn

ʿArabi's teaching is the consummate expression of Sufi gnosis and experience,[16] then we should indeed dismiss his detractors as misguided impostors. This conclusion, however, is unsatisfactory since it rests on one possible abstract definition of Sufism rather than on concrete historical data.

To explain the astounding longevity of the Ibn ʿArabi controversy, one has to admit that it involved something vital for his advocates and detractors who continually clashed over the religious idea he came to represent. In the process, the historical Ibn ʿArabi was fictionalized into a polemical image that the polemicists on both sides used as their benchmark. The elements of this image range from rumors and anecdotes, to authoritative logia and literary topoi, which were used by both parties to dramatize either Ibn ʿArabi's virtues or errors. Inevitably, as with any great system of ideas that has become public property, Ibn ʿArabi's teaching was seriously distorted and reduced to a set of catchy propositions that were, in turn, countered by clichéd formulas. Once the rules of the debate had been established by a few authoritative scholars, they were, some exceptions and variations apart, meticulously observed by both parties to the debate, leading, as it were, to the routinization and stabilization of the polemical discourse. Consequently, it is in vain that one rummages through later Islamic theology for fresh and original assessments of Ibn ʿArabi's complex worldview. What one finds is a repertoire of authoritative logia, standardized polemical arguments, and anecdotes relevant to the matter at hand. The result is an impoverished, castrated version of Ibn ʿArabi's legacy that consistently privileges peripheral issues over the gist.

In a drive to account for the origins of Ibn ʿArabi's "delusion", his critics, especially those in the Muslim West, made him part of a broad monistic conspiracy that was started by al-Hallaj, continued by the semilegendary al-Shudhi and his Andalusi disciples, and brought to fruition by the larger-than-life figure of Ibn Sabʿin. Even in the absence of a specialized study of this monistic "conspiracy," one can argue that it never existed except in the fantasy of Ibn ʿArabi's critics, although, of course, one cannot deny the continuity and interdependence of various types of mystical speculation.

On many points the fate of Ibn ʿArabi's teaching and of his posthumous image bears a close resemblance to that of al-Hallaj's. Yet, the Greatest Master definitely lacked the tragic aura of martyrdom that enveloped his controversial predecessor. If Ibn ʿArabi was ever persecuted for his views (as al-Ghubrini tried to convince us), this was just a minor episode that did not leave any deep trace on his psyche or subsequent career. In spite of his disregard for exoteric *ʿulamaʾ*, Ibn ʿArabi recognized their importance for upholding the established social order and public morals and shunned open confrontation with the religious establishment. In other words, unlike al-Hallaj, Ibn ʿArabi was no victim or sufferer—a fact that accounts for the substantial differences in the images of the two great mystics. While, for many Sufis, al-Hallaj was an active martyr who sacrificed his life for the sake of his mystical beliefs, they viewed Ibn ʿArabi as a great, aloof sage who was too deeply immersed in the sublime mysteries of the universe to be disturbed by his petty foes.

The same difference can be observed in the hostile images of two Sufi masters constructed by their detractors. While al-Hallaj's critics portrayed him as a psychopathic rebel or charlatan, whose open defiance of the societal conventions and the revealed law, brought upon him a cruel, if well-deserved retribution,[17] Ibn ʿArabi's detractors pictured him as a quiet sapper, who put a powerful mine under the community of Islam. The difference between al-Hallaj and Ibn ʿArabi was acutely perceived by Western students of their legacy. In Massignon's subjective opinion, Ibn ʿArabi's convoluted metaphysics and technical terminology are contrasted with the supposed directness and spontaneity of al-Hallaj's mystical experience.[18] On this view, the artificiality of Ibn ʿArabi's mysticism stems from his attempts to adulterate the primitive mystical experience of classical Sufism with the abstract speculation of the *falasifa*—an idea which, as we now know, was expressed already by Ibn al-Khatib and Ibn Khaldun, who argued that Ibn ʿArabi's thought was impregnated with Greek wisdom.

Other medieval critics of Ibn ʿArabi rightfully emphasized his dependence on Muʿtazili and Ashʿari *kalam* in his treatment of nonexistent things.[19] In a similar vein, Ibn ʿArabi's opponents correctly stressed the commonality between Ibn ʿArabi and the Ismaʿili thinkers, which is to the fore in his use of allegorical exegesis, symbolism, and more importantly, in his concept of the messianic world-restorer of Fatimi extraction. Anticipating modern discussions of Ibn ʿArabi's legacy, his medieval critics shrewdly pointed to the centrality of imagination to his epistemology and metaphysics. Many other incisive observations made by his critics were cited in the main body of this study and need not be repeated here. Briefly put, despite their obvious bias and dogmatism, Ibn ʿArabi detractors were able to pinpoint many crucial aspects of Ibn ʿArabi's weltanschauung.

As I mentioned in the introduction to this study, Western scholars have been quick to discard the assessments of the Greatest Master by his medieval critics as hostile, superficial, and outright slanderous. This is all the more surprising since, after years of painstaking research, they often arrive at essentially the same conclusions as his "bigoted" detractors. Western scholars' deep-seated distrust of the medieval *ʿulamaʾ* is dictated in part by their liberal commitment to the freedom of expression and to the unalienable right of individual to speak and think differently. Correct as this attitude is in principle, it cannot be mechanically transplanted onto the medieval Muslim society. At the risk of lapsing into an apologia for religious inquisition and persecution of intellectual nonconformity I suggest that contemporary ethical standards should not be applied to the remote historical epochs we have discussed. With regard to Ibn ʿArabi, this means that his teaching was rejected by the majority of authoritative scholars not because of their personal wrongheadedness or obscurantism but rather because they were acutely aware of the potential dangers of his daring mystical insights for the morals and faith of their correligionists. In the eyes of his detractors, Ibn ʿArabi, whose vast scholarly expertise and literary talent they implicitly acknowledged, was guilty first and foremost of crafting a teaching which, if misinterpreted, could ruin the very foundations of Muslim communal life.

To reiterate, there are several possible ways of looking at the long polemic over Ibn ʿArabi's legacy. The most obvious one would be to consider it yet another expression of the perennial conflict between the stern adherents of *nomos* (= the Muslim legists) and the emancipated champions of eros (= the mystics),[20] which is often seen as personified by Ibn Taymiyya at one extreme and Ibn ʿArabi at the other. Concrete evidence, however, shows that the situation was much more complex. Between the extremes there lies a vast no-man's-land that is strewn with innumerable nuances, personal predilections, pragmatic calculations of one's interest, pious reservations, and bet-hedging. In general, the problem faced by scholars who dealt with Ibn ʿArabi was one of taxonomy.[21] The multifaceted figure of the Greatest Master—a reputable *hadith* scholar, saint, visionary, theologian, and poet, who combined extreme literalism with thoroughgoing esotericism—defied all classificatory schemes routinely applied to other Muslim divines. This difficulty, which tormented already Ibn ʿArabi's first biographers, has haunted Muslim scholars ever since.

NOTES

Introduction

1. A vivid example of Ibn ʿArabi's appeal to the Western public is the Muhyiddin Ibn ʿArabi Society that was founded at Oxford in 1977. The society, which includes scholars as well as lay members of diverse backgrounds, is committed to the propagation, study, translation, and publication of Ibn ʿArabi's legacy. The society has branches in Turkey, on both U.S. coasts, and in Australia. For details see the *Journal of the Muhyiddin Ibn ʿArabi Society* and the society's *Newsletter* published in Oxford. Among the society's latest publications is a commemorative volume dedicated to Ibn ʿArabi, which comprises eighteen contributions by Western and Muslim scholars (see Hirtenstein and Tiernan. *Muhyiddin Ibn ʿArabi*).

2. See Chapter 1 of this study.

3. Mottahedeh. Review of Bulliet. "The Patricians of Nishapur," in *Journal of American Oriental Society,* vol. 95 (1975), p. 495; my approach to the *ʿulamaʾ* class is based on, or formulated in opposition to, the research of Lapidus, Bulliet, Petry, and Chamberlain.

4. Humphreys. *Islamic History,* pp. 187–208.

5. Ibid., pp. 197–201.

6. My sources are detailed in Chapter 1 of this study.

7. See, e.g., Chittick. "Ibn ʿArabi and His School," pp. 54–57.

8. See, e.g., Gordlevski. *Izbrannye sochineniya,* vol. 1, pp. 200–201, 219–225, 428, 435, and 467; Hussaini. *The Pantheistic Monism,* pp. xii-xiii; Holbrook. "Ibn ʿArabi"; Shelley. "Abdullah Effendi"; Knysh. "Ibrahim al-Kurani"; Brockelmann. *Geschichte,* vol. 1, pp. 571–582; and idem. *Supplement,* vol. 1, pp. 790–802.

9. See Ménage. *Kemal pasha-zade*—EI², vol. 4, pp. 879–881. For the text of his legal ruling in defense of Ibn ʿArabi's orthodoxy, see Ibn al-ʿImad.

Shadharat, vol. 5, p. 195. According to Lings, Kemal Pasha-zade's writings evince his heavy indebtedness to the monistic mysticism of al-Hallaj and Ibn ʿArabi; see Lings. *A Sufi Saint,* p. 96.

10. Shaykh Makki. *Al-Janib al-gharbi.*

11. Aïni. *La quintessence,* pp. 29–30; Brockelmann. *Geschichte,* vol. 1, pp. 571–582; idem. *Supplement,* vol. 1, pp. 790–802.

12. See Shmidt. *ʿAbd al-Wahhab;* Winter. *Society and Religion;* cf. Gordlevski. *Izbrannye sochineniya,* vol. 1 and "index" under "Muhyiddin Ibn ʿArabi."

13. For the 19th century see Aïni. *La quintessence;* Findley. *Ottoman Civil Officialdom,* pp. 179–181. For a more recent manifestation of the Ibn ʿArabi debate in Egypt see Homerin. "Ibn ʿArabi in the People's Assembly"; cf. al-Zayyin. *Ibn ʿArabi* and the numerous apologetic works by Mahmud Ghurab.

14. Landolt. "Die Briefwechsel"; Corbin. *La philosophie iranienne;* Rizvi. *Muslim Revivalist Movements;* idem. *A History of Sufism,* passim; Chittick and Wilson. *Fakhruddin,* esp. pp. 44–45 and 64, note 19; Friedmann. *Shaykh Ahmad Sirhindi,* passim; Algar. "Reflections of Ibn ʿArabi"; Waley. "Najm al-Din Kubra," pp. 96–100; Chittick. "Ibn ʿArabi and His School," pp. 56–57; idem. "Notes on Ibn ʿArabi's Influence"; O'Fahey and Radtke. "Neo-Sufism," pp. 57, 67, and 71–73; Radtke. "Erleuchtung," p. 54; Gramlich. *Die schiitischen Derwischorden,* vols. 2 and 3 and "index" under "Ibn ʿArabi."

15. For an explanation of the two versions of Ibn ʿArabi's name see al-Maqqari. *Nafh,* vol. 2, p. 373; Austin. *Sufis,* p. 21 and a plate between pp. 20 and 21.

16. See Bosch-Vila. *Ibn Mardanish*—EI^2, vol. 3, pp. 864–865; cf. Addas. *Ibn ʿArabi*, pp. 32–34.

17. See Urvoy. *Penseurs,* passim; Khalis. *La vie littéraire;* for an illuminating recent study of Islamic Seville see Lavallé. *Séville.*

18. Austin. *Sufis,* p. 24; Addas. *Ibn ʿArabi*, pp. 45–51.

19. Ibid., pp. 55–56.

20. Ibid. For curious parallels between Ibn ʿArabi's life and that of the great Spanish missionary and mystic Ramon Lull, see Bonner. *Selected Works,* pp. 10–52. Ibn ʿArabi's conversion bears striking resemblance to, and may have been patterned on, that of some earlier Muslim mystics; see, e.g., al-Sulami. *Tabaqat,* pp. 13–14; Arberry. *Muslim Saints,* pp. 63–66.

21. Ibn ʿArabi left several detailed descriptions of his Sufi friends and teachers in al-Andalus and in North Africa who were instrumental in shap-

ing his mystical personality; see Asin Palacios. *Vidas;* Austin. *Sufis;* Addas. *Ibn ʿArabi,* pp. 73–97. For a possible self-serving agenda pursued by Ibn ʿArabi in these writings see Urvoy. "Littérature et société," pp. 40–41.

22. On him see Marçais. *Abu Madyan*—EI², vol. 1, pp. 137–138; Austin. *Sufis,* index; Ibn ʿArabi. *Muhadarat,* passim.; Urvoy. "Littérature et société," p. 53; Addas. "Abu Madyan and Ibn ʿArabi."

23. See, e.g., Austin. *Sufis,* p. 30; Addas. *Ibn ʿArabi,* pp. 179–180. Since most of the accounts of the Andalusi and Maghribi period of Ibn ʿArabi's life are based exclusively on his own testimonies, one should take them with a grain of salt. In fact, apart from Ibn ʿArabi's own statements, we do not have any solid proof that in the West he was regarded as a Sufi master of the first rank. It appears that Ibn ʿArabi had to compete with the direct disciples of Abu Madyan, who must have been unwilling to treat the young Ibn ʿArabi as their peer. This lack of recognition may have eventually compelled Ibn ʿArabi to abandon the Maghrib for the East.

24. See Profitlich. *Die Terminologie;* and Gril. "Le 'Kitab al-inbah.'"

25. Corbin. *L'imagination,* pp. 55–58; Chittick. "Ibn ʿArabi and His School," p. 50.

26. *Futuhat,* vol. 4, pp. 547–548; and Austin. *Sufis,* pp. 42–43.

27. See Chapter 3 of this study.

28. By the term *monism* and its derivatives I understand a doctrine that asserts oneness, or unity, as the defining characteristic of reality (i.e., the Arabic equivalent of *wahda; ittihad;* and *wahdat al-wujud*). In accounting for the apparent multiplicity of existence, some Muslim thinkers came to view all things as manifestations or reflections of a unique and indivisible Absolute Reality—like the sun and its rays or its reflection in the moon. In other monistic systems, things are perceived as various forms of the same substance; see Homerin. *From Arab Poet,* p. 138.

29. Some feeling for the diversity of Ibn ʿArabi's subjects can be gained from Yahia's catalog of Ibn ʿArabi's legacy; see Yahia. *La classification.*

30. Hodgson. *The Venture of Islam,* vol. 2, p. 224.

31. Morris. "Ibn ʿArabi's 'Esotericism'"; Chodkiewicz. *An Ocean Without Shore,* passim.

32. This is finely demonstrated by Winkel, whose conclusions, however, are skewed by his partisan drive to defend Ibn ʿArabi against his "fundamentalist" detractors; see, e.g., Winkel. "Ibn ʿArabi's Fiqh," p. 72, note 13.

33. See, e.g., Mubarak. *Al-Tasawwuf,* pp. 119–154.

34. See, e.g., Nyberg. *Kleinere Schriften;* Knysh. *Mekkanskiye otkroveniya.*

35. Ibn ʿArabi's Andalusi and Maghribi predecessors are discussed in Knysh. "Mysticism and Messianic Movements in Islamic Spain" delivered to the seminar on Islamic Spain at Washington University in St. Louis, MO, February 2, 1993; see also Dreher. *Das Imamat;* Urvoy. "Littérature et société," pp. 53–54.

36. See, e.g., Deladrière. *La profession de foi,* passim. Deladrière's argument is not new: it simply reiterates Weber's idea that mystical knowledge is incommunicable insofar as it is not a knowledge of positive facts and doctrines, but rather an intuitive perception of the overall meaning of the world cast into myths, parables, and symbols.

37. Morris. "How to Study the 'Futuhat,'" p. 73.

38. Ibn ʿArabi's narrative method is discussed in the following studies: Sells. "Ibn ʿArabi's 'Garden'"; idem. "Ibn ʿArabi's 'Polished Mirror;" Austin. *Bezels,* pp. 16–21; Morris. "Ibn ʿArabi's 'Esotericism'"; idem. "How to Study the Futuhat." For a general discussion of the so-called mythic-visional style of writing that was current among Muslim mystics and poets of the age see Hodgson. *The Venture of Islam,* vol. 2, pp. 225–227 and 311–315; concerning the relationship between mystical experience and philosophical theory see Katz. "Language."

39. Hodgson. *The Venture of Islam,* vol. 2, p. 315.

40. Sells. "Ibn ʿArabi's 'Garden among the Flames'"; idem. "Ibn ʿArabi's 'Polished Mirror."

41. Morris. "How to Study the 'Futuhat'", p. 73.

42. See, e.g., Hirtenstein and Tiernan's "Preface" to *Muhyiddin Ibn ʿArabi,* p. XII.

43. *L'imagination,* passim. Corbin's conclusions regarding the underlying affinity between Shiʿi and Ismaʿili esotericism and Ibn ʿArabi's mysticism are to be treated with caution; see Knysh. "Sufizm," pp. 170–172; see also Chapter 1 of this study.

44. Bonner. *Selected Works,* vol. 1, p. 61; cf. Heath. *Allegory,* p. 186.

45. See, e.g., Nyberg. *Kleinere Schriften,* the German text, passim; cf. Knysh. "Ibrahim al-Kurani."

46. For a discussion of the historical roots of this theme see Takeshita. *Ibn ʿArabi's Theory* (which contains an extensive bibliography on the subject); see also Nasr. *An Introduction,* pp. 66–74; Conger. *Theories of Microcosms,* passim.

47. See Bonner. *Selected Works,* pp. 60–61; Heath. *Allegory,* p. 186.

48. See Austin. *Bezels,* pp. 25–27.

49. See Goldziher and Goichon. *Dahriyya.*—EI^2, vol. 2, pp. 95–97.

50. Austin. *Bezels,* pp. 31–32.

51. Bell. *Love Theory,* p. 207; for the origins of this theory in Muʿtazili and Ashʿari theology see Gimaret. *Théories,* pp. 3–20, passim.

52. Austin. *Bezels,* p. 37.

53. This theory is laid down in Ibn ʿArabi's early treatise, "The Phoenix Concerning the Seal of the Saints and the [Rise] of the Sun in the West" (*ʿAnqaʾ mughrib fi khatm al-awliyaʾ wa shams al-Maghrib*) which is discussed in Chapter 7 of this study. For a survey of *mahdi* theories in medieval Islam see Madelung. *Mahdi*—EI², vol. 5, pp. 1231–1238; Friedmann. *Prophesy Continuous,* passim.

54. See, e.g., al-Taftazani, Abu ʾl-Wafaʾ. "Al-Tariqa al-akbariyya," passim.

Chapter 1

1. For Muslim biographical literature see Gibb. "Islamic Biographical Literature"; Hafsi. "Recherches"; Makdisi. "The Genre of Tabaqat"; Humphreys. *Islamic History,* pp. 187–194.

2. The best biography of Ibn ʿArabi to date is Addas. *Ibn ʿArabi.* Drawing on autobiographical passages from Ibn ʿArabi's own works, Addas provided what can be described as a *self*-portrait of the Sufi rather than his critical biography. While it amply conveys Ibn ʿArabi's sense of self-importance and reformist ambition, it offers little insight into how he was assessed by his contemporaries outside his immediate circle of friends and followers. One should therefore be well advised not to treat Addas's work as an impartial account of Ibn ʿArabi's life-story; see reviews by Morris in *Studia Islamica,* vol. 70 (1989), pp. 185–187; and Landolt in *Bulletin Critique des Annales Islamologiques,* 7, (1990), pp. 47–49.

3. Chamberlain. *Knowledge,* p. 19.

4. See Nyberg. *Kleinere Schriften;* Afifi. *The Mystical Philosophy;* idem. "The Influence"; Landau. *The Philosophy;* and more recently, Netton. *Islamic Neoplatonism.*

5. See, e.g., Asin Palacios *El Islam cristianizado* idem. *La escatologia musulmana* (for a critical evaluation of these works see Morris. "Interpreters," pt. 1, pp. 542–545; Chodkiewicz. *Le sceau,* p. 15; and Knysh. "Sufizm," pp. 141–142 and 160–162; cf. Anawati-Gardet. *Mystique,* pp. 90–95). For a recent example of this "ecumenical" approach see D'Souza. "Jesus in Ibn ʿArabi's Fusus al-hikam"; and Houédard. "Ibn ʿArabi's Contribution." For Ibn ʿArabi's actual stance vis-à-vis the concrete Christians of Anatolia see Ibn ʿArabi. *Futuhat,* vol. 4, pp. 547–548; ibid. *Muhadarat,* vol. 2, p. 241;

Austin. *Sufis,* pp. 42–43. A balanced treatment of this issue can be found in Addas. *Ibn ʿArabi,* pp. 277–279.

6. Chittick. *The Sufi Path of Knowledge,* pp. IX-X and XVI-XX of the "Introduction"; see also Chodkiewicz. *Le sceau,* "index," under "Corbin" and "Izutsu"; and Knysh. "Sufizm," pp. 158–159.

7. Yahia. *La classification.*

8. Yahia's study finely shows that the opposition to Ibn ʿArabi in the Muslim scholarly *milieu* was provoked primarily by the *Fusus;* see *La classification,* vol. 1, pp. 114–122 and 240–257.

9. Corbin suggests an alternative translation of this title, "spiritual conquests"; see Corbin. *L'imagination,* pp. 63 and 278, note 215, which is feasible due to Ibn ʿArabi's propensity to pun and wordplay. It should be pointed out that *Futuhat* and some other less well-known works by Ibn ʿArabi, e.g., *Ruh al-quds, al-Durra al-fakhira,* and *Kitab al-israʾ*, were translated into Spanish by Asin Palacios; see *El Islam cristianizado, La escatologia musulmana,* and *Vidas.* However, due to the idiosyncrasies of his approach to Ibn ʿArabi, his conclusions are to be treated with extreme caution; see Morris. "Interpreters," pt. 1, pp. 542–545; Chodkiewicz. *Le sceau,* p. 15; Addas. *Ibn* ʿArabi, pp. 16–19, 25, 79–80, etc. Yahia's new edition of the *Futuhat* caused an uproar among conservative Egyptian scholars, who managed to arrange for a legislative ban on its internal distribution; see Homerin. "Ibn ʿArabi in the People's Assembly."

10. Chodkiewicz. *Le sceau.*

11. Chodkiewicz. *Les illuminations.* The other contributors to this volume are Chittick, C. Chodkiewicz, Gril, Morris, and Sells.

12. Chodkiewicz. *An Ocean Without Shore,* pp. 19–33, passim.

13. Chittick. *The Sufi Path of Knowledge.* See Knysh. Review of idem, in the *Journal of the Muhyiddin Ibn ʿArabi Society*, vol. 9 (1991), pp. 72–75; cf. Landolt. Review of idem, in *The Middle East Journal,* vol. 44 (1990), pp. 336–337.

14. See Chittick. *The Sufi Path of Knowledge,* pp. XX-XXII.

15. Ibid., pp. 289–290; and idem. "Rumi and *wahdat al-wujud,*" pp. 85–87.

16. Idem. *The Sufi Path of Knowledge,* pp. 27–28, 258–263, passim. Cf. Morris. "Ibn ʿArabi's 'Esotericism'."

17. See, e.g., Hodgson. *The Venture of Islam,* vol. 2, p. 241.

18. A similar method is pursued by Chodkiewicz in his *Ocean Without Shore,* passim.

19. Knysh. "Ibn ʿArabi: Advokat Sufizma."

20. For the reception of Ibn ʿArabi's legacy in different parts of the Muslim world see A. Ateş. *Ibn al-ʿArabi*—EI², vol. 3, pp. 707–711, esp. pp. 710–711; Nasr. "Ibn ʿArabi in the Persian Speaking World"; idem. *Sufi Essays,* passim; al-Taftazani, Abu ʾl-Wafaʾ. "Al-Tariqa al-akbariyya"; Chittick. *The Sufi Path of Knowledge,* pp. XVI-XX; idem. "Ibn ʿArabi and His School"; idem. "Notes on Ibn ʿArabi's Influence"; idem. "Rumi and *wahdat al-wujud*"; Chodkiewicz. "The Diffusion"; idem. *An Ocean Without Shore,* pp. 1–33, passim; Holbrook. "Ibn ʿArabi and Ottoman Dervish Traditions"; Algar. "Reflections of Ibn ʿArabi"; Knysh. "Ibn ʿArabi in the Later Islamic Tradition."

21. Morris. "Interpreters"; idem. *The Wisdom,* pp. 26–29. For Chittick's works see "Bibliography."

22. Chodkiewicz. "The Diffusion"; cf. idem. *An Ocean Without Shore,* pp. 1–33.

23. Addas. *Ibn ʿArabi,* pp. 230–232, 270, 295–299, etc. One can, however, argue that Ibn ʿArabi's autobiographical accounts are not exactly models of impartiality.

24. On the Muslim side similar apologies for Ibn ʿArabi were written by Mahmud Ghurab (see, e.g., *al-Radd ʿala Ibn Taymiyya*).

25. Massignon. *La Passion.* Henceforth an English translation of this work by H. Mason will be quoted.

26. For a critical assessment of Massignon's intellectual formation and his vision of Islam in general and Sufism in particular see Baldick. *Mystical Islam,* pp. 9, and 32–33; idem. "Massignon: Man of Opposites"; cf. Knysh. Review of idem, in *Narody Azii i Afriki,* vol. 5 (1990), pp. 193–197; Humphreys. *Islamic History,* pp. 194–195; and Knysh. "Sufizm," pp. 142–146; Ernst, "Traditionalism."

27. Humphreys. *Islamic History,* p. 194.

28. For a definition of these epistemological tools see Corbin. *L'imagination,* pp. 95, 102, 118–125, etc.

29. For some pertinent observations on the Mamluk historiography see Haarmann. *Quellenstudien,* pp. 159–175.

Chapter 2

1. According to Corbin, the *Futuhat* can be regarded as both a giant *summa theologica* and a *diarum spirituale;* see Corbin. *L'imagination,* p. 64.

2. For partial English translations see Austin. *Sufis;* cf. Asin Palacios. *Vidas* and Boase and Sahnoun. "Excerpts."

3. Urvoy. "Littérature et société," p. 41; Boase and Sahnoun. "Excerpts," pp. 47–54.

4. Ibn ʿArabi's lifelong friend and servant who wrote a synopsis of his oral teachings titled "The Book of Instruction on the Path to God" (*Kitab al-inbah ʿala tariq Allah*); see Gril. "Le 'Kitab al-inbah;'" Austin. *Sufis,* pp. 158–159; Fenton and Gloton. "The Book of the Description," p. 13.

5. Another close companion of Ibn ʿArabi who composed a dictionary of the technical terms that the Greatest Master used in his lectures; see Profitlich. *Die Terminologie.* For his life and work see al-Dhahabi. *Al-ʿIbar*, vol. 3, p. 254; Ibn al-ʿImad. *Shadharat,* vol. 5, p. 233; cf. Addas. *Ibn ʿArabi,* pp. 56–58, 195–197, and "index"; cf. al-Maqqari. *Nafh,* vol. 2, p. 364; cf. *Futuhat,* vol. 2, pp. 49 and 681, etc.

6. For al-Qunawi's role in the dissemination of Ibn ʿArabi's doctrines in Anatolia and Iran see Morris. "Interpreters," pt. 2, pp. 751–756; Chittick. "The Five Divine Presences"; idem. "The Last Will and Testament"; idem. "Mysticism versus Philosophy"; idem. "Sadr al-Din Qunawi"; idem. "Rumi and *Wahdat al-wujud,*" pp. 77–79.

7. An Anatolian author who wrote an influential commentary on the *Fusus al-hikam;* see Addas. *Ibn ʿArabi,* "index."

8. For al-Qunawi's much-cited description of his master's supernatural feats see Ibn al-ʿImad. *Shadharat,* vol. 5, pp. 196–197; the most comprehensive collection of Ibn ʿArabi's *karamat* can be found in al-Nabhani. *Jamiʿ karamat,* vol. 1, pp. 118–125; and Gordlevski. *Izbrannye sochineniya,* vol. 1, pp. 200–201 and 219–225.

9. Muhammad b. ʿAbd al-Ghani al-Baghdadi, better known as Ibn Nuqta, enjoyed the reputation of a reliable transmitter of *hadith* reports. All his works are devoted to *hadith* criticism and biographies of *hadith* transmitters; see Ibn Kathir. *Al-Bidaya,* vol. 3, p. 143; Brockelmann. *Geschichte,* vol. 1, pp. 355 and 358, and idem. *Supplement,* vol. 1, p. 609. For his father, a popular Sufi preacher patronized by Caliph al-Nasir's mother see Laoust. *Pluralismes,* p. 54.

10. On Ibn ʿArabi's life in Anatolia see Addas. *Ibn ʿArabi,* pp. 279–288.

11. Al-Dhahabi. *Ta'rikh,* tab. 64, p. 353 (for *ittihad* see my article in IES, pp. 116–117). From the poetical excerpts adduced by al-Dhahabi in support of his comment it is evident that he referred to Ibn ʿArabi's poetical *diwan,* "The Interpreter of Desires" (*Tarjuman al-ashwaq*). Its ostensibly sensual imagery and daring allusions incited the suspicion of some Syrian scholars who declared it blasphemous and profane. Consequently, Ibn ʿArabi had to write an extensive commentary on his poems protesting his innocence and explaining that they were nothing but allegorical expressions of mystical love for God; see Nicholson. *The Tarjuman,* pp. 3–8; Addas. *Ibn ʿArabi,* pp. 250–253, 285, and 308; and Menocal. *Shards,* pp. 74–89.

12. On his life and work that "constitute the final summation of the science of *hadith,*" see Rosenthal. *Ibn Hadjar al-ʿAskalani*—EI², vol. 3, pp. 776–778. Ibn Hajar's attitude toward Ibn ʿArabi is discussed in Chapter 5 of this study.

13. Nicholson. *The Tarjuman,* pp. 66–67; cf. Sells. "Ibn ʿArabiʾ 'Garden.'"

14. Ibn Hajar. *Lisan,* vol. 5, p. 313; cf. al-Suyuti. *Tabaqat,* p. 38.

15. See Rosenthal. *Ibn al-Dubaythi*—EI², vol. 3, p. 756.

16. As with many medieval Muslim historians, Ibn al-Dubaythi "continued"(*dhayyal*) the history of al-Samʿani (d. 562/1166), who, in turn, had written a continuation of the famous *Taʾrikh Baghdad* by al-Khatib al-Baghdadi (d. 463/1071).

17. Rosenthal. *Ibn al-Dubaythi*—EI², vol. 3, p. 756. This method was common among Muslim biographers, e.g., al-Sakhawi (d. 902/1497).

18. Henceforth Ibn ʿArabi's full name, when mentioned in the biographical accounts, will be abbreviated, except where it differs from the traditional.

19. See Arnaldez. *Maʿrifa*— EI², vol. 5, pp. 568–570; cf. Chittick. *The Sufi Path of Knowledge,* pp. 145–189.

20. I.e., the Sufis.

21. On the meaning of these Sufi terms see Chittick. *Faith and Practice,* pp. 170–171.

22. For Ibn ʿArabi's own accounts of his meetings with the Prophet see Austin. *Bezels,* pp. 45–46; and al-Kutubi. *Fawat,* vol. 3, p. 437.

23. Ibn al-Dubaythi. *Al-Mukhtasar al-muhtaj ilayhi,* vol. 1, p. 102; cf. Ibn al-Sabuni. *Takmilat al-ikmal,* p. 73; cf. an [intentionally?] abridged version of the entry in al-Dhahabi. *Taʾrikh,* tab. 64, p. 353; and Ibn Hajar. *Lisan,* vol. 5, p. 314.

24. Abu Tahir al-Silafi (d. 575/1179), a native of Isfahan who spent most of his life in Alexandria, was a renowned transmitter of *hadith* reports and an expert on their transmission (*isnad*). He wrote a number of influential books on *ʿilm al-rijal* and was a teacher of almost every renowned *hadith* scholar of the late 6th/12th and the first half of the 7th/13th centuries, al-Dhahabi. *Al-ʿIbar,* vol. 3, p. 71.

25. This method of transmission does not involve a direct contact between the receiver and the transmitter, whereas the normal procedure requires the former to read the texts to a licensed transmitter, who makes corrections in the student's notes. Some well-established scholars could occasionally receive an *ijaza in absentia,* by correspondence. In such cases, transmitters often granted a general authorization, allowing their

colleagues to teach all works by the same writer; cf. Addas. *Ibn ʿArabi,* p. 65, note 9; Khalidov. *Arabskiye,* pp. 108–121; Berkey. *The Transmission,* "index" under "ijazas."

26. Al-Dhahabi. *Taʾrikh,* tab. 64, p. 353. Al-Qari al-Baghdadi (the late 8th/14th century-early 9th/15th centuries), whose spirited apologia for Ibn ʿArabi in discussed in Chapter 5 of this study, was apparently dissatisfied with Ibn al-Dubaythi's dry tone and his lack of enthusiasm for Ibn ʿArabi's spectacular achievements. Therefore, he sought to enhance Ibn al-Dubaythi's report by adding the following phrase to the already positive portrait of the Sufi thinker: "I met him and found out that he was too sublime to be described and too great to be understood." Al-Qari al-Baghdadi. *Manaqib,* p. 32. This "positive" censorship by an admirer is the exact opposite of al-Dhahabi's negative corrections of the original texts that were just cited.

27. This is, incidentally, the name by which Ibn ʿArabi signed his works or authorized his students to transmit and teach them. According to al-Maqqari (d. 1041/1577), "His [name] was known in the West with the *alif* and the *lam* (i.e., with the definite article "al-"); however, the people in the East have agreed to call him without the *alif* and the *lam* in order to distinguish him from the *qadi* Abu Bakr b. al-ʿArabi," al-Maqqari. *Nafh,* vol. 2, p. 373; Ibn al-Sabuni. *Takmilat al-ikmal,* p. 37; cf. Austin. *Sufis,* a plate with a photograph of Ibn ʿArabi's signature, between pp. 20 and 21. On his namesake, the renowned judge and scholar of Seville see J. Robson. *Ibn al-ʿArabi*—EI,[2] vol. 3, p. 707.

28. I.e., "The Holy Spirit" (*Ruh al-quds*) and "The Precious Pearl" (*al-Durra al-fakhira*); see Austin. *Sufis.*

29. To make musk smell better, it was often mixed with some other fragrance; see Lane. *Lexicon,* vol. 1, pt. 5, p. 1947.

30. Ibn al-Najjar. *Al-Mustafad,* p. 27; cf. al-Safadi. *Al-Wafi,* vol. 4, p. 178; Ibn Hajar. *Lisan,* vol. 5, p. 314. Qasyun is a mountain overlooking Damascus. Ibn ʿArabi was buried at its foot, in the al-Salihiyya neighborhood.

31. He may have used an expanded version of the biography, which is no longer extant. This, however, is unlikely. As with al-Dhahabi's citation of Ibn al-Dubaythi's report, al-Maqqari heavily edited the original text of Ibn ʿArabi's obituary in order to present Ibn ʿArabi in a favorable light. The same pattern is seen in the biographical account of Ibn ʿArabi by al-Qari al-Baghdadi (see *Manaqib,* p. 31), who lavishly laced earlier biographies of the Greatest Master with details that are absent from the sources he quoted. For further instances of such apologetically "improved" narratives see a free rendition of Ibn al-Najjar's biography of Ibn ʿArabi by al-Safadi; see *al-Wafi,* vol. 4, p. 178; cf. al-Maqqari. *Nafh,* vol. 2, p. 366.

32. A Qurʾanic word that is applied to accomplished Sufi masters; cf. *Qurʾan,* 50:37; and *Qurʾan,* 2:179, 3:7, 3:190, 5:100, etc.; cf. Knysh. "Abu Nasr al-Sarraj," p. 162, note 15.

33. On two different dates of Ibn ʿArabi's birth see Austin. *Sufis,* p. 21, note 2.

34. Al-Maqqari. *Nafh,* vol. 2, p. 362. Similar reports on Ibn al-Najjar's authority are given in al-Safadi. *Al-Wafi,* vol. 4, p. 178; and Ibn Hajar. *Lisan,* vol. 5, p. 314; cf. Addas. *Ibn ʿArabi,* p. 285.

35. Upon Sibt Ibn al-Jawzi's death, an unfinished draft of his history was completed by Qutb al-din al-Yunini (d. 726/1326). Hence Ibn ʿArabi's obituary may have been written by al-Yunini who used Sibt's notes. Al-Kutubi (d. 764/1363), al-Maqqari (d. 1042/1632) and other authors attribute this note to al-Yunini; see al-Kutubi. *Fawat,* vol. 3, p. 436; al-Maqqari. *Nafh,* vol. 2, p. 364. Cf. Addas. *Ibn ʿArabi,* pp. 336–337.

36. Sufi gnosis, an experiential, supersensory knowledge as opposed to one obtained through rational argumentation or authoritative tradition.

37. On God's "Most Beautiful Names," including the one considered to be the greatest; see Gardet. *Al-Asmaʾ al-Husna*—EI², vol. 1, pp. 714–717.

38. Sibt Ibn al-Jawzi. *Mirʾat al-zaman,* vol. 8, pt. 1, p. 736.

39. Al-Maqqari. *Nafh,* vol. 2, p. 365. There is some confusion as to the identity of the donor. Al-Qari al-Baghdadi, an enthusiastic advocate of Ibn ʿArabi, maintained that this pension was allocated to him by Shams al-din al-Khuwayy (d. 637/1239), who had held the office of the chief *qadi* of the Shafiʿi *madhhab* of Damascus prior to Muhyi al-din Ibn al-Zaki; see al-Qari. *Manaqib,* p. 30; cf. al-Maqqari. *Nafh,* vol. 2, p. 378. This seems feasible, since Ibn al-Zaki became the chief *qadi* only *after* Ibn ʿArabi's death. For a discussion of the possible origin of such reports see Addas. *Ibn ʿArabi,* pp. 294–295. Ibn ʿArabi's friendship with al-Khuwayy is corroborated by a passage from the *Futuhat,* vol. 3, p. 508.

40. The Ibn al-Zaki family *(banu al-Zaki)* were hereditary judges of Damascus since the first half of the 6th/12th centuries. Among many members of this clan, Muhammad b. ʿAli b. al-Zaki al-Qurashi (d. 598/1202), the chief *qadi* of the Shafiʿi *madhhab* deserves a special note. According to Ibn Kathir, Muhammad b. ʿAli was hostile to "ancient" sciences, such as logic, philosophy, and speculative theology and used to tear up books that contained any rationalist or pre-Islamic ideas; Ibn Kathir. *Al-Bidaya,* vol. 13, p. 36. Cf. Pouzet. *Damas,* p. 121 and index under "Ibn al-Zaki." Muhammad b. ʿAli's strict convictions are in stark contrast with the broad-mindedness of his successor, Muhyi al-din Yahya Ibn al-Zaki, who acquired the reputation as a covert Shiʿi. He was appointed chief *qadi* only in 641/1242, i.e., after Ibn ʿArabi's death, a fact that contradicts the oft-cited statement that he patronized Ibn ʿArabi in his capacity of the supreme judge of Damascus; see Addas. *Ibn ʿArabi,* p. 296. Ibn ʿArabi was on friendly terms with yet another member of the Ibn al-Zaki clan, Zaki al-din Tahir (d. 617/1220), who took under his wing the controversial Andalusi mystic ʿAtiq al-Lawraqi. Thus,

Muhyi al-din Yahya's support for Ibn ʿArabi appears to have been part of the family tradition; cf. Addas. op. cit., pp. 299–300.

41. His pro-ʿAlid position is evidenced by his verses, quoted in Ibn Kathir. *Al-Bidaya,* vol. 13, pp. 272–273. It seems, however, that his Shiʿi inclinations were grossly exaggerated by the stringently Sunni historians associated with Ibn Taymiyya (d. 728/1328). Thus Ibn al-Suqaʿi (d. 726/1325), an official of the Mamluk administration, who was "a good Christian and a chronicler worthy of trust" (J. Sublet. *Ibn al-Sukaʿi*—EI², *Supplement,* p. 400; and Ibn as-Suqaʿi. *Tali,* p. XVI of the French Introduction) makes no mention of his pro-Shiʿi leanings. His verses demonstrate a sympathy for ʿAli that was common among many moderate Sunni scholars.

42. "He maintained that ʿAli should be given precedence over ʿUthman in keeping with the opinion of his master, Muhyi al-din Ibn ʿArabi"; Ibn Kathir. *Al-Bidaya,* vol. 13, p. 272; cf. Addas. *Ibn ʿArabi,* pp. 300–301. Ibn Kathir's conjecture that Ibn ʿArabi was a Shiʿi is ill-founded, especially since al-Dhahabi, himself no friend of the Greatest Master, saw no connection between Ibn al-Zaki's alleged pro-Shiʿi tendencies and his friendship with Ibn ʿArabi; al-Dhahabi. *Al-ʿIbar,* vol. 3, pp. 318–319.

43. According to the well-informed Ibn al-Suqaʿi, himself an experienced diplomat, Ibn al-Zaki's mission to Hulagu's camp, which was presented by Ibn Kathir and by other historians as high treason, was the only possible way to save Damascus from the impending pillage by the Mongol army; Ibn al-Suqaʿi. *Tali,* p. 169 (French text).

44. Abu Shama. *Tarajim,* p. 206; Pouzet. *Damas,* p. 451.

45. See Pouzet. *Damas,* pp. 23–148.

46. Abu Shama. *Tarajim,* pp. 205–206; cf. Addas. *Ibn ʿArabi,* pp. 300–301.

47. See Ahmad. *Abu Shama*—EI², vol. 1, p. 150. According to Pouzet, Abu Shama was married to a Maghribi woman and was on friendly terms with the immigrants from the Muslim West who had settled in Damascus in the aftermath of the *Reconquista.* Pouzet points out that Abu Shama made friends with Ibn ʿArabi and his two sons; see Pouzet. *Damas,* p. 179, note 181; and idem. "Maghrébins."

48. Al-Kutubi gives the date of his death as 28th *rabiʿ al-akhar, Fawat,* vol. 3, p. 436.

49. Abu Shama. *Tarajim,* p. 170.

50. The other man mentioned by Abu Shama is ʿAbdallah b. al-Nahhas (d. 654/1256). An offspring of a noble Damascene family, he withdrew from the world and became a recluse. Despite his deafness, he was considered a reliable transmitter of *hadith;* see Abu Shama. *Tarajim,* p. 189; Ibn Kathir. *Al-Bidaya,* vol. 13, p. 206; Pouzet. *Damas,* p. 365. We shall return to him later

on. The third washer was one al-Jamal b. ʿAbd al-Khaliq, whose identity remains obscure, Addas. *Ibn ʿArabi,* pp. 336–337.

51. See Ateş. *Ibn al-ʿArabi*—EI², vol. 3, p. 708.

52. At the end of his life he was disgraced and exiled to Egypt by the victorious Mamluks; see Ibn al-Suqaʿi. *Tali,* p. 169; al-Dhahabi. *Al-ʿIbar,* vol. 3, p. 319.

53. Ibn Taymiyya. *MRM,* vol. 1, pp. 170–171; vol. 4, pp. 24 and 76; cf. al-ʿAzzawi. "Muhyi al-din Ibn ʿArabi," passim.

54. See Chapter 5 of this study.

55. Al-Qari al-Baghdadi. *Manaqib,* p. 24.

56. See Chapter 4 of this study.

57. Ibn Taymiyya. *MRM,* vol. 4, p. 77.

58. A native of Valencia, Ibn al-Abbar was forced out of his homeland by the Christian *Reconquista* and settled in Bougie (*Bijaya*), a town in present-day Algeria, where he entered the service of a local Hafsid sovereign. After two years, the sultan, enraged by Ibn al-Abbar's intellectual independence and his scathing satire, had him brutally executed and burned together with his books and diplomas. Ibn al-Abbar's principal claim to fame is his "Continuation of the *al-Sila*" (*al-Takmila li-kitab al-sila*), i.e., of the famous biographical dictionary by Ibn Bashkuwal (d. 578/1183), whom Ibn ʿArabi listed among his teachers, see al-Mundhiri. *Al-Takmila,* vol. 3, p. 555; Ben Cheneb and Pellat. *Ibn al-Abbar*—EI², vol. 3, p. 673. Ibn al-Abbar's *Takmila* forms the basis of an interesting historio-sociological study of the Andalusi *ʿulamaʾ* by Urvoy; see Urvoy. *Le monde;* cf. Humphreys. *Islamic History,* pp. 190–191 and 207–208.

59. On al-Harastani, the chief *qadi* of Damascus and renowned *muhaddith* see Abu Shama. *Tarajim,* p. 106; Ibn al-ʿImad. *Shadharat,* vol. 5, p. 60.

60. Muslim b. al-Hajjaj (d. 261/865) was a celebrated *muhaddith,* whose collection of traditions entitled *Sahih,* along with its namesake by al-Bukhari (d. 256/870), are considered by Sunni scholars to be the most authoritative and reliable.

61. See note 73 of this chapter.

62. Ibn al-Abbar. *Al-Takmila,* no. 1023.

63. Cf. Urvoy. *Le monde,* p. 201.

64. See Chapter 7 of this study.

65. For this biographical genre in the Maghrib, see, e.g., Lévi-Provençal. *Les Historiens des Chorfa,* passim.

66. I.e., one who has memorized the whole text of the Qurʾan.

67. I.e., one who has realized fully (*tahaqqaq*) the divine reality (*haqiqa*); Chittick (*Faith and Practice,* p. 177) translates this term as "verifier."

68. See *Futuhat,* vol. 2, p. 18; cf. al-Ghubrini. *'Unwan,* pp. 80–82; and Addas. *Ibn 'Arabi,* pp. 216–217.

69. I.e., their influence on individual human destinies.

70. This story is related by Ibn 'Arabi himself in his *Kitab al-ba'*, pp. 10–11, though al-Ghubrini probably heard it in an oral rendition, since he begins his story with the phrase "I was told" *(dhukira li);* cf. Addas. *Ibn 'Arabi,* p. 216.

71. *Fiha ma fiha,* a slightly altered version of the famous phrase—*fihi ma fihi* ('in it is what is in it'), which is often ascribed to Ibn 'Arabi. Jalal al-din Rumi (d. 672/1273) used it as the title for his collection of wise sayings; see Ritter. *Djalal al-din Rumi*—EI[2], vol. 2, pp. 393–396. For an English translation of Rumi's work see Arberry. *Discourses.*

72. For al-Hallaj's trial and martyrdom see Massignon. *The Passion.* For other instances in which Muslim mystics fell victim to their ecstatic utterances see Ernst. *Words of Ecstasy.*

73. A noted Maliki jurist and ascetic from Bijaya who traveled as far as Bukhara and Hadramawt in search of *hadith.* He was regarded as a reliable transmitter of traditions and his lessons of *hadith* attracted numerous pupils from different parts of the Maghrib. He died in Bijaya in 652/1254 with the reputation of a saint, see al-Ghubrini. *'Unwan,* pp. 138–142.

74. On *ta'wil*—an allegorical interpretation of the Qur'an and the Sunna that was often used by Muslim philosophers, rational thinkers, mystics, and some Shi'is see Knysh. *Ta'wil,* in IES, pp. 218–219. In the context of the controversy between the adherents of the inner meaning of the Islamic revelation as opposed to their literalist opponents, *ta'wil* was sometimes, though not always, juxtaposed with *tafsir*—an historical, philological, and juridical commentary on the Muslim Scripture that focuses on its literal meaning.

75. These terms carry strong Christian overtones, since they were used by Arab Christians in their discussions of the doctrine of Incarnation. This made them extremely suspicious in the eyes of Muslim scholars; see Arnaldez. *Lahut/nasut*—EI[2], vol. 5, pp. 611–614; cf. Knysh. *Hulul and Ittihad* and *Lahut/nasut,* in IES, pp. 292–293 and 147. Al-Hallaj is believed to have been the first to introduce the pair *lahut/nasut* as well as the related concept of divine presence in human nature (*hulul*) into Sufi theosophical speculations. Since Ibn Taymiyya (d. 726/1326), and perhaps even earlier, accusations of *hulul* were leveled against Ibn 'Arabi and his followers; see Ibn Taymiyya. *MRM* vol. 1, pp. 66–67, 170–172, vol. 4, pp. 6–101, etc.

76. See Knysh. *Shath,* in IES, pp. 294–295; and Ernst. *Words of Ecstasy,* passim.

77. Al-Ghubrini. *ʿUnwan,* pp. 156–158.

78. Abu Shama. *Tarajim,* p. 230; al-Safadi. *Al-Wafi,* vol. 1, p. 230; Al-Maqqari. *Nafh,* vol. 2, pp. 269–270; Ibn al-ʿImad. *Shadharat,* vol. 5, pp. 310–311.

79. Addas. *Ibn ʿArabi,* p. 231.

80. One of the main gates of Damascus. See Pouzet. *Damas,* index, under "Bab al-Faradis."

81. *Al-Wafi,* vol. 4, p. 175; cf. French translation in Addas. *Ibn ʿArabi,* p. 231.

82. These predictions constitute the subject matter of the book *al-Shajara al-nuʿmaniyya fi ʾl-dawla al-ʿuthmaniyya;* see Yahia. *La classification,* vol. 2, pp. 456–457, which, in all likelihood, is a forgery; see Chodkiewicz. *An Ocean Without Shore,* pp. 17 and 137, note 55.

83. Addas. *Ibn ʿArabi,* pp. 231–232. Given Ibn ʿArabi's opposition to the ecstatic utterances (which he viewed as a sign of spiritual and intellectual immaturity), Addas is justified in questioning the veracity of al-Ghubrini's report. Her misgivings are further corroborated by the fact that Ibn ʿArabi himself never mentioned this dramatic episode either in the *Futuhat* or in any other work, while he did give a description of his short sojourn in Egypt; see, e.g., Austin. *Sufis,* pp. 91–91 and 94. Taking the lead from al-Ghubrini's testimony al-Dhahabi also states that "[Ibn ʿArabi] was charged [with a crime], but managed to escape"; *Siyar,* vol. 23, p. 48.

84. Ibn al-Musdi's *Muʿjam* remains in manuscript; see Kahhala. *Muʿjam,* vol. 12, p. 140. His obituary of the Greatest Master is quoted by most of the latter's biographers, e.g., al-Safadi, al-Kutubi, Ibn Hajar, al-Fasi, and al-Maqqari. Al-Dhahabi provides what appears to be an unabridged quotation from Ibn Musdi's work, which is repeated *verbatim* by al-Fasi (d. 832/1429), who, as a student of al-Dhahabi's son, Abu Hurayra, apparently inherited the great historian's negative attitude to the Greatest Master; see al-Fasi. *ʿIqd,* vol. 2, pp. 185–186; and Chapter 5 of this study.

85. For the language of allusions, which the Muslim mystics juxtapose with a literal expression (*ʿibara*), see Nwyia. *Ishara*—EI^2, vol. 4, p. 114; cf. Knysh. *Ramz*—EI^2, vol. 8, pp. 428–430.

86. Abu Bakr Muhammad b. al-Jadd (d. 586/1190), a distinguished theologian and jurisconsult, who counted among his teachers the leading scholars of his age, e.g., Ibn Rushd (d. 595/1198) and the *qadi* Abu Bakr b. al-ʿArabi (d. 543/1148); see Ibn al-ʿImad. *Shadharat,* vol. 4, p. 286; Monés. *Ibn al-Djadd*—EI^2, vol. 3, p. 348; and Urvoy. *Le monde,* pp. 181–183.

87. Muhammad b. Saʿid b. Zarqun (d. 586/1190), a Maliki theologian and *muhaddith* who was famous for his hostility to Ibn Hazm (d. 456/1064); see Ibn al-Abbar. *Al-Takmila,* no. 821 and Urvoy. *Le monde,* pp. 181–184.

88. Abu ʾl-Hasan Najba b. Yahya, a famous Andalusi *muhaddith* and Maliki *faqih,* who lived in the late 6th/12th—early 7th/13th centuries, see Urvoy. *Le Monde,* pp. 181–182.

89. ʿAbd al-Haqq b. ʿAbd al-Rahman al-Ishbili, a famous Andalusi jurisconsult, theologian, and philologist, whose works were widely studied and taught in al-Andalus and the Maghrib. According to al-Dhahabi, shortly after he had settled in Bijaya later in life, he fell victim to the ire of the local prince and died in 581/1185, in the aftermath of the beatings and humiliations inflicted on him on the prince's orders. Al-Ghubrini, however, omits (deliberately?) this gruesome episode from his biography; see al-Dhahabi. *Al-ʿIbar,* vol. 3, p. 82; al-Ghubrini. *ʿUnwan,* pp. 41–44; Ibn al-ʿImad. *Shadharat,* vol. 4, p. 271; al-Yafiʿi. *Mirʾat,* vol. 3, p. 422.

90. Al-Talqani was a popular Persian preacher and *faqih* of the Shafiʿi *madhhab;* see Ibn Kathir. *Al-Bidaya,* vol. 13, p. 11; al-Dhahabi. *Al-ʿIbar,* vol. 3, pp. 100–101; al-Yafiʿi. *Mirʾat,* vol. 3, p. 466. Al-Dhahabi's terse remark, interpolated in Ibn Musdi's narrative, is typical of a *hadith* expert whose task was to examine chains of transmitters attached to every *hadith* report. In this case, he has a good case: Ibn ʿArabi, whose first visit to Iraq falls on 601/1204–1205, simply could not have studied with al-Talqani, who had died in 590/1193–1194.

91. The Zahiri legal and theological school, founded by Dawud b. ʿAli b. Khalaf (d. 270/884), emphasized the literal *(zahir),* interpretation of the Qurʾan and the Sunna and discouraged any attempt to explain the Scriptures allegorically or rationally. It also opposed the exercise of one's personal discretion in the application of scriptural norms and rulings. The Zahiri teaching initially gained a wide following in Iraq, but later lost ground to the four orthodox *madhhabs* and is now defunct. It experienced a revival of sorts in al-Andalus, where it was vigorously propagated by Ibn Saʿid al-Balluti (d. 355/966) and by Ibn Hazm (d. 456/1064), whose works were familiar to Ibn ʿArabi. Under the Almohads, who sought to curtail the influence of Maliki jurists, Zahirism was for some time recognized as an official *madhhab* of the Almohad state, see Goldziher. *Die Zahiriten;* for an updated account see Prozorov. *Az-Zahiriyya*—IES, pp. 76–77. Ibn ʿArabi's solicitous concern for the letter of the revealed texts may have been a result of his sympathy for the doctrines of Ibn Hazm and his Andalusi followers; cf., however, Morris. "Ibn ʿArabi's 'Esotericism,'" where Ibn Hazm's influence on Ibn ʿArabi is questioned. For a recent discussion of Ibn ʿArabi's position vis-à-vis Zahirism see Chodkiewicz. *An Ocean Without Shore,* pp. 54–55 and 149, note 63.

92. Al-Dhahabi. *Taʾrikh,* tab. 64, pp. 352–353; cf. al-Fasi. *Al-ʿIqd,* vol. 2, pp. 185–186; al-Safadi. *al-Wafi,* vol. 4, p. 173; al-Kutubi. *Fawat,* vol. 2, p. 241;

Ibn Hajar. *Lisan,* vol. 5, p. 314. Al-Maqqari provides a slightly different list of Ibn ʿArabi's teachers; see *Nafh,* vol. 2, p. 363.

93. According to Massignon, Ibn Musdi was an opponent of the Greatest Master (*The Passion,* vol. 3, p. 264)—a fact that makes his empathetic treatment of the Sufi even more significant.

94. For a comprehensive study of Ibn ʿArabi's terminology see Hakim. *Al-Muʿjam.*

95. Chittick. *Faith and Practice,* pp. 174–175; cf. Boase and Sahnoun. "Excerpts", pp. 47–49, passim.

96. This term was kindly suggested to me by Chittick as an alternative to "esotericism" and to its derivations. Henceforth they are used interchangeably.

97. Ibn ʿArabi presented this *ijaza,* which enumerates in various manuscript versions from 270 to 290 works, to the Damascene ruler al-Malik al-Muzaffar Baha' al-din (d. 635/1237) in 632/1234; see Yahia. *La classification,* vol. 1, pp. 48–56; Addas. *Ibn ʿArabi,* pp. 124–130; Badawi. "Autobibliografía."

98. Al-Maqqari. *Nafh,* vol. 2, p. 363; cf. Badawi. "Autobibliografía," pp. 114–115.

99. For al-Qazwini see Kratchkovski. *Izbrannye sochineniya,* vol. 4, pp. 359–366.

100. I.e., the catastrophes that befell the tribes of unbelievers mentioned in the Muslim Scripture, e.g., the tribes ʿAd and Thamud, the people of Nuh (Noah), etc.

101. Al-Qazwini. *Athar al-bilad,* p. 497.

102. Ibid., p. 269.

103. See Chapter 3 of this study.

104. For Ibn Abi ʾl-Mansur see Gril. *La Risala;* cf. Ibn al-Ahdal. *Kashf,* pp. 273–274.

105. According to a more comprehensive (augmented?) version by al-Maqqari: "He combined the sciences acquired through learning with those bestowed on him [by God]." *Nafh,* vol. 2, p. 367.

106. In al-Maqqari's version, "His rank (*manzila*) was great. . . . " ibid.

107. A reference to Sufi ecstatics and visionaries who are absorbed in the direct contemplation of God to such an extent that they become incapable of conveying their subtle experiences to the others. For the *mawajid* (sing. *tawajud*) and the related notions of Sufi psychology, see Gramlich. *Das Sendschreiben,* pp. 115–118.

108. Abu 'l-'Abbas al-Hariri, or, according to some sources, al-Harrar or, occasionally, even al-Jarrar (d. 616/1219), was Ibn 'Arabi's compatriot from Seville, who later settled in Egypt to become a popular Sufi master; see Gril. *La Risala,* pp. 3–22 of the Arabic text and 83–110 and 209 of the French text. His close association with the Greatest Master is attested by the latter's works, e.g., *al-Futuhat,* vol. 1, pp. 376, 410, etc.; Austin. *Sufis,* pp. 91–95; cf. Addas. *Ibn 'Arabi,* pp. 233–236.

109. Gril. *La Risala,* p. 115. Al-Maqqari adds " who travelled together in the early mornings and the late nights"; see *Nafh,* vol. 2, p. 367.

110. See Ibn al-Suqa'i. *Tali,* pp. 82 and 118 of the Arabic text; al-Dhahabi. *Al-'Ibar,* vol. 3, pp. 372–373; Ibn Kathir. *Al-Bidaya,* vol. 13, p. 345; Ibn al-'Imad. *Shadharat,* vol. 5, pp. 412–413; and Nwyia. "Une cible."

111. See al-Dhahabi. *Al-'Ibar,* vol. 3, p. 336; Ibn Kathir. *Al-Bidaya,* vol. 13, pp. 299–304; Ibn al-'Imad. *Shadharat,* vol. 5, p. 359; cf. Pouzet. *Damas,* pp. 220–222.

112. See al-Dhahabi. *Al-'Ibar,* vol. 3, p. 368; al-'Ayni. *'Iqd al-juman,* p. 44; Ibn al-Kathir. *Al-Bidaya,* vol. 13, pp. 337–338; cf. Pouzet. *Damas,* p. 218, note 54.

113. Similar self-serving agendas lurk behind many Sufi narratives, whose authors were anxious to exaggerate the accomplishments of their shaykhs and to downplay those of their rivals. Hence the proliferation of the stories of spectacular Sufi miracles, which enthusiastic *murids* routinely ascribe to their teachers. Indirectly, the disciples benefited from the wide circulation of such miracle-narratives by basking in the light of the shaykh's glory; see Knysh. *Karama,* in IES, pp. 131–132.

114. Al-Khidr, or al-Khadir (Khizir) is a popular personage of the Sufi literature and Middle Eastern folklore who is often identified with the prophet Elijah (Ilyas). Al-Khidr is believed to be immortal; he travels freely across land and sea, helping those in need. He is particularly important for the Sufi lore that portrays him as a paragon of the friend of God (*wali Allah*), who ministers to Sufi novices, enlightening them on various ethical or theological dilemmas; see Wensinck. *Al-Khadir*—EI^2, vol. 4, pp. 902–905. For Ibn 'Arabi's own accounts of his meetings with al-Khidr see Addas. *Ibn 'Arabi,* "index"; cf. Netton. "Theophany as Paradox," passim.

115. Gril. *La Risala,* p. 15.

116. Ibid, pp. 32–33. The story is not devoid of chronological inconsistencies. To wit, according to al-Mundhiri, al-Harrar died in 616/1218–1219, i.e., prior to Ibn 'Arabi's arrival in Damascus (see Addas. *Ibn 'Arabi,* pp. 357–358), while in Ibn Abi 'l-Mansur's story he writes to al-Harrar from that city. The episode, however, might have occurred during Ibn 'Arabi's short visit to Damascus.

117. On him see Chapter 5 of this study.

118. According to al-Safadi (a pro-Ibn ʿArabi scholar), al-Qastallani's treatise targeted his personal foe, ʿAbd al-Haqq Ibn Sabʿin, who used his influence with the Meccan governor to banish al-Qastallani from the city in retaliation for the latter's criticism of his views and behavior. In al-Safadi's words, al-Qastallani opens his treatise with a sharp denunciation of al-Hallaj and concludes it with an attack on the mystical poetry of al-Tilimsani; see al-Safadi. *Al-Wafi,* vol. 2, p. 134; Rosenthal. *A History,* 505–506.

119. On Ibn Sabʿin see Chittick. "Rumi and *wahdat al-wujud,*" pp. 82–83; Kattoura. *Mystische und Philosophishe System;* and Chapter 7 of this study.

120. On this personage see Chapter 7 of this study.

121. Meaning Arabia.

122. In reality, Ibn ʿArabi left the Maghrib for the East in 598/1201; see Addas. *Ibn ʿArabi,* pp. 352–353.

123. Rosenthal. *A History,* p. 586 (Arabic text).

124. See, e.g., al-Safadi. *Al-Wafi,* vol. 4, p. 173; cf. Addas. *Ibn ʿArabi,* pp. 276–277.

125. In support of his suggestion al-Safadi quoted the following lines from al-Qastallani's poem:

> When I saw You shining through my very essence,
> I hastened to cleanse my spiritual state of
> all blameworthy features,
> While my innermost thought prostrated itself
> before
> The beauty, which I had never seen before in
> my whole life
> I recited a chapter (*sura*) from [the book of]
> your beauty
> And its [chapter's] goodness penetrated my
> entire body. . . .
>
> Al-Safadi. *Al-Wafi,* vol. 2, pp. 134–135

126. Al-Safadi. *Al-Wafi,* vol. 2, p. 135.

127. See, e.g., Chodkiewicz. *An Ocean Without Shore,* pp. 4–5 and 132, note 16.

128. Chittick. "Rumi and *wahdat al-wujud,*" pp. 87–88.

129. Cf. Addas. *Ibn ʿArabi,* p. 302.

Chapter 3

1. Haarmann. *Misr. Pt. 5. The Mamluk Period*—EI², vol. 6, pp. 166–177 and an extensive bibliography therein. Note Haarmann's conclusion that, during that period, Egypt and Syria formed a closely knit whole, both politically and culturally.

2. On Baybars (r. 658/1260-676/1277) and his military campaigns see Khowaiter. *Baibars the First;* Irwin. *The Middle East,* "index"; Thorau. *The Lion of Egypt* (and Little. Review of Thorau. *The Lion of Egypt,* in *Journal of Semitic Studies,* vol. 38/2 [autumn 1993], pp. 340–348).

3. Runciman. *History of the Crusades,* vol. 3, pp. 412–422; Irwin. *The Middle East,* pp. 77–78.

4. See Wilber. *The Architecture of Islamic Iran,* pp. 84–87; cf., however, Abu Lughod. *Before European Hegemony,* pp. 153–244.

5. Bloom. "The Mosque of Baybars," pp. 58–59.

6. See, e.g., Ibn Taymiyya. *Majmuʿat al-rasaʾil wa ʾl-masaʾil,* (henceforth MRM), vol. 1, pp. 170–171 and 179–180, vol. 4, p. 24; idem. *Fatawa,* vol. 11, pp. 447–448 and 457.

7. See, e.g., Howorth. *History of the Mongols,* pp. 402–403; Spuler. *Die Mongolen,* pp. 241–242.

8. The first Mongolian converts did indeed display considerable laxity in religious affairs, and their Islam was of a "superficial" nature; see Morgan. *The Mongols,* pp. 160–162. Moreover, their pro-Shiʿi leanings aroused the revulsion of the Sunni *ʿulamaʾ*, especially in view of Nasir al-din al-Tusi's role—probably greatly exaggerated—in the obliteration of the Sunni Caliphate in Baghdad; see Molé. "Les kubrawiyya," p. 70.

9. Ibn Taymiyya. *MRM,* vol. 4, pp. 24 and 28; cf. Little. "Religion," pp. 178–180. A similar view of the "corruptive" influence of the Mongol invasions was adopted—uncritically—by some modern Islamicists, e.g., Rahman. *Islam,* p. 153; cf. Karamustafa. "The Antinomian Dervish," pp. 249–252.

10. For a bibliography of scholarly literature on the Mamluk sultanate see Lapidus. *Muslim Cities,* pp. 217–242. Recent monographic studies of the period are Holt. *The Age of the Crusades;* Irwin. *The Middle East;* and Thorau. *The Lion of Egypt;* cf. also Petry. *The Civilian Elite;* and Humphreys. *From Saladin to the Mongols.* For a critical review of sources see Haarmann. *Quellenstudien;* Little. *An Introduction;* idem. *History and Historiography.*

11. Abu Shama. *Tarajim,* p. 208; cf. Haarmann. *Misr,* p. 167.

12. For Baybars's religious views see Bloom. "The Mosque of Baybars." On his cultivation of "antinomian dervishes" of the Qalandariyya brotherhood see Karamustafa. *God's Unruly Friends,* p. 52.

13. Al-Mihrani's early career was tarnished by an adulterous affair, as a result of which he had to flee from Upper Iraq to Aleppo and, thence, to Damascus. His conduct did not seem to change later in his life and grew even more scandalously Rasputinian after he became Baybars's spiritual counselor. He was finally accused of embezzlement, sodomy, and fornication, and landed in prison, where he died soon afterward; Irwin. *The Middle East,* pp. 53–55; cf. al-Dhahabi. *Siyar,* vol. 1, p. 14.

14. See Karamustafa. *God's Unruly Friends,* pp. 52–53; cf. Meier, *Abu Saʿid,* pp. 511–512.

15. On al-Badawi see Vollers and Littman. *Ahmad al-Badawi*—EI^2, vol. 1, pp. 280–281. He was the founder of the popular mystical order, al-Ahmadiyya (see Winter. *Society and Religion,* pp. 93–101), whose members were often criticized for its "non-Islamic" rites; see, e.g., Urvoy. "Le Genre 'Manaqib,'" passim. This is not to say that Baybars had an exclusive preference for the Sufi masters. He humbly accepted the admonitions of the respected *ʿulamaʾ*, notably Ibn ʿAbd al-Salam al-Sulami and Ibn bint al-Aʿazz, even when they went against his grain; Al-Subki. *Tabaqat,* vol. 8, pp. 215–217; cf. Homerin. *From Arab Poet,* pp. 40–44; Bloom. "The Mosque of Baybars," pp. 62–63.

16. Ibid.; Winter. *Society and Religion,* p. 19; al-Shaʿrani. *Tabaqat.* vol. 1, p. 15.

17. See Ibn Taymiyya's letter to al-Manbiji in *MRM,* vol. 1, pp. 161–183; and Ibn Kathir. *Al-Bidaya,* vol. 14, pp. 51–52. Cf. Little. "The Detention," pp. 324–325; and Irwin. *The Middle East,* p. 95; see also Chapter 4 of this study.

18. See Haarmann. *Misr,* p. 169.

19. Chodkiewicz. *Le sceau,* pp. 21 and 25; Holt. *The Age of the Crusades,* p. 80. In this connection historians often cite an anecdote about the righteous sultan Nur al-din Zengi (d. 569/1174), who was famous for his love of Sufi elders. While preparing for a decisive campaign against the Franks, one of his advisors suggested that he should cut subsidies to Sufi lodges in order to save money for the military effort. The sultan, so goes the story, angrily dismissed this advice, pointing out the miraculous efficacy of the Sufi prayers, which, in his view, far surpassed the power of the swords and arrows. Abu Zahra. *Ibn Taymiyya,* p. 206; on Nur al-din see Elisseeff. *Nur al-din.*

20. On this and other antinomian Sufi brotherhoods of Syria see Little. "Religion," pp. 176–177; Memon. *Ibn Taimiya's Struggle,* pp. 62–64; Karamustafa. *God's Unruly Friends,* passim.

21. See Laoust. "Le hanbalisme," pp. 60–61.

22. Little. "Religion," p. 174; Holt. *The Age of the Crusades,* pp. 152–153; Fernandes. *The Evolution of a Sufi Institution.* The erection of the giant

"royal" *khanaqa* near Siryaqus, north of Cairo, on the orders of Sultan al-Nasir Muhammad, is described in Ibn Taghribirdi. *Al-Nujum,* vol. 9, pp. 79–80. In all, in Mamluk Cairo there were sixty-one Sufi hospices and monasteries; Schimmel. "Some Glimpses," p. 376.

23. See Winter. *Society and Religion,* pp. 92–125.

24. Zarruq. *Qawa'id,* p. 35. According to this classification, Ibn 'Arabi's was the Sufism of the "wise man" (*al-hakim*). For al-Zarruq see Istrabadi. *The Principles of Sufism,* pp. 1–51.

25. Al-Ghazali was only one of a larger group of Muslim thinkers who contributed to the process of the incorporation of mystical experience into mainstream Sunnism. Similar attempts were made by al-Sarraj, al-Kalabadhi, al-Sulami, al-Qushayri, Abu Talib al-Makki, 'Abd al-Qadir al-Jilani, Abu Hafs 'Umar al-Suhrawardi, and other Sunni theologians.

26. Like any compromise, al-Ghazali's syncretism failed to satisfy either the adherents of the literal understanding and implementation of the revealed law (*ahl al-zahir*) or those who emphasized its inner aspects (*ahl al-batin*); see Nwyia. *Ibn 'Ata' Allah,* p. 9; Bell. *Love Theory,* pp. 206–207.

27. Many Muslim scholars pointed out the affinity between Sufism and the other esoteric traditions within Islam, notably "extreme" Shi'ism and Isma'ilism. They were quick to identify the common "fabricated" *hadith* that both the Sufis and the Shi'is used in support of their respective visions of the Islamic religion. Despite his high repute as a jurist and theologian, al-Ghazali himself was often accused of filling his writings with Sufi-Shi'i "fabrications"; see Ibn al-Jawzi. *Talbis,* p. 166, passim.

28. See Makdisi. "Hanbalite Islam," esp. pp. 251–254; idem. "Ash'ari and the Ash'arites"; idem. "The Non-Ash'arite Shafi'ism"; cf. Prozorov. "Pravoverie" and Knysh. "Orthodoxy" and "Heresy"; for the persecutions of Ash'arism in the Saljuq epoch see Bulliet. "The Political-Religious History."

29. See Hodgson. *The Venture of Islam,* vol. 1, pp. 384–392, vol. 2, pp. 192–195, passim.

30. See Landolt. *Walaya* in *The Encyclopedia of Religion.* Edited by Eliade. London-New York, 1987 vol. 15, pp. 321–323. On al-Hakim al-Tirmidhi and his doctrine of sainthood see Radtke. *Al-Hakim at-Tirmidi.* For its later development in the teaching of Ibn 'Arabi see Chodkiewicz. *Le sceau,* passim; idem. *An Ocean Without Shore,* pp. 38, 43–44, 46, etc.

31. Hodgson. *The Venture of Islam,* vol. 2, pp. 193–194 and 469–471.

32. This, of course, inevitably brings up the problem of "genuine" as opposed to "heretical" Sufism, which I will address in the context of the Ibn 'Arabi controversy. One should, however, remember that even the pious Sufis of old were not immune to persecutions by the contemporary secular and re-

ligious authorities that often considered them to be dangerous troublemakers; see Ibn al-Jawzi. *Talbis,* pp. 162–163, passim; Knysh. "Hanbalitskaya kritika"; Bell. *Love Theory,* pp. 88–90; Ernst. *Words of Ecstasy,* passim.

33. See, e.g., Russell. *Dissent and Order.*

34. See Ibn Kathir. *Al-Bidaya,* vol. 13, pp. 355, vol. 14, pp. 19, 36, 119, 127, 201–202, and 262; cf. Laoust. "Le hanbalisme," p. 59.

35. Haarmann. *Misr,* pp. 165–166.

36. Bloom. "The Mosque of Baybars," p. 62.

37. Petry. *The Civilian Elite,* p. 312; Holt. *The Age of the Crusades,* p. 150; Lapidus. *Muslim Cities,* p. 81; Hodgson. *The Venture of Islam,* vol. 2, pp. 62–69 and 91–135.

38. See Makdisi. *The Rise of Colleges;* for a critique of Makdisi's conclusions see Humphreys. *Islamic History,* pp. 199–202, and a bibliography mentioned therein; cf. Chamberlain. *Knowledge,* passim.

39. See Berkey. *The Transmission of Knowledge.*

40. Glick. *Islamic and Christian Spain,* p. 155.

41. Chamberlain. *Knowledge,* pp. 90–92; cf. Bulliet. *Islam,* pp. 101–114.

42. Humphreys. *Islamic History,* p. 187.

43. Sadeque. *Baybars,* p. 18; cf. Lapidus. *Muslim Cities,* p. 143.

44. For a more nuanced view of the situation that discerns three major occupational categories within the learned elite, namely, the bureaucrats, the jurist-scholars, and the religious functionaries, see Petry. *The Civilian Elite,* pp. 312–314; cf. Glick. *Islamic and Christian Spain,* p. 157.

45. See, e.g., Ibn Kathir. *Al-Bidaya,* vols. 13–14, passim (at the beginning of each year); cf. Little. *An Introduction;* idem. "Al-Safadi"; Mottahedeh. *Loyalty,* p. 140, passim.

46. According to Petry, the jurist-scholars constituted a distinct group within the *ʿulamaʾ* class, "who shared a universal vision of faith, a uniform scholastic method, a self-serving conception of recruitment, and a defensive attitude toward political authority"; *The Civilian Elite,* p. 314.

47. For a view of the chief judges that de-emphasizes their intermediary function and relegates them to a rubber stamp of the royal will, see ibid., p. 322.

48. See, e.g., Bloom. "The Mosque of Baybars," pp. 62–63.

49. Petry, who calls this group of *ʿulamaʾ* the "religious functionaries," stresses their greater influence on the masses, yet describes this influence as purely spiritual—a thesis that I do not share; ibid., pp. 323–324.

50. Glick. *Islamic and Christian Spain,* p. 156.

51. The importance of the *'ulama'* as spokesmen for the masses under the Ayyubids is evidenced by the career of Ibn 'Abd al-Salam al-Sulami (d. 660/1262), discussed in this chapter; see also al-Subki. *Tabaqat,* vol. 8, pp. 209–255. In the Mamluk epoch, the most vivid example is Ibn Taymiyya (d. 728/1328), whose profound influence on the Mamluk strongmen and the Syrian commoners stands in sharp contrast to his humble position as a teacher of *fiqh* at a Hanbali *madrasa* in Damascus; see Little. "The Detention."

52. Cf. Lapidus. *Muslim Cities,* p. 143.

53. See al-Sha'rani. *Tabaqat,* vol. 1, p. 15; Escovitz. "The Establishment of Four Chief Judgeships;" Little. "Religion," p. 174; Sadeque. *Baybars,* pp. 16–23 and 72; Bloom. "The Mosque of Baybars," pp. 62–63.

54. Chamberlain. *Knowledge,* pp. 90–92.

55. Glick. *Islamic and Christian Spain,* p. 157.

56. For an illuminating description of the rivalry among the scholars of Islamic Spain, see Monès. "Le rôle," passim; cf. Lévi-Provençal. *Histoire,* vol. 1, pp. 473–488.

57. Little. "The Detention," pp. 323 and 327.

58. On al-Munawi see al-Muhibbi. *Khulasat al-athar,* vol. 2, pp. 193–195 and 412–416; Ibn al-'Imad. *Shadharat,* vol. 7, p. 312; Saleh Hamdan. *Al-Munawi*—EI², vol. 7, p. 565; as a disciple of 'Abd al-Wahhab al-Sha'rani, he inherited his teacher's pro-Ibn 'Arabi stance.

59. A reference to the blind, unquestioning loyalty to one's tribe or kinship group that Muslim scholars often associated with the pagan Arabian society before Islam; see Gabrieli. *'Asabiyya*—EI², vol. 1, p. 681; Lawrence. *Ibn Khaldun,* passim.

60. Quoted in Ibn al-'Imad. *Shadharat,* vol. 5, p. 193.

61. On him see Laoust. *Ibn Kathir.* —EI², vol. 3, pp. 52–53; Little. *An Introduction,* pp. 69–73.

62. Lit. "the house of felicity," a palace of Damascus located near the city citadel that often served as a residence for the governor of the province as well as for the lesser Ayyubid princes who maintained no regular palace in Damascus. The "court of justice" was apparently a chamber or a hall, adjacent to the Dar al-Sa'ada, where court hearings took place; see Humphreys. *From Saladin to the Mongols,* pp. 248–249; Brinner. "Dar al-Sa'ada."

63. Or al-Shalghamani; according to Massignon, his name was Muhammad b. 'Ali b. Abi 'l-'Azaqir. A contemporary of al-Hallaj, whom he disliked, he reportedly espoused "extreme" Shi'i doctrines that he propagated freely due to the patronage of an influential Shi'i statesmen at the Caliph's court.

When the patron withdrew his support, al-Shalmaghani was arrested, condemned as a proponent of the doctrine of incarnation (*hulul*), and executed in 322/933. Ibn Kathir. *Al-Bidaya,* vol. 11, p. 191; Massignon. *The Passion,* vol. 1, pp. 34, 37, 316–320, and "index"; Prozorov. *Kniga,* p. 186; Ch. Pellat. *Muhammad b. ʿAli al-Shalmaghani*—EI², vol. 7, p. 397.

64. This sect derived its name from the Muslim esotericist al-Bajariqi, or al-Bajarbaqi, who, according to Ibn Khaldun (d. 808/1406), "belonged to the Sufi group known as Qalandariyya—the people who practiced the innovation of shaving heads." The great Arab historian describes al-Bajarbaqi as a fortune-teller who predicted "the future events through [mystical] unveiling." Al-Bajarbaqi's versified predictions gained wide currency among the commoners (see Ibn Khaldun. *Al-Muqaddima,* vol. 2, pp. 199–200; cf. Ibn Khaldun. *The Muqaddimah,* vol. 2, pp. 299–230). Al-Dhahabi and Ibn Kathir described al-Bajarbaqi as a notorious heretic who was condemned to death by a Maliki chief *qadi.* He managed to escape from Damascus to Egypt (or to Persia, according to Ibn Kathir). He is said to have entered the service of Satan, who rewarded him with a "satanic unveiling" (*kashf shaytani*). Ibn Kathir claimed that al-Bajarbaqi "led astray many people," including a few famous scholars. He died at al-Qabun near Damascus in 724/1324. Ibn Kathir. *Al-Bidaya,* vol. 13, p. 119; Ibn al-ʿImad. *Shadharat,* vol. 6, pp. 64–65; on the Bajarbaqiyya see Karamustafa. "The Antinomian Dervish," p. 242, note 65.

65. Yusuf b. al-Zaki ʿAbd al-Rahman al-Mizzi (d. 742/1341), a leading Syrian traditionalist and a friend of Ibn Taymiyya. In spite of his Shafiʿi background, al-Mizzi became an enthusiastic supporter of the Hanbali scholar. When the latter was imprisoned for his radical views, al-Mizzi's vociferous protests landed him in jail. Interestingly, at an early stage of al-Mizzi's career, Ibn Taymiyya is said to have dissuaded him from an unspecified Sufi teaching. Ibn Kathir, al-Mizzi's student and son-in-law, also became Ibn Taymiyya's admirer; see Ibn Kathir. *Al-Bidaya,* vol. 14, pp. 200–201 and 203–204; Juynboll. *Al-Mizzi*—EI², vol. 7, pp. 212–213.

66. Muhammad b. ʿUthman al-Dhahabi (d. 748/1347), an outstanding Arab historian, theologian, biographer, and author of numerous historical chronicles and biographical dictionaries. Al-Dhahabi's works contain at least five obituaries of Ibn ʿArabi, the longest of which is included in his recently published "History of Islam" (*Taʾrikh al-islam,* tab. 64, pp. 352–359). The other obituaries are basically abridgments of this longer one. Al-Dhahabi's fame rests primarily upon his expertise as *muhaddith.* He studied with the greatest scholars of his age, e.g., al-Mizzi, Ibn Daqiq al-ʿId (d. 702/1302), and Ibn Taymiyya. The latter had a profound impact on al-Dhahabi, and may have determined his negative attitude to Ibn ʿArabi and his followers. Significantly, al-Dhahabi was a teacher of Ibn Kathir, who made extensive use of the former's historical works in his massive *Bidayya.* For al-Dhahabi's life and work see. Ben Cheneb-[de Somogyi]. *Al-Dhahabi*—EI²,

vol. 3, pp. 214–216; for a recent (uncritical) evaluation of his personality and religious outlook see the Introduction to a new edition of *Ta'rikh al-Islam;* cf. *al-ʿIbar,* vol. 1, pp. "dal"-"ʿayn"; and Rosenthal. *A History,* "index". Al-Dhahabi's views of Ibn ʿArabi are discussed in Chapter 5 of this study.

67. Zayn al-din (d. 747/1347), the third and the youngest brother of Ibn Taymiyya. Although he received a solid theological education, he earned his living as a merchant. He was very loyal to his elder brother and accompanied him in his exile to Egypt; see Ibn al-ʿImad. *Shadharat,* vol. 6, p. 152; cf. Laoust. *Pluralismes,* pp. 69 and 122.

68. Ibn Kathir. *Al-Bidaya,* vol. 14, pp. 201–202. The investigation was presided over by the governor Altunbugha al-Nasiri; see Strauss. "L'inquisition," pp. 16–17.

69. See Laoust. "Le hanbalisme," p. 59.

70. For a comprehensive list of Ibn Taymiyya's followers see Laoust. "L'influence," pp. 23–30.

71. See ibid., p. 24; idem, "Le hanbalisme," p. 58. Al-Dhahabi's admiration for Ibn Taymiyya was, however, tempered by his rejection of the latter's extremist tendencies; see, e.g., Little. "Did Ibn Taymiyya Have a Screw Loose?"

72. For similar trials see Ibn Kathir. *Al-Bidaya,* vol. 14, p. 119. On the tribulations suffered by the Murcian thinker ʿAli al-Harrali (d. 638/1241) at the instigation of ʿIzz al-din Ibn ʿAbd al-Salam, see al-Ghubrini. *ʿUnwan,* pp. 145–146; al-Maqqari. *Nafh,* vol. 2, pp. 387–389; and Pouzet. "Maghrébins," p. 179; cf. Addas. *Ibn ʿArabi,* pp. 229–230.

73. Al-Shaʿrani. *Al-Yawaqit,* vol. 1, p. 9. On al-Fayruzabadi's attitude toward Ibn ʿArabi see Chapters 5 and 9 of this study.

74. A famous *faqih* and member of the Rifaʿi brotherhood, who wrote a treatise in defense of Ibn ʿArabi entitled "The Removal of the Shroud from the Mysteries of Shaykh Muhyi al-din's Teaching" (*Kashf al-ghita' ʿan asrar kalam al-shaykh Muhyi l-din*), which is extensively quoted in al-Shaʿrani's *Yawaqit,* vol. 1, pp. 6–11; see also Brockelmann. *Supplement,* vol. 2, p. 229; al-Zirikli. *Al-Aʿlam,* vol. 6, p. 238; Kahhala. *Muʿjam,* vol. 10, pp. 234–235.

75. Al-Shaʿrani. *Al-Yawaqit,* vol. 1, p. 9.

76. What may be the earliest refutation of Ibn ʿArabi entitled "A Condemnation of Ibn ʿArabi" (*Risala fi dhamm Ibn ʿArabi*) was written by the Damascene scholar Muhammad b. ʿUmar al-Kamili (d. 652/1254), who may have known him personally; see Yahia. *La classification,* vol. 1, p. 114. This work does not seem to have had any significant effect on the later polemic; at least, it is invoked by neither Ibn ʿArabi's supporters nor his detractors.

77. For Ibn ʿAbd al-Salam, whose "rare rectitude of conscience" was highly praised by Massignon, see Pouzet. *Damas,* pp. 29, 101, and "index". Pouzet, however, is more restrained in his evaluation of this scholar, indicating his intolerance and narrow-minded zealotry. On his life see Abu Shama. *Tarajim,* pp. 170–171; Ibn Kathir. *Al-Bidaya,* vol. 13, pp. 248–249; Ibn al-ʿImad. *Shadharat,* vol. 5, pp. 301–302. Ibn ʿAbd al-Salam's detailed biography by his son ʿAbd al-Latif is quoted by al-Subki in his *Tabaqat,* vol. 8, pp. 209–255—a principal source of my information on ʿIzz al-din, cf. Brockelmann. *Geschichte,* vol. 1, pp. 554–555; idem. *Supplement,* vol. 1, pp. 766–767. For an updated bibliography on the scholar see an otherwise unsatisfactory study of one of his works by Ridwan Mukhtar b. Gharbiyya, *Al-Imam fi bayan adillat al-ahkam;* see Ibn ʿAbd al-Salam. *Al-Imam*

78. To fight his theological opponents more effectively, Ibn Taymiyya did employ the terminology and methods of *kalam* speculation—a feature that sets him apart from the earlier Hanbalis, whose strictly fideist stance caused them to rely exclusively on the authoritative precedents set by the pious ancestors. Because of Ibn Taymiyya's atypical polemical tactics, he is sometimes characterized by modern scholars as a "neo-Hanbalite"; see, e.g., Bell. *Love Theory,* pp. 54–56 and 207–209; cf. Abrahamov. "Ibn Taymiyya on the Agreement."

79. The Ashʿaris and the Hanbalis diverged on whether the concrete copy of the Qurʾanic text and its recitation are created or uncreated. The former generally considered its "letter" and "sound" (but not articulate meaning) to be originated in time (*muhdath*), while the latter regarded them as eternal and uncreated—an occasion on which Hanbali literalism is pushed to its extreme limits. For a synopsis of the Ashʿari position on this problem by the leading Ashʿari *mutakallim* of his age see al-Subki. *Tabaqat,* vol. 8, pp. 218–229; cf. Peters. *God's Created Speech,* passim.

80. See al-Subki. *Tabaqat,* vol. 8, pp. 229–241.

81. On al-Harrali and his exegetical work, *al-Hikam,* see Nwyia. *Ibn ʿAtaʾ Allah,* pp. 56–62. Contrary to medieval authors, Nwyia believed that Ibn ʿAbd al-Salam insisted on expelling al-Harrali from Cairo to Syria, not the other way around; cf. Pouzet. *Damas,* p. 218. Not without malice, al-Maqqari, who always supported Sufis against their critics, pointed out that Ibn ʿAbd al-Salam was himself banished from Syria shortly after his altercation with al-Harrali. The latter stayed on and spent his last years in peace under the patronage of the Ayyubid ruler of Hama; see al-Maqqari. *Nafh,* vol. 2, p. 391. Al-Dhahabi describes al-Harrali as a "philosopher of Sufism" (*falsafi al-tasawwuf*), a derogatory term, in al-Dhahabi's mind; see al-Sakhawi. *Al-Daw*ʾ, vol. 1, p. 108.

82. Al-Hariri was the founder of the controversial dervish group al-Haririyya that was widely suspected of antinomian tendencies. For al-Hariri see al-Dhahabi. *Al-ʿIbar,* vol. 3, p. 252; al-Yafiʿi. *Mirʾat,* vol. 4, p. 112; Ibn

Kathir. *Al-Bidaya,* vol. 13, p. 185; Ibn al-ʿImad. *Shadharat,* vol. 5, p. 232; Pouzet. *Damas,* pp. 220–222; Meier. *Abu Saʿid,* p. 507, note 226. Several decades later Ibn Taymiyya issued a special *fatwa* condemning al-Harrali's foremost disciple, the poet Ibn Israʾil (d. 677/1278) for adhering to the doctrine of incarnation and unification; see Massignon. *Haririyya*—EI², vol. 3, p. 222. For samples of Ibn Israʾil's poetry in the tradition of *wahdat al-wujud* see Ibn Kathir. *Al-Bidaya,* vol. 13, pp. 299–304.

83. Abu Shama. *Tarajim,* p. 180.

84. Sources give two main reasons for Ibn ʿAbd al-Salam's expulsion. On the one hand, the new sultan is said to have cast his lot with the Hanbali party whose members bore a bitter grudge against their Shafiʿi detractor; see, e.g., al-Subki. *Tabaqat,* vol. 8, p. 241. A more immediate factor was Ibn ʿAbd al-Salam's opposition to the new sultan's concord with the Crusaders. This deal, under which the Muslims ceded a few strongholds and towns to the Franks in exchange for their military support, drew Ibn ʿAbd al-Salam's sharp criticism that led to his expulsion; see. ibid. vol. 8, pp. 243–245; and Ibn al-ʿImad. *Shadharat,* vol. 5, p. 302. Both versions of this event reflect a typical intertwining of religious and political factors.

85. Al-Subki. *Tabaqat,* vol. 8, pp. 216–217.

86. Ibid., vol. 8, pp. 215–216.

87. Ibid., p. 210.

88. On al-Suhrawardi, a typical representative of so-called *sharʿi* Sufism see Gramlich. *Die Gaben.*

89. Al-Subki. *Tabaqat,* vol. 8, pp. 215 and 248; Brockelmann. *Geschichte,* vol. 1, pp. 554–555. Ibn ʿAbd al-Salam composed at least six treatises on Sufism, most of which remain in manuscript.

90. Apud Ibn al-ʿImad. *Shadharat,* vol. 5, p. 302; cf. Gramlich. *Die Wunder,* pp. 125 and 241.

91. See, e.g., Ibn al-Jawzi. *Talbis,* pp. 218–250; Hujwiri. *Kashf,* pp. 393–420; Robson. *Tracts on Listening to Music.*

92. For a recent discussion of a mystical interpretation of this encounter see Netton. "Theophany as Paradox."

93. See Chapter 4 of this study.

94. Regarding Ibn ʿAbd al-Salam's advocacy of Sufi *karamat* see Gramlich. *Die Wunder,* pp. 125 and 241.

95. It should, however, be noted that objectively their understanding of "the correct Islam of the pious ancestors" was as little grounded on the practices and beliefs of the early Islamic community as were the doctrines of their opponents.

96. Rahman. *Prophesy,* pp. 102–103.

97. This is, however, not the impression one is likely to gain from a somewhat confused discussion of the provenance of this theme in Addas's *Ibn ʿArabi,* pp. 297–299. From what is said there, one might assume that it was the later biographers, and not Ibn Taymiyya himself, who introduced the theme of Ibn ʿAbd al-Salam's condemnation of the Greatest Master.

98. Nasir al-din Abu Bakr b. Salar, or al-Salar (d. 716/1317), a *muhaddith* of some renown, who, however, held neither important teaching positions nor administrative posts and was therefore largely ignored by the historians of the epoch; for a notable exception see Ibn al-Suqaʿi. *Tali,* p. 49 of the Arabic text.

99. Muhammad b. ʿAli Ibn Daqiq al-ʿId (d. 702/1302), an acclaimed *muhaddith* and prolific writer on *hadith* and *ʿilm al-rijal.* Although Ibn Daqiq al-ʿId studied Shafiʿi jurisprudence under Ibn ʿAbd al-Salam, he was also proficient in Maliki *fiqh.* He served as chief *qadi* of the Shafiʿi school in Egypt, where he met the exiled Ibn Taymiyya, who made a great impression on him. Ibn Daqiq al-ʿId taught *hadith* to al-Dhahabi and to many other leading scholars of the next generation; see al-Dhahabi. *Al-ʿIbar,* vol. 4, p. 6; Ibn al-ʿImad. *Shadharat,* vol. 6, pp. 5–6; and Ebeid and Young. *Ibn Daqiq al-ʿId*—EI^2, *Supplement,* p. 383.

100. In another reading—*shaykh sawʾ* (i.e., "vicious master"), which, in the end, conveys the same meaning. Several sources replace "suʾ" with "Shiʿi," a charge that tallies well with Ibn Taymiyya's critique of Ibn ʿArabi's doctrine of sainthood to be discussed in the next section. A more comprehensive list of the different versions of this episode is given in al-Biqaʿi. *Tanbih,* pp. 151–153.

101. Ibn Taymiyya. *MRM,* vol. 4, pp. 73 and 75; new edition, vol. 4, pp. 84 and 86; cf. Ibn al-Ahdal. *Kashf,* p. 207.

102. "I was told about this by many *fuqahaʾ*," Ibn Taymiyya. *MRM,* vol. 4, p. 75, new ed., vol. 4, p. 84.

103. For Muslim theological debates around the problem of the origination of the material universe see Goldziher and Goichon. *Dahriyya*—EI^2, vol. 2, pp. 95–97; Arnaldez. *Kidam*—EI^2, vol. 5, pp. 95–99; Davidson. *Proofs for Eternity,* passim; Leaman. *An Introduction,* pp. 25–86. As we shall see, Ibn Taymiyya considered the anticreationist thesis to be central to Ibn ʿArabi's teaching; e.g., *MRM,* vol. 4, pp. 6–16.

104. Lewinstein. "Notes," pp. 597–598.

105. See Madelung and Hodgson. *Ibaha*—EI^2, vol. 3, pp. 662–663.

106. On al-Safadi's approach to biographical writing see Little. "Al-Safadi."

107. See Rosenthal. *Ibn Sayyid al-Nas*—EI[2], vol. 3, pp. 932–933.

108. The first difference may be attributed to a scribal error. While in al-Safadi's recension, Ibn ʿArabi is called "teacher of evil, disgusting liar" (*shaykh suʾ kadhdhab*); al-Dhahabi's text has "a Shiʿi, disgusting liar" (*shiʿi kadhdhab*). Most of the published versions of Ibn ʿArabi's biography follow al-Safadi, except for Ibn Hajar (*Lisan,* vol. 5, p. 311), which is a word-for-word quotation from al-Dhahabi's *Mizan al-iʿtidal,* vol. 3, p. 659. However, the other biographical notes by al-Dhahabi cite al-Safadi's version, corroborating our conjecture that we are dealing with either a copyist or an editor's error; see, e.g., *Siyar,* vol. 23, p. 48; and *Taʾrikh al-islam,* tab. 64, p. 358.

109. *Al-Wafi,* vol. 4, p. 174.

110. Al-Dhahabi. *Mizan,* vol. 3, p. 656.

111. Al-Fasi. *ʿIqd,* vol. 2, p. 182.

112. *MRM,* vol. 4, p. 75.

113. Little. "Did Ibn Taymiyya Have a Screw Loose?" idem. "The Historical and Historiographical Significance."

114. "He never married, which is, of course, highly unusual for a Muslim, nor did he take concubines" Little. "Did Ibn Taymiyya Have a Screw Loose?" p. 105, quoting Ibn Rajab. *Dhayl,* vol. 2, p. 395. In Little's view, Ibn Taymiyya's single-minded focus on his goal bordered on obsession.

115. Cf. Little. "The Detention," p. 327. For some valuable observations on the editorial methods of medieval Muslim biographers see Little. *An Introduction;* and Haarmann. *Quellenstudien.*

116. Ibn Taymiyya. *MRM,* vol. 4, p. 75.

117. According to Muslim theologians, the Qurʾanic Pharaoh identified himself with God; see Qurʾan 79:24.

118. Ibn Taymiyya. *MRM,* new edition, vol. 4, p. 82; cf. Ibn al-Ahdal. *Kashf,* p. 207.

119. See Chapter 2 of this study.

120. Rizwan Ali,"Two Contemporaries," p. 196.

121. Little. "Did Ibn Taymiyya Have a Screw Loose?" p. 105. For a less generous evaluation of al-Dhahabi's treatment of his contemporaries see Rosenthal. *A History,* pp. 374–375. According to his disciple, Taj al-din al-Subki, in consequence of Ibn Taymiyya's influence, al-Dhahabi was prone to belittle Ashʿari theologians and to exalt *hadith* scholars, especially the Hanbalis.

122. This moderation is even more striking in view of his close ties with Ibn Taymiyya. In his work, al-Dhahabi was consistently critical of philo-

sophical mysticism à la Ibn ʿArabi and Ibn Sabʿin—an attitude enshrined in his terse characterization of the Damascene mystic Ibn Hud (d. 699/1300), a fervent partisan of Ibn Sabʿin, as "the erring Sufi unificationist" (*al-sufi al-ittihadi al-dall*); see *al-ʿIbar,* vol. 3, p. 398; cf. Ibn al-ʿImad. *Shadharat,* vol. 5, p. 446. He passed similar harsh verdicts on the other followers of Ibn ʿArabi and Ibn Sabʿin; see, e.g., *al-ʿIbar,* vol. 4, p. 98; for details see Chapter 5 of this study.

123. Al-Shaʿrani, who was well aware of al-Dhahabi's negative prejudice vis-à-vis Ibn ʿArabi, enthusiastically quoted this disclaimer as a proof of the ambiguity of the issue; see *al-Yawaqit,* vol. 1, p. 8.

124. Al-Dhahabi. *Mizan,* vol. 3, p. 659.

125. Al-Fasi. *ʿIqd,* vol. 2, p. 182.

126. The theory described here is usually attributed to Ibn Sina and his followers, whom Ibn Taymiyya treated under a separate heading; see, e.g., *MRM,* vol. 1, pp. 66–68.

127. Al-Fasi. *ʿIqd,* vol. 2, p. 170.

128. The holy individuals mentioned in the title of this work constitute the unseen hierarchy of the Muslim saints. Many Sufi authors describe them as the true masters of the universe, through whom divine grace is channeled to humanity; see Lockhart. *Abdal*—EI², vol. 1, pp. 94–95; Macdonald. *Ghawth*—EI², *Supplement,* p. 323; Jong. *Al-Kutb*—EI², vol. 5, pp. 543–546; Blochet. *Études sur l'esoterisme;* Fenton. "The Hierarchy of the Saints." For a possible origin of the concept, see Baldick. *Imaginary Muslims,* pp. 28–31. The *abdal* are the forty holy individuals charged with running the affairs of the world. The "Succor" is usually identified with the supreme saint of the age, also known as "Mystical Pole"(*al-qutb*).

129. For Ibn ʿArabi's detailed discussion of the hierarchy see *Futuhat,* vol. 2, pp. 2–139; cf. Fenton. "The Hierarchy of the Saints," pp. 20–22.

130. In several passages, Ibn ʿArabi identified himself with "the seal of the saints," or with the "seal of Muhammadan sainthood"(see Chodkiewicz. *Le sceau,* pp. 159–179; cf. Addas. *Ibn ʿArabi,* pp. 191–195; Austin. *Bezels,* pp. 38–39; Friedmann. *Prophesy Continuous,* pp. 70–76). Although cast in obscure symbols, this bold contention infuriated his adversaries, who accused him of abrogating the prophetic mission of Muhammad and replacing it with the sovereignty of the supreme Sufi saint; for details see Chapters 4 and 6 of this study.

131. Ibn ʿAbd al-Salam is referring to the rapid proliferation of the mystical "poles" in popular Sufi lore. While earlier Sufi writers maintained that each epoch has only one *qutb* (or *ghawth*), in later Sufism and Shiʿi mysticism, we find an increasing number of claimants to this title. Ibn ʿArabi himself contributed to this tendency by claiming that every local Muslim

community and every station on the mystical Path has its pole; see Knysh. *Kutb*—IES, pp. 144–145.

132. See note 30 of this chapter.

133. Sa'd al-din Muhammad b. Hamawayh, or Ibn Hammuya (d. 649/1252 or 658/1260), a noted Sufi from Khurasan, who resided in Damascus for a while. A disciple of the great Persian mystic Najm al-din Kubra, he became a leading exponent of mystical philosophy, which made him the target of Ibn 'Abd al-Salam's condemnation. Ibn Hamawayh is said to have corresponded with Ibn 'Arabi and evidently shared some of his views on sainthood and on the seal of the saints. Al-Dhahabi, following Ibn Taymiyya, stigmatized Ibn Hamawayh as a proponent of monism (*ittihad*); see Ibn Taymiyya. *MRM*, vol. 4, pp. 34–35; al-Dhahabi. *Al-'Ibar*, vol. 3, p. 265; Landolt, "Le paradoxe," pp. 167–174; Gril. *La Risala*, pp. 233–234.

134. For innovation in doctrine, behavior, or practice, as seen by mainstream Muslim theology, see Robson. *Bid'a*—EI², vol. 1, p. 1199. Accusations of *bid'a* figure prominently in anti-Sufi treatises; e.g., Ibn al-Jawzi. *Talbis* and al-Turkumani. *Kitab al-luma'*.

135. Ibn 'Abd al-Salam. "Risala fi 'l-abdal," pp. 13–14; for an earlier critique of the Sufi doctrine of sainthood by Ibn al-Jawzi (d. 597/1201) see Friedmann. *Prophesy Continuous*, p. 78.

136. See Morris. *The Wisdom of the Throne*, p. 19, where the situation in later Shi'i Islam is described; cf. Bulliet's comments on the Shafi'i-Hanafi debates over Sufism in 11th-century Nishapur, *Islam*, p. 111.

137. See Brockelmann. *Geschichte*, vol. 1, pp. 554–555; and al-Subki. *Tabaqat*, vol. 8, p. 248.

138. See, e.g., Nieli. *Wittgenstein*, pp. 6–15, passim.

139. See *MRM*, vol. 1, pp. 49–52, and new edition, vol. 1, pp. 57–64; cf. ibid., vol. 4, pp. 52–70, etc.

140. Already in Hajji Khalifa's bibliographical dictionary *Kashf al-zunun* this epistle is attributed to Ibn 'Abd al-Salam. According to Hajji Khalifa, the epistle "disclosed the falsehood of the popular views regarding them [the Pole, the Succor, and the Substitutes] and denied the fact of their existence." Hajji Khalifa. *Kashf al-zunun*, vol. 3, p. 429; cf. Rizwan Ali. "Two Contemporaries," p. 201.

141. That this indeed was the case is evident from the rejection of Ibn Taymiyya's creed (*'aqida*) by many contemporary scholars, who imputed to him innovations in legal theory and dogma; see Ibn al-Dawadari. *Kanz al-durar*, pp. 139–142; cf. Rosenthal. *A History*, pp. 376–377; and Little. "Did Ibn Taymiyya Have a Screw Loose?" pp. 102–103.

142. See, e.g., remarks to this effect in al-Biqaʿi. *Tanbih al-ghabi,* pp. 136–137; and Chapter 5 of this study.

143. Rizwan Ali. "Two Contemporaries," p. 198; cf. Addas. *Ibn ʿArabi,* p. 297.

144. In Muslim educational tradition these two functions often overlap. Many outstanding Muslim theologians and Sufi masters started their careers as servants to their teachers, which often meant keeping their master's house and doing household chores. The idea was always to be around in order not to miss even a single moment of the teacher's instruction; see Berkey. *The Transmission,* pp. 34–43.

145. Rizwan Ali. "Two Contemporaries," p. 198; Addas. *Ibn ʿArabi,* p. 297.

146. See Fleisch. *Al-Firuzabadi*—EI², vol. 2, p. 927. His role in the controversy is discussed in Chapters 5 and 9 of this study.

147. Al-Sakhawi. *Al-Dawʾ*, vol. 11, pp. 78–79.

148. Chodkiewicz. *An Ocean Without Shore,* p. 4.

149. Al-Qari al-Baghdadi. *Manaqib,* pp. 27–29; cf. al-Suyuti. *Tanbih,* fol. 48a; al-Shaʿrani. *Al-Yawaqit,* vol. 1, p. 10; al-Maqqari. *Nafh,* vol. 2, pp. 376–377; Ibn al-ʿImad. *Shadharat,* vol. 5, p. 193. The last source quotes the story on the authority of the celebrated Sufi and *muhaddith* al-Munawi (d. 1031/1621); cf. Rizwan Ali. "Two Contemporaries," pp. 197–198.

150. Al-Suyuti. *Tanbih,* 48a-b; cf. al-Maqqari. *Nafh,* vol. 2, p. 382, *apud* al-Yafiʿi (d. 728/1328).

151. Chodkiewicz. *An Ocean Without Shore,* pp. 1–2.

152. Rizwan Ali. "Two Contemporaries," p. 198. I have made minor stylistic changes to Rizwan Ali's translation of the passage.

153. For the conventions of this genre see Pellat. *Manakib*—EI², vol. 6, pp. 349–357; cf. Urvoy. "Le genre "manaqib.""

154. Al-Qari. *Manaqib,* p. 29.

155. On al-Fasi see Chapter 5 of this study.

156. This term is routinely used by Muslim heresiographers to designate the trends within Sufism that they regarded as deviating from the letter of the *shariʿa* and dispensing with conventional morality and religious obligations. The emergence of extreme tendencies in Sufism is usually associated with such controversial figures of early Sufi history as al-Bistami and al-Hallaj. Later on, this term was applied to the "intoxicated" Persian mystics: al-Kharaqani, Abu Saʿid Mayhani, ʿAyn al-Qudat al-Hamadhani, and, occasionally, to Ibn ʿArabi and to the proponents of monistic views. As Sufism's history shows, the borderline between the "moderate" and "extreme" types of

Islamic mysticism is artificial, and, on many instances, blurred; see Knysh. *Tasawwuf*—IES, p. 228.

157. Al-Fasi refers to Ibn ʿArabi's possible retraction of his views at the end of his life. This motif will be discussed later in this study.

158. A famous center of Islamic learning in Upper Egypt.

159. Al-Fasi. *ʿIqd,* vol. 2, pp. 184–185.

160. Ibn ʿAbd al-Salam. *Hall al-rumuz,* pp. 8–13. What follows is a paraphrase of this passage.

161. Meaning, "I am identical with God!"

162. Ibn ʿAbd al-Salam. *Hall al-rumuz,* pp. 9–10; cf. Ibn al-Ahdal. *Kashf,* p. 17.

163. Medieval writers deferentially referred to him as "Sultan of the Scholars." The fact that his books are widely edited and published in present-day Saudi Arabia is the best testimony to his acceptance even by the most conservative scholarly circles.

164. Al-Iskandari. *Lataʾif al-minan,* pp. 141–142; cf. Rizwan Ali. "Two Contemporaries," p. 199.

165. *Lataʾif al-minan,* pp. 141–143; cf. Nwyia. *Ibn ʿAtaʾ Allah,* p. 33; cf. Gramlich. *Die Wunder,* p. 125.

166. See Winter. *Society and Religion,* p. 89. On al-Mursi see Nwyia. *Ibn ʿAtaʾ Allah,* passim.

167. Al-Suyuti. *Tanbih,* 46b-47a; cf. Rizwan Ali. "Two Contemporaries," p. 199. For al-Shadhili and his followers in Alexandria who were the real institutors of the Shadhili *tariqa* see Nwyia. *Ibn ʿAtaʾ Allah.* Ibn ʿAtaʾ Allah's encounter with Ibn Taymiyya is discussed in Chapter 4 of this study.

168. See *Lataʾif al-minan,* pp. 252–253.

169. This, at least, is a conclusion reached by Nwyia (*Ibn ʿAtaʾ Allah,* pp. 25–26), who argued that, in his famous collection of pious supplications *The Book of Wisdom* (*Kitab al-hikam*), al-Iskandari consistently distanced himself from the controversial monistic metaphysics associated with Ibn ʿArabi and his followers. He was more concerned with world-renouncing piety, moralizing, and ascetic exercises than with the theoretical Sufism of Ibn ʿArabi and his school; see Nwyia. *Ibn ʿAtaʾ Allah,* pp. 38–43; for an English translation of the *Hikam* see Danner. *The Book of Wisdom.* This difference in outlooks is exemplified by al-Shadhili's reported encounter with Sadr al-din al-Qunawi (*Lataʾif al-minan,* pp. 163–164) which shows al-Shadhili's mystical state to be superior to that of al-Qunawi, whose preoccupation with the monistic metaphysics is implicitly denounced.

170. Ibn Taymiyya. *MRM,* vol. 4, p. 76; new edition, vol. 4, p. 85.

171. Rizwan Ali. "Two Contemporaries," p. 199.

172. For Ibn ʿArabi's views on sainthood see Chodkiewicz. *Le sceau;* Fenton. "The Hierarchy of the Saints." In developing this concept both Ibn ʿArabi and the Shadhili leaders drew upon the works of al-Hakim al-Tirmidhi, who is credited with articulation of the *wilaya* doctrine; see al-Iskandari. *Lata'if al-minan,* pp. 180 and 192.

173. For a recent study of al-Shaʿrani see Winter. *Society and Religion.* This work should, however, be treated with caution due to the author's static assumptions about Sufism and the Sufis. Throughout his study, Winter draws a rigid line between the "moderate" and "extremist" trends in Islamic mysticism—a dichotomy that evidently springs from "the obstinate notion that Sufism and *shariʿa* have represented polar opposites throughout Islamic history." Algar. "Reflections," p. 45; cf. Chittick. *Faith and Practice,* pp. 1–21. A dated, yet still helpful, introduction to al-Shaʿrani's life and thought is Shmidt. *Abd al-Wahhab.* Much of al-Shaʿrani's work is dedicated to the defense of Ibn ʿArabi and to the popularization of his legacy.

174. Meaning the Sufis.

175. Al-Shaʿrani. *Al-Yawaqit,* vol. 1, p. 11; cf. Rizwan Ali. "Two Contemporaries," p. 197.

176. Ibn Rajab. *Dhayl,* vol. 2, p. 140.

177. Rizwan Ali. "Two Contemporaries," p. 194, *apud* al-Qusi.

178. Died in 636/1238; see Abu Shama. *Tarajim,* p. 166.

179. In Ibn ʿArabi's dreams and visions, personages often communicate by allusions, signs, and gestures.

180. See Ibn ʿArabi. *Diwan,* pp. 256–257. A partial French translation is given in Addas. *Ibn ʿArabi,* p. 299.

Chapter 4

1. For a standard account of his life and work see Laoust. *Essai;* idem. "La biographie"; For more recent studies, see Michel. *Ibn Taymiyya's al-Jawab al-Sahih;* Bell. *Love Theory,* pp. 46–91, passim; Memon. *Ibn Taymiyya's Struggle;* Makdisi. "Hanbalite Islam," pp. 251–264; idem. "The Hanbali School"; idem. "Ibn Taymiyya"; Rahman. *Islam,* pp. 193–197, passim; Abrahamov. "Ibn Taymiyya on the Agreement"; Jackson. "Ibn Taymiyyah on Trial." Of the numerous studies on Ibn Taymiyya in Arabic one can mention ʿAbd al-Majid. *Naqd* and Hilmi. *Ibn Taymiyya wa 'l-tasawwuf.*

2. In my discussion of Ibn Taymiyya's critique of Ibn ʿArabi, the terms *monistic* and *unificationist* correspond respectively to the Arabic

ittihadiyya, wahdat al-wujud, hulul, and their derivatives. The problems involved in the use of these "alien and inappropriate interpretative categories" are addressed in Chittick's "Rumi and *wahdat al-wujud,*" esp. pp. 85–91, and need not be discussed here; cf. "Introduction" to this study, note 28.

3. Chittick. "Rumi and *wahdat al-wujud,*" pp. 85–87

4. Chittick, however, dismisses it as "simplistic"; "Rumi and *wahdat al-wujud,*" p. 86.

5. See Rahman. *Islam,* pp. 206 and 239; Makdisi. "The Hanbali School"; idem. "Ibn Taymiyya"; idem. "The Non-Ash'arite Shafi'ism," pp. 256–257; Homerin. "Ibn Taimiyah's *al-Sufiyah.*" Yet, his unqualified attribution to Sufism by Makdisi and, to a lesser extent by Rahman, was questioned—rightly it seems to me—by Michel (see "Ibn Taymiyya's *Sharh*"); for another persuasive argument against Ibn Taymiyya's affiliation with Sufism, see Meier. "Das sauberste"; cf. O'Fahey and Radtke. "Neo-Sufism," pp. 55, 59, and 61. A solution to this problem lies largely in one's definition of Sufism; see Knysh. "Hanbalitskaya kritika."

6. Hodgson. *The Venture of Islam,* vol. 2, p. 470; cf. Ibn Taymiyya. *MRM,* new edition, vol. 1, pp. 32–74.

7. In this respect at least, Ibn Taymiyya is a faithful follower of al-Ghazali, who also sought to rid Sufism of its elitist tenor and to play down its esoteric metaphysics; see Makdisi. "The Non-Asha'arite Shafi'ism," pp. 256–257. Unlike al-Ghazali, however, Ibn Taymiyya was skeptical that Sufi mystics had, as it were, direct line to God through which they received revelations similar to those of the Prophet—a viewpoint that makes his affiliation with the Sufi tradition superficial; see, e.g., O'Fahey and Radtke. "Neo-Sufism," p. 61. Similarly, Ibn Taymiyya resented the theoretical bent of speculative Sufism as inconsistent with "a catholicity of salvation accessible to all faithful," Makdisi. "The Non-Asha'arite Shafi'ism," p. 256.

8. For his harsh criticism of the Ahmadiyya-Rifa'iyya dervishes of Damascus, see Ibn Taymiyya. *MRM,* new edition, vol. 1, pp. 131–155; cf. Karamustafa. *God's Unruly Friends,* pp. 54–55.

9. Homerin. "Ibn Taimiyah's *al-Sufiyah,*" p. 220.

10. *Ibtal wahdat al-wujud wa 'l-radd 'ala 'l-qa'ilin biha;* see *MRM,* new edition, vol. 1, pp. 75–85.

11. *Al-Ihtijaj bi 'l-qadar 'ala 'l-ma'asi*—ibid., vol. 1, pp. 86–132.

12. *Kitab shaykh al-islam Ibn Taymiyya ila 'l-'arif bi-'llah al-shaykh Nasr al-Manbiji;* ibid., vol. 1, pp. 169–190.

13. *Haqiqat madhhab al-ittihadiyin, aw wahdat al-wujud,* ibid., vol. 4, pp. 3–112.

14. Chittick. "Rumi and *wahdat al-wujud,*" p. 86.

15. See Irwin. *The Middle East,* p. 97; cf. Little. "The Detention," passim.

16. Ibn al-Jawzi. *Talbis,* pp. 150–377; for his refutation of Sufism see Knysh. "Hanbalitskaya kritika."

17. On him see Adams. *Islam and Modernism,* pp. 177–204; Laoust. *Le califat;* Esposito. *Islam,* pp. 131–132 and "index"; Ende. *Rashid Rida*— EI^2, vol. 9, pp. 446–448.

18. On the Salafiyya see Esposito. *Islam,* "index"; and Adams. *Islam and Modernism;* a helpful, if schematic typology of the modern Islamic movements is given in Shepard. "Islam and Ideology."

19. See Esposito. *Islam,* "index." For Rida's sympathy for the so-called *shuhudi* mysticism, which casts doubt on his unconditional attribution to the camp of anti-Sufi scholars, see Jomier. *Le comméntaire;* Bell. *Love Theory,* 182; on *shuhudi* mysticism see Chittick. "Rumi and *wahdat al-wujud,*" pp. 89–91.

20. Awhad al-din Kirmani (d. 635/1238), a popular Sufi master, who met Ibn ʿArabi in Damascus and perhaps fell under his influence. A typical charismatic shaykh, he was prone to ecstatic outbursts that scandalized his learned contemporaries but attracted to him a broad popular following; see Weischer. *Kirmani*—EI^2, vol. 5, p. 166; Gril. *La Risala,* "index."

21. On Ibn Sabʿin (d. 668/1268) see Ghubrini. *ʿUnwan,* pp. 237–238; Badawi. *Rasaʾil;* "Introduction" to Ibn Sabʿin. *Budd al-ʿarif;* Kattoura. *Mystische und Philosophische System;* Urvoy. "Les thèmes"; Chittick. "Rumi and *wahdat al-wujud,*" pp. 82–83; the specificity of Ibn Sabʿin's mysticism in relation to that of Ibn ʿArabi is discussed further on.

22. On this early mystic, who was active in the second half of the 4th/10th centuries, see Arberry. *The Mawaqif and Mukhatabat.* Al-Niffari's writings display the experiential insights that prefigure the ideas of the espousers of *wahdat al-wujud.*

23. A famous mystical poet of Egypt who died between 694/1294 and 696/1297; see (ed.). *Al-Busiri*—EI^2, "Supplement," pp. 158–159.

24. On this important representative the *wahdat al-wujud* tradition, who studied under Sadr al-din al-Qunawi, see Chittick. "Wahdat al-wujud," pp. 14–15; idem. "Spectrums"; idem. "Ibn ʿArabi and His School"; idem. "Rumi and *wahdat al-wujud,*" pp. 79–81. Al-Farghani was the author of what appears to be the earliest monistic commentary on Ibn al-Farid's "Poem of the Way" (*Nazm al-suluk*), which was often cited by Ibn ʿArabi's opponents as a succinct statement of his line of thought. He may have been the first to make systematic use of the phrase *wahdat al-wujud* that was later applied to the Ibn ʿArabi school as a whole. Al-Farghani died around 699/1299–1300.

25. ʿAli b. ʿAbdallah al-Shushtari, a famous Sufi poet and close friend of Ibn Sabʿin. Unlike his teacher who was a philosopher par excellence,

al-Shushtari had a more practical turn of mind and developed a large retinue of disciples whom he instructed in his teacher's monistic principles during his travels in al-Andalus, North Africa, and Egypt. He wrote a few mystical treatises and a long poem in which he presented Ibn Sab'in's philosophy as the culmination of a long tradition of monistic thought. Upon Ibn Sab'in's death, al-Shushtari assumed the leadership of the mystical school known as al-Tariqa al-Shushtariyya. He died at Dumyat (Damietta) around 668/1268; see al-Ghubrini. *'Unwan,* pp. 239–242; Ibn al-Khatib. *Al-Ihata,* vol. 4, pp. 205–212; al-Maqqari. *Nafh,* vol. 2, pp. 388–390; Massignon. "Recherches sur Shushtari."

26. Awhad al-din al-Balabani, or al-Balyani (d. 686/1288), a Sufi master of strong monistic leanings and the author of "The Treatise on Unity," which was recently translated into French by Chodkiewicz (see Balyani. *Epître*). Although al-Balyani has been viewed as a faithful exponent of Ibn 'Arabi's doctrine, his understanding of *wahdat al-wujud* "cannot be put in the same category as that of Ibn 'Arabi,. . . . who took care to offset expressions of God's similarity with descriptions of His incomparability"; Chittick. "Wahdat al-wujud," p. 17.

27. See Chapter 2 of this study.

28. Chittick. "Rumi and *wahdat al-wujud,*" p. 85.

29. For a succinct synopsis of the Mu'tazili concept of *ma'dumat / ma'lumat* and its influence on Ibn 'Arabi's metaphysics see Nyberg. *Kleinere Schriften,* pp. 44–56; 'Afifi. "Al-A'yan al-thabita."

30. See, e.g., Gimaret. *Théories,* passim.

31. For Ibn Taymiyya's concept of human free will versus divine predestination and of theodicy see Bell. *Love Theory,* esp. pp. 61–73; cf. Rahman. *Islam,* pp. 146–147 and 194–195.

32. Rashid Rida's "critical edition" of Ibn Taymiyya's works is riddled with editorial blunders, misreadings, and mistaken comments to the extent that one begins to doubt his aptitude for the task at hand.

33. Cf. Knysh. *Ramz*—EI², vol. 8, pp. 428–430.

34. Baybars Jashnikir was a top-level Mamluk statesman who in 709/1309 usurped the Mamluk throne and proclaimed himself sultan. His reign, however, was short-lived. He was ambushed and murdered by the Mamluks loyal to the deposed sultan al-Nasir Muhammad; see Little. "The Detention," pp. 324–325; for Baybars Jashnikir's political career see Ibn Taghribirdi. *Al-Nujum,* vol. 8, pp. 232–282; Ibn Kathir. *Al-Bidaya,* vol. 14, pp. 51–58; Wiet. *Baybars II*—EI², vol. 1, p. 1126; Holt. *The Age of the Crusades,* pp. 110–113; Haarmann. *Quellenstudien,* pp. 71, 171, 179, and 227. On al-Manbiji see al-Dhahabi. *Al-'Ibar,* vol. 4, p. 55; Ibn Taghribirdi. *Al-Nujum,* vol. 9, pp. 244–245; Ibn al-Jazari. *Ghayat al-nihaya,* vol. 2, pp. 335–336; Ibn al-

ʿImad. *Shadharat,* vol. 6, p. 52; Laoust. *Pluralismes,* pp. 81, 84, and 95; cf. Massignon. *The Passion,* vol. 2, p. 324; Laoust. "Le hanbalisme," pp. 19 and 22.

35. On his life and work see Haarmann. *Quellenstudien,* pp. 61–84.

36. Ibn al-Dawadari. *Kanz al-durar,* vol. 9, pp. 143–144; cf. Nwyia. *Ibn ʿAtaʾ Allah,* pp. 24–25. With regard to al-Manbiji's strong attachment to Ibn ʿArabi, al-Dhahabi wrote: "His behavior was praiseworthy and he possessed many good qualities; however, he exceeded all bounds in his veneration of Ibn ʿArabi and his like. Perhaps he simply did not understand the [true] meaning of the doctrine of unification *(ittihad)*"; *al-ʿIbar,* vol. 4, p. 55.

37. On Ibn Makhluf see Ibn Kathir. *Al-Bidaya,* vol. 14, p. 93. The Malikis of Egypt were, as a rule, in opposition to Ibn Taymiyya.

38. He was a close associate or perhaps a teacher of Ibn ʿAtaʾ Allah al-Iskandari, whose attitude toward Ibn ʿArabi was discussed in Chapter 3 of this study.

39. Nwyia. *Ibn ʿAtaʾ Allah,* p. 25.

40. Ibn Kathir. *Al-Bidayya,* vol. 14, pp. 36, 37, 38, 47, etc.

41. For details see Bell. *Love Theory,* passim.

42. Homerin. "Ibn Taimiyah's *al-Sufiyah,*" p. 240; cf. Bell. *Love Theory,* p. 82. On *fanaʾ* see Knysh. *Fanaʾ*—IES, pp. 251–252 and "Bibliography."

43. Elsewhere, however, Ibn Taymiyya thoroughly separates these two tendencies, claiming that unificationism *(ittihad)*, which he attributes to Ibn ʿArabi and his exponents, postulates an absolute and undifferentiated unity of being that ignores the critical boundary between God and man. Incarnationalism *(hulul)*, on the other hand, is the philosophy of al-Hallaj and of other ecstatic Sufis, who kept God and man separate, yet who allowed for the possibility for one to "dwell" in the other. As Ibn Taymiyya demonstrates, the two theories tend to intermingle; Ibn Taymiyya. *MRM,* vol. 4, pp. 4–5; new edition, vol. 4, pp. 6–7.

44. ʿAbd al-Majid. *Naqd,* p. 157.

45. Ibn Taymiyya. *MRM,* vol. 4, p. 114.

46. See Bell. *Love Theory,* pp. 200–210.

47. See Austin. *Bezels,* pp. 264–266.

48. Meaning *al-Futuhat al-makkiyya.*

49. "The Essence of What Is Necessary for the Beginner [on the Sufi Path]" *(Al-Kunh ma la budda minhu li ʾl-murid)*; see Yahia. *La classification,* vol. 2, pp. 338–339. This work details the ascetic and spiritual discipline

incumbent on the *murid.* For a partial Spanish translation see Asin Palacios. *El Islam cristianizado,* pp. 371–377.

50. *Kitab [al-amr] al-muhkam al-marbut,* a treatise on Sufi discipline; for a partial Spanish translation see Asin Palacios. *El Islam cristianizado,* pp. 300–351.

51. *Al-Durra al-fakhira fi dhikr man intafaʿtu bih fi tariq al-akhira* "The Precious Pearl Concerned with the Mention of Those from Whom I Have Derived Benefit in the Way of the Hereafter." Yahia. *La classification,* vol. 1, pp. 192–193. This is Ibn ʿArabi's autobiographical work that details his meetings with the spiritual masters of al-Andalus, the Maghrib, and the Muslim East; see Austin. *Sufis.*

52. *Mataliʿ al-nujum* (var. *Mawaqiʿ al-nujum*). See Yahia. *La Classification,* vol. 2, pp. 375–376. A treatise devoted to the spiritual discipline of the Sufi novice, which was written in Almeria in 595/1199; see Ibn ʿArabi. *Futuhat,* vol. 1, p. 334 and vol. 4, p. 263; cf. Addas. *Ibn ʿArabi,* pp. 194 and 198.

53. *MRM,* new edition, vol. 4, p. 179.

54. I.e., the conflict between Ibn Taymiyya and the *ʿulamaʾ* in Egypt and Syria.

55. Ibn al-Dawadari. *Kanzal-durar,* p. 143; cf. ʿAbd al-Majid. *Naqd,* p. 157.

56. See *MRM,* new edition, vol. 4, p. 178. It should be remembered that Ibn Taymiyya took an active part in organizing several Muslim expeditions against the approaching Mongol armies and incited the civilians of Damascus to take the field against Mongols during a siege of the city.

57. Ibid., p. 179.

58. I.e., God.

59. I.e., without interpreting them away allegorically. In view of Ibn Taymiyya's insistence on the literal understanding of the Qurʾan and the Sunna this is no small praise.

60. *MRM,* new edition, vol. 1, p. 183.

61. Ibn Taymiyya. *MRM,* new edition, vol. 4, p. 8. Interestingly, in this passage Ibn Taymiyya implicitly concurs with those scholars who recommended to defer judgment on Ibn ʿArabi's infidelity to God. This, however, does not seem to have been Ibn Taymiyya's principal position, for elsewhere he condemns Ibn ʿArabi in no uncertain terms.

62. For Ibn Sabʿin's doctrine see Badawi. *Rasaʾil,* passim; Kattoura. *Mystische und Philosophische System.*

63. Ibn Taymiyya. *MRM,* new edition, vol. 1, pp. 91–92; ibid. vol. 4, p. 48.

64. Ibn Taymiyya. *MRM,* new edition, vol. 1, pp. 95–96; cf. Chittick. "Wahdat al-wujud," pp. 19–21.

65. Jamal al-din Muhammad b. Salim Ibn Wasil (d. 697/1298), a prominent historian and man of religion who wrote a famous history of the Ayyubid dynasty; see el-Shayyal. *Ibn Wasil*—EI², vol. 3, p. 967; Haarmann. *Quellenstudien,* "index."

66. Mahmud b. ʿAbd al-Rahman al-Isfahani (d. 749/1348), a famous Shafiʿi *faqih* and Sufi, who started his scholarly career in Damascus, whereupon he moved to Cairo to head a Sufi lodge in the vicinity of al-Qarafa. Al-Isfahani distinguished himself by long fasting and protracted retreats, which indicates his close association with Sufism; see al-Dhahabi. *Al-ʿIbar,* vol. 4, p. 150; Ibn al-ʿImad. *Shadharat,* vol. 6, p. 165.

67. I have been unable to identify the story in question. It may be one of the numerous anecdotes—similar to Ibn ʿArabi's marriage to the she-jinni—which adhered to Ibn ʿArabi's name either in his lifetime or after death.

68. Ibn Taymiyya. *MRM,* vol. 4, p. 83.

69. Al-Dhahabi. *Al-ʿIbar,* vol. 3, p. 364; Ibn Kathir. *Al-Bidaya,* vol. 13, p. 331. Al-Shaʿrani, who dedicates to al-Jaʿbari a long obituary notice, portrays him as a saint and miracle-worker who enjoyed great popularity with the Egyptian masses. He, however, makes no mention of al-Jaʿbari's hostility to the Greatest Master; see *al-Tabaqat,* vol. 1, p. 177.

70. Ibn Taymiyya. *MRM,* new edition, vol. 4, p. 85; cf. ibid., p. 81.

71. Ibid., p. 86.

72. Ibn Taymiyya. *MRM,* new edition, vol. 4, p. 7; cf. ibid., vol. 1, pp. 90–91; Memon. *Ibn Taymiyya's Struggle,* p. 34.

73. For an interesting parallel with the Christian mysticism of John Ruysbroeck (1293–1381) see Katz. "Language," p. 41.

74. Ibn Taymiyya. *MRM,* vol. 4, pp. 86–88.

75. Bell. *Love Theory,* p. 89.

76. There are several possible translations of this term. A German scholar suggests "Bestand habend," or "Bestehendes," as opposed to "seienden," (van Ess. *Die Erkenntislehre,* pp. 192 and 198–199). Cf. Nyberg's "logisches Sein" as against "Dasein," *Kleinere Schriften,* p. 46. Cf. also "intelligible, noumenal being" versus "sensual, phenomenal being," in Ibrahim and Sagadeev. *Classical Islamic Philosophy,* p. 332.

77. For a succinct account of the epistemological roots of this notion see Nyberg. *Kleinere Schriften,* pp. 44–56; van Ess. *Die Erkenntislehre,* pp. 192–202.

78. Ibn Taymiyya. *MRM,* new edition, vol. 4, p. 8 and vol. 1, p. 81. For a general discussion of relative versus absolute nonexistence see Wolfson. *The Philosophy of the Kalam,* pp. 362–366; Sagadeev and Ibrahim. *Classical Islamic Philosophy,* pp. 60–64. Occasionally, Ibn ʿArabi takes up the line of thinking introduced by the Muʿtazili al-Shahham who held that all intelligibles (*maʿlumat*) should be regarded as "things" (*ashyaʾ*) *tout court*. He however did not go as far as proclaiming them "bodies" (*ajsam*)—a view advanced by another Muʿtazili, al-Khayyat; see van Ess. *Die Erkenntislehre,* p. 192; cf. Nyberg. *Kleinere Schriften,* pp. 45–47.

79. Ibn Taymiyya. *MRM,* new edition, vol. 1, p. 81. Cf. Memon. *Ibn Taymiya's Struggle,* p. 37. One should keep in mind that in setting out Ibn Taymiyya's understanding of the *aʿyan thabita,* Memon continually confused Ibn ʿArabi's view of existence with that of Ibn Sina, whose ontology emphasizes the difference between necessary and possible existence. For a discussion of Ibn Sina's concepts of necessarily existent as against possible existent see Davidson. *Proofs for Eternity,* pp. 289–304; cf. Heath. *Allegory,* pp. 36–40.

80. Ibn Taymiyya's interpretation seems strained if one looks into Ibn ʿArabi's theory of the divine names, which allots them a predominant role in his metaphysical system; see, e.g., Fenton and Gloton. "The Book of the Description."

81. Cf. Chittick. *The Sufi Path of Knowledge,* pp. 33–44.

82. Ibn Taymiyya. *MRM,* new edition, vol. 4, pp. 61–62.

83. Ibid., vol. 4, pp. 21 and 87; cf. Addas. *Ibn ʿArabi,* p. 174.

84. See *Qurʾan*, 1:2.

85. Ibn Taymiyya. *MRM* new edition, vol. 4, pp. 21–22; cf. pp. 8 and 87.

86. Ibid, vol. 4, pp. 59–60.

87. Ibid., pp. 82–83. Most Muslim thinkers believed that the punishment for infidels in hellfire is everlasting; see Chittick. *Faith and Practice,* pp. 53 and 197; cf. Madelung's review of Chittick. Faith and Practice, in the *Journal of the Royal Asiatic Society,* vol. 4/1 (1994), p. 101.

88. He was a teacher of the great later Muʿtazili Abu ʿAli al-Jubbaʾi (d. 305/915), see Gardet. *Al-Djubbaʾi*—EI[2], vol. 2, pp. 569–570; cf. Nyberg. *Kleinere Schriften,* pp. 45–47.

89. Ibn Taymiyya. *MRM,* new edition, vol. 4, p. 8. For Memon's paraphrase see his *Ibn Taymiyya's Struggle,* p. 38.

90. Ibn Taymiyya's critique of Ibn ʿArabi's concept of existence is somewhat facile. In an early treatise, Ibn ʿArabi discerns four modes of existence: in speech, in script, *in concreto,* and in the mind. Elsewhere, following Ibn Sina, he speaks of two major types of existence, the eternal (necessary),

which belongs to God alone, and the temporal (possible), which is shared by all other existents, see Fenton and Gloton. "The Book of the Description," pp. 19–22; Knysh. *Mekkanskiye otkroveniya,* pp. 50–59; cf. Davidson. *Proofs for Eternity,* pp. 289–304. As always, his own position is hard to nail down.

91. Ibn Taymiyya. *MRM,* new edition, vol. 4, pp. 19–20.

92. A discursive strategy that consists of forcing (*ilzam*) the imaginary opponent to admit the absurdity of his views by inferring from his faulty propositions.

93. Ibid., p. 32.

94. Ibid., p. 33.

95. The origins of this concept is perhaps to be sought in al-Nazzam's theory of latency (*kumun*)—the innate predisposition of originated beings that determines the causal relationships between them; see Wolfson. *The Philosophy of the Kalam,* pp. 495–517.

96. According to Ibn Taymiyya, Ibn ʿArabi considered the "niche" of sainthood to be as eternal as the "lamp" of prophethood (Qurʾan 24:34).

97. Ibn ʿArabi refers to the fact that the term *wali* ("guarantor," "close friend") is applied to both God and man, whereas the word "prophet" is attributed exclusively to man; see Fenton and Gloton. "The Book of the Description," p. 34.

98. See Austin. *Bezels,* pp. 168–171.

99. See Friedmann. *Prophesy Continuous,* pp. 53–54.

100. See Austin. *Bezels,* pp. 66–67.

101. See Radtke. *Al-Hakim al-Tirmidi,* 89–94.

102. Ibn Taymiyya. *MRM,* new edition, vol. 4, pp. 56–57 and 66–79.

103. See Austin. *Bezels,* pp. 71–81; cf. Ibn Taymiyya. *MRM,* new edition, vol. 4, pp. 49–51.

104. Ibid., vol. 4, pp. 88–94.

105. Ibid., vol. 1, pp. 172–173.

106. Captured in his boastful statement "I am your Lord, the Most High," *Qurʾan,* 79:24.

107. Cf. Ibn Taymiyya's discussion of Ibn ʿArabi's interpretation of the Qurʾanic passage "And when thou throwest, it was not thyself that threw, but God threw" (8:17); *MRM,* new edition, vol. 1, pp. 108–110.

108. See the studies of Ibn Taymiyya by Laoust, Little, Makdisi, Michel, and Homerin.

109. Cf. Nyberg. *Kleinere Schriften,* pp. 45–47.

110. While al-Qunawi was indeed a disciple of Ibn ʿArabi, Ibn Sabʿin vigorously protested his indebtedness to the Greatest Master. As Ibn Taymiyya justly indicated, his views are much more consistently monistic than Ibn ʿArabi's. Ibn Sabʿin regarded his doctrine of absolute unity as unprecedented and bluntly dismissed all earlier mystical and philosophical systems as immature and short of the goal; see Kattoura. *Mystische und Philosophische System;* Badawi. *Rasaʾil,* pp. 14–15; Chittick. "Wahdat al-wujud," pp. 15–16; Urvoy. "Les thèmes." Although an erstwhile disciple of al-Qunawi, al-Tilimsani apparently considered Ibn Sabʿin's doctrine to be more congenial to his own understanding of monistic philosophy.

111. See, e.g., the works of Chittick, Deladrière, Morris, and Sells.

112. Toynbee. *An Historian's Approach,* p. 123.

113. See, e.g., Chittick. "Rumi and *wahdat al-wujud,*" p. 86.

114. The same approach to the *aʿyan thabita* is uncritically adopted by Memon, who consistently juxtaposes Ibn Taymiyya's "extreme nominalism" with Ibn ʿArabi's "realistic stand"; see Memon. *Ibn Taymiyya's Struggle,* pp. 34–37; The briefest of looks at Ibn ʿArabi's works shows that his *aʿyan thabita* defy the crisp realists-versus-nominalist classification imposed on his system by European scholars. Nyberg, who, like Memon, attempted to treat Ibn ʿArabi's position in terms of this familiar Western dichotomy, eventually admitted its inadequacy in accounting for Ibn ʿArabi's original goal: one moment the Sufi thinker presents himself as a realist, another as a nominalist, see *Kleinere Schriften,* pp. 31–33 and 47–48.

115. Chittick. *The Sufi Path of Knowledge,* p. 84.

116. Ibid.

117. Ibid. For some parallels with al-Shahham, al-Fuwati, and some other Muʿtazila see van Ess. *Die Erkenntnislehre,* pp. 192–196.

118. That is not to say that the problem of the relationship between the genera and the species, the universal and the particular was of no concern to the Greatest Master. It occupies a prominent place in his earlier works; see e.g., Nyberg. *Kleinere Schriften,* pp. 1–34; Fenton and Gloton. "The Book of the Description," passim. Yet, in these works, Ibn ʿArabi, to my knowledge, did not use the term *aʿyan thabita* to describe either the genera or the universals. In the *Fusus,* which seems to have been the major source of Ibn Taymiyya's information on the *aʿyan thabita* theory, this term is consistently used in the sense that I have just outlined. Cf. Ibn Khaldun. *The Muqaddimah,* vol. 3, pp. 89–90.

119. Briefly put, Ibn ʿArabi denies its temporal nature, describing it as a purely logical one.

120. The Hanbali approach is best understood in light of the concept of "human advantage" (*maslaha*) which seeks to accommodate a strictly *shari'a*-minded religious orientation to the exigencies of everyday life and to interpret the *shari'a* in terms of social utility. See Hodgson. *The Venture of Islam,* vol. 2, pp. 469–470; on Ibn Hanbal see the studies by Laoust.

121. See Davidson. *Proofs for Eternity,* passim.

122. Chodkiewicz. "The Diffusion," pp. 44–45; O'Fahey and Radtke. "Neo-Sufism," pp. 71–73; Vikør. *Sufi and Scholar,* pp. 114–115 and 271; on Ibn Idris see O'Fahey. *Enigmatic Saint.*

123. Chodkiewicz. "The Diffusion" pp. 44–45.

124. For the use of Ibn 'Arabi's concept of *wilaya* by the founder of this order see Abun-Nasr. *The Tijaniyya,* pp. 28–31; Chodkiewicz. "The Diffusion," pp. 41, 43–44.

125. In his study of the Ahmadiyya movement, Friedmann unequivocally states that Ibn 'Arabi "served as a primary source of inspiration for Ahmadi prophetology," which "cannot be properly understood and put into correct perspective without reference to the thought of Ibn 'Arabi and of thinkers who were influenced by him." Friedmann. *Prophesy Continuous,* pp. 70 and 72.

126. For recent studies of the ideological foundations of Wahhabism see Cook. "On the Origins"; and Peskes. *Muhammad b. 'Abdalwahhab.*

127. 'Abd al-Salam Faraj, the twenty-seven year-old ideologue of the movement *al-Jihad al-Islami,* was a diligent student of Ibn Taymiyya's condemnatory *fatwas;* see Sivan. "Ibn Taymiyya: Father of the Islamic Revolution," pp. 41–42.

128. Cf. Halliday. "Orientalism," pp. 155–156.

Chapter 5

1. Rosenthal. *A History,* p. 430, note 7.

2. The lengthiest biographies of the Greatest Master were written by al-Dhahabi (d. 748/1348), "History of Islam" (*Ta'rikh al-islam*), *tabaqa* (i.e., "class") no. 64 (corresponding to vol. 64 of the printed edition), pp. 352–359; al-Safadi (d. 764/1362), "A Complete [Roster] of the Deceased" (*al-Wafi bi 'l-wafayat*), vol. 4, pp. 173–178; al-Fasi (d. 832/1429), "The Precious Necklace" (*al-'Iqd al-thamin*), vol. 2, pp. 160–199; Muhammad al-Dawudi (d. 945/1538), "The Classes of Qur'anic Commentators" (*Tabaqat al-mufassirin*), vol. 2, pp. 204–210); al-Maqqari (d. 1041/1632) "The Breath of Perfume" (*Nafh al-tib*), vol. 2, pp. 365–388; Ibn al-'Imad (d. 1089/1679), "The Tiny Drops of Gold" (*Shadharat al-dhahab*), vol. 5, pp. 190–202; Yusuf

al-Nabhani (d. ca. 1345/1926),"The Collection of the Miracles of the Saints" (*Jamiʿ karamat al-awliyaʾ*), vol. 2, pp. 118–125.

3. For a comprehensive list of Ibn Taymiyya's followers and partisans see Ibn Nasir al-din. *Al-Radd al-wafir;* cf. Laoust. "L'influence."

4. On al-Dhahabi's posthumous importance for the later Mamluk historiography see Haarmann. *Quellenstudien,* "index."

5. For al-Dhahabi's critique of Ibn Taymiyya's extremism see Rosenthal. *A History,* pp. 376–378.

6. For praise of al-Dhahabi's fairness by al-Sakhawi (d. 902/1497), see Rosenthal. *A History,* pp. 348–351 and 376–378; cf., however, a critique of al-Dhahabi's bias toward the Hanbalis and resultant enmity toward Ashʿarism by al-Subki (d. 771/1369), ibid., pp. 374–375.

7. His opposition to monistic Sufism is evident from his sharp denunciation of the Sufi poet Ibn al-Farid as "the mainstay of the people of [absolute] oneness, whose poetry bleats with unification, pure and simple," who concealed under the guise of Sufism "the vipers of [monistic] philosophy," *al-ʿIbar,* vol. 3, p. 313; idem. *Mizan,* vol. 3, pp. 24–25.

8. For general observations regarding al-Dhahabi's position on Sufi philosophy see Pouzet. *Damas,* pp. 207–208, note 2; al-Dhahabi. *Al-ʿIbar,* vol. 4, pp. 55, 98, etc; cf. Homerin. *From Arab Poet,* pp. 57–58. It should be noted that apart from monistic Sufism al-Dhahabi was also bitterly opposed to Ashʿari *kalam,* which he, following Ibn Taymiyya, viewed as an illegitimate inquiry into aspects of religion that should be taken on trust.

9. *Ta'rikh,* tab. 64, p. 358.

10. See, e.g., Al-Azmeh. "Orthodoxy and Hanbalite Islam," passim.

11. Al-Dhahabi. *Mizan,* vol. 3, p. 660; Ibn Hajar. *Lisan,* vol. 5, p. 312; Ibn al-Ahdal. *Kashf,* p. 277; cf. Knysh. "Ibn ʿArabi in the Later Islamic Tradition," p. 313.

12. Al-Dhahabi. *Siyar,* vol. 23, pp. 48 and 49.

13. Al-Dhahabi is referring here to the she-jinni story discussed in Chapter 3 of this study.

14. Al-Dhahabi. *Mizan,* vol. 3, p. 659; cf. Ibn Hajar. *Lisan,* vol. 5, p. 312; and Knysh. "Ibn ʿArabi in the Later Islamic Tradition," p. 312.

15. Al-Dhahabi. *Taʾrikh,* tab. 64, p. 354. A slightly different version of this account is given by al-Fasi on the authority of the famous Hanbali traditionalist Abu Bakr Ibn al-Muhibb al-Tabari (d. 789/1387); on the latter see al-Suyuti. *Tabaqat al-huffaz,* p. 539; Ibn al-ʿImad. *Shadharat,* vol. 6, p. 309.

16. Al-Dhahabi. *Taʾrikh,* tab. 64, pp. 354–355.

17. On the meaning of this term see Hodgson. *The Venture of Islam,* vol. 2, "index" under "jamaʿi-sunni"; Prozorov. *Ahl al-sunna wa ʾl-jamaʿa*—IES, pp. 29–30; idem. "Pravoveriye," passim.

18. See Madelung. *Murdjiʾa*—EI², vol. 7, pp. 605–607; cf. Prozorov. *Al-Murjiʾa*—IES, p. 172.

19. Al-Dhahabi. *Taʾrikh,* tab. 64, p. 357; idem. *Siyar,* vol. 24, p. 49

20. Al-Dhahabi. *Mizan,* vol. 3, pp. 659–660.

21. Al-Dhahabi. *Taʾrikh,* tab. 64, pp. 358–359.

22. On al-Ashʿari (d. 324/935), see Gimaret. *Al-Ashʿari.* Al-Safadi's defense of Ibn Arabi by deriving his creed from Ashʿarism is so extraordinary that I can do no better than reproduce it here. "In the first volume of this book [i.e., the *Futuhat*]," wrote al-Safadi in his *al-Wafi* (vol. 4, pp. 174–175), "Ibn ʿArabi made explicit his views, which are, to my mind, from beginning to end identical with those of Abu ʾl-Hasan al-Ashʿari. Nay, he did not diverge from [al-Ashʿari] by one iota. An acquaintance of mine asked me to send him a copy of Ibn ʿArabi's [statement of] creed. At that time, he lived in Safad, while I was in Cairo. So, I copied it, that is the creed, in a pad, on the cover of which I inscribed [the following verses]:

> There is nothing in this creed that would
> draw disapproval or vilification.
> Nothing at all! And there is nothing
> here that contradicts either reason or
> The tidings brought by the Qurʾan!
> Al-Ashʿari is this creed's pivot
> And it is from his teaching that it draws
> its strength.
> Its scope is precisely that [of al-Ashʿari's],
> All it does is to give him [al-Ashʿari] further support.
> And yet, people continue to vilify him [Ibn ʿArabi],
> for man, alas, is never free from an envious grudge!

Al-Safadi's argument is tenuous, since he, wittingly or not, disregarded the fact that Ibn ʿArabi, in the introduction to the *Futuhat,* unequivocally described his creedal statement as one pertaining to "the commoners (*ʿumum*) among the people of outward submission (*Islam*), the people of tradition (*taqlid*), and rational speculation (*nazar*)." In other words, the creed in question is by no means identical with the esoteric truths that he pledged to unveil in the main body of his magnum opus, see Morris. "Interpreters," pt. 2, p. 733; cf. Knysh. "Ibn ʿArabi in the Later Islamic Tradition," p. 311.

23. Al-Safadi. *Al-Wafi,* vol. 4, p. 175.

24. A native of Yemen, al-Yafiʿi resided in Mecca, where he was recognized as the leader of the local Sufi community. Biographers, who highly praise his righteousness and humility, describe him as a partisan of Ashʿarism and a bitter critic of Ibn Taymiyya. On this account he became embroiled in a fierce theological dispute with the followers of the Hanbali doctor in Mecca; see Ibn al-ʿImad. *Shadharat,* vol. 6, pp. 210–212. A great admirer of Sufi *awliya*ʾ, he celebrated their prodigious deeds and exemplary piety in numerous writings. Al-Yafiʿi's pro-Sufi position was severely criticized by a fellow Ashʿari theologian who accused him of leniency toward the heresies of Ibn ʿArabi and his followers, see Ibn al-Ahdal. *Kashf,* pp. 274–277. Later still, his Sufi leanings were condemned by the Arabian reformer Ibn ʿAbd al-Wahhab (d. 1212/1792); see Peskes. *Muhammad b. ʿAbdalwahhab,* pp. 71–72.

25. Ibn al-Zamlakani acquired notoriety as a major Shafiʿi opponent of Ibn Taymiyya, whose views he refuted in several polemical treatises (for his biography see al-Safadi. *Al-Wafi,* vol. 4, pp. 214–221; Ibn al-ʿImad. *Shadharat,* vol. 6, pp. 78–79; and Ibn Kathir. *Al-Bidaya,* vol. 14, pp. 136–137; cf. Jackson. "Ibn Taymiyyah on Trial," pp. 48–49). Supporters of Ibn Taymiyya accused Ibn al-Zamlakani of instigating persecutions against the Hanbali in Syria. Curiously, a later adherent of Ibn Taymiyya who came from Shafiʿi background argued that, deep in his heart, Ibn al-Zamlakani was an admirer of Ibn Taymiyya and opposed him in solidarity with the other Shafiʿi scholars; see Ibn Nasir al-din. *Al-Radd,* pp. 56–58. Cf. Brockelmann. *Geschichte,* vol. 2, p. 71. The existence of Ibn al-Zamlakani's commentary on the *Fusus,* which, unfortunately has not come down to us, is attested by Hajji Khalifa. *Kashf,* p. 426; Kahhala. *Muʿjam,* vol. 11, p. 25; and Yahia. *La classification,* vol. 1, p. 133.

26. Ibn al-Ahdal, a major Yemeni critic of Ibn ʿArabi, doubted that Ibn al-Zamlakani had ever composed this work; see Ibn al-Ahdal. *Kashf,* pp. 276–277. The point however remains moot, for Ibn al-Ahdal apparently confounded two different members of the large Ibn Zamlakani family.

27. Cf. al-Yafiʿi's long account of Ibn al-Farid's life, which was "arranged to elicit feelings of awe and reverence on behalf of the mystical poet"; Homerin. *From Arab Poet,* p. 56.

28. Al-Yafiʿi. *Mirʾat,* vol. 4, p. 101; for a later version of the story see al-Qari. *Manaqib,* p. 29; on al-Suhrawardi see Gramlich. *Die Gaben.* Ibn ʿArabi did not seem to have personal knowledge of al-Suhrawardi; see *Futuhat,* vol. 1, p. 609 and vol. 4, p. 192; cf. Addas. *Ibn ʿArabi,* pp. 284–285.

29. Ibn al-Ahdal. *Kashf,* p. 274.

30. E.g., his "Garden of Sweet Basils" (*Rawd al-rayahin*), which extols the virtues of the greatest Sufi masters from the earliest time until his own

age. Al-Yafiʿi's biographical dictionary of the mystics, "The Book of Guidance" (*Kitab al-irshad*), contains an apology for Ibn ʿArabi; see Yahia. *La classification,* vol. 1, p. 118; Brockelmann. *Geschichte,* vol. 2, p. 227, nos. 4, 5, 8, 9, 10, 11, etc.; idem, *Supplement.* vol. 2, p. 228. Passages on Ibn ʿArabi from the *al-Irshad* are extensively quoted, and rebuffed, in Ibn al-Ahdal. *Kashf,* pp. 273–277.

31. Al-Qari. *Manaqib,* pp. 35–42. Apart from al-Yafiʿi, this category included such scholars as Sibt Ibn al-Jawzi (d. 654/1256) and al-Khazraji (d. 812/1410), on the latter see Bosworth. *Al-Khazradji*—EI², vol. 4, p. 1188.

32. See Sartain. *Jalal al-Din* and Chapter 3 of this study.

33. See Chapter 8 of this study.

34. Al-Suyuti, *Tanbih,* fol. 47a-b; cf. Knysh. "Ibn ʿArabi in the Later Islamic Tradition," p. 312.

35. Al-Fasi belonged to the historiographical and biographical school established by al-Dhahabi. He is said to have studied in Damascus with al-Dhahabi's son Abu Hurayra, whom he cites in his critical biography of Ibn ʿArabi; see al-Fasi. *ʿIqd,* vol. 2, p. 186; cf. vol. 1, p. 334.

36. Al-Fasi evidently refers to the laudatory "biography" of Ibn ʿArabi, "The Precious Pearl in the Glorious Deeds of the Shaykh Muhyi al-din" (*al-Durr al-thamin fi manaqib al-shaykh Muhyi al-din*) by al-Qari al-Baghdadi, which is discussed further on.

37. Al-Fasi. *ʿIqd,* vol. 2, p. 199.

38. Ibid., p. 171.

39. On Ibn ʿArabi's visionary meeting with the Prophet, who commissioned him to write the *Fusus,* see Austin. *Bezels,* pp. 45–46.

40. For Ibn ʿArabi's original argument that turns on the Arabic homonym *insan* (meaning both "man" and "pupil") see Austin. *Bezels,* p. 51; cf. Nicholson. *Studies,* pp. 151–152.

41. Cf. Austin. *Bezels,* pp. 73–81.

42. See Qur'an 71:23.

43. Austin. *Bezels,* p. 78.

44. Ibid.

45. Ibid., p. 74; this rendering of Ibn ʿArabi's thesis is a bit simplistic, see *Fusus,* pp. 85–87, 132, 238–239, etc.

46. Qur'an 1:5; Austin. *Bezels,* pp. 79–80; cf. p. 170.

47. See, e.g., Qur'an 2:7; 2:10; 2:90; 3:105, etc.

48. Ibn ʿArabi's interpretation of the relevant Qurʾanic passages rests on the connotations of the Arabic root *ʿdhb,* which may mean both "torment" (*ʿadhab*) and "sweetness" or "pleasure" (*ʿadhb*); see Austin. *Bezels,* pp. 110 and 132.

49. For the importance of wording in the *istiftaʾ* procedure see Homerin. *From Arab Poet,* p. 71.

50. We can only speculate about the identity of the compilers of the questionnaire. Al-Biqaʿi (*Tanbih,* pp. 151 and 179) mentions among them the Sufi shaykh ʿAbd al-Latif b. Balaban al-Saʿudi (d. 736/1336)—a fact that once again shows that we are dealing with more than a simple "Islam"-versus-"Sufism" dichotomy emphasized in Western studies; see, e.g., Rahman. *Islam,* passim; for a more recent example see Vikør. *Sufi and Scholar,* pp. 270–273.

51. For Ibn ʿArabi's discursive method and "mystical dialectics" see Sells. "Ibn ʿArabi's "Garden" '; idem. "Ibn ʿArabi's 'Polished Mirror'"; Chittick. *The Sufi Path of Knowledge,* pp. 28–30 passim.; Morris. "Ibn ʿArabi's Esotericism.'"

52. In commenting on Ibn ʿArabi's rendition of the Nuh story, his later opponent angrily exclaimed: "By God, the very presence of the *Fusus* among the Muslims is a gross injustice to Islam," Ibn al-Ahdal. *Risala fi shaʾn,* fol. 2a.

53. Al-Fasi. *ʿIqd,* vol. 2, p. 171; for similar charges leveled at Ibn al-Farid see Homerin. *From Arab Poet,* p. 64.

54. Ibn Jamaʿa was, at various times, chief *qadi* of the Shafiʿi *madhhab* in Egypt and Damascus, head of the corporation of the Damascene Sufis (*shaykh al-shuyukh*), and preacher at the Umayyad mosque in Damascus. In addition, he taught Shafiʿi *fiqh* at a number of prestigious religious colleges, see Ibn Kathir. *Al-Bidaya,* vol. 14, p. 171; al-Kutubi. *Fawat,* vol. 3, pp. 297–298; al-Safadi. *Al-Wafi,* vol. 2, pp. 18–20; al-Yafiʿi. *Mirʾat,* vol. 4, p. 287; Ibn al-ʿImad. *Shadharat,* vol. 6, pp. 105–106; Kahhala. *Muʿjam,* vol. 8, pp. 201–202; Pouzet. *Damas,* pp. 214–215; Salibi. *Ibn Djamaʿa*—EI^2, vol. 3, pp. 248–249. For further references see Ibn Jamaʿa. *Tahrir al-ahkam.*

55. That Ibn Jamaʿa's negative evaluation of Ibn ʿArabi in this *fatwa* does not necessarily reflect his personal attitude to monistic Sufism can be surmised from his deep respect for Hasan Ibn Hud (d. 699/1300), that "*impie majeur de l'islam,*" whom Massignon considered to be a foremost exponent of the doctrine of oneness in Damascus; see Massignon. "Ibn Sabʿin," p. 676; Pouzet. "De Murcie à Damas"; idem. *Damas,* p. 219.

56. Al-Fasi. *ʿIqd,* vol. 2, p. 171; cf. al-Biqaʿi. *Tanbih,* p. 153.

57. See al-Dhahabi. *Al-ʿIbar,* vol. 4, pp. 30–31; Ibn Kathir. *Al-Bidaya,* vol. 14, p. 67; Ibn al-ʿImad. *Shadharat,* vol. 6, pp. 28–29; Ibn Rajab. *Dhayl,* vol. 2, p. 362.

58. Al-Fasi. *ʿIqd,* vol. 2, pp. 172–173; cf. Al-Azmeh. "Orthodoxy and Hanbali Fideism," pp. 264–266.

59. A renowned *faqih,* who held several teaching positions at prestigious religious colleges in Cairo and served as preacher and prayer leader at the celebrated Ibn Tulun mosque. Apart from the traditional Qurʾanic sciences and *hadith,* al-Jazari took a keen interest in logic, medicine, mathematics, and poetry; see al-Safadi. *Al-Wafi,* vol. 5, p. 263; Kahhala. *Muʿjam,* vol. 12, p. 128; on the Jazari family see Haarmann. *Quellenstudien,* pp. 12–13.

60. Al-Fasi. *ʿIqd,* vol. 2, pp. 173–174.

61. A teacher of *hadith* at several Cairene colleges, al-Kattan was notorious for his bellicose temper and intolerance of what he considered heretical manifestations of popular religiosity. Chronicles also stress his presumptuousness through which he eventually alienated his friends and peers. He was prone to publicly ridicule his colleagues, thus making a lot of enemies among Egyptian *ʿulamaʾ*. Al-Kattan was a disciple of Ibn Daqiq al-ʿId, the greatest Egyptian *muhaddith* of his epoch, who, as we remember, figured prominently in the story of Ibn ʿArabi's condemnation by ʿIzz al-din Ibn ʿAbd al-Salam. On al-Kattan see Al-Dhahabi. *Al-ʿIbar,* vol. 4, p. 111; Ibn Kathir. *Al-Bidaya,* vol. 14, p. 194; cf. Yahia. *La classification,* vol. 1, p. 124, where his name is erroneously rendered as "al-Kattani."

62. Al-Fasi. *ʿIqd,* vol. 2, pp. 174–175; al-Biqaʿi. *Tanbih,* pp. 155–156.

63. Al-Bakri went on record as a bitter opponent of Ibn Taymiyya. Together with several other scholars, he volunteered to testify against the Hanbali doctor and insisted on his imprisonment. Al-Bakri's career came to an abrupt end when a Mamluk ruler of Cairo, incensed by his outspokenness, banished him to a small village, where he died, reportedly, of chagrin; see al-Dhahabi. *Al-ʿIbar,* vol. 4, pp. 69–70; Ibn Kathir. Al-Bidaya, vol. 14, pp. 118–119; al-Safadi. *Al-Wafi,* vol. 22, pp. 331–332; Ibn al-ʿImad. *Shadharat,* vol. 6, p. 64; cf. Yahia. *La classification,* vol. 1, p. 123.

64. See Katz. "Visionary Experience," passim; for a detailed bibliography on this issue see pp. 111–112 of Katz's study.

65. According to an oft-cited report put in the mouth of Prophet: "Whoever has seen me [in sleep] has seen me truly, for Satan cannot impersonate me," Katz. "Visionary Experience," p. 11, note 5.

66. Al-Fasi. *ʿIqd,* vol. 2, pp. 176–177; al-Biqaʿi. *Tanbih,* pp. 158–159; cf. Ibn al-Ahdal, see *Kashf,* pp. 275–276.

67. See Yahia. *La classification,* vol. p. 124. Al-Zawawi owed his fame to his long commentary on al-Bukhari's *Sahih;* see Brockelmann. *Supplement,* vol. 2, p. 961; al-Zirikli. *Al-Aʿlam*, vol. 5, p. 961.

68. Al-Fasi. *ʿIqd,* vol. 2, pp. 176–177; cf. al-Biqaʿi. *Tanbih,* pp. 157–158.

69. A more comprehensive list of legal opinions against Ibn ʿArabi was later compiled by al-Sakhawi (d. 902/1497); see Yahia. *La classification,* vol. 1, pp. 123–124. In addition to the *muftis* on al-Fasi's list, al-Sakhawi mentions many other critics of Ibn ʿArabi, who produced *fatwas* against him at about the same time. Among them were Ibrahim b. Miʿdad al-Jaʿbari (d. 687/1288)—the Egyptian Sufi whom we mentioned in connection with Ibn Taymiyya's critique, Ibrahim b. Ahmad al-Raqqi (d. 703/1303), Ahmad al-Wasiti (d. 711/1311)—Ibn Taymiyya's close associate, Ahmad b. ʿAli al-Qurashi (d. 715/1315), the Hanbali scholar Musa b. Ahmad (d. 726/1326), ʿAli b. Ismaʿil al-Qunawi (d. 729/1329), Ahmad b. Muhammad al-Samʿani (d. 736/1336), and Ahmad al-Ghubrini (d. 714/1314). Al-Sakhawi's listing should, however, be taken with a grain of salt, for he indiscriminately lumped together both the authors of full-scale anti-Ibn ʿArabi *fatwas* and those whose criticism of the Sufi master was incidental to their main purpose. Moreover, al-Sakhawi's accuracy may also be called into question. For instance, one can hardly imagine that al-Ghubrini issued a condemnatory *fatwa* against Ibn ʿArabi in view of his favorable treatment of the Greatest Master in his *ʿUnwan al-diraya;* see Chapter 2 of this study.

70. I have been unable to identify the corresponding passage in al-Dhahabi's works. On Ibn al-Ahdal see Chapter 9 of this study.

71. Meaning Ibn ʿArabi and his followers.

72. Meaning the *ʿulamaʾ*.

73. Chief *qadi* of the Maliki *madhhab* in that epoch.

74. Ibn al-Ahdal. *Risala fi shaʾn*, fol. 30b; cf. al-Habshi. *Al-Sufiyya,* p. 148.

75. See, e.g., Homerin. *From Arab Poet,* pp. 31–32.

76. Al-Fasi. *ʿIqd,* vol. 2, pp. 177–178.

77. Wiet. *Barkuk*—EI², vol. 1, pp. 1050–1051.

78. Al-Biqaʿi. *Tanbih,* pp. 150–151.

79. Al-Bulqini held many honorable teaching posts, and was, for a short term, appointed the grand *qadi* of Damascus; see al-Sakhawi. *Al-Dawʾ*, vol. 5, pp. 85–90; Brockelmann. *Geschichte,* vol. 2, p. 93; idem., *Supplement,* vol. 2, p. 110; Gibb. *Bulkini*—EI², vol. 1, p. 1308.

80. On this prominent *muhaddith* and biographer, often considered to be the greatest *ʿalim* of his generation, see al-Sakhawi. *Dawʾ*, vol. 2, pp. 36–40; Haarmann. *Quellenstudien,* "index"; Rosenthal, *Ibn Hadjar al-ʿAskalani*—EI², vol. 3, pp. 776–778.

81. Ibn Hajar. *Lisan,* vol. 4, 317–319; al-Fasi. *ʿIqd,* vol. 2, p. 178; cf. al-Biqaʿi. *Tanbih,* p. 176. Al-Bulqini took a more cautions view of Ibn al-Farid,

but when pressed admitted that the latter was an unbeliever too; see Homerin. *From Arab Poet,* p. 59.

82. Similar efforts were later exerted by al-Sakhawi, a disciple of Ibn Hajar's, who sought to present his master as a bitter critic of Ibn ʿArabi and his school; see Yahia. *La classification,* vol. 1, p. 130.

83. See, e.g., Ibn Hajar. *Tabsir al-muntabih,* vol. 3, p. 940; idem. *Lisan,* vol. 5, pp. 311–315.

84. See, e.g., Rosenthal. *A History,* pp. 375–376.

85. A vivid example of Ibn Hajar's cautions approach is his biography of the Sufi master in the *Lisan al-mizan,* which simply rehashes quotations from the previous authors, both pro- and anti-Ibn ʿArabi, while never making explicit the author's own view. A similar tactics is evident in Ibn Hajar's obituary of Ibn al-Farid; see Homerin. *From Arab Poet,* p. 116, note 17.

86. *Lisan,* vol. 5, pp. 312–313.

87. Ibid., p. 315.

88. Ibn Hajar referred to the knowledge of the occult properties of the letters of the Arabic alphabet claimed by Ibn ʿArabi; see Fahd. *ʿIlm al-huruf*—EI[2], vol. 3, pp. 595–596; cf. Knysh. *Mekkanskiye otkroveniya,* pp. 68–84.

89. Ibn Hajar. *Lisan,* vol. 5, p. 315; for a French translation of some passages from the *Futuhat* dealing with gematria and isopsephy (numeric value of Arabic words) see Chodkiewicz (ed.). *Les illuminations,* pp. 385–487. It should be noted that in the context of Islamic theological discourse the adjectives "strange" (*gharib*) and "unusual," or "unheard-of" (*ʿajib*) carry deprecatory connotations. All these and some other terms are closely linked to the notion of innovation (*bidʿa*) in theory or practice, which was routinely condemned by mainstream Muslim scholars.

90. See Knysh. "Ibn ʿArabi in the Later Islamic Tradition," pp. 313–314. On Ibn Hajar's pains to explain and condone Ibn ʿArabi's "heresies" see al-Biqaʿi. *Tanbih,* pp. 138–139. Two of Ibn Hajar's disciples, al-Sakhawi and al-Biqaʿi, became leaders of the antimonistic faction after his death; see Chapter 8 of this study.

91. See Ibn Kathir. *Al-Bidaya,* vol. 14, p. 252; al-Suyuti. *Tabaqat al-huffaz,* pp. 525–526; Ibn al-ʿImad. *Shadharat,* vol. 6, p. 180; Brockelmann. *Geschichte,* vol. 2, pp. 106–107.

92. See, e.g., Laoust. *Ibn Taymiyya*—EI[2], vol. 3, p. 954.

93. Al-Fasi. *ʿIqd,* vol. 2, p 187.

94. On this individual see note 15 of this chapter.

95. Al-Fasi. *ʿIqd,* vol. 2, p. 189.

96. Al-Qunawi was a disciple of the Shaykh al-Manbiji, who was instrumental in bringing Ibn Taymiyya to trial over his condemnation of Ibn ʿArabi (see Chapter 4 of this study). Apart from holding the office of preacher and professor at the Ibn Tulun mosque in Cairo, al-Qunawi was also in charge of the *Dar saʿid al-suʿada'*, the principal Sufi lodge of Egypt, whose directors traditionally maintained pro-Ibn ʿArabi position (e.g., Karim al-din al-Amuli, d. 710/1310, mentioned in Chapter 4 of this study). Toward the end of his life al-Qunawi became the chief Shafiʿi *qadi* of Damascus; see Brockelmann. *Geschichte,* vol. 2, p. 105; Laoust. *Pluralismes,* p. 95; cf. pp. 81 and 84.

97. Al-Fasi. *ʿIqd,* vol. 2, p. 191; al-Biqaʿi. *Tanbih,* pp. 66–67; Ibn al-Ahdal. *Kashf,* pp. 275–276. In mainstream Sunni theology, *ʿisma* is usually reserved to the prophets and messengers of God. The Shiʿis and some Sufi theorists, however, ascribed it respectively to their *imams* and *awliya'*. See Madelung and Tyan. *ʿIsma*—EI², vol. 4, pp. 181–184.

98. Al-Fasi. *ʿIqd,* vol. 2, pp. 190; cf. al-Biqaʿi. *Tanbih,* p. 66–67.

99. Al-Fasi. *ʿIqd,* vol. 2, p. 190.

100. Ibid., p. 197.

101. In the medieval Islamic tradition, this practice was known as "mutual curse" (*mubahala*).

102. Al-Fasi. *ʿIqd,* vol. 2, p. 198. A longer version of this anecdote, quoted in al-Biqaʿi's *Tanbih,* places it in a more specific social and chronological framework. In al-Biqaʿi's version, the episode in question occurred in 787/1385, i.e., during the reign of al-Zahir Barquq, who had among his closest confidants one Shaykh Safa. Ibn Hajar's opponent, Ibn al-Amin, threatened to complain to the powerful Shaykh Safa about Ibn Hajar's disrespect for the men of God (i.e., the Sufis). Fearful that the sultan might use this complaint as an excuse for confiscating his property, Ibn Hajar suggested that the dispute be resolved through the *mubahala;* see al-Biqaʿi. *Tanbih,* pp. 149–150.

103. Rosenthal. *Al-Fasi*—EI², vol. 2, p. 828.

104. See al-Fasi. *ʿIqd,* vol. 1, pp. 337–338, 341; Löfgren. *Arabische Texte,* pp. 199–200.

105. See Chapter 9 of this study.

106. See Löfgren. *Makhrama*—EI², vol. 6, pp. 132–133, and Knysh. *Ba Makhrama* for *Encyclopedia of Arabic Literature,* Routledge, forthcoming.

107. The *tarjama* in question must have been identical with the one we have just discussed. Alternatively, it was its enlarged version that circulated under the title "The Awakening of the Aware and of the Unaware to the Temptation by Ibn ʿArabi" (*Tanbih al-nabih wa 'l-ghabi min iftitan bi-Ibn ʿArabi*). This treatise appears to be lost (see al-Fasi. *ʿIqd,* vol. 2, p. 162, note

1; al-Biqaʿi. *Tanbih,* p. 195), although it was extensively quoted by later writers such as al-Biqaʿi (anti-Ibn ʿArabi) and al-Suyuti (pro-Ibn ʿArabi).

108. Löfgren. *Arabische Texte,* vol. 2, p. 200; and Chapter 9 of this study.

109. According to Yahia, his full name was "Ahmad b. Ibrahim b. ʿAbdallah al-Qadiri." Yahia puts his death in 821/1418. His *nisba* indicates his affiliation with the Sufi order Qadiriyya, although we have no other evidence to support this conjecture; see Yahia. *La classification,* vol. 1, p. 113; cf. Brockelmann. *Supplement,* vol. 1, p. 791. What information we have on al-Qari al-Baghdadi is culled from his laudatory biography of the Greatest Master, "The Precious Pearl in the Glorious Deeds [or Virtues] of the Shaykh Muhyi al-din" (*Al-Durr al-thamin fi manaqib al-shaykh Muhyi al-din*), henceforth *Manaqib.* The editor of the *Manaqib,* Salah al-din al-Munajjid, was unaware of the exact date of al-Qari's death; he tentatively placed it at the turn of the 9th/15th centuries. Significantly, the name of the author at the close of the *Manaqib* differs from that cited by Yahia. In his work, al-Qari al-Baghdadi described himself as a pupil of al-Fayruzabadi, whose lectures he attended during a visit to Delhi in 784/1382 (see *Manaqib,* pp. 7–8). The *Manaqib's* indebtedness to al-Fayruzabadi is further attested by several direct quotations from the latter's *fatwa* in defense of Ibn ʿArabi; see ibid., pp. 63–72.

110. See al-Qari al-Baghdadi. *Manaqib,* p. 11; al-Fasi. *ʿIqd,* vol. 2, p. 162, note 1; Yahia. *La classification,* vol. 1, p. 118; Addas. *Ibn ʿArabi,* p. 295.

111. Al-Sakhawi. *Al-Dawʾ*, vol. 10, pp. 79–86.

112. The *Manaqib* seems to be his only known work; see al-Qari al-Baghdadi. *Manaqib,* pp. 7–8.

113. See *Manaqib,* pp. 21–22. Al-Qari al-Baghdadi, who wrote his book almost 150 years after Ibn ʿArabi's death, simply could not have possibly been aware of the Ibn ʿArabi's physical portrait, which is found neither in his own works nor in those of his followers. No wonder that al-Qari's description of the physical characteristics of the Sufi master consists of such banalities as "[he was] neither tall, nor short," with "hair, neither long nor short; neither lank nor curly," etc. (cf. the portrait of the Prophet in Ibn ʿArabi. *Muhadarat al-abrar,* pp. 61–67). The parallel with the Prophet is not fortuitous, for, in al-Qari's phrase,"such a composition can pertain to no one but the Messenger of God, and it was precisely one of Shaykh Muhyi al-din"; see *Manaqib,* p. 22.

114. Cf. Addas. *Ibn ʿArabi,* pp. 208–218.

115. Such, e.g., as his marriage to the mother of his foremost disciple Sadr al-din al-Qunawi; see *Manaqib,* p. 25; cf. pp. 35 and 38. That this marriage really took place was doubted by some scholars; see, e.g., Ateş. *Ibn al-ʿArabi*—EI^2, vol. 3, p. 708; cf., however, Addas. *Ibn ʿArabi,* pp. 269–270.

116. See Chapter 2 of this study.

117. Al-Qari al-Baghdadi. *Manaqib,* p. 24. This seems to be an exaggeration. Ibn ʿArabi's original shrine in Damascus was a pretty modest construction that acquired prominence only during the Ottoman epoch, when it was rebuilt and enlarged on the orders of the Ottoman sultan Selim the Grim after his conquest of Syria. Since then, Ibn ʿArabi and his tomb came under the patronage of the Ottoman rulers, who held him in high regard on account of his putative prediction of the triumphal rise of the Ottoman state.

118. It is not clear which member of the great Ibn ʿAsakir family is meant here. Apart from the great historian ʿAli Ibn ʿAsakir, who died in 571/1176 and could not have possibly met Ibn ʿArabi, there were other eminent members of this clan; see Elisséeff. *Ibn ʿAsakir*—EI^2, vol. 3, pp. 713–715. Ibn ʿArabi himself listed al-Qasim Ibn ʿAsakir (d. 600/1203) among his *hadith* instructors (see al-Qari al-Baghdadi. *Manaqib,* p. 31, note 1).

119. On these biographers see Chapter 2 of this study.

120. See Ibn ʿArabi. *Rasaʾil,* separate pagination, vol. 1, pp. 1–14. Ibn ʿArabi wrote two epistles to al-Razi, in which he attempted to persuade him of the superiority of mystical gnosis over the purely rationalist outlook of the *mutakallimun.* I am, however, unaware of al-Razi's reply to Ibn ʿArabi's letters. The latter's statements imply that the two men had not met (e.g., pp. 3–4). For a subsequent development of the mysticism-versus-rationalism theme in the correspondence between al-Qunawi and Nasir al-din al-Tusi see Chittick. "Mysticism versus Philosophy."

121. Al-Qari al-Baghdadi. *Manaqib,* pp. 25–26.

122. Ibid., pp. 33–34.

123. According to Addas, the stipend in question was established by Muhyi al-din Ibn Zaki; furthermore she considers al-Qari's mention of al-Khuwayy as the donor to be a result of confusion between the two *qadis.* Addas. *Ibn ʿArabi,* p. 301.

124. Al-Qari al-Baghdadi. *Manaqib,* p. 30; cf. later versions of the story that claim that the *qadi* served Ibn ʿArabi "as if he were his slave" (*yakhdamuhu khidmat al-ʿabid*); see al-Maqqari. *Nafh,* vol. 2, p. 382; al-Shaʿrani. *Al-Yawaqit,* p. 9; Addas. *Ibn ʿArabi,* pp. 294–295.

125. See, e.g., Ibn ʿArabi. *Futuhat,* vol. 3, p. 508.

126. Al-Qari al-Baghdadi. *Manaqib,* p. 30; cf. al-Maqqari. *Nafh,* vol. 2, p. 382.

127. Escovitz. "The Establishment of Four Chief Judgeships;" Little. "Religion," p. 174; Irwin. *The Middle East,* p. 43; Bloom. " The Mosque of Baybars," pp. 61–63.

128. On the other hand, Addas thinks that Ibn ʿArabi was married to a woman from the Ibn Zaki family; see Addas. *Ibn ʿArabi,* p. 301. If so, then al-Qari must have confounded al-Zawawi with Ibn Zaki.

129. Al-Qari al-Baghdadi. *Manaqib,* pp. 41–42.

130. Al-Sakhawi. *Al-Dawʾ*, vol. 11, pp. 78–79; cf. Knysh. "Ibn ʿArabi in the Later Islamic Tradition," pp. 318–319; idem. "Ibn ʿArabi in the Yemen," pp. 50–51.

131. Al-Qari al-Baghdadi. *Manaqib,* pp. 68–70.

132. Ibid., pp. 76–82.

133. Austin. *Bezels,* p. 18.

134. See, e.g., Yahia. *La classification,* vol. p. 113.

Chapter 6

1. See Barthold. "Ulugbek i ego vremya," p. 59; Hodgson. *The Venture of Islam,* vol. 2, pp. 386–436.

2. Barthold. "Ulugbek i ego vremya" pp. 46–47 and 59.

3. Ibid. p. 47; Hodgson. *The Venture of Islam,* vol. 2, pp. 428–429; Manz. *The Rise and Rule,* p. 47.

4. See Barthold. ibid., p. 60; Hodgson. *The Venture of Islam,* vol. 2, pp. 430–435.

5. Barthold. "Ulugbek i ego vremya," pp. 45–46.

6. Translated from Arabic by Woods in Woods. "The Rise of Timurid Historiography," p. 82. On Ibn ʿArabshah see Pedersen, EI^2, vol. 3, pp. 711–712.

7. See, e.g., Molé. "Les Kubrawiyya," passim.

8. Barthold. "Ulugbek i ego vremya," passim; Fischel. *Ibn Khaldun and Tamerlane,* p. 47.

9. Van Ess. *Die Erkenntnislehre,* p. 7.

10. Barthold. "Ulegbek i ego vremya," p. 46; Ibn ʿArabshah, whose testimony has just been quoted, was one such honorable captive.

11. For the cultural and religious atmosphere of Timur's epoch, see Nagel. *Timur.*

12. Barthold. "Ulugbek i ego vremya," p. 60; Fischel. *Ibn Khaldun and Tamerlane,* p. 47.

13. Browne. *Literary History of Persia,* vol. 3, p. 353.

14. For alternative dates of his birth see ʿUmayra. "Muqaddimat al-muhaqqiq," pp. 75–76.

15. Al-Iji's theological views are discussed in van Ess. *Die Erkenntnislehre;* for a brief introduction to al-Iji's thought see Watt. *Islamic Philosophy,* p. 137.

16. Ibn al-ʿImad. *Shadharat,* vol. 6, p. 321.

17. See, e.g., al-Shawkani. *Al-Badr,* vol. 2, p. 303.

18. For a list of al-Taftazani's works see Storey. *Al-Taftazani*—EI, vol. 7, pp. 605–606; ʿUmayra. "Muqaddimat al-muhaqqiq," pp. 109–120.

19. See Storey. ibid., p. 605; ʿUmayra. ibid., p. 115.

20. Al-Jurjani, whose scholarly interests in many respects mirrored those of al-Taftazani, was the author of many popular manuals on *kalam,* rhetoric, *usul* and *furuʿ*, grammar, and technical terminology of Islamic sciences; see al-Sakhawi. *Al-Dawʾ*, vol. 5, p. 328; al-Shawkani. *Al-Badr,* vol. 1, p. 488; Tritton. *Al-Djurdjani*—EI², vol. 2, pp. 602–603. The episode in question may have been invented by al-Taftazani's biographers in order to dramatize the subsequent hostility between the two scholars.

21. Among the points of disagreement between the two scholars were such, from our perspective, insignificant issues as the authenticity of the *hadith* about love of the pussy cat, see Smith. "Al-Birrah," p. 134.

22. Ibn al-ʿImad. *Shadharat,* vol. 6, pp. 321–322; al-Shawkani. *Al-Badr,* vol. 2, pp. 304–305; van Ess. *Die Erkenntnislehre,* pp. 6–7.

23. Ibid., p. 7.

24. Ansari. "Taftazani's Views," p. 65.

25. Watt. *Islamic Philosophy,* pp. 136–138; Hodgson. *The Venture of Islam,* vol. 2, p. 472; Ansari. "Taftazani's Views," pp. 65–66; Madelung. *Maturidiyya*—EI², vol. 6, pp. 847–848.

26. Hodgson. *The Venture of Islam,* p. 472.

27. Ansari. "Taftazani's Views," p. 65.

28. Tritton. *Al-Djurdjani*—EI², vol. 2, p. 602.

29. For a scheme illustrating the filiation of the philosophical and theological trends that contributed to al-Taftazani's intellectual formation see van Ess. *Die Erkenntnislehre,* pp. 34 and 35; cf. Ansari. "Taftazani's Views," pp. 64–65.

30. For a list of his disciples see ʿUmayra. "Muqaddimat al-muhaqqiq," pp. 123–135.

31. I modified the translation of this passage in Elder. *A Commentary on the Creed of Islam,* p. XXI. Cf. Ibn Khaldun. *The Muqaddimah,* vol. 3, p. 117.

32. Elder. *A Commentary on the Creed of Islam,* p. XXI.

33. Hodgson. *The Venture of Islam,* vol. 2, p. 472.

34. See, e.g., Elder. *A Commentary on the Creed of Islam,* p. XX.

35. See, e.g., Lewinstein. "Notes," passim.

36. Watt. *Islamic Philosophy,* p. 313; Ansari. "Taftazani's Views," p. 65; Madelung. *Maturidiyya*—EI², vol. 6, pp. 847–848.

37. Ansari. "Taftazani's Views," passim.

38. Watt. *Islamic Philosophy,* p. 138; cf. Elder. *A Commentary on the Creed of Islam,* p. XX. Elder provided an annotated English translation of this seminal work.

39. Elder. *A Commentary on the Creed of Islam,* p. XXI; cf. Wolfson. *The Philosophy of the Kalam,* pp. 714–717. For a comparison between the two schools see Watt. *The Formative Period,* pp. 314–316.

40. See Story. *Al-Taftazani*—EI, vol.7, pp. 604–605.

41. See Chapter 3 of this study; and Nagel. "Ibn al-ʿArabi"; cf. Austin. *Bezels,* pp. 153–155 and 193.

42. Al-Taftazani. *Sharh al-maqasid,* vol. 1, p. 191.

43. On the concept of "states" or "modes" of divine existence that most Ashʿari *mutakallimun* identified with divine "attributes" see Frank. *Beings,* "index," under "hal."

44. At-Taftazani. *Sharh al-maqasid,* p. 188. For various definitions of *kalam* and its subject matter see Wolfson. *The Philosophy of the Kalam,* pp. 1–58; Ibrahim and Sagadeev. *Classical Islamic Philosophy,* pp. 17–21; and Watt. *The Formative Period,* passim.

45. Meaning humanity.

46. Al-Taftazani. *Sharh al-maqasid,* vol. 1, p. 190.

47. Bulliet. *Islam,* p. 111.

48. Elder. *A Commentary on the Creed of Islam,* p. XXIV. Al-Taftazani's discussion of Sufi "inspiration" bears close resemblance to the views of his teacher, al-Iji. For some striking parallels see van Ess. *Die Erkenntislehre,* pp. 121–123, cf. p. 162. Both al-Iji and his disciple concurred with the mainstream Ashʿari view that admitted the existence of inspired Sufi knowledge and Sufi miracles.

49. Al-Taftazani. *Risala fi wahdat al-wujud,* pp. 7, 8, and 30–33.

50. *Risala fi wahdat al-wujud* (henceforth *RWW*). This title was given to it by an anonymous Turkish editor in Istanbul (?). Al-Taftazani's text forms part of a longer collection of anti-Ibn ʿArabi treatises (pp. 1–47). Manuscripts of the *Risala* known to me bear different titles. The title of a Berlin manuscript (Ahlwardt, no. 2891) is "The Humiliation of the Heretics" (*Fadihat al-mulhidin*), which is considered "doubtful" by Storey (*Al-Taftazani*—EI, vol. 7, p. 606). A second manuscript in the Yahuda collection of Princeton University Library (Yahuda 276, fol. 1b-40a) is titled "The Refutation and Defamation of the *Fusus al-hikam*" (*al-Radd wa ʾl-tashniʿ ʿala Fusus al-hikam*). Manuscripts of al-Taftazani's works in Turkish collections listed by Yahia bear the title "The Refutation of the Lies of the *Fusus*" (*Radd abatil al-Fusus*); see *La classification,* vol. 1, p. 115. The original title of the work, mentioned by the author himself in the text of the treatise (see p. 10 of the printed edition, fol. 9a of the Yahuda manuscript), reads "The Humiliation of the Heretics and the Friendly Admonition of the Adherents of God's Unity" (*Fadihat al-mulhidin wa nasihat al-muwahhidin*)—i.e., exactly the one that Storey dismissed as "doubtful." I shall be using the title of the printed edition.

51. A Qurʾanic allusion; see Qurʾan 83:14.

52. Al-Taftazani. *RWW,* p. 2.

53. I.e., *al-Futuhat al-makkiyya,* "The Meccan Revelations."

54. Al-Taftazani, *RWW,* p. 6; idem. *Al-Radd,* fol. 5b; cf. Knysh. "Ibn ʿArabi in the Later Islamic Tradition," pp. 312–313.

55. An "extreme" Shiʿi sect, see Massignon. *Nusairi*—EI, vol. 6, pp. 963–967; idem. "Les Nusayris."

56. See al-Biqaʿi. *Tanbih* pp. 79–80. Al-Jurjani's position vis-à-vis the Greatest Master was ambiguous. In his celebrated dictionary of the technical terms of Islamic sciences, he made extensive use of Ibn ʿArabi's *Futuhat* as well as the work of his noted exponent, al-Qashani; see Flügel. *Definitiones.*

57. See Austin. *Bezels,* pp. 45–46.

58. Al-Taftazani. *RWW,* p. 6; idem. *Al-Radd* fol. 5b.

59. Cf. al-Taftazani's commentary on al-Nasafi's creed, where he categorically excluded any possibility for a saint (*wali*) to achieve the rank of the prophet. Moreover, unlike the prophets, whom al-Taftazani regarded as infallible, he viewed the saints as susceptible to error and thus accountable for their sins; see Elder. *A Commentary on the Creed of Islam,* pp. 157–158.

60. This objection jibes well with al-Taftazani's conviction that the texts of the holy writings should be interpreted "in accordance with their external meaning unless a decisive proof requires [an allegorical interpretation], as in case of the verses whose external meaning implies a specific direction [in which God is located] or [God's] corporeality." Those who assert that they

know the inner meaning of the Scripture, which is at odds with its literal interpretation, are, in al-Taftazani's view, rank heretics similar to the Shiʿi *batiniyya*. At the same time, al-Taftazani remained faithful to the Ashʿari view that there are "hidden allusions to fine points (*daqa'iq*)" which are accessible only to the perfected Sufis (*arbab al-suluk*); see Elder. *A Commentary on the Creed of Islam,* pp. 158–159.

61. Yet, unlike Sufi writers who squarely placed *ahl al-maʿrifa* above the *ʿulama'*, al-Taftazani implicitly treated them as inferior to the accomplished *mutakallimun*. It was the latter whom he described as "the verifiers"—ones whose understanding of religion rests on an irrefutable syllogistic reasoning. See Elder. *A Commentary on the Creed of Islam,* pp. 65, 68, 111, 118, etc.; cf. al-Biqaʿi. *Tanbih* p. 81.

62. Al-Taftazani. *RWW,* pp. 3 and 8–9 .

63. Ibid., p. 36.

64. Ibid., p. 7.

65. Cf. Böwering's observation that "Ibn ʿArabi's theory transformed the early Sufis' psychological experience of mystical union into an ontological speculation on the unity of being, propelling the idea of *tawhid* to a dynamic conclusion"; "Ibn al-ʿArabi's Concept of Time," p. 75.

66. Al-Taftazani, *RWW,* pp. 33–34.

67. See Knysh. *Fayd*—MIES, pp. 248–249.

68. For a superb account of al-Ghazali's attempt to reconcile the doctrine of emanation with the creationism of the mainstream Sunni dogma see Landolt. "Ghazali and "Religionswissenschaft,"" passim. Here Landolt argues that al-Ghazali was not an implacable opponent of neo-Platonic philosophy, as many Muslim writers and Western Islamicists still claim; cf. Makdisi. "The Non-Ashʿarite Shafiʿism," passim.

69. Al-Taftazani. *RWW,* pp. 9–10. For an analysis of the term *taʿayyun* in Ibn ʿArabi's metaphysics see Chittick. *The Sufi Path of Knowledge,* p. 83.

70. Al-Taftazani. *RWW,* pp. 10–11; cf. idem. Al-*Radd,* fol. 9b-10a.

71. Al-Taftazani. *RWW,* p. 10.

72. See, e.g., al-Taftazani. *RWW,* p. 12; idem. Al-*Radd,* fol. 11a.

73. Al-Taftazani. *RWW,* p. 12.

74. Ibid.

75. According to Chittick, this term literally signifies "to be or to become an entity" or "the state of being specified and particularized." While, as Chittick points out, in Ibn ʿArabi's own works the concept of *taʿayyun* "assumes no special importance," it is central to the works of the later

representatives of his school of thought, e.g., Sadr al-din al-Qunawi; see Chittick. *The Sufi Path of Knowledge,* p. 83.

76. Al-Taftazani. *RWW,* p. 12; cf. idem. Al-*Radd,* fol. 11a.

77. ʿAfifi. "Al-Aʿyan al-thabita," passim. For a discussion of the ways in which Ibn ʿArabi's teaching was interpreted by his later followers see Morris. "Interpreters"; cf. Knysh. "Irfan Revisited."

78. "If you wish to see this meaningless gibberish for yourself, read the interpretation of the *surat al-Fatiha* by al-Sadr al-Qunawi"; al-Taftazani. *RWW,* p. 13. On al-Qunawi's commentary on the first Qurʾanic chapter, which Chittick described as one of his "most important works," see Chittick. "The Last Will and Testament," pp. 48 and 55–56.

79. For definitions of *intelligibilia* (*maʿqulat*) in the *kalam* literature of the epoch see van Ess. *Die Erkenntnislehre,* "index" under "maʿqulat."

80. Al-Taftazani. *RWW,* p. 13, cf. idem., Al-*Radd,* fol. 11b.

81. Al-Taftazani referred to the so-called construct status (*idafa*) which is widely used in such Arabic phrases as, "Zayd's money" (*mal Zayd*), "Zayd of the horse" (*Zayd al-faras),* etc.

82. Al-Taftazani. *RWW,* p. 22.

83. Ibid., p. 20; idem. Al-*Radd,* fol. 12a.

84. Chittick. *The Sufi Path of Knowledge,* pp. 297–289. This conclusion is sometimes drawn from Ibn ʿArabi's notion of the immutable essences, which he shares with some Muʿtazili thinkers. For a detailed discussion of the intellectual background that determined al-Taftazani's rejection of this and related concepts see van Ess. *Die Erkenntislehre,* pp. 191–202; Nyberg. *Kleinere Schriften,* pp. 44–47.

85. Al-Taftazani. *RWW,* p. 14; idem. Al-*Radd,* fol. 12a-12b.

86. *RWW,* pp. 14–15.

87. Chittick. *The Sufi Path of Knowledge,* p. 289.

88. Al-Taftazani. *RWW,* p. 23.

89. Ibid., p. 24.

90. Ibid., pp. 38–47.

91. See, Prozorov. *Kniga,* passim; for a brief summary of the medieval Islamic concepts of heresy and heretics see Prozorov. "Pravoveriye," pp. 48–52; cf. Kraemer. "Heresy."

92. See Qur'an 4:61, 4:88, 4:138, 8:49, 9:64, etc.

93. On the Druse see Makarem. *The Druse Faith;* Rodionov and Polosin. *Rasa'il al-hikma.*

94. On the traditional Muslim conceptions of the people of the Book see Watt. *Muslim-Christian Encounters,* pp. 9–51.

95. "Time" is one of the epithets attributed to God in some *hadith,* which may have taken their origin in the veneration of time by pre-Islamic Arabs. For Ibn ʿArabi's conception of *dahr* see Chittick. *The Sufi Path of Knowledge,* p. 395, note 7 and Böwering. "Ibn Al-ʿArabi's Concept of Time," passim. Cf. Prozorov. *Kniga,* "index" under "dahriyya"; Böwering. "Ideas of Time," passim. In medieval Muslim theology, the espouser of *dahr* (*dahri*) is an individual who denies the existence of the Lord, his creation, reward and punishment, religious laws, and doctrines; he heeds only his own desires and sees evil only in what prevents him from gratifying them; he recognizes no difference between man, the domestic animal, and the wild beast; see Goldziher and Goichon. *Dahr*—EI², vol. 2, pp. 95–97. This definition tallies well with the "abominations" of the *wujudiyya* described by Ibn Taymiyya and al-Taftazani.

96. *Zandaqa* is usually treated alongside apostasy (*ridda*) by Muslim heresiologists who concurred that "an apostate who has secretly fallen away from Islam under the cloak of outward conformity . . . must be beheaded." The distinctive feature of the *zindiq* as opposed to the other miscreants is his concealment of his true beliefs: "there is thus no way to be certain of the truth of his statements, and especially of the sincerity of his repentance"; see Fierro. "Heresy in al-Andalus," p. 899. For special studies of *zandaqa* and *zindiqs* see Badawi. *Al-Ilhad,* pp. 27–40; Vajda. "Les zindiqs"; Gabrieli. "La zandaqa""; Kraemer. "Heresy"; Prozorov. "Pravoveriye," pp. 49–51.

97. Austin. *Bezels,* p. 249.

98. Ibid., p. 255.

99. According to the concordances of the Qur'an I have consulted, Pharaoh is mentioned in twenty-seven *suras;* see, e.g., Kassis. *Concordance,* pp. 431–432.

100. "Why then was there no town which believed, and its belief profited it except the people of Jonah? When they believed, We lifted away from them the punishment of humiliation in this present life and gave them enjoyment of life for a season"; see Qur'an 10:98; cf. Austin. *Bezels,* pp. 264–26; al-Taftazani. *RWW,* p. 40.

101. Al-Taftazani. *RWW,* pp. 39–42.

102. Austin. *Bezels,* p. 265.

103. Ibid., p. 250.

104. "I believe in what the Children of Israel believe in," Qur'an, 10:90.

105. Al-Taftazani. *RWW,* pp. 41–42. Ibn ʿArabi foresaw this objection and took pains to respond to it; see Austin. *Bezels,* p. 265. Elsewhere, however, he

admitted that Pharaoh's profession of faith was indeed a blind imitation. Ibid., pp. 194–195.

106. Al-Taftazani. *RWW,* pp. 41–46.

107. Ibid., pp. 46–47.

108. Ibid., p. 13.

109. See, e.g., Knysh. "Ibrahim al-Kurani," p. 39. Among the other Sufi authorities cited by al-Taftazani are Jalal al-din Rumi (d. 672/1273) and the Hanbali mystic al-Ansari (d. 481/1089), *RWW,* pp. 8 and 37.

110. See, e.g., al-Taftazani. *RWW,* p. 38.

111. The oft-mentioned reference to the theme of the bricks in the "wall of prophecy" can hardly be classified as a direct quotation, especially since it was misinterpreted by al-Taftazani, betraying his remarkable ignorance of its real place within the context of Ibn ʿArabi's teaching; see *RWW,* p. 7.

112. A typical example is Ibn ʿArabi's idea that idolaters worship no one but God. Al-Taftazani could have borrowed it from Ibn ʿArabi's interpretation of the *surat Nuh* (Qur'an 71; Austin. *Bezels,* pp. 71–81), although it is featured in the other writings of the Greatest Master; see Chittick. *The Sufi Path of Knowledge,* pp. 356–381.

113. See Chapter 8 of this study.

114. On al-Dawani's contribution to Muslim speculative sciences and political theory see Lambton. *Al-Dawani*—EI², vol. 2, p. 174; Rosenthal. *Political Thought,* pp. 210–223; Hodgson. *The Venture of Islam,* vol. 2, pp. 472–473; Watt. *Islamic Philosophy,* p. 139.

115. See Al-Dawani. *Iman Firʿawn,* pp. 11 and 23, where the author accuses Ibn ʿArabi's detractors of unbelief. From the titles of al-Dawani's unpublished works one may surmise that he supported Ibn ʿArabi on other issues also; see Brockelmann. *Geschichte,* vol. 2, p. 282.

116. He wrote three long treatises against Ibn ʿArabi; see Yahia. *La classification,* vol. 1, pp. 116–117; cf. Schacht. *Al-Halabi*—EI², vol. 3, p. 90.

117. Born in Herat, Mulla ʿAli al-Qari spent most of his life in Mecca, where he was buried. He was a prolific writer who, throughout his life, attacked the Shafiʿi and Maliki schools of law, thereby incurring the wrath of their adherents; see Brockelmann. *Geschichte,* vol. 2, pp. 394–398; idem., *Supplement,* vol. 2, pp. 539–543; al-Muhibbi. *Khulasat al-athar,* vol. 3, pp. 185–186; al-Shawkani. *Al-Badr,* vol. 1, pp. 445–446; al-Zirikli. *Al-Aʿlam,* vol. 5, pp. 12–13; for a more benign aspect of his work see Smith. "Al-Birrah."

118. For a list of al-Qari's refutations of the Greatest Master see Yahia. *La classification,* vol. 1, p. 117. Two of them were published in *Majmuʿat al-rasa'il,* pp. 52–114 and 116–123; cf. al-Dawani. *Iman Firʿawn,* pp. 25–85.

119. Yahia. *La classification,* vol. 1, pp. 116–117.

120. See Knysh. "Ibrahim al-Kurani."

121. Manuscripts of al-Kurani's works can be found in the Yahuda Collection of Princeton University, N.J., under nos. 3869, 3114, 4440, 5656, etc. To date, none of them has been published, which is also true of the numerous works by his opponents; see Yahia. *La classification,* vol. 1, p. 117.

122. Ibid., vol. 1, pp. 116–117, and 120–121; al-Nabhani. *Jamiʿ karamat,* vol. 1, pp. 118–125.

123. E.g., "The Manifest Victory in the Refutation of the Objections Raised by the Opponent of Muhyi al-din" (*Al-Fath al-mubin fi radd iʿtirad al-muʿtarid ʿala Muhyi al-din*). On this work, published in Egypt in 1304 A.H., see Brockelmann. *Supplement,* vol. 1, p. 802. Al-ʿAttar was also the author of several commentaries on the *Fusus* and editor of a collection of mystical litanies attributed to Ibn ʿArabi; see Kahhala. *Muʿjam,* vol. 7, pp. 286–287.

124. See, e.g., al-Taftazani. *RWW,* p. 33.

Chapter 7

1. See, e.g., Zarruq. *Qawaʿid,* pp. 14, 35, 41, 52, and 129; Ibn al-Qadi. *Jadhwat al-iqtibas,* p. 282; Istrabadi. *The Principles of Sufism,* pp. 17 and 35; Chodkiewicz. *An Ocean Without Shore,* pp. 6–12.

2. For al-Shaʿrani's abridgments of the *Futuhat,* see Chodkiewicz. *An Ocean Without Shore,* p. 10; cf. Knysh. *Ash-Shaʿrani*—IES, pp. 291–292.

3. Chodkiewicz. "The Diffusion," pp. 44–45; cf. idem. *An Ocean Without Shore,* pp. 4–5.

4. See Lévi-Provençal. *Histoire de l'Espagne Musulmane,* vol. 3, pp. 454–488.

5. Chodkiewicz. "The Diffusion," pp. 38–39; idem. *An Ocean Without Shore,* pp. 6–16. For the history of Sufism in al-Andalus and North Africa see the works of Asin Palacios and Nwyia. For more recent accounts see Cornell. "Mirrors of Prophethood" (North Africa); Addas. "Andalusi Mysticism" (al-Andalus); Austin. *Sufis;* Urvoy. *Penseurs;* idem. *Le monde.*

6. A typical view of Ibn ʿArabi in the Maghribi scholarly milieu is outlined by the famous *faqih* and litterateur Ibn al-Qadi (d. 1025/1616); on him see Lévi-Provençal. *Les Historiens des Chorfa,* pp. 77, 90, 100–112, and 247–250. Citing a number of authoritative North African scholars, Ibn al-Qadi argues that although Ibn ʿArabi's statements are often ambiguous, one should refrain from condemning him as an unbeliever. He suggests that his

colleagues suspend judgment regarding Ibn ʿArabi's orthodoxy and think well of his intentions (*taslim*). Ibn al-Qadi suggests the same circumspect approach with regard to other controversial Sufi masters, e.g., Ibn al-Farid, al-Shushtari, Ibn Ahla, Ibn Sabʿin, al-Harrali, and al-Tilimsani; see Ibn al-Qadi. *Jadhwat al-iqtibas,* vol. 2, p. 282.

7. Massignon. "Ibn Sabʿin," p. 664; cf. Addas. *Ibn ʿArabi,* p. 176.

8. See the opinions of Ibn al-Abbar and al-Ghubrini discussed in Chapter 2 of this study.

9. Al-Dhahabi. *Al-ʿIbar,* vol. 4, pp. 19–20; Ibn al-ʿImad. *Shadharat,* vol. 6, p. 16; Pellat. *Ibn al-Zubayr*—EI², vol. 3, p. 976. Ibn al-Zubayr distinguished himself as a staunch opponent of charismatic individuals of Sufi inspiration, who instigated persecutions against two influential Sufi "magicians," first in Malaga, then in Granada.

10. This work is no longer extant. According to Pellat, the first word of the title should be *radd*—i.e, "repulsion," see Pellat. *Ibn al-Zubayr*—EI², vol. 3, p. 976. For Ibn al-Zubayr's active role in the Western scholarly campaign against the monistic "heresy" see Kattoura. *Mystische und Philosophische System,* pp. 15 and 20.

11. Named after Abu ʿAbdallah al-Shudhi (d. ca 600/1203), an Ashʿari *mutakallim* and mystic, who held the post of *qadi* in Seville. His teachings were proclaimed heretical by some scholars of Seville, causing him to emigrate to North Africa. He settled in Tlemsen, where he earned his living selling sweetmeats. In Tlemsen he continued to preach his ideas, occasionally posing as a madman, possibly out of fear of further prosecutions; see *Rawdat al-taʿrif,* p. 604, note 1422; Ibn Sabʿin. *Budd al-ʿarif,* pp. 17–22. Ibn al-Zubayr, Qutb al-din al-Qastallani (d. 686/1287) and other authors credited al-Shudhi with the introduction of the doctrine of absolute unity into Western Islam; see, e.g., Rosenthal. *A History,* p. 585. Al-Shudhi's ideas were later propagated by Ibn Dahhaq (Ibn al-Marʾa), Ibn Ahla, and Ibn Sabʿin, all of whom viewed themselves as his disciples; see Massignon. *The Passion,* vol. 2, pp. 308–330; Kattoura. *Mystische und Philosophische System,* pp. 7–11.

12. See, Massignon. "Ibn Sabʿin," pp. 664–665.

13. Kattoura. *Die Mystische und Philosophische System,* p. 15.

14. The Andalusi scholar al-Fakhkhar (d. 723/1323) names al-Saffar among the three greatest Andalusi "heresiarchs"; see Fierro. "Heresy," p. 895; cf. Massignon. "Ibn Sabʿin," p. 665. Ibn al-Zubayr and Abu Hayyan considered al-Saffar to be a follower of the famous monistic thinker Ibn Ahla. Pellat, however, describes al-Saffar as an ordinary magician, see Pellat. *Ibn al-Zubayr*—EI², vol. 3, p. 976. In another account, al-Saffar was stoned to death on the orders of the Nasrid sultan ʿAbdallah Ibn al-Ahmar; see Kattoura. *Mystische und Philosophische System,* pp. 19–20; *apud* al-Sakhawi's *al-Qawl al-munbi,* p. 94a.

15. Abu Hayyan's other teacher was Qutb al-din (Ibn) al-Qastallani (d. 686/1287), whose polemical obituary of the Greatest Master was discussed in Chapter 2 of this study.

16. Ibn Kathir. *Al-Bidaya,* vol. 14, p. 224; al-Dhahabi. *Al-ʿIbar,* vol. 4, p. 134; Ibn al-ʿImad. *Shadharat,* vol. 6, pp. 145–147; Glazer. *Abu Hayyan*—EI[2], vol. 1, p. 126. Abu Hayyan seems to have had the same pugnacious temper as his teacher, with whom he soon ran afoul. Ostracized by his Andalusi contemporaries, he fled to the East, where he was soon embroiled in a heated debated with Ibn Taymiyya over the credibility of the celebrated Arab linguist Sibawayh. Characteristically, Ibn al-ʿImad describes Abu Hayyan as a staunch supporter of Sunni Islam who was tireless in stamping out the "innovations" of the Muslim philosophers and of other "heretics."

17. Muhammad b. ʿAli Ibn Ahla (d. 645/1247), a native of Murcia and famous *mutakallim,* who is credited with adhering to an unspecified monistic doctrine. Following in the steps of the Sufi rebel Ibn Qasi, he instituted a semiclandestine movement at Lorca, combining promises of spiritual guidance with claims to political leadership. A disciple of Ibn al-Marʾa and a presumed teacher of Ibn Sabʿin, Ibn Ahla is usually counted by Muslim heresiographers among the "people of oneness" (*ahl al-wahda*), although he may also have entertained the Ismaʿili (*batini*) belief in the impending advent of the messianic world-restorer, which prompted him to make a bid for power in Lorca. As with Ibn Qasi, he was soon deposed and fled to Murcia where he died two years after the capture of the city by the Christians, see Ibn Sabʿin. *Budd al-ʿarif,* pp. 20–21; Kattoura. *Die Mystische und Philosophische System,* pp. 14–22; cf. Massignon. "Ibn Sabʿin," pp. 669–670; Fierro. "Heresy," p. 895.

18. On them see the next section; cf. Massignon. "Ibn Sabʿin," pp. 665–666; al-Biqaʿi. *Tanbih al-ghabi,* pp. 156–157.

19. Abu Hayyan. *Al-Nahr al-madd,* vol. 1, p. 564; cf. al-Biqaʿi. *Tanbih al-ghabi,* pp. 156–157.

20. In the earlier period, Maliki critics of Sufism in the Muslim West usually focused on its practical "excesses," especially the popular infatuation with miracles, encouraged by some Sufi leaders. At any rate, unlike later scholars, such early critics were much less concerned with mystical doctrines, although some seem to have rejected Sufism altogether; see, e.g., Fierro. "The Polemic"; Nwyia. *Ibn ʿAbbad,* pp. XXXII-XXXV.

21. His condemnatory "biography" of Ibn ʿArabi was mentioned in Chapter 2 of this study. His life and work are described in al-Dhahabi. *Al-ʿIbar,* vol. 3, pp. 362–363; Ibn Kathir. *Al-Bidaya,* vol. 13, p. 328; al-Safadi. *Al-Wafi,* vol. 2, pp. 132–135; al-Kutubi. *Fawat,* vol. 2, pp. 310–312; al-Yafiʿi. *Mirʾat,* vol. 4, p. 202; Ibn al-ʿImad. *Shadharat,* vol. 5, p. 397; al-Shaʿrani. *Tabaqat,* vol. 5, p. 137; Brockelmann. *Geschichte,* vol. 1, p. 451; idem. *Supplement,* vol. 1, p. 809; for his role in the antimonistic polemic see Kattoura. *Mystische und Philosophische System,* pp. 18–22; and Homerin. *From Arab Poet,* pp. 30–31.

22. Al-Safadi. *Al-Wafi,* vol. 2, pp. 132–135; al-Fasi. *Al-ʿIqd,* vol. 2, p. 186; al-Biqaʿi. *Tanbih al-ghabi,* p. 153; Ibn al-ʿImad. *Shadharat,* vol. 5, p. 397; Yahia. *La classification,* vol. 1, p. 114; Massignon. "Ibn Sabʿin," pp. 662–664; idem. *The Passion,* vol. 2, pp. 34, 64, and 309–315; Addas. *Ibn ʿArabi,* pp. 175–176. A fragment of al-Qastallani's unpublished polemical treatise is quoted by Abu Hayyan; see Rosenthal. *A History,* pp. 584–586.

23. Addas. *Ibn ʿArabi,* pp. 175–176.

24. Ibn Taymiyya quotes al-Qastallani's treatise on several instances; see Ibn Taymiyya. *MRM* (new edition), vol. 1, p. 91; vol. 4, p. 84; cf. Kattoura. *Mystische und Philosophische System,* pp. 21–22.

25. Chodkiewicz. "The Diffusion"; idem. *An Ocean Without Shore,* pp. 4–16.

26. See Lomax. *The Reconquest,* pp. 160–172.

27. Watt. *A History,* p. 136.

28. See Talbi. *Ibn Khaldun*—EI², vol. 3, p. 826; Ibn al-Khatib. *Rawdat al-taʿrif,* p. 18; for a firsthand account to the meetings between two scholars see Ibn Khaldun. *The Muqaddimah,* vol. 3, p. 396 and vol. 1, pp. XLIV-XLV.

29. All three started their careers at royal chanceries. For a general account of the religious life in the Maghrib and al-Andalus in that epoch see Nwyia. *Ibn ʿAbbad,* pp. IX-LX; see Jayyusi. *The Legacy,* passim; cf. Ibn al-Khatib. *Al-Ihata.*

30. For his laudatory biography with long extracts from his poetry and prose see Ibn al-Khatib. *Al-Ihata,* vol. 1, pp. 239–259; and idem. *Al-Katiba,* pp. 239–245.

31. Gibert. *Ibn al-Khatima*—EI², vol. 3, p. 837. Almeria was an important center of Andalusi Sufism and home to such outstanding mystics as Ibn al-ʿArif (d. 536/1141) and Muhammad al-Ghazzal; see Asin Palacios. *The Mystical Philosophy,* pp. 120–123; see also "Introduction" to *Diwan Ibn Khatima* by Muhammad Ridwan al-Daya, in Ibn Khatima. *Diwan,* pp. 7–8. According to Asin Palacios, Almerian Sufis adhered to the esoteric tradition of Ibn Masarra (d. 319/931), whom he portrayed—wrongly it seems—as "a follower of pseudo-Empedocles," see Stern. "Ibn Masarra"; Addas. *Ibn ʿArabi,* pp. 73–75 and 79–80; Cornell. "Mirrors of Prophethood," pp. 171–173 and 180–181.

32. See Ibn ʿArabi. *Futuhat,* vol. 1, p. 334.

33. In his *Nafh al-tib,* al-Maqqari provides long excerpts from the correspondence between Ibn Khatima and Ibn al-Khatib following the vizier's forced flight from al-Andalus in 773/1371–2; see *Nafh,* vol. 8, pp. 174–184; (ed.) Ihsan ʿAbbas, vol. 6, pp. 28–38; Ibn Khatima was an instructor to Ibn al-Khatib's son ʿAli; see Ibn Khatima. *Diwan,* pp. 10–11.

34. Al-Maqqari. *Azhar,* vol. 3, p. 54. It appears that the first part of Ibn Khatima's notice was a verbatim quotation from the earlier biography of the Sufi master by Ibn al-Abbar (see Chapter 2 of this study). As Ibn al-Abbar, Ibn Khatima seems to have been aware only of those Ibn ʿArabi's works that were written in the West. At least he did not mention Ibn ʿArabi's controversial masterpieces, the *Fusus* and the *Futuhat,* which were written in the East. As with Ibn al-Abbar, this indicates Ibn al-Khatima's lack of awareness of Ibn ʿArabi's notoriety following his departure to the East.

35. On the role of symbol in the Sufi tradition see Knysh. *Ramz*—EI^2, vol. 8, pp. 428–430.

36. In contrast to a normal metaphor with a paired subject.

37. Al-Maqqari. *Azhar,* vol. 3, pp. 54–55; for a shorter version of the same account that omits (intentionally?) Ibn Khatima's criticism see al-Maqqari. *Nafh,* vol. 2, p. 378; cf. Ibn Khatima. *Diwan,* p. 11.

38. See an analysis of his literary style and poetical imagery in Ibn Khatima. *Diwan,* pp. 19–22.

39. This section is based in part on my contribution "Ibn al-Khatib" for *Cambridge History of Arabic Literature: The Literature of al-Andalus,* forthcoming.

40. Al-Maqqari. *Nafh* (ed. Ihsan ʿAbbas), vol. 5, pp. 189–251 and 350–603.

41. Ibn al-Khatib. *Al-Ihata,* vol. 1, p. 22 and vol. 2, pp. 17–18.

42. Ibid., vol. 1, pp. 23–24.

43. Ibn al-Khatib. *Ta'rikh al-Maghrib,* p. "lam."

44. Idem. *Al-Ihata,* vol. 1, pp. 25–27.

45. Idem. *Ta'rikh al-Maghrib,* pp. "lam" and "mim"; Arié. *L'Espagne,* p. 440.

46. Ibid., p. 441; Ibn al-Khatib. *Al-Ihata,* vol. 1, p. 30.

47. For these individuals see Arié. *L'Espagne,* "index."

48. Al-Maqqari. *Nafh,* (ed. Ihsan ʿAbbas), vol. 5, pp. 118–122.

49. Bencheneb. "Mémoires," p. 77.

50. Ibn al-Khatib. *Al-Ihata,* vol. 1, pp. 33–36.

51. Idem. *Al-Katiba,* pp. 146–153; cf., however, idem. *Al-Ihata,* vol. 1, pp. 40–41, which contains a laudatory biography of al-Nubahi.

52. Al-Maqqari. *Nafh* (ed. Ihsan ʿAbbas), vol. 5, pp. 110–111.

53. A pun based on the ambiguity of the word *ʿizam,* which means both "nobility" and "bones."

54. Ibn al-Khatib. *Diwan,* vol. 1, p. 185; cf. al-Maqqari. *Nafh* (ed. Ihsan ʿAbbas), vol. 5, pp. 111–112.

55. Ibn al-Khatib took a sympathetic approach to Sufism, which he shared with many great *ʿulamaʾ* of the Marinid epoch, who, in Nwyia's phrase, "regarded their education as incomplete, if they had not attended the classes offered by a Sufi shaykh." In general, many Maghribi and Andalusi jurists of the age supported al-Ghazali's intention to marry exoteric religion (*ʿilm al-zahir*) with the scrupulous moral discipline and mystical gnosis of the Sufis (*ʿilm al-batin*); see Nwyia. *Ibn ʿAbbad,* pp. XLII-XLIII; Mahdi. "The Book and the Master," passim; de Santiago Simon. "¿Ibn al-Jatib, mistico?"

56. Giffen translates this Arabic title as "The Anthology of Ardent Love"; see Giffen. *Theory of Profane Love,* p. 38.

57. Bell. *Love Theory,* p. 182. Born in Tlemsen of the family of a famous Maghribi holy man, Ibn Abi Hajala grew up in Damascus, which was his home for the greater part of his life. Later, he moved to Cairo, where he became head of a Sufi monastery; Ibn Hajar. *Inbaʾ*, vol. 1, pp. 81–82; see also Robson and Rizzitano. *Ibn Abi Hadjala*—EI^2, vol. 3, p. 686; Rizzitano. "Il Diwan"; and Giffen. *Theory of Profane Love,* pp. 38–39.

58. Ibn al-Khatib. *Rawdat al-taʿrif,* p. 38; al-Maqqari. *Nafh* (ed. Ihsan ʿAbbas), vol. 7, p. 100; cf. Ibn Khaldun. *The Muqaddimah,* vol. 3, pp. 98–99.

59. According to Ibn al-ʿImad, Ibn Abi Hajala used to tell the Shafiʿis that he was a follower of their rite, while to the Hanafis he presented himself as a Hanafi. On certain issues he adhered to the position advocated by the Hanbalis; see Ibn al-ʿImad. *Shadharat,* vol. 6, pp. 241–242.

60. *Kana kathir al-hatt ʿala ʾl-ittihadiyya,* Ibn Hajar. *Inbaʾ*, vol. 1, p. 81.

61. Homerin. *From Arab Poet,* p. 58.

62. Al-Biqaʿi. *Tahdhir al-ʿibad,* pp. 215–216; Ibn Hajar. *Inbaʾ*, vol. 1, p. 81. Ibn al-ʿImad. *Shadharat,* vol. 6, p. 241. Among the other Sufis condemned by Ibn Abi Hajala were Ibn ʿArabi, Ibn Sabʿin, al-Qunawi, al-Tilimsani, al-Shushtari, Hasan Ibn Hud, al-Hariri, and Ibn Ahla. Aside from his principal target, Ibn al-Farid, Ibn Abi Hajala seems to have been particularly ill-disposed to Ibn Sabʿin, whom he sought to discredit by circulating anecdotes harmful to his reputation; see al-Maqqari. *Nafh* vol. 2, pp. 403–404.

63. Massignon. "Ibn Sabʿin," p. 668; de Santiago Simon. "¿Ibn al-Jatib, mistico?"

64. Ibn al-Khatib. *Rawdat al-taʿrif,* p. 38. Neither topic is new in Islamic theological literature. Ibn Abi Hajala's work was preceded, e.g., by Ibn al-Jawzi's "Censure of Passion" (*Dhamm al-hawaʾ*), which recounts anecdotes

aimed at demonstrating the darker side of carnal desire. Love of God, along with its profane counterpart, are the subject matter of the works of Ibn Taymiyya's noted disciple, Ibn Qayyim al-Jawziyya (d. 751/1350), analyzed in Bell. *Love Theory,* pp. 92–181.

65. For uses of tree symbolism in Ibn Khatib's work see Knysh. "Ibn al-Khatib," in *Cambridge History of Arabic Literature.* L. Giffen, who seems to have had no direct knowledge of Ibn al-Khatib's work, bluntly dismissed it as "illogical" and "confusing" (see *Theory of Profane Love,* p. 40)—an assessment that I do not share.

66. I.e., standard accusations that Muslim *ʿulamaʾ* leveled at the *falasifa;* see Arnaldez. *Falsafa*—EI², vol. 2, pp. 769–775; cf. Leaman. *An Introduction,* passim.

67. For some parallels between Ibn al-Khatib's concept of love of God and the teaching of the great Catalan thinker Ramon Lull, see Lull. *Blanquerna,* pp. 409–468. For possible Sufi influences on Lull see Bonner. *Selected Works,* vol. 2, pp. 1217–1222.

68. Massignon, who had at his disposal an unpublished manuscript of the *Rawdat al-taʿrif,* reads *muntammin;* see Massignon. "Ibn Sabʿin," p. 668.

69. *Rawdat al-taʿrif* seems to be Ibn al-Khatib's only work that deals specifically with Sufi motifs, giving us an insight into yet another dimension of his well-rounded personality; see "Introduction" to the *Rawdat al-taʿrif,* pp. 48–49; cf. de Santiago Simon. "¿Ibn al-Jatib, mistico?" passim.

70. See a list of Ibn al-Khatib's sources by Muhammad al-Kattani, editor of the *Rawdat al-taʿrif,* pp. 46–47.

71. This fact alone indicates that Ibn al-Khatib was much better conversant with Ibn ʿArabi's work than his friend and colleague Ibn Khatima. Although the editor of the *Rawdat al-taʿrif* attempted to identify the sources used by Ibn al-Khatib, he sometimes neglected indirect references to, and quotations from, Ibn ʿArabi's writings; see, e.g., *Rawdat al-taʿrif,* pp. 584 and 595.

72. de Santiago Simon. "¿Ibn al-Jatib, mistico?" p. 228.

73. Ibn al-Khatib. *Rawdat al-taʿrif,* pp. 50–52.

74. For Ibn ʿArabi concept of love see Chittick. *The Sufi Path of Knowledge,* "index" under "love" and "lover," p. 460; cf. Knysh. *Mekkanskiye otkroveniya,* pp. 30–33 and 176–211.

75. Ibn al-Khatib. *Rawdat al-taʿrif,* p. 54.

76. Ibid., pp. 54–59.

77. Ibid, pp. 494, 498–499, 507, and 532.

78. Ibid., pp. 157, 309, 404, 427, 462, 500, etc.

79. Chodkiewicz. *An Ocean Without Shore,* pp. 1–18.

80. For this term see, e.g., Cornell. "Mirrors of Prophethood," pp. 160, 371–372, passim. As the present study shows, the borderline between the "Sharʿi" and "heterodox" Sufism can be extremely fine.

81. The founder of the influential Rifaʿiyya Sufi brotherhood, see al-Shaʿrani. *Tabaqat,* vol. 1, pp. 161–165; Trimingham. *Sufi Orders,* pp. 37–40 and "index."

82. On this Hanbali mystic and preacher of Baghdad see Braune. *Die Futuh al-gaib;* and Chabbi. *ʿAbd al-Qadir al-Jilani.*

83. On this Maghribi saint see al-Shaʿrani. *Tabaqat,* vol. 1, pp. 133–135; and Knysh. *Abu Madyan*—IED, pp. 9–10. A detailed account of his life and work is given in Cornell. "Mirrors of Prophethood," pp. 313–354. A hagiographical portrait of Abu Madyan and his North African disciples was provided by the Maghribi scholar Ibn Qunfudh (d. 810/1408) in his *Uns al-faqir.*

84. This seems to have eluded Massignon, who believed that Ibn al-Khatib included in this category only the classical Sufis of the 4th/10th and 5th/11th centuries. For the history and teachings of the Shadhili mystical order see Nwyia. *Ibn ʿAtaʾ Allah;* idem. *Ibn ʿAbbad;* Danner. *The Book of Wisdom;* Cornell. "Mirrors of Prophethood," pp. 418–474.

85. *Rawdat al-taʿrif,* pp. 620–631.

86. See Chittick. "Wahdat al-wujud," pp. 14–15; idem. "Rumi and *wahdat al-wujud,*" pp. 79–81; idem. "Spectrums."

87. See Chapter 2 note 5 of this study.

88. A noted Andalusi mystic who had a large following among the population of Almeria and its environs. His popularity irritated the local religious authorities, who reported his activities to the Almoravid ruler. Accused of fomenting a revolt against the Almoravid state, Ibn al-ʿArif was summoned to the Almoravid capital in Marrakesh, where he died under obscure circumstances; see Ibn al-Zayyat. *Al-Tashawwuf,* no. 18; Ibn Bashkuwal. *Kitab al-sila,* no. 175. Ibn al-ʿArif's religious and political ideas have been recently reassessed by Cornell, who showed Ibn al-ʿArif to be a typical "Sharʿi Sufi" with little or no interest in mystical philosophy; see Cornell. "Mirrors of Prophethood," pp. 173–202. Cornell's conclusion, however, appears to be at odds with Ibn al-Khatib's view, which associated this Sufi master with the religiously suspect "philosophy of [divine] manifestation." Ibn ʿArabi held Ibn al-ʿArif in high esteem and often mentioned him in his works; see Chittick. *The Sufi Path of Knowledge,* pp. 398–399, note 5; cf. Halff. "Mahasin"; and Urvoy. "Les thèmes," pp. 99–100; Nwyia. "Note"; Addas. "Andalusi Mysticism," pp. 920–924.

89. A popular Andalusi mystic, who gained prominence on the eve of the final dissipation of the Almoravid state. Like Ibn al-ʿArif, Ibn Barrajan was

accused of conspiring to overthrow the Almoravids, summoned to the Almoravid capital, and died in prison; see Ibn al-Zayyat. *Al-Tashawwuf,* pp. 169–170; al-Munawi. *Al-Kawakib,* p. 91; Faure. *Ibn Barradjan*—EI², vol. 3, p. 732; Cornell. "Mirrors of Prophethood," pp. 177–178. Ibn ʿArabi knew his works well and quoted them in his writings; see Chittick. *The Sufi Path of Knowledge,* p. 398, notes 15 and 16; Ibn ʿArabi. *Fusus,* pp. 255–256. On the relationship between Ibn al-ʿArif and Ibn Barrajan see Nwyia. "Note," and idem. "Rasaʾil." For a reevaluation of the roles of Ibn al-ʿArif, Ibn Barrajan, and Ibn Qasi in the history of Andalusi mysticism see Addas. "Andalusi Mysticism," pp. 921–926.

90. A renowned Sufi master, who after a period of intense training, proclaimed himself the *mahdi* of the age and led a Sufi rebellion in the Algarve (*gharb al-Andalus,* present-day Portugal). Ibn Qasi's spectacular political achievements (for a short time he carved out for himself an independent state) and mystical doctrines that justified his messianic claims by using the Sufi notion of supreme sainthood had a strong impact on Ibn ʿArabi. Ibn Qasi's esoteric views have been examined in Goodrich. "A 'Sufi' Revolt;" Lagardère. "La tarîqa"; Dreher. *Das Imamat.* Ibn ʿArabi wrote a commentary on Ibn Qasi's only extant work "The Removal of the Sandals" (*Khalʿ al-naʿlayn*); see Addas. *Ibn ʿArabi,* pp. 77–78.

91. A famous occultist and fortune-teller with Sufi connection, whose predictions in poetry and prose gained wide popularity throughout the Muslim world; see Ibn Khaldun. *The Muqaddimah,* vol. 3, p. 172, note 807; idem. *Shifaʾ* pp. 51–54; Dietrich. *Al-Buni*—EI², "Supplement," pp. 156–157; Ullmann. *Die Natur- und Geheimwissenschaften,* pp. 234 and 390.

92. *Rawdat al-taʿrif,* p. 584. Traditions of this type, known as *hadith qudsi*, are ascribed directly to God, and thus can be viewed as a sort of Muslim apocrypha; see Graham. *Divine and Prophetic Word.* The "Hidden Treasure" *hadith* was widely cited by Sufis in support of their cosmological speculations. It has many variants, one of which is quoted by Ibn al-Khatib: "I [God] was a hidden treasure and I loved to be known. Therefore I created creatures so that they might know Me." For Ibn ʿArabi's use of this *hadith,* see Chittick. *The Sufi Path of Knowledge,* p. 391, notes 14 and 17; cf. Ibn Khaldun. *The Muqaddimah,* vol. 3, p. 88, note 495.

93. This cosmological conception receives its classical formulation in Chapter 1 of the *Fusus;* see Austin. *Bezels,* pp. 50–57.

94. *Rawdat al-taʿrif,* pp. 555–564. Ibn al-Khatib discusses the teachings of the *falasifa* in a special chapter of his work.

95. E.g., *al-ahadiyya, al-wahidiyya, al-hadra al-ʿamaʾiyya, hadrat al-habaʾ, al-barzakh, tajalli, al-nafas al-rahmani, al-taʿayyun al-habaʾi, al-ʿunsur al-aʿzam, haqiqat al-haqaʾiq,* etc. For these terms see al-Hakim. *Al-Muʿjam,* and Chittick. *The Sufi Path of Knowledge,* "index."

96. Ibn al-Khatib. *Rawdat al-ta'rif,* pp. 585–598. Ibn al-Khatib's treatment of the oneness of being as opposed to the manyness of knowledge (ibid., p. 597) suggests his intimate familiarity with the works of al-Farghani, the foremost disciple of Sadr al-din al-Qunawi; see Chittick. "Spectrums," passim; idem., "Rumi and *wahdat al-wujud,* pp. 80–81.

97. Syrier. "Ibn Khaldun and Islamic Mysticism," p. 290.

98. This is the principle theme of Ibn 'Arabi's *Fusus;* see, e.g. Austin. *Bezels,* p. 18; cf. Ibn 'Arabi. *'Anqa' mughrib*, passim.

99. *Rawdat al-ta'rif,* pp. 597–598.

100. Ibid., pp. 555–564.

101. Ibid., pp. 602–603.

102. See note 11 of this chapter.

103. Ibrahim Ibn Yusuf Ibn Dahhaq (Dihaq), better known as Ibn al-Mar'a, was a renowned Ash'ari theologian and philosopher who studied with al-Shudhi and propagated the latter's teachings among his contemporaries. During his stay in Malaga, he was charged with heresy by the *qadi* Ibn al-Murabit and forced to leave for Murcia, where he spent the rest of his life; see Ibn al-Khatib. *Al-Ihata,* vol. 1, pp. 325–326; Ibn al-Qadi. *Jadhwat al-iqtibas,* pp. 87 and 406; Ibn Sab'in. *Budd al-'arif,* pp. 18–22; Massignon. "Ibn Sab'in," p. 669. Rosenthal. *A History,* pp. 585–586. Ibn Mar'a wrote extensively on the nature of divine names and refuted Ibn Masarra's thesis that the plurality of divine attributes should be seen as real. For him, the plurality of the empirical world was but an illusion. In his translation of Ibn Khaldun's *Muqaddima,* Rosenthal neglects the fact that Ibn Mar'a and Ibn Dahhaq are the same individual; see Ibn Khaldun. *The Muqaddimah,* vol. 3, pp. 90–91 and note 500. In most later accounts Ibn al-Mar'a is depicted as a proponent of outright solipsism that treats the empirical world as a pure illusion; see Kattoura. *Mystische und Philosophische System,* pp. 11–14. He could not have been a master of Ibn Sab'in, as claimed by al-Maqqari (*Nafh,* vol. 2, p. 406), since Ibn Sab'in was born in 614 A.H., i.e., three years after the death of Ibn Dahhaq/Ibn Mar'a. There is, however, no reason to doubt that Ibn Mar'a's exercised profound influence on Ibn Sab'in through his numerous disciples in Murcia, especially Ibn Ahla.

104. See Chapter 2 of this study, note 119.

105. A famous Andalusi mystic and poet whose remarkable poetic account of the history of the monistic trend in Islam is reproduced in Ibn al-Khatib's *Rawdat al-ta'rif,* pp. 609–618. Al-Shushtari was one of Ibn Sab'in's closest associates who, upon the latter's death, succeeded him at the head of a *tariqa* and even drew up a code of behavior for his followers; see al-Maqqari. *Nafh,* vol. 2, pp. 185–187 and 205–207; Massignon. "Ibn Sab'in," pp. 677–679.

106. A Mursian student of Ibn Ahla, who propagated his doctrine of absolute oneness in the mosques of Lorca and Murcia. He is said to have allowed his followers to drink wine and to take more than four wives; see al-Sakhawi. *Al-Qawl al-munbi,* fol. 93b; Ibn al-Khatib. *Rawdat al-taʿrif,* p. 604, note 1424; Kattoura. *Mystische und Philosophische System,* pp. 18–19; Massignon. "Ibn Sabʿin," p. 670.

107. See note 17 of this chapter.

108. A black surgeon of Maghribi origin, who died in Damascus; Ibn al-ʿImad. *Shadharat,* vol. 5, p. 403. I have found no information on his theological views.

109. A wadi located northwest of Murcia (the Spanish Ricate), Ibn al-Khatib. *Al-Ihata,* vol. 4, p. 31, note 2; Massignon. "Ibn Sabʿin," p. 668. Ibn al-Khatib seems to have referred to the Shudhiyya, whose adherents concentrated in Murcia and its environs. All these and a few other members of the Shudhiyya (e.g., Ibn al-Labbaj, Abu ʾl-Hasan al-Muqim, and Ibn ʿAyyash al-Malaqi) figure in the lists of monistic thinkers compiled by Ibn al-Zubayr and Abu Hayyan; see Kattoura. *Mystische und Philosophische System,* p. 27, note 80.

110. "Ibn Sabʿin," pp. 666–668.

111. *Rawdat al-taʿrif,* pp. 604–605.

112. Ibid., p. 620. Unlike many *ʿulamaʾ* before him, Ibn al-Khatib was well aware of the fact that *Aflatun* (Plato) and *Aflatin* (Plotinus) were two different thinkers; ibid., p. 534.

113. Ibn al-Khatib seems to refer here to the mystic-cum-philosopher type of thinker, who combines rationalist speculation with supersensory "unveiling." If so, the term *hakim* may apply to Ibn Masarra and Ibn ʿArabi as well as Ibn Sina; see, e.g., Addas. "Andalusi Mysticism," pp. 916–918.

114. *Rawdat al-taʿrif,* pp. 630–631.

115. For Ibn Khaldun's life and work see al-Sakhawi. *Al-Dawʾ*, vol. 4, pp. 145–149. For early studies of his thought in Europe see von Kremer. *Ibn-Chaldun;* Schmidt. *Ibn Khaldun;* Bouthoul. *Ibn Khaldoun;* Fischel. *Ibn Khaldun and Tamerlane;* idem. *Ibn Khaldun in Egypt;* and the introduction to the English translation of the *Muqaddima* by Franz Rosenthal: Ibn Khaldun. *The Muqaddimah,* vol. 1, pp. XXIX-LXXXVII; Hodgson. *The Venture of Islam,* vol. 2, pp. 476–484. For a contemporary Muslim perspective see Baali and Wardi. *Ibn Khaldun and Islamic Thought-Styles.* For a revisionist approach see Al-Azmeh. *Ibn Khaldun;* Lawrence. *Ibn Khaldun and Islamic Ideology;* cf. Talbi. *Ibn Khaldun*—EI[2], vol. 3, pp. 825–31.

116. The only studies of Ibn Khaldun's views on Sufism are, to my knowledge, Syrier. "Ibn Khaldun and Islamic Mysticism" and Batsyeva. "Shifaʾ al-saʾil."

117. For a view of Ibn Khaldun as a "sociologist" par excellence see Schmidt. *Ibn Khaldun;* Bouthoul. *Ibn-Khaldoun,* Lacoste. *Ibn Khaldun;* cf. Hodgson. *The Venture of Islam,* vol. 2, p. 482. For an attempt to strip the great Maghribi historian of his sociological credentials see Al-Azmeh. *Ibn Khaldun,* p. 170, passim.

118. For Ibn al-Khatib's disenchanted vision of history see my contribution "Ibn al-Khatib" for *Cambridge History of Arabic Literature: The literature of al-Andalus,* forthcoming.

119. See, e.g., Syrier. "Ibn Khaldun and Islamic Mysticism," p. 265, quoting an influential study of Islam by von Kremer. Al-Azmeh, describes Ibn Khaldun's attitude as the "vernacular" realism of a politician rather than the "reflective" realism of a philosopher; see Al-Azmeh. *Ibn Khaldun,* p. 149.

120. Syrier. "Ibn Khaldun and Islamic Mysticism," p. 268.

121. *The Muqaddimah,* vol. 3, pp. 37–39 and 246–258.

122. For a handy, if somewhat impressionistic synopsis of Ibn Khaldun's attitude toward Islamic philosophy see Al-Azmeh. *Ibn Khaldun,* pp. 115–117. Hodgson, however, describes Ibn Khaldun as a *faylasuf* par excellence; see *The Venture of Islam,* vol. 2, pp. 479–483. In a similar vein, Rosenthal questions the sincerity of Ibn Khaldun's rejection of philosophical thinking; see Rosenthal. "Ibn Khaldun and His Time," p. 23.

123. See, e.g., Al-Azmeh who defines Ibn Khaldun's world-outlook as "a robust stance of realism," adding that in his work we find "an everyday commonsensical realism, one which does little more than register things as they appear to happen . . . and which . . . refutes the claims to knowledge by philosophers, astrologers, magicians and alchemists because their claims go beyond that which is possible for human knowledge"; Al-Azmeh. *Ibn Khaldun,* pp. 149–150; cf. the opinion of Anderson, who describes Ibn Khaldun's realism as "tragic," ("Conjuring with Ibn Khaldun," p. 119)—an opinion that resonates with the view of many 19th-century Orientalists, who emphasized Ibn Khaldun's "skepticism," "cold detachment," and "positivistic approach." Cf., however, Syrier. "Ibn Khaldun and Islamic Mysticism," pp. 265, 267, and 271.

124. Fischel. *Ibn Khaldun in Egypt,* pp. 27–28. One should not, however, put much stock in his affiliation with this Sufi institution, since his main responsibility was the oversight of the pious endowment (*waqf*) bestowed upon it by the wealthy donors and not the training of the Sufis who resided there.

125. Ibn Khaldun. *The Muqaddimah,* vol. 3, pp. 76–103. For a rather superficial analysis of this chapter see Shehadi. "Theism, Mysticism, and Scientific History." This chapter is also analyzed in Syrier. "Ibn Khaldun and Islamic Mysticism," which depicts Ibn Khaldun as a crypto-Sufi thinker who carefully disguised his mystical leanings; cf. also *The Muqaddimah,* vol. 2, pp. 186–192.

126. This work has been discussed in the following studies: Nwyia. *Ibn ʿAbbad,* pp. L-LV; Batsyeva. "Shifaʾ al-saʾil"; cf. Mahdi. "The Book and the Master," passim; Al-Azmeh. *Ibn Khaldun,* p. 7, note 8. The *Shifaʾ* presents a summary of Ibn Khaldun's attitude toward Sufism, which is preceded by a brief survey of the rise and evolution of mystical theory and practice. Summarizing the contents of this work, Rosenthal remarks that it "leads to the conclusion that only moderate, traditional mysticism is to be tolerated according to Muslim law"; see Rosenthal. "Ibn Khaldun and His Time," p. 23. This conclusion bespeaks the "Ibn Khaldun as a Sufi" thesis of Syrier, who ascribed to Ibn Khaldun "undeniable leanings to Absolute Monism" which he allegedly shared with Ibn ʿArabi and Ibn Sabʿin; see Syrier. "Ibn Khaldun and Islamic Mysticism," p. 300, passim.

127. The first draft of the *Muqaddima* was completed in 779/1377.

128. Nwyia. *Ibn ʿAbbad,* pp. XLVIII-XLIX; Mahdi. "The Book and the Master," pp. 3–4. Al-Shatibi did not address his question specifically to Ibn Khaldun. Rather it was directed to al-Shatibi's teacher, the Maliki *faqih* Abu ʾl-ʿAbbas al-Qabbab (d. 779/1377) and the celebrated Maghribi mystic Ibn ʿAbbad al-Rundi (d. 792/1390). The fact that Ibn Khaldun volunteered an answer demonstrates his interest in the problem of Sufi education; see Mahdi. "The Book and the Master," pp. 5–9. On al-Shatibi and Ibn ʿAbbad see "Introduction" to Nwyia's. *Ibn ʿAbbad,* passim.

129. Very little is known about this "great Spanish saint"; see Ibn Khaldun. *The Muqaddimah,* vol. 3, p. 94; Massignon. "Ibn Sabʿin," p. 668; Syrier. "Ibn Khaldun and Islamic Mysticism," p. 284; cf. Al-Azmeh. *Ibn Khaldun,* p. 7, note 8.

130. See, e.g., *The Muqaddimah,* vol. 3, pp. 98–99—a passage that is quoted verbatim from *Rawdat al-taʿrif,* p. 488. For al-Ansari, the Hanbali mystic whose bold formulations of *tawhid* were often cited by the members of the Ibn ʿArabi school and their critics, see de Beaurecueil. *Khwadja ʿAbdullah Ansari;* Danner. *The Book of Wisdom,* which contains a translation of al-Ansari's "Intimate Conversations." For al-Ansari's role in Western Sufism see, Halff. "Mahasin"; cf. Lings. *A Sufi Saint,* p. 128; Addas. "Andalusi Mysticism," p. 926.

131. Syrier. "Ibn Khaldun and Islamic Mysticism," passim; Batsyeva. "Shifaʾ al-saʾil," passim.

132. Ibn Khaldun. *Shifaʾ*, p. 48.

133. Ibid.

134. For this early exponent of Sufi "psychology" see Smith. *An Early Mystic of Baghdad;* Sezgin. *Geschichte,* vol. 1, pp. 639–642; van Ess. *Die Gedankenwelt;* Roman. *Al-Muhasibi.*

135. See Syrier. "Ibn Khaldun and Islamic Mysticism," p. 298.

136. *The Muqaddimah,* vol. 3, pp. 82 and 102. See Gramlich. *Das Sendschreiben;* and Halm. *Al-Kushayri*—EI², vol. 5, pp. 526–527; cf. von Schlegell. *Principles of Sufism.*

137. Ibn Khaldun. *Shifa'*, p. 48; cf. Syrier. "Ibn Khaldun and Islamic Mysticism," pp. 286–287.

138. Ibn Khaldun. *The Muqaddimah,* vol. 3, p. 100.

139. Ibid., pp. 54 and 253–254.

140. Mahdi. "The Book and the Master," p. 11.

141. Ibid.; cf. Syrier. "Ibn Khaldun and Islamic Mysticism," p. 286.

142. Mahdi. "The Book and the Master," p. 14.

143. Ibn Khaldun. *Shifa'*, pp. 48–49; idem. *The Muqaddimah,* vol. 3, pp. 99–102.

144. Ibn Khaldun. *Shifa',* p. 56; cf. *The Muqaddimah,* vol. 3, p. 102.

145. See Al-Azmeh. *Ibn Khaldun,* p. 107.

146. *The Muqaddimah,* vol. 3, p. 85. I have slightly modified Rosenthal's translation; cf. *Shifa'*, p. 50. In another instance, Ibn Khaldun censured "recent extremist Sufis" for having "confused the problems of [metaphysics and speculative theology] with their [Sufi] path," which, in his opinion, is a serious error, because "intuitive experience is absolutely different from scientific perceptions and ways," *The Muqaddimah,* vol. 3, p. 155. The same argument was advanced in al-Taftazani's "Epistle."

147. On this notion see Gardet. *'Alam*—EI², vol. 1, pp. 350–352; Knysh. *Malakut*—IES, pp. 154–155.

148. Ibn Khaldun. *Shifa'*, p. 56.

149. Syrier. "Ibn Khaldun and Islamic Mysticism," p. 293.

150. *The Muqaddimah,* vol. 3, pp. 86–87.

151. Syrier. "Ibn Khaldun and Islamic Mysticism," p. 293.

152. In his translation of the *Muqaddima,* Rosenthal renders this Arabic term as "revelation." This is misleading, given the word's complex connotations in the later Sufi thought; see Knysh. *Tajalli*—IES, pp. 219–220.

153. See note 86 of this chapter.

154. Ibn Khaldun. *The Muqaddimah,* vol. 3, pp. 87–88; cf. al-Fasi. *'Iqd,* vol. 2, pp. 180–181. This seems to be a fairly accurate description of al-Farghani's cosmology; see, e.g., Chittick. "Spectrums," passim; cf. idem. "The Five Divine Presences." Al-Farghani's tripartite manifestation corresponds to the triplicity (*tathlith*) of divine Being in relation to becoming, i.e.: 1. Be-

ing that is self-identified with its own oneness and its own knowledge of it (*ʿayn al-wahda*); 2. Being that knows itself as one in relation to itself (*ahadiyya*); 3. Being that knows itself as one in relation to the many (*wahdaniyya*). This triad, as Syrier rightly pointed out ("Ibn Khaldun and Islamic Mysticism," p. 290), is a distinctive feature of the thinkers of the Ibn ʿArabi school. Yet it does not necessarily accurately represent the views of its eponym.

155. *The Muqaddimah,* vol. 3, p. 89.

156. *Shifa*ʾ, pp. 56–57; *The Muqaddimah,* vol. 3, p. 89; cf. Rosenthal. "Ibn Khaldun and His Time," p. 23; Syrier. "Ibn Khaldun and Islamic Mysticism," pp. 291–293.

157. Al-Fasi could only meet Ibn Khaldun in Egypt, since he never traveled to the Maghrib. Moreover, al-Fasi explicitly referred to him as "[chief] judge of the community of Egypt" (*qadi ʾl-jamaʿa bi ʾl-diyar al-misriyya*), see *ʿIqd,* vol. 2, p. 178.

158. Although this term normally designates practitioners of Sufism, in certain contexts it may assume pejorative overtones, i.e., "pseudo-Sufis," "those who ostensibly practice Sufism [in order to disguise their heretical views]."

159. An allusion to Qurʾan 102:7. Possibly, a work of Ibn Barrajan, see Brockelmann. *Geschichte,* vol. 1, p. 434; Addas. "Andalusi Mysticism," pp. 925–926.

160. Al-Fasi. *ʿIqd,* vol. 2, pp. 180–181.

161. Ibn Khaldun. *Shifa*ʾ, pp. 49–50 and 110–111; cf. al-Dhahabi. *Mizan,* vol. 3, p. 109.

162. Ibn Khaldun. *Shifa*ʾ, p. 52; cf. Ibn al-Khatib. *Rawdat al-taʿrif,* pp. 604–605.

163. Ibn Khaldun. *The Muqaddimah,* vol. 2, pp. 187–188; vol. 3, p. 92.

164. Ibid., vol. 2, p. 187.

165. Ibid., vol. 3, pp. 93–94.

166. Ibid., vol. 2, pp. 187–188; idem. *Shifa*ʾ, p. 52. For Ibn ʿArabi's conception of the Muhammadan Reality that indeed displays strong eschatological tendencies see Ibn ʿArabi. *ʿAnqaʾ mughrib*, pp. 48 and 50–51. For details see the unpublished Ph. D. dissertation by Elmore of Yale University, "The Fabulous Gryphon: Ibn ʿArabi's *ʿAnqaʾ mughrib*."

167. According to Rosenthal, this treatise is not directly linked to the *mahdi* predictions (see *The Muqaddimah,* vol. 3, p. 189, note 960). This is incorrect, since the whole work is an exposition of the rise of the Fatimi *mahdi.* Some similar works attributed to Ibn ʿArabi are mentioned in Fahd. *Malhama*—EI^2, vol. 6, p. 247.

168. Nothing is known about this individual beyond the fact that he was a disciple of Ibn Sab'in (and not of Ibn 'Arabi), who wrote a commentary on Ibn Qasi's "Removal of the Sandals." Ibn Khaldun. *The Muqaddimah,* vol. 3, p. 188.

169. Ibn Khaldun. *The Muqaddimah,* vol. 3, p. 188; Al-Azmeh. *Ibn Khaldun,* p. 91. The brevity of Ibn Khaldun's exposition of this important doctrine prevented Al-Azmeh from grasping the central point of his argument. As a result, he confounds the intermediate messiah (i.e., the Fatimi harbinger of the sainthood era) with the ultimate *mahdi,* whom Muslim eschatology identifies with the Qur'anic Jesus; see, e.g., Friedmann. *Prophesy Continuous,* pp. 63 and 112; for Ibn 'Arabi's treatment of this issue see Ibn 'Arabi. *Futuhat,* vol. 2, pp. 100, 111 and 337; cf. *Futuhat* (ed. Yahia), vol. 1, pp. 47 and 59, vol. 2, p. 341, vol. 8, pp. 177 and 179, etc.; idem. *'Anqa' mughrib,* passim; Chodkiewicz. *Le sceau,* passim.

170. Unlike the restricted lawgiving prophecy, universal prophecy (or universal saintship), in Ibn 'Arabi's view, subsumes both legislative prophesy and its inner dimension, sainthood; see Austin. *Bezels,* p. 168.

171. Nor does it appear in the other manuscript copies of the *'Anqa'*, as Dr. Elmore has kindly communicated to me.

172. Austin. *Bezels,* pp. 66–67.

173. Ibid. pp. 168–171.

174. Ibid., p. 66.

175. Ibn Khaldun. *The Muqaddimah,* vol. 3, pp. 190–192.

176. See Ibn 'Arabi. *'Anqa' mughrib,* p. 77, where Ibn 'Arabi gives the putative date for the *imam's* advent as *kh-d-b,* i.e., 692 (A.H.), whereas Ibn Khaldun, *apud* Ibn Abi Watil, has *kh-f-j,* i.e., 683, see *The Muqaddimah,* vol. 3, p. 190.

177. Ibn Khaldun. *The Muqaddimah,* vol. 3, p. 172, note 807. Al-Buni was often accused of infringing on the God's prerogative to the knowledge of the unseen (*al-ghayb*), see Knysh. *Al-Ghayb*—IES, p. 53.

178. See Chodkiewicz. *Les illuminations,* pp. 385–487.

179. Ibn Khaldun. *Shifa'*, pp. 53–55; idem. *The Muqaddimah,* vol. 2, p. 190; cf. vol. 3, pp. 172–182.

180. See, e.g., ibid. vol. 2, pp. 192–220, where Ibn Khaldun questions the authenticity of the eschatological *hadith* which predicted the imminent rise of the Fatimi *mahdi;* cf. Al-Azmeh. *Ibn Khaldun,* p. 90.

181. See Ferhat and Triki. "Faux prophètes;" García-Arenal. "Le conjonction du soufisme et sharifisme"; Fletcher. "Al-Andalus." These studies are largely based on the analysis of relevant sections from the *Muqaddima;* cf. Fierro. *La heterodoxia,* passim.

182. See Ibn Khaldun. *The Muqaddimah,* vol. 3, pp. 182–227, for a detailed elucidation of the letter magic known as *za'iraja;* cf., however, ibid., pp. 180–182; and Al-Azmeh. *Ibn Khaldun,* pp. 91–92.

183. Ibn Khaldun. *The Muqaddimah,* vol. 3, pp. 100–101, 182, etc.

184. Rosenthal. "Ibn Khaldun and His Time," p. 23; cf. Syrier. "Ibn Khaldun and Islamic Mysticism," passim.

185. Al-Azmeh explains Ibn Khaldun's negative attitude to later visionary Sufism by his profound hostility to the Shiʿis (see *Ibn Khaldun,* p. 7, note 8). To my mind, the argument should be reversed. His hostility to Shʿism and certain aspects of Sufism stems from his deep concern for the community's welfare and stability which, in his view, were threatened by both the chiliastic theories of Shiʿism and by their Sufi analogs.

186. On the latter see Morris. "The Spiritual Ascension."

187. This view corresponds closely to Ibn Sabʿin's self-image; see Kattoura. *Mystische und Philosophische System,* passim.

188. For a study of the origins and spread of this term in the Muslim East see Chittick. "Rumi and *wahdat al-wujud.*"

189. See Syrier. "Ibn Khaldun and Islamic Mysticism," passim; for different reading of Ibn Khaldun's position see Ateş. *Ibn ʿArabi*—EI^2, vol. 3, p. 711.

Chapter 8

1. *Apud* al-Biqaʿi. *Tanbih,* p. 165; on the author see Fleisch. *Ibn Hisham*—EI,^{2} vol. 3, pp. 801–802.

2. Of the works written in the 7th/13th centuries mention should be made of "The Epistle on the Condemnation of Ibn [al-] ʿArabi" (*Risala fi dhamm Ibn al-ʿArabi*) by an obscure Syrian author, Muhammad b. ʿUthman al-Kamili al-Dimashqi (d. 652/1254); "The Book of Connection" (*Kitab al-irtibat*); and "The Sincere Admonition" (*Nasiha sariha*) by al-Qastallani (d. 686/1287); three short treatises by the antimonistic Sufi Ahmad al-Wasiti (d. 711/1311), a friend and follower of Ibn Taymiyya (on al-Wasiti see Ibn al-ʿImad. *Shadharat,* vol. 6, pp. 24–25; cf. Yahia. *La classification,* vol. 1, p. 114). In the 8th/14th centuries the following works were written by Ibn ʿArabi's critics: "The Elucidation of the Judgement Regarding the Corrupt Tenets of the *Fusus*" (*Bayan hukm ma fi 'l-Fusus min al-iʿtiqadat al-mafsuda*) by ʿAbd al-Latif al-Suʿudi (d. 736/1336); "The Epistle on the Oneness/Unity of Being" (*Risala fi wahdat al-wujud*) by al-Taftazani (d. 792/1390); "Encircling the Irresponsible Statements of the *Fusus* by the Wall of [Authoritative] Texts" (*Tasawwurat al-nusus ʿala tahawwurat al-Fusus*) by Muhammad b.

Muhammad al-Ayzari al-Shafiʿi (d. 808/1404), Yahia. *La classification,* vol. 1, p. 115.

3. Yahia. *La classification,* vol. 1, pp. 115–116; to this one should add the polemical "biography" of Ibn ʿArabi by al-Fasi (d. 831/1429) discussed in Chapter 5 of this study, as well as the book-size refutations of Ibn ʿArabi by Siraj b. Musafir al-Qaysari (d. 856/1452) and Muhammad b. Muhammad b. Mansur Ibn Imam al-Kamiliyya (d. 864/1459) mentioned in al-Sakhawi's *al-Dawʾ*, vol. 3, p. 244 and vol. 9, pp. 94–95; cf. Rosenthal. *A History,* p. 606.

4. Some of these *fatwas* have already been discussed in Chapter 5 of this study; for a list of eighty-two *fatwas* issued by Ibn ʿArabi's theological opponents see Yahia. *La classification,* vol. 1, pp. 126–132; *apud* al-Sakhawi's *al-Qawl al-munabbi / al-munbi.*

5. See Yahia. *La classification,* vol. 1, pp. 113, 118, and 133. To the apologies on Yahia's list one should add an apologetic (?) treatise by the chief *qadi* of the Egyptian Malikis Muhammad b. Ahmad al-Bisati (d. 842/1438) and a work composed by the Rifaʿi Shaykh Siraj al-din Muhammad b. ʿAli al-Makhzumi (d. 885/1480); see al-Sakhawi. *Al-Dawʾ*, vol. 7, p. 7; Brockelmann. *Supplement,* vol. 2, p. 229; al-Zirikli. *Al-Aʿlam,* vol. 6, p. 238; Kahhala. *Muʿjam,* vol. 10, pp. 234–235. No treatises in defense of the Greatest Master were written in the late 7th/13th centuries.

6. Al-Sakhawi put together a collection of anti-Ibn ʿArabi *fatwas* titled "The Statement, Clarifying [the Facts] of Ibn ʿArabi's Biography" (*Al-Qawl al-munbi [al-munabbi] ʿan tarjamat Ibn ʿArabi*), a Berlin manuscript, spr. 790/fols. 1–250. Additionally, he frequently referred to the Ibn ʿArabi polemic in his monumental collection of scholarly biographies titled "The Shining Light" (*al-Dawʾ al-lamiʿ*); see, e.g., vol. 1, pp. 108 and 114, vol. 3, pp. 31–33, 222, and 244, vol. 9, pp. 95, 194, 250, 292–294, and 296, vol. 10, pp. 84, 199, 201, and 256, vol. 11, p. 78; cf. Rosenthal. *A History,* pp. 584–586.

7. Al-Sakhawi's haughty treatment of the uncouth Turkoman *faqih* is motivated by his sense of superiority over non-Arab scholars, whom many Arab authors of the Mamluk period often treated as slow-witted bumpkins. Cf., however, Haarmann. "Arabic in Speech, Turkish in Lineage"; idem. *Misr*—EI², vol. 5, pp. 173–175. On the other hand, oftentimes "the tentative immersion of the [Turkic] military elite in the world of higher Islamic learning could engender complications" (Berkey. *The Transmission,* p. 152). Overenthusiastic newcomers such as Taghri Birmish could occasionally upset the established balance of power within the predominantly Arab and Persian scholarly establishment; for an instance of successive "immersion," see ibid., pp. 154–155.

8. Al-Sakhawi. *Al-Dawʾ*, vol. 3, pp. 31–32; cf. Nagel. *Timur,* p. 292.

9. Al-Sakhawi. *Al-Dawʾ*, vol. 3, p. 33.

10. See Chapter 5 of this study; and al-Sakhawi. *Al-Daw'*, vol. 3, p. 32, who contends that symbolic "executions" of Ibn ʿArabi's works "continued to recur over and over again" (*wa takarrar dhalika ʿasr*^{an} *baʿd ʿasr*).

11. Knysh. "Ibn ʿArabi in the Later Islamic Tradition," p. 315; for a similar treatment of the works of Ibn Hazm and al-Ghazali in al-Andalus see Kassis. "Muslim Revival," pp. 106–107.

12. A middle-ranking official in the Mamluk administration.

13. An Egyptian historian who wrote a continuation of Ibn Kathir's *Al-Bidaya wa 'l-nihaya;* see Haarmann. *Quellenstudien,* p. 124.

14. Ibn Muzhir was private secretary to the sultan Qa'it Bay, who took active part in the resolution of the debate over Ibn al-Farid and Ibn ʿArabi in 874/1469–875/1470; see the next section and Homerin. *From Arab Poet,* pp. 69–71.

15. I.e., dismissed from his post.

16. Nothing is known about this personage.

17. Ibn Iyas. *Bada'iʿ al-zuhur,* vol. 3, p. 203.

18. As I argue elsewhere ("Ibn Arabi in the Later Islamic Tradition," p. 315), some details of this story indicate that the Ibn ʿArabi issue was deliberately exploited by al-Hulaybi's rivals to ruin his career in the hope of obtaining his office.

19. See, e.g., al-Sakhawi. *Al-Daw'*, vol. 9, p. 250, and vol. 10, p. 199.

20. See al-Sakhawi. *Al-Daw'*, vol. 9, p. 194 and vol. 10, p. 199; Ibn al-ʿImad. *Shadharat,* vol. 7, p. 206; Nagel. *Timur,* pp. 290–293.

21. al-Sakhawi. *Daw'*, vol. 3, p. 170; cf. Nagel. *Timur,* p. 292.

22. Al-Sakhawi, ibid., p. 244.

23. E.g., the Indian Hanafi ʿUmar b. Ishaq Siraj al-din (d. 774/1372); see Nagel. *Timur,* pp. 290–292.

24. He is often confused with his namesake Khawaja ʿAla' al-din Muhammad al-Bukhari (d. 802/1400), who was the chief organizational successor of Baha' al-din Naqshband. Unlike the subject of this chapter, the other al-Bukhari held a high opinion of Ibn ʿArabi and his teaching; see Algar. "Reflections of Ibn ʿArabi," pp. 50–51.

25. The following account of al-Bukhari's life is based on al-Sakhawi (*al-Daw'*, vol. 9, pp. 291–294) and Ibn al-ʿImad (*Shadharat,* vol. 7, pp. 241–242); a less flattering biography of this scholar was written by his theological opponent; see Ibn Nasir al-din. *Al-Radd al-wafir,* p. "qaf"; cf. Brockelmann. *Supplement,* vol. 1, p. 794.

26. For manuscripts of this treatise see Yahia. *La classification,* vol. 1, pp. 115–116; Brockelmann. *Supplement,* vol. 1, p. 794.

27. On this Shafiʿi scholar of Hanbali leanings, see Ibn al-ʿImad. *Shadharat,* vol. 7, pp. 243–245. His refutation of al-Bukhari contains a long list of the non-Hanbali followers of Ibn Taymiyya; see Ibn Nasir al-din. *Al-Radd al-wafir,* passim.

28. Ibn Hajar al-ʿAsqalani, *apud* al-Sakhawi. *Al-Dawʾ*, vol. 9, p. 294.

29. For this episode see al-Sakhawi. *Al-Dawʾ*, vol. 1, pp. 113–115.

30. See al-Biqaʿi. *Tanbih,* pp. 182–195.

31. Ibid., pp. 186–189.

32. Al-Sakhawi. *Al-Dawʾ*, vol. 9, p. 291.

33. Ibid., vol. 9, p. 294; cf. ibid., p. 291.

34. On the art of scholarly dispute in medieval Islam see Makdisi. *The Rise of Colleges,* "index" under "munazara" and Wagner. *Munazara*—EI², vol. 6, pp. 656–568.

35. I.e., Ibn Hajar al-ʿAsqalani, whom al-Sakhawi regarded as his master par excellence.

36. I.e., al-Bisati, the chief *qadi* of the Maliki *madhhab* in Egypt.

37. Al-Sakhawi. *Al-Dawʾ*, vol. 9, pp. 291–292; for a paraphrase of al-Sakhawi's account, see Homerin. *From Arab Poet,* pp. 59–60; note, however, that Ibn al-Farid's orthodoxy was not at issue in this incident.

38. For a full list of its members see al-Biqaʿi. *Tanbih,* p. 139.

39. Although in theory the four Sunni *madhhabs* were declared equal by Baybars I, in practice the Shafiʿi legal school, as the most numerous, still enjoyed more weight than the others.

40. Al-Biqaʿi. *Tanbih,* p. 139.

41. Ibid., pp. 170–174. It should, however, be noted that al-Biqaʿi, an outspoken critic of Ibn ʿArabi, deliberately ignores al-Bisati's altercation with al-Bukhari, portraying both as bitter opponents of monistic Sufism.

42. Homerin. *From Arab Poet,* pp. 59–60.

43. Ibid. and al-Biqaʿi *Tanbih,* pp. 174–175.

44. Al-Suyuti later wrote that it was only through divine interference that al-Bisati managed to retain his post after this scandal; see al-Suyuti. *Tanbih* (printed ed.), p. 40.

45. Ibn al-ʿImad. *Shadharat,* vol. 7, pp. 339–340.

46. Homerin. *From Arab Poet,* pp. 120–121, note 58.

47. Giffen. *Theory of Profane Love,* p. 41, note 123; see al-Sakhawi. *Al-Daw*ʾ, vol. 1, pp. 101–111. For a more balanced outline of al-Biqaʿi's life and work see Ibn al-ʿImad. *Shadharat,* vol. 7, pp. 339–340, although this biographer too stresses al-Biqaʿi's haughtiness and self-conceit; cf. Ibn Iyas. *Badaʾiʿ al-zuhur,* vol. 3, p. 169; Brockelmann. *Geschichte,* vol. 2, pp. 142–143.

48. More precisely, the campaign was triggered by a public reading of al-Farghani's famous commentary on the *al-Taʾiyya,* which drew al-Biqaʿi's criticism; see Homerin. *From Arab Poet,* p. 62.

49. I have, however, found no evidence of al-Biqaʿi's opposition to al-Ghazali in his own writings; see, e.g., al-Biqaʿi. *Sirr al-ruh,* pp. 109–112; cf. Homerin. *From Arab Poet,* p. 118, note 32. It seems probable that al-Sakhawi deliberately circulated this rumor to besmirch the reputation of his rival.

50. According to Homerin, "another contemporary, al-Khatib al-Jawhari (819–900–1416–95), also noted that al-Biqaʿi was of extremely bad character and was quick to slander others"; op. cit., p. 68.

51. Al-Sakhawi. *Al-Daw*ʾ, vol. 1, p. 107; cf. Homerin. *From Arab Poet,* p. 118, note 37.

52. For a brief description of his treatise on the calamities of lovers and the vicissitudes of profane love see Giffen. *Theory of Profane Love,* pp. 41–42; samples of his poetic work are cited in his biography by al-Sakhawi. See also Rosenthal. *A History,* pp. 107 and 398.

53. Little. "Did Ibn Taymiyya Have a Screw Loose?," p. 108.

54. Homerin. *From Arab Poet,* p. 62.

55. Ibid., p. 68; this remark is to be taken with a grain of salt, since Homerin largely relies on the partial evidence from al-Sakhawi.

56. Al-Sakhawi. *Al-Daw*ʾ, vol. 1, pp. 108–109; according to Homerin, al-Biqaʿi succeeded in dragging into the controversy the reclusive scholar Ibn Imam al-Kamiliyya who normally shunned noisy disputes; see *From Arab Poet,* p. 62. The real cause of al-Biqaʿi's failure lies in an unfavorable alignment of social and political forces and vested interests in the Mamluk kingdom that determined the eventual defeat of the anti-Ibn al-Farid party; for details see ibid, pp. 55–75.

57. See, ibid., pp. 60–62, passim.

58. By al-Biqaʿi's time the tomb of Ibn al-Farid had become an object of pious visits and popular worship, which was generously supported through pious endowments bequeathed to it by high-ranking Mamluk officials; see Boullata. "Toward a Biography," passim; Homerin. *From Arab Poet,* pp. 60–62 and 76–92.

59. See, e.g., a poetic ridicule of Ibn al-Shihna, another Syrian detractor of the Sufi poet, Homerin. *From Arab Poet,* p. 66.

60. See Ibn Iyas. *Bada'iʿ al-zuhur*, vol. 3, p. 214; Ibn al-ʿImad. *Shadharat,* vol. 7, p. 349; Sourdel. *Ibn al-Shihna*—EI², vol. 3, p. 938. Al-Sakhawi's long biography of Ibn al-Shihna indicates that the latter's attitude to Ibn ʿArabi underwent a dramatic change from an uncompromising opposition to a wholehearted endorsement, *al-Daw'*, vol. 9, pp. 295–305, esp. pp. 296 and 301. To explain this sudden change of heart, al-Sakhawi cites Ibn al-Shihna's senility.

61. Interestingly, this opinion was condoned even by al-Sakhawi (himself a sworn enemy of monistic Sufism), who admitted that the few blasphemous statements in Ibn al-Farid's poetry are not enough to pronounce him a bone fide *kafir.* When the news of al-Sakhawi's position had reached al-Biqaʿi, the latter reportedly accused him of being a covert Sufi sympathizer, thereby aggravating the already strong animosity between the two men; see al-Sakhawi. *Al-Daw'*, vol. 1, p. 108. Al-Sakhawi's sincerity in this episode is highly suspect given his profound hostility toward monistic Sufism. His uncharacteristic support of the Ibn al-Farid faction must have been dictated by his rivalry with al-Biqaʿi or perhaps by his awareness of the pro-Ibn al-Farid stance taken by Barquq and the sultan's entourage—considerations which, in this case at least, outweighed his personal convictions.

62. Both works were edited in 1372/1953 by an anti-Sufi Egyptian scholar ʿAbd al-Rahman al-Wakil under the pretentious title "The Destruction of Sufism" (*Masraʿ al-tasawwuf*). In the introduction, the editor expressed his personal abhorrence to Islamic mysticism and its followers, accusing them of fostering bygone superstitions and of contributing to the overall economic and cultural decline of Muslim societies. Al-Wakil's position, which is obvious from the bulky and tendentious annotations to the text, is typical of the liberal Egyptian intellectuals of the 1950s; see, e.g., Gilsenan. "Trajectories." For the manuscripts of the other anti-Ibn al-Farid's treatises by al-Biqaʿi see Homerin. *From Arab Poet,* pp. 143–144.

63. See, e.g., al-Sakhawi. *Al-Daw'*, vol. 9, p. 250, regarding the famous scholar Muhammad b. Muhammad al-Kinani, known as Ibn al-Qattan (d. 879/1473), who, prior to al-Biqaʿi's campaign, had concealed his admiration for Ibn ʿArabi, but then "came out" and defended him publicly; cf. Homerin. *From Arab Poet,* p. 118, note 37, regarding Amin al-din al-Aqsara'i (d. 880/1475).

64. For a list of members of the Ibn ʿArabi/Ibn al-Farid faction see ibid., pp. 67–69.

65. Ibn Iyas. *Bada'iʿ al-zuhur,* vol. 3, p. 45; for more poems of this kind see Homerin. *From Arab Poet,* p. 66.

66. Ibid., pp. 69–71.

67. See ibid., p. 67.

68. Al-Suyuti. *Tanbih* (printed ed.), pp. 20–21; Ibn al-ʿImad. *Shadharat,* vol. 5, p. 191.

69. According to al-Biqaʿi, the original title of his treatise was "The Texts [That Demonstrate] the Unbelief of the *Fusus*" (*Al-Nusus min kufr al-Fusus*), al-Biqaʿi. *Tanbih,* p. 22.

70. Al-Biqaʿi discerned the following types of unbelief: those of the *zindiqs,* of the *mulhidun,* of the *ashab al-bidʿa,* of the *ashab al-dalala,* and, finally, of the *kuffar* per se; cf. Prozorov. "Pravoveriye," pp. 50–52.

71. Among the sources used by al-Biqaʿi are al-Ghazali, the celebrated *sharʿi* mystic and *muhaddith* Muhyi al-din al-Nawawi (d. 676/1277), the influential Maliki theologian al-Qadi ʿIyad (d. 544/1149), and the great Muslim heresiographer al-Shahrastani (d. 548/1153).

72. The frustrated editor of the *Tanbih* sought to remedy this drawback by supplying titles and notes to the different sections of al-Biqaʿi's narrative. These titles, however, are often misleading, and reflect the editor's own anti-Sufi agenda.

73. "The *Taʾiyya,*" according to al-Biqaʿi, "is the same as the *Fusus* and there is no difference between the two," *Tanbih,* pp. 55–56. In an oft-cited anecdote, Ibn al-Farid is said to have acknowledged that Ibn ʿArabi's *Futuhat* was the best commentary on his *Taʾiyya;* see, e.g., Boullata. "Toward a Biography," p. 55.

74. *Tanbih,* pp. 55–56, 70–72, 88–92, 100–103, 114–116, and 126–127.

75. Apart from al-Farghani, commentaries on Ibn al-Farid's poems were written by ʿAbd al-Razzaq al-Qashani (d. 730/1330) and, later on, ʿAbd al-Ghani al-Nabulusi; see Scattolin. "The Mystical Experience," p. 274.

76. Al-Biqaʿi. *Tanbih,* pp. 70–73 and 86–88; cf. Kamada. "Nabulusi's Commentary" and Knysh. *Ibn al-Farid*—IES, pp. 86–87.

77. Al-Biqaʿi. *Tanbih,* pp. 66–67. Abu Zurʿa was famous as a reliable *muhaddith* and leading jurist of his age. He wrote on diverse religious subjects and held the office of chief *qadi* of the Shafiʿi school in Egypt after al-Bulqini. While in office, he was renouned for his uprightness and personal modesty; see al-Sakhawi. *Al-Dawʾ*, vol. 1, pp. 336–344; al-Shawkani. *Al-Badr,* vol. 1, p. 72; al-Suyuti. *Tabaqat al-huffaz,* p. 548; Brockelmann. Geschichte, vol. 2, pp. 66–67; Yahia. *La classification,* vol. 1, pp. 128; *Abu Zurʿa*—EI^2, "Supplement," p. 39.

78. Al-Biqaʿi. *Tanbih,* pp. 135–136; cf. pp. 140–141.

79. He was a well-traveled and prolific scholar who counted among his disciples such great figures as Ibn Hajar al-ʿAsqalani; see al-Sakhawi. *Al-Dawʾ*, vol. 4, pp. 171–178; Ibn al-ʿImad. *Shadharat*, vol. 7, pp. 55–57; Brockelmann. *Geschichte,* vol. 2, pp. 65–66.

80. Qur'an: 19:53 and 20:94–95.

81. Elsewhere in the *Fusus* Ibn ʿArabi went even further, arguing that Moses punished Aaron for *preventing* his people from worshiping the calf because he knew of God's immanent presence in any object of worship; see Austin. *Bezels,* pp. 244–245.

82. See Qur'an, 17:23.

83. In Ibn ʿArabi's view, this Qur'anic passage is an affirmative statement rather than a commandment; see, e.g., Chittick. *The Sufi Path of Knowledge,* pp. 342–343; for a lengthy criticism of Ibn ʿArabi's interpretation of this verse by a later scholar see Ibn al-Ahdal. *Kashf,* pp. 192–193.

84. I.e., for protesting against the veneration of the calf.

85. Al-Biqaʿi. *Tanbih,* pp. 121–122.

86. Ibid., p. 123.

87. Bell. *Love Theory,* pp. 200–210; for Christian parallels see O'Grady. *Heresy,* passim.

88. Cf. Morris. "Interpreters," pt. 2, pp. 741–744.

89. Al-Biqaʿi. *Tanbih,* p. 56.

90. Our sources portray Ibn al-Naqqash as a prodigy, whose early death in Damascus (at either 39 or 43 years of age) reportedly prevented him from becoming the greatest scholar of the age. Among his principal teachers were Abu Hayyan al-Gharnati and Taqi al-din al-Subki, both of whom, as we know, were bitter critics of Ibn ʿArabi's teachings. Ibn al-Naqqash's Qur'anic commentary was by all accounts an original work, since it contained no quotations or borrowings from the earlier commentaries. Ibn al-Naqqash's sharp mind also shines in his brief but penetrating assessment of Ibn ʿArabi's work. For Ibn al-Naqqash's biographies see al-Shawkani. *Al-Badr,* vol. 2, p. 211; al-Dawudi. *Tabaqat,* vol. 2, pp. 202–204.

91. See Chapter 7 of this study.

92. Concerning Ibn ʿArabi's concept of imagination and its role in cognitive and metaphysical processes see Corbin. *L'imagination,* passim; Chittick. *The Sufi Path of Knowledge,* pp. 14–16 and 116–117.

93. See Ibn ʿArabi. *Futuhat,* vol. 1, pp. 126–131; Addas. *Ibn ʿArabi,* pp. 147–148. According to Ibn ʿArabi, this land was created from the leftovers of the clay that God had used in shaping Adam's body.

94. Cf. Chittick. *The Sufi Path of Knowledge,* pp. 59, 67, 112 and 115.

95. ʿUthman b. ʿUmar Ibn al-Hajib (d. 646/1249), a prominent Maliki jurist and grammarian, who probably met Ibn ʿArabi during his stay in Damascus (from 617/1220 to 639/1241), where he taught Maliki *fiqh.* Al-

though usually named among Ibn ʿArabi's detractors, I am unaware of any lengthy refutation of the Greatest Master ascribed to him; see Yahia. *La classification,* vol. 1, p. 122; Fleisch. *Ibn al-Hadjib*—EI², vol. 3, p. 781.

96. Al-Biqaʿi. *Tanbih,* pp. 163–164.

97. On him see Chapter 9 of this study.

98. Probably, *Rawd al-talib fi ʾl-fiqh*—Ibn al-Muqri's compendium of Shafiʿi *fiqh;* see Brockelmann. *Geschichte,* vol. 2, p. 244.

99. Al-Biqaʿi. *Tahdhir,* p. 253; cf. idem. *Tanbih,* pp. 201–202.

100. E.g., Shaykh al-Matbuli and ʿIzz al-din al-Kinani; see Homerin. *From Arab Poet,* pp. 62 and 65–67.

101. Al-Biqaʿi. *Tahdhir,* pp. 209–212.

102. Bell. *Love Theory,* p. 178.

103. Al-Biqaʿi. *Tahdhir*, pp. 265–268.

Chapter 9

1. On the history of Zaydism see Strothmann. *Kultus;* idem. "Die Litteratur"; idem. *Das Staatsrecht;* Van Arendonck. *Les débuts de l'imâmat;* Tritton. "The Mutarrifiya;" idem. *The Rise of the Imams;* Serjeant. "A Zaydi Manual"; idem. "The Interplay"; idem. "Society and Trade"; Zabara. *Aʾimmat al-Yaman*; Madelung. *Der Imam;* idem. *Religious Trends,* pp. 86–92; Abrahamov. *Al-Kasim b. Ibrahim;* Subhi. *Al-Zaydiyya;* al-ʿAmri. *Al-Imam al-Shawkani;* Gochenour. *The Penetration;* Dresch. *Tribes;* Coussonnet. "Les assises"; Haykel. "Al-Shawkani." For a bibliography on the history of the Ismaʿili community of Yemen see Poonawala. *Bio-bibliography.* Of the major studies of Yemeni Ismaʿilism mention should be made of Strothmann. *Gnosis-texte;* Hamdani, Husayn. *Al-Sulayhiyyun;* Hamdani, ʿAbbas. "The Daʿi"; idem. "Evolution;" Geddes. "The Apostasy"; Madelung. *Ismaʿiliyya*—EI², vol. 4, pp. 200–201; Stern. "The Succession"; Fyzee. "Three Sulaymani Daʿis"; Maqalih. *Qiraʾa*, pp. 133–170. A succinct overview of the history of the three Islamic communities of Yemen—the Zaydis, the Ismaʿilis, and the Sunnis—is given in Madelung. "Islam in Yemen" and Gochenour. "Towards a Sociology." For a political history of the Yemeni confessions in the early Middle Ages (i.e., until the 5th/11th centuries) see Piotrovsky. *Yuzhnaya Araviya.*

2. See, e.g., El-Shami and Serjeant. "Regional Literature: The Yemen." A noteworthy exception is Messick's *The Calligraphic State,* which, however, deals mainly with the modern period.

3. El-Shami and Serjeant. "Regional Literature: The Yemen," p. 460; cf. Coussonnet. "Les assises," passim; Varisco. "Texts and Pretexts," passim.

4. El-Shami and Serjeant. "Regional Literature: The Yemen," pp. 444–445.

5. The religious map of Yemen and South Arabia changed over the centuries. The traveler and geographer al-Maqdisi, writing around 378/988, reported that the majority of Yemenis adhered to the Hanafi rite, though there also were some Malikis and other legal and theological schools, e.g., the Ibadis. Throughout the 5/11th centuries, the area from Ibb to the South Arabian coast witnessed a rapid dissemination of the Shafi'i *madhhab.* With time, Shafi'sm became well entrenched in Janad, Sana'a', Aden, Lahj, and the Tihama, ousting the non-Sunni allegiances as well as the other Sunni *madhhabs;* Ibn al-Ahdal. *Tuhfat al-zaman,* pp. 110, 114–115, and 171; El-Shami and Serjeant. "Regional Literature: The Yemen," p. 445; Madelung. "Islam in Yemen," pp. 174–175. Hanafism continued to hold ground against the Shafi'i encroachment well into the Rasulid era (7/13th-9/15th centuries; Ibn Samura. *Tabaqat,* p. 74; and Ibn al-Ahdal. *Tuhfat al-zaman,* pp. 292–293), when the Hanafi school was represented by several colleges in Zabid, Ta'izz, and Aden (see al-Janadi. *Al-Suluk,* p. 549; al-Burayhi. *Tabaqat,* p. 310, note 1; al-Habshi. *Hayat al-adab,* p. 206; and al-Akwa'. *Madaris,* passim) and by many renowned scholars; see, e.g., Ibn al-Ahdal. *Tuhfat al-zaman,* pp. 241–242. Malikism seems to have been quite widespread in the earlier epochs, but had finally given way to Shafi'ism by the 6th/12th centuries, ibid., pp. 299–300. From that time onward we hear only of visiting Maghribi Malikis who came to Yemen to teach their *madhhab* to local students, which indicates that Yemeni Malikism was no longer indigenous; see al-Janadi. *Al-Suluk,* p. 460; al-Burayhi. *Tabaqat,* pp. 343, 345, 347, and 349; al-Akwa'. *Madaris,* passim.

6. On the Ibadis see Lewicki. *Al-Ibadiyya*—EI², vol. 3, pp. 648–660. The last mention of the Ibadi community in Hadramawt (South Arabia) dates back to the mid-7th/13th centuries. From then on, Hadramawt and most of Lower Yemen, became a bastion of Shafi'ism that produced many outstanding exponents of the *madhhab;* see El-Shami and Serjeant. "Regional Literature: The Yemen," p. 445; Knysh. "Ocherk religioznoy zhizni." Valuable observations on the religious situation in medieval Yemen can be found in Serjeant's *Studies in Islamic History and Civilization.* A brief and perfunctory overview of Yemeni Islam is Renaud. "Histoire et la pensée," which, characteristically, allots much more space to the Zaydis and Isma'ilis than to the Yemeni Sunnis. Ahmad Sharaf al-din's *Ta'rikh al-fikr al-islami* is also heavily biased in favor of the Zaydis; the same applies to a more recent work, Maqalih. *Qira'a,* which celebrates the "open-mindedness" of Zaydi Islam, all but ignoring the Shafi'i tradition. The only exception is 'Abdallah al-Habshi's (al-Hibshi's) *Masadir al-fikr al-islamic* (henceforth *Masadir*), which provides a relatively evenhanded overview of the vast corpus of Yemeni religious literature.

7. See al-Habshi. *Masadir;* idem. *Hayat al-adab;* a helpful bibliography of the Yemeni historiographical tradition is Sayyid. *Masadir ta'rikh al-Yaman;* cf. Serjeant. "Materials"; Piotrovsky. *Yuzhnaya Araviya,* pp. 185–192.

8. For the social and economic factors that contributed to the rapid proliferation of the Islamic *madrasas* from the 5th/11th centuries on see Makdisi. *The Rise of Colleges.*

9. Chelhod. "Histoire de Zabid," pp. 72–73; idem. "L'Islam," p. 43; Madelung. "Islam in Yemen," p. 175. For the situation in the Zaydi ares see Coussonnet. "Les assises," pp. 29–30 and 32.

10. See, e.g., Ibn al-Ahdal, *Tuhfat al-zaman,* p. 307; al-Sharji. *Tabaqat al-khawass,* pp. 67, 79, 97, etc.

11. See, e.g., al-Burayhi. *Tabaqat,* pp. 72–82; al-Sharji. *Tabaqat al-khawass,* p. 244, passim; cf. Madelung. "Islam in Yemen," p. 176.

12. Al-Burayhi. *Tabaqat,* pp. 72–82 and 136–142; al-Sharji. *Tabaqat al-khawass,* pp. 97, 134, 147, 410, etc.

13. Ibn al-Ahdal. *Tuhfat al-zaman,* pp. 284–289; Ibn Hajar. *Inba'*, vol. 3, pp. 177–178; al-Habshi. *Masadir,* p. 303; idem. *Al-Sufiyya,* passim.

14. See, e.g., al-Habshi. *Al-Sufiyya,* passim.

15. For Western accounts of Yemeni Sufism see Wüstenfeld. *Die Çufiten;* Serjeant. *The Sayyids;* de Jong. "Les confréries," pp. 230–234; Madelung. "Islam in Yemen," pp. 175–176; cf. al-ʿAqili. *Al-Tasawwuf;* al-Habshi. *Al-Sufiyya;* on Sufism in Hadramawt and South Arabia see al-Shilli. *Al-Mashraʿ* and al-ʿAlawi. *Ta'rikh Hadramawt,* vol. 2, passim.

16. See, e.g., Varisco. "Texts and Pretexts," p. 15.

17. See, e.g., Ibn Hajar. *Al-Durar,* vol. 2, p. 190.

18. On the Rasulid state-building under al-Malik al-Muzaffar Yusuf (r. 647/1249–694/1295) see Varisco. "Texts and Pretexts."

19. Al-Habshi. *Mu'allafat,* pp. 54–56.

20. See, Smith. *The Ayyubids;* idem. "The Ayyubids and Rasulids;" idem. "The Political History," pp. 135–137; Chelhod. "L'Islam," pp. 42–47; idem. *Neuf siècles;* Varisco. "Texts and Pretexts"; al-Khazraji. *Al-ʿUqud;* Yajima. *A Chronicle;* Ibn al-Daybaʿ. *Qurrat al-ʿuyun;* al-Fasi. *ʿIqd,* vol. 6, pp. 339–349.

21. For an illuminating study of al-Muzaffar's political strategy see Varisco. "Texts and Pretexts."

22. Smith. "The Political History," p. 137.

23. Ibid., p. 136; cf. Varisco. "Texts and Pretexts," p. 21; Browne, "Preface" to al-Khazraji's *al-ʿUqud,* vol. 2, pp. xxii-xiv.

24. See al-Habshi. *Hayat al-adab,* p. 50.

25. See, e.g., Varisco. "Texts and Pretexts," p. 21; for the literary output of the Rasulid sultans see al-Habshi. *Mu'allafat,* passim.

26. E.g., al-Muzaffar Yusuf (d. 694/1295) was proficient in *fiqh, hadith,* and Qur'anic exegesis; al-Ashraf 'Umar (d. 696/1297) composed works on biography, medicine, astronomy, agriculture, and genealogy; al-Afdal 'Abbas (d. 778/1377) distinguished himself as an historian; al-Ashraf Isma'il (d. 803/1400) excelled in the belle-lettres and historical writing; see al-Khazraji. *Al-'Uqud,* vol. 2, p. 378; Sayyid. *Masadir ta'rikh al-Yaman,* pp. 148–150 and 157–158; El-Shami and Serjeant. "Regional Literature: The Yemen," pp. 461–462. Many Rasulid sultans and princes studied under the guidance of the foremost scholars and litterateurs of their time; see, e.g., al-Burayhi. *Tabaqat,* p. 312; al-Habshi.*Masadir,* pp. 605–610; idem. *Mu'allafat,* pp. 55–58, 61–62, 78–84, passim.

27. Chelhod. "Histoire de Zabid," pp. 72–74; Varisco. "Texts and Pretexts," p. 21. As a vivid illustration of the Rasulids' love of learning one may note that the sultan al-Malik al-Muzaffar (r. 647/1249–694/1295) sent a special messenger to Herat in order to obtain an autograph of Fakhr al-din al-Razi's *Commentary on the Qur'an* because he found too many mistakes in the copy at his disposal; see Browne, "Preface" to al-Khazraji's *al-'Uqud,* vol. 2, p. xiii; cf. ibid., p. 278 of the Arabic text.

28. Varisco. "Texts and Pretexts," p. 21.

29. Al-Burayhi. *Tabaqat,* pp. 339–340. The Rasulid sultan repeatedly invited this renowned Egyptian scholar to take up the post of the supreme *qadi* of Yemen, but Ibn Hajar persistently declined his overtures; see Ibn Hajar. *Inba',* vol. 3, p. 178; al-Sakhawi. *Al-Daw',* vol. 1, p. 261.

30. He flourished under the sultans al-Ashraf Isma'il II and al-Nasir Ahmad (r. 803/1400–827/1424); see al-Burayhi. *Ta'rikh,* pp. 296–297; for further details see the next section.

31. Al-Fasi. *'Iqd,* vol. 1, pp. 338 and 341 and Chapter 5 of this study; Löfgren. *Arabische Texte,* vol. 2, pp. 199–200; al-Burayhi. *Tabaqat,* pp. 349–350.

32. Ben Cheneb. *Ibn al-Djazari*—EI[2], vol. 3, p. 753; for his stay in Yemen see al-Burayhi. *Tabaqat,* pp. 342–347.

33. Miquel. *Ibn Battuta*—EI[2], vol. 3, pp. 735–736; on Ibn Battuta's description of the Rasulid Yemen see Sayyid. *Masadir ta'rikh al-Yaman,* pp. 150–151; Chelhod. "L'Islam," p. 44; idem. "Histoire de Zabid," pp. 74–75; and Dunn. *The Adventures,* pp. 109–118. For some other eminent visitors to Rasulid Yemen see al-Burayhi. *Tabaqat,* pp. 339–352.

34. Morris. "Interpreters", pt. 3, p. 108; Chittick. "Ibn 'Arabi and His School," p. 56; Zaydan. *Al-Fikr al-sufi,* passim.

35. See, e.g., al-Khazraji. *Al-ʿUqud,* vol. 1, pp. 223 and 263; Zaydan. *Al-Fikr al-sufi,* pp. 33–46.

36. Ibid.; cf. Ibn al-Ahdal. *Kashf,* p. 214; for some other eminent Sufi visitors to the Rasulid Yemen see al-Burayhi. *Tabaqat,* pp. 340–342.

37. Ibn ʿAlwan. *Al-Tawhid al-aʿzam,* pp. 34–35; al-Habshi. *Masadir,* pp. 305–306 and idem. *Hayat al-adab,* pp. 225–235; idem. *Al-Sufiyya,* passim.

38. Zaydan. *Al-Fikr al-sufi,* pp. 38–41.

39. See, e.g., Yahia's introduction to the new edition of the *Futuhat,* vol. 1, p. 36.

40. See, e.g., Ibn Hajar. *Inbaʾ*, vol. 3, p. 178; Yahya b. al-Husayn. *Ghayat al-amani,* vol. 2, p. 569; al-Habshi. *Al-Sufiyya,* passim; and idem. *Masadir,* p. 303.

41. Al-Khazraji. *Al-ʿUqud,* vol. 1, p. 110; vol. 2, pp. 248–249; al-Sharji. *Tabaqat al-khawass,* p. 244; Ibn al-Ahdal. *Tuhfat al-zaman,* p. 357; Ibn al-Muqri. *Majmuʿ*, pp. 16–19; al-Habshi. *Hayat al-adab,* pp. 225–226; idem. *Al-Sufiyya,* p. 33, passim.

42. See, al-Habshi. *Hayat al-adab,* p. 225.

43. See, e.g., al-Burayhi. *Tabaqat,* pp. 65 and 199; Ibn al-Ahdal. *Kashf,* pp. 217 and 220–221; idem. *Tuhfat al-zaman,* p. 357; Ibn al-Muqri. *Majmuʿ*, pp. 4–19; for an eloquent apology for *samaʿ* see Ibn ʿAlwan. *At-Tawhid al-aʿzam,* pp. 133–137.

44. Ibn al-Muqri. *Majmuʿ*, pp. 10, 12–14, 20, 25, etc.; Ibn Hajar. *Inbaʾ*, vol. 3, p. 178; al-Habshi. *Hayat al-adab,* p. 226.

45. Boase and Sahnoun. "Excerpts", pp. 51–52.

46. This, at least, is an impression I gained from the conversations with contemporary Yemeni historians and religious scholars in 1986–1989; cf. Ba Fadl. *Daʿwat al-khalaf,* passim.

47. For his life and work see: al-Sakhawi. *Al-Dawʾ*, vol. 3, pp. 145–147; al-Shawkani. *Al-Badr,* vol. 1, pp. 218–219; Brockelmann. Geschichte, vol. 2, p. 235; idem. *Supplement,* vol. 2, 238; al-Zirikli. *Al-Aʿlam,* vol. 2, p. 240; Kahhala. *Muʿjam,* vol. 4, pp. 15–16; Sayyid. *Masadir taʾrikh al-Yaman,* pp. 178–183. For further references see al-Habshi. *Masadir*, p. 132 and "Introduction" to Ibn al-Ahdal. *Tuhfat al-zaman,* pp. 5–13. For some eminent Sufis in the Ibn al-Ahdal family see al-Khazraji. *Al-ʿUqud,* vol. 1, p. 263; al-Sharji. *Tabaqat al-khawass,* pp. 195–198; Ibn ʿAlwan. *Al-Tawhid al-aʿzam,* pp. 18 and 30.

48. On the al-Ahdal sayyids see al-Muhibbi. *Khulasat al-athar,* vol. 1, pp. 67–68; Löfgren. *Al-Ahdal*—EI[2], vol. 1, pp. 255–256; al-Habshi. *Masadir,* p. 132; Baʿkar. *Kawakib,* pp. 521–526; Voll. "The Mizjaji Family," pp. 79–80.

49. For a list of Ibn al-Ahdal's teachers see al-Sakhawi. *Al-Daw'*, vol. 3, pp. 145–146.

50. Ibn al-Ahdal. *Tuhfat al-zaman,* pp. 6–7.

51. Ba'kar. *Kawakib,* p. 522. Ibn al-Raddad's career will be discussed further on.

52. See al-Sakhawi. *Al-Daw'*, vol. 3, pp. 146–147.

53. See, e.g., *Tuhfat al-zaman,* pp. 285–291.

54. In Western scholarship, Ibn al-Ahdal is known primarily as an historian of medieval Yemen. His two major historical works are adaptations of the earlier Yemeni chronicles, *al-Suluk fi tabaqat al-'ulama' wa 'l-muluk* by al-Janadi (d. 732/1331) and *Mir'at al-janan* by al-Yafi'i. For Ibn al-Ahdal's exposition of the goals of historical writing see Rosenthal. *A History,* pp. 317–318; for a list of his historical and biographical works see Brockelmann. *Geschichte,* vol. 2, p. 235.

55. Al-Sakhawi, who mentions eighteen works attributed to Ibn al-Ahdal, describes the *Kashf* as "an enormous volume" (*mujallad dakhm*); *al-Daw'*, vol. 3, p. 146. Judging from the frustratingly sloppy edition of this work by the Tunisian scholar Ahmad Bakir (Bukayr) Muhammad, the manuscript of this work consisted of 172 fols., which corresponds to 316 pages in the printed edition.

56. See *Tuhfat al-zaman,* pp. 266–268.

57. A manuscript of this work, titled *Risala fi sha'n Ibn 'Arabi, aw Mukhtasar fi bayan hal Ibn 'Arabi,* is located in the library of the Institute for Oriental Studies, Russian Academy of Sciences, St. Petersburg, ref. no. B4642. It may be identical with Ibn al-Ahdal's other work on al-Sakhawi's list—i.e., *Bayan hukm al-shalh wa 'l-nass 'ala muruq Ibn al-'Arabi wa Ibn al-Farid;* al-Sakhawi. *Al-Daw'*, vol. 3, p. 146.

58. Abu 'l-Ghayth, known in Yemen as "The Greatest Sun [of the mystical way]" (*shams al-shumus*), is said to have been a brigand who was converted to Sufism in an episode that is closely patterned on the conversion story of the early ascetic al-Fudayl Ibn 'Iyad (d. 187/803); see Arberry. *Muslim Saints,* pp. 53–57. Abu 'l-Ghayth's miraculous biography is featured in most Yemeni histories and bio/hagiographical dictionaries; see e.g., al-Sharji. *Tabaqat al-khawass,* pp. 406–410, passim; al-Janadi. *Al-Suluk,* pp. 383–386 and 456–457; al-Yafi'i. *Mir'at,* vol. 4, p. 136; al-Khazraji. *Al-'Uqud,* vol. 1, p. 110; Ibn al-Ahdal. *Tuhfat al-zaman,* pp. 280–291 and 353–354; al-Burayhi. *Tabaqat,* "index"; see also al-Habshi. *Masadir,* p. 305; idem. *Al-Sufiyya,* pp. 15–16; 53–55, 70–72; El-Shami and Serjeant. "Regional Literature: The Yemen," p. 468.

59. See, e.g., al-Khazraji. *Al-'Uqud,* vol. 1, p. 109; Zaydan. *Al-Fikr al-sufi,* pp. 36–37; on the *shatahat* see Chapter 2 of this study.

60. Ibn al-Ahdal. *Kashf,* pp. 214, 252, 255, etc.; idem. *Tuhfat al-zaman,* pp. 287–291; cf. al-Maqbali. *Al-ʿAlam,* p. 299.

61. See, e.g., al-Janadi. *Al-Suluk,* pp. 385–386; Ibn al-Ahdal. *Tuhfat al-zaman,* pp. 280–282, 286–288, and 290–291; al-Habshi. *Al-Sufiyya,* pp. 53–55 and 70–72. Many of the sayings in question are reminiscent of those attributed to the classical Sufis; see Ibn al-Ahdal. *Tuhfat al-zaman,* pp. 290–291.

62. Ibn al-Ahdal. *Kashf,* pp. 279–280; idem. *Tuhfat al-zaman,* p. 275.

63. See Zaydan. *Al-Fikr al-sufi,* p. 36.

64. To substantiate this claim, Ibn al-Ahdal argues that Abu ʾl-Ghayth Ibn Jamil was illiterate and therefore left behind no writings. Hence, the blasphemous sayings must have been inserted into the records of his oral teachings which were taken by his disciples; see Ibn al-Ahdal. *Kashf,* pp. 220 and 279–280; idem. *Tuhfat al-zaman,* pp. 285–286. This explanation is rebuffed by a modern Yemeni researcher, who viewed Ibn Jamil's sayings to tally with what is known about his personality; al-Habshi. *Al-Sufiyya,* p. 71; cf. al-Maqbali. *Al-ʿAlam,* p. 299.

65. Al-Habshi. *Al-Sufiyya,* p. 33.

66. See al-Janadi. *Al-Suluk,* pp. 385–386 and 455–458; al-Sharji. *Tabaqat al-khawass,* pp. 69–71; al-Yafiʿi. *Mirʾat,* vol. 4, p. 257; al-Khazraji. *Al-ʿUqud,* vol. 1, pp. 160–162; Ibn al-Ahdal. *Kashf,* pp. 281–290; idem. *Tuhfat al-zaman,* pp. 246 and 353–357; al-Burayhi. *Tabaqat,* "index"; al-Habshi. *Masadir,* p. 306; Brockelmann. *Geschichte,* vol. 1, p. 449; El-Shami and Serjeant. "Regional Literature: The Yemen," p. 468; and Messick. *The Calligraphic State,* pp. 50 and 276, note 40; for a recent edition of Ibn ʿAlwan's mystical treatise see Ibn ʿAlwan. *Al-Tawhid al-aʿzam.*

67. Al-Sharji. *Tabaqat al-khawass,* pp. 363–364.

68. Ibn al-Ahdal. *Tuhfat al-zaman,* pp. 354–356; cf. al-Habshi. *Al-Sufiyya,* pp. 72 and 73.

69. Al-Khazraji. *Al-ʿUqud,* vol. 1, p. 161; al-Sharji. *Tabaqat al-khawass,* p. 69.

70. Ibid.; see also al-Janadi. *Al-Suluk,* pp. 456–457; Ibn al-Ahdal. *Tuhfat al-zaman,* pp. 354–355.

71. Ibn al-Ahdal, however, had no doubts about Ibn ʿAlwan's intellectual affinity with of the Greatest Master; see, e.g., *Tuhfat al-zaman,* pp. 289 and 355.

72. Al-Sharji. *Tabaqat al-khawass,* pp. 70–71; cf. Ibn al-Ahdal. *Tuhfat al-zaman,* pp. 355–356.

73. Massignon. *The Passion,* vol. 2, pp. 293–294; cf. al-Habshi. *Al-Sufiyya,* p. 72.

74. Concerning the Ayyubid position vis-à-vis Sufism see: Chodkiewicz. *Le sceau,* pp. 19–22. Some facts illustrating the Rasulids' leniency toward their Sufi subjects are mentioned in al-Habshi. *Al-Sufiyya,* pp. 42–50. At the same time, both the Ayyubids and the Rasulids were acutely aware of the potential political dangers presented by organized mystical movements and ruthlessly suppressed any attempts to use mysticism for political goals; see e.g., Smith. "The Political History," p. 36.

75. Al-Khazraji. *Al-ʿUqud,* vol. 1, p. 409.

76. For the Rifaʿiyya (Ahmadiyya) see Trimingham. *Orders,* pp. 37–40 and "index." The presence of this order in Yemen, documented in al-Sharji's *Tabaqat al-khawass,* is totally neglected in Madelung. "Islam in Yemen," p. 176.

77. Al-Sharji. *Tabaqat al-khawass,* p. 245.

78. Ibn al-Ahdal. *Kashf,* p. 217; cf. Zaydan. *Al-Fikr al-sufi,* p. 40.

79. Some Yemeni sources spell his name as "al-Bana," "al-Baba," or even "Ibn al-Taʾih"; see al-Khazraji. *Al-ʿUqud,* vol. 2, p. 428; cf. vol. 1, pp. 206–207 (in the latter passage his death is dated 677/1278, which may indicate a confusion between two different scholars).

80. Yajima. *A Chronicle,* p. 25; for a more comprehensive bibliography on those rulers see Sayyid. *Masadir taʾrikh al-Yaman,* p. 396. It should be noted that al-Muzaffar's voluntary abdication came as the result of his disillusionment with his mundane pursuits and was followed by his conversion to Sufism.

81. He taught *fiqh* at the Madrasa al-Ashrafiyya in Zabid and counted many prominent Yemeni scholars among his students; see, e.g., al-Khazraji. *Al-ʿUqud,* vol. 1, pp. 256, 337 and 412, vol. 2, pp. 15 and 37.

82. Ibn al-Ahdal. *Tuhfat al-zaman,* p. 347; cf. al-Khazraji. *Al-ʿUqud,* vol. 1, p. 412.

83. Interestingly, similar condemnations were brought up by the scholars of Aden against the quite conventional Ashʿari doctor from Persia named al-Baylaqani (mid-7/13th centuries). In general, Yemeni *ʿulamaʾ* were suspicious of *kalam* speculation, which they viewed as the domain of their principal opponents, the Zaydis, who espoused a version of the Muʿtazili doctrine. A strong opposition to rational and philosophical theology on the part of the conservative Yemeni legists explains why Ashʿarism took more than two centuries to establish itself as a legitimate doctrinal persuasion in Yemen; see Ibn al-Ahdal. *Tuhfat al-zaman,* pp. 240–242; cf. Madelung. "Islam in Yemen," p. 175.

84. For the text of al-Muzaffar's letter see Ibn al-Ahdal. *Kashf,* p. 219; al-Habshi. *Al-Sufiyya,* p. 114; al-Akwaʿ. *Madaris,* p. 69.

85. Ibn al-Ahdal. *Kashf,* p. 219.

86. Ibid., p. 216; cf. al-Khazraji. *Al-ʿUqud,* vol. 1, pp. 206–207, where Ibn al-Naba's death is given as 677/1278.

87. Ibn al-Ahdal. *Tuhfat al-zaman,* p. 289; al-Khazraji. *Al-ʿUqud,* vol. 1, pp. 389–390; Baʿkar. *Kawakib,* pp. 543–546.

88. One of al-Yahyawi's teachers was Ibn al-Naba, who may have introduced his disciple to Ibn ʿArabi's ideas; see al-Habshi. *Al-Sufiyya,* pp. 73–74.

89. Al-Khazraji. *Al-ʿUqud,* vol. 1, p. 389.

90. Ibn al-Ahdal. *Kashf,* p. 217.

91. On the bibliography of this period see Sayyid. *Masadir taʾrikh al-Yaman,* p. 396; cf. ʿAbd al-ʿAl. *Banu Rasul,* pp. 166–175. Concerning the ties of friendship between the sultan and Abu ʾl-ʿAtiq see Ibn al-Ahdal. *Kashf,* p. 218; al-Khazraji. *Al-ʿUqud,* vol. 1, p. 389; cf. al-Habshi. *Al-Sufiyya,* p. 74; Baʿkar. *Kawakib,* pp. 544–545.

92. According to al-Khazraji, "the sultan never opposed anything he [i.e. al-Yahyawi] wanted to do, on the assumption that whatever he did was correct," *al-ʿUqud,* vol. 1, p. 389.

93. Al-Yahyawi's prognostication skill reportedly allowed him to predict the rise and fall of al-Muʾayyad's rebellious brother, the prince al-Ashraf, who deposed the sultan but was unable to enjoy the fruits of his triumph as he died soon afterwards; see Baʿkar. *Kawakib,* p. 544.

94. Ibn al-Ahdal. *Kashf,* p. 218.

95. He is said to have transferred the supervision of *awqaf* endowments from semi-independent judges to the officials of the royal chancery; see al-Khazraji. *Al-ʿUqud,* vol. 1, p. 389.

96. Ibn al-Ahdal. *Kashf,* p. 218. Despite these measures, consumption of date wine was widespread both among the rulers and the commoners; see Chelhod. "Histoire de Zabid," p. 75.

97. *Kashf,* p. 218; similar charges were leveled at another leader of the Ibn ʿArabi party, Abu Bakr Ibn al-Raddad, see Ibn Hajar. *Inbaʾ*, vol. 3, p. 178.

98. Ibn al-Ahdal. *Kashf,* pp. 217 and 218; cf. al-Habshi. *Al-Sufiyya,* pp. 74–75. For al-Nashiri's biography see al-Sharji. *Tabaqat al-khawass,* pp. 32–33; Ibn Hajar. *Inbaʾ*, vol. 2, p. 525; al-Sakhawi. *Al-Dawʾ*, vol. 1, p. 257; Ibn al-ʿImad. *Shadharat,* vol. 7, p. 109; and al-Habshi. *Masadir,* p. 206.

99. Ibn al-Ahdal. *Kashf,* p. 218. Al-Yahyawi's younger brother Muhammad (d. 712/1312), who succeeded him as the grand *qadi* of Yemen, was also a Sufi ascetic, although he seemed to have adhered to a more conventional form of Sufism; see Baʿkar. *Kawakib,* p. 545.

100. For his biography and work see Ibn Hajar. *Inba'*, vol. 2, pp. 272–273; al-Sharji. *Tabaqat al-khawass,* pp. 101–107; al-Sakhawi. *Al-Daw'*, vol. 2, pp. 282–284; al-Nabhani. *Jami' karamat,* vol. 1, p. 358; al-Habshi. *Al-Sufiyya,* passim; idem., *Hayat al-adab,* pp. 226–227; al-Akwa'. *Madaris,* pp. 212, 213, and "index"; Zaydan. *Al-Fikr al-sufi,* pp. 37–43.

101. For his rule see Sayyid. *Masadir ta' rikh al-Yaman,* p. 397.

102. Ibn Hajar. *Inba'*, vol. 2, p. 272; al-Sakhawi. *Al-Daw'*, vol. 2, pp. 282–283; al-Shawkani. *Al-Badr,* vol. 2, p. 139.

103. Al-Jabarti, however, was not the illiterate bumpkin his foes tried to portray him as. He began his career by teaching the Qur'an at an elementary school (al-Sakhawi. *Al-Daw'*, vol. 2, p. 283), whereupon he turned to an austere asceticism and mystical meditation. Having made rapid progress on the Sufi Path, he received Sufi investiture from the leading masters of his time. When al-Jabarti's detractors mention his "illiteracy," they mean that he did not receive formal religious education and expressed himself in colloquial Arabic; see, e.g., Ibn al-Ahdal. *Kashf,* p. 215. Al-Jabarti's proficiency in the Islamic sciences is attested by Ibn Hajar who made his personal acquaintance on a visit to Zabid; *Inba'*, vol. 2 p. 272.

104. I.e., *sura* 36. Al-Jabarti's alleged lack of formal theological training is also mentioned by Ibn al-Ahdal, who, however, considered this to be relatively unimportant in comparison with al-Jabarti's monistic "delusions"; see *Kashf,* pp. 215–216.

105. Al-Shawkani. *Al-Badr,* vol. 2, pp. 214–225; cf. Brockelmann. *Supplement,* vol. 2, pp. 818–819.

106. Al-Shawkani. *Al-Badr,* vol. 2, p. 139. Al-Sakhawi's harsh treatment of al-Jabarti naturally flowed from his relentless opposition to the Greatest Master, which found its most notable expression in his polemical treatise titled *al-Qawl al-munbi 'an tarjamat Ibn 'Arabi.*

107. Zaydan. *Al-Fikr al-sufi,* pp. 40–42.

108. E.g., al-Khazraji. *Al-'Uqud,* vol. 2, p. 248; cf. al-Habshi. *Hayat al-adab,* p. 227.

109. Ibn Hajar. *Inba'*, vol. 2, p. 272; al-Sakhawi. *Al-Daw'*, vol. 2, pp. 382–383; al-Shawkani. *Al-Badr,* vol. 1, p. 139; al-Akwa'. *Madaris,* pp. 213–214. A similar respect for Ibn 'Arabi was demonstrated by al-Jabarti's successors at the head of the Sufi school; see Ibn al-Muqri. *Majmu'*, p. 34; Ibn Hajar. *Inba'*, vol. 3, p. 178.

110. According to a hostile observer, in al-Jabarti's lectures the *Fusus* assumed the place of the Qur'an; see Ibn al-Muqri. *Majmu'*, pp. 32–33; cf. also 13 and 14.

111. For al-Qashani and his place within the Ibn ʿArabi tradition see Macdonald. *ʿAbd al-Razzak al-Kashani*—EI², vol. 1, pp. 88–89; Izutsu. *A Comparative Study;* Landolt. "Der Briefwechsel;" Morris. "Interpreters," pt. 3, pp. 101–108.

112. Dawud al-Qaysari (d. 751/1350), a disciple of al-Qashani and the author of an influential commentary on the *Fusus,* see Chittick. "The Five Divine Presences"; cf. Knysh. "Irfan Revisited," pp. 631–635.

113. Mu'ayyad al-din al-Jandi (d. 690/1291), the author of an early commentary on the *Fusus* that formed "the basis for most of the numerous commentaries that were written later," Chittick. "Rumi and *wahdat al-wujud,*" p. 79.

114. The editor's reading of the text makes only a confusing sense. In view of the overall inaccuracy of his edition of the *Kashf,* I was forced, throughout, to provide alternative readings. In this case, I read *la'in taʿtini al-ka's la-arsalak ila khalqi,* though other variants are possible.

115. *Subhanak*—an epithet normally applied to Allah.

116. Ibn al-Ahdal. *Kashf,* p. 214.

117. Cf. Morris. "Interpreters," pt. 2, pp. 738–741.

118. See Knysh. "Ibrahim al-Kurani."

119. See Chittick. "Rumi and *wahdat al-wujud.* "

120. Al-Sharji. *Tabaqat al-khawass,* pp. 104–105.

121. Ibn al-Ahdal. *Kashf,* pp. 214 and 215; cf. Zaydan. *Al-Fikr al-sufi,* pp. 36–37.

122. Ibid., p. 214; for similar accusations leveled at Ibn ʿArabi and his followers by a contemporary Muslim writer see al-Zayyin. *Ibn ʿArabi,* pp. 44–54, passim.

123. Zaydan. *Al-Fikr al-sufi,* p. 37.

124. Ibn al-Ahdal. *Kashf,* p. 215, quoting Ibn al-Raddad's book on the transmission of the Sufi frock (*khirqa*), which is still in manuscript; see al-Habshi. *Masadir,* p. 312.

125. See Massignon. *The Passion,* vol. 2, p. 6, note 6; Zaydan. *Al-Fikr al-sufi,* p. 37.

126. For Ibn ʿArabi's stance on the transcendency/immanence issue see Chittick. *The Sufi Path of Knowledge,* p. 358 and Sells. "Ibn ʿArabi's 'Garden,'" idem. "Ibn ʿArabi's Polished Mirror." Note, however, that in a famous passage from the *Fusus* Ibn ʿArabi explicitly stated that God "bears the name of Abu Saʿid al-Kharraz [a famous early Sufi] and all the other names

given to relative beings"; Austin. *Bezels,* p. 86, cf. 95 and 108--an idea which al-Jabarti made his own.

127. See, e.g., al-Sharji. *Tabaqat al-khawass,* pp. 101–102 and 104.

128. This argument falls to the ground if we remember that al-Jabarti's successor, Ibn al-Raddad, was a formally trained scholar.

129. Ibn al-Ahdal. *Kashf,* p. 215.

130. Ibid., p. 216.

131. Ibid.

132. Judging by his *nisba* "al-Qurashi," Ibn al-Raddad's family came from the Prophet's native tribe Quraysh. His other *nisba,* al-Bakri, indicates that he belonged to the descendants of the first Islamic caliph Abu Bakr; see al-Burayhi. *Tabaqat,* p. 298; al-Habshi. *Masadir,* p. 312.

133. He studied under the leading scholars of his time in Mecca and Medina see Ibn Hajar. *Inba'*, vol. 3, pp. 177–178; al-Sakhawi. *Al-Daw'*, vol. 1, p. 261.

134. Al-Habshi. *Al-Sufiyya,* p. 26. For the mystical pedigree of this frock starting from al-Jabarti all the way back to the founder of the Qadiriyya order see al-Sakhawi. *Al-Daw'*, vol. 1, p. 262.

135. I.e., Ibn ʿArabi's teaching.

136. Ibn Hajar. *Inba'*, vol. 3, pp. 177–178; cf. al-Sakhawi. *Al-Daw'*, vol. 1, p. 261.

137. See, e.g., al-Khazraji. *Al-ʿUqud,* vol. 2, pp. 225–227.

138. *Al-Daw'*, vol. 1, p. 261.

139. Ibn Hajar. *Inba'*, vol. 3, p. 178.

140. Al-Habshi. *Masadir,* p. 312; for a list of Ibn al-Raddad's works see Zaydan. *Al-Fikr al-sufi,* p. 45.

141. Al-Sharji. *Tabaqat al-khawass,* pp. 90–91.

142. Al-Burayhi. *Tabaqat,* pp. 301–302.

143. Meaning Ibn ʿArabi's teaching.

144. Ibn Hajar. *Inba'*, vol. 3, p. 178; cf. al-Sakhawi. *Al-Daw'*, vol. 1, p. 261.

145. This is especially remarkable since al-Jabarti's sons were also active Sufis of no mean repute, e.g., Radi al-din Abu Bakr (d. 823/1420) who "followed his father's path in all respects" (al-Sharji. *Tabaqat al-khawass,* p. 39; cf. Ibn al-Ahdal. *Tuhfat al-zaman,* p. 357). After al-Jabarti's death many Sufis of Zabid retained their loyalty to the Jabarti family with Radi al-din at

its head. The Jabartis remained active until around 875/1470, when Isma'il al-Jabarti Jr., the last distinguished Sufi in the al-Jabarti line, died without a successor. His death coincided with the decline of the Ibn 'Arabi school in Yemen. Al-Sharji mentions a few Sufi shaykhs named al-Jabarti, who were active in Ta'izz in the late 9th/15th centuries (*Tabaqat al-khawass,* p. 422), but it is not clear whether they came from the same al-Jabarti clan.

146. Al-Burayhi. *Tabaqat,* p. 299; according to Ibn al-Ahdal (*Kashf,* p. 221), Ibn al-Raddad was offered the post of the chief *qadi* of Yemen shortly before his death in 821/1418; cf. Abu Zayd. *Isma'il,* pp. 21 and 22; al-Habshi. *Al-Sufiyya,* pp. 138 and 139. Ibn al-Hajar explained the temporal gap between the death of al-Fayruzabadi (817/1415) and the appointment of Ibn al-Raddad by the fact that al-Nasir wanted him (i.e., Ibn Hajar) to take the office and kept it vacant for two years. When Ibn Hajar finally declined, al-Nasir gave it to Ibn al-Raddad; see Ibn Hajar. *Inba'*, vol. 3, p. 178; cf. al-Sakhawi. *Al-Daw'*, vol. 1, p. 261.

147. For al-Jili's life and work see Zaydan. *Al-Fikr al-sufi;* Morris. "Interpreters," pt. 3, p. 108; Ritter. *'Abd al-Karim al-Djili*—EI^2, vol. 1, p. 71; al-Baghdadi. *Hadiyat al-'arifin,* vol. 1, pp. 610–611; Brockelmann. *Geschichte,* vol. 2, pp. 205–206; Kahhala. *Mu'jam,* vol. 5, pp. 313–314; Bannerth. *Das Buch.* For a standard, if somewhat dated, account of al-Jili's philosophical views see Nicholson. *Studies,* pp. 82–148.

148. Al-Khazraji, e.g., mentioned him only in connection with the Yemeni Sufis who had received instruction under his guidance, see *al-'Uqud,* vol. 1, pp. 82, 223 and 263; cf., however, al-Habshi. *Al-Sufiyya,* p. 131.

149. Ibn al-Ahdal. *Kashf,* p. 214; cf. Ibn al-Muqri. *Majmu'*, p. 29.

150. See Zaydan. *Al-Fikr al-sufi,* pp. 23–26.

151. For some renowned members of the Bijli family see al-Sharji. *Tabaqat al-khawass,* pp. 198–202 and 239.

152. Ibn al-Ahdal. *Kashf,* p. 214.

153. Bannerth. *Das Buch,* p. 37.

154. Ibid., pp. 35–37.

155. Zaydan. *Al-Fikr al-sufi,* pp. 35–36.

156. Al-Sharji. *Tabaqat al-khawass,* p. 385; cf., however, al-Sakhawi. *Al-Daw'*, vol. 2, pp. 283–284.

157. See, e.g., Ritter. *'Abd al-Karim al-Djili*—EI^2, vol. 1, p. 71; Nicholson. *Studies,* p. 81. Concerning al-Hakkak see al-Sharji. *Tabaqat al-khawass,* p. 385; al-Burayhi. *Tabaqat,* pp. 284–285; al-Habshi. *Masadir,* p. 362.

158. Morris. "Interpreters," pt. 2, pp. 741–744; Zaydan. *Al-Fikr al-sufi,* pp. 38–43; cf. al-Taftazani, Abu 'l-Wafa'. "Al-Tariqa al-akbariyya," passim.

159. See al-Jili. *Al-Insan.*

160. Al-Jili referred to the primordial, cosmic essence of the Prophet Muhammad (*al-haqiqa al-muhammadiyya*) rather than to his "limited" historical manifestation; see al-Hakim. *Al-Mu'jam,* pp. 347–352.

161. Burckhardt. *Al-Jili,* p. XX. I have modified Burckhardt's translation of this passage (for the original Arabic text see al-Jili. *Al-Insan,* vol. 2, p. 48). For an analysis of this concept within the context of "an Islamic Logos doctrine" see Nicholson. *Studies,* pp. 86–89.

162. Zaydan. *Al-Fikr al-sufi,* p. 37.

163. Ibid., p. 37.

164. Ibid., pp. 23 and 38.

165. Ibid., p. 40.

166. Morris. "Interpreters," pt. 2, p. 753.

167. See, e.g., *Kashf,* p. 214.

168. Ibid.

169. Zaydan. *Al-Fikr al-sufi,* passim.

170. Al-Sharji. *Tabaqat al-khawass,* p. 244.

171. Al-Khazraji. *Al-'Uqud,* vol. 2, pp. 248–249; al-Habshi. *Hayat al-adab,* pp. 226–227.

172. Or "al-Makki," according to al-Khazraji, see *al-'Uqud,* vol. 2, p. 273. Despite his opposition to al-Jabarti, al-Misri was himself a mystic of moderate leanings—a fact that belies al-Habshi's view of these events as a confrontation between the *sufiyya* and the *fuqaha'* par excellence; see al-Sakhawi. *Al-Daw',* vol. 2, p. 283; al-Shawkani. *Al-Badr,* vol. 1, p. 139.

173. Al-Khazraji. *Al-'Uqud,* vol. 2, pp. 272–273. Madelung mistakenly reverses the situation, claiming that it was al-Jabarti who was expelled to India; see "Islam in Yemen," p. 176.

174. One scholar, Muhammad b. Musa al-Dhu'ali (d. 790/1388), wrote a refutation (*radd*) of al-Jabarti and was about to pass it onto the preacher of a Friday mosque to be read from the pulpit. However, upon hearing about the fate of al-Misri, he withdrew his pamphlet; al-Habshi. *Al-Sufiyya,* p. 98. When the storm blew over, al-Dhu'ali bemoaned the expulsion of Salih al-Misri and al-Jabarti's "outrageous" behavior; see al-Sakhawi. *Al-Daw,* vol. 2, p. 283.

175. Al-Habshi. *Mu'allafat,* p. 90.

176. See al-Sakhawi. *Al-Daw',* vol. 11, pp. 78–79; al-Burayhi. *Tabaqat,* pp. 117–120; Ibn al-'Imad. *Shadharat,* vol. 7, p. 91; al-Habshi. *Masadir,* p. 217; al-Akwa'. *Madaris,* pp. 154–155.

177. See al-Qari al-Baghdadi. *Manaqib,* pp. 64–65; al-Maqqari. *Nafh,* vol. 2, p. 379.

178. According to al-Burayhi, Ibn al-Khayyat's response was five pages in length, *Tabaqat,* p. 119.

179. Al-Qari al-Baghdadi. *Manaqib,* p. 66; cf. al-Maqqari. *Nafh,* vol. 2, p. 379.

180. Ibid.; al-Qari al-Baghdadi. *Manaqib,* p. 65; cf. O'Fahey. *Enigmatic Saint,* p. 103.

181. See al-Sakhawi. *Al-Daw'*, vol. 10, p. 85.

182. Cf. Zakariya al-Ansari's (d. 926/1519) ruling in favor of Ibn al-Farid and Ibn ʿArabi in the al-Biqaʿi episode; Homerin. *From Arab Poet,* pp. 69–73.

183. In a sense, al-Fayruzabadi's *fatwa* anticipates the official prohibition to publicly debase the Greatest Master under some Ottoman sultans; see Ibn al-ʿImad. *Shadharat,* vol. 5, p. 165.

184. Al-Sakhawi. *Al-Daw'*, vol. 10, p. 86.

185. For Ibn Hajar's position vis-à-vis the Ibn ʿArabi debate see Chapter 8 of this study.

186. Al-Sakhawi. *Al-Daw'*, vol. 10, p. 85.

187. See note 98 of this chapter.

188. Al-Habshi. *Masadir,* p. 312.

189. Ibn al-Ahdal. *Kashf,* p. 216; al-Habshi. *Al-Sufiyya,* pp. 99 and 128–129.

190. Al-Sakhawi. *Al-Daw'*, vol. 1, p. 258.

191. Al-Sharji. *Tabaqat al-khawass,* p. 92.

192. Our sources usually refer to him as "Ibn Nur al-din"; see al-Burayhi. *Tabaqat,* pp. 268–269. Al-Sakhawi dedicates to him only a few lines, mentioning his opposition to Ibn ʿArabi's followers, *al-Daw'*, vol. 8, p. 223; cf. al-Habshi. *Masadir,* pp. 218 and 312.

193. Al-Burayhi. *Tabaqat,* p. 269; al-Habshi. *Masadir,* p. 218. According to Ibn al-Ahdal (*Kashf,* p. 216), it was the young Persian Sufi al-Kirmani, and not Ibn al-Raddad, who was al-Khatib's opponent in the dispute.

194. Al-Burayhi. *Tabaqat,* pp. 268–269; al-Habshi. *Masadir,* p. 312; idem. *Hayat al-adab,* p. 100; idem. *Al-Sufiyya,* pp. 134–135.

195. Ibn al-Ahdal. *Kashf,* p. 217.

196. He died in 837/1433. In modern Yemeni scholarship, Ibn al-Muqri is often viewed as an embodiment of the cultural florescence of Yemen

under the Rasulids. On his biography see al-Sakhawi. *Al-Daw'*, vol. 2, pp. 292–295; al-Burayhi. *Tabaqat,* pp. 300–305; Ibn al-ʿImad. *Shadharat,* vol. 7, pp. 220–222; al-Shawkani. *Al-Badr,* vol. 1, pp. 142–145. For a fine introduction to Ibn al-Muqri's life and thought by a contemporary Arab scholar see Abu Zayd. *Ismaʿil;* cf. al-Habshi. *Dirasat,* pp. 27–43; idem. *Hayat al-adab,* pp. 269–281; idem. *Masadir,* p. 220.

197. Al-Sakhawi. *Al-Daw'*, vol. 2, p. 293.

198. Ibn al-ʿImad. *Shadharat,* vol. 5, p. 192.

199. Meaning Sufi concerts in the mosques.

200. I.e., distinguished scholars.

201. Ibn al-Muqri. *Majmuʿ*, p. 9; cf. al-Habshi. *Dirasat,* pp. 35–36.

202. Ibn al-Muqri's poetic legacy includes two long anti-Sufi poems, *al-Dhariʿa ila nasr al-shariʿa,* which consists of 162 verses; and *al-Hujja al-damigha li-rijal al-Fusus al-ra'igha,* which consists of 241 verses, see Brockelmann. *Geschichte,* vol. 2, pp. 243–244. Both poems are included in Ibn al-Muqri. *Majmuʿ*.

203. Ibn al-Muqri. *Majmuʿ*, pp. 11–12; I relied on the text of Ibn al-Muqri's *Diwan* that I collated with the lengthy quotations from Ibn al-Muqri's poems by al-Fasi and Salih al-Maqbali (d. 1108/1696).

204. For Ibn ʿArabi's treatment of the relationships between God (*ilah*) and "divine thrall" (*ma'luh*) as well as Lord (*rabb*) and his "vassal" (*marbub*) see Chittick. *The Sufi Path of Knowledge,* pp. 60, 275, etc.

205. The anonymous editor of Ibn al-Muqri's *Majmuʿ* has *ja'ir*, "rascal," "scoundrel." In al-Fasi's *ʿIqd,* this word is rendered as *ha'ir,* i.e., "confused, perplexed," whereas the text of al-Maqbali has *fajir,* i.e., "shameless liar"; see al-Fasi. *ʿIqd,* vol. 2, p. 193; al-Maqbali. *Al-ʿAlam,* p. 327.

206. In the Muslim tradition, the profession of faith is said to consist of two parts, the negation and the affirmation. The first part denies the existence of any deities (*aliha,* sing. *ilah*) other than God, while the second asserts the existence of the one and only Deity, Allah.

207. The editor of al-Maqbali's text reads: *mustajhilan li-mugha'ir*, i.e., "accusing of ignorance anyone who dares to object [to his statements]"; see al-Maqbali. *Al-ʿAlam,* p. 327; cf. Ibn al-Muqri. *Majmuʿ*, p. 11.

208. See Austin. *Bezels,* p. 110.

209. A reference to Ibn ʿArabi's statement that "God does not take a man, unless he be a believer, insofar as the divine warning has reached him. For this reason sudden death and the killing of man unawares are abhorred," Austin. *Bezels,* p. 265.

210. Ibn al-Muqri. *Majmu'*, pp. 10–11; al-Fasi. *'Iqd,* vol. 2, pp. 192–193; al-Maqbali. *Al-'Alam,* p. 327.

211. Ibn al-Ahdal. *Kashf,* p. 217.

212. See, e.g., Ibn al-Muqri. *Majmu'*, pp. 23–24.

213. Ibn al-Ahdal. *Kashf,* p. 217. Ibn al-Ahdal, however, admits that some *muftis* withheld judgment, arguing that it was impossible to prove whether the statements in question were indeed made by Ibn 'Arabi or interpolated into his works at a later date. Others, according to Ibn al-Ahdal, refrained from judgment out of fear for Ibn al-Raddad's reprisals.

214. Ibn al-Muqri. *Majmu'*, pp. 36–37.

215. *Kashf,* p. 221.

216. I.e., 'Afif al-din al-Tilimsani (d. 690/1291).

217. Ibn al-Muqri. *Majmu'*, p. 10; cf. Ibn al-Ahdal. *Kashf,* p. 221.

218. See al-Sakhawi. *Al-Daw'*, vol. 9, pp. 188–189; al-Sharji. *Tabaqat al-khawass,* pp. 332–334; al-Burayhi. *Tabaqat,* pp. 291–292; al-Habshi. *Al-Sufiyya,* pp. 153–154; idem. *Masadir,* p. 313. For the role of this family in the religious life of Arabia see Voll. "The Mizjaji Family," which, however, makes no mention of the earlier history of the Mizjaji clan.

219. I have not consulted this work, which was widely used in al-Habshi. *Al-Sufiyya.* According to Ibn al-Ahdal, it "was marred by excessive praise for Ibn 'Arabi, al-Hallaj and other monists"; see Ibn al-Ahdal. *Kashf,* p. 222.

220. Abu Zayd. *Isma'il,* pp. 295–296; for Ibn al-Muqri's poetic admonition addressed to al-Mizjaji, see *Majmu'*, pp. 41–50.

221. Al-Zahir was married to his daughter; al-Burayhi. *Tabaqat,* p. 292.

222. Al-Habshi. *Al-Sufiyya,* p. 148.

223. Al-Burayhi. *Tabaqat,* pp. 196–197; al-Sakhawi. *Al-Daw'*, vol. 10, p. 225; al-Habshi. *Al-Sufiyya,* pp. 153–154; cf. Ibn al-Muqri. *Majmu'*, pp. 30–32. There are some interesting parallels in the composition of the monistic factions in Egypt and in Yemen. They both included *'ulama'* as well as professional courtiers, who were ever eager to cater to the ruler's whims.

224. See Ibn al-Muqri. *Majmu'*, pp. 243–245.

225. Ibid., pp. 30–32.

226. Ibid., p. 31.

227. Al-Habshi. *Al-Sufiyya,* pp. 154–168; Abu Zayd. *Isma'il,* p. 22.

228. Ibn al-Muqri. *Majmu'*, p. 31.

229. Nicholson, who apparently was unaware that al-Jili died in Yemen, gave an earlier date for his death; see *Studies,* p. 82.

230. Ibn al-Ahdal explains al-Nasir's mystical propensities by his interest in Isma'ili philosophy which, in Ibn al-Ahdal's view, was quite congruent with the esoteric content of Ibn 'Arabi's teachings; see Ibn al-Dayba'. *Qurrat al-'uyun,* vol. 2, pp. 124–125.

231. Ibn al-Muqri. *Majmu'*, pp. 36–37.

232. On this family and its founder see al-Janadi. *Al-Suluk,* p. 478; al-Burayhi. *Tabaqat,* pp. 314–315; al-Khazraji. *Al-'Uqud,* vol. 1, pp. 257–260; Ba'kar. *Kawakib,* pp. 527–532; al-Sharji. *Tabaqat al-khawass,* pp. 57–64. For the institution of the sacred territory in Arabia that no one (at least in theory) dared to violate see Serjeant. "Haram and Hawta"; cf. Knysh. "The Cult of Saints," pp. 137–139.

233. Ibn al-Ahdal. *Kashf,* p. 222; al-Habshi. *Al-Sufiyya,* pp. 151– 152.

234. Ibn al-Muqri. *Majmu'*, p. 36.

235. Ibn al-Jazari, a disciple of al-Bulqini, visited Yemen as both a scholar and a merchant. He subsidized his travels by selling the goods he carried with him; see al-Sakhawi. *Al-Daw'*, vol. 9, pp. 255–260; Ibn al-'Imad. *Shadharat,* vol. 7, pp. 204–206; al-Burayhi. *Tabaqat,* pp. 54–55; al-Shawkani. *Al-Badr,* vol. 2, p. 257–259; al-Akwa'. *Madaris,* p. 205; for the text of Ibn al-Jazari's *fatwa* see Ibn al-Ahdal. *Kashf,* pp. 223–224. It should be noted that during his sojourn in Yemen Ibn al-Jazari was wined, dined, and housed by Ibn al-Muqri; see Ibn al-Muqri. *Majmu'*, pp. 74–75.

236. See *Kashf,* pp. 225–230.

237. The preacher, Musa b. Muhammad al-Duja'i (d. 851/1447), was an erstwhile student of al-Nashiri and a bitter critique of the Ibn 'Arabi party, al-Burayhi. *Tabaqat,* p. 309; Ibn al-Ahdal. *Kashf,* p. 220; al-Habshi. *Al-Sufiyya,* p. 135.

238. Ibn al-Muqri. *Majmu'*, p. 35.

239. See, e.g., ibid. pp. 24, 26, 34, 52, 56–58, etc.

240. See al-Habshi. *Al-Sufiyya,* pp. 161–164.

241. See, e.g., Ibn al-Muqri. *Majmu'*, pp. 28–32.

242. Ibn al-Dayba'. *Qurrat al-'uyun,* vol. 2, p. 128; 'Abd al-'Al. *Banu Rasul,* pp. 232–233; Smith. "The Political History," p. 137

243. Al-Habshi. *Al-Sufiyya,* pp. 165–166.

244. In Ibn al-Muqri's *Majmu'*, p. 38, his name is spelled "Ibn Fakhr."

245. See al-Sakhawi. *Al-Daw'*, vol. 5, p. 312; al-Burayhi. *Tabaqat,* pp. 309–310; al-Habshi. *Masadir,* p. 223; idem. *Al-Sufiyya,* p. 153.

246. Al-Burayhi. *Tabaqat,* pp. 351–352.

247. Ibn al-Daybaʿ. *Qurrat al-ʿuyun,* vol. 2, pp. 124–125.

248. The ascendancy of monistic Sufism in Yemen was well-known to Muslim scholars outside Arabia, as attested by al-Biqaʿi's complaints about the plight of the *shariʿa* in that country at the hands of the "heretical" followers of Ibn ʿArabi and Ibn al-Farid, Homerin. *From Arab Poet,* p. 64. His complaints, however, have nothing to do with the activities of the local Qarmati community, as suggested by Homerin see ibid., p. 118, note 33.

249. See, e.g., al-Habshi. *Fihrist,* which lists dozens of manuscript works by Ibn ʿArabi and his followers copied in Yemen and Hadramawt; cf. idem. *Masadir,* pp. 303–344.

250. On the fate of Ibn ʿArabi's legacy in Arabia in the 11/17th and 12th/18th centuries see Knysh. "Ibrahim al-Kurani."

General Conclusion

1. I.e., at the notion that the universe functions in strict accordance with causal relations—a view espoused by the *falasifa* and some rationalist theologians, especially the Muʿtazilis.

2. They consider God to be similar to his creatures, as opposed to the first group, which views him as absolutely transcendent and dissimilar.

3. Cf. Knysh. *Mekkanskiye otkroveniya,* p. 159.

4. See, e.g., Chittick. *Faith and Practice,* p. 4; for some parallels with Christian theology see O'Grady. *Heresy,* pp. 152–153.

5. Bell. *Love Theory,* passim.

6. Bürgel. "Ecstasy and Control," pp. 628–629; idem. *The Feather,* pp. 8–19, 47–50, passim.

7. This opposition is routinely invoked in most modern studies of Ibn ʿArabi and his thought.

8. Burckhardt. *An Introduction,* passim; cf. Morris. "Ibn ʿArabi's 'Esotericism.'"

9. Stepaniants. *Sufi Wisdom,* pp. 13–32, passim.

10. Dermenghem. *Le culte,* passim; Urvoy. "Le genre 'Manaqib,'" passim.

11. As an example one may cite the inscription on the cover page of al-Shawkani's (d. 1250/1834) *al-Sawarim al-hidad,* in which the author pleads with God to pardon him for his derogatory treatment of the Greatest

Master earlier in life. Written forty years after the completion of the original draft, al-Shawkani's disclaimer bears witness to his intense fear of the impending reckoning as well as to his lack of conviction of the soundness of his earlier intellectual position. The inscription in question was kindly brought to my attention by Dr. Bernard Haykel of St. John's College, Oxford, who has al-Shawkani's manuscript in his private collection.

12. This, according to Professor Sells of Haverford College, PA, was the position of the late prof. Fazlur Rahman, who, in his books and public lectures denounced Ibn ʿArabi for adulterating Islam with "foreign elements," yet praised him highly in front of a small group of his graduate students. I am grateful to Professor Sells for this information.

13. See Denny. *Islam,* pp. 11–12; cf. Laoust. *Les schismes,* pp. 458–461. More recently, an attempt to juxtapose Islam and Christianity on account of the former's alleged indifference to abstract theological issues and correct belief was undertaken in Asad. "Medieval Heresy," passim; cf. idem. *Genealogies of Religion,* pp. 47–48.

14. In fact, no universal *ijma*ʿ on this or on any other issue was possible in the absence of an institutionalized church or church councils. In Christianity, even these powerful and structured mechanisms have been unable to impose and enforce a uniform religious creed; see, e.g., Russell. *Dissent and Order,* passim.

15. Chittick. *Faith and Practice,* pp. 1–21.

16. Ibid., p. 177.

17. See Massignon. *The Passion,* passim.

18. Ibid., vol. 2, pp. 395–399.

19. For similar conclusions reached by a contemporary Islamicist see Nagel. "Ibn al-ʿArabi."

20. See Bell. *Love Theory,* pp. 200–210.

21. Cf. O'Grady. *Heresy,* pp. 150–151.

BIBLIOGRAPHY

ʿAbd al-ʿĀl, Aḥmad Muḥammad, *Banū Rasūl wa banū Ṭāhir wa ʿalāqāt al-khārijiyya fī ʿahdihimā:* Alexandria, al-Hayʾa al-Miṣriyya al-ʿĀmma li ʾl-Kitāb, 1980.

ʿAbd al-Majīd, Shawqī Bashīr, *Naqd Ibn Taymiyya li ʾl-taṣawwuf:* Khartoum, Dār al-Fikr, 1987.

ʿAbd al-Wahhāb Ibn Manṣūr, *Aʿlām al-Maghrib al-ʿarabī:* Rabat, al-Maṭbaʿa al-Malikiyya, 1978.

Abrahamov, Binyamin (ed.), *Al-Ḳāsim b. Ibrāhīm on the Proof of God's Existence:* Leiden, E. J. Brill, 1990.

Abrahamov, Binyamin, "Ibn Taymiyya on the Agreement of Reason With Tradition." In *The Muslim World* (Hartford), 82 (July/October 1992): pp. 256–273.

Abū Ḥayyān, Muḥammad b. Yūsuf, *Al-Nahr al-mādd min al-baḥr al-muḥīṭ fī tafsīr al-Qurʾān:* 8 vols., Riyadh, Maktabat wa Maṭābiʿ al-Nashr al-Ḥadītha, 1969.

Abu-Lughod, Janet L., *Before European Hegemony: The World System A. D. 1250–1350:* New York, Oxford University Press, 1989.

Abun-Nasr, Jamil M., *The Tijaniyya: A Sufi Order in the Modern World:* London, issued under the auspices of the Royal Institute of International Affairs by Oxford University Press, 1965.

Abū Shāma, ʿAbd al-Raḥmān b. Ismāʿīl, *Tarājim rijāl al-qarnayn al-sādis wa ʾl-sābiʿ: al-maʿrūf bi ʾl-dhayl ʿalā al-rawḍatayn:* Cairo, no publisher, 1947.

Abū Zahra, Muḥammad, *Ibn Taymiyya: ḥayātuh wa-ʿaṣrah, ārāʾuh wa-fiqhuh:* Cairo, Dār al-Fikr al-ʿArabī, 1952.

Abū Zayd, Ṭāḥā Aḥmad, *Ismāʿīl al-Muqrī: ḥayātuh wa shiʿruh:* Sanaa, Markaz al-Dirāsāt wa ʾl-Buḥūth al-Yamanī and Dār al-Adab, 1986.

Adams, Charles Clarence, *Islam and Modernism in Egypt; A Study of the Modern Reform Movement Inaugurated by Muhammad ʿAbduh:* reprint of the 1932 edition, American University at Cairo Oriental Studies, New York, Russell & Russell, 1968.

Addas, Claude, *Ibn ʿArabi, ou La quête du soufre rouge:* Paris, Gallimard, 1989.

Addas, Claude, "Andalusi Mysticism and the Rise of Ibn ʿArabi." In *The Legacy of Muslim Spain:* Ed. by Salma Jayyusi, Leiden, E. J. Brill, 1992: pp. 909–933.

Addas, Claude, "Abu Madyan and Ibn ʿArabi." In *Muhyiddin Ibn ʿArabi: A Commemorative Volume:* Ed. by Stephen Hirtenstein and Michael Tiernan, Brisbane, Element, 1993: pp. 163–180.

Affifi, Abul Ela, *The Mystical Philosophy of Muhyid Din Ibnul ʿArabi:* Cambridge (Eng.), Cambridge University Press, 1939.

Affifi, Abul Ela, "The Influence of Hermetic Literarture on Moslem Thought." In *BSOAS,* 13/4 (1951): pp. 840-849.

ʿAfīfī, Abū ʾl-ʿAlā, "Al-Aʿyān al-thābita fī madhhab Ibn ʿArabī wa ʾl-maʿlūmāt fī madhhab al-muʿtazila." In *Al-Kitāb al-tidhkārī: Muḥyī ʾl-dīn Ibn ʿArabī fī dhikrā al-miʾawiyya al-thāmina li-mīlādih 1165–1240:* Cairo, al-Hayʾa al-Miṣriyya al-ʿĀmma li ʾl-Kitāb, 1969: pp. 209–220.

Aïni, Mehemmed-Ali, *La quintessence de la philosophie de Ibn-i-Arabî:* Trans. by Ahmed Réchid. Libraire Orientaliste, Paul Geuthner, Paris, 1926.

al-Akwaʿ, Ismāʿīl, *Al-Madāris al-islāmiyya fī ʾl-Yaman:* Maktabat al-Jīl al-Jadīd, Sanaa, 1986.

al-ʿAlawī, Ṣāliḥ al-Ḥāmid, *Taʾrīkh Ḥaḍramawt:* 2 vols., Jeddah, Maktabat al-Irshād, 1968.

Albergoni, Gianni and Bédoucha, Geneviève, "Hiérarchie, médiation et tribalisme en Arabie du Sud: la hijra yéménite." In *L'Homme* (Paris), 118 (1991): pp. 7–35.

Algar, Hamid, "Reflections of Ibn ʿArabî in Early Naqshbandî Tradition." In *Journal of the Muhyiddin Ibn ʿArabi Society* (Oxford), 10 (1991): pp. 45–66.

al-ʿAmrī, Ḥusayn b. ʿAbdallāh, *Al-Imām al-Shawkānī: dirāsa fi fiqhih wa fikrih:* Beirut, Dār al-Fikr al-Muʿāṣir and Damascus, Dār al-Fikr, 1990.

Anawati, Georges C. and Gardet, Louis, *Mystique musulmane; aspects et tendances, expériences et techniques:* 3d ed., Études Musulmanes, 8, Paris, J. Vrin, 1976.

Anderson, Jon, "Conjuring with Ibn Khaldūn: From an Anthropological Point of View." In *Ibn Khaldūn and Islamic Ideology;* Ed. by Bruce Lawrence, Leiden, E. J. Brill, 1984: pp. 111–121.

Ansari, Zafar Ishaq, "Taftazānī's Views on *taklīf, ğabr,* and *qadar:* A Note on the Development of Islamic Theological Doctrines." In *Arabica* (Paris), 16/1 (1969): pp. 65–78.

al-ʿAqīlī, Muḥammad b. Aḥmad, *Al-Taṣawwuf fī Tihāma:* Jeddah, Maktabat al-Irshād, 1964.

Arberry, Arthur J., *The Mawāqif and Mukhāṭabāt of Muḥammad Ibn ʿAbdi ʾl-Jabbār al-Niffarī:* printed by Cambridge University Press for the trustees of the "E. J. W. Gibb Memorial," London, Luzac and Co., 1935.

Arberry, Arthur J., *Discourses of Rumi:* reprint of the 1961 edition, London, J. Murray, 1993.

Arberry, Arthur J., *Muslim Saints and Mystics:* London, Routledge and Kegan Paul, 1966.

Arié, Rachel, *L'Espagne musulmane au temps des naṣrides (1232–1492):* Paris, Éditions de Boccard, 1973.

Asad, Talal, "Medieval Heresy: An Anthropological View." In *Social History,* 11 (1986): pp. 354–362.

Asad, Talal, *Genealogies of Religion: Discipline and Reasons of Power in Christianity and Islam:* Baltimore, The John Hopkins University Press, 1993.

Asín Palacios, Miguel, *La escatología musulmana en la Divina Comedia; seguida de la historia y critica de una polémica:* 2d ed., Madrid and Granada, 1943.

Asín Palacios, Miguel, *El Islam cristianizado; estudio del "sufismo" a través de las obras de Abenarabi de Murcia:* Madrid, Editorial Plutarco, 1931.

Asín Palacios, Miguel, *The Mystical Philosophy of Ibn Masarra and His Followers:* Trans. by Elmer H. Douglas and Howard W. Yoder, Leiden, E. J. Brill, 1978.

Asín Palacios, Miguel, *Vidas de santones andaluces; la "Epístola de la santidad" de Ibn ʿArabi de Murcia:* Madrid, E. Maestre, 1933.

Austin, R. W. J., *Ibn al-ʿArabi. The Bezels of Wisdom:* The Classics of Western Spirituality, New York, Paulist Press, 1980.

Austin, R. W. J., *Sufis of Andalusia. The "Ruh al-quds" and "Al-Durat al-fakhira" of Ibn ʿArabi:* 2d ed., Berkeley, University of California Press, 1977.

ʿAynī, Badr al-dīn Maḥmūd b. Aḥmad, *ʿIqd al-jumān fī taʾrīkh ahl al-zamān:* 4 vols., Cairo, al-Hayʾa al-Miṣriyya al-ʿĀmma li ʾl-Kitāb, 1987–1992.

Al-Azmeh, Aziz, *Ibn Khaldūn in Modern Scholarship: A Study in Orientalism:* London, Third World Centre for Research and Publishing, 1981.

Al-Azmeh, Aziz, "Orthodoxy and Ḥanbalite Fideism". In *Arabica* (Paris), 35 (1988): pp. 253–266.

al-ʿAzzāwī, ʿAbbās, "Muḥyī al-dīn Ibn ʿArabī wa ghulāt al-taṣawwuf." In *Al-Kitāb al-tidhkārī: Muḥyī al-dīn Ibn ʿArabī fī dhikrā al-miʾawiyya al-thāmina li-mīlādih,* al-Hayʾa al-Miṣriyya al-ʿĀmma li ʾl-Kitāb, 1969: pp. 155–179.

Baali, Fuad and Wardi, Ali, *Ibn Khaldun and Islamic Thought-Styles: A Social Perspective:* Boston, Mass., G. K. Hall, 1981.

Badawī, ʿAbd al-Raḥmān, "Autobibliografía de Ibn ʿArabi." In *Al-Andalus* (Madrid), 20 (1955): pp. 107–128.

Badawī, ʿAbd al-Raḥmān, ed., *Rasā ʾil Ibn Sabʿīn:* Turā thunā Series, Cairo, al-Muʾassasa al-Miṣriyya al-ʿĀmma li ʾl-Taʾlīf wa ʾl-Anbāʾ wa ʾl Nashr, 1965.

Badawī, ʿAbd al-Raḥmān, *Min taʾrīkh al-ilḥād fī ʾl-islām:* 2d. ed, Beirut, al-Muʾassasa al-ʿArabiyya, 1980.

Bā Faḍl, Muḥammad ʿAlī, *Daʿwat al-khalaf ilā ṭarīqat al-salaf:* Riyadh, no publisher, 1979.

Baghdādī, Ismāʿīl, *Hadiyat al-ʿārifīn:* 2 vols., Istambul, Milli Egtim Basivemi, 1951.

Baʿkar, ʿAbd al-Raḥmān, *Kawākib yamaniyya fī samāʾ al-islām:* Beirut, Dār al-Fikr al-Muʿāṣir, and Damascus, Dār al-Fikr, 1990.

Baldick, Julian, *Imaginary Muslims: The Uwaysi Sufis of Central Asia:* London, I. B. Tauris, 1993.

Baldick, Julian, "Massignon: Man of Opposites." In *Religious Studies,* (London), 23 (March 1987): pp. 29–39.

Baldick, Julian, *Mystical Islam: An Introduction to Sufism:* London, Tauris, 1989.

Balyānī, Awḥad al-dīn, *Epître sur l'unicité absolue:* Preface and trans. by Michel Chodkiewicz, Paris, Les Deux Océans, 1982.

Bannerth, Ernest, *Das Buch der vierzig Stufen von ʿAbd al-Karim al-Ǧili. Nach einer Bagdader Handschrift herausgegeben, übersetzt und mit Erlaüterungen versehen von Ernst Bannerth:* Vienne, R. M. Rohrer, 1956.

Barthold, V. V., "Ulugbek i ego vremia." In *Sochineniya,* 2/2, Moscow, Nauka, 1964: pp. 27–196.

Batsyeva, Svetlana M., "Shifa' al-sa'il li-tahdhib al-masa'il—traktat Ibn Khalduna o sufizme." In *Blizhnii i Srednii Vostok: istoriya, kul'tura, istochnikovedeniye:* Moscow, Nauka, 1968: pp. 40–46.

Beaurecueil, Serge de, *Khwādja ʿAbdullāh Anṣārī; mystique hanbalite:* Université Saint-Joseph, Institut de Lettres Orientales, Recherches, 26, Beirut, Impr. Catholique, 1965.

Bell, Joseph Norment, *Love Theory in Later Hanbalite Islam:* Albany, SUNY Press, 1979.

Bencheneb, S. "Mémoires, tableaux historiques et portraits dans l'oeuvre de Lisan ad-Din Ibn al-Khatib." In *Revue d'histoire et civilization du Maghreb* (Algiers), 2 (1967): pp. 54–85.

Berkey, Jonathan P., *The Transmission of Knowledge in Medieval Cairo: A Social History of Islamic Education:* N.J., Princeton, Princeton Studies on the Near East, Princeton University Press, 1992.

al-Biqāʿī, Ibrāhīm b. ʿUmar, *Maṣraʿ al-taṣawwuf, aw, Tanbīh al-ghabī ilā takfīr Ibn ʿArabī wa Taḥdhīr al-ʿibād min ahl al-ʿinād:* Ed. by ʿAbd al-Raḥmān al-Wakīl, Cairo, 1953.

al-Biqāʿī, Ibrāhīm b. ʿUmar, *Sirr al-rūḥ:* Ed. by ʿAbd al-Jalīl al-ʿAṭā, Damascus, Dār al-Bashā'ir, 1994.

Blochet, M. E., *Études sur l'esotèrisme musulman:* Tradition islamique, 7, Paris, Michel Allard Editions Orientales, 1979.

Bloom, Jonathan, "The Mosque of Baybars al-Bunduqdārī in Cairo." In *Annales Islamologiques* (Cairo), 18 (1982): pp. 45–79.

Boase, Roger and Sahnoun, Farid, "Excerpts from the *Epistle on the Spirit of Holiness* (*Risâlah Rûh al-Quds*)." In *Muhyiddin Ibn ʿArabi: A Commemorative Volume:* Ed. by Stephen Hirtenstein and Michael Tiernan, Brisbane, Element, 1993, pp. 44–72.

Bonner, Anthony, *Selected Works of Ramón Llull:* 2 vols., Princeton, N.J., Princeton University Press, 1985.

Boullata, Issa, "Toward a Biography of Ibn al-Farid." In *Arabica* (Paris), 38/1 (1981): pp. 38–56.

Bouthoul, Gaston, *Ibn Khaldoun, sa philosophie sociale:* Paris, Paul Geuthner, 1936.

Böwering, Gerhard, "Ideas of Time in Persian Sufism." In *Iran* (London), 30 (1992): pp. 77–98.

Böwering, Gerhard, "Ibn al-ʿArabī's Concept of Time." In *Gott ist schön und Er liebt die Schönheit:* Ed. by Alma Giese and J. Christoph Bürgel, Bern, Peter Lang, 1994.

Böwering, Gerhard, *The Mystical Vision of Existence in Classical Islam: The Qurʾānic Hermeneutics of the Ṣūfī Sahl at-Tustarī:* Studien zur Sprache, Geschichte und Kultur des islamischen Orients, 9, Berlin and New York, W. de Gruyter, 1980.

Braune, Walther, ed., *Die Futūḥ al-gaib des ʿAbd al-Qādir:* Berlin and Leipzig, W. de Gruyter, 1933.

Brinner, William M., "Dār al-saʿāda and dār al-ʿadl in Mamluk Damascus." In *Studies in Memory of Gaston Wiet:* Ed. by M. Rosen-Ayalon, Jerusalem, 1977: pp. 235–247.

Brockelmann, Carl, *Geschichte der arabischen Litteratur:* 2 vols., Leiden, E. J. Brill, 1943–1949.

Brockelmann, Carl, *Geschichte der arabischen Litteratur: Supplementband:* 3 vols., Leiden, E. J. Brill, 1936–1942.

Browne, Edward G., *A Literary History of Persia:* 4 vols., Cambridge (Eng.), The University Press, 1928.

Bukhārī, Muḥammad b. Ismāʿīl, *Ṣaḥīḥ:* Le recueil des traditions mahométanes par Abou Abdallah Mohammad ibn Ismail el-Bokhari. Publié par M. L. Krehl et continué par Th. W. Juynboll: 4 vols., Leiden, E. J. Brill, 1866–1908.

Bulliet, Richard W., *Islam: The View from the Edge:* New York, Columbia University Press, 1994.

Bulliet, Richard W., *The Patricians of Nishapur; A Study in Medieval Islamic Social History:* Harvard Middle Eastern Studies, 16, Cambridge (Mass.), Harvard University Press, 1972.

Bulliet, Richard W., "The Political-Religious History of Nishapur in the Eleventh Century." In *Islamic Civilization 950–1150:* Ed. by D. S. Richards, Oxford, Cassirer, 1973: pp. 71–91.

al-Burayhī (al-Barayhī), ʿAbd al-Wahhāb b. ʿAbd al-Raḥmān, *Ṭabaqāt ṣulaḥāʾ al-Yaman:* Ed. by ʿAbdallāh Muḥammad al-Ḥabshī (al-Ḥibshī), Beirut, Dār al-Adab, 1983.

Burckhardt, Titus (trans.), *ʿAbd al-Karîm al-Jîlî: The Universal Man:* English translation by Angela Culme-Seymour, Beshara Publications, Sherborne, UK, 1983.

Burckhardt, Titus, *An Introduction to Sufi Doctrine:* Trans. by D. M. Matheson, Wellingsborough, Northamptonshire, 1976.

Bürgel, Johann, "Ecstasy and Control in Andalusi Art: Steps Toward a New Approach." In *The Legacy of Muslim Spain:* Ed. by Salma Kh. Jayyusi, Leiden, E. J. Brill, 1992: pp. 626–638.

Bürgel, Johann, *The Feather of Simurgh: The "Licit Magic" of the Arts in Medieval Islam.* New York, New York University Press, 1988.

Chabbi, Jacqueline, *'Abd al-Qadir al-Jilani, idées sociales et politiques:* Paris, Sorbonne, 1971.

Chamberlain, Michael, *Knowledge and Social Practice in Medieval Damascus, 1190–1350:* Cambridge, Cambridge University Press, 1994.

Chelhod, Joseph, *Neuf siècles d'histoire de l'Arabie du Sud: 622–1517. Le souhait de celui qui s'interesse aus événements de la ville Zabid:* The Yemeni Center for Research and Studies, Sanaa, 1973.

Chelhod, Joseph, "Introduction à l'histoire sociale et urbaine de Zabid." In *Arabica* (Paris), 25/1 (1978): pp. 48–88.

Chelhod, Joseph, "L'Islam en Arabaie du Sud." In *L'Arabie du Sud: histoire et civilization:* Ed. by Chelhod J. et al., Vol. 2. *La société yéménite de l'Hégire aux idéologies modernes:* Paris, G. P. Maisonneuve, 1984: pp. 13–55.

Chittick, William, *Faith and Practice of Islam: Three Thirteenth Century Sufi Texts:* New York, SUNY Press, 1992.

Chittick, William and Wilson, P. L., *Fakhruddin 'Iraqi: Divine Flashes:* New York, Paulist Press, 1981.

Chittick, William C., "The Five Divine Presences: From al-Qūnawī to al-Qayṣarī." In *The Muslim World* (Hartford), 72 (April 1982): pp. 107–128.

Chittick, William C., "Ibn 'Arabi and His School." In *Islamic Spirituality: Manifestations,* ed. by S. H. Nasr, New York, Crossroad, 1991: pp. 49–79.

Chittick, William C., "The Last Will and Testament of Ibn 'Arabi's Foremost Disciple and Some Notes on Its Author." In *Sophia Perennis* (London), 4/1 (1978): pp. 43–58.

Chittick, William C., "Mysticism Versus Philosophy in Earlier Islamic History: The al-Ṭūsī, al-Qūnawī Correspondence." In *Religious Studies* (Cambridge), 17 (Mar 1981): pp. 87–104.

Chittick, William C. "Notes on Ibn al-'Arabī's Influence in the Subcontinent." In *The Muslim World,* vol. 82/3–4 (July-October 1992): pp. 218–241.

Chittick, William C., "Sadr al-Din Qunawi on the Oneness of Being." In *International Philosophical Quarterly* (New York), 21/2 (June 1981): pp. 171–184.

Chittick, William C., "Spectrums of Islamic Thought: Saʿīd ul-Dīn Farghānī on the Implications of Oneness and Manyness." In *The Legacy of Medieval Persian Sufism:* Ed. by Leonard Lewisohn, London and New York, Khaniqahi Nimatullahi Publications, 1992: pp. 203–217.

Chittick, William C., *The Sufi Path of Knowledge: Ibn al-ʿArabi's Metaphysics of Imagination:* Albany, SUNY Press, 1989.

Chittick, William C., "Wahdat al-wujud in Islamic Thought." In *Bulletin of the Henry Martyn Institute of Islamic Studies* (Hyderabad), 10 (January–March 1991): pp. 7–27.

Chodkiewicz, Michel, "The Diffusion of Ibn ʿArabi's Doctrine." In *Journal of the Muhyiddin Ibn ʿArabi Society,* 9 (1991): pp. 36–57.

Chodkiewicz, Michel (ed.), *Les illuminations de la Mecque. Textes choises:* La Biblioteque de l'Islam, Paris, Sindbad, 1989.

Chodkiewicz, Michel, *An Ocean Without Shore: Ibn Arabi, the Book, and the Law:* Albany, SUNY Press, 1993.

Chodkiewicz, Michel, *Le sceau des saints: prophétie et sainteté dans la doctrine d'Ibn Arabi:* Paris, Gallimard, 1986.

Conger, George Perrigo, *Theories of Macrocosms and Microcosms in the History of Philosophy:* New York, Russell & Russell, 1967.

Cook, Michael, "On the Origins of Wahhābism." In *Journal of the Royal Asiatic Society* (London), 2/2 (1992): pp. 191–202.

Corbin, Henry, *L'imagination créatrice dans le soufisme d'Ibn ʿArabi:* Paris, Flammarion, 1958.

Corbin, Henry, *La philosophie iranienne islamique aux XVIIe et XVIIIe siècles:* Paris, Buchet/Chastel, 1981.

Cornell, Vincent Joseph, "Mirrors of Prophethood: The Evolving Image of the Spiritual Master in the Western Maghrib from the Origins of Sufism to the End of the Sixteenth Century": Unpublished Ph.D. dissertation, Los Angeles, University of California, 1989.

Coussonnet, Nahida, "Les assises du pouvoir zaydite au xii-e siècles." In *REMMM,* 67/1 (1993): pp. 25–37.

Danner, Victor, *Ibn ʿAtaʾ Allah, The Book of Wisdom:* The Classics of Western Spirituality, New York, Paulist Press, 1978.

Davidson, Herbert A., *Proofs for Eternity, Creation, and the Existence of God in Medieval Islamic and Jewish Philosophy:* New York, Oxford University Press, 1987.

al-Dawānī, Muḥammad b. Asʿad, *Īmān Firʿawn li-Jalāl al-dīn al-Dawānī wa ʾl-radd ʿalayh li-ʿAlī b. Sulṭān Muḥammad Qārī; wa taʾyīd Sayyidī*

Muḥyī 'l-dīn Ibn al-ʿArabī li 'l-īmān: Ed. by Ibn al-Khaṭīb: Cairo, al-Maṭbaʿa al-ʿAṣriyya wa Maktabaṭuhā, 1964.

Dāwūdī, Muḥammad b. ʿAlī, *Ṭabaqāt al-mufassirīn:* 2 vols., ed. by ʿAlī Muḥammad ʿUmar, Cairo, Maktabat Wahba, 1972.

Deladrière, R., *La profession de foi d'Ibn ʿArabi: Texte, traduction et commentaire de la Tadkira:* Lille, Université de Lille 3, 1975.

Denny, Frederick, *Islam and the Muslim Community:* San Francisco, Harper and Collins, 1987.

Dermenghem, Emile, *Le culte des saints dans l'Islam maghrébin:* 6th ed., Paris, Gallimard, 1954.

al-Dhahabī, Muḥammad b. Aḥmad, *Al-ʿIbar fī khabar man ghabar:* 4 vols., ed. by Abū Ḥājir Muḥammad Zaghlūl, Beirut, Dār al-Kutub al-ʿIlmiyya, 1985.

al-Dhahabī, Muḥammad b. Aḥmad, *Mīzān al-iʿtidāl fī naqd al-rijāl:* 4 vols., ed. by ʿAlī Muḥammad Bajāwī, Cairo, ʿĪsā al-Bābī al-Ḥalabī, 1963.

al-Dhahabī, Muhammad b. Aḥmad, *Siyar aʿlām al-nubalāʾ:* 23 vols., ed. by Shuʿayb al-Arnāūṭ and Ḥusayn al-Asad, Beirut, Muʾassat al-Risāla, 1985.

al-Dhahabī, Muḥammad b. Aḥmad, *Taʾrīkh al-islām wa ṭabaqāt al-mashāhīr wa 'l-aʿlām:* 43 vols., ed. by ʿUmar ʿAbd al-Salām Tadmurī, Beirut, Dār al-Kitāb al-ʿArabī, 1987–1993.

Dreher, P. Joseph, *Das Imāmat des islamischen mystikers Abūlqāsim Aḥmad Ibn al-Ḥusain Ibn al-Qasī (gest. 1151):* Inaugural-Dissertation, Bonn, 1985.

Dresch, Paul, *Tribes, Government, and History in Yemen:* Oxford, Clarendon Press, 1989.

D'Souza, Andreas, "Jesus in Ibn ʿArabi's *Fusus al-hikam.*" In *Islamochristiana / Dirāsāt Islāmiyya Masīḥiyya* (Vatican), 8 (1982): pp. 185–200.

Dunn, Ross E., *The Adventures of Ibn Battuta: A Muslim traveller of the 14th century:* Berkeley, University of California Press, 1989.

Elder, Earl Edgar, *A Commentary on the Creed of Islam:* Record of Civilization, Sources and Studies, New York, Columbia University Press, 1950.

Elisséeff, Nikita, *Nur ad-Din, un grand prince musulman de Syrie au temps des croisades:* 3 vols., Damascus, Institut Français de Damas, 1967.

El-Shami, A. and Serjeant, Robert, "Regional Literature: The Yemen." In *Religion, Learning, and Science in the Abbasid Period:* Cambridge, Cambridge University Press, 1990: pp. 442–468.

Ernst, Carl W., *Words of Ecstasy in Sufism:* SUNY Series in Islam, Albany, SUNY Press, 1985.

Ernst, Carl W., "Traditionalism, The Perennial Philosophy, and Islamic Studies." In *MESA Bulletin* (Cambridge University Press), 28 (1994): pp. 176–180.

Escovitz, Joseph H., "The Establishment of Four Chief Judgeships in the Mamluk Empire." In *Journal of the American Oriental Society,* 102/3 (July–October 1982): pp. 529–531.

Esposito, John L., *Islam: The Straight Path:* Oxford and New York, Oxford University Press, 1991.

Ess, Josef van, see Van Ess.

al-Fāsī, Taqī al-dīn Muḥammad b. Aḥmad, *Al-ʿIqd al-thamīn fī taʾrīkh al-Balad al-Amīn:* 8 vols., ed. by Muḥammad Ḥāmid al-Faqī, Fuʾād Sayyid, and Maḥmūd Muḥammad Ṭanāhī, Cairo, Maṭbaʿat al-Sunna al-Muḥammadiyya, 1958–1969.

Fenton, Paul B. and Gloton, Maurice, "The Book of the Description of the Encompassing Circles." In *Muhyiddin Ibn ʿArabi: A Commemorative Volume:* Ed. by Stephen Hirtenstein and Michael Tiernan, Brisbane, Element, 1993: pp. 12–43.

Fenton, Paul B., "The Hierarchy of the Saints in Jewish and Islamic Mysticism." In *Journal of the Muhyiddin Ibn ʿArabi Society,* 10 (1991): pp. 12–34.

Ferhat, Halima and Triki, Hamid, "Faux Prophètes et mahdis dans le Maroc médiévale." In *Hespéris tamuda* (Rabat), 26–27 (1988–1989): pp. 5–23.

Fernandes, Leonor E., *The Evolution of a Sufi Institution in Mamluk Egypt: The Khanqah:* Islamkundliche Untersuchungen, 134, Berlin, K. Schwartz, 1988.

Fierro, Maribel, "Heresy in al-Andalus." In *The Legacy of Muslim Spain:* Ed. by Salma Jayyusi, Leiden, E. J. Brill, 1992: pp. 895–908.

Fierro, Maribel, *La heterodoxia en al-Andalus durante el período omeya:* Madrid, Instituto Hispano-Arabe de Cultura, 1987.

Fierro, Maribel, "The Polemic about the *karāmāt al-awliyāʾ* and the Development of Sufism in al-Andalus." In *BSOAS,* 55/2 (1992): pp. 236–249.

Findley, Carter V., *Ottoman Civil Officialdom: a Social History:* Princeton, N.J., Princeton University Press, 1989.

Fischel, Walter Joseph, *Ibn Khaldūn and Tamerlane, Their Historic Meeting in Damascus, 1401 A. D. (803 A. H.); A Study Based on Arabic Manu-*

scripts of Ibn Khaldūn's "Autobiography": Berkeley, University of California Press, 1952.

Fischel, Walter Joseph, *Ibn Khaldun in Egypt; His Public Functions and His Historical Research, 1382–1406; A Study in Islamic Historiography:* Berkeley, University of California Press, 1967.

Fletcher, Madeleine, "Al-Andalus in the Almohad Ideology." In *The Legacy of Muslim Spain:* Ed. by Salma Kh. Jayyusi, Leiden, E. J. Brill, 1992: pp. 235–258.

Flügel, Gustav, ed., *Definitiones viri meritissimi scherif Ali Ben Mohammed Dschordschani. Accedunt definitiones theosophi Mohji-ed-din Mohammed ben Ali vulgo Ibn Arabi dicti:* Leipzig, 1845.

Frank, Richard M., *Beings and Their Attributes: The Teaching of the Basrian School of the Muʿtazila in the Classical Period:* Studies in Islamic Philosophy and Science, Albany, SUNY Press, 1978.

Friedmann, Yohanan, *Prophesy Continuous: Aspects of Ahmadi Religious Thought and Its Medieval Background:* Comparative Studies on Muslim Societies, 3, Berkeley, University of California Press, 1989.

Friedmann, Yohanan, *Shaykh Ahmad Sirhindi: An Outline of His Thought and a Study of His Image in the Eyes of Posterity:* McGill Islamic Studies, 2, Montreal, McGill University, Institute of Islamic Studies, 1971.

Fyzee, Asaf, "Three Sulaymani Daʿis: 1936–1939." In *Journal of the Bombey Branch of the Royal Asiatic Society* (Bombey), 14 (1940): 101–104.

Gabrieli, Francesco, "La 'zandaqa' au 1er siècle abbaside." In *L'Elaboration de l'Islam. Colloque de Strasbourgh, 12–13–14 Juin, 1959:* Paris, Presses Universitaires de France, 1961: pp. 23–38.

García-Arenal, Mercedes, "La conjonction du sufisme et sharifisme au Maroc: le Mahdi comme saveur." In *REMMM* (Aix-en-Provence), 55–56/1–2 (1990–1991): pp. 233–256.

Geddes, Charles L., "The Apostasy of ʿAli b. al-Fadl." In *Arabian and Islamic Studies. Articles Presented to R. B. Serjeant:* Ed. by Robert L. Bidwell and G. Rex Smith, London, Longman, 1983: pp. 80–85.

al-Ghubrīnī, Aḥmad b. Aḥmad, *ʿUnwān al-dirāya fī man ʿurifa min al-ʿulamāʾ fī al-miʾa al-sābiʿa bi-Bijāya:* Ed. by Rābin Bū Nār, Algeria, al-Shirka al-Waṭaniyya li ʾl-Nashr wa ʾl-Tawzīʿ, 1970.

Ghurāb, Maḥmūd, *Al-Radd ʿalā Ibn Taymiyya min kalām Muḥyī ʾl-dīn Ibn ʿArabī:* Damascus, Maṭbaʿat Zayd Ibn Thābit, 1981.

Gibb, Hamilton, "Islamic Biographical Literature." In *Historians of the Middle East:* ed. by B. Lewis and P. M. Holt, London, Oxford University Press, 1962: pp. 54–58.

Giffen, Lois, *The Theory of Profane Love Among the Arabs:* New York, New York University Press, 1971.

Gilsenan, Michael, "Trajectories of Contemporary Sufism." In *Islamic Dilemmas: Reformers, Nationalists, and Industrialization:* Ed. by Ernst Gellner, Amsterdam, Mouton, 1985: pp. 187–198.

Gimaret, Daniel, *Théories de l'acte humain en théologie musulmane:* Paris, J. Vrin, 1980.

Gimaret, Daniel, *La Doctrine d'al-Ashʿarī:* Patrimoines, Islam, Paris, Cerf, 1990.

Glick, Thomas E., *Islamic and Christian Spain in the Early Middle Ages:* Princeton, N.J., Princeton University Press, 1979.

Gochenour, David Th., "The Penetration of Zaydi Islam Into Early Medieval Yemen": Unpublished Ph.D. dissertation, Harvard University, 1984.

Gochenour, David Th., "Towards a Sociology of the Islamization of Yemen." In *Contemporary Yemen: Politics and Historical Background:* Ed. by B. R. Pridham, London, Croom Helm, 1984: pp. 1–19.

Goldziher, Ignaz, *Die Zahiriten: ihr Lehrsystem und ihre Geschichte:* Leipzig, O. Schulze, 1884.

Goodrich, David Raymond, "A 'Ṣūfī' Revolt in Portugal: Ibn Qasī and His 'Kitāb Khalʿ al-Naʿlayn'": Unpublished Ph.D. dissertation, Columbia University, April 1979.

Gordlevski, Vladimir A., *Izbrannye sochineniya:* 4 vols., Moscow, Nauka, 1960–1968.

Graham, William A., *Divine Word and Prophetic Word in Early Islam: A Reconsideration of the Sources, With Special Reference to the Divine Saying or Hadith Qudsi:* The Hague, Mouton, 1977.

Gramlich, Richard, *Die schiitischen Derwischorden Persiens:* 3 vols., Wiesbaden, Franz Steiner, 1965–1981.

Gramlich, Richard, *Die Gaben der Erkenntnisse des ʿUmar as-Suhrawardī (ʿAwārif al-maʿārif):* Freiburger Islamstudien, 6, Wiesbaden, F. Steiner, 1978.

Gramlich, Richard, *Das Sendschreiben al-Qušayris über das Sufitum:* Freiburger Islamstudien, 12, Stuttgart, F. Steiner, 1989.

Gramlich, Richard, *Die Wunder der Freunde Gottes: Theologien und Erscheinungsformen des islamischen Heiligenwunders:* Freiburger Islamstudien, 11, Wiesbaden, F. Steiner, 1987.

Gril, D., "Le kitāb al-inbāh ʿalā ṭarīq Allāh de ʿAbdallāh Badr al-Ḥabašī: un témoignage de l'enseignement spirituel de Muḥyī-l-dīn Ibn ʿArabī." In *Annales Islamologiques* (Cairo), 15 (1979): pp. 87–164.

Gril, D., *La Risāla: biographies des maîtres spirituels connus par un cheikh égyptien du VIIe / XIIIe siècle:* Textes Arabes et Études Islamiques, 25, Cairo: Institut Français d'Archeologie Orientale, 1986.

Haarmann, Ulrich, *Quellenstudien zur frühen Mamlukenzeit:* Freiburg, D. Robischon, 1969.

Haarmann, Ulrich, "Arabic in Speech, Turkish in Lineage: Mamluks and Their Sons in the Intellectual Life of Fourteenth Century Egypt and Syria." In *Journal of Semitic Studies* (Manchester/Cambridge), 33 (1988): pp. 81–114.

al-Ḥabshī (al-Ḥibshī), ʿAbdallāh, *Fihrist al-makhṭūṭāt al-yamaniyya fī Ḥaḍramawt:* Aden, Al-Markaz al-Yamanī li ʾl-Abḥāth al-Thaqāfiyya, 1975.

al-Ḥabshī, ʿAbdallāh, *Al-Ṣūfiyya wa ʾl-fuqahāʾ fī ʾl-Yaman:* Sanaa, Markaz al-Dirāsāt wa ʾl-Buḥūth al-Yamanī, 1396/1976.

al-Ḥabshī, ʿAbdallāh, *Dirāsāt fī ʾl-turāth al-yamanī:* Beirut, Dār al-ʿAwda, 1977.

al-Ḥabshī, ʿAbdallāh, *Muʾallafāt ḥukkām al-Yaman:* Ed. by Elke Niewöhner-Eberhard, Wiesbaden, Otto-Harassowitz, 1979.

al-Ḥabshī, ʿAbdallāh, *Ḥayāt al-adab al-yamanī fī ʿaṣr banī Rasūl:* 2d ed., Sanaa, Wizārat al-Aʿlām, 1980.

al-Ḥabshī, ʿAbdallāh, *Maṣādir al-fikr al-islāmī fī ʾl-Yaman,* Saida/Beirut, al-Maktaba al-ʿAṣriyya, 1988.

Hafsi, I., "Recherches sur le genre 'Tabaqat' dans la littérature arabe." In *Arabica,* 21 (1977): pp. 1–41.

al-Ḥakīm, Suʿād, *Al-Muʿjam al-ṣūfī: Al-Ḥikma fī ḥudūd al-kalima:* Beirut, Dandara li ʾl-Ṭibāʿa wa ʾl-Nashr, 1981.

Halff, Bruno, "Maḥāsin al-Mağālis d'Ibn al-ʿArīf et l'oeuvre du ṣoufi ḥanbalite al-Anṣārī." In *Revue des Études Islamiques* (Paris), 39/2 (1971): pp. 321–335.

Halliday, Fred, "Orientalism and Its Critics." In *British Journal of Middle Eastern Studies* (London), 20/2 (1930): pp. 145–163.

Hamdānī, ʿAbbās, "The Dāʿī Ḥātim ibn Ibrāhīm al-Ḥāmidī." In *Oriens* (Leiden), 23–24 (1974): pp. 258–300.

Hamdānī, ʿAbbās, "Evolution of the Organizational Structure of the Fāṭimī Daʿwah." In *Arabian Studies* (Cambridge), 3 (1976): pp. 85–114.

Hamdānī, Ḥusayn, *Al-Ṣulayḥiyyūn wa ʾl-ḥaraka al-fāṭimiyya fī ʾl-Yaman:* Cairo, Maktabat Miṣr, 1955.

Haykel, Bernard, "Al-Shawkani and the Jurisprudential Unity of Yemen." In *REMMM,* 67/1 (1993): pp. 53–66.

Heath, Peter, *Allegory and Philosophy in Avicenna: With a Translation of the Book of the Prophet Muhammad's Ascent to Heaven:* Philadelphia, University of Pennsylvania Press, 1992.

Ḥilmī, Muṣṭafā, *Ibn Taymiyya wa 'l-taṣawwuf:* Alexandria, Dār al-Daʿwa, 1982.

Hirtenstein, Stephen and Tiernan, Michael (eds.), *Muhyiddin Ibn ʿArabi: A Commemorative Volume:* Brisbane, Element, 1993.

Hodgson, Marshall G. S., *The Venture of Islam: Conscience and History in a World Civilization:* 3 vols., Chicago, University of Chicago Press, 1974.

Hoenerbach, Wilhelm, *Islamische Geschichte Spaniens:* Zürich, Artemis Verlag, 1970.

Holbrook, Victoria Rowe, "Ibn ʿArabî and Ottoman Dervish Traditions: The Melâmî Supra-order." In *Journal of the Muhyiddin Ibn ʿArabi Society* (Oxford), 9 (1991): pp. 18–35.

Holt, Peter Malcolm, *The Age of the Crusades: The Near East from the Eleventh Century to 1517:* History of the Near East, London and New York, Longman, 1986.

Homerin, Th. Emil, "Ibn ʿArabi in the People's Assembly: Religion, Press, and Politics in Sadat's Egypt." In *The Middle East Journal* (Washington D.C.), 40 (Summer 1986): pp. 462–77.

Homerin, Th. Emil, *From Arab Poet to Muslim Saint: Ibn al-Fāriḍ, His Verse and His Shrine:* Columbia, University of South Carolina Press, Columbia, S.C., 1994.

Homerin, Th. Emil. "Ibn Taimīyah's *al-Ṣūfīyah wa-l-fuqarā'*." In *Arabica* (Paris), 32/2 (1985): pp. 219–244.

Houédard, Dom Sylvester, "Ibn ʿArabi's Contribution to the Wider Ecumenism." In *Muhyiddin Ibn ʿArabi: A Commemorative Volume:* Ed. by Stephen Hirtenstein and Michael Tiernan, Brisbane, Element, 1993: pp. 291–306.

Howorth, Henry H., Sir, *History of the Mongols, From the Ninth to the Nineteenth Century:* 4 vols., London, Longmans, Green, and Co., 1876–1927.

Hujwīrī, ʿAlī b. ʿUthmān, *The Kashf al-maḥjūb, The Oldest Persian Treatise on Sufism:* Trans. by Reynold A. Nicholson, with a foreword by Shahidullah Faridi, Lahore, Islamic Book Foundation, 1976.

Humphreys, R. Stephen, *From Saladin to the Mongols: The Ayyubids of Damascus, 1193–1260:* Albany, SUNY Press, 1977.

Humphreys, R. Stephen, *Islamic History: a Framework for Inquiry:* Rev. ed., Princeton, N.J., Princeton University Press, 1991.

Husseini, Abdul Qadir Saiyid, *The Pantheistic Monism of Ibn ʿArabi:* Lahore, Muhammad Ashraf, 1970.

Ibn al-Abbār, Muḥammad b. ʿAbdallāh, *Al-Takmila li-kitāb al-ṣila:* Ed. by F. Codera, Madrid, 1886.

Ibn ʿAbd al-Salām, ʿIzz al-dīn, "Risāla fī ʾl-abdāl wa ʾl-ghawth." In *Majmūʿ al-rasāʾil:* Aleppo, al-Maṭbaʿa al-ʿIlmiyya, 1345 A. H.: pp. 11–16.

Ibn ʿAbd al-Salām, ʿIzz al-dīn, *Ḥall al-rumūz wa mafātīḥ al-kunūz:* Silsilat al-Thaqāfa al-Islāmiyya, Maṭbaʿat Nūr al-Amal, 1961.

Ibn ʿAbd al-Salām, ʿIzz al-dīn, *Al-Imām fī bayān adillat al-aḥkām:* Ed. by Riḍwān Mukhtār b. Gharbiyya, Beirut, Dār al-Bashāʾir, 1989.

Ibn al-Ahdal, al-Ḥusayn, *Risāla fī shaʾn Ibn ʿArabī aw Mukhtaṣar fī bayān ḥāl Ibn ʿArabī:* ms. in the collection of the Institute for Oriental Studies, St. Petersburg, number B4642.

Ibn al-Ahdal, al-Ḥusayn, *Kashf al-ghiṭāʾ ʿan ḥaqāʾiq al-tawḥīd wa ʾl-radd ʿalā Ibn ʿArabī al-faylasūf al-ṣūfī:* Ed. by Aḥmad Bukayr Muḥammad, Tunis, 1964.

Ibn al-Ahdal, al-Husayn, *Tuḥfat al-zamān fī taʾrīkh al-Yaman:* Ed. by ʿAbdallāh al-Ḥabshī, Dār al-Tanwīr, Beirut, 1986.

Ibn ʿAlwān, Ahmad, *Al-Tawḥīd al-aʿẓam al-mubligh man la yaʿlam ilā rutbat man yaʿlam:* Ed. by ʿAbd al-ʿAzīz al-Manṣūb, Markaz al-Dirāsāt wa ʾl-Abḥāth al-Yamanī, Sanaa, 1990.

Ibn ʿArabī, Muḥyī al-dīn, *ʿAnqāʾ mughrib fī khātam al-awliyāʾ wa shams al-maghrib:* Egypt, Muḥammad ʿAlī Ṣubayḥ, 1954.

Ibn ʿArabī, Muḥyī al-dīn, *Dīwān Ibn ʿArabī:* Baghdad, Maktabat Muthannā, 1963.

Ibn ʿArabī, Muḥyī al-dīn, *Fuṣūṣ al-ḥikam:* Ed. by Abū ʾl-ʿAlā ʿAfīfī, Cairo, ʿĪsā al-Bābī al-Ḥalabī, 1946.

Ibn ʿArabī, Muḥyī al-dīn, *Al-Futūḥāt al-makkiyya:* photoreproduction of Cairo 1867 ed.: 4 vols., Beirut, Dār Ṣādir, 1968.

Ibn ʿArabī, Muḥyī al-dīn, *Al-Futuḥāt al-makkiyya:* Ed. by ʿUthmān Yaḥyā, Cairo, al-Hayʾa al-Miṣriyya al-ʿĀmma li ʾl-Kitāb, 1972–.

Ibn ʿArabī, Muḥyī al-dīn, *Kitāb al-bāʾ*: O. Yahia, *Historie et classification de l'oeuvre d'Ibn ʿArabi:* Damascus, Institut Français de Damas, 1964, Vol. 1: pp. 180–181.

Ibn ʿArabī, Muḥyī al-dīn, *Kitāb al-isrā ʾ ilā ʾl-maqām al-asrā , aw, Kitāb al-miʿrāj:* Ed. by Suʿā d al-Ḥakīm, Beirut, Dandara li ʾl-Ṭibā ʿa wa ʾl-Nashr, 1988.

Ibn ʿArabī, Muḥyī al-dīn, *Mekkanskiye otroveniya (al-Futuhat al-makkiyya):* Introduction, translation, commentaries, and bibliography by Alexander Knysh. St. Petersburg, St. Petersburg Center for Oriental Studies, 1995.

Ibn ʿArabī, Muḥyī al-dīn, *Muḥāḍarat al-abrār wa musāmarat al-akhyār:* Ed. by Muḥammad Mursī al-Khūlī, Cairo, Dār al-Kitāb al-Jadīd, 1972.

Ibn ʿArabī, Muḥyī al-dīn, *Rasāʾil Ibn ʿArabī:* 2 vols., Hayderabad-Deccan, Dāʾirat al-Maʿārif al-ʿUthmāniyya, 1948.

Ibn ʿArabī, Muḥyī al-dīn, *Risālat rūḥ al-quds f ī muḥāsabat al-nafs:* Damascus, Muʾassasat al-ʿIlm li ʾl-Ṭibāʿa wa ʾl-Nashr, 1964.

Ibn ʿArabī, Muḥyī al-dīn, *Al-Shajara al-nuʿmāniyya f ī ʾl dawla al-ʿuthmāniyya:* In O. Yahia, *Histoire et classification de l'*oeuvre *d'Ibn ʿArabi*: Damascus, Institut Français de Damas, 1964, vol. 2: pp. 456–57.

Ibn ʿArabī, Muḥyī al-dīn, *The Tarjumān al-ashwāq, A Collection of Mystical Odes, by Muḥyi'ddīn Ibn al-ʿArabī:* Ed. and trans. by R. A. Nicholson, Publications of the Oriental Translation Fund, 20, London, Royal Asiatic Society, 1911.

Ibn ʿAṭā Allāh al-Sakandarī, Aḥmad b. Muḥammad, *The Book of Wisdom:* see Danner *The Book of Wisdom*.

Ibn ʿAṭā Allāh al-Sakandarī, Aḥmad b. Muḥammad, *Laṭāʾif al-minan.* See al-Iskandari, *Laṭāʾif al-minan.* Cairo, 1974.

Ibn Bashkuwā l, Khalaf b. ʿAbd al-Mālik, *Kitāb al-ṣila f ī taʾrīkh aʾimma:* 2 vols., Cairo, al-Dār al-Miṣriyya li ʾl-Taʾlīf wa ʾl-Tarjama, 1966.

Ibn al-Dawādārī, Abū Bakr b. ʿAbdallāh, *Kanz al-durar wa jāmiʿ al-ghurar:* Maṣādir Taʾrīkh Miṣr al-Islāmiyya, Cairo, Qism al-Dirāsāt al-Islāmiyya, al-Maʿhad al-Almānī li ʾl-Āthār bi ʾl-Qāhirah, Wiesbaden, F. Steiner, 1960–1982.

Ibn al-Daybaʿ, ʿAbd al-Raḥmān, *Qurrat al-ʿuyūn f ī akhbār al-Yaman al-maymūn:* 2 vols., ed. by Muḥammad b. ʿAlī al-Akwaʿ, Cairo, al-Maṭbaʿa al-Salafiyya, 1977.

Ibn al-Dubaythī, Muḥammad b. Saʿīd, *Al-Mukhtaṣar al-muḥtāj ilayh min taʾrīkh Abī ʿAbdallāh Muḥammad Saʿīd b. Muḥammad b. al-Dubaythī:* 2 vols., ed. by Muṣṭafā Jawād, Baghdad, al-Majmaʿ al-ʿIlmī al-ʿIrāqī, 1951.

Ibn al-Fāriḍ, ʿUmar b. ʿAlī, *Dīwān Ibn al-Fāriḍ:* Beirut, Dār al-Kutub al-ʿIlmiyya, 1990.

Ibn Ḥajar al-ʿAsqalānī, Aḥmad b. ʿAlī, *Al-Durar al-kāmina fī aʿyān al-miʾa al-thāmina:* 4 vols., ed. by Muḥammad Sayyid Jād al-Ḥaqq, Cairo, Dār al-Kutub al-Ḥadītha, 1966–1967.

Ibn Ḥajar al-ʿAsqalānī, Aḥmad b. ʿAlī, *Lisān al-mīzān:* 7 vols., Multān, Idāra Taʾlīfāt Ashrafiyya, 1911–1912.

Ibn Ḥajar al-ʿAsqalānī, Aḥmad b. ʿAlī, *Inbāʾ al-ghumr bi-anbāʾ al-ʿumr:* 3 vols., ed. by Ḥasan Ḥabashī, Cairo, Lajnat al-Iḥyāʾ al-Turāth al-Islāmī, 1968–1972.

Ibn Ḥajar al-ʿAsqalānī, *Tabṣīr al-muntabih bi-taḥ rīr al-mushtabih:* 4 vols., ed. by ʿAlī Muḥammad al-Bajawī and Muḥammad ʿAlī al-Najjār, Cairo, Dār al-Miṣriyya li ʾl-Taʾlīf wa ʾl-Tarjama, 1964–1967.

Ibn al-ʿImād, ʿAbd al-Ḥayy b. Aḥmad, *Shadharāt al-dhahab fī akbār man dhahab:* 8 vols., Beirut, al-Maktab al-Tijārī li ʾl-Ṭibāʿa wa ʾl-Nashr wa ʾl-Tawzīʿ, 1966.

Ibn Iyās, Muḥammad b. Aḥmad, *Badāʾiʿ al-zuhūr fī waqāʾiʿ al-duhūr:* 4 vols., ed. by Paul Kahle and Muḥammad Muṣṭafā, Franz Steiner and Cairo, 1963–1972.

Ibn Jamāʿa, Badr al-dīn, *Taḥrīr al-aḥkām fī tadbīr ahl al-Islām li ʾl-imām Badr al-dīn Ibn Jamāʿa al-mutawaffā sanat 733:* Ed. by Fuʾād ʿAbd al-Munʿim Aḥmad, Qatar, Dār al-Thaqāfa, 1408/1988.

Ibn al-Jawzī, Abū ʾl-Faraj ʿAbd al-Raḥmān b. ʿAlī, *Talbīs Iblīs:* Beirut, Dār al-Kutub al-ʿIlmiyya, 1368 A.H.

Ibn al-Jazarī, Muḥammad b. Muḥammad, *Kitāb ghāyat al-nihāya fī ṭabaqāt al-qurrāʾ*: 2 vols., ed. by Gotthelf Bergsträsser and Otto Prezl, Egypt, Nasharāt al-Islāmiyya, 1933–35.

Ibn Kathīr, Ismāʿīl b. ʿUmar, *Al-Bidāya wa ʾl-nihāya:* 14 vols., ed. by Aḥmad Abū Muslim, new ed., Beirut, Dār al-Kutub al-ʿIlmiyya, 1985.

Ibn Khaldūn, *Al-Muqaddima:* 2 vols., Beirut, Dār al-Qalam, 1981.

Ibn Khaldūn, *The Muqaddimah:* 3 vols., trans. by F. Rosenthal, Bollingen Series XLIII, Princeton N.J., Princeton University Press, 1958.

Ibn Khaldūn, *Shifāʾ al-sāʾil li-tahdhīb al-masāʾil:* Ed. by Ighnāṭīyūs ʿAbduh Khalīfa, Beirut, Imprimerie Catholique, 1959.

Ibn al-Khaṭīb, Lisān al-dīn, *Al-Lamḥa al-badriyya fī ʾl-dawla al-naṣriyya:* Ed. by Muḥibb al-dīn al-Khaṭīb, Cairo, 1347 A.H.

Ibn al-Khaṭīb, Lisān al-dīn, *Al-Katība al-kāmina fī man laqiynāh bi 'l-Andalus min shu'arā' al-mi'a al-thāmina:* Ed. by Iḥsān 'Abbās, Dār al-Thaqāfa, Beirut, 1963.

Ibn al-Khaṭīb, Lisān al-dīn, *Ta'rīkh al-Maghrib al-'arabī fī al-'aṣr al-wasīṭ:* Ed. by Aḥmad al-'Abbādī and Muḥammad al-Kattānī, Casablanca, Dār al-Kutub, 1964.

Ibn al-Khaṭīb, Lisān al-dīn, *Rawḍat al-ta'rīf bi 'l-ḥubb al-sharīf:* 2 vols., ed. by Muḥammad al-Kattānī, Beirut, Dār al-Thaqāfa, 1970.

Ibn al-Khaṭīb, Lisān al-dīn, *Al-Iḥāṭa fī ta'rīkh Gharnāṭa:* 2d ed., 4 vols., ed. by Muḥammad 'Inān, Cairo, Maktabat al-Khānjī, 1973–1978.

Ibn al-Khaṭīb, Lisān al-dīn, *Dīwān Lisān al-dīn Ibn al-Khaṭīb al-Salamānī:* 2 vols., ed. by Muḥammad Miftāḥ, Casablanca, Dār al-Thaqāfa, 1989.

Ibn Khātima, *Dīwān Ibn Khātima al-Anṣārī wa Risālat al-Faḍl al-'Ādil bayn al-raqīb wa 'l-wāshī al-'ādhil:* Ed. by Muḥammad Riḍwān al-Dāyā, Beirut and Damascus, Dār al-Fikr al-Mu'āṣir, 1994.

Ibn al-Muqrī, Ismā'īl, *Majmū' al-qāḍī al-fāḍil...Sharaf al-dīn Ismā'īl Ibn Abū Bakr al-Muqrī,* Bombey, Maṭba'at Nukhbat al-Akhbār, 1305 A.H.

Ibn al-Najjār al-Baghdādī, *Al-Mustafād min Dhayl Ta'rīkh Baghdād li 'l-Ḥāfiẓ Muḥibb al-dīn Ibn al-Najjār al-Baghdādī:* Ed. by Bashshār 'Awwād Ma'rūf and introd. by Muḥammad Mawlid Khalaf, Beirut, Mu'assasat al-Risāla, 1986.

Ibn Nāṣir al-dīn al-Dimashqī, Muḥammad, *Al-Radd al-wāfir:* Ed. by Zuhayr al-Shāwīsh, Beirut, Al-Maktab al-Islāmī, 1393 A.H.

Ibn al-Qāḍī, Aḥmad b. Muḥammad, *Jadhwat al-iqtibās fī dhikr man ḥalla min al-a'lām madīnat Fās:* 2 vols., ed. by Aḥmad Ibn al-Qāḍī al-Maknāsī, Rabat, Dār al-Manṣūr, 1973–74.

Ibn al-Qunfudh, Aḥmad b. Ḥusayn, *Uns al-faqīr wa 'izz al-ḥaqīr:* Ed. by A. Faure and M. al-Fāsī, al-Markaz al-Jāmi'īli 'l-Baḥth al-'Ilmī, Rabat, 1965.

Ibn Rajab, 'Abd al-Raḥmān b. Aḥmad, *Al-Dhayl 'alā Ṭabaqāt al-ḥanābila:* 2 vols., ed. by Muḥammad Ḥamīd al-Faqī, Cairo, Maṭba'at al-Sunna al-Muḥammadiyya, 1952–1953.

Ibn Sab'īn, 'Abd al-Ḥaqq b. Ibrāhīm, *Rasā'il.* See Badawī, *Rasā'il Ibn Sab'īn.*

Ibn Sab'īn, 'Abd al-Ḥaqq b. Ibrāhīm, *Budd al-'ārif:* Ed. by George Kattoura, Beirut, Dār al-Andalus and Dār al-Kindī, 1978.

Ibn al-Ṣabūnī, Muḥammad b. 'Alī, *Kitāb takmilat al-ikmāl fī 'l-ansāb wa 'l-asmā' wa 'l-alqāb:* Beirut, 'Ālam al-Kutub, 1986.

Ibn Samura, ʿUmar b. ʿAlī, *Ṭabaqāt fuqahāʾ al-Yaman:* Ed. by Fuʾād Sayyid, Cairo, Maṭbaʿat al-Sunna al-Muḥammadiyya, 1957.

Ibn al-Suqāʿī, Faḍl Allāh b. Abī al-Fakhr, *Tālī Kitāb wafāyāt al-aʿyān:* Ed. and trans. by Jacqueline Sublet, French and Arabic ed., Damascus, Institut Français de Damas, 1974.

Ibn Taghrībirdī, Abū ʾl-Maḥāsin Yūsuf, *Al-Nujūm al-zāhira fī mulūk Miṣr wa ʾl-Qāhira:* 10 vols., Cairo, Dār al-Kutub al-Miṣriyya, 1929–1949.

Ibn Taymiyya, Aḥmad b. ʿAbd al-Ḥalīm, *Majmūʿ fatāwā shaykh al-Islām Aḥmad Ibn Taymiyya:* 35 vols., ed. by ʿAbd al-Raḥmān . . . al-Najdī al-Ḥanbalī, Riyadh, no date.

Ibn Taymiyya, Aḥmad b. ʿAbd al-Ḥalīm, *Majmūʿat al-rasāʾil wa ʾl-masāʾil:* 5 vols., reprint of the 1923–1930 Cairo edition, Cairo, Lajnat al-Turāth al-ʿArabī, 1976.

Ibn Taymiyya, Aḥmad b. ʿAbd al-Ḥalīm, *Majmūʿat al-rasāʾil wa ʾl-masāʾil:* 4 vols., ed. by Muḥammad Rashīd Riḍā, Cairo, Maṭbaʿat al-Manār, 1341 A.H.

Ibn al-Zayyāt, Yūsuf b. Yaḥyā, *Al-Tashawwuf ilā rijāl al-taṣawwuf:* Ed. by A. Faure, Rabat, Maṭbūʿāt Ifrīqiyya al-Shimāliyya al-Fanniyya, 1958.

Ibrahim, Tawfiq and Sagadeev, Arthur, *Classical Islamic Philosophy:* Trans. by H. Campbell Creighton, Moscow, Progress Publishers, 1990.

Irwin, Robert, *The Middle East in the Middle Ages: The Early Mamluk Sultanate, 1250–1382:* London, Croom Helm, 1986.

al-Ishbīlī, ʿAbd al-Ḥaqq b. ʿAbd al-Raḥmān, *Kitāb al-tahajjud:* Ed. by Masʿad ʿAbd al-Ḥamīd al-Saʿdūnī and Muḥammad b. al-Ḥasan b. Ismāʿīl, Beirut, Dār al-ʿIlmiyya, 1994.

al-Iskandarī [Ibn ʿAṭāʾ Allāh al-Sakandarī], Aḥmad b. Muḥammad, *The Book of Wisdom:* See Danner, *Ibn ʿAtaʾ Allah.*

al-Iskandarī [Ibn ʿAṭāʾ Allāh al-Sakandarī], Aḥmad b. Muḥammad, *Laṭāʾif al-minan:* Ed. by Maḥmūd ʿAbd al-Ḥalīm, Cairo, 1974.

Istrabadi, Zaineb S., "'The Principles of Sufism' (Qawaʾid al-Tasawwuf): An Annotated Translation": Unpublished Ph.D. dissertation, Bloomington, Indiana, 1989.

Izutsu, Toshihiko, *A Comparative Study of the Key Philosophical Concepts in Sufism and Taoism:* 2 vols., Tokyo, Keio Institute of Cultural and Linguistic Studies, 1966–1967.

Jackson, Sherman, "Ibn Taymiyyah on Trial in Damascus." In *Journal of Semitic Studies* (Cambridge), 29/1 (1994): pp. 41–85.

al-Janadī, Muḥammad b. Yūsuf al-Sakasikī, *Al-Sulūk fī ṭabaqāt al-ʿulamāʾ wa ʾl-mulūk:* Ed. by Muḥammad b. ʿAlī al-Akwaʿ, Wizārat al-Aʿlām, Sanaa, 1983.

Jayyusi, Salma Kh. (ed.), *The Legacy of Muslim Spain:* Leiden, E. J. Brill, 1992.

al-Jīlānī, ʿAbd al-Qādir, *Die Futuh al-gaib.* See Braune, *Die Futūḥ al-gaib.*

al-Jīlī, ʿAbd al-Karīm, *Al-Insān al-kāmil fī maʿrifat al-awākhir wa ʾl-awāʾil:* 2 vols., Cairo, Būlāq, 1304 A.H.

al-Jīlī, ʿAbd al-Karīm, *Qaṣīdat al-nādirāt al-ʿayniyya:* Ed. by Yūsuf Zaydān, Dār al-Jīl, Beirut, 1988.

Jomier, Jacques, *Le comméntaire coranique du Manâr:* Islam d'hier et d'aujourd'hui, 11, Paris, G.-P. Maisonneuve, 1954.

de Jong, Frederik, "Les confreries mystiques musulmanes au Machreq arabe." In *Les ordres mystiques dans l'Islam: Cheminements et situation actuelle:* Ed. by A. Popovic and G. Veinstein, Paris, Éditions de l'École des Hautes Études en Sciences Sociales, 1985: pp. 205–243.

Kaḥḥāla, ʿUmar Riḍā, *Muʿjam al-muʾallifīn, tarājim muṣannifī al-kutub al-ʿarabiyya:* 15 vols., Damascus, al-Maktaba al-ʿArabiyya, 1957–1961.

Kamada, Shigeru, "Nabulusi's Commentary on Ibn al-Farid's Khamriyya." In *Orient* (Tokyo), 18 (1982): pp. 19–40.

Karamustafa, Ahmet T., "The Antinomian Dervish as Model Saint." In *Modes de transmission de la culture religieuse en Islam,* Cairo, Institut Français d'Archeologie Orientale du Caire, 1993: pp. 241–260.

Karamustafa, Ahmet T., *God's Unruly Friends: Dervish Groups in the Islamic Later Middle Period, 1200–1550:* Salt Lake City, University of Utah Press, 1994.

Kassis, Hanna, *A Concordance of the Qurʾan:* Berkeley, University of California Press, 1983.

Kassis, Hanna, "Muslim Revival in Spain in the Fifth/Eleventh Century." In *Der Islam* (Strassburg), 67/1 (1990): pp. 78–110.

Kattoura, George, *Das Mystische und Philosophische System des Ibn Sabʿin:* Unpublished Ph.D. dissertation, Tübingen, Eberhard-Karls-Universität, 1977.

Katz, Jonathan, "Visionary Experience, Autobiography, and Sainthood in North African Islam." In *Princeton Papers in Near Eastern Studies* (Princeton, N.J.), 1 (1991): pp. 85–118.

Katz, Steven. "Language, Epistemology, and Mysticism." In *Mysticism and Philosophical Analysis:* Ed. by Steven Katz, New York, Oxford University Press, 1978: pp. 22–74.

Khalidov, Anas B., *Arabskiye rukopisi i arabskaya rukopisnaya traditsiya:* Moscow, Nauka, 1985.

Khalifah, Ha(j)ji, *Kashf al-zunun: Lexicon bibliographicum et encyclopaedicum a Mustafa ben Abdallah Katib Jelabi, dicto et nomine Haji Khalifa, celebrato compositum. Ad codicum Vinlobonensium, Parisiensium et Berolinensis fidem primum edidit Latine vertiti et commentario indicibusque instruxit Gustavus Fluegel:* 7 vols., ed. by Gustav Flügel, London, Printed for the Oriental Translation Fund, 1835–1858.

Khalis, Salim, *La vie littéraire à Séville au XIe siècle:* Alger, SNED, 1977.

al-Khaṭīb al-Baghdādī, Abū Bakr Aḥmad b. ʿAlī, *Taʾrīkh Baghdād:* 14 vols., Cairo, no publisher, 1931.

al-Khazrajī, ʿAlī b. Ḥasan, *Al-ʿUqūd al-luʾluʾiyya fī taʾrīkh al-dawla al-rasūliyya:* 2 vols., ed. by Shaykh Muḥammad ʿAsal, Leiden, E. J. Brill, 1913–1918.

Khowaiter, Abdul Aziz, *Baibars the First: His Endeavours and Achievements:* London, Green Mountain Press, 1978.

Knysh, Alexander, "Mirovozzreniye Ibn ʿArabi: k istorii sufiyskikh uchenii." In *Religii mira:* Moscow, Nauka, 1984: pp. 87–95.

Knysh, Alexander, "Ibn ʿArabi: Advokat Sufizma." In *Narodnye dvizheniya i ikh ideologiya v pred-industrial'nykh obshchestvakh Azii:* Moscow, Institute for Oriental Studies, 1985: pp. 33–36.

Knysh, Alexander, "Ucheniye Ibn ʿArabi v pozdnei musul'mankoi traditsii." In *Sufizm v kontekste musul'manskoi kul'tury:* Ed. by N. Prygarina, Moscow, Nauka, 1989: pp. 6–19.

Knysh, Alexander, "Hanbalitskaya kritika sufizma (po materialam 'Talbis Iblis' Ibn al-Jawzi)." In *Pis'mennye pamyatniki narodov Vostoka:* Moscow and Leningrad, Nauka, 1989: pp. 6–19.

Knysh, Alexander, "Sufizm." In *Islam: Istoriograficheskiye ocherki:* Ed. by S. M. Prozorov, Moscow, 1991: pp. 109–207.

Knysh, Alexander, "Ibn ʿArabi in the Yemen: His Admirers and Detractors." In *Journal of the Muhyiddin Ibn ʿArabi Society* (Oxford), 11 (1992): pp. 38–63.

Knysh, Alexander, "Kul't svyatykh i ideinaya bor'ba v islame." In *Traditsionnoe mirovozzreniye u narodov Peredney Azii:* Ed. by M. Rodionov, Moscow, Nauka, 1992: pp. 47–49.

Knysh, Alexander, "Irfan Revisited: Khomeini and the Legacy of Islamic Mystical Philosophy." In *The Middle East Journal* (Washington D.C.), 46 (Autumn 1992): pp. 631–53.

Knysh, Alexander, "'Orthodoxy' and 'Heresy' in Medieval Islam: An Essay an Reassessment." In *The Muslim World* (Hartford), 83 (January 1993): pp. 48–67.

Knysh, Alexander, "Ibn ʿArabi in the Later Islamic Tradition." In *Muhyiddin Ibn ʿArabi (A.D. 1165–1240): Volume of Translations and Studies Commemorating the 750th Anniversary of His Life and Work:* Ed. by Stephen Hirtenstein and Michael Tiernan, Brisbane, Element, 1993: pp. 307–327.

Knysh, Alexander, "The Cult of Saints in Hadramawt: An Overview." In *New Arabian Studies* (Exeter), 1 (1993): pp. 137–152.

Knysh, Alexander, "Abu Nasr al-Sarraj al-Tusi, Kitab al-lumaʿ fi ʾl-tasawwuf." In Stanislav Prozorov. *Khrestomatiya po islamu:* Moscow, Nauka, 1994: pp. 138–166.

Knysh, Alexander, "Ibrāhīm al-Kūrānī (d. 1101/1690), An Apologist for *waḥdat al-wujūd.*" In *Journal of the Royal Asiatic Society,* 3d series, 5/1 (April 1995): pp. 39–47.

Knysh, Alexander, *Mekkanskiye otkroveniya;* see Ibn al-Arabi. *Mekkanskiye otkroveniya*

Knysh, Alexander, "Ocherk religioznoi zhizni Khadramauta v pozdnee srednevekov'e." In *Ocherki istorii i kul'tury Khadramauta:* Ed. by Piotr Gryaznevich, Moscow, Nauka, forthcoming.

Kratchkovskii, Ignatii Yulianovich, *Izbrannye Sochineniya:* 6 vols., Moscow, Akademiya Nauk SSSR, 1955–1960.

Kraemer, Joel, "Heresy versus the State in Medieval Islam." In *Studies in Judaica, Karaitica and Islamica Presented to Leon Nemoy on His Eightieth Birthday:* Ed. by Sheldon R. Brunswick, Bar-Ilan University Press, 1982: pp. 167–180.

von Kremer, Alfred, *Ibn Chaldun und seine Culturgeschichte der Islamischen Reiche:* Vienna, Akademie der Wissenschaften, 1879.

al-Kutubī, Muḥammad b. Shākir, *Fawāt al-wafāyāt wa ʾl-dhayl alayhā:* 4 vols., ed. by Iḥsān ʿAbbās, Beirut, Dār al-Ṣādir, 1973–1974.

Lacoste, Yves, *Ibn Khaldun: The Birth of History and the Past of the Third World:* London, Verso, 1984.

Lagardère, Vincent, "La tarîqa et la révolte des murîdûn." In *Revue de l'Occident musulman et de la Méditerranée,* 35 (1983): pp. 157–170.

Landau, Rom, *The Philosophy of Ibn ʿArabī:* London, Allen and Unwin, 1959.

Landolt, Hermann, "Der Briefwechsel zwischen Kāšānī und Simnānī über Waḥdat al-Wuǧūd." In *Der Islam* (Stuttgart) 50/1, (1973): pp. 29–81.

Landolt, Hermann, "Ghazali and 'Religionswissenschaft'." In *Asiatische Studien/Études Asiatiques: Zeitschrift der Schweizerischen Asien Gesellschaft/Révue de la Société Suisse d'Études Asiatiques,* 45/1 (1991): pp. 19–72.

Landolt, Hermann, "Le paradoxe de la 'face de Dieu': 'Aziz-e Nasafi (VIIe/XIIIe siècle) et la 'monisme ésoterique' de l'Islam." In *Studia Iranica* (Paris), 25/2 (1996): pp. 163–192.

Lane, Edward William, *An Arabic-English Lexicon:* 8 vols., ed. by Stanley Lane-Poole, Beirut, Libraire du Liban, 1980.

Laoust, Henri, *Le califat dans la doctrine de Rašīd Riḍā*: Beirut, Institut Français de Damas, 1938.

Laoust, Henri, *Essai sur les doctrines sociales et politiques de Taḳī-d-Dīn Aḥmad b. Taimīya canonisteḥanbalite, né à Harran en 661/1262 mort à Damas en 728/1328:* Cairo, Institut Français d'Archeologie Orientale, 1939.

Laoust, Henri, "La biographie d'Ibn Taymīya d'après Ibn Katīr." In *Bulletin d'études orientales* (Beirut), 9 (1942–1943): pp. 115–162.

Laoust, Henri, ed. and trans., *Le Traité de droit public d'Ibn Taimīya:* Beirut, 1948.

Laoust, Henri, "Le hanbalisme sous les mamlouks bahrides." In *Revue des Études Islamiques* (Paris), 28 (1960): pp. 1–71.

Laoust, Henri, *Les schismes dans l'Islam: Introduction à une étude de la religion musulmane:* Paris, Payot, 1965.

Laoust, Henri, "L'influence d'Ibn Taymiyya." In *Islam: Past Influence and Present Challenge:* Ed. by Alford T. Welch, Pierre Cachia, and Michael V. McDonald, Edinburgh, Edinburgh University Press and Albany, SUNY Press, 1979: pp. 15–33.

Laoust, Henri, *Pluralismes dans l'Islam:* reprint of articles from *Revue des Études Islamiques,* 1932–1978, Paris, Libraire Orientaliste, P. Geuthner, 1983.

Lapidus, Ira Marvin, *Muslim Cities in the Later Middle Ages:* Harvard Middle Eastern Studies, 11, Cambridge, (Mass.), Harvard University Press, 1967.

Lavallé, Bernard, ed., *Séville: Vingt siècles d'histoire:* Bordeaux, Maison des Pays Ibériques, 1992.

Lawrence, Bruce, ed., *Ibn Khaldūn and Islamic Ideology,* Leiden, E. J. Brill, 1984.

Leaman, Oliver, *An Introduction to Medieval Islamic Philosophy:* Cambridge, Cambridge University Press, 1985.

Lévi-Provençal, Evariste, *Les Historiens des Chorfa: essai sur la littérature historique et bibliographique au Maroc du XVIe au XXe siècle:* Paris, E. Larose, 1922.

Lévi-Provençal, Evariste, *Histoire de l'Espagne Musulmane:* 3 vols., Paris, G. P. Maisonneuve, Paris, 1950–1953.

Lewinstein, Keith, "Notes on Eastern Hanafite Heresiography." In *Journal of the American Oriental Society* (Michigan), 114/4 (1994): pp. 583–598.

Lings, Martin, *A Sufi Saint of the Twentieth Century: Shaikh Aḥmad al-'Alawī: His Spiritual Heritage and Legacy:* 2d ed., revised and enlarged, Berkeley, University of California Press, 1971.

Little, Donald, "Did Ibn Taymiyya Have a Screw Loose?" In *Studia Islamica* (Paris), 41 (1975): pp. 93–111.

Little, Donald, "The Historical and Historiographical Significance of the Detention of Ibn Taymiyya." In *International Journal of Middle Eastern Studies* (Cambridge), 4 (1973): pp. 320–327.

Little, Donald, *History and Historiography of the Mamluks:* London, Variorum Reprints, 1986.

Little, Donald, *An Introduction to Mamluk Historiography; An Analysis of Arabic Annalistic and Biographical Sources for the Reign of al-Malik an-Nāṣir Muḥammad b. Qalā'un:* Freiburger Islamstudien, 2, Montreal, McGill-Queens University Press, 1970.

Little, Donald, "Religion Under the Mamluks." In *The Muslim World* (Hartford), 73/3–4 (1983): pp. 165–181.

Little, Donald, "Al-Ṣafadī as Bigrapher of His Contemporaries," In *Essays on Islamic Civilization Presented to Niyazi Berkes:* Ed. by Donald Little, Leiden, E. J. Brill, 1976: pp. 190–210.

Löfgern, Oskar (ed.), *Arabische Texte zur Kenntnis der Stadt Aden im Mittelalter:* 2 vols., Uppsala, Otto Harassowitz, 1936–1950.

Lomax, Derek W., *The Reconquest of Spain:* London and New York, Longman, 1978.

Lull, Ramon, *Blanquerna:* Trans. by E. A. Peers, ed. by Robert Irwin, new ed., London, Dedalus and New York, Hippocrene Books, 1987.

Madelung, Wilferd, *Der Imām al-Qāsim b. Ibrāhīm und die Glaubenslehre der Zayditen:* Berlin, W. de Gruyter, 1965.

Madelung, Wiferd, *Religious Trends in Early Islamic Iran:* Albany, Persian Heritage Foundation, 1988.

Madelung, Wilferd, "Islam in Yemen." In *Yemen: 3000 Years of Art and Civilization:* Ed. by Werner Daum, Innsbruck, Pinguin and Frankfurt/Main, Umschau, 1988: pp. 174–176.

Mahdi, Muhsin, "The Book and the Master as Poles of Cultural Change in Islam." In *Islam and Cultural Change in the Middle Ages:* Ed. by S. Vryonis Jr., Wiesbaden, 1975: pp. 3–15.

Makarem, Sami Nasib, *The Druse Faith:* New York, Delmar, 1974.

Makdisi, George, "Ashʿari and the Ashʿarites in Islamic Religious History." In *Studia Islamica* (Paris), 17 (1962): pp. 37–80 and 18 (1963): pp. 19–39.

Makdisi, George, "Ibn Taymiyya: A Ṣūfī of the Qādirīya Order." In *American Journal of Arabic Studies* (Leiden), 1 (1973): pp. 118–129.

Makdisi, George, "The Hanbali School and Sufism." In *Humaniora Islamica* (The Hague), 2 (1974): pp. 61–72.

Makdisi, George, "Hanbalite Islam." In *Studies on Islam:* Ed. and trans. by M. Swartz, London, Oxford University Press, 1981: pp. 216–274.

Makdisi, George, *The Rise of Colleges: Institutions of Learning in Islam and the West:* Edinburgh, Edinburgh University Press, 1981.

Makdisi, George, "The Non-Ashʿarite Shāfiʿism of Abū Ḥāmid al-Ghazzālī." In *Revue des Études Islamiques* (Paris), 54 (1986): pp. 239–257.

Makdisi, George, "The Genre of Tabaqat: Law and Orthodoxy in Classical Islam." In *Islamic Studies* (Islamabad), 32/4 (1993): pp. 371–396.

Manz, Beatrice Forbes, *The Rise and Rule of Tamerlane:* Cambridge Studies in Islamic Civilization, Cambridge (Eng.) and New York, Cambridge University Press, 1989.

Maqāliḥ, ʿAbd al-ʿAzīz, *Qirāʾa fī fikr al-zaydiyya wa ʾl-muʿtazila:* Beirut, Dār al-ʿAwda, 1982.

al-Maqbalī, Ṣāliḥ b. Mahdī, *Al-ʿAlam al-shāmikh fī īthār al-ḥaqq ʿalā ʾl-abāʾ wa ʾl-mashāʾikh:* Beirut, Dār al-Ḥadīth, 1985.

al-Maqqarī, Aḥmad b. Muḥammad, *Azhār al-riyāḍ fī akhbār ʿIyāḍ:* reprint and completion of 1939 edition published by Bayt al-Maghrib, Cairo, of which only 3 vols. appeared; 4 vols., Rabat, Sundūq Iḥyāʾ al-Turāth al-Islāmī al-Mushtarak bayna al-Mamlaka al-Maghribiyya wa Dawlat al-Imārāt al-ʿArabiyya al Muttaḥida, 1978.

al-Maqqarī, Aḥmad b. Muḥammad, *Nafḥ al-ṭīb min ghusn al-Andalus al-raṭīb:* 10 vols., Beirut, Dār al-Fikr, 1986; or ed. Iḥsān ʿAbbās, 8 vols., Beirut, Dār Ṣādir, 1968.

Massignon, Louis, "Recherches sur Shushtari, poète andalou enterré à Damiette." In *Mélanges offerts à William Marçais:* Paris, Éditions G.-P. Maisonneuve, 1950: pp. 253–276.

Massignon, Louis, "Les Nusayris." In *L'Élaboration de l'Islam: Colloques de Strasbourg 12–13–14 Juin, 1959:* Paris, Presses Universitaires de Françe, 1961: pp. 110–114.

Massignon, Louis, "Ibn Sab'īn et la 'conspiration anti-hallağienne' en Andalousie et en Orient du XIIIe siècle." In *Études d'orientalisme dédiées à la mémoire de Lévi-Provençal:* Paris, G.-P. Maisonneuve et Larose, 1962, vol. 2: pp. 661–683.

Massignon, Louis, *The Passion of al-Hallāj: Mystic and Martyr of Islam:* 4 vols., trans. by Herbert Mason, Bollingen Series, 98, Princeton, N.J., Princeton University Press, 1982.

Massignon, Louis, *La Passion de Hosayn b. Mansour Hallâj: martyr mystique de l'Islam exécuté à Baghdad le 26 mars 922:* 4 vols., New ed., Bibliothèque des Idées, Paris, Gallimard, 1975.

Meier, Fritz, *Abū Sa'īd Abū l-Ḫayr: Wirklichkeit und Legende:* Acta Islamica, 11, Teheran-Liège, Bibliothèque Pahlavi & Leiden, Diffusion E. J. Brill, 1976.

Meier, Fritz, "Das sauberste über die vorbestimmung. Ein stück Ibn Taymiyya." In *Saeculum* (Freiburg), 32 (1981): pp. 74–89.

Memon, Muhammad Umar, *Ibn Taimīya's Struggle Against Popular Religion:* Religion and Society, 1, The Hague, Mouton, 1976.

Menocal, Maria Rosa, *Shards of Love: Exile and the Origins of the Lyric:* Durham, Duke University Press, 1994.

Messick, Brinkley, *The Calligraphic State: Textual Domination and History in a Muslim Society:* Berkeley, University of California Press, 1993.

Michel, Thomas, *A Muslim Theologian's Response to Christianity: Ibn Taymiyya's Al-Jawab al-Sahih:* Delmar, Caravan, 1984.

Michel, Thomas, "Ibn Taymiyya's *Sharḥ* on the *Futūḥ al-Ghayb* of 'Abd al-Qādir Jīlānī." In *Hamdard Islamicus* (Karachi), 4/2 (1981): pp. 3–12.

Molé, M., "Les Kubrawiya entre sunnisme et chiisme aux VIII-e et IX-e siècles de l'hégire." In *Revue des Études Islamiques* (Paris), 29 (1961): pp. 61–142.

Monès, Hussain, "Le rôle des hommes de religion dans l'histoire de l'Espagne musulmane jusqu'à la fin du Califat." In *Studia Islamica* (Paris), 20 (1964): pp. 47–88.

Morgan, David, *The Mongols: Peoples of Europe:* Oxford and New York, B. Blackwell, 1986.

Morris, James Winston, *The Wisdom of the Throne: An Introduction to the Philosophy of Mulla Sadra:* Princeton N.J., Princeton Library of Asian Translations, Princeton University Press, 1981.

Morris, James Winston, "Ibn ʿArabī and His Interpreters." In *Journal of the American Oriental Society* (Michigan), 106/3 (1986): pp. 539–64, 106/4 (1986): pp. 733–56 and 107/1 (1987): pp. 101–120.

Morris James Winston, "The Spiritual Ascension: Ibn ʿArabī and the *miʿrāj.*" In *Journal of the American Oriental Society,* 107 (1987): pp. 629–652 and 108 (1988): pp. 63–77.

Morris, James Winston, "Ibn ʿArabi's 'Esotericism': The Problem of Spiritual Authority." In *Studia Islamica* (Paris), 71 (1990): pp. 37–64.

Morris, James Winston, "How to Study the 'Futûhât': Ibn ʿArabi's Own Advice." In *Muhyiddin Ibn ʿArabi. A Commemorative Volume:* Ed. by Stephen Hirtenstein and Michael Tiernan, Brisbane, Element, 1993: pp. 73–89.

Mottahedeh, Roy, *Loyalty and Leadership in an Early Islamic Society:* Princeton, N.J., Princeton University Press, 1981.

Mubārak, Zakī, *Al-Taṣawwuf al-islāmī fī ʾl-adab wa ʾl-akhlāq:* 2 vols., Beirut, Dār al-Jīl, 1975.

al-Muḥibbī, Muḥammad Amīn b. Faḍl Allāh, *Khulāṣat al-athar fī aʿyān al-qarn al-ḥādī ʿashar:* 4 vols., Beirut, Maktabat al-Khayyāṭ, 1966.

al-Munāwī, Muḥammad ʿAbd al-Raʾūf, *Al-Kawākib al-durriyya fī tarājim al-sāda al-ṣūfiyya:* Cairo, Maṭbaʿat al-Anwār, 1938.

al-Mundhirī, ʿAbd al-ʿAẓīm b. ʿAbd al-Qawī, *Al-Takmila li-wafayāt al-naqala:* 6 vols., ed. by Bashshār ʿAwwād Maʿrūf al-Najaf, Cairo, Maṭbaʿat al-ʿĪsā al-Ḥalabī, 1968–1969.

al-Mundhirī, ʿAbd al-ʿAẓīm b. ʿAbd al-Qawī, *Al-Targhīb wa ʾl-tarhīb min al-ḥadīth al-sharīf:* 4 vols., ed. by Muḥyī al-dīn Dīb Mistū et al., Damascus, Dār Ibn Kathīr, 1993.

Muslim, Ibn al-Ḥajjāj al-Qushayrī, *Ṣaḥīḥ Muslim:* 3d ed., 18 vols., Beirut, Dār Iḥyāʾ al-Turāth al-ʿArabī, 1984.

al-Nabhānī, Yūsuf b. Ismāʿīl, *Jāmiʿ karāmāt al-awliyāʾ*: 2 vols., ed. by Ibrāhīm ʿAtwah ʿAwaḍ, Egypt, Maṭbaʿat al-Bābī al-Ḥalabī, 1962.

Nagel, Tilman, "Ibn al-ʿArabi und das Aschʿaritentum." In *Gottes ist der Orient, Gottes ist der Okzident: Festschrift für Abdoljavad Falaturi zum 65. Geburtstag:* Ed. by Udo Tworuschka, Cologne and Vienna, Böhlau Verlag, 1991: pp. 206–245.

Nagel, Tilman, *Timur der Erober und die islamische Welt des späten Mittelalters:* Munich, C. H. Beck, 1993.

Nasr, Seyyed Hossein, *An Introduction to Islamic Cosmological Doctrine: Conceptions of Nature and Methods Used for Its Study by the Ikhwan al-Safa'*, al-Biruni, and Ibn Sina: Cambridge (Mass.), Belknap Press of Harvard University Press, 1964.

Nasr, Seyyed Husain, "Ibn ʿArabi in the Persian Speaking World." In *Al-Kitāb al-tidhkārī: Muḥyī 'l-dīn Ibn ʿArabī fī dhikrā al-miʾawiyya al-thāmina li-mīlādih 1165–1240:* Cairo, al-Hayʾa al-Miṣriyya al-ʿĀmma li 'l-Kitāb, 1969: pp. 257–263.

Nasr, Seyyed Hossein, *Sufi Essays:* London, Allen & Unwin, 1972.

Netton, Ian Richard, *Muslim Neoplatonists: An Introduction to the Thought of the Brethren of Purity:* London and Boston, Allen & Unwin, 1982.

Netton, Ian Richard, "Theophany as Paradox: Ibn al-ʿArabî's Account of al-Khadir in His Fusûs al-Hikam." In *Journal of the Muhyiddin Ibn ʿArabi Society* (Oxford), 11 (1992): pp. 11–22.

Nicholson, Reynold Alleyne, *The Turjumān al-ashwāq, a Collection of Mystical Odes by Muḥyi'ddīn Ibn al-ʿArabī:* Oriental Translation Fund, 20, London, Royal Asiatic Society, 1911.

Nicholson, Reynold Alleyne, *Studies in Islamic Mysticism:* Cambridge, Cambridge University Press, 1921.

Nieli, Russell, *Wittgenstein: From Mysticism to Ordinary Language. A Study of Viennese Positivism and the Thought of Ludwig Wittgenstein:* Albany, SUNY Press, 1987.

Nwyia, Paul, "Note sur quelques fragments inédits de la correspondance d'Ibn al-ʿArif avec Ibn Barrajan." In *Hespéris* (Paris), 43 (1956): pp. 217–221.

Nwyia, Paul, *Ibn ʿAbbād de Ronda, 1332–1390; un mystique prédicateur à la Qarawīyīn de Fès:* Université Saint-Joseph, Institut de Lettres Orientales, Recherches, 17, Beirut, Imprimerie Catholique, 1961.

Nwyia, Paul, *Ibn ʿAtāʾ Allāh et la naissance de la confrérie šādilite:* Recherches, Nouvelle Serie A, Langue arabe et pensée islamique, 2, Beirut, Dar al-Machreq, 1972.

Nwyia, Paul, "Une cible d'Ibn Taimiya: le moniste al-Tilimsânî (m. 690/1291)". In *Bulletin d'Études Orientales* (Beirut), 30 (1978): pp. 127–145.

Nwyia, Paul, "Rasāʾil ibn al-ʿArīf ilā aṣḥāb thawrat al-murīdīn fī 'l-Andalus." In *Al-Abḥāth* (Beirut), 27 (1979): pp. 43–56.

Nyberg, H. S., *Kleinere Schriften des Ibn al-ʿArabī, nach Handschriften in Uppsala und Berlin zum ersten Mal hrsg. und mit Einleitung und Kommentar versehen von H. S. Nyberg:* Leiden, E. J. Brill, 1919.

Obermeyer, G.-J., "La formation de l'imamate et de l'état au Yémen: Islam et culture politique." In *La Péninsule arabique d'aujourd'hui:* Ed. by P. Bonnenfant, vol. 2, Paris, CNRS, 1982: pp. 31–46.

O'Fahey, Rex S., *Enigmatic Saint: Ahmad Ibn Idris and the Idrisi Tradition:* Evanston, Ill., Northwestern University, 1990.

O'Fahey, Rex S. and Radtke, Bernd, "Neo-Sufism Reconsidered." In *Der Islam* (Strassburg), 70 (1993): pp. 52–87.

O'Grady, Joan, *Heresy: Heretical Truth or Orthodox Error?*: Element, Dorset, 1985.

Peskes, Esther, *Muḥammad b. ʿAbdalwahhāb (1703–1792) im Widerstreit:* Beirut and Stuttgart, Beirute Texte und Studien, 1993.

Peters, J. R. T. M., *God's Created Speech: A Study in the Speculative Theology of the Muʿtazilī Qāḍī l-quḍāt Abū l-Ḥasan ʿAbd al-Jabbār b. Aḥmad al-Hamadānī:* Leiden, E. J. Brill, 1976.

Petry, Carl F., *The Civilian Elite of Cairo in the Later Middle Ages:* Princeton, N.J., Princeton University Press, 1980.

Piotrovsky, Mikhail B., *Yuzhnaya Araviya v ranneye srednevekovʾe: stanovleniye srednevekovogo obshchestva,* Moscow, Nauka, 1985.

Poonawala, Ismail, *Bio-bibliography of Ismaʿili Literature:* Malibu, Undena Publications, 1977.

Pouzet, Louis, *Damas au VIIe-XIIIe siècle: vie et structures religieuses d'une métropole islamique:* Recherches, Nouvelle series A, Langue arabe et pensée islamique, 15, Beirut, Dar al-Machreq, 1988.

Pouzet, Louis, "De Murcie à Damas: le chef des Sabʿiniens Badr ad-Dīn al-Ḥasan Ibn Hūd." In *Islão e Arabismo na Peninsula Ibérica:* Évora, Universidade de Évora, 1986: pp. 317–330.

Pouzet, Louis, "Maghrébins à Damas au VIIe-XIIIe siècle." In *Bulletin d'Études Orientales* (Damascus), 28 (1975): pp. 167–199.

Profitlich, Manfred, *Die Terminologie Ibn ʿArabī's im Kitāb wasāʾil as-sāʾil des Ibn Saudakīn:* Freiburg, Schwartz, 1973.

Prozorov, Stanislav M., *Ash-Shahrastani. Kniga o religiyakh i sektakh:* Moscow, Nauka, 1984.

Prozorov, Stanislav M., "'Pravoverie' i 'zabluzhdenie' v rannem islame." In *Vostok* (Moscow), 6 (1991): pp. 44–55.

al-Qārī al-Baghdādī, Abū Ḥasan ʿAlī, *Manāqib Ibn ʿArabī:* Ed. by Ṣalāḥ al-dīn al-Munajjid, Beirut, Muʾassasat al-Turāth al-ʿArabī, 1959.

al-Qazwīnī, Zakarīyā b. Muḥammad, *Athār al-bilād:* Beirut, Dār Ṣādir li ʾl-Ṭibāʿa wa ʾl-Nashr, 1960.

al-Qushayri, *Principles of Sufism*. See von Schlegell, *Principles of Sufism*.

Radtke, Bernd, *Al-Ḥakīm al-Tirmidī: ein islamischer Theosoph des 3./9. Jahrhunderts:* Islamkundliche Untersuchungen, 58, Freiburg, Schwartz, 1980.

Radtke, Bernd, "Erleuchtung und Aufklärung: Islamische Mystik und Europäischer Rationalismus." In *Die Welt des Islams* (Leiden), 34 (1994): pp. 48–66.

Rahman, Fazlur, *Islam:* 2d ed., Chicago, University of Chicago Press, 1979.

Rahman, Fazlur, *Prophecy in Islam; Philosophy and Orthodoxy:* London, Allen & Unwin, 1958.

Renaud, Etienne, "Histoire et la pensée religieuse au Yémen." In Joseph Chelhod et al., *L'Arabie du Sud: histoire et civilization. Vol. 2, La société yéménite de l'Hégire aux idéologies modernes:* Paris, G.-P. Maisonneuve, 1984: pp. 57–68.

Rizvi, Athar Abbas, *A History of Sufism in India:* 2 vols., New Delhi, Munshiram Manoharlal, 1978.

Rizvi, Athar Abbas, *Muslim Revivalist Movements in Northern India in the Sixteenth and Seventeenth Centuries:* Agra, India, Agra University, 1965.

Rizwan Ali, Sayyid, "Two Great Contemporaries of the Thirteenth Century: Sulṭān al-ʿulamāʾ al-ʿIzz Ibn ʿAbd al-Salām and Ibn ʿArabī." In *Islamic Culture* (Hyderabad), 45/3 (1971): pp. 193–201.

Rizzitano, Umberto, "Il Diwan as-Sababa dello scrittore magrebino Ibn Abi Hağala." In *Rivista degli Studi Orientali* (Rome), 28 (1953): pp. 35–70.

Robson, James, *Tracts on Listening to Music, Being Dhamm al-malāhī, by Ibn Abī 'l-Dunyā, and Bawāriq al-ilmāʿ, by Majd al-Dīn al-Ṭūsī al-Ghazālī:* Oriental Translation Fund, 34, London, The Royal Asiatic Society, 1938.

Rodionov, Mikhail and Polosin, Valeri, *Rasaʾil al-hikma:* I-XIV (*Poslaniya mudrosti*): St. Petersburg, St. Petersburg Center for Oriental Studies, 1995.

Roman, André (trans.), *Al-Muḥāsibī: Kitāb al-tawahhum:* Paris, Libraire C. Klincksieck, 1978.

Rosenthal, Erwin Isak Jakob, *Political Thought in Medieval Islam; An Introductory Outline:* Cambridge (Eng.), Cambridge University Press, 1958.

Rosenthal, Franz, *A History of Muslim Historiography:* 2d ed., Leiden, E. J. Brill, 1968.

Rosenthal, Franz, "Ibn Khaldūn and His Time." In *Ibn Khaldūn and Islamic Ideology:* Ed. by Bruce Lawrence, Leiden, E. J. Brill, 1984: pp. 14–26.

Runciman, Steven, Sir, *A History of the Crusades:* 3 vols., New York, Harper & Row, 1964.

Russell, Jeffrey, *Dissent and Order in the Middle Ages: The Search for the Legitimate Authority:* New York, Twayne Publishers, 1992.

Sadeque, Syedah Fatima, *Baybars I of Egypt:* reprint of the 1956 edition published by Oxford University Press, New York, AMS Press, 1980.

al-Ṣafadī, Khalīl b. Aybak, *Kitāb al-wāf ī bi 'l-wafāyāt:* 24 vols., ed. by Hellmut Ritter, Nasharāt al-Islāmiyya, 6, Istanbul, Maṭbaʿat al-Dawla, 1931.

al-Sakhāwī, Muḥammad b. ʿAbd al-Raḥmān, *Al-Dawʾ al-lāmiʿ li-ahl al-qarn al-tāsiʿ:* 12 vols., Cairo, Maktabat al-Qudsī, 1934–36.

al-Sakhāwī, Muḥammad b. ʿAbd al-Raḥmān, *Al-Qawl al-munbī (al-munabbī) ʿan tarjamat Ibn ʿArabī:* a manuscript in the Library of Berlin, 2849 spr. 790, fols. 1–250.

de Santiago Simon, E., "¿Ibn al-Jatib, mistico?" In *Homenaje a don José Maria Lacarra de Miguel:* Saragossa, Anubar, 3, 1977: pp. 217–228.

Sartain, E. M., *Jalal al-din al-Suyuti.* Vol. 1 *Biography and Background:* Cambridge, Cambridge University Press, 1975.

Sayyid, Ayman Fuʾād, *Maṣādir taʾrīkh al-Yaman fi ʿaṣr al-islāmī:* Cairo, French Institute in Cairo, 1974.

Scattolin, Guiseppe, "The Mystical Experience of ʿUmar ibn al-Farid." In *The Mulsim World* (Hartford), 82 (1992): pp. 274–286.

Schimmel, Annemarie, "Some Glimpses of Religious Life in Egypt During the Later Mamluk Period." In *Islamic Studies* (Karachi), 4 (1965): pp. 352–392.

Schlegell, B. R. von (trans.), *Al-Qushayri. Principles of Sufism:* Berkeley, Mizan Press, 1990.

Schmidt, Nathaniel, *Ibn Khaldun: Historian, Sociologist, Philosopher:* reprint: Lahore, Universal Books, 1978.

Sells, Michael A., "Ibn ʿArabi's 'Garden Among the Flames': A Reevaluation." In *History of Religions* (Chicago), 23 (May 1984): pp. 287–315.

Sells, Michael A., "Ibn ʿArabi's 'Polished Mirror': Perspective Shift and Meaning Event." In *Studia Islamica* (Paris), 67 (1988): pp. 121–149.

Serjeant, Robert, "Materials for South Arabian History: Notes on new MSS from Hadramawt." In *BSOAS* (London), 13 (1950): pp. 281–307 and 581–601.

Serjeant, Robert, "A Zaydi Manual of hisba of the 3d Century." In *Revista degli Studi Orientali* (Rome), 28 (1957): pp. 1–34.

Serjeant, Robert, *The Sayyids of Hadramawt:* London, SOAS, University of London, 1957.

Serjeant, Robert, "Haram and hawta: The Sacred Enclave in Arabia." In *Mélanges Taha Husayn:* Ed. by ʿAbd al-Raḥmān Badawī, Cairo, Dār al-Maʿārif, 1962: pp. 41–58.

Serjeant, Robert, "Historians and Historiography of Hadramawt." In *BSOAS* (London), 25 (1962): pp. 239–261.

Serjeant, Robert, "South Arabia." In *Commoners, Climbers, and Notables:* Ed. by Chistoffle A. O. Nieuwenhuijze, Leiden, E. J. Brill, 1977: pp. 226–247.

Serjeant, Robert, *Studies in Islamic History and Civilization:* London, Variorum Reprints, 1981.

Serjeant, Robert, "The Inteplay Between Tribal Affinities and Religious (Zaydi) Authority in the Yemen." In *Al-Abḥāth* (Beirut), 30 (1982): pp. 11–50.

Serjeant, Robert, *Society and Trade in South Arabia:* Ed. by G. Rex Smith, London, Variorum Reprints, 1996.

Sezgin, Fuat, *Geschichte der Arabischen Schrifttums:* Vol. 1., Leiden, E. J. Brill, 1967.

Sharaf al-dīn, Aḥmad Ḥusayn, *Taʾrīkh al-fikr al-islāmī fī ʾl-Yaman: Cairo, Maṭbaʿat al-Kīlānī,* 1968.

al-Shaʿrānī, ʿAbd al-Wahhāb b. Aḥmad, *Al-Ṭabaqāt al-kubrā al-musammā bi-lawāqiḥ al-anwār fī ṭabaqāt al-akhyār:* 2 vols., Cairo, Maktabat wa Maṭbaʿat Muḥammad Ṣubayḥ wa Awlāduh, no date.

al-Shaʿrānī, ʿAbd al-Wahhāb b. Aḥmad, *Al-Yawāqīt wa ʾl-jawāhir fī bayān ʿaqāʾid al-akābir:* reprint of the 1899 Cairo edition, 2 vols., Beirut, no publishers 1974.

al-Sharjī, Aḥmad b. Aḥmad, *Ṭabaqāt al-khawāss ahl al-ṣidq wa ʾl-ikhlāṣ:* Beirut, al-Dār al-Yamaniyya, 1986.

al-Shawkānī, Muḥammad b. ʿAlī, *Al Badr al-ṭāliʿ bi-maḥāsin min baʿad al-qarn al-sābiʿ*: 2 vols., Cairo, Maṭbaʿat al-Saʿāda, 1929–1930.

Shaykh-i Makkī, Abū ʾl-Fatḥ Muḥammad, *Al-Jānib al-gharbī fī ḥall mushkilāt al-Shaykh Muḥyī al-dīn Ibn ʿArabī,* Tehran, Intishā rāt-i Mawlā , 1985.

Shehadi, Fadlou, "Theism, Mysticism and Scientific History in Ibn Khaldun." In *Islamic Theology and Philosophy: Studies in Honor of George*

F. Hourani: Ed. by Michael E. Marmura, Albany, SUNY Press, 1984: pp. 265–279.

Shelley, Christopher, "Abdullah Effendi: Commentator on the *Fusus al-hikam.*" In *Journal of the Muhyiddin Ibn ʿArabi Society* (Oxford), 17 (1995): pp. 75–83.

Shepard, William, "Islam and Ideology: Towards a Typology." In *International Journal of Middle Eastern Studies* (Cambridge), 19 (1987): pp. 307–336.

al-Shillī, Muḥammad Ibn Abī Bakr, *Al-Mashraʿ al-rawī fī manāqib al-sāda al-kirām Āl Abī ʿAlawī:* 2 vols., Cairo, al-Maṭbaʿa al-Sharafiyya, 1319 A.H.

Shmidt, Aleksandr, *ʿAbd al-Wahhab al-Sharaniy i ego Kniga razsypannykh zhemchuzhyn:* St. Petersburg, 1914.

Sibṭ Ibn al-Jawzī, Yūsuf b. Qizughlī, *Mirʾāt al-zamān fī taʾrīkh al-aʿyān:* Hyderabad, Maṭbaʿat Majlis Dāʾirat al-Maʿārif al-ʿUthmāniyya, no date.

Sivan, Emmanuel, "Ibn Taymiyya: Father of the Islamic Revolution." In *Encounter* (London) (May 1983): pp. 41–50.

Smith, G. Rex, "The Ayyubids and Rasulids: The Transfer of Power in 7th/13th Century Yemen." In *Islamic Culture* (Hyderabad), 43 (1969): pp. 175–188.

Smith, G. Rex, *The Ayyubids and Early Rasulids in the Yemen:* 2 vols., London, Luzac (Gibb Memorial Series, n.s. 26), 1974–1978.

Smith, G. Rex, "Al-Birrah fī ḥubb al-hirrah: A 10th/16th century Arabic text on pussy cats." In *Arabian and Islamic Studies Presented to R.B. Serjeant:* Ed. by Robert Bidwell and G. Rex Smith, London, Longman, 1983: pp. 134–145.

Smith G. Rex, "The Political History of the Islamic Yemen Down to the First Turkish Invasion (1–945/622–1538)." In *Yemen: 3000 Years of Art and Civilization in Arabia Felix:* Ed. by Werner Daum, Innsbruck, Pinguin and Frankfurt/Main, Umschau, 1988: pp. 129–139.

Smith, Margaret, *An Early Mystic of Baghdad: A Study of the Life and Teaching of Harith b. Asad al-Muhasibi:* London, The Sheldon Press, 1935.

Spuler, Berthold, *Die Mongolen in Iran:* 2d enlarged ed., Berlin, Akademie-Verlag, 1955.

Stepaniants, Marietta, *Sufi Wisdom:* Albany, SUNY Press, 1994.

Stern, Samuel, "The Succession of the Fatimid Imām al-ʿĀmir." In *Oriens* (Leiden), 4/2 (1951): pp. 193–255.

Stern, Samuel, "Ibn Masarra, Follower of Pseudo-Empedokles—An Illusion." In *Actas de IV cogresso de estudios arabes e islamicos: Coimbra-Lisbon, 1968:* Leiden, E. J. Brill, 1971: pp. 325–337.

Strauss, E., "L'inquisition dans l'état mamlouke." In *Revista degli Studi Orientali* (Rome), 25 (1950): pp. 16–17.

Strothmann, Rudolf, "Die Litteratur der Zaiditen." In *Der Islam* (Strassburg-Berlin), 1 (1910) and 2 (1911): pp. 354–368 and 49–78.

Strothmann, Rudolf, *Das Staatsrecht der Zaiditen:* Strassburg, K. J. Tübner, 1912.

Strothmann, Rudolf, *Kultus der Zaiditen:* Strassburg, K. J. Tübner, 1912.

Strothmann, Rudolf, *Gnosis-Texte der Isma'iliten:* Göttingen, Vandenhoeck, 1943.

Ṣubḥī, Aḥmad Maḥmūd, *Al-Zaydiyya:* 2d ed., Alexandria, Munsha'at al-Ma'ārif, 1984.

al-Subkī, Tāj al-dīn 'Abd al-Wahhāb b. 'Alī, *Ṭabaqāt al-shāfi'iyya al-kubrā:* 10 vols., ed. by Maḥmūd Muḥammad al-Tanāhī and 'Abd al-Fattāḥ Muḥammad al-Ḥilw, Cairo, 'Īsā al-Bābī al-Ḥalabī, 1964–1976.

al-Sulamī, Abū 'Abd al-Raḥmān Muḥammad, *Kitāb ṭabaqāt al-ṣūfiyya.* Texte arabe avec une introduction et un index par Johannes Pedersen: Leiden, E. J. Brill, 1960.

al-Suyūṭī, Jalāl al-dīn, *Ṭabaqāt al-mufassirīn:* Ed. by 'Alī Muḥammad 'Umar, Cairo, 1976.

al-Suyūṭī, Jalāl al-dīn, *Tanbīh al-ghabī fī tanzīh Ibn 'Arabī:* A ms in the Library of the Institute for Oriental Studies, St. Petersburg, no. 2508 D539. Recently published by 'Abd al-Raḥmān Ḥasan Maḥmūd as *Tanbīh al-ghabī fī takhṭī'at Ibn 'Arabī:* Cairo, Maktabat al-Adab, 1990.

al-Suyūṭī, Jalāl al-dīn, "Qam' al-mu'āriḍ fī nuṣrat Ibn al-Fāriḍ." In 'Abd al-Khāliq Maḥmūd 'Abd al-Khāliq, *Jalāl al-dīn al-Suyūṭī wa 'l-taṣawwuf al-islāmī:* Cairo, no publisher, 1987: pp. 48–102.

al-Suyūṭī, Jalāl al-dīn, *Ṭabaqāt al-ḥuffāẓ:* Cairo, Maktabat al-Waḥda, 1973.

Syrier, Miya, "Ibn Khaldun and Islamic Mysticism." In *Islamic Culture* (Hyderabad), 21/3 (1947): pp. 264–302.

Taftāzānī, Mas'ūd b. 'Umar, *A Commentary on the Creed of Islam.* See Elder, *A Commentary on the Creed of Islam.*

al-Taftāzānī, Abū 'l-Wafa', "Al-ṭarīqa al-akbariyya." In *Al-Kitāb al-tidhkārī: Muḥyī 'l-dīn Ibn 'Arabī. Fī dhikrā al-mi'awiyya al-thāmina li-*

mīlādih: Cairo, al-Hay'a al-Miṣrīyya al-'Āmma li 'l-Ta'līf wa 'l-Nashr, 1389/1969: pp. 295–353.

al-Taftāzānī, Sa'd al-dīn Mas'ū d, *Al-Radd wa 'l-tashnī' 'alā 'l-Fuṣūṣ:* A ms in the Garrett Collection of Princeton University, nos. 276 and 5939.

al-Taftāzānī, Sa'd al-dīn, *Risāla fī waḥdat al-wujūd:* Istanbul, no publisher, 1294 A.H.

al-Taftāzānī, Sa'd al-dīn, *Sharḥ al-maqāṣid:* 5 vols., ed. by 'Abd al-Raḥmān 'Umayra, Beirut, 'Ālam al-Kutub, 1989.

Takeshita, Masataka, *Ibn 'Arabī's Theory of the Perfect Man and Its Place in the History of Islamic Thought:* Tokyo, Institute for the Study of Languages and Cultures of Asia and Africa, 1987.

Thorau, Peter, *The Lion of Egypt: Sultan Baybars I and the Near East in the Thirteenth Century:* Trans. by P. M. Holt, London and New York, Longman, 1992.

Toynbee, Arnold Joseph, *An Historian's Approach to Religion:* 2d. ed., Oxford, Oxford University Press, 1979.

Trimingham, J. Spencer, *The Sufi Orders in Islam:* Oxford, The Clarendon Press, 1971.

Tritton, Arthur, "The Mutarrifiyya." In *Le Muséon* (Louvain), 63 (1950): pp. 59–67.

Tritton, Arthur, *The Rise of the Imams of Sanaa:* reprint, Hyperion Press, Westpoint, Conn., 1981.

Turki, Abdelmagid, "Lisān al-Dīn Ibn Ḫaṭīb (713–76/1313–74), juriste d'après son oeuver inédite Muthlā al-ṭarīqa fī dhamm al-wathīqa." In *Arabica* (Paris), 16/2 (1969): pp. 155–211.

al-Turkumānī, Idrīs Ibn Baydakīn, *Kitāb al-luma' fī 'l-ḥawādīth wa 'l-bida':* 2 vols., ed. by Ṣubḥi Labīb, Cairo, Qism al-Dirāsāt al-Islāmiyya bi 'l-Ma'had al-Almānī li 'l-Athār, 1986.

Ullmann, Manfred, *Die Natur und Geheimwissenschften im Islam:* Wiesbaden, Handbuch der Orientalistik, erste Abtailung, Ergänzungsband VI, zweiter Abschnitt, 1972.

'Umayra, 'Abd al-Raḥmān, "Muqaddimat al-muḥaqqiq." In Sa'd al-dīn Mas'ūd al-Taftāzānī, *Sharḥ al-maqāṣid:* Ed. by 'Abd al-Raḥmān 'Umayra, Beirut, 'Ālam al-Kutub, 1989: pp. 17–44.

Urvoy, Dominique, "Les thèmes chrétiens chez Ibn Sab'in et la question de la spécificité de sa pensée." In *Studia Islamica* (Paris), 44 (1976): pp. 99–121.

Urvoy, Dominique, *Le monde des ulémas andalous du Ve-XIe au VIIe-XIIIe siècle: Étude sociologique:* Geneva, Libraire Droz, 1978.

Urvoy, Dominique, "Les emprunts mystiques entre Islam et Christianisme et la veritable portée du Libre d'Amie." In *Estudios Lulianos* (Majorca), 23 (1979): pp. 37–44.

Urvoy, Dominique, "Littérature et société dans le Séville Musulmane." In *Séville: Vingt siècles d'histoire:* Ed. by Bernard Lavallé, Bordeaux, Maison des Pays Ibériques, 1992: pp. 37–56.

Urvoy, Dominique, *Penseurs d'al-Andalus: la vie intellectuelle à Cordoue et Séville au temps des empires berbères:* Paris, Éditions du Centre National de la Recherche Scientifique, 1990.

Urvoy, Marie-Thérèse, "Le Genre 'Manaqib' comme auto-analyse collective." In *Arabica* (Paris), 38/3 (1991): pp. 307–325.

Vajda, George, "Les zindiqs en pays d'Islam au début de la période abbaside." In *Rivista degli Studi Orientali* (Rome), 17 (1938): pp. 173–229.

Van Arendonck, Cornelis, *Les débuts de l'imamate zaidite au Yémen:* Trans. by J. Ryckmans, Leiden, E. J. Brill, 1961.

Van Ess, Josef, *Die Gedankenwelt des Ḥārit al-Muḥāsibī:* Bonn, Selbstverlag des Orientalistischen Seminar Universität Bonn, 1961.

Van Ess, Josef, *Die Erkenntnislehre des 'Aḍudaddīn al-Īcī:* Wiesbaden, Franz Steiner, 1966.

Varisco, Dan, "Texts and Pretexts: The Unity of the Rasulid State Under al-Malik al-Muzaffar." In *REMMM* (Aix-en-Provence) 67/1 (1993): pp. 13–24.

Vikør, Knut, *Sufi and Scholar on the Desert Edge: Muhammad b. 'Ali al-Sanusi and His Brotherhood:* London, Hurst & Co, 1995.

Voll, John, "The Mizjaji Family in Yemen." In *Eighteenth Century Renewal and Reform in Islam:* Ed. by Nehemia Levtzion and John Voll, Syracuse, Syracuse University Press 1987: pp. 69–92.

Waley, Mohammad I., "Najm al-Din Kubra and the Central Asian School of Sufism." In *Islamic Spirituality: Manifestations:* Ed. by S. H. Nasr, vol. 2, London, SCM Press: pp. 80–104.

Watt, W. Mongomery, *A History of Islamic Spain:* Edinburgh, Edinburgh University Press, 1965.

Watt, W. Montgomery, *The Formative Period of Islamic Thought:* Edinburgh, Edinburgh University Press, 1973.

Watt, W. Montgomery, *Islamic Philosophy and Theology: an Extended Survey:* 2d ed., Edinburgh, Edinburgh University Press, 1985.

Watt, W. Montgomery, *Muslim-Christian Encounters: Perceptions and Misperceptions:* London and New York, Routledge, 1991.

Wilber, Donald Newton, *The Architecture of Islamic Iran: The Il Khanid Period:* Princeton, N.J., Princeton Oriental Studies, 17, Princeton University Press, 1955.

Winkel, Eric, "Ibn ʿArabî's Fiqh: Three Cases From the 'Futûhât'." In *Journal of the Muhyiddin Ibn ʿArabi Society* (Oxford), 13 (1993): pp. 54–74.

Winter, Michael, *Society and Religion in Early Ottoman Egypt: Studies in the Writings of ʿAbd al-Wahhab al-Shaʿrani:* Studies in Islamic Culture and History, 4, New Brunswick, N.J., Transaction Books, 1982.

Wolfson, Harry Austryn, *The Philosophy of the Kalam:* Cambridge (Mass.), Harvard University Press, 1976.

Woods, John E., "The Rise of Timurid Historiography." In *Journal of Near Eastern Studies* (Chicago), 46 (April 1987): pp. 81–108.

Wüstenfeld, F, *Die Çufiten in Süd-Arabien im XI (XVIII) Jahrhundert:* Göttingen, Dieterich, 1883.

al-Yāfiʿī, ʿAbdallāh b. Asʿad, *Mirʾāt al-janān wa ʿibrat al-yaqẓān:* 4 vols., Hyderabad, Dāʾirat al-Maʿārif al-Niẓāmiyya, 1918.

al-Yāfiʿī, ʿAbdallāh b. Asʿad, *Rawḍ al-rayāḥīn fī ḥikāyāt al-ṣāliḥīn al-mulaqqab nuzhat al-ʿuyūn al-nawādir:* 2d ed., Egypt, Maktabat wa Maṭbaʿat Muṣṭafā al-Bābī al-Ḥalabī wa Awlādih, 1955.

Yahia, Osman, *Histoire et classification de l'oeuvre d'Ibn ʿArabi:* 2 vols., Damascus, Institut Français de Damas, 1964.

Yaḥyā b. al-Ḥusayn, *Ghāyat al-amānī fī akhbār al-quṭr al-yamānī:* 2 vols., ed. by Saʿīd ʿĀshūr, Cairo, al-Hayʾa al-Miṣriyya al-ʿĀmma li ʾl-Kitāb, 1968.

Yajima, Hikoichi, *A Chronicle of the Rasulid Dynasty of Yemen from the Unique MS Paris, no. Arabe 4609:* Tokyo, Institute for the Study of Languages and Cultures of Asia and Africa, 1976.

Zabāra, Muḥammad, *Aʾimmat al-Yaman:* Sanaa, Dār al-Yamaniyya, 1984.

Zarrūq, Aḥmad b. Aḥmad, *Qawāʿid al-taṣawwuf:* Ed. by Muḥammad Zahrī Najjār, 2d ed., Cairo, Maktabat al-Kulliyya al-Azhariyya, 1976.

Zaydān, Yūsuf, *Al-Fikr al-ṣūfī ʿind ʿAbd al-Karīm al-Jīlī:* Beirut, Dār al-Nahda al-ʿArabiyya, 1988.

al-Zayyin (al-Zayn), Sāmiḥ ʿĀṭif, *Ibn ʿArabī: dirāsa wa taḥlīl:* Beirut, al-Sharika al-ʿĀlamiyya li ʾl-Kitāb, Beirut, 1988.

al-Ziriklī, Khayr al-dīn, *Al-Aʿlām, qāmūs tarājim li-ashhar al-rijāl wa ʾl-nisāʾ min al-ʿarab wa ʾl-mustaʿribīn wa ʾl-mustashriqīn:* 4th ed., 8 vols., Beirut, Dār al-ʿIlm li ʾl-Malāyīn, 1979.

GENERAL INDEX

INDEX OF TERMS

abdal (supreme saints who run the affairs of the world), 309n. 128
adab (polite literature), 27, 172, 237
ahl al-ma'rifa (people of divine gnosis; Sufis), 150, 339n. 61
ahl al-sunna wa 'l-jama'a (orthodox Sunni community), 116
ahl al-wahda (people of unity, or oneness), 180, 345n. 17
'alim (scholar), 330n. 80
See also *'ulama'*
'ama' (nebulous presence), 190
'aqida (profession of faith; doctrinal statement), 235m 310n. 141
'arif , pl. *'arifun* (Sufi gnostic), 25, 53, 106, 165
ashab al-tajalli (proponents of divine self-manifestation), 192, 196, 198
ashab al-wahda (proponents of the unity of being), 192, 196
See also *wahda*
a'yan thabita (immutable entities, i.e., archetypes of empirical beings), 13, 94, 101–04, 106, 108, 109, 154, 320n. 79, 322nn. 114, 118

baqa' (subsistence in God), 206
al-batiniyya (esotericists), 213, 339n. 60, 345n. 17
bid'a (reprehensible innovation), 257, 310n. 134, 331n. 89, 365n. 70

chief *qadi*. See *qadi al-qudat*
continuation. See *dhayl*

dahr (aeon; time), 341n. 95
al-dahriyya (espousers of the doctrine of the eternity of the world), 14, 341n. 95
dhayl (continuation), 27
dhikr (invocation of the divine name(s)), 178, 180, 233
diwan (collection of poetry), 10, 82, 286n. 11
diwan (bureau; state department), 56

ecstatic utterances, 117, 236
See also *shatahat*

falasifa ([Muslim] philosophers), 157, 174, 179, 181, 185, 208, 276, 349n. 66, 351n. 94, 354n. 122, 385n. 1
falsafa ([Islamic] philosophy), 53, 71, 144, 172, 189
fana' (passing away of one's self; self-annihilation [in God]), 93, 150, 151, 206
faqih, pl. *fuqaha'* (Muslim jurisprudent), 37, 44, 63, 71, 76, 84, 85, 137, 218, 229, 232, 233, 239, 240, 242, 252, 255, 267, 274, 304n. 74, 307n. 102, 319n. 66, 329n. 59, 343n. 6, 355n. 128, 360n. 7, 380n. 172

in al-Andalus, 6, 197, 291n. 58
in Damascus, 8, 83, 318n. 54
in Egypt, 202, 203, 209, 210–11, 213, 318n. 54, 329n. 61
in the Maghrib, 35, 169, 175, 197, 348n. 55
and the Mongols, 50, 142
in the Ottoman Empire, 4
in Yemen, 132, 227–28, 233, 235–36, 238–39, 248, 252, 255, 257, 264, 266–67, 269, 276, 374n. 83
and Ibn ʿArabi, 8, 21, 46, 106, 116, 118–21, 137–39, 168, 198, 204, 222, 233, 225, 228, 273
and rulers, 57, 231, 264
and *shariʿa,* 56, 78
and Sufism, 52–54, 73, 183, 188, 191, 218, 222, 238, 252, 339n. 61
Western study of, 3, 17, 277, 279n. 3
umma (Muslim community), 5
See also *ahl al-sunna wa ʾl-jamaʿa*
unification, 98, 107, 148, 152, 306n. 82, 313n. 2
See also *ittihad; wahda (mutlaqa); wahdat al-wujud*
unity of being, 5, 149, 151
unity of witnessing, 5
usul (principles of jurisprudence), 336n. 20
wahda [mutlaqa] (doctrine of [absolute] unity; oneness), 91, 92, 98, 150–51, 179, 190, 281n. 28, 357n.154
wahdat al-wujud (unity of being), 90, 115, 123, 153, 198, 244, 281n. 28, 306n. 82, 314n. 2, 315n. 24, 316n. 26
wahid shakhsi (individual entity), 156–57
wali, pl. *awliyaʾ* ("friend of God"; saint), 53, 80, 81, 236, 296n. 114, 321n. 97, 326n. 24, 332n. 97, 338n. 59
Ibn ʿArabi as, 15, 65, 67, 71, 85, 220
waqf, pl. *awqaf* (Islamic charitable foundation), 55, 354n. 124, 375n. 95
wilaya ("friendship with God;" sainthood), 53, 54, 81, 178, 192–93, 323n. 124, 312n. 172
world-restorer. See *mahdi*
wujud (empirical existence), 101
wujudiyya (proponents of *wahdat al-wujud*), 123, 149, 151–52, 154, 156–58, 162, 180, 341n. 95

zandaqa (heresy; atheism), 159, 239, 341n. 96
zindiq, pl. *zanadiqa* (Manichean; heretic), 159, 265, 341n. 95, 365n. 70
Ibn ʿArabi as, 75, 100, 126, 149

INDEX OF BOOK TITLES